The Golden Age of American Law

THE

GOLDEN AGE

OF

AMERICAN

LAW

Selected and edited

with an introduction and notes by

CHARLES M. HAAR

GEORGE BRAZILLER

New York

Illustrations by David Levine

PREFACE

The period from 1820 to 1860 has a special appeal for Americans. It stands as a golden age—a halcyon era of sturdy yeomanry, simple virtue, a universally acceptable morality, and confidence in a future of expanding prosperity. In a far more complex world, caught in the no-man's-land between rejected older values and new ones yet unformed, many Americans have turned to this era in search of inspiration or comfort and, not surprisingly, have found it. But it is lawyers in particular who have felt its attraction, since it was then that law moved into a dominant role in structuring social affairs. The interaction of law with the ideals, technology, and physical conditions of these formative years, as reflected in contemporary writings of the legal profession, is the theme of this book.

There is a tendency to gild the past with uncritical generosity, but this period did indeed witness a proliferation of institutions destined to have permanent effect. A whole panoply of modern arrangements—political parties, public education, trade unions, and national corporations among them—was then forged. Permanent changes were fashioned in the law as well, as it was molded to the needs of American society. This age produced much of the nation's important legal literature, for the problems of social ordering posed by life in a new country were met by legal craftsmanship of the highest caliber. Indeed, the remarkable development of legal institutions in the pre–Civil War years moved Roscoe Pound to name the period the "Formative Era of American Law," while others have aptly described its classic manner of reasoning and rhetoric as the "Grand Style of the Common Law."

Law is as indispensable and natural a part of the environment of men in society as the air they breathe. It may be simply the projection of one man's will, or the pronouncements of a small class; it may be broadly based, as on the consensus of the adult population; it may be a purely oral tradition, or entirely written, or somewhere between the two extremes —but by whatever means, rules will always be established to govern the inevitable relations of men with each other and with their possessions.

When people are creating afresh, as Americans were after the War for Independence, this tendency of a society to establish institutionalized procedures for settling matters of common concern is brought out most sharply. The first Europeans to colonize the New World brought with them the law of their country, just as they brought its language. Although each group carried a different culture (and legal system), the law of England was dominant. As long as colonial ties existed, Americans looked to English law to ascertain their rights and duties. But after the war they were free to—and indeed needed to—develop a body of law peculiarly suited to America, so that by and large American law may be regarded as the offspring of the marriage between English common law and the people and conditions of the new country.

But independence alone is not enough: sustained and conscious attention to legal institutions demands also a national excess of energy which can be devoted to such an intellectual luxury. The end of the Revolution was hardly a time of leisure and affluence. The initial period of independence was occupied with basic considerations, legal and nonlegal; such creative legal energies as existed went into fashioning the new nation's political structure and its organic law. This was the era of Constitution-making.

By 1820 the essential task of clearing and preparing the ground for legal institutions had been completed, and a period of intense legal development began which lasted until approximately 1860. The quality of the nation's legal architects has been tested and proved by the institution they created, by its durability, and by its capacity to grow and flex with changed physical conditions, technologies, and ideals. Subsequent generations were to put the finishing touches to the structure, live in it, repair and extend it; but it was the men of this era who laid the foundation and erected the framework.

These men and their creation illuminate the age in which they lived and worked, for they encountered fundamental problems of political and social ordering. Dissolution of the vestiges of feudal society in the New World created the need for a fresh analysis of goals, as well as for a legal framework to establish the conditions necessary for community life and order consistent with the approved goals. A study of this framework must also be a study of the era.

This book is an attempt to recreate the legal experiences of the years between 1820 and 1860, and to set forth firsthand evidence that they did in fact constitute a golden age. The writings are those of participants in the work of law and contemporary observers of it, as revealed in judicial opinions, statutes, debates, diaries, essays, speeches, letters, and, occasionally, works of fiction. Over a hundred years have passed since the close of that period; the reader will not be surprised to find materials quaint in language or substance; what is surprising is the degree to which they retain pertinence. In selecting and editing the extracts I have tried to convey the temper of the time, its spirit and flavor. My choice of material has been guided by several considerations, the major criterion being the extent to which a document reveals the intellectual climate of the time; law is taken in a broad sense ranging from what may be termed "lawyer's law," such as codification or procedure, to its cultural presuppositions and interaction with mainstreams of thought. Contemporary relevance was another guide: I prefer materials on problems still alive today to those dealing with themes that have lost the power to excite any save antiquarian interest. Other items are included simply because they are amusing. Unavoidably, the wealth of available material had to be compressed into manageable proportions, and some highly relevant documents from this period are omitted or abbreviated because they are well known and readily available elsewhere.

The materials are divided into five parts. The first and last probe the special identity of American law and the legal profession, while the three middle sections consider the growth of the law as a response to the political, social, and economic transformations of the society.

Part I sketches the lawyer in the context of his time: what he was like as a person and how he dressed and behaved; how he viewed society and how it saw him; the role he played in the community and how he stood in relation to his fellow attorneys; what forces, educational and professional, shaped him.

Part II deals with the separation and division of political power. It shows how under the pressure of solving immediate problems, whether in the political forum or through public opinion, the general principles and broadly stated powers of the organic law acquired a detailed connotation.

Part III analyzes reforms in the practice and substance of law from two vantage points: the law as it appeared to lawyers, who had both the advantages and disadvantages of close involvement with the subject matter; and the law as seen by the more critical, albeit sometimes unsophisticated, eyes of the layman. These appraisals were debated not only in the context of the legal reforms on which much of the enduring fame of this period rests, but in that of social reform as well.

Part IV focuses on the interrelation of law and economic change; it traces legal developments in corporations, banking, usury, labor, and urban land-use controls. The role of law during this period of rapid economic development in the United States is of special interest for those currently concerned with raising the standards of living in underdeveloped countries and creating the institutional structure for change.

The fifth and final part concentrates on the degree to which the law of the United States is unique and the reasons underlying its special evolution.

In seeking out common themes which tie this near half-century together, the dynamism, the exuberance of those years stands out. The national government was busy extending its jurisdiction and winning popular acceptance of its authority. The peace achieved by the Treaty of Ghent in 1814 opened the way to a burgeoning of business enterprise. Crèvecœur's "new man," the American, was conquering the West. The emergence of the common man was evidenced by Andrew Jackson's attack on the Bank of the United States as a monopoly; he hit upon a far

more popular theme than Nicholas Biddle and Henry Clay realized, to
their later chagrin. The restlessness of this new nation made itself felt
in other ways; property qualifications for voting, established religion on
the state level, the regulation of entrance into the professions by elite
groups—all traditional notions—were rejected in this period. And from
1820 onwards, almost every factor in the development of American society—land settlement, slavery, banking, railroads, corporations, foreign
relations—brought the legal profession into closer relation with the life
of the United States. Despite an international reputation as a burly young
giant best characterized by its lawless West, the country chose to entrust
the guidance of its affairs to the sanity of law, unlike other societies undergoing similar stresses of political change or economic expansion.

In this swollen river of agitation, what was the role of the lawyer?
Did he moderate popular passion and try to channel it in more fruitful
directions? Did he stand on the bank of the river and try to chart its
course? Or was he a part of the agitation himself, carried along by the
current? Was there a unique structure of American law? Was there a deep
concern for the beneficent use of law in the public interest? And what
function did law, appeal to reason, and distillation of legal experience play
in changing the face of America?

I am indebted to many for valuable advice and suggestions. My colleagues, John P. Dawson and Mark deWolfe Howe, reviewed portions of
these materials. Professors Bernard Bailyn and William Letwin read
through the introductory chapters with much care. Three students of the
Harvard Law School, Stephen Schlissel, Stephen Subrin, and Anthony
Vernava, participated in the joint enterprise of examining and selecting
the source materials.

Joanna Gould, Barbara Hering, and Stephen Lefkowitz helped in
organizing the chapters and in editorial work. Allan Feld, Joseph Kett,
and Lloyd L. Weinreb contributed to shaping the arrangement of the materials. Finally, Edwin Seaver's encouragement throughout the preparation of the book went far beyond the call of duty.

—CHARLES M. HAAR

Harvard Law School
January, 1965

CONTENTS

Contents xiii

Illustrations by David Levine

For Nan

Part I

THE
LEGAL
PROFESSION

Lemuel Shaw.

Introduction

There were many lawyers in Colonial America. But a legal profession in the modern sense did not come into being until after the colonies had wrested their freedom from England. The origin and rapid growth of the American bar was a by-product of the tremendous energies expended to fill the legal vacuum created by the rupture of political ties.

Until the War for Independence the law governing the colonies consisted in part of enactments adopted locally, subject to the veto of the mother country. The balance and larger part was the common law of England as "found" by judges, and those statutes of Parliament which extended to this country by virtue of its colonial status. Thus one of the most pressing needs in the wake of military victory was to re-examine the body of legal doctrine left at the end of the war, and to develop the law afresh wherever it was found to be inadequate.

An obvious, though only partial, solution was to readopt voluntarily the English law with all its merits and defects. "Reception" statutes enacted for that purpose by the now sovereign states served as one starting point for the evolution of the law. Another was the organic law, the Articles of Confederation, superseded a few years later by the Constitution.

From these meager beginnings the next few generations, led by the rising legal profession, were to fashion the legal institutions which are the inheritance of today. In the process of unfolding the powers of the Constitution John Marshall's Supreme Court laid the legal foundations of the nation. Certainly the higher reaches of constitutional law reveal the creative process, but it can be seen even more clearly in sections of private law, such as property and contracts, and on the state rather than on the federal level; during this period large sectors of national life were organized on a local basis. State legislatures and courts, preparing the groundwork for industrialism and democracy in a new country, adjusted English doctrines to meet the flood of changing conditions. They attempted to simplify the technicalities of procedure and to eliminate the most egregious roadblocks to the administration of justice. Not the least of their accomplishments was the popular identification of democratic government with law.

So rapidly did they build the legal superstructure that by 1830, when de Tocqueville took his prophetic soundings of the United States, he described it as a law-dominated society. The general public shared the pride of men like Chief Judge Shaw that the United States was "peculiarly, exclusively and emphatically a government of laws." The rhetorical sweep of language current in the age of Shaw has dropped from fashion, but the core idea remains as vital as ever. What he called the "absolute and entire supremacy of law" is still a foundation of political rights and freedoms. Often by law was meant the law enunciated by individual judges, the common law as contrasted with the civil law "under which," in the words of Chief Judge Gibson of Pennsylvania, "justice may be unceremoniously snatched by the hands of power."

As the law grew, so too did the role of the lawyer. The presence of written constitutions on both the federal and state levels thrust lawyers into the heart of the issue of accountable power. "The discussion of constitutional questions," wrote Mr. Justice Story, "throws a lustre round the bar, and gives a dignity to its functions which can rarely belong to the profession in any other country."

Attainment of such status by the profession was surprising in an environment which was plainly hostile to any small group assuming a dominant role in the direction of societal affairs. Powerful forces opposed the formulation of a self-conscious, structured profession. The expansiveness and ruggedness of life in America mocked the lawyer's traditional role of gentleman and scholar and, much more so, that of leader of affairs. Frontier conditions aggravated the difficulties of a new bar: witness its virtues and shortcomings presented in *Flush Times* by Judge Baldwin, with his kaleidoscopic view of lawyers who trusted for success to their audacity and their lungs.

Somewhat paradoxically, the popular interest in politics and public affairs, which de Tocqueville saw as a hallmark of democratic society, hindered the attainment by the legal profession of what some supposed to be its proper dignity. A trial, as well as a political debate, was likely to attract large crowds. A society still predominantly rural tended to turn an event like the arrival of the circuit-riding judge into a social gathering, a rare opportunity for meeting neighbors. Court day, as recaptured in Senator Hoar's recollection of the Worcester bar, meant that "people came in from the country round in their covered wagons, simply for the pleasure of attending Court and seeing the champions contend with each other"; it was the occasion for social entertainment and interchange of gossip: "Everybody, with or without business, generally attends," wrote David Davis of the Illinois circuit; the Kentucky court of Clay's day presented a Hogarthian scene of brawls and drunken spectators.

The lawyer occupied the center of a stage and legal oratory had to take on a popular tone. As Lincoln knew, and as Choate complained, a lawyer's success depended more upon his popular appeal than on his technical expertise. Such a standard of values—witness the career of S. S. Prentiss or of William Wirt—attached greater weight to eloquence than to substance. In such a society the lawyer had difficulty establishing himself as part of a specially trained elite. Further, the popular democratic rhetoric which marked political discussions in Jacksonian America poured scorn on the notion that specialized training made any man a member of a privileged elite. To the extent that history can be segmented, 1830 may be taken as a dividing point in the profession's public standing. Before that date the prestige and expertise of the lawyer had been rarely questioned. Thereafter society, except for the lawyers, began to react ambivalently, as it will to any powerful and ambitious group; references to the ill repute of the legal profession multiply after 1830.

The regulations of the time permitted anyone to practice law, medicine, or any other occupation, without being officially licensed by the state. To raise the prestige of their calling, the more learned and dignified practitioners of such arts began to establish voluntary associations intended to operate as private licensing authorities, collective warrantors of their members' abilities. But these self-appointed professional elites did not enjoy the confidence of the public. Distrust of privilege was strong, and so too was the belief that all callings were equally meritorious. Vocal elements were aggressively hostile to all forms of special privilege—medical associations, chartered banks, and other organized groups were attacked as well as bar associations. Opposition to lawyers in particular as a professional group sprang from the twin beliefs that a lawyer could not possibly be the better for belonging to a fancy organization, and that lawyers had purposely made the administration of justice an intricate matter in order to preserve a monopoly. Popular opinion was clear: to speak of a "profession" and set standards for admission to it was un-American.

The suspicion that legal technicalities were a mark of professional cunning, "playing of the nurse to villains," a trap for the virtuous, intensified the public's fear of a monopoly. Many of today's familiar complaints—and the standard rebuttals—arose in the conversation of the time: advocacy for a cause in which the lawyer did not believe, the great expense of legal proceedings, the uncertainty of the law, the interminable delays, the courtroom seen as the site for shearing lambs—often with the implication that the members of the profession were alone responsible. To many watching the spectacular fortunes which some amount of legal learning, especially if parlayed with speculation in land titles, could amass, the law seemed obviously to be a rascal's way to paper fortunes. Then, as today, there was the inescapable fact, pointed out by John Pickering in 1830 in a lecture before the Boston Society for the Diffusion of Useful Knowledge, that in a lawsuit one of the two contending parties has to lose, and that the loser will naturally feel he has a right to complain of the law. Pickering could have added that in any event, since men's contacts with the legal system occur chiefly when calamities overtake them, lawyers tend to be associated in the public mind with pain and trouble, for they act upon relations that are already strained and irritated.

Lay criticism apprised the profession that its public image had deteriorated. "Lawyers have been the subjects of more honor and more obloquy, of more confidence and more suspicion, than popular estimation has allotted to persons of any other employment," is the opening sentence of an address in 1851 by Judge Charles P. Jones at the Law School of Cincinnati College. A note of apology, of defensiveness, occasionally crept into the statements of lawyers, as in David Dudley Field's paper delivered at Albany Law School in 1855.

But the criticism did not completely destroy the legal fraternity's self-image; the picture it drew of itself was startlingly different from that of popular imagination. A powerful element in this self-portrait was the identification of professional tasks with public service—the whole community was the client. The self-esteem and sense of public service that lawyers enjoyed when they dealt as legislators, judges, or commentators with constitutional issues and questions of public law, they also felt as practitioners of private law. Were they not then too making law? Was not the nation's law the final product of the lawyers' pleadings in innumerable private cases? Some lawyers even affirmed that the standing of the legal profession was an index of the civilization of a people. This sense of their peculiar importance as the shepherds and representatives of the nation led them to assume a pose always popular with lawyers: that of preservers of the fabric of society. Though this pose was not entirely convincing, many contemporary writers pointed out the need for a body of priests whose peculiar business it should be to understand, elucidate, and enforce the principles of law. By this was understood the pinnacle of the profession, the judiciary, with its paternal role as arbiter of the moral tone of the entire community.

Although the attack against monopoly elements in professional groups did not damage the amour-propre of lawyers, it did produce some casualties; these were mainly among the bar associations which appeared after the Revolution. The bar initially possessed few of the accoutrements of a formal organization, and even fewer toward the end of the period than before. So far as corporate unity is concerned, the years 1830 to 1850 were in Dean Pound's words "a period of decadence." What few associations there were weakened during these years and went into an accelerated decline toward the end of the period.

Jacksonian reformers thought they could achieve great ends by opening the practice of the profession to all. Ironically, the belief that law was just another means of livelihood turned it in that very direction. By encouraging an influx of new, often untrained lawyers, professional standards were depressed to levels which justified complaints about the inadequacy of the legal profession. "Every man his own lawyer" was the slogan. And conditions at that time were favorable as never since, for specialization was at low ebb. One form of specialization in the craft had ended after the Revolution, when American lawyers jettisoned the English distinction between barristers, who appeared in court, and solicitors, who did not. Specialization by subject—admiralty, corporation law, criminal law—had not yet dimmed the excitement of general practice with its variety of experience.

It is difficult to see how the legal profession could survive, much less thrive, under the pressure of forces geared so strongly toward mediocrity. Yet the records show that its achievements at this time were of the highest quality. Lawyers had a sweeping success as leaders in many fields, and wielded enormous influence on a professional basis. How is this apparently paradoxical state of affairs to be explained?

In turn, this inquiry raises the problem of defining professional status in a democratic society. There is no simple definition of a profession; in a broad sense it encompasses any vocation in which a man habitually earns his living. The *Oxford Universal Dictionary* suggests a narrower, and for our purposes a more helpful, definition: "a vocation in which a professed knowledge of some department of learning is used in its application to the affairs of others." The guiding notion is that the professional is not confined to his own narrow area of expertise, but that he applies his special tools to a wide range of fields. Mr. Justice Holmes put it more pithily in his injunction to "teach law in the grand manner," and said on another occasion that a lawyer should "wreak" himself upon the subject by seeing it in relation to "the frame of the universe."

This view of the nature of a profession pervaded the thinking of Jacksonian lawyers, despite the disappearance of formalized organization. Personality, strong character, education, or social class apparently generated enough power, even if not reinforced by official delegation to a private group, to stimulate the aspirations and activity of the young lawyer. The enormous achievement of lawyers in business, society, and politics, notwithstanding the decay of formal guild organization, suggested that a formal organization with rigid licensing practices was not a necessity; for lawyers—or at least a hard core—did in fact constitute a profession *ipso facto*, whether by common cast of mind, by selfish closed-shop needs, or by special functions in the market place and government. It was perhaps as a reaction to the centrifugal forces which opposed the establishment of a legal profession that lawyers displayed a growing concern with the paraphernalia of professionalism as a learned activity: schools, ethical codes, and publications.

Among these concerns, legal education naturally absorbed a large share of professional introspection. Two themes recurred. One was the need for rigorous training in the law. The duty of the young lawyer was to apply himself to systematic study of "the amiable and admirable secrets of the law." To gain the confidence of the community the science demanded industry, perseverance, and learning. "Never yet has jurisprudence twined her wreath around a sluggard's brow" was the substance of a valedictory address to the graduates of the law class of Cincinnati College in 1838.

The other and related theme stressed during these formative years was condemnation of the narrow learning of the typical lawyer, a sore point with those seeking liberal and cultivated men. In speaking of courtroom advocacy, the question was asked:

> Can anything be more jejune, feeble and commonplace? Anything more unworthy to be called eloquence? This dearth of oratory is attributable in part to the number of inferior men who crowd themselves within the bar. But it must also be assigned in large measure, to utter want of literary furnishment in the great mass of the profession. They study law . . . and they study nothing else. . . . They are content to know the verbiage of the law, and they bow reverently to the ipse dixit of ancient compilers of rules, and modern digesters of precedents. As to studying the classics, they were bored sufficiently with them at college. As to Burke and Milton, they throw no light upon the Rule of Shelley's case, and a lawyer should not waste time upon them. Such members of the profession . . . will never cultivate eloquence themselves, nor encourage its growth in others.

Preparation for the law according to this school of thought should, in addition to legal learning, comprehend literature, the rules of rhetoric, and other fields of knowledge. "They spend their lives in active toil, wrestling forever in the flames of litigation," said Henry Warner in his *Discourse on Legal Science* delivered at the New York Law Institute in 1832, "and actually wanting leisure for better things." Wirt's letters reveal an interesting though possibly idealistic view of the education needed by the young lawyer. The advice of Henry Clay, quoted below, adds another dimension to the portrait.

Much of the agitation about lawyers' education may in retrospect seem to have been baseless. Perhaps each era is haunted by the giants of earlier days and by the illusion of a golden age that will never recur. But few today will equate with a deterioration of learning and eloquence the society which produced Benjamin, Binney, Choate, Clay, Evarts, Harper, Mason, O'Connor, Taney, Webster, and Lincoln.

The year 1821 saw the beginning of Professor David Hoffman's struggle to establish a law institute at the University of Maryland, in which he proposed to deliver three hundred and one lectures for a fee of one hundred dollars. Benjamin F. Butler's plan for the organization of the Law Faculty opened a serious inquiry into the nature of scientific law schools and methods of instruction. Harvard Law School was opened in 1817 and the Yale Law School in 1824. The enduring value of these events may not have been immediately evident. The story of Lincoln as a bar examiner and the resignations of Professors Parker and Stearns from the Harvard

Law Faculty for lack of pupils both make the same point: that law in this period was still learned largely through practice—and, there was reason to believe, at the expense of the novice's first clients. What formal education there was had serious defects. In perspective, however, the beginning of law teaching by universities must be seen as a major achievement. Much of the current outlook of law schools can be traced directly to the plan fathered by Butler.

Here again the views of the profession were not those of the public. Lawyers who decried the level of educational standards and proclaimed the need for schooling in the classical liberal arts ran into popular opposition. Charges were made that the lawyers were too pedantic, too engrossed in sesquipedalian terminology. The charge of the New York Legislature to its Commissioners on Practice and Pleadings called "for the abandonment of all Latin and other foreign tongues." William Seward commented often on the prolixity of bills in chancery which were paid for by the folio; "one day, he took a mortgage foreclosure just completed, counted the words, found that there were 4,500; taking his pen he drew up one a tenth the length, comprising everything required on law or facts." The apparent contradictions in the testimony of contemporary observers—some felt that lawyers must have an even wider education and some that lawyers were already becoming overeducated—can be seen as an example of the larger struggle over whether there should be professions at all in a democratic society.

A similar disagreement arose over the role of the lawyer in politics. It is not consistent with the dignity of a profession that a man enter it only as a steppingstone to something higher; he then becomes something of a renegade in the eyes of his former companions. And yet the law was the best preparation for politics. Hence this period produced Timothy Walker's strictures on the lawyer who did not devote his whole life to the law; he viewed politics as a sad misuse of a glorious calling, and denied that any man could aspire to become an eminent lawyer who did not confine himself rigidly to his profession. At the same time others urged that lawyers were too Olympian, too out of touch with the masses—the very reverse of claiming that the lawyer was overinvolved in politics. Once again, conflicting attitudes toward professionalization of the law explain these disparate points of view.

More politely conceived, politics becomes statecraft, and Walker's fear of involvement betrays the fallacy of the undistributed middle. Public service, even where mixed with the motivation of personal advancement, came to be the hallmark of the American lawyer, and this period cemented the identification of the legal with the political career. The lawyer's education, his extensive relations with private citizens, and the discipline of public speaking led to his prominence on the floor of Congress or in the state legislature. Law was the avenue of success for the poor boy, and politics was a natural byroad. Not surprising, then, that the political path continued to be heavily traveled despite the occasional warnings posted by eminent jurists.

The appearance of codes of ethics was another sign of the lawyers' attempt to achieve group identification. These self-policing efforts may also be regarded as an attempt to forestall more drastic remedies. Early codes of ethics reveal that the bar's reaction to public criticism was equivocal. It rejected imputations that law was a business. Law was a noble and elevated pursuit, a peaceful remedy for social ills, that substituted reason and justice for passion and violence. It promoted the release of the individual's creative energies and the assertion of his will. Apart from the sonorities and self-congratulations which always seemed to attend an occasion for speechmaking, a heavy, almost solemn sense of responsibility and obligation was felt by many members of the profession.

They accepted as just, however, the censure of the practice of law as carried on by some of their fellows. Indeed, they could hardly have done otherwise. There were embarrassing individual cases, which evoke Macaulay's aphorism that English lawyers "with wigs on their heads and bands round their necks, would do, for a guinea, what, without these appendages, they would think wicked and infamous to do for an empire." *Bennet* v. *Hargus*, an early case from Nebraska, is an extreme instance. After losing a murder case, in which he acted as counsel for defendant, a Judge Bradford secured the passage of an act through the legislature— of which he was a member—"to repeal certain acts of the legislative assembly of Nebraska, passed at the first session thereof." When the act was vetoed on the ground that this meant the repeal of the entire Criminal Code, Bradford winked and blinked "like a toad under a harrow" and assured the legislature that repeal meant only recourse to the common law. Relying upon the dignified judge, his fellow legislators overrode the veto, thereby unwittingly permitting his client to escape paying the penalty for his crime.

Such wayward incidents probably reinforced the stress on moral self-discipline, which, as Durkheim points out, is a part of professional self-identification. The first attempt in the United States to develop a formal guide to morality in legal practice is embodied in Judge George Sharswood's *Code of Ethics*. Dealing with the perplexities, duties, and temptations of the lawyer, it contained principles of conduct for lawyers as officers of the court. "To a young lawyer, character is everything." In all his dealings with the court a practitioner should "use no deceit, imposition, or evasion." This issue of lawyers' honor is a recurring sore point, as witnessed by the defense in a nonlegal periodical, *The American Review*: "While we presume that the Bar does not offer any more than its fair proportional share of virtue, we utterly deny that its members, as a body, are guilty of extraordinary departure from the path of integrity in the pursuit of their calling."

Many of the leaders of the bar strove to better their profession—to enable, or force, the lawyer to perform his function, in Chief Judge Shaw's words, "in a manner most honorable to himself and useful to his age and country." There was sharp criticism of what was regarded as the then prevailing opinion that the lawyer's duty to his client swallowed up other responsibilities, including those due to the court and to the state. The leaders, in the East at any rate, shared the view of the lawyer's public responsibilities which Greenleaf stressed at Harvard Law School.

> While our aid should never be withheld from the injured or the accused, let it be remembered that all our duties are not concentrated in conducting an appeal of the law; that we are not only lawyers, but citizens and men; that our clients are not always the best judges of their own interests at our hands. It is for us to advise to what course, which will best conduct to their permanent benefit, not merely as solitary individuals, but as men connected with society by enduring ties.

But if these adjurations did not fall entirely on deaf ears, neither did they produce the desired result. In 1850 David Dudley Field expressed unhappiness with the profession of law as a public calling, for he detected in it a tendency to sacrifice broader values to the client's interests. Perhaps there was this much merit in Field's observation: that American lawyers at this time seemed to be associating themselves, or at least were accused of associating themselves, with the interests of the wealthy. If this were so, the lawyers were certainly failing to perform their proper function of representing all the interests in the community.

The social position of the lawyer in this period is difficult to assess. In the East, in the early part of this period, lawyers were considered an elite. According to de Tocqueville, the profession constituted the only aristocratic element in the Republic. Commonly lawyers were thought to subscribe as a class to the philosophy of Choate, that the function of law is to tame the fitful will of the crowd or divert it into appropriate channels. Whether this philosophy was due to a professional cast of mind that valued antiquity over novelty, or to the nature of a vocation which adjusted rather than constructed, is not clear. What is clear is that it presupposes the social and moral supremacy of lawyers. Jacksonian reformers, harshly interpreting the Choate approach, charged lawyers with strangling the rights of the common man. They characterized the practice of law as a masquerade by which the wealthy East—a privileged group of patronage and power—oppressed the rest of the nation.

Lawyers' conservatism does not necessarily indicate that they failed to play a major role in social change. The despotism of numbers is a recurring issue in American thought; democracy constantly teeters on the brink of "arithmocracy," to use Matthew Arnold's expression, and some check upon arbitrary majority rule is necessary. There was a feeling during this period that reform had been achieved: the Revolution had redistributed privilege and reparceled property. Whether it was self-delusion or not, this premise led directly to the conclusion that the residuary task of the law was to conserve. Nor should the conditioning imposed by the lawyer's job be overlooked: to him falls the task of making visions concrete; making the descent into details always tests the validity of erstwhile grand schemes and reveals any flaws there may be. To a certain extent, Fenimore Cooper, with his curious blend of a novelist's imagination and a patrician's conservatism, articulated the crusty suspicion of a law dominated by the masses.

The practitioners who opposed the Choate philosophy held the view that the purpose of law was to facilitate change—to create the framework for a fresh society that was coping with novel conditions on a newly discovered continent. Hence people believed, sometimes unexpectedly, that law should sweep away the legal traditions of aristocratic England—especially the law of real property with its ancient manorial customs and feudal rights—and start afresh under a republican form of government.

The key to reconciling the view of lawyers as an aristocratic element with the occasional portraits of them as reformers may lie in the traditional Fabian role of the lawyer: a concern for neatness and symmetry in applying law to new situations has the effect, in many instances, of reconstructing the forms of social arrangements. The lawyer's professional desire for technical order may thus unwittingly reinforce and gain acceptance for social change. If recorded observations from this period are to be believed, lawyers recognized themselves as part of a new society which demanded startling transformations in the social and economic fabric. But though they welcomed the wind of change, they sought to regulate it. This was the true position of the moderates of the legal profession. Here Lincoln is typical: though plainly not opposed to reform, he looked for gradual evolution in other contemporary problems as well as slavery.

These opposing views toward the job of law in a physically and socially mobile society stem from the problem of professionalism. The lawyer, through direct association and the vicarious experience of cases, deals with the emergencies of other people as a matter of routine. *Nil admirari* becomes the protective shell of the hard-working practitioner. While the objectivity gained through familiarity is the core of the lawyer's expertise, it is an attribute which may in turn gain for him his client's suspicions.

In brief, the lawyer's status in this period was determined by his effort to rise above the level of a trade and reach that of a profession. The effort ran into opposition from those forces in American life which wanted no part of the specially trained and specially privileged elites who were trying to map out for themselves a broad control over society. From this conflict, both sides learned. The profession gained a greater awareness of common interests, and its character as a public servant improved by benefiting from Jacksonian criticisms. When faced by serious threats to the old order of common law, many members of the profession displayed a skillful willingness to adapt that order to the new needs. The Jacksonian legal ideal that unlettered wisdom and practical good sense could lead to more astute judgment than knowledge of black-letter law bore positive fruit. A wide-open profession tended to bring more of the experiences of ordinary people to bear on the developing law; it meant that a legal meritocracy evolved in which success depended on talent and energy.

At the same time, the egalitarian "folk" ethos gave way to the realities of a complex society where the lawyer's skills and discipline were needed. With its usual disregard for consistency, the public, while deprecating practitioners of law for inattention to truth and fairness, continued to bestow upon them its offices of trust. Thirteen of the first sixteen Presidents were lawyers. This can be attributed at least in part to the fact that no one came up with a viable alternative to the existing legal order. The scheme of law elaborated at great length by Story, Kent, and Walker was clear, authoritative, impressive—and rushed in to fill the legal vacuum of the new country. No layman became proficient enough in the problem areas to assert his qualifications against those of the lawyers. The lawyer's knowledge of the drafting and interpretation of laws made him indispensable on all sides; as holder of political office, adviser to commerce and industry, intermediary in personal and social affairs, he assumed a commanding position. The successful emergence and endurance of a professional identity was bound at times to be synonymous with a monopoly of the practice of law and a failure to serve the public interest. Nevertheless, at the best levels of professional achievement, lawyers formed what Holmes called "the little army of specialists," from whom "men learn that bustle and push are not the equivalent of . . . serene mastery." As democratic ideology ceased to reject professionalism the Jacksonian conflict developed wider ramifications: the idea of a profession became far more inclusive than in Europe, and other vocations avidly scrambled for grounds upon which to justify their professional status.

The accomplishment of the legal profession in the formative era was prodigious. It succeeded in accommodating the English law to the spirit of the new age and the conditions of a pioneer country far different from those of the mother country. With little precedent at hand, and that frequently remote from the issues to be resolved, new substantive doctrines of law had to be evolved. The genius of the American bar was that it effected the transition by building as best it could on the past, rather than by breaking with it and starting anew.

The results are even more impressive when assessed in the light of conditions prevailing in the early years. The legal profession, itself newly emergent, had little straw with which to make bricks. The contents of the law were but imperfectly perceived. There was no formal system of education, no Inns of Court to which the bar had been previously attached. Texts were few. There was not even a system of printed reports of court opinions, those essential links in the common-law chain. Nevertheless, by 1829 more than one hundred and fifty volumes of reports of decisions had been published, and states were appointing official reporters. Story, Greenleaf, Parsons, and Bishop, among others, prepared texts. Legal periodicals, albeit with uncertain fates, were launched to help to find and analyze the law and to discuss issues. Academic training began. Lawyers, numerous and powerful during this period, overflowed the confines of their profession into society, business, and, most notably, into politics. By appointment or election they sat in the legislatures, held cabinet posts, and occupied every type of public office conceivable. Where law governs, the lawyer flourishes.

The profession reaped many benefits from the talents of the remarkable lawyers of the period. Despite intermittent sniping, the group as a whole earned the respect and confidence which it was accorded. Nor was this due solely to craftsmanship and competence. Then as now, law was a pathway to wealth, distinction, and political influence; many of its practitioners felt deeply responsible toward the society to which they owed their eminence, and helped to create a tradition of public service. An emerging sense of duty and unity of interest led to the formulation of professional standards of competence and morality.

Lawyers of that day were more flamboyant than they are now. Their style of legal discourse was often impassioned; they unfolded their arguments grandly and comprehensively. Although they were not prone to question the assumptions underlying their elaborate structures of eloquence and logic, the results they achieved were solid and substantial. They laid the foundations for jurisprudence and government. Their expositions, as Story wrote of Marshall in 1833, in his dedication to the *Commentaries on the Constitution*, "remind us of some mighty river of our own country which, gathering in its course the contributions of many tributary streams, pours at last its own current into the ocean, deep, clear, and irresistible."

There was great work to be done, and it is remarkable how often lawyers met the challenge. Those heights could not have been attained without the breadth of view which characterizes this golden age of American law. Its major spokesmen projected law not simply as a trade, but as a social agency for shaping rules and adjudicating disputes, as a philosophy of government in the broadest sense. The lawyer was cast not in the role of a scrivener or a pedantic dealer in words, but in that of a man grappling with the problems of men. Lawyers became the cement of the young society. Story's eloquent call to a more reticent and irreverent generation, not overfond of rhetoric, is a typical statement of the creed of his times:

> May our successors in the profession look back upon our times, not without some kind regrets, and some tender recollections. May they cherish our memories with that gentle reverence which belongs to those who have laboured earnestly, though it may be humbly, for the advancement of the law. May they teach a holy enthusiasm from the review of our attainments, however limited they may be, which shall make them aspire after the loftiest possessions of human learning. And thus may they be enabled to advance our jurisprudence to that degree of perfection which shall make it a blessing and protection to our country, and excite the just admiration of mankind.

1. The Lawyer's Role in a New Nation

LAWYERS UNDER A REPRESENTATIVE
FORM OF GOVERNMENT

Lemuel Shaw

The pre-eminence of Lemuel Shaw (1781–1861) as spokesman for the golden age of American law could be challenged by no one except Mr. Justice Story. As Chief Justice of the Supreme Court of Massachusetts for thirty years, Shaw exerted a profound influence on commercial and constitutional law throughout the country. He combined a vigorous intellect with a personality bordering on the majestic, and spoke in a tone that was overwhelming to his contemporaries. He tended to be impatient with exhaustive collections of precedents—of a case Shaw had argued as a young lawyer, the court remarked that the point had "been urged by the counsel . . . with as much force as zeal and eloquence without authority" could give. Many political and economic issues of the day, undecided and of first impression, came to him. He helped the common law to accommodate itself to changes in business and social habits; it was this judicial adaptation to modern conditions that made other techniques unnecessary to bring law up-to-date, especially the competing one of statutory reform. In the following extract Shaw develops the theme of law as a restraint on power.

LET US THEN, gentlemen, proceed to consider the condition, the importance and utility of the profession of the law, in the actual situation and prospects of the United States. The proposition which I wish to maintain, and which I think may be fully established, is this; that in a free, representative government, founded upon enlarged and liberal views, designed to secure the rights, to promote the industry and to advance the happiness of a great community, and adapted to a high state of civilization and improvement, it is of the highest importance that there should be a body of men, trained, by a well adapted course of education and study, to a thorough and profound knowledge of the law, and practically skilled in its application, whose privilege and duty it is, in common with their fellow citizens, to exert a fair share of influence in the enactment of laws, and

Lemuel Shaw, "Profession of the Law in the United States," *American Jurist* (January, 1832), **VII**, p. 56.

whose peculiar duty and exclusive occupation it is, to assist in the application of them to practice in the administration of justice, in its various departments. May I not go farther, and add, that the utility of this profession, the benefits which it is capable of conferring, and the respect in which it shall be held, in any community, will be in a great measure proportioned to the degree, in which the government and institutions of such community, are founded upon free principles.

There are, obviously, two very different modes of governing mankind; the one, by the will of a superior, either absolute, as in the case of a naked despotism, or more or less modified and restrained, as in the case of a limited monarchy; the other, by laws fixed and certain, binding upon the whole people, being the will of the whole people, deliberately expressed in the mode established by fundamental laws, and openly promulgated, by which, and by which alone, every citizen is entitled to seek his rights, and bound to regulate his conduct. And this description applies not only to his civil rights, but emphatically to those, which in a much higher degree awaken the interest and engage the affections of freemen, because they are the only safe pledge and guaranty of all the rest; I mean his political rights.

In a mere naked, absolute despotism, whatever appearance it may exhibit of splendor or of greatness, it is manifest that law and its professors, would be entirely out of place. A stern, inexorable, or capricious will, stands in the place of reason, of justice, and principle. Both legislation and jurisprudence are lamentably concise. *Sic volo, sic jubeo; stat pro ratione voluntas.* . . .

But whilst a simple despotism, as the extreme of arbitrary government, seems incompatible with the very existence of laws, yet fortunately for the dignity and happiness of mankind, it can hardly exist in a state of society, advanced beyond the first steps in the progress of civilization. The possession of property, though held by the frailest tenure, the necessary participation of military power, the influence which even inferior agents may acquire, must, to a certain extent, soften the most odious features of absolute despotism. Still it is obvious, that where arbitrary and uncontrolled power forms the basis, and determines the predominant character of government; where the people have imbibed its principles, acknowledged its maxims, and submitted to its dominion; although laws may exist, and although they may be administered with some decent regard to equitable principles, and the dictates of natural justice, so far as they regard the personal and civil rights of subjects, they are either silent or treacherous, in regard to every principle and maxim which affects their political rights, and the relation between sovereign and subject. Stripped of her highest prerogative, that of regulating and limiting the powers of the government, and establishing the rights and duties of subjects, upon fixed principles, the law ceases to be regarded with that entire respect and veneration, which she so justly commands, in the hearts of freemen. . . .

Under the early feudal institutions of Europe, originating in a state of society, little advanced beyond that of barbarism, in which military authority alone was regarded with much respect, there were some rude notions of liberty and equal rights, and some restraint was imposed upon the unlimited powers of the monarch, by the privileges asserted on the part of the feudal aristocracy, supported by military force. In most of the continental nations of Europe, where the powers of the feudal aristocracy have gradually yielded to the increasing power of the throne, until the principle of unlimited monarchy has been fully established, the civil law has been received and adopted as an entire system, and acknowledged as of absolute authority. In England, on the contrary, where, from her insular situation, and from a series of fortunate and extraordinary events, which it is unnecessary to recapitulate, a free government has been established upon the basis of a similar feudal monarchy and aristocracy, the civil law, from its first introduction, was regarded by her barons with extreme jealousy. Their stern determination to reject what they considered as its corrupting influence, was expressed in the memorable response, *nolumus leges Angliæ mutare*. So jealous, indeed, were the good people of England, of the political heresies of the civil law, that they resisted, with great earnestness, the adoption of those principles of equity, in the private relations of society, which have since been acknowledged as of unquestionable soundness. . . .

In thus pointing out the marked and radical distinction, between the theory and principle of free and arbitrary forms of government, I am far from intimating that the one is wholly destitute of good, or the other free from imperfection. The existence of arbitrary government presupposes an entire control of the military strength of a country, the capacity to enforce a strict execution of the criminal law, and the most rigorous regulations of police, all calculated to secure an internal tranquillity, which is not without its charms, to the cautious, the timid, and the weak. On the other hand, a free government, whatever be its forms, and however wisely framed, is still subject to the weakness and imperfection incident to all human productions. It depends essentially for its execution and utility, upon the general intelligence of the people, upon public virtue and moderation, a noble disregard of private, selfish, and personal interests, and a sincere respect for the equal rights of others, and the best good of the whole. The unbounded latitude of public discussion, which its condition implies, upon all those subjects, which most deeply engage the passions and interests of men, may sometimes lead to a blind and enthusiastic zeal, which may be productive of great violence, oppression, and injustice.

But the true point of view in which the obvious distinction in the principle and practice of the two systems, ought to be regarded by freemen, and which must always cherish the hopes and sustain the efforts of freemen, is this. Under an arbitrary government, the corrupting influence of uncontrolled power on the hearts of those who exercise it, the discouragement of education and general intelligence, among the great body of the people, the debasing effect produced by the employment of physical force and coercion as the means and instrument of governing, the discouragement of patriotism and public virtue, by rendering them useless or contemptible, the repression of enterprise, industry, and intellectual exertion, by the establishment of artificial ranks; these circumstances produce a perpetual tendency on the part of the people to degradation, and on the part of the government to corruption and degeneracy.

Whilst, under a free government, every advance in general intelligence and improvement, adds something to the strength, security, and perfection of its institutions; all the aspirings of the most gifted minds are awakened and encouraged, all the efforts of enterprise are sustained by the assurance that its rewards are near and certain, that all the honors and privileges which society can confer, are open to those who, by their virtues, talents, and public services, shall best deserve them. These circumstances have a constant tendency to advance society to the highest state of moral and intellectual improvement, of which it is capable, and to ensure the greatest happiness of the greatest numbers.

Perhaps, gentlemen, in thus enlarging upon the nature and principles of government, it may appear that I am departing too widely from that range of topics, which properly belong to the place and to the occasion. But, if I am not entirely mistaken, the practical consequences, to be drawn from this view of the supremacy of law, in a free government, and the immediate and direct influence which this consideration must necessarily exert upon the character, condition, and duties of those who are professionally engaged in its actual administration, this must be a subject of deep and peculiar interest to the American lawyer. Our government, throughout its entire fabric, professes to be a free, representative government. It is peculiarly, exclusively, and emphatically a government of laws. The constitutions of the United States, and of the several states, with all their provisions and limitations, are regarded, and very properly regarded, as a part of the laws. Indeed they possess this character in a peculiar and eminent degree, because they are of general obligation, of a fixed and determinate character, controlling and modifying all the ordinary acts of legislation, binding and imperative upon all courts and tribunals of justice, and subject to be repealed or changed only by a peculiar and complicated mode, in which the deliberate will of the whole people is cautiously expressed. To these fundamental laws, every individual citizen has a right to appeal, and does constantly appeal, in the discussion and establishment of his rights, civil as well as political. In an equal degree, they regulate and control the highest functions of government, determine the just sources and limits, and regulate the distribution of all powers, executive, legislative, and judicial. These principles may, at any time, be drawn in question before the tribunals of justice, and are subject to the same rules of judicial interpretation, with all other legal provisions. It is difficult to conceive of the vast extent, to which this consideration enlarges the field of American jurisprudence, and increases the functions, and elevates the duties and character of the American lawyer.

AN INSTRUMENTALITY OF THE STATE

Rufus Choate

The fame of great advocates, so far as it rests on courtroom performance, has a precarious basis. Their reputation rarely outlives the generation which witnessed their triumphs.

Rufus Choate (1799–1859) was a legend in his own day. His political positions were conservative: "I do not believe that it is the greatest good to the slave or the free that four million of slaves should be turned loose in all their ignorance, poverty and degradation to trust to luck for a home and a living." Nevertheless, he emerges as a stormy, impetuous person, "Southern and Italian" in temperament with an "unearthly glance of the eye." He was a master at cross-examination. He was popularly supposed to fascinate the jury as a snake does a bird, and the story is told that no client he defended in a criminal action was ever convicted. Though Wendell Phillips said he was "a monkey in convulsions," his spectacular dramatic effects contributed largely to his fame as an orator and he was constantly in demand as a lecturer on the lyceum platform.

In the speech which follows, Choate expresses his respect for "the jurist as jurist." For him the practice of the law came before politics, judgeships, and a professorship of law at Harvard. It seemed to him at once the most stimulating career and the best way of serving the state. His career was closely identified with Webster—from the time the Dartmouth College peroration made a lasting impression, through Webster's attendance at the valedictory address Choate delivered at Dartmouth in 1819, his filling the Senate seat vacated by Webster in 1841 when he became Secretary of State, his defense of Webster's conduct in the McLeod case, and his dramatic appeal in 1852 to the Whigs for the nomination of Webster for the Presidency.

As a lawyer he did not rely on inspiration alone; his preparation for trial was famous: he once defined a lawyer's vacation as the period between putting a question to the witness and hearing the answer. Although Choate's services were much in demand—his largest recorded fee for a single case was $2,500, and his greatest annual income $22,000—his cases were not important in writing legal history as were those of his teachers Webster and Wirt. He captured the imagination of his contemporaries, but he now holds a position he would not particularly have relished—a figure

*gifted with a poetic intensity and eloquence, which the recorded words
alone are not sufficient to convey.*

THERE ARE REASONS without number why we should love and honor our
noble profession, and should be grateful for the necessity or felicity or
accident which called us to its service.

But of these there is one, I think, which, rightly apprehended, ought to
be uppermost in every lawyer's mind, on which he cannot dwell too thought-
fully and too anxiously; to which he should resort always to expand and
erect his spirit and to keep himself up, if I may say so, to the height of his
calling; from which he has a right to derive, in every moment of weariness
or distaste or despondency—not an occasion of pride, but—ceaseless admonitions to duty and incentives to hope. And that reason is, that better
than any other, or as well as any other position or business in the whole
subordination of life, his profession enables him to *serve the State.* As well
as any other, better than any other profession or business or sphere, more
directly, more palpably, it enables and commands him to perform certain
grand and difficult and indispensable duties of patriotism,—certain grand,
difficult, and indispensable duties to our endeared and common native land.

Turning for the present, then, from other aspects of the profession,
survey it under this. Certainly it presents no nobler aspect. It presents none
so well adapted—I do not say, to make us vain of it, but—to make us fit
for it, to make us equal to it, to put us on turning it to its utmost account,
and working out its whole vast and various and highest utilities. It raises it
from a mere calling by which bread, fame, and social place may be earned,
to a function by which the republic may be served. It raises it from a
dexterous art and a subtle and flexible science—from a cunning logic, a
gilded rhetoric, and an ambitious learning, wearing the purple robe of the
sophists, and letting itself to hire—to the dignity of almost a department of
government,—an instrumentality of the State for the well-being and conservation of the State. Consider then the position and functions of the American Bar in the Commonwealth.

I make haste to say that it is not at all because the legal profession
may be thought to be peculiarly adapted to fit a man for what is technically
called "public life," and to afford him a ready, too ready an introduction to
it,—it is not on any such reason as this that I shall attempt to maintain the
sentiment which I have advanced. It is not by enabling its members to leave
it and become the members of a distinct profession,—it is not thus that
in the view which I could wish to exhibit, it serves the State. It is not the
jurist turned statesman whom I mean to hold up to you as useful to the
republic,—although jurists turned statesmen have illustrated every page,

Rufus Choate, "The Position and Functions of the American Bar, as an Element
of Conservatism in the State (1845)," *The Works of Rufus Choate*, I (1862), p. 414.

every year of our annals, and have taught how admirably the school of
the law can train the mind and heart for the service of constitutional liberty
and the achievement of civil honor. It is not the jurist turned statesman; it
is the jurist as jurist; it is the jurist remaining jurist; it is the bench, the
magistracy, the bar,—the profession as a profession, and in its professional
character,—a class, a body, of which I mean exclusively to speak; and my
position is, that as such it holds, or may aspire to hold, a place, and per-
forms a function of peculiar and vast usefulness in the American Commonwealth.

Let me premise, too, that instead of diffusing myself in a display of all
the modes by which the profession of the law may claim to serve the State,
I shall consider but a single one, and that is its agency as an element of
conservation. The position and functions of the American Bar, then, as an
element of conservation in the State,—this precisely and singly is the topic
to which I invite your attention.

And is not the profession such an element of conservation? Is not this
its characteristical office and its appropriate praise? Is it not so that in its
nature, in its functions, in the intellectual and practical habits which it
forms, in the opinions to which it conducts, in all its tendencies and influences of speculation and action, it is and ought to be professionally and
peculiarly such an element and such an agent,—that it contributes, or ought
to be held to contribute, more than all things else, or as much as any thing
else, to preserve our organic forms, our civil and social order, our public
and private justice, our constitutions of government,—even the Union itself?
In these crises through which our liberty is to pass, may not, must not, this
function of conservatism become more and more developed, and more and
more operative? May it not one day be written, for the praise of the American Bar, that it helped to keep the true idea of the State alive and germinant
in the American mind; that it helped to keep alive the sacred sentiments of
obedience and reverence and justice, of the supremacy of the calm and
grand reason of the law over the fitful will of the individual and the crowd;
that it helped to withstand the pernicious sophism that the successive
generations, as they come to life, are but as so many successive flights of
summer flies, without relations to the past or duties to the future, and
taught instead that all—all the dead, the living, the unborn—were one
moral person,—one for action, one for suffering, one for responsibility,—
that the engagements of one age may bind the conscience of another; the
glory or the shame of a day may brighten or stain the current of a thousand
years of continuous national being? . . .

There are nations, I make no question, whose history, condition, and
dangers call them to a different work. There are those whom every thing
in their history, condition, and dangers admonishes to reform fundamen-
tally, if they would be saved. . . . But with us the age of this mode and this
degree of reform is over; its work is done. . . . We need reform enough,
Heaven knows; but it is the reformation of our individual selves, the better-

ing of our personal natures; it is a more intellectual industry; it is a more diffused, profound, and graceful, popular, and higher culture; it is a wider development of the love and discernment of the beautiful in form, in color, in speech, and in the soul of man,—this is what we need,—personal, moral, mental reform,—not civil—not political! No, no! Government, substantially as it is; jurisprudence, substantially as it is; the general arrangements of liberty, substantially as they are; the Constitution and the Union, exactly as they are,—this is to be wise, according to the wisdom of America.

To the conservation, then, of this general order of things, I think the profession of the Bar may be said to be assigned, for this reason, among others,—the only one which I shall seek to develop,—that its studies and employments tend to form in it and fit it to diffuse and impress on the popular mind a class of opinions—one class of opinions—which are indispensable to conservation. Its studies and offices train and arm it to counteract exactly that specific system of opinions by which our liberty must die, and to diffuse and impress those by which it may be kept alive. . . . There are sentiments concerning the true idea of the State, concerning law, concerning liberty, concerning justice, so active, so mortal, that if they pervade and taint the general mind, and transpire in practical politics, the commonwealth is lost already. . . .

And now what are these sentiments and opinions from which the public mind of America is in danger, and which the studies and offices of our profession have fitted us and impose on us the duty to encounter and correct?

In the first place, it has been supposed that there might be detected, not yet in the general mind, but in what may grow to be the general mind, a singularly inadequate idea of the State as an unchangeable, indestructible, and, speaking after the manner of men, an immortal thing. . . . The tendency appears to be to regard the whole concern as an association altogether at will, and at the will of everybody. Its boundary lines, its constituent numbers, its physical, social, and constitutional identity, its polity, its law, its continuance for ages, its dissolution,—all these seem to be held in the nature of so many open questions. . . . It might almost seem to be growing to be our national humor to hold ourselves free at every instant, to be and do just what we please, go where we please, stay as long as we please and no longer; and that the State itself were held to be no more than an encampment of tents on the great prairie, pitched at sundown, and struck to the sharp crack of the rifle next morning, instead of a structure, stately and eternal, in which the generations may come, one after another, to the great gift of this social life.

On such sentiments as these, how can a towering and durable fabric be set up? To use the metaphor of Bacon, on such soil how can "greatness be sown"? How unlike the lessons of the masters, at whose feet you are bred! The studies of our profession have taught us that the State is framed for a duration without end,—without end—till the earth and the heavens be no more. *Sic constituta civitas ut eterna!* In the eye and contemplation of law, its masses may die; its own corporate being can never die. . . .

In the next place, it has been thought that there was developing itself in the general sentiment, and in the practical politics of the time, a tendency towards one of those great changes by which free States have oftenest perished,—a tendency to push to excess the distinctive and characteristic principles of our system, whereby, as Aristotle has said, governments usually perish,—a tendency towards transition from the republican to the democratical era, of the history and epochs of liberty.

Essentially and generally, it would be pronounced by those who discern it a tendency to erect the actual majority of the day into the *de jure* and actual government of the day. . . .

It is said, then, that you may remark this tendency, first, in an inclination to depreciate the uses and usurp the functions of those organic forms in which the regular, definite, and legally recognized powers of the State are embodied,—to depreciate the uses and usurp the function of written constitutions, limitations on the legislature, the distribution of government into departments, the independence of the judiciary, the forms of orderly proceeding, and all the elaborate and costly apparatus of checks and balances, by which, as I have said, we seek to secure a government of laws and not of men. . . .

And now am I misled by the influence of vocation, when I venture to suppose that the profession of the Bar may do somewhat—should be required to do somewhat—to preserve the true proportion of liberty to organization,—to moderate and to disarm that eternal antagonism?

These "organic forms" of our system,—are they not in some just sense committed to your professional charge and care? In this sense, and to this extent, does not your profession approach to, and blend itself with, one, and that not the least in dignity and usefulness, of the departments of statesmanship? Are you not thus statesmen while you are lawyers, and because you are lawyers? These constitutions of government by which a free people have had the virtue and the sense to restrain themselves,—these devices of profound wisdom and a deep study of man, and of the past, by which they have meant to secure the ascendency of the just, lofty, and wise, over the fraudulent, low, and insane, in the long run of our practical politics,—these temperaments by which justice is promoted, and by which liberty is made possible and may be made immortal,—and this *jus publicum*, this great written code of public law,—are they not a part, in the strictest and narrowest sense, of the appropriate science of your profession? More than for any other class or calling in the community, is it not for you to study their sense, comprehend their great uses, and explore their historical origin and illustrations,—to so hold them up as shields, that no act of legislature, no judgment of court, no executive proclamation, no order of any functionary of any description, shall transcend or misconceive them,—to so hold them up before your clients and the public, as to keep them at all times living, intelligible, and appreciated in the universal mind?

Something such has, in all the past periods of our history, been one of the functions of the American Bar. To vindicate the true interpretation of the charters of the colonies, to advise what forms of polity, what systems of jurisprudence, what degree and what mode of liberty these charters permitted,—to detect and expose that long succession of infringement which grew at last to the Stamp Act and Tea Tax, and compelled us to turn from broken charters to national independence,—to conduct the transcendent controversy which preceded the Revolution, that grand appeal to the reason of civilization,—this was the work of our first generation of lawyers. To construct the American constitutions,—the higher praise of the second generation. I claim it in part for the sobriety and learning of the American Bar; for the professional instinct towards the past; for the professional appreciation of order, forms, obedience, restraints; for the more than professional, the profound and wide intimacy with the history of all liberty, classical, mediæval, and, above all, of English liberty,—I claim it in part for the American Bar that, springing into existence by revolution,—revolution, which more than any thing and all things lacerates and discomposes the popular mind,—justifying that revolution only on a strong principle of natural right, with not one single element or agent of monarchy or aristocracy on our soil or in our blood,—I claim it for the Bar that the constitutions of America so nobly closed the series of our victories! These constitutions owe to the Bar more than their terse and exact expression and systematic arrangements; they owe to it, in part, too, their elements of permanence; their felicitous reconciliation of universal and intense liberty with forms to enshrine and regulations to restrain it; their Anglo-Saxon sobriety and gravity conveyed in the genuine idiom, suggestive of the grandest civil achievements of that unequalled race. To interpret these constitutions, to administer and maintain them, this is the office of our age of the profession. Herein have we somewhat wherein to glory; hereby we come into the class and share in the dignity of founders of States, of restorers of States, of preservers of States.

A SEPARATE RANK IN SOCIETY

Alexis de Tocqueville

Alexis de Tocqueville was the keenest observer of the United States during its formative era. Democracy in America *was originally published in two volumes in French in 1835 and 1840. The design of his work: "I do not*

*know whether I have succeeded in making known what I saw in America,
but I am certain that such has been my sincerest desire, and that I have
never, knowingly, molded facts to ideas, instead of ideas to facts." After
brilliant accomplishments at the lycée in Metz, de Tocqueville returned to
Paris to pursue the study of law. At twenty, he completed his legal preparation, and at twenty-two was appointed, by royal patent, to a judgeship
in the law courts of Versailles. Assigned the task of studying the American
penal system, de Tocqueville departed for America in 1831 with his
fellow magistrate and friend, Gustave de Beaumont. Their subsequent
study,* The American Penal System and Its Application in France, *satisfied
even the French demand for precise analysis and detail, and established
de Tocqueville as an authority on prison systems and penal law. When
de Tocqueville resigned his magistracy to write* Democracy in America *he
was already well qualified by training and experience to speak on the
subject of law and lawyers in the new world.*

IN VISITING the Americans and studying their laws, we perceive that the
authority they have entrusted to members of the legal profession, and
the influence that these individuals exercise in the government, are the
most powerful existing security against the excesses of democracy. This
effect seems to me to result from a general cause, which it is useful to
investigate, as it may be reproduced elsewhere. . . .

Men who have made a special study of the laws derive from this occupation certain habits of order, a taste for formalities, and a kind of
instinctive regard for the regular connection of ideas, which naturally
render them very hostile to the revolutionary spirit and the unreflecting
passions of the multitude.

The special information that lawyers derive from their studies ensures
them a separate rank in society, and they constitute a sort of privileged
body in the scale of intellect. This notion of their superiority perpetually
recurs to them in the practice of their profession: they are the masters of a
science which is necessary, but which is not very generally known; they
serve as arbiters between the citizens; and the habit of directing to their
purpose the blind passions of parties in litigation inspires them with a
certain contempt for the judgment of the multitude. Add to this that they
naturally constitute *a body*; not by any previous understanding, or by an
agreement that directs them to a common end; but the analogy of their
studies and the uniformity of their methods connect their minds as a common interest might unite their endeavors.

Some of the tastes and the habits of the aristocracy may consequently
be discovered in the characters of lawyers. They participate in the same
instinctive love of order and formalities; and they entertain the same repugnance to the actions of the multitude, and the same secret contempt of the
government of the people. I do not mean to say that the natural propensities

Alexis de Tocqueville, *Democracy in America* (1956), p. 272.

of lawyers are sufficiently strong to sway them irresistibly; for they, like most other men, are governed by their private interests, and especially by the interests of the moment. . . .

I do not, then, assert that *all* the members of the legal profession are at *all* times the friends of order and the opponents of innovation, but merely that most of them are usually so. In a community in which lawyers are allowed to occupy without opposition that high station which naturally belongs to them, their general spirit will be eminently conservative and anti-democratic. When an aristocracy excludes the leaders of that profession from its ranks, it excites enemies who are the more formidable as they are independent of the nobility by their labors and feel themselves to be their equals in intelligence though inferior in opulence and power. But whenever an aristocracy consents to impart some of its privileges to these same individuals, the two classes coalesce very readily and assume, as it were, family interests. . . .

The government of democracy is favorable to the political power of lawyers; for when the wealthy, the noble, and the prince are excluded from the government, the lawyers take possession of it, in their own right, as it were, since they are the only men of information and sagacity, beyond the sphere of the people, who can be the object of the popular choice. If, then, they are led by their tastes towards the aristocracy and the prince, they are brought in contact with the people by their interests. They like the government of democracy without participating in its propensities and without imitating its weaknesses; whence they derive a twofold authority from it and over it. The people in democratic states do not mistrust the members of the legal profession, because it is known that they are interested to serve the popular cause; and the people listen to them without irritation, because they do not attribute to them any sinister designs. The lawyers do not, indeed, wish to overthrow the institutions of democracy, but they constantly endeavor to turn it away from its real direction by means that are foreign to its nature. Lawyers belong to the people by birth and interest, and to the aristocracy by habit and taste; they may be looked upon as the connecting link between the two great classes of society.

The profession of the law is the only aristocratic element that can be amalgamated without violence with the natural elements of democracy and be advantageously and permanently combined with them. I am not ignorant of the defects inherent in the character of this body of men; but without this admixture of lawyer-like sobriety with the democratic principle, I question whether democratic institutions could long be maintained; and I cannot believe that a republic could hope to exist at the present time if the influence of lawyers in public business did not increase in proportion to the power of the people.

This aristocratic character, which I hold to be common to the legal profession, is much more distinctly marked in the United States and in England than in any other country. This proceeds not only from the legal

studies of the English and American lawyers, but from the nature of the
law and the position which these interpreters of it occupy in the two countries. The English and the Americans have retained the law of precedents;
that is to say, they continue to found their legal opinions and the decisions
of their courts upon the opinions and decisions of their predecessors. In
the mind of an English or American lawyer a taste and a reverence for
what is old is almost always united with a love of regular and lawful
proceedings. . . .

The French codes are often difficult to comprehend, but they can be
read by everyone; nothing, on the other hand, can be more obscure and
strange to the uninitiated than a legislation founded upon precedents. The
absolute need of legal aid that is felt in England and the United States, and
the high opinion that is entertained of the ability of the legal profession,
tend to separate it more and more from the people and to erect it into a
distinct class. The French lawyer is simply a man extensively acquainted
with the statutes of his country; but the English or American lawyer re-
sembles the hierophants of Egypt, for like them he is the sole interpreter
of an occult science. . . .

In America there are no nobles or literary men, and the people are
apt to mistrust the wealthy; lawyers consequently form the highest political
class and the most cultivated portion of society. They have therefore nothing to gain by innovation, which adds a conservative interest to their
natural taste for public order. If I were asked where I place the American
aristocracy, I should reply without hesitation that it is not among the rich,
who are united by no common tie, but that it occupies the judicial bench
and the bar.

The more we reflect upon all that occurs in the United States, the more
we shall be persuaded that the lawyers, as a body, form the most powerful,
if not the only, counterpoise to the democratic element. In that country we
easily perceive how the legal profession is qualified by its attributes, and
even by its faults, to neutralize the vices inherent in popular government.
When the American people are intoxicated by passion or carried away by
the impetuosity of their ideas, they are checked and stopped by the almost
invisible influence of their legal counselors. These secretly oppose their
aristocratic propensities to the nation's democratic instincts, their super-
stitious attachment to what is old to its love of novelty, their narrow views
to its immense designs, and their habitual procrastination to its ardent
impatience.

The courts of justice are the visible organs by which the legal profession is enabled to control the democracy. The judge is a lawyer who,
independently of the taste for regularity and order that he has contracted
in the study of law, derives an additional love of stability from the inalien-
ability of his own functions. His legal attainments have already raised him
to a distinguished rank among his fellows; his political power completes

the distinction of his station and gives him the instincts of the privileged classes.

Armed with the power of declaring the laws to be unconstitutional, the American magistrate perpetually interferes in political affairs. He cannot force the people to make laws, but at least he can oblige them not to disobey their own enactments and not to be inconsistent with themselves. I am aware that a secret tendency to diminish the judicial power exists in the United States; and by most of the constitutions of the several states the government can, upon the demand of the two houses of the legislature, remove judges from their station. Some other state constitutions make the members of the judiciary elective, and they are even subjected to frequent re-elections. I venture to predict that these innovations will sooner or later be attended with fatal consequences; and that it will be found out at some future period that by thus lessening the independence of the judiciary they have attacked not only the judicial power, but the democratic republic itself.

It must not be supposed, moreover, that the legal spirit is confined in the United States to the courts of justice; it extends far beyond them. As the lawyers form the only enlightened class whom the people do not mistrust, they are naturally called upon to occupy most of the public stations. They fill the legislative assemblies and are at the head of the administration; they consequently exercise a powerful influence upon the formation of the law and upon its execution. The lawyers are obliged, however, to yield to the current of public opinion, which is too strong for them to resist; but it is easy to find indications of what they would do if they were free to act. The Americans, who have made so many innovations in their political laws, have introduced very sparing alterations in their civil laws, and that with great difficulty, although many of these laws are repugnant to their social condition. The reason for this is that in matters of civil law the majority are obliged to defer to the authority of the legal profession, and the American lawyers are disinclined to innovate when they are left to their own choice.

It is curious for a Frenchman to hear the complaints that are made in the United States against the stationary spirit of legal men and their prejudices in favor of existing institutions.

The influence of legal habits extends beyond the precise limits I have pointed out. Scarcely any political question arises in the United States that is not resolved, sooner or later, into a judicial question. Hence all parties are obliged to borrow, in their daily controversies, the ideas, and even the language, peculiar to judicial proceedings. As most public men are or have been legal practitioners, they introduce the customs and technicalities of their profession into the management of public affairs. The jury extends this habit to all classes. The language of the law thus becomes, in some measure, a vulgar tongue; the spirit of the law, which is produced in the schools and courts of justice, gradually penetrates beyond their walls into the bosom of society, where it descends to the lowest classes, so that at last

the whole people contract the habits and the tastes of the judicial magistrate. The lawyers of the United States form a party which is but little feared
and scarcely perceived, which has no badge peculiar to itself, which adapts
itself with great flexibility to the exigencies of the time and accommodates
itself without resistance to all the movements of the social body. But this
party extends over the whole community and penetrates into all the classes
which compose it; it acts upon the country imperceptibly, but finally
fashions it to suit its own purposes.

THE INDEX OF CIVILIZATION

David Dudley Field

The career of David Dudley Field (1805–1894) is one of the more intri-
guing at the American bar, and still awaits its proper evaluation. He was
the first-born son of a gifted family: his brother Cyrus laid the Atlantic
cable, his brother Stephen became a Justice of the United States Supreme
Court, and he himself was prominent as a lawyer for sixty years. Early in
his career, Field was a passionate reformer; his work on the New York
codes is a lasting monument to his enthusiasm. In ironic contrast to the
following admonitions to the profession never to "prostitute itself to a bad
cause" is his post–Civil War career. He was counsel for Jay Gould and
"Jim" Fisk in the Erie Railroad litigation; from 1873 to 1878 he acted as
counsel for Boss Tweed, after a falling out with the Committee of Seventy
which initiated the prosecution of the Tweed ring. Although he was not
formally reprimanded, Field was subsequently charged with unprofessional
conduct in distorting the processes of law and in corrupting state legisla-
tures. How did the powerful energies of the young idealist come to be
directed to the amassing of personal wealth and the unscrupulous wielding
of power?

WHAT WE ARE GOING TO SAY may not accord exactly with either the popular
notions, or those which prevail among the legal profession; but we say it
confidently, nevertheless, as the result of much reflection. Some persons
look with jealousy upon the lawyers as a class, and think that whatever
they say of themselves, or of their science, should be received with a certain distrust; while there are others, who conceive that the law is perfect,
and the profession as nearly so as it can be, in the nature of things. We are
of neither class. We think the profession does, at this time, hold certain
grave errors, while we think, also, that it is naturally and in fact the first of

David Dudley Field, "The Study and Practice of the Law," *Democratic Review*
(1844), XIV, p. 345.

professions, and its proper employments the noblest which the citizen can exercise in a free state.

It is changed, greatly changed, from what it was, whether for better or worse we need not inquire. They who can recollect the men of the last generation, will recall very different figures from those which now occupy the courts. To judge from the portraits and anecdotes of a remoter period, the difference then was still greater. We have a certain veneration for an old-fashioned lawyer, such as we can ourselves recollect having seen in our boyhood. Well do we remember the powdered hair, the small-clothes, the silver knee-buckles, the silk stockings, the gold-headed cane, the steady, upright gait, the solemn countenance. There was none of the bustle of our period. Moderation and gravity were the two words written most strongly on the faces of the venerable men who walked quietly into court in the morning, spoke, when they had anything to say, earnestly and to the point, and then walked home as serene as they came. Some few portraits of the old lawyers are still hanging in the court rooms, with their placid faces regarding the new spectacle, as if they scarcely knew what to make of it. There is, for instance, a full length portrait of the late Abraham Van Vechten, hanging in the Supreme Court room at Albany; the exact image of the man, as we last saw him. Learned, good, venerable, you felt instinctively a respect for him. When we saw him last, he was arguing a motion before the Chancellor. His full Dutch face, his fine figure, for so old a man, his sonorous voice, deliberate utterance, and earnest logical argument, made a strong impression on our then young imagination. Was he the last of his race?

The bar is now crowded with bustling and restless men. Those who have the best practice, are tasked almost beyond endurance. The multiplication of law-books, and, above all, the multiplication of courts, have quadrupled their labors. The quiet, decorous manners, the gravity, and the solid learning, so often conjoined in a former generation, are now rarely seen together. A new race has sprung up and supplanted the old. A feverish restlessness, and an overtasked mind, are the present concomitants of a leading position in the profession.

But we must not be detained from the main purpose we had in view. We maintain, then, at the outset, as a fact as well established as any in the history of the race, that the condition of the legal profession is an index of the civilisation of a people. The following are some of the reasons of this opinion:

1. As the relations of men multiply, the rules which regulate them, multiply also. These relations increase with the increase of population, property, commerce, and the arts. In the primitive condition of the race there were few laws, and those of the simplest description. . . .

2. So soon as there exists a profession of lawyers, not only is their advice necessary in the more difficult transactions of private life, but their intervention is also necessary to represent the suitor and advocate his claims

before the courts. In this position everything is confided to their integrity and honor. The magnitude of the interests placed in their hands, property, character, liberty, life, the responsibility which they assume, the confidence which they receive, all demand and presuppose the highest qualities and character. No dishonest or dishonorable man could retain the confidence of honest and honorable men. The most intimate relation, in fact, subsists between the character of the community and the character of the bar. An unscrupulous bar could not exist among an upright, high-minded community; and if you find anywhere a corrupt legal profession, you find it in the midst of a corrupt and corrupting people.

This is even more true of lawyers than of public officers. Various causes may happen to put bad men into public office; a defective system of nomination; perverse party spirit, or something else. The elector may be obliged to choose between two candidates, neither of whom he respects. But the choice of an adviser and advocate, is the choice of each person for himself from a numerous body, constantly changing, and susceptible of indefinite increase, according to the demands of society. He chooses for the qualities on which he can most rely. If he be worthy of confidence himself, he never can confide in an unworthy character. They who calumniate the lawyers they consult, calumniate themselves. Just so far, then, as a nation consists of high and noble spirits, so far will the legal profession which it cherishes in its bosom, be high and noble also.

3. The judicial department is necessarily recruited from the legal profession. Judges must be lawyers, and chosen only from among lawyers. This circumstance alone, the bare fact that one of the great departments of government, co-ordinate in power, equal in dignity, and that one, moreover, upon which, more than the others, the safety of the citizen depends, is, by the very law of its condition, eligible only out of the ranks of one profession, is enough to give it a pre-eminence over every other.

The condition of the judiciary is one of the surest tests of progress. The officers of justice come into direct contact with the people, decide their disputes, know their causes, protect them, right them. Their integrity is a better evidence of the soundness of the national mind, we venture to say, than that of any other class of magistrates. The character of the judges is however the character of the lawyers. They are made at the bar; their moral characters take their complexion there. To degrade the bar leads directly and inevitably to the degradation of the bench.

Does not the actual condition of the different nations of the world furnish proof of our position? Who are the lawyers of Turkey or Egypt? What is their condition in Russia or the states of Austria? In France we know that the advocates, since the revolution, have become a powerful body: and in England they are next to the nobles.

If it be true, as we think we have shown, that the condition of the legal profession is an index of civilisation, then its learning, its integrity, its character, are matters of public concernment. With this view we propose to inquire how far it now fulfils the true ends of its institution.

But let us explain what we consider those ends to be. We conceive them to be threefold: *First.* When an opinion is asked, to state the law truly. *Secondly.* When advice is asked, to advise justice. And *Thirdly.* When co-operation is asked, to assist the right and oppose the wrong. If there be any further duties devolving on the lawyer, we do not perceive them, and less than these, we cannot think will satisfy the just demands of society.

We will now explain wherein we think the profession falls short of these ends, and the reasons of it, which we shall consider together. The sources of the complaints against lawyers we conceive to be these: . . .

First.—It has been said, we know not how many times, that a lawyer is not at liberty to refuse any one his services, and that when engaged he may properly do all he can for his client. The great English moralist took this ground, and supported it by an ingenious but an imperfect argument. Lord Brougham has even gone so far as to say, in a speech in the English House of Lords, within a year or two, that the advocate is bound to carry his zeal for his client so far, as to forget that there is any other person in the world beside him, and to lose sight of every other consideration than the one of his success.

Now to our view a more revolting doctrine scarcely ever fell from any man's lips. We think it unsound in theory and pernicious in practice. It assumes that a man has a right to whatever the law will give him, that the law itself is so clear that it cannot be mistaken or perverted, and that he may rightfully avail himself of every defect in an adversary's proof which the rules of evidence, or accident, or time, may have caused; three propositions, every one of which is without foundation. . . .

A strong mind at the bar, and a weak one on the bench, lead but too often to erroneous judgments, by which honest causes fail, and good men suffer. The argument we are combating takes for granted the infallibility of judges, and the certainty of law. Who, conversant with the proceedings of courts, does not know that neither can be counted on? Before ordinary tribunals, a great deal more depends on the advocate than most men are aware of. Truth is sometimes difficult to find. There are advocates who

> "Could make the worse appear
> The better reason, to perplex and dash
> Maturest counsels."

Let us not be misunderstood. We by no means assert that an advocate may not take upon himself the defence of a man whom he knows to be guilty. He may. He may not undertake to show him to be innocent; but he may undertake to show the circumstances of his case; to present the palliating circumstances of temptation, or of provocation, or anything else, that may affect the moral quality of the action, or determine the degree of punishment. He may also in civil cases present defences recognized and provided by law, although he may himself disapprove of the principle and policy of the law.

We have no doubt that the extent of the alleged indifference among lawyers to the moral aspects of causes is greatly exaggerated. In our own observation, we have not discovered anything like the loose notions which Brougham maintains for the whole profession. But there are instances of it undoubtedly. Brougham's speech is itself evidence enough of that—"Forget that there is any other person in the world than his client." What a monstrous declaration! sacrifice everything, every relation, every consideration, to save his client! Forget that there is a society whose welfare the advocate is bound by the highest sanctions to promote; that there are other parties, whose interests are at stake, that there are duties to society, to every member of it, as well as to the one who has retained him! How *can* a man forget these, and retain his conscience or his memory?

The comprehensive answer to the maxim we conceive to be, that the law and all its machinery are means, not ends; that the purpose of their creation is justice; and, therefore, he who in his zeal for the maintenance of the means, forgets the end, betrays not only an unsound heart, but an unsound understanding.

The next source of the complaints against lawyers, is a vicious system of procedure. How far the common law system of practice is capable of amendment, so as to adapt itself to the wants of society, need not now be discussed. The different communities which sprang out of the English people, have made more or less changes from the old plan, so that in some of them there is now a very simple, if not a very rational system of legal practice. Our observations point particularly to the practice as it exists in this State. And of that we say, that a system more clumsily devised for the accomplishment of its end, and more inconvenient in practice, could scarcely be imagined. It is an artificial, complex, technical system, inherited from our forefathers, and now grown so obsolete, and so burdensome, as no longer to command the respect or answer the wants of society. Its principal characteristics are a great many forms of an antique phraseology, according to which every controversy in the ordinary courts must be carried on; forms, the reasons of which perished long ago, and which are now become inadequate, uncouth, and distasteful. By reason of the prevalence of these forms in the ordinary courts, another system of courts has grown up, called courts of equity, practising upon another plan, professing to supply the deficiencies of the former, and yet become themselves so artificial, and withal so dilatory, that their delays and expense have passed into a proverb.

The great evil of all this can be seen at a glance. The whole course of legal proceedings has become a reproach among the people. And although the lawyers are not responsible for the whole of them, they are generally considered so. The administration of the law does not receive the confidence which it would otherwise command, and which is particularly desirable in a popular government. Causes are determined upon technical reasons so often, that a plain man may almost despair of justice.

Upon the lawyers the effect is still worse. To say nothing of the influence upon their own minds—a very serious consideration—it condemns a considerable class among them to the merest drudgery in the world. So numerous are these forms, so complicated the proceedings, that they occupy a large portion of the time of the most numerous class of practitioners, the attorneys, whose time and talents are thus nearly thrown away. There is no real utility in these services; in fact, if nine-tenths of them were dispensed with, justice would be the gainer, because she would be disburthened of a great many clogs and hindrances in her way. The labor is thrown away, and so many fine heads and strong hands are condemned to the servile, the belittleing employment of writing out old jingles of words, invented somewhere about the times of the Edwards.

The remedy for this is as simple as the evil itself is discernible; and that is, to strike out all the jargon, and substitute a plain and rational system of procedure, a thing of no more intrinsic difficulty than the forms of proceeding in other business, or before other public bodies. If that were now done, the number of lawyers might be less, but the occupations of those who remained would be more worthy of the liberal profession they belong to, and would escape the censure which they now receive.

The third source of complaint, is the tendency of their studies and practice to make lawyers satisfied with them as they are, and indisposed to change. That such is their tendency must be admitted upon the concurrent testimony of all observers. The reasons of it might not be explained with the same unanimity. Whether it be because the nature of a lawyer's practice confines his inquiries to what the law is, instead of what it ought to be, as most persons who have speculated on the subject, have asserted, or whether it be owing to something else, the fact is indisputable that practising lawyers exhibit that tendency. We say *practising* lawyers as distinguished from others. Legal writers and professors of law whose minds have not been narrowed by the practice, the faculties of Law in the foreign universities, have as enlarged views respecting their science as the writers or professors of any other of the sciences.

The mere practising lawyer, accustomed to dictate the *responsa prudentum* to listening clients, to confine his vision to single cases, to find the law only applicable to them, comes somehow or other to regard the law, as the geologist regards the earth, or the astronomer the heavens, as a fixed system, which it is his highest ambition to comprehend.

Nothing will ever change this tendency, but a more liberal course of study. Comparative anatomy has done wonders for surgery and natural history. Why might we not have *comparative law,* to place the legal systems of different countries and ages, side by side, that the lawyer may profit by the history of the world. He is, perhaps, the only man of science, who does not look beyond his own commonwealth, and to whom the history of other countries is as a sealed book.

Lastly. There appears to be a strange misconception of the relations between the Bar and the Bench. The judges too often put themselves in a false position towards the bar. The Bench is, as we have said, necessarily recruited from the Bar. It is instructed and supported by the Bar. Now, with this relation actually existing between them, it seems incredible that they should ever stand in positions antagonistic to each other; but yet this is often, if not always the fact.

We think the bar have great reason to complain of the manners of the judges. With some remarkable exceptions, there is not that suavity of deportment, that gentlemanly bearing, which, while it inspires respect, never forgets what is due to others. The language which judges sometimes indulge in, speaking to the practitioners before them, would ill become a superior to an inferior, and certainly is disreputable in an equal, elevated it may be by office, but still among equals. That such manners should have been borne so long is not a little remarkable. It cannot be for want of spirit at the bar, for no man who knows its members can doubt that, but from an unwillingness to engage in personal altercations with a judge. For no other reasons can we conceive it to have happened, that the rudeness of some of our judges has not been rebuked and repressed.

This misunderstanding between it and the judiciary, injures the profession seriously in the public estimation. The people, seeing the treatment which it receives from the judges, and supposing that they know it better than others, naturally conclude that it deserves all it receives. . . .

If we were addressing the judges, we should remind them that their success and the maintenance of their power depends much on their professional brethren. Without the arguments of counsel their opinions would lose a great part of their value. The ideas, which constitute the merit of the judgment, commonly originate with the advocate. Originality is not always an attribute of the bench. The reasons are discovered and prepared in the lawyer's closet: they are examined and weighed in the judge's seat. Perhaps the bar requires the higher talent; certainly, it has existed there always. There has never been a judge in this country who has not had superiors in his court.

We should remind them further, that of all magistracies they are intrinsically the weakest. If they have been strong, it is because they had a hold on men's opinions. For that they are indebted chiefly to the legal profession. In a popular excitement, on occasions of the exercise of an unpopular judgment, where should they find their best support? Where they have always found it, in the lawyers themselves. Let them imagine the consequence, if these were to take part against them. If it were so, it is easy to foresee that the judges could not stand the collision. Even now the tendency of the times is to shorten the tenure and lessen the power of the judiciary. As yet the legal profession has formed a wall about it, and protected it. If this wall were thrown down, the judicial establishment as it now stands, with its honor and its power, could not remain.

To these reasons, thus briefly developed, we think the profession of the law owes whatever of censure has been cast upon it. None of them, however, are necessarily permanent. The evil is remediable by the profession itself. They can establish their own maxims, and regulate their own conduct; their united recommendation would produce a reform in the course of procedure; a more liberal and enlarged course of study would dissipate the narrow prejudices which make them bar their gates against all reforms; and a resolute spirit, acting in concert, would speedily reduce a rude judge into submission to the laws of decorum.

The true lawyer is he, who has mastered the science of jurisprudence in its elements and its details, from the foundation to the summit; who has compared the laws of his country with the laws of other countries and with the wants of his own; who is always ready to enlarge and beautify and make more commodious the edifice which generations have raised, without subverting its foundations; who holds his learning and eloquence at the service of the injured; who never prostitutes them to a bad cause; and who everywhere approves himself the friend of order and the adviser of peace.

A MORE INTIMATE PORTRAIT

The diversity of conditions in those years—and points of view very different from those of the New England lawyers—may be seen in the following sketches. They include a description of law in frontier society, two novelists' pictures of the lawyer, discussions on money and the law, and a British traveler's comments on the Boston courts.

Rough and Tumble of Law

JOSEPH G. BALDWIN

Joseph Glover Baldwin (1815–1864) was born in Virginia, where he studied law as a young man. In 1836 he set out to make his fortune in Alabama and Mississippi. Here he spent the next eighteen years; this was

Joseph G. Baldwin, *Sketches of the Flush Times of Alabama* (1858), p. 47.

the setting for the frantic speculation and wild resort to law described in Flush Times. *Perhaps the only way to make palatable the grim, almost anarchic dispensation of justice was to season well with frontier humor.*

Baldwin eventually became restless again, and in 1854 he migrated to California where, in 1858, he became an associate justice of the Supreme Court.

THOSE WERE JOLLY TIMES. Imagine thirty or forty young men collected together in a new country, armed with fresh licenses which they had got gratuitously, and a plentiful stock of brass which they had got in the natural way; and standing ready to supply any distressed citizen who wanted law, with their wares counterfeiting the article. I must confess it looked to me something like a swindle. It was doing business on the wooden nutmeg, or rather the patent brass-clock principle. There was one consolation: the clients were generally as sham as the counsellors. For the most part, they were either broke or in a rapid decline. They usually paid us the compliment of retaining us, but they usually retained the fee too, a double retainer we did not much fancy. However, we got as much as we were entitled to and something over, *videlicet,* as much over as we got at all. The most that we made was experience. We learned before long, how every possible sort of case could be successfully lost; there was no way of getting out of court that we had not tested. The last way we learned was *via* a verdict: it was a considerable triumph to get *to* the jury, though it seemed a sufficiently easy matter to get away from one again. But the perils of the road from the writ to an issue or issues—for there were generally several of them—were great indeed. The way was infested and ambushed, with all imaginable points of practice, quirks and quibbles, that had strayed off from the litigation of every sort of foreign judicature,—that had been successfully tried in, or been driven out of, regularly organized forums, besides a smart sprinkling of indigenous growth. Nothing was settled. Chaos had come again, or rather, had never gone away. Order, Heaven's first law, seemed unwilling to remain where there was no other law to keep it company. I spoke of the thirty or forty barristers on their first legs—but I omitted to speak of the older members who had had the advantage of several years' practice and precedence. These were the leaders on the Circuit. They had the law—that is the practice and rulings of the courts—and kept it as a close monopoly. The earliest information we got of it was when some precious dogma was drawn out on us with fatal effect. They had conned the statutes for the last fifteen years, which were inaccessible to us, and we occasionally, much to our astonishment, got the benefit of instruction in a clause or two of "the act in such cases made and provided" at a considerable tuition fee to be paid by our clients. Occasionally, too, a repealed statute was revived for our especial benefit. The courts being forbidden to charge except as specially asked, took away from us, in a great measure, the protection of the natural guardians of our ignorant innocence: there could be no prayer for general relief, and we did not—many of us—know how to pray specially, and always ran great risks of prejudicing our cases before the jury, by having instructions refused. It was better to trust to the "uncovenanted mercies" of the jury, and risk a decision on the honesty of the thing, than blunder along after charges. As to reserving points except as a bluff or scarecrow, that was a thing unheard of: the Supreme Court was a perfect *terra incognita:* we had all heard there was such a place, as we had heard of Heaven's Chancery, to which the Accusing Spirit *took up* Uncle Toby's oath, but we as little knew the way there, and as little expected to go there. . . .

The leaders were sharp fellows—keen as briars—*au fait* in all trap points—quick to discern small errors—perfect in forms and ceremonies— very pharisees in "anise, mint and cummin—*but neglecting judgment and the weightier matters of the law."* They seemed to think that judicature was a tanyard—clients' skins to be curried—the court the mill, and the thing "to work on their leather" with—*bark:* the idea that justice had any thing to do with trying causes, or sense had any thing to do with legal principles, never seemed to occur to them once, as a possible conception.

Those were quashing times, and they were the *out quashingest* set of fellows ever known. They moved to quash every thing, from a *venire* to a *subpœna:* indeed, I knew one of them to quash the whole court, on the ground that the Board of Police was bound by law to furnish the building for holding the Court, and there was no proof that the building in which the court was sitting was so furnished. They usually, however, commenced at the *capias*—and kept quashing on until they got to the forthcoming bond which, being set aside, released the security for the debt, and then, generally, it was no use to quash any thing more. In one court, forthcoming bonds, to the amount of some hundred thousands of dollars, were quashed, because the execution was written "State of Mississippi"—instead of *"the* State of Mississippi," the constitution requiring the style of process to be the State of Mississippi: a quashing process which vindicated the constitution at the expense of the foreign creditors in the matter of these bonds, almost as effectively as a subsequent vindication in respect of other bonds, about which more clamor was raised. . . .

They had put an old negro, Cupid, in C—— county, in question for his life, and convicted him three times, but the conviction never would stick. The last time the jury brought him in guilty, he was very composedly eating an apple. The sheriff asked him how he liked the idea of being hung. "Hung," said he—"hung! You don't think they are going to *hang* me, do you? I don't mind these little circuit judges: wait till old *Shurkey* says the word in the High Court, and then it will be time enough to be getting ready."

But if quashing was the general order of the day, it was the special order when the State docket was taken up. Such quashing of indictments! It seemed as by a curious display of skill in missing, the pleader never could get an indictment to hold water. I recollect S., who was prosecuting *pro tem.* for the State, convicted a poor Indian of murder, the Indian having only counsel volunteering on his arraignment; S. turned around and said with emphatic complacency: "I tell you, gentlemen, there is a fatality attending my indictments." "Yes," rejoined B., "they *are* generally quashed."

It was in criminal trials that the juniors flourished. We went into them with the same feeling of irresponsibility that Allen Fairfield went into the trial of poor Peter Peeble's suit *vs.* Plainstaines, namely—that there was but little danger of hurting the case. Any ordinary jury would have acquitted nine cases out of ten without counsel's instigating them thereto—to say nothing of the hundred avenues of escape through informalities and technical points. In fact, criminals were so unskilfully defended in many instances, that the jury had to acquit in spite of the counsel. Almost any thing made out a case of self-defence—a threat—a quarrel—an insult—going armed, as almost all the wild fellows did—shooting from behind a corner, or out of a store door, in front or from behind—it was all self-defence! The only skill in the matter, was in getting the right sort of a jury, which fact could be easily ascertained, either from the general character of the men, or from certain discoveries the defendant had been enabled to make in his mingling among "his friends and the public generally,"—for they were all, or nearly all, let out on bail or without it. Usually, the sheriff, too, was a friendly man, and not inclined to omit a kind service that was likely to be remembered with gratitude at the next election.

The major part of criminal cases, except misdemeanors, were for killing, or assaults with intent to kill. They were usually defended upon points of chivalry. The iron rules of British law were too tyrannical for free Americans, and too cold and unfeeling for the hot blood of the sunny south. They were denounced accordingly, and practically scouted from Mississippi judicature, on the broad ground that they were unsuited to the genius of American institutions and the American character. . . .

A goodly youth, . . . Jim T. by name . . . was the best lawyer of his age I had ever seen. He had accomplished himself in the elegant science of special pleading,—had learned all the arts of confusing a case by all manner of pleas and motions, and took as much interest in enveloping a plain suit in all the cobwebs of technical defence as Vidocq ever took in laying snares for a rogue. He could "entangle justice in such a web of law," that the blind hussey could have never found her way out again if Theseus had been there to give her the clew. His thought by day and his meditation by night, was special pleas. He loved a demurrer as Domine Dobiensis loved a pun—with a solemn affection. He could draw a volume of pleas a night, each one so nearly presenting a regular defence, that there was scarcely any telling whether it hit it or not. If we replied, ten to one he demurred to the replication, and would assign fifteen special causes of demurrer in as many minutes. If we took issue, we ran an imminent risk of either being caught up on the facts, or of having the judgment set aside as rendered on an immaterial issue. It was always dangerous to demur, for the demurrer being overruled, the defendant was entitled to judgment final. Cases were triable at the first term, if the writ had been served twenty days before court. It may be seen, therefore, at a glance, that, with an overwhelming docket, and without books, or time to consult them if at hand, and without previous knowledge, we were not reposing either on a bed of roses or of safety. Jim T. was great on variances, too. If the note was not described properly in the declaration, we were sure to catch it before the jury: and, if any point could be made on the proofs, he was sure to make it. How we trembled when we began to read the note to the jury! And how ominous seemed the words "I object"—of a most cruel and untimely end about being put to our case. How many cases where, on a full presentment of the legal merits of them, there was no pretence of a defence, he gained, it is impossible to tell. . . .

I never thought Jim acted altogether fairly by squire A. The squire had come to the bar rather late in life, and though an excellent justice and a sensible man, was not profoundly versed in the metaphysics of special pleading. He was particularly pleased when he got to a jury on "a plain note," and particularly annoyed when the road was blocked up by pleas in abatement and demurrers or special pleas in bar. He had the most unlimited admiration of Jim. Indeed, he had an awful reverence for him. He looked up to him as Boswell looked up to Sam Johnson, or Timothy to Paul. The squire had a note he was anxious to get judgment on. He had declared with great care and after anxious deliberation. Not only was the declaration copied from the most approved precedent, but the common counts were all put in with all due punctilios, to meet every imaginable phase the case could assume. Jim found a variance in the count on the note: but how to get rid of the common counts was the difficulty. He put a bold face on the matter, however, went up to A. in the court-house, and threw himself into a passion. "Well," said he, with freezing dignity—"I see, sir, you have gone and put the common counts in this declaration—do I understand you to mean them to stand? I desire to be informed, sir?" "Why, y-e-s, that is, I put 'em there—but look here, H——, what are you mad at? What's wrong?" "What's wrong?—a pretty question! Do you pretend, sir, that my client ever borrowed any money of yours—that yours ever paid out money for mine? Did your client ever give you instructions to sue mine for borrowed money? No, sir, you know he didn't. Is that endorsed on the writ? No, sir. Don't you know the statute requires the cause of action to be endorsed on the *capias ad respondendum*? I mean to see whether an action for a malicious suit wouldn't lie for this; and shall move to strike out all these counts as multifarious and incongruous and heterogeneous." "Well, Jim, don't get mad about it, old fellow—I took it from the books." "Yes, from the English books—but didn't you know we don't govern ourselves by the British statute?—if you don't, I'll instruct you." "Now," said A., "Jim, hold on—all I want is a fair trial—if you will let me go to the jury, I'll strike out these common counts." "Well," said Jim, "*I will this time*, as it is you; but let this be a warning to you, A., how you get to suing my clients on promiscuous, and fictitious, and pretensed causes of action."

Accordingly they joined issue on the count in chief—A. offered to read his note—H. objected—it was voted out, and A. was nonsuited. "Now," said Jim, "that is doing the thing in the regular way. See how pleasant it is to get on with business when the rules are observed!"

Elements of a Successful Professional Income

HENRY CLAY

Henry Clay (1777–1852) recalled that when he set up in practice as a lawyer in Lexington, Kentucky, he did not have the means of paying his weekly board. But he proved successful from the start. An optimist, a booster, he took legal fees in horses and land, and invested in land speculations and manufacturing. Westerners would not all agree with Clay on the nature of legal practice in their region as expressed in the following letter. David Davis, Lincoln's campaign manager and later appointed by him to the Supreme Court, wrote: "The practice of the law in Illinois nowadays is not a very easy business, and withal not very profitable. I am satisfied that no professional man ought ever to locate himself in a county purely agricultural. It is only where manufacturing or commercial business is done, that a lawyer can expect to have plenty to do." But as Kentucky's accredited representative at Washington—he was even Presidential candidate of the National Republican and Whig parties in 1824—Henry Clay was regarded as the spokesman of the new ambitions of the West.

DEAR SIR

I have read your favor of the 28th Aug. requesting my opinion as to a suitable place to establish yourself, in your profession, West of the Mountains. There is some difficulty in advising, on such a subject, without knowing whether you mean to dedicate yourself exclusively to the Law, or to combine with the practice present or ultimate views to politics. The observations which I will make may be applied to both.

The elements of a successful professional income are population and wealth. Where both are united, in a great degree, there is consequently much business and great demand for members of the profession. A poor

Henry Clay, Letter of September 11, 1831. Library of Congress, *Burton Harrison Papers*, Box 2.

but highly dense population may supply adequate professional employment, as a great accumulation of wealth, with a sparse population, may also do. The objection to Lynchburg, I should think, is that neither of these elements exists in sufficient degree. The same objection applies to Natchez, where however there is more wealth. The society is very good in that city. There is not much serious competition in the profession, but the practice is very laborious, requiring excursions from 50 to 150 miles.

If I were to make a selection for myself I should think of Columbus and Cincinnati in Ohio, Louisville and N. Orleans. Columbus offers greater political and pecuniary advantages than either. It will in 15 or 20 years contain a population of 10 or 12 thousand, now it has about 2 or 3. . . . Society there is plain but respectable. A man who would establish himself there, live economically and industriously, throw his surplus gains into town property, . . . in 15 or 20 years would find himself rich, and, if he had a popular turn, might secure any political elevation which the State affords.

Cincinnati is the most rising City of the West, is much better than Columbus for business, society and enjoyment, and is not much inferior as a political location. There is however a numerous bar at that place, and professional services I believe are not very highly rewarded.

There is less competition at Louisville, which is, next to Cincinnati, the Western city that is most rapidly increasing. A greater amount of business is probably transacted at the former than the latter place. It is in fewer hands, and I believe that professional services are much better paid there. There are several respectable members of the Bar at Louisville but not one who is first rate. It was formerly unhealthy but is otherwise now. Society is pretty good. The character of the population is more decidedly commercial than that of Cincinnati.

There is a numerous, though I do not think generally, a very talented Bar at N. Orleans. Magureau, among the French lawyers, and Grimes among the American stand at the head. Both are eminent. The former would be regarded so at the Court of Capetian. Neither is popular. Neither profess in the public confidence in their pecuniary transactions. There are other lawyers in N.O. who make more money, but none occasionally obtain such high fees. In a single case, including his fees and commissions, Magureau some time ago received $19,000. Business is immense at N. Orleans, and it is rapidly increasing, and must inevitably increase. The repeal of the duty on sugar would give businessmen a severe shock, but the business of N.O. would still augment. Your knowledge of French and Spanish would be of great advantage to you. They are almost indispensable. Sometimes, to obviate the inconvenience of a want of them, a connexion is formed between a French and an American lawyer, but all partnerships are bad and unequal.

N. Orleans has the air, manner, language and fashions of an European Continental City. Society upon the whole is very good, and you may have any sort, gay or grave, American, Creole, or Foreign, learned or unlearned, commercial or professional, black, white, yellow or red.

Twelve years ago I had a thought of going to that city, and they offered to guaranty a practice of $18,000 per annum, and I believe I could have made it. Should I not have done better than to have been the greater part of the intervening time running the gauntlet of politics? Last winter, my opinion was asked professionally upon a novel case of insurance. I gave it, and a check was handed to me for $500 with a promise of $500 more, if it should be settled according to my opinion. It has been since compromised on that basis.

The courts are generally shut the sickly months, so that you could come to the West or go to the North, as unquestionably you ought to do, if you go there, during their continuances.

Practice is very simple. The flummery of special pleading is entirely dispensed with. Every man's complaint or defense is stated just as it is, without any regard to technical forms.

Upon the whole, I think if I had your youth and attainments I should go to N.O. and, if I did not, to Louisville.

But, my dear sir, your own eye and your own observations should decide alone for you. You ought to reconnoitre and judge for yourself. Should you determine to do so, I hope I may have the pleasure of seeing you here. . . .

Louisiana does not, I need hardly remark, offer such advantages for high political elevation, as several other States.

What Has the Lawyer Done?

JOHN W. PITTS

Fees have always been a delicate matter; in many of the colonies, persons acting as attorneys were forbidden compensation. Typical of the passionate broadside against lawyers is the following excerpt from the eleven numbers "written and printed expressly for the benefit of the people" by John W. Pitts. In his preface the author states that his first scheme was to publish his exposé through the medium of a common newspaper. "Everybody acknowledges with all frankness the propriety and correctness of the sentiments couched in them, yet the editors as is too much the case with many other people are afraid to express their sentiments publicly, lest the Lawyers should be mad." He therefore had them printed in pamphlet form (forty-eight pages) at the price of twelve and one-half cents each.

John W. Pitts, *Eleven Numbers against Lawyer Legislation and Fees at the Bar* (1843), p. 5.

To the Editors of the Recorder:

Gentlemen:—In a country like this, a country which is professed to be a country of freedom, it becomes every patriot to watch with jealousy over its liberties, and to report forthwith every evil principle or practice in vogue, that tends in the least to bring it into bondage. Under a sense of this duty, I feel it incumbent on me to notify the public, through the medium of your very valuable and widely circulating paper, of a practice in our country which, if it has not already absorbed the current of our liberties, is tending rapidly to it; and as this communication is intended expressly for the public good, I desire that you and all the editors in the State will weigh well the matter couched in it, and use all laudable means to arrest the evil, and to put a stop to that stone which is rolling recklessly through the land, desolating city and hamlet, people and liberty, and casting all indiscriminately and relentlessly into an unfathomable grave. . . .

The sin to which I allude is the exceeding lameness of our laws. We profess to live in a free country, and to be heirs of liberty, when in reality there is nothing more false, nothing more untrue: indeed, it is a libel upon the terms. But whilst we have to gaze upon and mourn over the visage of our almost deceased freedom, and to listen with horror to the knell of departed liberty, the consoling thought arises, a remedy is at hand: and may the God of Heaven help us to apply it. If I understand the term correctly, *Liberty is the power of enjoying rights without paying for them.* After the indispensable claims of a government are satisfied, if impartial justice awards $100 to me, for property, damage, or any thing else, that hundred dollars are mine to all intents and purposes; and for the same reason that any other property is mine. And if I have to pay a portion of that hundred dollars in order to get the remainder, I certainly pay tribute; and yet such is unfortunately the case in all the laws of Georgia. I burn a man's corn house, and thereby, according to the verdict of an impartial and sworn jury, damage the man $500; he cannot, by the laws of Georgia, realize the verdict. He must pay a tribute of $150 to a lawyer for pleading for him. Again, you hold my note for $1,000 for value received. I confess the claim to be just; yet you cannot collect it by the laws of Georgia without paying a tribute of fifty dollars to a lawyer. . . . Why, what has the lawyer done to entitle him to any part of the claimant's property? Why, he read the law, and made that profession his study; and it was taken for granted by the people, that he was better qualified to make laws for the good of community than a man of any other profession; consequently, the people sent him to the Legislature to enact laws for them; and what is the result? He leaves the interest of his confiding constituents out of mind; consults his own individual interest; makes the laws as complicated as his ingenuity can devise; come[s] home and declares he has done the best he could for the land; and yet the laws are so complicated that no conjuror can ferret them, nor any two lawyers agree upon one point. With this much fair speech he approaches the gentleman, and observes: "Mr. Claimant, your cases require much mental labor and talk, but I will nevertheless attend to them for $400. The sum is small for cases so complicated, but I think I can gain them; at all events I will do my best." The claimant admits the laws to be complicated, and sees himself placed between two losses, $1,600 and $400; and as a wise man he chooses the least.

We learn from this how it is that the lawyer becomes entitled to the $400 of the claimant's money. In short it is claimed on the ground of his infidelity, his ingenuity in framing laws without meaning, his little anecdotes to the jurors, and his *palavering* upon points that have no bearing upon the case under debate.

Thus *millions of dollars* are annually thrown away upon a class in the community, who, if they were awarded according to their sayings and doings, would live in a fine brick house with a fine brick wall around it. Many a poor vagrant lives on bread and water, and sleeps in the Penitentiary, that never did half the mischief to society that many of these honorable Esquires have done. And if the flood of evil is not stayed, every other class in community will be consumed with utter destruction. A poor tailor saves a few dollars together over the midnight lamp; and the next morning it is demanded of him by a lawyer to defend him in a case that he is a perfect stranger to. The farmer may delve in brier-beds and swamps until the last drop of sweat excludes [sic] from his melting frame, in order to support his family, or to provide for himself in his grey hairs; and the whole of it is demanded the next hour by a lawyer to rescue it from a robber who was detected in stealing it the night before. The pathetic cry of the perishing orphan for bread restrains not the avaricious hand of the attorney; but his ears to the mournful tale are deaf as to the zephyr of a distant clime, that passes unheeded and unknown. Known assassins, high-way robbers, and midnight thieves, are all sustained against justice, with all the eloquence and zeal worthy of a better cause; and all right, nothing wrong! when if the same doings and sayings had been done and expressed by a saint, he would be considered accessory! . . .

The remedy is simply this: Let the people of each county in the State assemble at a convenient time in their respective districts, and elect delegates to meet in general convention at the court-house in the county in which they live, for the purpose of nominating candidates for the Legislature; let these delegates be instructed by their constituents not to nominate a lawyer under any circumstances; and if one should be nominated, not to vote for him.—When these delegates shall have assembled in general convention at the court-house, let these salutary injunctions be repeated by some competent member of the body, or by some other person selected by them, or by their constituents for that purpose; and let this individual state also his reasons for thus acting. Make it also his province and duty to lay before the convention a synopsis of the laws of the land, and the burdens under which we, our fathers, and our father's fathers, have groaned from time immemorial up to this hour. Let him also show that these evils are founded in the influence which the lawyers wield in the Legislature; and if their wily sports are not checked, we shall soon be hostages to destruction and the joint heirs of ruin.

With this picture before them, the will of their constituents, their own interests, the interests of their children and of their children's children, of their country and of millions unborn, will prompt them to do right; and in so doing, they will leave the names of lawyers off their tickets; and whomsoever the delegates nominate let the people support. . . .

But perhaps it will be urged by some that the farmers, have never made political matters and law their study, and therefore they cannot legislate upon matters so intricate. To this I reply, that laws and politics, when drifting along their natural channel, are as easily understood as the ordinary transactions of neighbor with neighbor; and if on inspection they are found to be otherwise, it is because they have been perverted from their ancient course, and rendered intricate for speculation. In proof of this I refer you to Washington, Franklin, Wm. Henry Harrison, and a host of others, who never saw a law book; yet whose sayings and doings have immortality won, and established them a character for ability in all departments of state, that shall stand plumed in perpetual day, whilst thousands of jurists shall lie "covered in shameful spewing."

An Eminently *Safe* Man

HERMAN MELVILLE

Herman Melville enjoyed a long and close relationship with Chief Justice Lemuel Shaw. The two families were friends of many years standing; the Justice had once been engaged to an aunt of Melville's, who had died during their betrothal; as a child, Melville played regularly at the Shaw household. In 1845 Melville dedicated Typee: *"To Lemuel Shaw, Chief Justice of the Commonwealth of Massachusetts, this little work is affectionately inscribed by the author." Melville added in a later letter, "For the world would hardly have sympathised to the full extent of those feelings with which I regard my father's friend, and the constant friend of all his family." Two years later he married Elizabeth Shaw. Melville's admiration for her father continued throughout his life, although he never became close to his brothers-in-law, especially Lemuel Shaw, Jr. There must have been present an underlying ambivalence; his respect for the Chief Justice obviously did not extend to all members of the profession.*

Herman Melville, "Bartleby," *The Piazza Tales* (1853), p. 20.

IMPRIMIS: I am a man who, from his youth upwards, has been filled with
a profound conviction that the easiest way of life is the best. Hence, though
I belong to a profession proverbially energetic and nervous even to turbu-
lence at times, yet nothing of that sort have I ever suffered to invade my
peace. I am one of those unambitious lawyers who never addresses a jury
or in any way draws down public applause, but, in the cool tranquillity of a
snug retreat, do a snug business among rich men's bonds, and mortgages,
and title deeds. All who know me consider me an eminently *safe* man. The
late John Jacob Astor, a personage little given to poetic enthusiasm, had
no hesitation in pronouncing my first grand point to be prudence, my next,
method. I do not speak it in vanity, but simply record the fact that I was
not unemployed in my profession by the late John Jacob Astor, a name
which, I admit, I love to repeat, for it hath a rounded and orbicular sound
to it, and rings like unto bullion. I will freely add that I was not insensible
to the late John Jacob Astor's good opinion.

Some time prior to the period at which this little history begins my
avocations had been largely increased. The good old office, now extinct in
the State of New York, of a Master in Chancery, had been conferred upon
me. It was not a very arduous office, but very pleasantly remunerative.
I seldom lose my temper, much more seldom indulge in dangerous indignation at wrongs and outrages, but I must be permitted to be rash here and
declare that I consider the sudden and violent abrogation of the office of
Master in Chancery, by the new Constitution, as a premature act, inasmuch
as I had counted upon a life lease of the profits, whereas I only received
those of a few short years. But this is by the way.

A Veteran Lawyer

JOHN PENDLETON KENNEDY

*Like William Wirt, whose biography he wrote in 1849, the ambition of
John Pendleton Kennedy (1795–1870) was to combine law with letters. In
spite of early successes at the bar, a dabbling in politics which included
two terms in Congress and was capped by the Secretaryship of the Navy
under President Fillmore in 1852, and the publication of over half a dozen
books, a certain dilettantism seems to have pervaded all of Kennedy's
activities.*

*The leisurely sketches of Swallow Barn are a classic exercise in local
color description; he casts a mellow glow even on the lawyer. Philly Wart
is a charming anachronism, but undoubtedly drawn from life: the whimsy
is redeemed—rather, startlingly inverted—by the underlying shrewdness of
the characterization.*

John P. Kennedy, *Swallow Barn* (1832), p. 210.

PHILPOT WART . . . is a practitioner of some thirty or forty years' standing, during the greater part of which time he has resided in this district. . . . His dress is that of a man who does not trouble himself with the change of fashions; careless, and, to a certain degree, quaint. It consists of a plain, dark coat, not of the finest cloth, and rather the worse for wear; dingy and faded nankeen small clothes; and a pair of half boots, such as were worn at the beginning of this century. His hat is old, and worn until the rim has become too pliable to keep its original form; and his cravat is sometimes, by accident, tied in such a manner, as not to include one side of his shirt collar;—this departure from established usage, and others like it, happen from Mr. Wart's never using a looking-glass when he makes his toilet.

His circuit takes in four or five adjoining counties, and, as he is a regular attendant upon the courts, he is an indefatigable traveller. His habit of being so much upon the road, causes his clients to make their appointments with him at the several stages of his journeyings; and it generally happens that he is intercepted, when he stops, by some one waiting to see him. Being obliged to pass a great deal of his time in small taverns, he has grown to be contented with scant accommodation, and never complains of his fare. But he is extremely particular in exacting the utmost attention to his horse.

He has an insinuating address that takes wonderfully with the people; and especially with the older and graver sorts. This has brought him into a close acquaintance with a great many persons, and has rendered Philly Wart,—as he is universally called,—a kind of cabinet-counsellor and private adviser with most of those who are likely to be perplexed with their affairs. He has a singularly retentive memory as to facts, dates, and names; and by his intimate knowledge of land titles, courses and distances, patents, surveys and locations, he has become a formidable champion in all ejectment cases. In addition to this, Philly has such a brotherly and companionable relation to the greater number of the freeholders who serve upon the juries, and has such a confiding, friendly way of talking to them when he tries a cause, that it is generally supposed he can persuade them to believe anything he chooses.

His acquirements as a lawyer are held in high respect by the bar, although it is reported that he reads but little law of later date than Coke Littleton, to which book he manifests a remarkable affection, having perused it, as he boasts, some eight or ten times; but the truth is, he has not much time for other reading, being very much engrossed by written documents, in which he is painfully studious. He takes a great deal of authority upon himself, nevertheless, in regard to the Virginia decisions, inasmuch as he has been contemporary with most of the cases, and heard them, generally, from the courts themselves. Besides this, he practised in the times of old Chancellor Wythe, and President Pendleton, and must necessarily have absorbed a great deal of that spirit of law-learning which has evaporated in the hands of the reporters. As Philly himself says, he understands the currents of the law, and knows where they must run; and, therefore, has no need of looking into the cases.

Philly has an excellent knack in telling a story, which consists in a caustic, dry manner, that is well adapted to give it point; and sometimes he indulges this talent with signal success before the juries. When he is at home,—which is not often above a week or ten days at a time,—he devotes himself almost entirely to his farm. He is celebrated there for a fine breed of hounds; and fox-hunting is quite a passion with him. This is the only sport in which he indulges to any excess; and so far does he carry it, that he often takes his dogs with him upon the circuit, when his duty calls him, in the hunting season, to certain parts of the country where one or two gentlemen reside who are fond of this pastime. On these occasions he billets the hounds upon his landlord, and waits patiently until he dispatches his business; and then he turns into the field with all the spirit and zest of Nimrod. He has some lingering recollections of the classics, and is a little given to quoting them, without much regard to the appropriateness of the occasion. It is told of him, that one fine morning, in December, he happened to be with a party of brother sportsmen in full chase of a gray fox, under circumstances of unusual animation. The weather was cool, a white frost sparkled upon the fields, the sun had just risen and flung a beautiful light over the landscape, the fox was a-foot, the dogs in full cry, the huntsmen shouting with exuberant mirth, the woods re-echoing to the clamor, and every one at high speed in hot pursuit. Philly was in an ecstasy, spurring forward his horse with uncommon ardor, and standing in his stirrups, as if impatient of his speed, when he was joined in the chase by two or three others as much delighted as himself. In this situation he cried out to one of the party, "Isn't this fine; don't it put you in mind of Virgil? Tityre tu patulæ recubans sub tegmine fagi." Philly denies the fact; but some well authenticated flourishes of his at the bar, of a similar nature, give great semblance of truth to the story. . . .

Philly's universal acquaintance through the country and his preeminent popularity have, long since, brought him into public life. He has been elected to the Assembly for twenty years past, without opposition; and, indeed, the voters will not permit him to decline. It is, therefore, a regular part of his business to attend to all political matters affecting the county. His influence in this department is wonderful. He is consulted in reference to all plans, and his advice seems to have the force of law. He is extremely secret in his operations, and appears to carry his point by his calm, quiet, and unresisting manner. He has the reputation of being a dexterous debater, and of making some sharp and heavy hits when roused into opposition; though many odd stories are told, at Richmond, of his strenuous efforts, at times, to be oratorical. He is, however, very much in the confidence of the political managers of all parties, and seldom fails to carry a point when he sets about it in earnest.

Courtroom Spittoons

WILLIAM HANCOCK

I VISITED SEVERAL of the law courts in Boston, which here, as elsewhere, are held in fine large commodious apartments with abundant accommodations for the public, and a roomy enclosure for the clerks and counsel. In fact everybody has so much room, and is so little distinguished by position or appearance from anybody else, that the effect on entering, while a case is in progress, is at first rather bewildering. The seats for the jury are but slightly elevated from the floor, and both judges and counsel wear neither wig nor gown. For the rest there is but little difference between Boston and Westminster, except that in the former place counsel, perhaps, brow-beat the witnesses and banter each other a little less than at the latter, and expectorate a great deal more—which latter tendency in the judge, jury, counsel, prisoner, and audience, accounts for the spittoons—generally about the size and pattern of a church font—with which the court room, and the passages leading thereto, and the staircases, and the lobbies, and every portion of the building are liberally supplied, but which, unfortunately, not a few disdain to use.

TO DESERVE SUCCESS IN YOUR PROFESSION

Timothy Walker

Part and parcel of the industrious and overworked nation commented on by both Dickens and Mrs. Trollope is the feeling, so strongly expressed in this lecture by Walker, that a man should be and do something. The life story of Timothy Walker (1806–1856) could be narrated as a homily on the virtues of industry. At the age of sixteen he could look back on years of work on the family farm in Wilmington, Massachusetts, but no time spent on formal education. Yet when he graduated from Harvard

William Hancock, *An Emigrant's Five Years in the Free States of America* (1860), p. 166.

Timothy Walker, "Professional Success," *Western Law Journal* (1844), I, p. 544.

College in 1826 he was first in his class. Three years later he entered Harvard Law School as a member of the first class since its reorganization. There he studied under Joseph Story, to whom he later dedicated his famous treatise on American law. One of his classmates was the elder Holmes, whose sharply critical son was to comment that Walker's book was the best general practical approach to the law that he could find in his student days.

Walker was of Pilgrim stock, and it may not be a distortion to view him as a latter-day pilgrim transplanting the legal culture of the East to the then Western section of the country. In evaluating the hypothesis of the Western frontier's influence on democratic culture, this type of Eastern export—people and patterns of life—must be heavily weighted. He emigrated to Cincinnati, Ohio, in 1830, where he later established the first law school in the West and the fourth oldest presently existing law school in the country. In 1843 he launched a scholarly legal publication, the Western Law Journal. *This was a major vehicle through which the newer society confronted Eastern legal ideas, and was the forum for many articles agitating for reform in legal procedures and institutions.*

THE QUESTION, THEN, is reduced to this—How are you to deserve success in your profession? Undoubtedly the first requisite is a competent knowledge of the law. This, indeed, is absolutely indispensable. No strength of intellect, no brilliancy of imagination, no powers of eloquence, no amount of other learning, can supply the want of a knowledge of the law. Nor is it enough to know where to look for this knowledge, in case of need. You must have it at your tongue's end. Otherwise the best lawyer would be he who had the largest library. I say again, this will not suffice. You must have your law knowledge in your heads, not in your book cases. You must be prepared to answer questions as they present themselves, at least in common matters; otherwise your wit will come too late for use. The client will be gone, and the case lost. Knowledge then, ready, available knowledge of the law, is the first and indispensable condition of succss. And this, I need not add, can only be acquired by vast labor. Our profession allows no borrowed capital. We must ourselves create the stock we trade upon; not by hand-work, but by head-work; long continued, unremitted head-work. Years hence you will feel this more sensibly that you can now. Then you will be convinced, that there is no danger of exaggerating the toil required to make an accomplished lawyer; and if you are worthy of success, the strongest statement will not damp your ardor even now. But at all events, the truth must be told; and the truth is, that you could not have selected a profession requiring more laborious research. You are indeed admitted to the bar at the end of two years; but you may thank your stars, if you become accomplished lawyers at the end of ten. The limit fixed by the ancient sages is twenty; and if perfection in jurisprudence be the aim, it is not too distant. But I do not believe perfection possible. I do not believe there ever was a lawyer who could say, there was nothing more for him to learn. But I am not speaking of perfection. I am speaking only of the amount of learning necessary to make a good, ready minded lawyer. And I repeat, that you will have done well, if you shall have compassed this in ten years of assiduous devotion to study. You have, however, this consolation, that your knowledge must necessarily increase with your business.—Every case will be a lesson; your whole professional life must be one of progressive improvement; item after item will be daily added to the pre-existing sum, until the final aggregate becomes immense. To me this is one of the most encouraging considerations connected with the profession. Few would have patience to undertake it, if all the knowledge must be acquired before commencing practice. But as it is, we do not feel the vast labor we undertake. We are hardly conscious, except from a comparison of our minds at distant periods, how much we are daily learning. Whereas, in fact, we are paid by our clients for improving our own minds; and the fatigue of occupation is alleviated by the pleasure arising from new acquisitions. . . .

But while a profound knowledge of the law is the first condition of professional success, it is not the only condition. The most learned lawyer in the world would not get business, if he did not attend to it. The question with the client is, not who knows the most law, but who will manage a cause the best; and, all other things being equal, he will manage a cause the best, who devotes most attention to it. A habit of strict attention to business, therefore, is, next to legal knowledge, the most important requisite for success. Your clients must know where to find you, and when to find you. Once establish a reputation for attending diligently and faithfully to whatever you undertake, and you cannot fail to have employment. This alone, without great talents or extensive attainments, will give you a respectable standing. You may not, on this account be employed in great and difficult cases; but you will be certain to have a good share of the current professional business. And this is the kind of business from which most emolument is made, since it more than makes up in quantity, what it lacks in quality. And here let me urge it upon you, as an invariable rule, to prepare your cases thoroughly before you go into Court. This is said to have been the great secret of William Pinckney's success. He never appeared in Court without complete preparation; and therefore never appeared but to the highest advantage.—He was armed at all points, and could not be taken by surprise. And this careful preparation, so beneficial to a veteran, is absolutely indispensable for a young lawyer. . . .

I will further add, on this head, that to be successful lawyers, you must be nothing but lawyers. By this I mean, that the law must be your exclusive pursuit. You cannot be men of all work, and lawyers beside; any more than you can be in two places at the same time.—The law is said to be a jealous mistress, and in this respect you will find her so. She must and will have your exclusive devotion, or else she will discard you altogether. In this country lawyers are lured from their calling chiefly in two ways—by speculation, and by politics. They wish to make money faster than by fees, and therefore embark in speculation; or they wish to gain reputation faster than by regular practice, and therefore plunge into politics. I regard either as fatal to distinguished professional success. The law cannot be put on and taken off like a garment. It requires all the time and talents you can command; and just in proportion as you divert them to other absorbing pursuits, you discourage clients from employing you, because you disable yourselves from attending to their interests. Of the two temptations, that of politics is far the greater. Yet I confess I cannot see why. What can be more ephemeral than the reputation thus acquired? The popular favorite to-day is the object of reproach to-morrow. The idol of one party is libelled by the other. The greatest lover of the people must admit that they are exceedingly capricious in their likes and dislikes. They smile and frown, applaud and hiss, almost in the same breath. And yet—strange infatuation!—the law is deserted for such fame as this, although the great lawyer is remembered and honored when the great politician has been long forgotten. It is a noble attribute of our profession, that its great achievements are imperishably preserved in judicial reports; and thus the memory of every great lawyer is handed down, from generation to generation, to remotest ages. And yet such enduring fame as this is given up, for the transient breeze of popular applause! Well be it so. But for myself, I am content with the law: I would rather stand well even in a county Court, than be at the very head of stump politicians. And had I the most burning thirst for fame, and the power to choose what kind it should be, I would be a Mansfield rather than a Pitt, a Marshall rather than a Jefferson. But I labor in vain upon this theme; there is some unaccountable fascination in political life, to most persons, against which it is useless to reason. Be assured of this, however, that professional and political success rarely go together. To obtain the one, you must renounce all hope of the other. There may be some exceptions, but they are exceedingly rare. Devote yourselves then undividedly to the law, if you mean to be successful lawyers; and reserve politics to retire upon, when the purpose of professional life has been attained.

And now what comes next? If you have the requisite knowledge, and attend strictly to business, is any thing more wanted? Yes, you must have integrity. I know of no profession in which success depends so much upon public confidence; and nothing but the strictest integrity can secure this confidence. Much of our business consists in giving professional advice. Our opinions are purchased, that our clients may be guided by them; and to answer their purpose, such opinions should not only be learnedly, but honestly given. . . . I would dwell upon the necessity of integrity with more emphasis, because we are not reputed to have a very high standard of professional ethics. That this is, to a great extent, a libel upon us, I have no doubt. But the effect of such an impression in the community is to create the very evil it imputes. A bribe is never offered without a belief that it will be accepted.—And, in like manner, it is because lawyers are supposed to be not over scrupulous in matters of conscience, that unprincipled clients dare to approach them. But so far as legal opinions are concerned, even the most unprincipled clients will consult those upon whose honesty they can rely. In this part of our profession, then, integrity is indispensable to any degree of success. Make it an invariable rule, therefore, never to advise a man contrary to your own convictions.—In the long run, a single frank opinion against going to law, will be worth more to you, than twenty opinions dishonestly given the other way. Thus far there can be no room for doubt. But now we come to a more difficult question. When a client has a bad cause, shall we prosecute it for him? This is a question which each of you must make up his mind upon, for it will often arise. After much reflection, I have arrived at the conclusion, that a lawyer is not accountable for the moral character of the cause he prosecutes, but only for the manner in which he conducts it. If he does no more than present the case to the Court and jury in the most favorable light, without falsehood, deception or misrepresentation, it seems to me that he only discharges his duty to himself, his client, and the community, and co-operates in promoting the great ends of justice. Any other conclusion would make lawyers their clients' conscience-keepers, and require them to prejudge a cause by declining to undertake it. The result would be, that a questionable case would find no advocates, and could not have a fair hearing. For if it be the duty of one lawyer to decline a prosecution, it is the duty of all to decline; and thus a cause is decided before it goes into Court. This reasoning may be fallacious, but it has satisfied my own mind. And if I have in the first place, frankly and explicitly stated my opinion to my client, so as not to mislead him; and if in the management of his case I have been guilty of no artifice or indirection, and taken no dishonorable advantage, I stand justified at the bar of my own conscience, whatever others may think of my conduct. I desire however to be distinctly understood. I abhor as much as any one the rascally maxim, that every thing is fair in litigation. On the contrary, I hold, that the greatest fee ever offered is no justification for attempting to gain a cause by trick or chicanery; and I look upon that lawyer as essentially a knave, who practises upon that doctrine. Such then are my views of professional integrity, as indispensable to professional success. I have considered it merely in a worldly point of view. And the result is, that if there were no such thing as religious or moral obligation—if this life were our whole existence, and death an everlasting sleep—it would still be true, that the strictest honesty is a lawyer's wisest policy. Confidence and trust are the life-blood of his being; and the all-wise Creator has ordained, that integrity alone can inspire confidence and trust. Set out, then, with the sublime resolution, that under all circumstances, you will hold fast to your integrity; that come what may, the world shall always know where to find you, by considering where you ought to be found.

2. *Organization of a Professional Bar*

EDUCATION, FORMAL AND INFORMAL

It is of the essence of a profession that it assumes a better knowledge than its clients of the nature and operation of matters within its field; hence the importance to the bar in this period of developing a high degree of systematic knowledge on which its advice and action could be based.

One reason for the founding of professional schools was to refine and transmit this knowledge. A similar phenomenon is easily identifiable in our current society: every marginal occupation with any pretensions seeks a university nexus.

In the early Republic, there was virtually no academic instruction in the law; a man trained for the bar by "reading" in the office of a practitioner. While so preparing in the office of Judge Johnson in Brooklyn, William Gardiner Hammond, later the renowned editor of Blackstone's Commentaries, *wrote to his father: "Few of the lawyers about here get beyond the* ita lex scripta est. *The more I see of the lawyers and the law students of the city, the more satisfied am I with my country education. A large proportion of the bar are educated, more rather uneducated, entirely in the lawyer's office, first as errand boy, then a copyist, with the privilege of learning what they can pick up of Latin, and grammar, etc., and so they finally get enough by rote to pass an examination without really knowing anything at all of the profession as a science. One told me that he was four years reading Blackstone through, and knew very little about it after all."*

No Excellence Without Great Labor

WILLIAM WIRT

In the long literature of advice to the novice, senior members of the bar tend to prove their all-round quality by stressing classical culture, philosophy, and literature fully as much as utilitarian knowledge. The letter of William Wirt (1772–1834) is typical for its combination of the elements of both an ethics and a success manual. A member of the Virginia bar, he was Attorney General of the United States for twelve years, in which capacity he initiated the practice of preserving official opinions. He also

William Wirt, *Southern Literary Messenger* (October, 1834), I, p. 34.

had a great literary reputation for his The Letters of the British Spy, *supposed to be the observations of an English traveler on Virginia society, and* Sketches of the Life of Patrick Henry. *His original equipment, it is said, consisted of "a rapid and indistinct enunciation, a considerable degree of shyness, a copy of* Blackstone, *two volumes of* Don Quixote, *and a copy of* Tristram Shandy." *He was the candidate of the Anti-Mason party for the Presidency in 1832.*

BALTIMORE, DECEMBER 20, 1833.

MY DEAR SIR:

Your letter, dated "University of ———, December 12," was received on yesterday morning—and although it finds me extremely busy in preparing for the Supreme Court of the United States, I am so much pleased with its spirit, that I cannot reconcile it to myself to let it pass unanswered. If I were ever so well qualified to advise you, to which I do not pretend, but little good could be done by a single letter, and I have not time for more. . . .

If your *spirit* be as stout and pure as your letter indicates, you require little advice beyond that which you will find within the walls of your University. A brave and pure spirit is more than *"half the battle,"* not only in preparing for life, but in all its conflicts. *Take it for granted, that there is no excellence without great labor.* No mere aspirations for eminence, however ardent, will do the business. Wishing, and sighing, and imagining, and dreaming of greatness, will never make you great. If you would get to the mountain's top on which the temple of fame stands, it will not do *to stand still,* looking, admiring, and wishing you were there. You must gird up your loins, and go to work with all the indomitable energy of Hannibal scaling the Alps. Laborious study, and diligent observation of the world, are both indispensable to the attainment of eminence. By the former, you must make yourself master of all that is known of science and letters; by the latter, you must know *man,* at large, and particularly the character and genius of your own countrymen. You must cultivate assiduously the habits of *reading, thinking,* and *observing.* Understand your own language grammatically, critically, thoroughly: learn its origin, or rather its various origins, which you may learn from Johnson's and Webster's prefaces to their large dictionaries. Learn all that is delicate and beautiful, as well as strong, in the language, and master all its stores of opulence. You will find a rich mine of instruction in the splendid language of Burke. His diction is frequently magnificent; sometimes too gorgeous, I think, for a chaste and correct taste; but he will show you all the wealth of your language. You must, by ardent study and practice, acquire for yourself a *mastery* of the language, and be able both to speak and to write it, promptly, easily, elegantly, and with that variety of style which different subjects, different hearers, and different readers are continually requiring. You must have such a command of it as to be able to adapt yourself, with intuitive quickness and ease, to every situation in which you may chance to be placed—and you will find no great difficulty in this, if you have the *copia verborum* and a correct taste. With this study of the language you must take care to unite the habits already mentioned—the diligent observation of all that is passing around you; and *active, close* and *useful thinking.* If you have access to Franklin's works, read them carefully, particularly his third volume, and you will know what I mean by *the habits of observing and thinking.* We cannot all be *Franklins,* it is true; but, by imitating his mental habits and unwearied industry, we may reach an eminence we should never otherwise attain. Nor would he have been *the Franklin* he was, if he had permitted himself to be discouraged by the reflection that we cannot all be *Newtons.* It is our business to make the most of our own talents and opportunities, and instead of discouraging ourselves by comparisons and imaginary impossibilities, to believe all things possible—as indeed almost all things are, to a spirit bravely and firmly resolved. Franklin was a fine model of *a practical man* as contradistinguished from a *visionary theorist,* as men of genius are very apt to be. He was great in that greatest of all good qualities, *sound, strong, common sense.* A mere book-worm is a miserable driveller; and a mere genius, a thing of gossamer fit only for the winds to sport with. Direct your intellectual efforts, principally, to the cultivation of the strong, masculine qualities of the mind. Learn (I repeat it) *to think—to think deeply, comprehensively, powerfully*—and learn the simple, nervous language which is appropriate to that kind of thinking. Read the legal and political arguments of Chief Justice Marshall, and those of Alexander Hamilton, which are coming out. Read them, *study them*; and observe with what an omnipotent sweep of thought they range over the whole field of every subject they take in hand—and *that* with a scythe so ample, and so keen, that not a straw is left standing behind them. Brace yourself up to these great efforts. Strike for this giant character of mind, and leave prettiness and frivolity for triflers. There is nothing in your letter that suggests the necessity of this admonition; I make it merely with reference to that tendency to efflorescence which I have occasionally heard charged to southern genius. It is perfectly consistent with these herculean habits of thinking, to be a laborious student, and to know all that books can teach. This extensive acquisition is necessary, not only to teach you how far science has advanced in every direction, and where the *terra incognita* begins, into which genius is to direct its future discoveries, but to teach you also the strength and the weakness of the human intellect—how far it is permitted us to go, and where the penetration of man is forced, by its own impotence and the nature of the subject, to give up the pursuit;—and when you have mastered all the past conquests of science, you will understand what Socrates meant by saying, that he knew only enough to be sure that *he knew nothing—nothing, compared with that illimitable tract that lies beyond the reach of our faculties.* You must never be satisfied with the surface of things: probe them to the bottom, and let nothing go 'till you understand it as thoroughly as your powers will enable you. Seize the moment of excited curiosity on any subject to solve your doubts; for if you let it pass, the desire may never return, and you may remain in ignorance. The habits which I have been recommending are not merely for college, but for life. Franklin's habits of constant and deep ex- cogitation clung to him to his latest hour. Form these habits now: learn all that may be learned at your University, and bring all your acquisitions and your habits to the study of the law, which you say is to be your profes- sion;—and when you come to this study, come resolved to master it—not to play in its shallows, but to sound all its depths. There is no knowing what a mind greatly and firmly resolved, may achieve in this department of science, as well as every other. Resolve to be the first lawyer of your age, in the depth, extent, variety and accuracy of your legal learning. Master the science of pleading—master Coke upon Littleton—and Coke's and Plowden's Reports—master Fearne on Contingent Remainders and Execu- tory Devises, 'till you can sport and play familiarly with its most subtle distinctions. Lay your foundation deep, and broad, and strong, and you will find the superstructure comparatively light work. It is not by shrinking from the difficult parts of the science, but by courting them, grappling with them, and overcoming them, that a man rises to professional greatness. There is a great deal of law learning that is dry, dark, cold, revolting—but it is an old feudal castle, in perfect preservation, which the legal architect, who aspires to the first honors of his profession, will delight to explore, and learn all the uses to which its various parts used to be put: and he will the better understand, enjoy and relish the progressive improvements of the science in modern times. You must be a master in every branch of the science that belongs to your profession—the law of nature and of nations, the civil law, the law merchant, the maritime law, &c. the chart and outline of all which you will see in Blackstone's Commentaries. Thus covered with the panoply of professional learning, a master of the pleadings, practice and cases, and at the same time a *great constitutional and philosophic lawyer,* you must keep way, also, with the march of general science. Do you think this requir- ing too much? Look at Brougham, and see what man can do if well armed and well resolved. With a load of *professional duties* that would, *of them- selves,* have been appalling to the most of *our* countrymen, he *stood, never- theless, at the head of his party in the House of Commons,* and, *at the same time, set in motion and superintended various primary schools and various periodical works, the most instructive and useful that ever issued from the British press, to which he furnished, with his own pen, some of the most masterly contributions,* and yet found time *not only to keep pace* with the progress of the *arts and sciences,* but *to keep at the head of those whose peculiar and exclusive occupations these arts and sciences were. There* is a model of *industry and usefulness* worthy of all your emulation. You must, indeed, be a great lawyer; but it will not do to be a mere lawyer—more especially as you are very properly turning your mind, also, to the political service of your country, and to the study and practice of eloquence. You must, therefore, be a political lawyer and historian; thoroughly versed in the constitution and laws of your country, and fully acquainted with *all its statistics*, and the history of all the leading measures which have distinguished the several administrations. You must study the debates in congress, and observe what have been the actual effects upon the country of the various measures that have been most strenuously contested in their origin. You must be a master of the science of political economy, and especially of *financiering*, of which so few of our young countrymen know any thing. The habit of observing all that is passing, and thinking closely and deeply upon them, demands pre-eminently an attention to the political course of your country. But it is time to close this letter. You ask for instructions adapted to improvement in eloquence. This is a subject for a treatise, not for a letter. Cicero, however, has summed up the whole art in a few words: it is—*"apte—distincte—ornate dicere"*—to speak *to the purpose*—to speak *clearly and distinctly*—to speak *gracefully*:—to be able *to speak to the purpose*, you must understand your subject and all that belongs to it:—and then your *thoughts and method* must be *clear in themselves* and *clearly and distinctly enunciated*:—and lastly, your voice, style, delivery and gesture, must be *graceful and delightfully impressive*. In relation to this subject, I would strenuously advise you to two things: *Compose much, and often, and carefully, with reference to this same rule of apte, distincte, ornate*; and let your *conversation* have reference to the same objects. I do not mean that you should be *elaborate and formal* in your ordinary conversation. Let it be *perfectly simple and natural,* but *always, in good time,* (to speak as the musician) and well enunciated.

Plan for Organizing a Faculty of Law

BENJAMIN FRANKLIN BUTLER

Butler (1795–1858) was a partner in Albany for four years in the office of Martin Van Buren, a lifelong friend. He entered Jackson's cabinet as Attorney General in 1833, and as was customary in those days, he continued private practice. In 1838 he organized the law department of the University of New York, and served as a professor for several years. The report which follows had great contemporary influence.

Benjamin Butler, *Plan for the Organization of a Law School* (1835), pp. 5, 15, 25.

NEW-YORK, JULY 6th, 1835.

To REV. J. M. MATHEWS, D. D., Chancellor of the University of the City of New-York.

SIR,

In compliance with your request, I proceed to commit to paper, the details of the Plan for organizing a FACULTY OF LAW, and for establishing a System of Instruction in Legal Science, in the University of the City of New-York, heretofore submitted to the consideration of yourself and your associates in the government of that Institution. . . .

It is true that an institution which should furnish even a moderate amount of sound instruction, to only a few of our Law Students, would under existing circumstances, deserve to be regarded as a public blessing. But though the means of professional education in this city, are at present so defective, as to render any relief, however partial, a matter of great importance; the wants, in this respect, of our great and growing metropolis, are not to be satisfied by any half-way provisions. They demand a Scientific Institution for Legal Education, founded on a plan at once stable, appropriate, and expansive: an Institution which shall be capable of supplying to all who may desire to resort to it,—and this not for a few years only, but so long as the Law shall be cultivated as a science—the means of acquiring an accurate knowledge of its Principles and Practice: an Institution which shall be fitted to elevate the standard of professional attainments, and to exert an extensive and healthful influence on the character and conduct of the Bar, and through them, on the great interests of legislation and justice, and on the other departments of social life with which Lawyers are, in our country, so intimately connected. . . .

The great principle of division of labor, adopted with so much success in other departments of industry and science, is equally applicable to a Law School. The science to be taught embraces a great number of branches, many of which have but little connection with each other, and some of which are so difficult and extensive, as to furnish to him who attempts their complete investigation, ample materials for years of laborious research. It admits, and to be taught with the utmost perfection, requires, as minute a subdivision of labor as Theology or Medicine. In the Law Faculties of those Universities on the continent of Europe in which the Law is taught in a scientific and thorough manner, we accordingly find a professor for each of the important divisions. In some cases there are nine or ten professors of Law, ordinary and extraordinary, at a single university.

Whilst it would be far in advance of our condition and necessities, to copy the extended organization of the institutions just referred to, it yet appears to me, . . . that you will not only find it safe in a financial view, but really indispensable to the success of your endeavors, to employ at least *three* regular Professors.

A suitable classification of the students, with a view to the adaptation of their studies to their respective years and attainments, is perhaps next in importance to a division of labor on the part of the Professors. . . .

In the further application of these principles, the following has occurred to me, as a suitable plan for the organization of the school, and for the courses and method of instruction to be adopted in it. . . .

Instruction in Law Schools is usually communicated through the medium of lectures; and when properly managed, this mode of teaching may undoubtedly be made extremely useful to the student. . . . The lectures in these cases have usually been in writing, and not unfrequently prepared with such accuracy and precision, as to fit them for the press on the completion of the series. This is an admirable method of composing institutional books; and we are indebted to it for the Commentaries of Blackstone and Kent, Wooddeson and Story; but it appears to me not well adapted to the business of instruction in a Law School. . . .

The most useful kind of Law lectures, (I had almost said the only kind from which much benefit can be derived) is that which is designed to elucidate a preparatory course of Text reading previously assigned to the student, and to impress on his mind and memory, its leading principles. And for this purpose the oral lecture is by all means to be preferred; for whoever undertakes to discuss, in writing, any particular Legal subject, will necessarily find himself compelled to write a treatise or dissertation. But if treatises or dissertations are to be read, the pupil had better do it for himself, and under such circumstances as to enable him to peruse and digest them at his leisure. Besides, the rules of Law on almost any given subject, are too numerous and sometimes too abstruse, to be treasured in the memory without the aid of notes and memoranda which cannot be made whilst listening to a fluent reader. Many legal principles are also so artificial and refined, and others qualified by distinctions so subtle, as not to be understood without the closest attention, even when presented to the mind in a written page—much less when pronounced with the rapidity of ordinary reading.

The oral lecture is not only far more attractive and inciting, but it furnishes the opportunity of supplying the defects of the Text books, and of giving much useful information which would never be incorporated in a written lecture. The speaker not being confined to the precision of written language, nor to a strictly scientific examination of his subject, and his great object being to expound and illustrate the Text reading, he may select such topics as are most important, and when necessary may amplify and repeat, in a manner which may be very useful to his hearers, but which would not be allowed in written composition. Lectures, more or less of this nature, are now taking the place of the written dissertations formerly read in our Law Schools; and as their superiority to the old method is too obvious to need further remark, I proceed to point out the mode in which I think they should be given.

Each course of instruction should be divided into a convenient number of lectures, a Syllabus of which should, from time to time be printed for the use of the School. After stating with suitable minuteness, the subject and divisions of each lecture, and the time when it is to be delivered, the Syllabus should carefully specify the preparatory studies. They should consist of appropriate selections from the most approved elementary books, with references to the Statute Law, if there be any applicable to the subject, and to one or more leading authorities from the Reports. This preparatory reading should not be so voluminous, but that an intelligent and industrious student may go through it with care, during the interval between the lectures, and at the same time attend with fidelity to his office duties. On the other hand, it should be sufficiently extensive, to impart to such a student, a general knowledge of the state of the Law on the given subject. The Professor to be qualified for his lecture, must not only be thoroughly acquainted with the preparatory Text reading, but he must also extend his researches to other kindred sources; and without attempting to write a formal dissertation, he should yet draw up such a brief, as may enable him to speak on the topics he may select, in a fluent, perspicuous and accurate manner. With this special preparation, added to his general learning and experience, he will be enabled to elucidate the Text-reading, and to communicate a large amount of valuable instruction. In his remarks he should endeavor to bring before the mind, in a distinct and forcible manner, the general principles which belong to his subject; to state the leading rules, with their exceptions; and to develope the history and reason of all; with such illustrations as may be likely to impress on the memory the substance both of the Text Books and of the Lecture.

To derive from such a lecture all the instruction it is capable of imparting, the preparatory course must have been faithfully studied and clearly understood; and to ascertain whether such be the fact, recourse must be had to personal examinations. These may, I think, be connected with the lecture, by interspersing it with appropriate questions, at the pleasure of the Professor, in such manner as to put at least one question, during the lecture, to each member of the class. If it be too large to admit an interrogatory to each pupil, the object may be sufficiently attained, by dividing the questions among the students at the pleasure of the Professor. These interrogatories should be connected with the points intended to be explained in the lecture; and should in no case be known to the student, except so far as his preparatory reading may have enabled him to anticipate and prepare for them. The answers to such interrogatories, if correct, will furnish instruction to the whole class; and in proportion to their fulness and accuracy, and to the promptitude and clearness with which they are given, will confer honor on the students from whom they come. If wrong in whole or in part, they will indicate the topics on which full and accurate illustration is particularly needed, and thus draw out such remarks from the Professor, as will be likely to make a lasting impression upon the understanding and memories of all.

Where the lecture is confined to the mere business of reading or speaking on the one side, and of listening on the other, it must soon become monotonous and tiresome, unless the teacher be endowed with considerable powers of language and elocution. And even when those advantages are possessed, though they may secure for the moment the attention of the audience, it is by no means certain that any lasting impression will be made on their memories. This sort of teaching is also defective in not sufficiently awakening and exercising the mental faculties of the students. The use of occasional interrogatories will not only give animation and excitement to the lecture; but accomplish other and more important purposes. It will compel the students to go through the preparatory course, in a careful manner; and to listen with interest to the lecture during its delivery. They will frequently be obliged to reflect, to reason, and to judge; their minds will be brought into contact with each other and with the mind of their teacher; and as the answers made to the questions which may be put to them, will furnish a decisive test of the industry and intelligence of those who give them, a generous and useful spirit of emulation will be excited in the class. Special recitations on the lectures as delivered, should also be attended to at stated intervals.

As a further means of promoting emulation, and with the higher view of preparing the students for speaking and writing on legal subjects, it will be useful to exercise their minds by forensic debates in moot courts, and by requiring from them written opinions on questions of law, and readings and dissertations on statutes and other themes, as circumstances may admit.

To avoid any interference with the attendance and duties of Law clerks in the offices of their principals, the exercises of the School may all be had in the afternoon and evening. Such an arrangement will also answer another valuable purpose: it will bring such students under the care of the Law Faculty, at hours when they least enjoy the supervision of their principals, and are most exposed to the temptations of a great city. The mornings of each day before office hours and the numerous intervals of leisure when in the offices, will be abundantly sufficient for reading and study.

To keep up with the lectures, to sustain with credit the examinations and other tests to which he will be subjected, and to derive any considerable advantage from the course of instruction here delineated, it will doubtless be necessary that the student apply himself with method and industry, to the studies and exercises of the School. For however able or unwearied may be the exertions of his teachers, his improvement will mainly depend on his own capacity and diligence. But this is an unavoidable condition of every scheme which may be projected for instruction in the science of the Law. Every man who is at all acquainted with the nature and history of the Legal Profession, will admit, that without a considerable degree of intellect, and a large amount of industry and perseverance, it is impossible to acquire even a moderate knowledge of its Principles and Practice. In a Law School well conducted on the plan above sketched, the intellectual and other qualifications of the students will very soon be developed; and those who are more than commonly deficient in natural endowments, in industry, or in any other requisite, will probably be induced to abandon the study of the Law, and to select some other calling more appropriate to their character and habits.

Harvard Law School: Its Advantages

COMMITTEE OF OVERSEERS

In 1832 the Dane Law College, Harvard University, was dedicated. Josiah Quincy, then President of Harvard, had himself undergone a desultory training in law by way of the apprentice system, and in his address he pleaded for a thoroughly professional training. Since the law must be considered a science, Quincy wondered "how it could ever have been deemed practicable to prosecute the study of it, successfully, elsewhere" than at a university. This report, and the one which follows it, indicate the nature of the Law School in Quincy's day.

THE ATTENTION of the Committee was first directed to the actual condition of the School, and its advantages as a place of legal education. Here there is occasion for lively satisfaction. The number of students is one hundred, assembled from all parts of the Union, and constituting a representation of the whole country. Their attendance upon the lectures and other exercises, though entirely voluntary, is full and regular; while their industry, good conduct, and intelligent reception of instruction is a source of gratification to their professors.

Lectures were given, during the current term, by Professor PARKER, upon Equity Pleadings, Bailments, and Practice,—by Professor PARSONS, upon Blackstone's Commentaries, Admiralty Jurisdiction, Shipping, Bills and Notes,—and by Professor ALLEN, upon Real Law and Domestic Relations. In treating most of these branches, the professors employed text-books of acknowledged authority, to which the attention of the students was especially directed. They also examined the students in these books, and in leading cases illustrating the subject.

This system, which, with substantial uniformity, has been continued

Report of the Committee of Overseers, *Character and History of the Law School of Harvard University* (1850).

in the School since its earliest foundation, appears well adapted to instruction in the law. It is essential that the student should be directed to certain text-books, which he must study carefully, devotedly. Nor can he properly omit to go behind these, and verify them by the decided cases, letting no day pass without its fulfilled task. In this way he is prepared for examination, and enabled to appreciate the explanations and illustrations of the lecture-room, throwing light upon the text, and showing its application to practical cases. The labors of the student will qualify him to comprehend the labors of the instructor. Still further, examinations in the text-books, accompanied by explanations and illustrations, interest the student in the subject, and bring his mind in contact with that of his instructor.

These same purposes are promoted by the favorite exercise of moot-courts, held twice a week by the different professors in succession. A case involving some unsettled question of law is presented by four students, designated so long in advance as to allow time for careful preparation; and at the close of the arguments an opinion is pronounced by the presiding professor, commenting upon the arguments on each side, and deciding between them. These occasions are found to enlist the best attention, not only of those immediately engaged, but of the whole School,—while some of the efforts they call forth show distinguished research and ability. On this mimic field are trained forensic powers destined to be the pride and ornament of the bar.

The advantages for study afforded by the extensive library of the Law School should not be forgotten. This is separate from the Public Library of the University, and contains about fourteen thousand volumes. Here are all the American Reports,—the Statutes of the United States, as well as those of all the several States,—a regular series of all the English Reports, including the Year-Books,—the English Statutes,—the principal treatises on American and English law,—also a large body of works in the Scotch, French, German, Dutch, Spanish, Italian, and other foreign law,—and an ample collection of the best editions of the Roman or Civil Law, with the works of the most celebrated commentators upon that ancient text. This library is one of the largest and most valuable, relating to law, in the country. As an aid to study, it cannot be estimated too highly. Here the student may range at will through all the demesnes of jurisprudence. Here he may acquire knowledge of law-books, learning their true character and value, which will be of incalculable service in his future labors. Whoso knows how to use a library possesses the very keys of knowledge. Next to knowing the law is knowing where to find it.

There is another advantage, of peculiar character, in the opportunity of kindly and profitable social relations among the students, and also between students and professors. Young men engaged in similar pursuits are instructors to each other. The daily conversation concerns their common studies, and contributes some new impulse. Mind meets mind, and each derives strength from the contact. The professor is also at hand. In the lecture-room, and also in private, he is ready for counsel and help. The students are not alone. At every step they find an assistant ready to conduct them through the devious and toilsome passes, and to remove the difficulties which throng the way. This twofold companionship of students with each other and with their appointed teachers is full of good influence, not only in the cordial intercourse it begets, but in the positive knowledge it diffuses, and its stimulating effect upon the mind.

In dwelling on the advantages of the Law School as a seat of legal education, the Committee therefore rank side by side with the lectures and exercises of the professors the profitable opportunities afforded by the library and the fellowship of persons engaged in the same pursuits, all echoing to the heart of the pupil, as from the genius of the place, constant words of succor, encouragement, and hope.

Harvard Law School: Cost and Curriculum

COMMITTEE OF OVERSEERS

THE DESIGN of this Institution is to afford a complete course of legal education for gentlemen destined for the bar in the different parts of the United States, and also elementary instruction for gentlemen not destined for the bar, but yet desirous of qualifying themselves for public life or for commercial business. The various branches of public and constitutional law, the common law, and admiralty, maritime, and equity law, are taught, with occasional illustrations of foreign law.

The School is under the immediate superintendence and direction of Mr. Greenleaf, Royall Professor of Law in the University. Mr. Justice Story, Dane Professor of Law in the University, resides in Cambridge, and during the intervals of his judicial duties assists in the superintendence. The Royall Professor gives instruction in the Common Law, and all the other juridical studies. In every week during the term, there are at least six private lectures, and usually more; at which the students are examined in their respective studies, and oral explanations and illustrations are given by the Professors. The private lectures are on Mondays, Tuesdays, Wednesdays, Thursdays, and Fridays. Public written lectures are also occasionally delivered by the Professors upon the more important topics of jurisprudence. The academic year commences in the beginning of September.

There are three terms and three vacations in the year, corresponding with those of the undergraduates.

Catalogue of Harvard Law School (1834).

Students may generally be accommodated with rooms in the college buildings upon the same terms as undergraduates, and may, if they choose, board in commons as resident graduates, at the rate of $1.90 per week. The fees for instruction are $100 per annum, for which the students have the use of lecture rooms, the library, and the privilege of attending all the public lectures of the University *gratis*; with the opportunity for instruction in the modern languages on the payment of $10 per annum for each language studied. Gentlemen, who are graduates of a college, will complete their education in three years; those who are not graduates, in five years. Instruction, however, will be given for stated periods, as may suit the convenience of students, but without subdividing any of the terms.

No previous examination is necessary for admission; but every student will be expected to bring from his parents or friends a certificate of his good character and some general statement of his previous studies. Bonds are required for the payment of all dues to the college.

Constant residence in Cambridge is not deemed indispensable; it is sufficient if attendance is given at the regular hours prescribed for lectures, examinations, and study.

The students have the use of an extensive law library, and access to the general library of the University, containing more than thirty-five thousand volumes. They are furnished with all the books used as class books, except where they prefer to supply themselves, as they frequently will, for the purpose of making references and notes, with a view to future study and practice.

In addition to the course of reading, the students occasionally write dissertations upon subjects of law. Once in every week a *moot court* is held before one of the Professors, at which in rotation four of the students argue some law case, which is previously given out, so that they may make suitable preparation; and at the close of the arguments the Professor delivers his own opinion, commenting upon the doctrines maintained on each side.

COURSE OF STUDY

The books marked thus (*) compose the course which is completed in *two* years. The studies of gentlemen who remain longer in the School are pursued in the remaining books in the *regular course*, to which others are added from time to time, as far as the leisure and progress of the students may permit. The *parallel course* is prescribed chiefly for private reading.

Regular Course.	*Parallel Course.*
*Blackstone's Commentaries.	Sullivan's Lectures.
*Kent's Commentaries.	Hale's Hist. of the Common Law.
Wooddeson's Lectures.	Reeves's Hist. of the English Law.
	Hoffman's Legal Outlines.

Regular Course.   Parallel Course.

LAW OF PERSONAL PROPERTY.

*Chitty on Pleading.
*Stephen on Pleading.
*Chitty on Contracts.
*Starkie on Evidence.
*Long on Sales.
Bingham on Infancy.
Angell and Ames on Corporations.
Williams on Executors.
Hammond on Parties.
Angell on Limitations.
Roper on Husband and Wife.

Select titles in the Abridgments of
  Dane and Bacon.
Collinson on Idiots and Lunatics.
Shelford on Lunatics, &c.
Hammond's *Nisi Prius*.
Kyd on Awards.
Reeve's Domestic Relations.
Roberts on the Statute of Frauds.
Roper on Legacies.
Gould's System of Pleading.
Starkie on Slander.
Saunder's Reports, (Williams' ed.)
Select Cases in the Reports.

COMMERCIAL AND MARITIME LAW.

*Abbott on Shipping.
*Bayley on Bills.
*Paley on Agency.
*Marshal on Insurance.
*Story on Bailments.
*Gow on Partnership.
Theobald on Principal and Surety.
Brown's Admiralty Law.

Phillips on Insurance.
Benecke on Insurance, by Phillips.
Stevens on Average, by Phillips.
Livermore on Agency.
Azuni's Maritime Law.
Fell on Guarantee.
Bacon's Abridgment, *tit*. Merchant.
Dane's Abridgment, select titles.
Pothier on Maritime Contracts.
Collier on Partnership.
Select Cases in the U.S. Courts.

LAW OF REAL PROPERTY.

*Cruise's Digest.
Fearne on Remainders.
Powell on Mortgages, (Rand's ed.)
Sanders on Uses and Trusts.
*Stearns on Real Actions.
Adams on Ejectment, by Tillinghast.
Sugden's Vendors.
Jackson on Real Actions.

Preston on Estates.
Runnington on Ejectment.
Powell on Devises.
Angell on Water Courses.
Woodfall's Landlord and Tenant.
Roscoe on Actions Respecting Real
  Property.
Coke upon Littleton.
Dane's Abridgment—Select titles.
Hayes on Limitations in Devises.
Select Cases in the Reports.

EQUITY.

Barton's Suit in Equity.
*Maddock's Chancery.
*Cooper's Pleadings.

Fonblanque's Equity.
Redesdale's Pleadings in Equity.
Beame's Pleas in Equity.

Regular Course.	*Parallel Course.*
Jeremy's Equity Jurisdiction.	Hoffman's Master in Chancery.
Newland on Contracts in Equity.	Blake's Chancery.
Eden on Injunctions.	Select Cases in the Reports.

CRIMINAL LAW.

East's Pleas of the Crown.	Chitty's Criminal Law.
Russell on Crimes.	Archbold's Pleading and Evidence.
	Select Cases in the Reports.

CIVIL LAW.

Gibbon's Roman Empire, Ch. 44.	Pothier on Obligations.
Justinian's Institutes.	Domat's Civil Law—Select titles.
	Brown's Civil Law.
	Butler's Horæ Juridicæ.
	Ayliff's Roman Law.

LAW OF NATIONS.

Marten's Law of Nations.	Ward's Law of Nations.
Rutheford's Institutes.	Vattel's do.
Wheaton on Captures.	Bynkershoek's Law of War.

CONSTITUTIONAL LAW.

American Constitutions.	The Federalist.
*Story's Commentaries on the Con-	Rawle on the Constitution.
stitution.	Select Cases and Speeches.

Advertisement for a Course of Lectures

WESTERN LAW JOURNAL

THE TWENTIETH ANNUAL COURSE OF LECTURES will commence on Wednesday, the 19th of October, 1853, and will continue till the 20th of April, 1854. . . .

The course of instructions is designed to prepare students for the practice of the law, so that gentlemen, immediately upon their graduation, can be admitted to the bar, and enter upon the practical duties of their profession. With this view a moot court will be holden by one of the professors once in each week, or oftener, at which students will be required to prepare pleadings, furnish briefs, and make oral arguments. Besides this, there will

Western Law Journal (August, 1853), X, p. 527.

be a daily exercise, consisting of lectures by the professors, and of recitations in the text-books, which are embraced in the course.

No examination, and no particular course of previous study, is required for admission.

The students will be expected to furnish themselves with the following text-books, the last editions of which are recommended: Walker's Introduction to American Law, (second edition;) Kent's Commentaries, (seventh edition;) Blackstone's Commentaries, of which Wendell's edition is recommended; Greenleaf on Evidence vol. 1; Smith's Mercantile Law, Holcombe and Gholson's edition of which is recommended; Stephen on Pleading; and Adams's Equity.

At the close of the term, the students will be examined by a Committee of the Bar of Cincinnati, consisting of at least five gentlemen, and upon those whom they report to be qualified to practice law, the Board of Trustees will confer the degree of Bachelor of Laws.

The requisites for admission to the Bar in Ohio, are citizenship, majority, good moral character, two years' study, and an examination by a committee of the Bar. But by the Charter of this College, that examination is dispensed with, as to those who have attended the full course of studies here, and have graduated, and have studied 15 months in addition to the term.

The course will embrace all the usual titles and subjects of Common and Statute Law, Equity and Admiralty.

The tuition fee is $60 for the term, in advance. An additional fee of $5 is charged as a graduation fee, to all who take a degree. Those who have matriculated for one term, may attend any subsequent terms free of charge.

Board and lodging may be had here, in respectable houses, at from $2.50 to $3 per week.

Any additional information in regard to the school will be cheerfully given, upon application, by letter or otherwise, to either of the professors, at Cincinnati.

Ardor for a Chosen Profession

CHARLES SUMNER

Despite the letters of his student days, Charles Sumner (1811–1874) was to find law practice weary and stale, before he entered upon his great career in the Senate. "Though I earn my daily bread," he complained, "I lay up none of the bread of life." For a time he was a lecturer at the Harvard Law School—his radical views apparently kept him from a professorship— where he was a devoted pupil and collaborator of Joseph Story.

Memoirs of Charles Sumner (ed. Pierce, 1877), I, pp. 111, 119.

Law School, Divinity Hall, No. 10, Sept. 29, 1831.

BUT, to stop this vague sermonizing, I am now a regular member of the Law School, have read a volume and a half of Blackstone, and am enamored of the law. Tower, we have struck the true profession; the one in which the mind is the most sharpened and quickened, and the duties of which, properly discharged, are most vital to the interests of the country, —for religion exists independent of its ministers; every breast feels it: but the law lives only in the honesty and learning of lawyers. Let us feel conscious, then, of our responsibility; and, by as much as our profession excels in interest and importance, give to it a corresponding dedication of our abilities. And yet I give back in despair when I see the vast weight which a lawyer must bear up under. Volumes upon volumes are to be mastered of the niceties of the law, and the whole circle of literature and science and history must be compassed. . . .

Tell me what law-books you have read and are reading, and whether you have taken notes of or "commonplaced" any of your study. I have taken some notes from Blackstone of the different estates, contingent remainders, &c. As to Blackstone, I almost feel disposed to join with Fox, who pronounced him the best writer in the English language. He is clear, fluent, and elegant, with occasionally a loose expression and a bad use of a metaphor; but what a good thing for our profession that we can commence our studies with such an author. His commentaries unfold a full knowledge by themselves of the law,—a knowledge to be filled out by further study, but which is yet a whole by itself. . . .

I never receive a letter from one of my old college friends without experiencing a most pleasing melancholy. Memory is always at hand, with her throng of recollections and associations, the shadows of past joys,— joys gone as irrevocably as time. Youth and college feelings have given way to manhood and its sterner avocations. The course is fairly commenced in the race of life, and every intellectual and corporal agency is bent to exertion. There are now no Saturdays bringing weekly respites from drudgery, allowing a momentary stop in the path of duty. All is labor. It mattereth not the day or hardly the hour, for duty is urgent all days and all hours. What, then, could bring up more pleasing recollections, and yet tinged with melancholy (because they are never more to be seen, except in memory's mirror) than a letter from one who was present and active in those scenes to which the mind recurs? I sometimes let a whole hour slip by unconsciously, my book unvexed before me, musing upon old times, feelings, and comrades. My eye sees, as exactly as if I had left it but yesterday, the old recitation-room and all its occupants. My ear seems yet to vibrate with the sound of the various voices which we heard so often. But the reverie has its end, for the present and future drive from the mind musings of the past.

Judge Story is at Washington, with the Supreme Court, for the winter.

Of course the school misses him. Our class, as yet, has had nothing to do with him. Those who do recite to him love him more than any instructor they ever had before. He treats them all as gentlemen, and is full of willingness to instruct. He gives to every line of the recited lesson a running commentary, and omits nothing which can throw light upon the path of the student. The good scholars like him for the knowledge he distributes; the poor (if any there be), for the amenity with which he treats them and their faults. . . .

I am now upon Kent's second volume. He is certainly the star of your State. I like his works, though less than most students. To me he is very indistinct in his outlines. This, perhaps, is the more observable, stepping, as I do, from the well-defined page of Blackstone. Truly, the English commentator is a glorious man; he brings such a method, such a flow of language and allusion and illustration to every topic! I have heard a sensible lawyer place Kent *above* him; but, in my opinion, sooner ought the earth to be above the clear and azure-built heavens! And yet the character of Kent, as told to me, bewitches me. His works, in fact, are crude, and made to publish and get money from (he has already cleared twenty thousand dollars from them) rather than to be admired and to last. A revision may put them in a little better plight for visiting posterity, and I understand he is giving them this. . . .

A successor has been appointed to Mr. Ashmun, who will commence his duties here in July, or next September. You have seen him announced in the papers,—Mr. Greenleaf, of Maine; a fine man, learned lawyer, good scholar, ardent student, of high professional character, taking a great interest in his profession: add to this, a gentleman, a man of manners, affability, and enthusiasm, nearly fifty years old; now has a very extensive practice in Maine, which he will wind up before he starts upon his new line of duties. It were worth your coming from New York to study under Judge Story and Greenleaf next term. I shall not be here after this year; not but I should like to be here,—for I could spend my life, I believe, in this, as some call it, monkish seclusion,—but because it is necessary to obtain a knowledge of practice in a lawyer's office, to come down from books and theory to men and writs; and one year, which will alone remain to me after Commencement, is usually considered little enough for that purpose.

How do you progress in law? Write me. How do you like Kent? I owe him much. I have had from him a great deal of elegant instruction. His Commentaries are not wholly appreciated by the student upon a first perusal; they are hardly elementary enough. Ashmun said that they were written as the judgments of a judge. But when one is a little advanced or familiar with them, he sees the comprehensive views they take of the law of which they treat, and the condensed shape into which the law on their several titles is thrown. Kent is one of the glories of your State, whether you look at him as a commentator or a judge. In the latter capacity, his opinions, for learning and ability, stand almost unrivalled. Judges Marshall and Story alone, of any judges in our country, may be compared with him.

No Excuse for the Presence of a Young Person

HENRY JAMES

Henry James's amusing and wry description of his collision with legal education exposes a feeling experienced by more students than would dare to admit to it. In his Autobiography, *Charles Francis Adams says: "I never took to the law; and I am sure the law never came my way. However, I tried, establishing myself first with my brother John, and later in a gloomy, dirty den in my father's building, 23 Court Street; and there I sat for the next year and a half, trying to think that I was going through an apprenticeship. I didn't realize it, but I was a round peg trying to get into a square hole. Still, my father was satisfied." Even the great Webster, while reading for the law, doubted if he possessed the "brilliancy, and at the same time penetration and judgement enough for a great law character."*

THE FORENOON LECTURES at Dane Hall I never in all my time missed, that I can recollect, and I look back on it now as quite prodigious that I should have been so systematically faithful to them without my understanding the first word of what they were about. They contrived—or at least my attendance at them did, inimitably—to be "life"; and as my wondering dips into the vast deep well of the French critic to whom all my roused response went out brought up that mystery to me in cupfuls of extraordinary savour, where was the incongruity of the two rites? That the Causeries du Lundi, wholly fresh then to my grateful lips, should so have overflowed for me was certainly no marvel—that prime acquaintance absolutely *having*, by my measure, to form a really sacred date in the development of any historic or aesthetic consciousness worth mentioning; but that I could be to the very end more or less thrilled by simply sitting, all stupid and sentient, in the thick company of my merely nominal associates and under the strange ministrations of Dr. Theophilus Parsons, "Governor" Washburn and Professor Joel Parker, would have appeared to defy explanation only for those by whom the phenomena of certain kinds of living and working sensibility are unsuspected. For myself at any rate there was no anomaly—the anomaly would have been much rather in any prompter consciousness of a sated perception; I knew why I liked to "go," I knew even why I could unabashedly keep going in face of the fact that if I had learned my reason I had learned, and was still to learn, absolutely nothing else; and that sufficiently supported me through a stretch of

Henry James, *Notes of a Son and Brother* (1914), p. 344.

bodily overstrain that I only afterwards allowed myself dejectedly to measure. The mere sitting at attention for two or three hours—such attention as I achieved—was paid for by sorry pain; yet it was but later on that I wondered how I could have found what I "got" an equivalent for the condition produced. The condition was one of many, and the others for the most part declared themselves with much of an equal, though a different, sharpness. It was acute, that is, that one was so incommoded, but it had broken upon me with force from the first of my taking my seat—which had the advantage, I acknowledge, of the rim of the circle, symbolising thereby all the detachment I had been foredoomed to—that the whole scene was going to be, and again and again, as "American," and above all as suffused with New England colour, however one might finally estimate that, as I could possibly have wished. Such was the effect of one's offering such a plate for impressions to play on at their will; as well as of one's so failing to ask in advance what they would matter, so taking for granted that they would all matter somehow. It would matter somehow for instance that just a queer dusky half smothered light, as from windows placed too low, or too many interposing heads, should hang upon our old auditorium—long since voided of its then use and, with all its accessory chambers, seated elsewhere afresh and in much greater state; which glimpse of a scheme of values might well have given the measure of the sort of profit I was, or rather wasn't, to derive. It doubtless quite ought to have confounded me that I had come up to *faire mon droit* by appreciations predominantly of the local chiaroscuro and other like quantities; but I remember no alarm—I only remember with what complacency my range of perception on those general lines was able to spread.

It mattered, by the same law, no end that Dr. Theophilus Parsons, whose rich, if slightly quavering, old accents were the first to fall upon my ear from the chair of instruction beneath a huge hot portrait of Daniel Webster should at once approve himself a vivid and curiously-composed person, an *illustrative* figure, as who should say—exactly with all the marks one might have wished him, marks of a social order, a general air, a whole history of things, or in other words of people; since there was nothing one mightn't, by my sentiment, do with such a subject from the moment it gave out character. Character thus was all over the place, as it could scarce fail to be when the general subject, the one gone in for, had become identical with the persons of all its votaries. Such was the interest of the source of edification just named, not one ray of whose merely professed value so much as entered my mind. Governor Washburn was of a different, but of a no less complete consistency—queer, ingenuous, more candidly confiding, especially as to his own pleasant fallibility, than I had ever before known a chaired dispenser of knowledge, and all after a fashion that endeared him to his young hearers, whose resounding relish of the frequent tangle of his apologetic returns upon himself, quite, almost always, to inextricability, was really affectionate in its freedom. I could

understand and admire that—it seemed to have for me legendary precedents; whereas of the third of our instructors I mainly recall that he
represented dryness and hardness, prose unrelieved, at their deadliest—
partly perhaps because he was most master of his subject. He was none
the less placeable for these things withal, and what mainly comes back
to me of him is the full sufficiency with which he made me ask myself
how I *could* for a moment have seen myself really browse in any field
where the marks of the shepherd were such an oblong dome of a bare
cranium, such a fringe of dropping little ringlets toward its base, and a
mouth so meanly retentive, so ignorant of style, as I made out, above a
chin so indifferent to the duty, or at least to the opportunity, of chins. If
I had put it to myself that there was no excuse for the presence of a
young person so affected by the idea of how people looked on a scene
where the issue was altogether what they usefully taught, as well as
intelligently learned and wanted to learn, I feel I should, after my first
flush of confusion, have replied assuredly enough that just the beauty of
the former of these questions was in its being of equal application everywhere; which was far from the case with the latter.

Preface to *Introduction to American Law*

TIMOTHY WALKER

The stress on American texts is most characteristic of this period. There
were no strict rules as to citation to the court as there were in England,
and these books served practitioners and teachers alike. In those days when
textbooks had major influence on the thinking of lawyers, Timothy Walker's
Introduction to American Law, *based on lectures delivered at his law*
school, was especially significant, going through eleven editions.

ACCORDING TO THE CUSTOM of the times, a preface usually takes the
form of an apology for adding to the multitude of books; and I shall so
far comply with this custom as to explain my reasons for making this
publication.

    While pursuing my legal studies, I found myself much in the con-
dition of a mariner without chart or compass. I experienced at every step
the want of a first book upon the law of this country. I felt that much time
would have been saved if I could have commenced my course with a
systematic outline of American, instead of English law; for, as the two
systems differ in nearly as many points as they correspond, and as I had
no means of distinguishing between the applicable and the inapplicable, I
necessarily acquired many false impressions, the more difficult to be

Timothy Walker, *Introduction to American Law* (1855), p. v.

subsequently corrected because they were first impressions. In a word, I came to the conclusion that fewer facilities have been provided for studying the elementary principles of American jurisprudence, than for perhaps any other branch of useful knowledge.

And these results of my experience as a student, have acquired additional confirmation from my experience as a teacher. In the year 1833, I became connected with the Cincinnati Law School, at first a private institution, but afterwards a department of the Cincinnati College; and here I was hourly called upon to remove the doubts and difficulties which I had myself encountered. In order to do this in the most convenient and effectual manner, and without a thought of publication, I commenced the preparation of the following Lectures, which I read to the students, as an introduction or accompaniment to the usual course of legal study. Such being my object, I endeavored to be clear and simple, rather than to seem profound or erudite; and instead of attempting to give a complete exposition of any single branch of law, I sought to bring together all the various branches, and present them to view under a comprehensive but systematic outline, which would exhibit their general bearings and relations only, and not their particular details; but, at the same time, in connection with each successive topic, I mentioned the books containing more detailed information. . . .

If an author may be allowed to express an opinion in his own case, I would say that the chief merits of this book will be found to consist in perspicuity and condensation. As to originality, unless it be in the arrangement and modes of illustration, it does not belong to such an undertaking; but it is proper to say, that I have quoted very sparingly the language of other writers, and never without giving credit. I have, moreover, scrupulously avoided giving long abstracts of cases, though this is a very convenient method of making or amplifying law books. In a word, I have crowded as many general principles as I could into the smallest compass compatible with clearness; and, to this end, I have sought to use just such words, and so many words, as would express my meaning, and no more.

A Review of Greenleaf's *Evidence*

LAW REGISTER

There were some rumblings of a case system: Bennet and Head's Leading Criminal Cases *in 1856 was believed by them to be "the first application of this plan of discussing legal questions [by selection of leading cases] to the Criminal Law." But by and large such works were attempts to organize*

Law Register (1842), V, p. 54.

and arrange the principles of the subject. Typical was the treatise on
Evidence *by Simon Greenleaf, dedicated to his colleague, Story.*

BUT IT IS TIME to give our readers some more accurate idea of Professor
Greenleaf's work. It is presented by the author to the profession with a
natural modesty, which suggests to him the necessity for some apology
for placing it side by side with the treatises of Starkie and Phillips. For
ourselves, we require no apology. The treatise of Mr. Starkie contains a
vast body of English law, with which the American lawyer has practically
nothing to do. What is really useful in this country, and what has been
decided here has indeed been added in notes, until Ossa has risen upon
Pelion. So it is with the work of Mr. Phillips. But there are no books more
clumsy in the use, and more troublesome in the digestion, than the
English treatises heaped up with notes of the American cases. We have
before us, at this moment, an edition of Chitty on Contracts, which was
originally a small work, that has grown to be a monster of this kind. A very
well executed monster it certainly is; but inasmuch as the method of an
editor is never the method of an author, especially if they write in different countries, the editor can never make his learning half so effective
and instructive, as if he took the same learning, and therewith turned author
on his account. We would not be misunderstood as if encouraging the
disuse of English treatises. We have only said, that there is much law in
England, ancient and modern, with which the American lawyer has nothing
to do practically. We have not said, that he has no concern with its
theory. The whole body of the law of England, is, and for centuries must
be, the chief source of all our knowledge and all our proficiency in this
great science. As well might the Musselman cease to look to Mecca, as the
professors of this science in all countries in which the common law is
implanted, cease to look to England. But we are not, however, of the
opinion which seems to govern an eminent counsellor and neighbor of
ours—himself an editor of prodigious learning—who rarely deigns in his
works to cite any thing but English authorities. We hold to instructing
the young American lawyer in what is the law of the spot where he dwells
and practises, lest he should find himself, on some fine day of his *debut*,
insisting on a doctrine which is administered only in Westminster Hall. To
as much of the learning peculiar to that ancient seat as he chooses to bring
to the aid of his studies, we do not object, and the more of it the better.

Mr. Greenleaf has aimed at this result, in his treatise. It has been
his object to treat the law of evidence with reference to our own jurisprudence. The law of evidence, however, is a system of English origin,
with its main principles and doctrines seated in the law of England. He
has accordingly chosen from the right sources in that law, while he shows
its application or modification in our own. Having to instruct young men
from all parts of the Union, he has stated the doctrines and rules common
to all the United States, omitting what is purely local law. This will render

the work valuable to the profession at large; and the comprehensive and at the same time accurate manner in which he has accomplished the object, will cause it to be eagerly sought for in every part of the country. As an elementary work, it is the best we have ever seen for students, and we have already had occasion to know its convenience as an accurate, and to enjoy its merits as an able and instructive treatise.

A Review of Story's *Conflict of Laws*

AMERICAN JURIST

Of all the text writers, the most prolific and important was Joseph Story (1779–1845), Dane Professor of Law at Harvard and erstwhile Associate Justice of the United States Supreme Court. "I am impatient for leisure to prepare some written lectures, for there is a terrible deficiency of good elementary books." And he proceeded to his eight-foot shelf of treatises, covering the whole field of commercial law, as well as constitutional law and equity. The Commentaries on the Constitution *became a classic in the North; the* Conflict of Laws *had the honor of being the first American law-book to be cited as authority in the courts of England. Like Chancellor Kent, Story relied heavily on civil law in the absence of capable English texts in the commercial field.*

Doctrinal writing made it possible for judicial decisions to be the growing point of the law. By a grand sweep and overview of legal principles, they became a nationalizing force, smoothing out what might have been an intolerable diversity of local laws. In a sense, too, the texts blunted the drive for codification in that they made the common law more systematic and more readily accessible.

By the end of the period there was a growing tradition of student participation in learning the law, and an English observer could write with approval of legal education in the United States: "It is curious to compare the silly moots, and bows to Benchers, which formed a part of the student's curriculum the other day in Lincoln's Inn, with the real mootings and debates which the students were on the same day carrying on, before that great Lawyer [Story], sitting in his Professor's chair." He contrasted "the enthusiasm and delight with which Story was followed, with the feelings which now exist in the pupil class in some of [the] Inns of Court."

WHEN WE SAY, that his works are wholly unlike and incomparably superior to the common run of modern law books, we allow to them, but a very small part of the merit to which they are entitled. The ordinary law publications of the present day, seem to be compiled, rather for the

American Jurist (April, 1834), XI, p. 366.

booksellers, than for the profession. They are generally nothing more, than mere collections of cases, or of marginal notes of cases, or scraps and extracts from other books, which under an hundred different forms and disguises with some imposing title, have from time to time, before been palmed upon the public as new and valuable works. Books of this sort have issued and are daily issuing from the press, in such countless and overwhelming numbers as to have become a grievous nuisance. We have often among many other vain things wished that, for the public benefit, the nature of the case would admit of some remedial process, whereby this nuisance might be abated and its continuance might be restrained or stayed forever by a perpetual injunction, or that there were some modern *Omar*, possessed of the exterminating spirit of the ancient *Khalif*, to whose special charge, we might recommend these catch-penny publications.

To say that the works of the learned professor, both in regard to matter and manner, far excel the very best English treatises, is, in our estimation, but moderate praise. For we are constrained to confess, that among those of the highest authority and greatest merit, scarcely any can be found, whose chief value and excellence does not consist merely in an accurate statement of the cases and points decided in the various courts of law and equity, upon the subjects of which they treat. If any new or un-settled questions are discussed, they are commonly only such as necessarily arise or are suggested in tracing out analogies, resemblances, and differ-ences between these decided cases. The authority of these cases is seldom questioned and more seldom tested by general reasoning, or reference to established elementary principles. Decisions are not often followed out to their collateral consequences. Where the courts have been silent, these writers preserve the most profound silence. They venture upon no un-trodden ground, no new field of inquiry. If the subject has been but partially explored, they leave it where they find it. If the matter be in-volved in ever so much doubt or obscurity, if the lights furnished by the scanty decisions of their domestic tribunals be ever so few or faint, they never think of going beyond the narrow limits of their own forum, and invoking the aid even of the greatest masters of the civil or foreign law to clear up or solve a doubt, establish a principle, or supply a manifest deficiency. Hence the barrenness of many branches of the common law. Hence the paucity of principles and rules adapted to the every-day business and affairs of an active, enterprizing, and enlightened age. Hence the obscurity, doubt, and perplexity, in which these principles and rules are involved. Hence too, the manifest and lamentable want of system, sym-metry, uniformity, and consistency, which has always characterized the English jurisprudence. . . .

The real value of treatises upon law depends not merely upon the erudition, but in a great degree also upon the practical experience and judgment of those by whom they are written. Such writers as Lord Chief Justice Coke, and Lord Chief Barons Gilbert and Comyns, in former days, and Mr. Chancellor Kent, and Mr. Justice Story in our own times, possessing exalted talents improved and ripened by the most extensive cultivation and experience, carry with them a weight of authority, which is universally and justly acknowledged and respected. Most treatises are only useful as indexes to the reports and authorities. No experienced lawyer ventures to rely on the soundness of their doctrines or the accuracy of their statements. But we may consult the works of such men as these as the oracles of jurisprudence. We rise from the perusal of them with the satisfaction, that we have learnt all which will repay the labor of research. We lament that such able interpreters of the law are not more numerous. Unfortunately in England, whence much of our jurisprudence is derived, of those who have been the most able to expound its mysteries, and let in gladsome light upon its darkest recesses, few have been willing to undertake the task. . . .

The work before us gives us fresh occasion to congratulate the public upon the inestimable advantages, which are flowing from the law institution over which he presides. To his appointment to the professorial chair in that institution, we are probably indebted, for these most excellent works; and if his life and health shall be continued, and we most earnestly hope that they may be for many years yet to come, we have reason to entertain the highest expectations of his future productions on other branches of jurisprudence. We have, moreover, reason to hope, that through his means the study of the civil and foreign law will become more common.

A Review of Story's *Equity and Jurisprudence*

AMERICAN LAW MAGAZINE

THIS IS ONE OF THE BEST, if not the best of the books published by its learned author, who certainly has not been unmindful of the debt which every lawyer is said to owe his profession. It may be said to be the most complete treatise on the subject—systematically arranged, treating upon almost every point which has arisen or may arise, and especially rich and delightful in its references to, and illustrations drawn from the civil law. It has one fault, common to this and his other works, which may, however, be excusable in a judge before whom the same questions may possibly afterwards arise. We mean the indeterminate mode in which most points are frequently discussed, throwing together the arguments and authorities, *pro* and *con*, and leaving the student's mind in a sad state of perplexity and unhappiness. This fault, however, is amply compensated by the assurance that he may feel, that he has before him all the light which can enable him to decide the question for himself. . . .

We have referred to the evidence which these volumes afford of the intimate acquaintance of the writer with the civil law and the law of continental Europe, and the richness of illustration with which he has thereby been enabled to adorn his subject. He has drawn upon it most copiously upon all occasions, and it is to be hoped that American students and jurists will be excited by the taste here afforded, to resort to the fountain of instruction to be found in this code of written reason. The education of American lawyers, though not so profound and systematic as that of their brethren at Westminster Hall, is more various and liberal. It is necessarily adapted to the nature of their functions. There are none in this country who apply themselves to any particular branch, and hence the professional mind is more elastic than in England. We have not the accuracy and familiarity which results from this subdivision of labour, and hence many mistakes and incongruities; yet our jurisprudence has a more growing and expansive character. Its portals are wider open for illustration and improvement from every other system.

ADMISSION TO THE BAR

The discipline of members and authority over standards are distinguishing characteristics of a profession. Yet the same casualness displayed toward education marked admission to the bar, with but few exceptions. When he was a member of the United States Supreme Court, Chase told the story of what happened after his examination for admission to the bar in open court:

> *The judge smiled and said, "We think, Mr. Chase, that you must study another year and present yourself again for examination." "Please, your honors," said I deprecatingly, "I have made all my arrangements to go to the western country and practice law." The kind judge yielded to the appeal, and turning to the Clerk said, "Swear in Mr. Chase."*

Charles Francis Adams in his Autobiography *confirms this practice. He knew well the then Chief Justice of the Massachusetts Supreme Court— a neighbor.*

> *I asked Bigelow to examine me. He ought to have asked me a few questions as to my length of study, etc., and then, in a good-natured, friendly way advised me to wait a while longer. Instead of that, however, he told me to come at a certain time into the Supreme*

Court room where he was then holding court; and he would examine me. . . . I remember well that on several of the subjects in question I knew absolutely nothing. A few days later I met the judge on the platform of the Quincy station, and he told me I might come up to the court room and be sworn in. I did so; and became a member of the bar. I was no more fit to be admitted than a child. The whole thing illustrated my supreme incompetence, and the utterly irregular way in which admission to the bar was then obtained.

On this, too, there is a famous Lincoln story:

> *I knocked at the door of his room, and was admitted, but I was hardly prepared for the rather unusual sight that met my gaze. Instead of finding my examiner in the midst of books and papers, as I had anticipated, he was partly undressed and, so far as the meager accommodations of the room permitted, leisurely taking a bath. . . .*
>
> *Motioning me to be seated, he began his interrogatories at once, without looking at me a second time to be sure of the identity of his caller. "How long have you been studying?" he asked. "Almost two years," was my response. "By this time, it seems to me," he said laughingly, "you ought to be able to determine whether you have in you the kind of stuff out of which a good lawyer can be made. What books have you read?" I told him, and he said it was more than he read before he was admitted to the bar. . . .*
>
> *He asked me in a desultory way the definition of a contract, and two or three fundamental questions, all of which I answered readily, and I thought, correctly. Beyond these meager inquiries, as I now recall the incident, he asked nothing more. As he continued his toilet, he entertained me with recollections—many of them characteristically vivid and racy—of his early practice and the various incidents and adventures that attended his start in the profession. The whole proceeding was so unusual and queer, if not grotesque, that I was at a loss to determine whether I was really being examined at all or not. After he had dressed we went downstairs and over to the clerk's office in the courthouse, where he wrote a few lines on a sheet of paper, and inclosing it in an envelope, directed me to report with it to Judge Logan, another member of the examining committee at Springfield.*
>
> *The next day I went to Springfield, where I delivered the letter as directed. On reading it, Judge Logan smiled, and, much to my surprise, gave me the required certificate without asking a question beyond my age and residence, and the correct way of spelling my name. The note from Lincoln read: "My dear Judge:—The bearer of this is a young man who thinks he can be a lawyer. Examine him, if you want to. I have done so, and am satisfied. He's a good deal smarter than he looks to be."*

The American Whig Review *provides still more evidence of the widespread lack of organized examinations.*

"Mr. C., Can You Swim?"

AMERICAN WHIG REVIEW

THE DEFECTS of the bar in this country may, for the present objects, be loosely classified under two heads: Defects of Preparatory Education, Defects of Professional Discipline.

In truth, we can hardly be said to have anything of a special education at all for this profession. The statutory provisions to that effect are notoriously waste-paper. The fact, the practice is this: A boy, say from 12 to 16 years of age, with the common-school accomplishment in "reading, writing and arithmetic," enters an attorney's office; which he perhaps sweeps for the first two years. The balance of the apprenticeship to seven years (the legal term in this State for students of this description) is instructively occupied in copying over a thousand times the same cabalistic forms, "running errands," and—*swearing to affidavits.* His studies do not often transcend the "Clerk's Assistant," and any instruction he receives relates but to the theory of "making up a bill of costs"—according to his equivocal expertness in which is estimated his proficiency and his promise in the Profession. After this profound and edifying initiation, he emerges a dapper Attorney-at-Law! This may be an extreme, but it is nevertheless, we aver, a common case. The necessary consequences, moral as well as mental, upon a considerable portion of our bar directly, and indirectly, by reflection, upon the *reputation* of the whole body, we leave the plain sense or the personal experience of the public to determine. As to the collegiate diploma receivable in lieu of a portion of this period, we all know it to be obtained commonly by persons incapable of reading its contents in Latin.

For the supplementary guaranty of our Examination is a still greater "sham" (if that be possible) than even the apprenticeship. Unmasked of technology, it reminds one of the Canonical programme of the middle ages, which began with the interrogatory, "Can you *read* the Four Gospels?" Nor does this resemblance between the candidates end with the examination, but extends, quite naturally, to the professions for which such examinations could be held to qualify; as witness the following account of the clerical body at the period alluded to, by a sarcastic contemporary: *Potius dediti* (says Alanus) *gulæ quam glossæ, potius* COLLIGUNT LIBRAS *quam* LEGUNT LIBROS, &c. Our examinations of at least the candidates for attorneyship, are exclusively upon Court rules and mere Practice. But besides being technical—as comports possibly with the ordinary capacity of the examiners—they are become so trite, that collections of the whole set, in manuscript, with the proper answers appended, are known to be

American Whig Review (September, 1846), IV, p. 256.

common among our Law students. So that the examination is reducible to a few hours' effort of mere memory. The writer can say, for his own part, that the sum of his preparation *with immediate reference to this ordeal,* was made within the single week preceding the event. Nor did he avail himself, in this feat, of the examination-made-easy catechism alluded to, but of the intelligent and methodical treatise of Mr. Burril, on Practice. It may be retorted, the practical proficiency was probably proportionable. Well, we will not gainsay an objection which only fortifies our argument. In fine, we think the actual scheme of Legal examination (and implicitly of course, of education) is well hit off in the following sketch, from a newspaper, which (for decency, doubtless) places the scene in the wild South-West.

"Judge P.," said Mr. C.'s friend, "is now in the village; will you go and stand your examination?"

Of course C. consented. He had been for several days anxiously waiting for the Judge at the —— Exchange, alias groggery, alias doggery. After the introduction the Judge said:

"Well, Mr. C., you want to be examined for admittance to the bar." "Yes, sir." "Well, sir, let us take something to drink: barkeeper, give us two juleps. Mr. C., can you swim?" "Yes, sir, I can," said C., greatly surprised. "Well, sir, let's take another drink: barkeeper, two cocktails." The cocktails vanished, and the judge said: "Mr. C., have you got a horse?" "Certainly, sir," said C. "Very good," said the Judge, as soberly as though charging a grand jury. "Mr. C., if you please, we'll take a drink: barkeeper, two toddies." The toddies disappeared, and C. owns he began to feel rather queer. "Mr. C.," said the Judge, "can your horse swim?" "Yes, sir, he can, for I have tried him from necessity." "Then, sir," said the Judge, with increasing gravity, "your horse can swim, and you can swim, and by G—d, I think you are well qualified for an Alabama lawyer. Give me your commission, and I will sign it. Meanwhile, barkeeper, give us two punches, for my friend Mr. C. and myself. Mr. C.," continued the Judge, "I drink success to your admission to the Bar."

This may be actual fiction, but it is ideal truth.

Fees and Admissions

RULES OF THE ESSEX BAR

The rules of the Essex Bar, a local bar association, indicate that despite a popular desire for the relaxing of standards, a few bar associations did control admissions and professional conduct.

Rules of the Bar of the County of Essex, Massachusetts (1831).

WHEREAS, in all the liberal professions, great mischiefs are caused to the public by unlearned and immoral persons assuming to perform duties, which can safely be entrusted to none, but to such as are competent in knowledge and pure in character; and as the surest safeguards against these evils it has been an ancient custom for those who exercise such professions, to unite themselves as a fraternity, to prescribe to themselves such rules as are found best adapted to secure their honor and usefulness, to judge of the qualifications of such as offer themselves to become members of the profession, and by their approbation, and by admission to their society, to distinguish those who have pursued a proper course of study and discipline, from such as intrude themselves without due preparation:—And whereas maintenance, barratry, and abuse of legal process are the usual consequences of unsuitable and unqualified persons assuming the practice of the law;—

The members of the Bar of Essex do agree upon and establish the following rules: . . .

ALL counsellors and attorneys, who have been regularly admitted to practise, and who now reside or usually practise in this county, may subscribe these rules at, or before, the next annual meeting. But after that day no person shall subscribe the same, unless upon being admitted, on the recommendation of this Bar, to practise as an attorney in the Court of Common Pleas.

No person who has been admitted to practise in any other county of this Commonwealth shall be considered a member of this Bar, nor allowed to subscribe these rules, until he shall have filed with the Secretary of this Bar a certificate of his having been so admitted, and shall have produced to the Standing Committee the recommendation of the Bar of the county, in which he shall have been so admitted. . . .

IT is considered improper and dishonorable, and tending greatly to the prejudice not only of practitioners at this Bar, but of the public, for any person, who is not a regularly admitted practitioner at the same, or at some other Bar in this State, to commence an action before any justice of the peace, or in the Court of Common Pleas, or Supreme Judicial Court, District or Circuit Court, and no gentleman of the Bar shall, upon any terms, nor under any circumstances whatever, assume the care of such action; nor shall any gentleman of this Bar, upon any terms, nor under any circumstances, be in any manner connected in his professional practice with any person who is not, as aforesaid, a regularly admitted practitioner. Nor shall any gentleman assume the care of any action originated in this county by a person practising therein, nor advise, nor consult, nor be in any manner associated in any case whatever with any person practising in this county, who shall not have subscribed these rules.

TAKING into consideration that the rules of the Supreme Judicial Court require that nine years, at least, should have been passed in literary and professional pursuits, to qualify a man for admission to that Court as an Attorney thereof, and two years practice therein as an attorney, to qualify him for admission as a counsellor thereof, and also that those who take upon themselves to perform professional duties are, and ought to be, holden in law and in honor to indemnify their clients for all losses or damages which are occasioned by negligence or want of professional knowledge; and lastly, that the members of the profession are never applied to, if the party can obtain, without their agency, the rights which the laws of the land secure to him;—

We, the subscribers, members of the Bar in the county of Essex, establish the following rates of compensation and fees as the lowest, which we can reasonably and honorably receive; and we bind ourselves not to receive less fees or compensation than are herein expressed, nor any commutation or substitute therefor, viz.

	Dols.	Cts.
For Summonses and Writs, &c. and commencing the action:		
Where the debt is under 50 dollars	3.	00
—————————— 50 or over	4.	00
—————————— 500 or over	5.	00
In Replevin and Trespass	5.	00
On the Trustee Process—		
where the debt is 50 dollars or less	4.	00
—————— over 50	5.	00
—————— over 500	6.	00
Appearance in the C. C. Pleas—		
For the first term	4.	00
For the second term	3.	00
And for each term after, not less than	2.	00
Provided that where the demand is under 100 dollars, the Attorney may take the bill of costs only.		
The appearance of a Trustee by his Attorney, at the first term, shall be equivalent to the personal appearance of the Trustee.		
Appearance at the Supreme Judicial Court, in all cases, not less, at any term, than	6.	00
In Real Actions, including Partition, and Petitions for the sale of Real Estate—		
For the Writ or Petition	5.	00
Attendance at a term in C. C. P. not less than	4.	00
Ditto in S. J. C. not less than	6.	00
For libels of Divorce, and appearance for the party, exclusive of costs, not less than	12.	00
Petition, &c. for Naturalization, exclusive of court and clerk dues, not less than	12.	00
Arguing fees, in actions commenced in the C. C. P. on any issue in fact or law, not less than	10.	00

Ditto in S. J. C. not less than 15.   00
Advice, in any case, not less than 3.   00
Letter requesting payment, &c. half the price of a writ in
    each case.
Commissions on money collected:
    For the first 300 dols. not less than two per centum.
    For all sums above 300, at the rate of one per cent.
    And on all money collected for Foreigners, not less than
        two and a half per cent.

THE sum which every student shall be required to pay for his law education, shall be at the rate of one hundred and fifty dollars for each year, to be paid, or satisfactorily secured to be paid, at the expiration of each year.

THE Committee, or a major part of them, shall examine all students who may be proposed for admission as attorneys of the Court of Common Pleas in this county, which examination shall be had at such time and place, and in such manner, as the Committee or the major part of them may determine, and within twenty days next preceding the commencement of the session of the court, at which such students may respectively intend to be admitted. And if the Committee, or the major part of them, before whom such examination is had, are of opinion that such students have complied with the rules of the Bar, and that they possess the qualifications necessary to entitle them to admission to the Court of Common Pleas, the Committee, or the major part of them, who made the examination, shall give a certificate thereof to the candidates respectively; which certificate being filed by the Secretary, such candidate shall thereupon be recommended by the President, or by one of the Committee in behalf of the Bar, for admission accordingly, provided he shall have been proposed for admission by a vote of the Bar at the preceding term, unless a major part of the Bar at a Bar meeting shall object thereunto.

THE qualifications of students for recommendation by the Bar for admission to the Court of Common Pleas shall be the following.—The applicant shall have been graduated at some college or university, and shall have diligently studied law three years in the office of a counsellor in the Supreme Judicial Court of this State, and the last of said years in the county of Essex, unless such student shall have passed such last year at the law school at Cambridge, and shall also have studied one year in this county, and shall produce a certificate of these facts, and that he is of good moral character.

And any person having a liberal education, and a regular degree as aforesaid, who shall afterwards have commenced and pursued the study of the law in any other State, in the office of a counsellor of the highest Judicial Court of such State, for two years, and afterwards shall pursue the study of the law in the office of a counsellor of the Supreme Judicial Court of this State, residing within the county of Essex, for one year, shall be entitled to a recommendation by the Committee of the Bar, for admission to the Court of Common Pleas, on producing certificates of these facts, and that he is of good moral character.

Or 2d. If the applicant shall not have been graduated at some university, he shall have had a good school education, equivalent to such education as would qualify him for admission at Harvard university in the freshman class; and he shall have devoted four years to the study of such sciences and literature, as are the subjects of instruction at the university, and shall have studied law three years besides in the office of a counsellor as aforesaid, and shall be certified to have so done, and to be of good moral character.

Or 3d. The applicant shall have such school education as aforesaid, and shall have devoted two years to scientific and literary attainments, and shall have diligently studied in the office of a counsellor five years besides as aforesaid, and shall be certified so to have done, and that he is of good moral character.

And the Committee of the Bar may, if they see fit, require of any applicant, who has not been graduated at some university, to submit to an examination before said Committee, as to his scientific, literary, and classical attainments. . . .

No student shall commence or defend any action, or do any professional business whatever on his own account.

THE standing rules and regulations shall be entered in the Bar-book, subscribed by every member of the Bar, and every gentleman of the Bar shall be bound in honor to give notice in writing to the President, of any transgression or breach of these rules by any gentleman belonging to the profession.

No person shall be recommended by the Bar for admission to practise as an attorney at the Court of Common Pleas, until he shall have in writing declared his assent to the Bar rules, and his determination to adhere to the same.

THE Committee shall inquire, on complaint of any member of the Bar, or other notice, of malpractice or infringement of the standing rules of the Bar, or of any unfair, oppressive, dishonorable, or illegal practices.

So much of these rules and regulations as respects fees, shall be printed on sheets of paper, with the names of those members who have subscribed the same, and one of these sheets shall be put up in some conspicuous place, in the office of every attorney and counsellor of the Supreme Judicial Court, and of the Court of Common Pleas, to the end that every gentleman may show to his clients, if there be any occasion so to do, the rules by which his practice is to be governed.

Brotherhood of the Bar

FREDERICK ROBINSON

*There were many bar associations but most of them, unlike that of the
Essex Bar, were social organizations. As J. S. Buckingham observed, the
"legal gentlemen" appeared "to congregate and herd together with members of their own profession, and especially to delight in the society of
clubs." A very different interpretation of the solidarity of the bar is manifested in this letter by Frederick Robinson. His hatred of any "priviledged"
group was to last all his life. In 1834 he was elected to the Massachusetts
Legislature. He was a declared enemy of the National Bank, and described
Jackson's famous veto as the stroke "which served to arouse the people."
He sponsored a bill to abolish imprisonment for debt, and was a supporter
of the General Trades Union and unionism in general. For him politics
was a class conflict between the producers—laborers—and the capitalists—
speculators.*

MARBLEHEAD, June 25, 1831.

Hon. RUFUS CHOATE,

Sir,—I told you yesterday that it was cowardly in you to pursue the
course which you did towards me. I have had a night to reflect on your
proceedings, and I now assert, that it was cowardly in the extreme not only
in you, but in the whole "brotherhood of the bar," to postpone the question of power and privilege, which you know is odious to the people, until
the court was ready to rise, and until the jury had been dismissed and all
the spectators had retired.

I asked you then, sir, and I ask you now, again, why, if you have the
right, as you say you have, to demand the authority by which I appear to
do business in our public courts you did not demand it when the actions,
which I entered were called? The reason to my mind is obvious. You
feared, that all in the court, who had not sworn allegiance to the bar,
would express in their countenances, at least, sympathy for a man, contending for one of *their* rights, and disapprobation towards a secret, powerfully organized fraternity determined to crush him. You therefore, supposed
it would be more prudent to consult with the court and your secret bar
association, and proceed according to the dictation of their united wisdom
and courage. But you must have thought me blind indeed, if you suppose,

---

Frederick Robinson, *A Letter to the Hon. Rufus Choate, Containing a Brief
Exposure of Law Craft, and Some of the Encroachments Upon the Rights and
Liberties of the People* (1831), p. 3.

that I should not see, that your proceeding towards me, was the result, of a preconcerted arrangement between the court and the bar. How else can I account for your conduct? When my actions were called, you suffered one of them to be defaulted, and asked for leave for the other to remain open on the docket. Why did you not then call for the power? You looked around the court house, and you saw it filled with people, whom you know, are jealous of their rights and liberties, and you feared to do it. . . .

But when the business of the court was nearly ended, I began to discover the plot. I began to observe an uncommon solicitude among the "brotherhood of the bar," by drawing themselves up, around the bench. Notice was given, that the public business was ended, the spectators retired and the judge dismissed the jury. Then it was, Sir, for the first time, you gave me notice, that you was ready to pay money into the court. Then, for the first time, you told me, you meant to make me produce my power of attorney, and when I remonstrated to you against the *double* course, which you had pursued towards me during the term, and against the cowardliness of waiting, before you proposed this measure, until all had retired, except the "secret brotherhood of the bar," then it was, for the first time you said, that if I attempted "to practice the law without being regularly admitted to the bar we'll put you down."* I told you, "I feared you not, not all your secret fraternity, that I was standing on broad constitutional ground, and no power on earth should put me down, until it put me in the grave." You called for my power, and I demanded by what authority. I said, that I claimed every right and every privilege, in our country, which any other individual can enjoy, that I claimed the same facility of doing business in our public courts, which any other man can have, that if there be any laws, which contravene the rights of my appearing as an attorney, on terms of equality with other men, I protested against such laws, as unconstitutional and void. But that I could easily conceive how such laws have been forced through our legislature, by a secret, interested, organized body, within the legislature. I therefore, protested against the operation of such laws on me. You know, the judge then said that the laws, to which I referred, were of too long standing for him to decide unconstitutional, (as if any length of time can render unconstitutional laws constitutional,) but that he gave me liberty to carry the question to the S. J. Court. But did you ever know a judge in this Commonwealth, who was not also, a member of your "secret bar association"? . . .

And now Sir, I ask what right have you to enforce the rules of your association on me? You told the judge, that I was not "a member of the

---

* You previously told me, you "could not respect me as a *brother*." I asked you "to treat me as a man." But how much is his respect worth, who respects not the rights and liberties of others?

bar," and therefore you demanded, by what authority, I appeared to do business in the court. Is the court and the bar one and the same thing? The people do not so understand it, I believe; though I am well convinced, that there is a close copartnership between them. I am more disposed to believe, that such a partnership exists, because I cannot conceive how the bar, a secret society, unknown in the law, could deprive me of my rights, by any rules or by laws of the association, did not the court adopt and enforce the rules of the bar. In this way, your fraternity have been enabled by little and little, to entrench itself behind an impassible barrier. And the only access now, is by a single door, which gives admittance only to him, who has been led on by the most *lengthy* process, with the most costly foundation. In the first place he must be regularly admitted into one of our aristocratic, incorporate colleges, or universities. He must there, spend at least four years either in study, or at his election, in a kind of costly monastic idleness. He is then, wise or foolish, learned, or ignorant, admitted to a *degree*, and honoured with a *title*. His name is then admitted to be enrolled on the archives of the bar, and after spending at least three years more in idleness or study, under the nominal tutor of a member of the bar to whom he must pay, at least one hundred and fifty dollars annually, he is then admitted, wise or foolish, learned or ignorant, without examination, into the secret fraternity of the bar. And no person can be admitted into "the holy alliance," of the court and the bar, even if he be more learned, than Johnson, a greater lawyer than Bacon, more eloquent than Cicero, if he have devoted his time till old age, with the most intense application to study, under the most learned instructors, unless he go step by step through all the formality, which I have described. Now, Sir, can you say that this is not a true description of "the rules of the court and the bar," with respect to the admission of attorneys? Who then, cannot see, that the object of these rules are to keep out of the profession every man of self-education, to exclude every such man as Patrick Henry, Roger Sherman, and Benjamin Franklin? whose names are now, the boast, the honour, and ornament of our country. But if they were alive now, in Massachusetts, could they be admitted to "the bar"? Would they be suffered to do business in our public courts? Can you suppose, then that the people, who like me, are jealous of their rights and liberties, will any longer countenance, a society whose object is to discourage self-education? . . .

I know that my chance of success is small. I know that the fraternity of the bar, which has waged war against me is powerful, beyond what is commonly conceived. I know that you have fortified yourselves, by alliance with the other learned professions. I know that you have interested every rich and powerful family in your favor. And I know that you have in this way established a proud, haughty, overbearing, four-fold aristocracy in our country.* The root of this aristocracy, which saps the liberties of the people, and has branched out and covered the land, is in our colleges. Into these you are initiated in infancy, your seclusion from the world, and your pursuits being different from the rest of society naturally excites your vanity, ambition and pride, and even in infancy you look upon yourselves as a "superior order," as the future lawyers, doctors, priests, judges and governors of mankind, and you look upon the rest of the world as inferior, plebeians, laborers, educated only for manual employment. You are there permitted even in infancy, to form secret associations, "Phi Beta Kappa Societies," &c. in which you are taught to recognize each other by signs and grips and passwords, and swear to stand by each other through life. Does not this sufficiently account, for the alliance, which I have mentioned, of the learned professions? But what induces the rich also, who are not of these "liberal orders,"† to join this "holy alliance"? Who are the parents, generally, of the youth, who fill our colleges and incorporate learned institutions? Is there a rich man in the land, the father of three booby boys, that does not, at least in his imagination discern a regular bred scrawler of writs at the bar, an adminstrator of doses to the sick, and an expounder of mysteries in the church? I know that the most of the offices of government are in your hands. Who are the presidents, the governors, the justices, the sheriffs, the judges, the solicitors and attorneys of the state? I know that the press is generally under your dictation and control, that the rich, the powerful and the learned are in your favor, yet with but truth law and justice on my side, I dare in our country to stand up, to assert and to defend my rights. And when the great disinterested body of the people hesitate to protect each other in their common rights and privileges, they are gone forever, and nothing but revolutions can redeem them. If the people have become careless of their rights, and refuse assistance, when they see them invaded in others, let them rest assured that their turn will come by and by.—If such is the uneasiness of the people, with respect to our common rights and privileges it is time for every one, who is determined to live free and equal to seek another country.—Ours can be the abode only, of the master and slave.

---

* "Good society," is the name, by which this fourfold aristocracy distinguish themselves. They have many other ways to exalt themselves and to degrade and debase the rest of our species. By leading the fashion, by expensive profusion and by making these essential to "good society," others, whose resources are more narrow, are induced to ape them and ruin themselves by ostentation. And by adopting certain rules and conventionalities, as essential to "high and costly manners," and by despising all, who have not been initiated into this kind of masonry, they have it in their power, still more, to distinguish themselves, from what they call "the common herd, the mob, the vulgar, the rabble," &c.

† It is a little remarkable, how in all ages, wicked and corrupt associations have always continued to cover their wickedness, under the mask of fair names, such as the holy wars, the holy inquisition, the holy alliance, and now in our country the only illiberal monopoly professions have assumed the name of "liberal professions"!

You say, that the bar is a "necessary evil." I know that it is an evil, that it is necessary I deny. I know of no good resulting to the community from the existence of your secret bar association. Public good was not the object of your combination. It is a conspiracy against the rights and liberties of the people. The same motives influence you to associate together into a fraternity denominated "the bar," which induce robbers to constitute a society called "a banditti," and one of these societies is as much "a necessary evil," as the other. And the *bar rules* of "these privileged orders," are not very dissimilar. The object of them both are to protect each other in their robberies, and extortions, and to "put down," and destroy every one, who will not submit to their "rules and regulations," and become sworn brothers of the banditti, or the bar. Of these secret societies however the bar is the most to be feared. The one robs us of our purse, openly and honourably in comparison, in the highway against law and at the risk of life. The other robs us not of our purse alone, but of our rights also, in the sanctuary and under the semblance of the law.

ETHICS OF THE PROFESSION

Distrust of lawyers has always been a part of the folklore of the United States. A Spanish conquistador-governor is said to have implored the king of Spain to send no lawyers to his new domains: "They are all devils."
"There is no greater curse to any community than a poor and unscrupulous lawyer," was the observation made to Tom Nichols in 1850 "by a lawyer who had been poor, was rich, and had not, it was said, been overburdened with scruples." And it is no mean tribute to the strength of this feeling that it should prove good material for more popular anecdotes.

Fit for a Lawyer

NEBRASKA ADVENTURER

AN OLD LADY walked into a lawyer's office, lately, when the following conversation took place:—

"Squire, I called to see if you would like to take this boy, and make a lawyer of him."

"The boy appears rather young, ma'am. How old is he?"

Nebraska Adventurer (October 25, 1856), p. 3.

"Seven years, sir."

"He is too young, decidedly too young. Have you no older boys?"

"Oh, yes, sir, I have several; but we have concluded to make farmers of the others. I told my husband I thought this little fellow would make a first-rate lawyer, and so I called to see if you would take him."

"No, madam, he is too young yet to commence the study of a profession. But why do you think this boy so much better calculated for a lawyer than your other sons? What are his particular qualifications?"

"Why, do you see, sir, he is just seven years old to-day. When he was only five he would lie like the devil; when he got to be six, he was sassy and impudent as any crittur could be; and now he will steal everything he can lay his hands on. Now if he ain't fit for a lawyer, I would like to know what he would have to learn?"

"Pretty well educated, I should think."

The Conduct of Attorneys

GEORGE SHARSWOOD

The mixed results of efforts to overcome this impression are indicated by the following extracts. George Sharswood (1810–1883) attempted to raise the ethical standards of his profession. He was associate judge of the District Court of Philadelphia for twenty-two years and later became chief justice of the State Supreme Court. He also served as professor of law at the University of Pennsylvania, and taught there for eighteen years following his appointment in 1850. It was said, presumably with mixed feelings, that often counsel did not fully understand his own case until he heard Judge Sharswood's charge to the jury. A Compendium of Lectures on the Aims and Duties of the Profession of Law *was published in 1854 and went through several editions.*

THERE IS, PERHAPS, no profession, after that of the sacred ministry, in which a high-toned morality is more imperatively necessary than that of the law. There is certainly, without any exception, no profession in which so many temptations beset the path to swerve from the line of strict integrity; in which so many delicate and difficult questions of duty are continually arising. There are pitfalls and mantraps at every step, and the mere youth, at the very outset of his career, needs often the prudence and self-denial, as well as the moral courage, which belong commonly to riper years. High moral principle is his only safe guide; the only torch to light

George Sharswood, *Professional Ethics* (1854), p. 55.

his way amidst darkness and obstruction. It is like the spear of the guardian
angel of Paradise:

> No falsehood can endure
> Touch of celestial temper, but returns
> Of force to its own likeness.

The object of this Essay is, to arrive at some accurate and intelligible
rules by which to guide and govern the conduct of professional life. It
would not be a difficult task to declaim in general propositions—to erect a
perfect standard and leave the practitioner to make his own application
to particular cases. It is a difficult task, however, as it always is in practice,
to determine the precise extent of a principle, so as to know when it is
encountered and overcome by another—to weigh the respective force of
duties which appear to come in conflict. In all the walks of life, men
have frequently to do this; in none so often as at the Bar.

The responsibilities, legal and moral, of the lawyer, arise from his
relations to the court, to his professional brethren, and to his client. . . .

The oath directed by law in this state to be administered upon the
admission of an attorney to the bar, "to behave himself in the office of
attorney according to the best of his learning and ability, and with all
good fidelity, as well to the court as to the client; that he will use no falsehood, nor delay any man's cause for lucre or malice," presents a comprehensive summary of his duties as a practitioner.

Fidelity to the court, fidelity to the client, fidelity to the claims of
truth and honor: these are the matters comprised in the oath of office.

It is an oath of office, and the practitioner, the incumbent of an
office—an office in the administration of justice—held by authority from
those who represent in her tribunals the majesty of the commonwealth, a
majesty truly more august than that of kings or emperors. It is an office,
too, clothed with many privileges—privileges, some of which are conceded to no other class or profession. It is therefore that the legislature
have seen fit to require that there should be added to the solemnity of the
responsibility, which every man virtually incurs when he enters upon the
practice of his profession, the higher and more impressive sanction of an
appeal to the Searcher of all Hearts.

Fidelity to the court requires outward respect in words and actions.
The oath, as it has been said, undoubtedly looks to nothing like allegiance
to the person of the judge; unless in those cases where his person is so
inseparable from his office, that an insult to the one is an indignity to the
other. In matters collateral to official duty, the judge is on a level with
the members of the bar, as he is with his fellow-citizens; his title to distinction and respect resting on no other foundation than his virtues and
qualities as a man. . . . There are occasions, no doubt, when duty to the
interests confided to the charge of the advocate demands firm and

decided opposition to the views expressed or the course pursued by the court, nay, even manly and open remonstrance; but this duty may be faithfully performed, and yet that outward respect be preserved, which is here inculcated. Counsel should ever remember how necessary it is for the dignified and honorable administration of justice, upon which the dignity and honor of their profession entirely depend, that the courts and the members of the courts, should be regarded with respect by the suitors and people; that on all occasions of difficulty or danger to that department of government, they should have the good opinion and confidence of the public on their side. Good men of all parties prefer to live in a country, in which justice according to law is impartially administered. Counsel should bear in mind also the wearisomeness of a judge's office; how much he sees and hears in the course of a long session, to try his temper and patience. Lord Campbell has remarked that it is rather difficult for a judge altogether to escape the imputation of discourtesy if he properly values the public time; for one of his duties is to "render it disagreeable to counsel to talk nonsense." Respectful submission, nay, most frequently, even cheerful acquiescence in a decision, when, as is most generally the case, no good result can grow to his cause from any other course, is the part of true wisdom as well as civility.

Duties of an Attorney

NEW YORK CODE

Canon No. 27 of the New York Bar states: "It is unprofessional to solicit professional employment by circulars, advertisements, through touters or by personal communications or interviews not warranted by personal relations." The extract following needs no background note.

THE DUTY of an attorney and counsellor [shall] be—

1. To support the Constitution and Laws of the United States, and of this State;

2. To maintain the respect due to the Courts of justice and judicial officers;

3. To counsel or maintain such actions, proceedings, or defences, only, as appear to him legal and just, except the defence of a person charged with a public offence;

4. To employ, for the purpose of maintaining the causes confided

---

Duties of Attorneys, *New York Code* (1849), #511.

to him, such means only as are consistent with truth, and never to seek to mislead the Judges by any artifice or false statement of fact or law;

5. To maintain inviolate the confidence, and, at every peril to himself, to preserve the secrets, of his clients;

6. To abstain from all offensive personality, and to advance no fact prejudicial to the honor or reputation of a party or witness, unless required by the justice of the cause with which he is charged;

7. Not to encourage either the commencement or the continuance of an action or proceeding, from any motive of passion or interest; and

8. Never to reject, for any consideration personal to himself, the cause of the defenceless or the oppressed.

Lawyers and Honesty

ABRAHAM LINCOLN

THERE IS a vague popular belief that lawyers are necessarily dishonest. I say vague, because when we consider to what extent confidence and honors are reposed in and conferred upon lawyers by the people, it appears improbable that their impression of dishonesty is very distinct and vivid. Yet the impression is common, almost universal. Let no young man choosing the law for a calling for a moment yield to the popular belief—resolve to be honest at all events; and if in your own judgment you cannot be an honest lawyer, resolve to be honest without being a lawyer. Choose some other occupation, rather than one in the choosing of which you do, in advance, consent to be a knave.

THE PINNACLE OF THE PROFESSION

The reward system in the profession depends not so much upon money as upon prestige and honor. Judgeships in this period began—though not entirely—to be regarded as such an emolument for professional achievement.

In those days there were truly judges and attendant lawyers on horseback. Judge Woodbridge, of the Supreme Court of the Territory of Michigan, complained in a letter in 1828 of the legislature's directing courts to be held in each of the organized counties, so that the judges have "to

Abraham Lincoln, "Notes for a Law Lecture (July 1, 1850)," *Collected Works,* II (1953), p. 80.

traverse, mostly on horseback, an immense country, over roads not yet half formed &, some of which are exceedingly dangerous." But Chief Justice Waite was recalled as a good companion in traveling the circuit: "He was always cheerful and our ride in the midst of the forest which was then nearly unbroken was always enlivened by his ready anecdotes." He was not alone in enjoying his obligatory travels: "In my opinion," wrote David Davis, "Lincoln was happy, as happy as he could be, when on his circuit— and happy no other place."

Solicitation of an Office

HORACE BINNEY

Horace Binney (1780–1875), a leader of the Philadelphia bar, declined the offer of a position on the Supreme Court of Pennsylvania in 1830. His national reputation rested in part on the Girard Trust case, when he prevailed against Webster's argument for the heirs. Binney's argument in the following extract, against the state constitutional amendment making the tenure of judges for a term of years instead of for life, did not succeed.

IN THE TIME of General Washington and of his immediate successor Mr. Adams, I think it would not have been thought less strange for a man to solicit a judgeship than for a lady to solicit a gentleman in marriage. Had such an instance occurred, it would have been universally held to imply a want of both dignity and capacity, to have been a self-puffing and a self-seeking, which wholly unfitted the applicant for a judicial station. Solicitation of such an office by the individual concerned, or at his instance, was wholly unknown. But [Jefferson] led the way to a change. From a tide-waiter to a minister plenipotentiary, from a marshall to the highest judge in the land, the people were enticed to interfere, by personal recommendations, in all appointments to office. They were sometimes prompted to do it by agents to the Executive, to divide or perhaps cast off the responsibility for an improper appointment. In the sequel every office became subject to the usage, and the interval was a short one between asking others to ask for you and asking directly of the appointing power. . . . I object to the practice in regard to any office. I abominate it in regard to judicial office, in which it can hardly be expected that the judge will stand erect and unbending between the parties after he has obtained his place by begging it as a favour from one of them.

Horace Binney, Letter (1827), Charles C. Binney, *The Life of Horace Binney* (1903), p. 89.

Every Quality and Attainment of Law

BENJAMIN R. CURTIS

Upon graduation from Harvard College in 1829, Benjamin R. Curtis entered the law school and worked under Joseph Story. He ascribed his skill as a common-law pleader to the habit of reciting Chitty's forms while walking the floor with a sick child in his arms. In 1851 he served in the Massachusetts Legislature. In the same year he was appointed to the United States Supreme Court by President Fillmore. During the trying period of compromise, Curtis supported conciliation (as represented in Webster's Seventh of March Address) *and opposed the Free Soilers. In the Dred Scott case Curtis dissented vigorously from Taney's majority opinion; the differences over this case led to Curtis's resignation in 1857. He returned to Boston to practice law, and in 1868 was counsel for President Johnson during the impeachment trial.*

DEAR SIR, But the recorded opinions of a judge, as you know, present only one side of his judicial character and mind. To write an able, learned, and satisfactory opinion of a case is certainly not easy; and in reference to the science of the law and to the ultimate decision of causes which have advanced to that stage, it is often very important. But it has seemed to me that a far more difficult and useful field of labor, speaking generally, is the safe, prompt, judicious, and wise controlling power of a judge on the Circuit. I have no doubt that every quality and attainment of which a judge is capable may there find their fullest exercise and their most difficult work. I presume you will agree with me, that there is no field for a lawyer which, for breadth and compass and the requisitions made on all the faculties, can compare with a trial by jury; and I believe it is as true of a judge as of a lawyer, that in the actual application of the law to the business of men, mingled as it is with all passions and motives and diversities of mind, temper, and condition, in the course of a trial by jury, what is most excellent in him comes out, and finds its fitting work, and whatever faults or weaknesses he has are sensibly felt.

Perhaps the necessities of the country may some day require that the judges of the Supreme Court should sit only as a court of error; but it will certainly be a loss to the country, and an injury to the judges themselves, when they cease to come directly in contact with the people on the

Mr. Justice Curtis, Letter (November 16, 1851), *Life and Writings of B. R. Curtis,* I (ed. Curtis, 1851), p. 157.

circuits, and when they are no longer required to apply the law of evidence of facts,—a process not very satisfactory to the mind, but, in my opinion, of eminent utility.

I Most Always Found Principles Suited to My Views

JAMES KENT

James Kent (1763–1847) felt called upon to engage in the strategic work of placing a seething urban democracy under the constraint of the common law. An ardent Federalist (and, later, Whig), he was profoundly distrustful of democracy with its "inflammatory appeals to the worst passions of the worst men." His opposition to the extension of the franchise at the constitutional convention of 1821 is taken as the model of American conservatism at bay. In 1814 he was appointed to the newly established Court of Chancery. Here he remained until 1823, when the constitutional convention, by imposing a mandatory retirement age of 60, forced him to retire. From 1826 to 1830 he wrote his monumental Commentaries on American Law, *published in four volumes. This work established him as the American Blackstone. It went through six editions before his death, eight more until the last one in 1873, edited by Holmes.*

IN 1814 I was appointed Chancellor. The office I took with considerable reluctance. It had no claims. The person who left it was stupid, & it is a curious fact that for the nine years I was in that office, there was *not a single decision, opinion or dictum of either of my two predecessors . . .* from 1777 to 1814 cited to me or even suggested. I took the court as if it had been a new institution, & never before known to the U. S. I had nothing to guide me, & was left at liberty to assume all such English chancery powers and jurisdiction as I thought applicable under our constitution. This gave me great scope, & I was only checked by the revision of the Senate & court of Errors. I opened the gates of the court immediately, & admitted almost gratuitously the first year 85 counsellors, though I found there had not been but 13 admitted for 13 years before. Business flowed in with a rapid tide. The result appears in the seven volumes of Johnson's Ch. reports.

My study in Equity jurisprudence was very much confined to the topics elicited by the cases. I had previously read, of course, the modern Equity reports, down to the time, & of course I read all the new ones

James Kent, "An American Law Student," *Bench and Bar,* pp. 837, 844.

as fast as I could procure them. . . . The business of the court of chancery oppressed me very much, but I took my daily exercise, & my delightful country rides among the Catskill or the Vermont mountains with my wife, & kept up my health and spirits. I always took up the cases in their order, & never left one until I had finished it. This was only *doing one thing at a time.* My practice was first to make myself perfectly & accurately (mathematically accurately) master of the facts. It was done by abridging the bill, & then the answers, & then the depositions, & by the time I had done this slow tedious process I was master of the cause & ready to decide it. I saw where justice lay and the moral sense decided the cause half the time, & I then set down to search the authorities until I had exhausted my books, & I might once & a while be embarrassed by a technical rule, but I *most always found principles suited to my views of the case*, & my object was to discuss a point as never to be teazed with it again, & to anticipate an angry & vexatious appeal to a popular tribune by disappointed counsel.

Talking Familiarly with Lawyers

PHILIP HONE

I PASSED A COUPLE OF HOURS this morning in the Chancellor's [Chancellor Walworth of New York City] court and was much pleased. It is held in a small office in the wing of his dwelling house, which serves as a law library, very extensive, and I should judge well selected. His honor sits at his desk on a platform raised about a foot, his habiliments not remarkably neat, pantaloons drawn half way up to his knees, drinking most intemperately of water (his only drink, as he is president of the teetotalers), talking familiarly with the lawyers on points as they arise in the case, and frequently interrupting the speaker in what appeared to me rather an abrupt manner, which I think must be a stumbling block in the way of young counselors, but I liked it very much. There were about twenty lawyers seated without order, some at a green table, but the greater number on chairs with their backs against the wall, and their legs cocked up; everything was easy and unconstrained, but quiet and decorous. The Chancellor does a great deal of the talking himself, but is treated with great respect. It looked very much like a schoolmaster and his pupils, only the boys were a little too big to answer the description of the latter.

The Diary of Philip Hone (1828–1851), I (ed. Nevins, 1927), p. 489.

The Supreme Court of the United States

GODFREY T. VIGNE

THE SUPREME COURT of the United States is a very high and honourable tribunal, composed of a chief justice, with a salary of 5000 dollars and six associate justices, with a salary of 4500 dollars each, who hold a sitting once a year, at Washington, commencing on the second Monday in January. The court sits five hours every day for two months, deciding in that time usually about eighty causes, which are reported as those of the law courts in England used, and ought still to be, by an officer of the court. . . .

All the Judges in the American courts enjoy an immunity from wigs, and the Judges of the Supreme Court alone are clothed in "silk attire." Their robes are black, and fashioned according to the taste of the wearer. I examined four or five of them which were hanging up in the court, and found that although perfectly judicial, they displayed no small attention to taste in their cut and general appearance. A proper degree of dignity is required and observed in the Supreme Court; business is there conducted as it ought to be in every court of justice; but some of the state courts are remarkably deficient in this respect: even in the Court-house at Philadelphia, during the sitting of the Circuit Court, I have seen a gentleman, a counsellor of eminence, coolly seat himself on the table whilst a judgment was being given, and in that attitude I have heard him address some interlocutory observations to the Court, and press them upon its attention with great earnestness and ability. I cannot understand why more dignity, both judicial and forensic, should not be observed in the courts of the United States. I have often been in the company of American lawyers, who, as individuals, were men of gentlemanly manners, and excellent general information, which they have ever evinced a readiness to impart; but I do not remember one who ever mentioned the subject at all, without admitting that a proper want of the respect due to the time and the place is frequently but too visible in the American courts; and yet there is no improvement.

Silence, being indispensable, is well preserved; but counsel and attorneys may be occasionally seen with their legs dangling over the back of a chair, or possibly resting on the table. A corresponding carelessness of manner is of course exhibited by the spectators. I have even observed persons with their hats on in court, and upon inquiry have been told they were Quakers; but once or twice I remember having taken the liberty of doubting the information. I hope I shall not be supposed to mean, that no greater decorum is observed in the principal courts of the larger cities than in those

Godfrey T. Vigne, Esq., of Lincoln's Inn, *Six Months in America* (1833), p. 68.

held at places of minor importance; I am speaking of them generally, as I found them when in travelling. I happened to arrive at some place where a court was sitting, and "just dropped in" for half an hour *en passant*; but still there is always a something even in the best of them, which, to an English eye, appears undignified and indecorous; although there can be no doubt that their appearance is not mended by the total absence of wigs and gowns from all of them.

The spirit of equality renders it allowable, and the impossibility in distant towns of making the profession answer by any other arrangement, renders it necessary, that a barrister and solicitor should frequently commence business as partners, and play into each other's hands. A Judge will frequently travel from town to town unattended, in his gig, or on horseback, with his saddle-bags before him, or in the stagecoach, and dine at the village table d'hôte with shopkeepers, pseudo majors, and advertising attorneys.

When it is considered that the Supreme Court has a federal jurisdiction extending over a union of twenty-four states, many of them as large or larger than England, whose humble and individual importance are increasing, and which are divided and subdivided by party, and by conflicting and annually arising interests, and which are becoming more and more democratic in every succeeding year, and consequently more and more opposed to the spirit in which the constitution was originally framed, some idea may be formed of the importance that is attached to the decisions of this court, whose authorities, from first to last, are intended as a safeguard to the Union. The independence of this court, and, in fact, of all the federal judiciary, may be termed the sheet anchor of the United States. Its power constitutes their chief hope; the abuse of it is the only medium of tyranny, and is therefore the principal source of apprehension. The Judges of all the federal courts hold their offices during good behaviour, and are removable only by impeachment. It would reasonably be supposed that the individual states would follow the example of the general government in the appointment of their Judges; but this is not the case. In seven of the states they are elected for a term of years only; in Rhode Island they are elected annually; in five of the states they are obliged to go out of office at sixty, sixty-five, or seventy years of age. This law in the enlightened state of New York has deprived it of the valuable services of Chancellor Kent, the author of the admirable Commentaries on the Laws of America. There are many democrats who actually wish that the Judges of the Supreme Court should be elected for a term of years only. This custom is notoriously productive of sufficient hardships in some of the more remote states, where, on account of the smallness of the salary, amounting to not more than two or three hundred pounds, the bench is sometimes filled by young and inexperienced men, who are the children of party, and whose decisions must be occasionally affected by the hope of re-election.

THE AMERICAN BAR IN 1851

Democratic Review

THE OPINION PREVAILS pretty generally, among the older class of lawyers, that the Bar of this country is deteriorating in learning, eloquence and character. This opinion is attributable in part to the reverence for by-gone days and by-gone men, which forms so prominent and harmless a trait in the habits of thought and expression indulged by those who are about to pass from the stage of action. They are always glorifying the golden years of their youth; and their auditors, catching some of their inspiration, are wont to regard the actors in those earlier times as superior to the every-day persons whom they see around them. In all this there is nothing peculiar to the present generation. It was ever thus, and ever will be thus, from age to age, "to the last syllable of recorded time."

Another source whence springs the opinion to which we have alluded, is the fact, that the bar in our day does not stand so far above the mass of the people in regard to general intelligence, oratorical gifts, and knowledge of the law itself, as it did fifty, or even thirty years ago. During this period the common mind of the country has received a mighty upward bound. Education is now widely diffused. The works of masters in the arts and sciences, and the productions of accomplished writers in every branch of literature, circulate through all the avenues of society, and at prices which bring them within the reach of the humbler classes. Newspapers, "the poor man's encyclopædia," and periodicals of every grade, and devoted to all conceivable subjects, are as omnipresent as the circumambient air. Then, too, the nation is converted into one great debating society, one grand mass convention, where nobody's seat is contested, where everybody is always in order, where the utmost freedom of speech is allowed, and where all sorts of questions, important, unimportant, and indifferent, are discussed, according to the several tastes of the disputants. Notwithstanding the abuses and absurdities that have been generated by this universal fermentation of the national mind, it has evolved many valuable principles, many rare facts, and has diffused through the masses of the community an incalculable amount of important information. . . .

If these things be so, then it may well be true, that though the American bar has not positively deteriorated in learning and eloquence, yet, because of the upward tendency of the whole body of the people, the relative distance between them may be very sensibly diminished, and, therefore, in the estimation of those who do not carefully survey the whole ground, the bar will seem to occupy a lower position than in the halcyon days of its

"The American Bar," *Democratic Review* (1851), XXVIII, p. 195.

undisputed supremacy, when Marshall took his seat on the Supreme bench at Washington, and Hamilton delighted select audiences by his luminous logic in the City Hall of New-York, while the people left the work of legislation to lawyers, and regarded the occult mysteries of jurisprudence as something too sacred for unlearned hands to touch, and too awful for uninitiated eyes to scan.

It may, nevertheless, be true, that owing to the undoubted increase of the number of legal practitioners, when compared with the increase of population, and owing to the greater ease with which admission to the bar is now gained, in consequence of the gradual diminution and relaxation of the tests of membership, we say, it may be true, that *every* lawyer in our day is not as learned as was every lawyer in those times when the rules of admission were more stringent in their nature and more rigidly enforced. Admitting this to be so, it may still be doubted whether the really-learned and competent members of the profession are injured in any way by the abolishment of the old monopoly of the bar, while it admits hardly of a question, that the legal reforms, and especially in the modes of procedure, of which this abolition was a part, tend powerfully to promote the ends of justice, by rendering the science of the law less occult, and its practice less difficult.

The age is gone by when the opinion will be tolerated, that the main end, or even *an* end to be sought by a system of jurisprudence, is the establishment of an abstruse science, and the creation of an "order" of men to practice it. It is now demanded, that the prime object of the law and its ministers, shall be, to mete out speedy and exact justice between man and man; that judges shall disregard the technicalities and crotchets of a scholastic age, and make forms yield to substance, in determining the merits of controversies; that precedents which have outlived the occasions that originated them, shall not obstruct the current of equity; that rules which have survived the reasons on which they were based, shall give place to others founded on the enlightened wants of our own times; and that causes shall be dismissed from the courts as rapidly as the substantial interests of the parties will permit.

In the accomplishment of these desirable objects, radical changes have been effected, and others are yet demanded in the three main agencies by which the judiciary supplies the multifarious wants of the people—*Pleading, Practice, and Evidence*. These constitute the working machinery of the profession and the courts. The common law system of *pleading*, simple at its origin, has, through the refinements of times and men eminently pedantic, acute, and technical, become too transcendental for the ordinary uses of a practical age. It is an exquisite scheme of logic, hard to be understood by the most subtile minds, and incomprehensible to the great majority of common-place intellects, who are compelled daily to deal with its nice distinctions. The code of *practice* which most of the courts of this country adopt, and which contains the leading features of the English system, consists of a series of inflexible rules, extremely arbitrary in their structure, and generally enforced with great rigor, to the special benefit of a race of small attorneys, with memories as exact as the multiplication table, but with minds utterly incapable of comprehending general principles, and who look upon the law as a cunningly devised scheme for playing tricks upon suitors, and swelling up bills of costs. By lodging too little discretion with the courts, so that they may adapt their proceedings to the ever-shifting exigencies of causes, this system often works the greatest injustice to suitors. Some of the states of the Union have swept it utterly away, leaving their tribunals to the guidance of a few general rules, while exercising a large discretion in cases unprovided for, and which they are to meet as they arise. The rules of *evidence* furnished by the common law, are only less technical in many of their essential features than the systems of pleading and practice. Within a few years they have been subjected to great modifications in several of the states, and must undergo still greater, ere they become a perfect medium, rather than a partial obstruction to the rays of truth.

It is these grand defects in the machinery of the judiciary, that have generated the very common opinion among the spectators of its workings, that the law, and especially the practice of the law, is a system of chicanery, or, at the best, of quackery, and that every lawyer is by profession either a knave or a charlatan, or a compound of both.

This opinion respecting lawyers is not confined to the vulgar. It permeates all classes, tinging even educated and liberal minds with prejudice. It has crept into literature. Be it tragedy, comedy, or farce, if a lawyer be introduced, he is the villain or dupe of the piece. How many despicable rogues, in the garb of attorneys, have novelists depicted? A grave historian, recording the incidents of the trial of Charles I., tells us, that the president of the tribunal was "one Bradshaw, a lawyer"! Even clergymen have been known to read, with special emphasis, the "wo" denounced against the lawyers of Judea, eighteen hundred years ago, by the Great Teacher; forgetting that the same wo was pronounced upon the "chief-priests" of that generation.

In a recent number, we pointed to some of the good traits in the character of the profession, while portraying the many defects of a vicious system. We will not repeat what we said then, but will merely add, that while we presume the Bar does not afford any more than its fair proportional share of virtue, we utterly deny that its members, as a body, are guilty of extraordinary departures from the path of integrity in the pursuit of their calling. That they combine together to enmesh clients in the net-work of litigation, for the sole purpose of picking their pockets, no well informed mind believes. That, through the ignorance, or caution, or willfulness of suitors, in stating their cases to counsel, the latter are often led to give erroneous opinions, is known to every member of the profession; and all persons competent to form a judgment in the matter, will tell you, that for every instance where a lawyer corruptly misleads his client, there are ten where a suitor misleads his counsel. The zeal with which an advocate will stand by to the end, what turns out to be a bad cause, has subjected the profession to much reproach; whereas, in the large majority of such cases, this conduct should entitle them to unmixed praise. The client is careful to fill the mind of his counsel with all the bright points of his side of the case, and all the dark features of the other side, while he leaves it for the trial to develop the antagonisms of his representations. He is sure to make himself out to be a deeply wronged man, and his opponent a very bad fellow, of whose arts and whose witnesses he cautions his counsel to beware. Thus prepossessed, the advocate becomes the representative of one whose mouth is to be closed while he passes the ordeal of justice, and in whose name and stead he is to do battle. He enters the arena, struggles to meet every adverse turn which the conflict takes, looks with suspicion upon every word of testimony that tells heavily upon his client, and it is only when the impartiality of the bench turns the scale against him, that he yields to the conviction, that he has been duped into the support of a bad cause by a dishonest man.

As to the science of jurisprudence, as distinguished from its practice, it is fated to encounter all the vulgar prejudices of other sciences, and some which are peculiar to itself. A good deal of its learning must ever lie beyond the ken of those who do not make it their study. This will excite suspicion. Many of its terms and phrases will always jar upon the unlearned ear. This will afford themes for ridicule. It vitally affects, and authoritatively determines, the most sensitive interests of society, regulating every man's conduct and interfering in every man's business. In this respect, so long as it gratifies the whims, enhances the prosperity, and avenges the wrongs of an individual, it receives his unqualified praise. But, every law-suit has two sides, one of which is destined to be beaten. In every contest there is the vanquished as well as the victor—the captive as well as the captor. And who ever knew the beaten to speak peaceably of the beater—the vanquished of the victor—the captive of the captor? Such rare magnanimity is not engendered by the heat and bitterness of litigation. Thus, almost every hotly-contested cause, raises up at least one new enemy of the law and the lawyers.

The abuses, errors, and absurdities of the legal profession are more promptly exposed, and therefore are more patent, than those of the professions of medicine and divinity. In the conflicts of the courts, each party has his champion, whose duty it is, not merely to defend his own side, but to demolish the other. In such an arena, unless both combatants, as well as the umpire, are deplorably ignorant, charlatans cannot play off their tricks without exposure on the spot. Put the professions of medicine and divinity to such a trial, and how would they endure the test? Let every prescription of the physician, and every homily of the clergyman, be subjected to a rigid cross-examination, and an acute analysis, by a disciple of some hostile school, while a competent umpire summed up the controversy, and twelve impartial men pronounced their verdict upon it, and how much of quackery and heresy would be laid bare to vulgar eyes? And it is through such an ordeal that the law and its practitioners are compelled to pass continually. To all other sciences and arts, professions and callings, may jurisprudence and its ministers appropriately say: "Let not him that girdeth on his harness boast himself as he that putteth it off."

To return to the question of the deterioration of the American bar in learning and eloquence. The number of elective and especially legislative offices in this country—the universality of the right of suffrage—the eligibility of almost every person to any station in the government—the frequency of elections,—all these tend to precipitate the great body of ambitious men into the whirlpool of politics. The legal profession is the highway to official distinction. Many enter it, not to practice its duties, and win its honors, but simply because it affords facilities for obtaining public stations. This has no doubt tended to lower the standard of learning within the pale of the bar. These fugitive lawyers impress much of their superficiality upon a profession of which they constitute so considerable a portion. It will, however, be borne in mind, that with occasional exceptions, our greatest lawyers have also been distinguished as politicians. Such names as the following will readily occur to the memory of the reader:—Jay, Sherman, Hamilton, Dexter, Pinckney, Burr, Ogden, Bayard, Sargeant, Livingston, Binney, Holmes, Clay, Webster, Wirt, Crittenden, Woodbury, J. C. Spencer, Van Buren, Barry, Legare, B. F. Butler, Grundy, Choate and Prentiss. The most eminent exceptions to this rule, not entirely unknown as politicians, but far better known as lawyers, have generally been elevated to the bench. We refer to such jurists as Marshall, Kent, Story, Parsons, Daggett, Parker, Tilghman, Tucker, Martin, Thompson, Spencer, Hopkinson, Gibson, Baldwin, McLane, Taney, Wayne, Shaw, Nelson and Cady.

The reputation of the first class of names we have mentioned, would tend to prove, that occasional indulgence in other pursuits than those of the law, is not incompatible with the highest attainments in the profession. Indeed, observation establishes the fact, that such indulgence rather aids than retards the *advocate*—him who practices chiefly at *Nisi Prius*—in reaching the loftiest position at the bar. Though the law is a jealous goddess, and is wont to bestow her choicest favors on those who worship most assiduously at her altars, the barrister who would win verdicts must frequently kneel at other shrines than hers. So acute and philosophical an observer as Edmund Burke, said, when sketching the character of Grenville: "He was bred to the law, which is, in my opinion, one of the first and noblest of human sciences; a science which does more to quicken and invigorate the understanding, than all other kinds of learning put together; *but is not apt, except in persons very happily born, to open and liberalize the mind exactly in the same proportion.*" To supply the defect pointed out by this great man, must be the purpose of every one who would mount the highest places in the profession. A *mere* lawyer, versed in the *dicta* of books, and tied down by red tape to time-honored precedents, but who knows nothing of other branches of learning, may be a valuable chamber adviser in common causes;

but he lacks many of the qualifications essential to eminence on the bench, and must utterly fail as an advocate at the bar.

Presuming the lawyer to possess the ordinary acquaintance with general science, bestowed by a liberal education, the two pursuits most conducive to success in the forensic field of the profession, are politics and literature. We do not mean politics in the vulgar sense, but statesmanship; the study of the philosophy of government; a participation in the conduct of public affairs. And we use the term literature in its restricted sense; the study of the best models, ancient and modern, in the department of *belles lettres*.

The disciples of Coke may be disposed to take issue with us on this latter point. But, we apprehend, there can be no greater mistake than to suppose, that a moderate indulgence in the cultivation of polite literature, both as a student and an author, will hinder one's success at the bar. It is useful as a means of relaxation from the dry drudgery of the profession; it expands and liberalizes the mind; it forms and refines the taste; it affords the choicest material for illustration and embellishment; it breaks up and dissipates the crabbed style of writing and speaking, which every close student of the ancient law is apt to contract; it is essential to the forming of a perfect, or even a respectable orator. . . .

It might naturally be supposed, that the juridical forum would be the chosen spot where eloquence would strike its deepest roots, throw up its loftiest branches, and bear its choicest fruits. Justice is the theme—rights to be vindicated, and wrongs to be redressed, innocence to be protected, and vice punished, are the ends to be attained—the reason of the judge is to be enlightened, and the feelings of the jury aroused, and their verdict won— the utmost freedom of discussion is allowed—and yet, visit our courts, and listen to the addresses ordinarily delivered there. . . .

There is a better, and even a worse class of lawyers, from whom eloquence has as little to hope as from these. The better class, to which we allude, are those who regard the law as a liberal science, and have a taste for literature. But they are deluded with the idea, that if they would become able and successful lawyers, they must study nothing but law. So they set their faces through life against everything which would tempt them into the pursuit, even for a day, of any other kind of knowledge. These disciples of "the black-letter school," being usually sound lawyers and honest men, but utterly incapable of cutting a second-rate figure as advocates, exert a pernicious influence upon the younger members of the bar. Their gifts and attainments too often define the boundaries of professional excellence, and among these, oratory finds no place. But the deleterious effects of their example do not stop here. A majority of the bench is generally selected from this class. When thus elevated, they are apt to discourage the display of those gifts in the advocate, of which they are destitute, either not appreciating their value, or ill-concealing their envy at the superior influence they exert upon jurors and auditors over their own bald exhibitions. Slovenly in their juridical performances, whether oral or written, they almost regard it as a personal affront when counsel, in addressing the bench, leave the citation of cases, and their application to the matter in hand, to course over the field of original speculation, and deduce arguments from first principles, or, in addressing the jury, refuse to confine themselves to the dry details of the testimony, but enlighten the reason and kindle the passions, clothing their thoughts in vigorous and polished diction, and enlivening and adorning the path they are treading with the flashes of wit and the flowers of fancy.

We shall dismiss the other class of the profession to which we have alluded—the worst class—very summarily. Neither eloquence nor honesty has anything to hope from them. Their highest ideas of the practice of the law, are, skill in gaining some technical advantage over an opponent by trickery, and swindling him out of a heavy bill of costs, by means of false affidavits. The radical reforms in pleading and practice, and the diminution in the length of the fee-bill, which are being introduced into most of the states, are rapidly sweeping away this race of vermin. . . .

And . . . as to text-books. Confining our observations to American authors, and excluding from the category such writers as Kent, Story, Hoffman, and Greenleaf, we are compelled to say, that many of these treatises have been executed in the most disorderly, vague, and jejune manner. Often they are mere digests of adjudicated cases, copied in the precise words of the head-notes of the reports, strung together at random by a feeble thread of common-place criticism, and requiring for their composition no more intellect than would be necessary to compile the indexes of a hundred volumes of the reports into one. The making of law-books is a trade. A bookseller enters into a contract with some student hardly out of his teens, or some attorney wholly out of business, to prepare a work on some branch of the law. The forthcoming treatise, "by a distinguished member of the profession," is extensively advertised in the newspapers, in catalogues, and on the covers of law magazines, ere pen is put to paper. At length it appears. The publisher employs some needy recipient of his bounty (perhaps the author himself) to eulogize the work through the same media that heralded its approach. The profession purchase it on the faith of these *ante* and *post* puffings, and never discover, till they consult its pages, that they have been duped into buying a shallow and worthless production. We recollect being present when one of the most eminent counsellors of the New-York bar was tumbling over the leaves of a new treatise, of the class we have described, for an hour or two, searching for some point; and having compared the doctrine in the text with the case on which it professed to be based, he threw down the volume, exclaiming in a rage, "This fellow is unfit to teach the A. B. C.'s in a common school, and yet he presumes to write a law-book!" We by no means intend to say, that the four American authors we have mentioned, compose all the names that should be exempted from our censure. We cite them as the heads of a class of text-book writers, whose works will bear comparison with those of the first class of English authors, while some of them have far surpassed trans-Atlantic productions in depth of learning, breadth of comprehension, vigor of reasoning, and purity and dignity of style.

As to the decisions of the courts, as embodied in the reports. These are almost invariably drawn up by the judges themselves. We have sketched the qualifications, for the performance of this task, of that great body of practitioners, who, loving the law and despising eloquence, furnish the majority of our judges. They have formed their style of writing upon the crabbed models of the ancient expositors of the common law—the Littletons, the Cokes, the Bractons, of the olden time. Having no acquaintance with elegant literature—never having devoted an hour's time even to the study of rhetoric since they came to the bar—incapable of writing in a vigorous, lucid, orderly, terse manner, many able American judges are constantly sending to the press productions which every lawyer is compelled to study, composed in a style so feeble, obscure, negligent and verbose, that respectable literary journals would not spread them upon their pages, even though the subject-matter were congenial to the tastes of their readers. Who ever heard of a man being elevated to the bench because he was a vigorous, clear, and elegant writer, as well as a learned, acute, and safe lawyer? Yet the reports of his judgments will derive a large share of their value with posterity from his capacity to clothe them in strong, terse, and luminous language. . . .

We have time and space barely to allude to those stores of knowledge, ranging over every science and art, every trade and calling, which a lawyer in extensive practice at *Nisi Prius* must possess, if he would acquit himself even respectably. Everything, from the construction of the United States Constitution to the construction of a fanning-mill, must pass in review before him. Breaches of the marriage contract, and of a warranty in the sale of horses—broken limbs unskillfully reduced by quack surgeons, and characters damaged by slanderous tongues or libellous pens—the science of the steam-engine, and the constituent elements of a patent elixir—whether somnambulism or an *alibi* is the best defence to an indictment for murder—marine insurance, and the drift of the trade winds—fire insurance and the combustible nature of oils—building contracts, and the mysteries of carpenters, bricklayers and painters—the tanning of leather, the erection of saw-mills, and the construction of railways—the usages of brokers, bankers, merchants and doctors—the rights of clergymen, school-masters, sea-captains, and militia colonels, and the duties of parishioners, scholars, sailors and soldiers:—in short, and omitting details, the lawyer in full business, in the space of a single month, is often compelled to familiarize himself with legal learning which lies scattered along the track of the last five hundred years, and with the various arts, sciences, professions, trades, and practices of his own times; be as patient as a scourged donkey, while working like a galley slave; be broad awake to all the defects of his own side of the case, and keen to detect the tricks of his "learned opponent";

keep his temper while a mercurial judge wrests the guidance of the trial out of his hands, and turns it into channels where defeat is almost certain to overtake him; listen to the ill-timed suggestions of an ignorant client, while put to the rack by the perversity or stupidity of a witness; and at the close of a protracted contest, with a pile of blotted manuscript before him, not one word of which he has had time to review, he must rise, bring order out of confusion, symmetry out of chaos, demolish this witness, support that, reconcile contradictions, anticipate and answer the objections of his adversary, smooth down the prejudices of the court, win the good will of the jury, and secure a verdict—if he can!

Surely, lawyers that *are* lawyers, need not be told, that they must study something beside Coke and Chitty.

Though the American Bar may be deficient in legal and general knowledge, and negligent in the cultivation of rhetoric and oratory, it has produced as many able lawyers and eloquent advocates, during the last thirty years, as the English. . . .

If this be true, (and we have no reason to doubt it,) then, at the present time, the American bar must be decidedly superior to the English. We think it would not be difficult to name hundreds of American lawyers, "who can now address a jury, in an important case, with average ability."

By the side of these eminent foreign names, we venture to place those of Pinckney, Webster, Clay, Wirt, Talcott, Sargeant, Williams, Binney, Storrs, Crittenden, Legare, Prentiss, and Choate, and to challenge a comparison between them in respect to depth and scope of legal attainments, capacity to enlighten judges by luminous argumentation, power to sway juries by informing the reason or arousing the passions, and the possession of all the gifts and graces which combine to make profound lawyers and eloquent advocates. Nor do we think the task would be hopeless of selecting thirteen other names that would pass the ordeal with honor. . . .

The truth undoubtedly is, that since the Revolution, the matured mind of America has been more exclusively devoted to the kindred subjects of jurisprudence and government, than to any other of the liberal sciences, and for the obvious reason, that much of the national intellect has, owing to the recent origin and peculiar structure of our institutions, been necessarily employed in founding, erecting, and administering a civil polity, partly of our own creation, and partly borrowed from our British ancestors. This has compelled our statesmen and lawyers to examine the groundwork as well as the details of the constitution and laws of England, so that they might mould and adapt to our uses such parts of them as were congenial to our republican system. And being desirous to obtain materials to perfect our institutions from all countries, they have extended their researches into the political and judicial polities of contemporary nations. Hence it is, that American writers on government and law have equalled, if not surpassed, in scope of comprehension, variety of learning, and freedom of speculation, those of England, since the advent of our Republic.

Part II

ALLOCATION
OF
POWER

Dan.l Webster

Introduction

The United States was still a child to the ways of sovereignty at the start of the period. The new political status of the country had not led to great changes in the private relationships of society, but in the domain of public law everything was unfamiliar. It was natural then that public-law questions, though few in number, when they did arise had a clear and urgent priority over questions of private law, the daily fare of the law courts.

After the Revolution, as before, individuals entered into relationships of employment, contract, property, and even of injury. The English common-law rules on the rights and duties incident to such relations had not occasioned any great dissatisfaction previously, proving on the whole an acceptable body of private law. It was felt that where changes were required by alterations in conditions and ideas they could be effected—as they were, perhaps at a slower rate, in England—by the process of gradual modification which is the essence of a common-law system.

Contrast with this the public-law situation. Here every relationship was new, not only in an obvious sense by reason of the country's recent independence, but often also in the absolute sense of being a first attempt to put into practice the abstractions of political theory. There was no body of public law whose rules could be borrowed to meliorate between the different powers of the Federal Government, or between the states individually or in combination with the Federal Government. Although there were some resemblances between the relations of the sister states to each other and those among independent sovereign nations, the differences were probably more numerous. In any attempt to come to terms with problems arising from these differences there was no body of experience on which to draw. Under the compulsion of originality, balance became the motif of many compromises reached in the emerging community. At times, this meant the application of fertile imaginations and creative powers to the full extent to devise middle courses which, although hardly inspiring, were the stuff of which national unity and workable arrangements were made.

The broad consensus before 1850 which made legal solutions to the problem of allocating governmental power possible can be traced to the characteristic which de Tocqueville found to be the key feature of America in the 1830's—the "general equality of condition" of its inhabitants. There were, of course, social gradations, but there were few depressed groups without any prospect of bettering their condition. This was partly due to the abundance of free land, but this physical condition alone does not seem a sufficient cause. More likely, the explanation of this felicitous situation lies in the interaction of such plentiful resources and the American legal order. Just as law and plenty had cooperated earlier to destroy such aristocratic European institutions as primogeniture and entail, the interaction now provided a broad base of economic democracy on which political democracy could be built. Whether the abundance of land or the thrust of the common law was more significant in leading to a democratically oriented society is a proposition which cannot be resolved empirically, though the example of what happened in Latin America seems to suggest an answer. They too had free land at the beginning of settlement. But latifundiary monoculture, centering on the large-scale cultivation of such crops as sugar and on the grazing of cattle, created conditions unlike those in most of the United States in a very short time. As land holdings grew larger, those who were unable to raise the massive amount of capital needed to enter profitable farming were often forced to accept work as hired hands. This was rarely true in the United States. In 1830 it did not require a vast amount of capital for a person to engage actively in farming in this country. With high social mobility built on the abundance of land and abetted by legal institutions, few men were likely to resort to revolution rather than law to improve their lot.

This helps to account both for the high esteem accorded to the law and for the prominence of lawyers at that time. The lawyer formulated the compromises which all Americans desired. The law provided the element of stability and balance in society which made it possible for men to pursue business or agricultural interests—interests which were beginning to provide the common man with a prosperity never dreamed of in Europe.

The major lesson of the delicate accommodation of powers during this era is that the keystone of law is reason. If it is in the interests of the majority to obtain reasonable solutions to a problem, law can prevail—but where reason goes, law too departs. From the 1820's to 1860 law and the Constitution were used by lawyers over and over again for hammering out compromises. But when the emotional issue became overriding as it did with slavery—when those who had ears heard not the reasoning of their opponents—the compromising ability of the law was unwanted and unheeded. The strength of the common law is that it lends itself readily to the reaching of approximate solutions. It is in the very nature of the lawyer's conservatism that he seeks to adjust conflicts between hostile elements in society, and to avoid the disproportionate growth of any single element. Only where compromises are totally unacceptable does the law cease to function.

It was thus inevitable that the focus of legal energies—as well as the key issue politically—was the establishment of an equilibrium within the constitutional framework. Dispute raged over the proper allocation of governmental powers. The now all-but-forgotten theory that the United States was a federation of sections, as well as a union of states, was vigorously urged, and as forcibly rejected.

Many of the important issues were joined and explored initially in connection with tariff policy. It was the question of tariffs, not slavery, which first made the South militant. But, as Bancroft suggests in *Calhoun and the South Carolina Nullification Movement*, the two issues were inter-related: the nexus was a fear that "a centralized Federal Government with a surplus reserve derived from protective tariffs would embark on schemes for compensated emancipation and colonization." Against this background, and the decline of the South Carolina cotton economy, Calhoun devised his theories of "Greek democracy," "state interposition," "concurrent majority," and the formula of a sectional veto on national policy. South Carolina's Ordinance of Nullification (1832) was countered by Jackson's Proclamation. But the question was still regarded as debatable—and debated it was, with vigor, conviction, and brilliance. Legal arguments about the essential nature of the federal union and the meaning of the "compact" were advanced in the Senate by Calhoun and Webster in their microscopic examination of the Constitution. Following their speeches, Clay's Compromise Tariff and the Force Bill, giving the Federal Government complete and summary control of cases arising under custom laws, were passed. Thus, in the words of Professor Summer, "the olive branch and the rod were bound up together."

The establishment of the national bank raised the same issues, and they were supported by similar arguments. The view that the Federal Government existed by the consent of the sovereign states and that Article X of the Constitution reserved to the states all powers not specifically delegated by the Constitution to the Federal Government was the basis for much of the opposition from Southern leaders to both the First and Second Banks of the United States. This issue, too, was settled by debate within the legal framework, ultimately by reference to John Marshall's Supreme Court. Marshall was Chief Justice for thirty-four years (1801–1835), and the Court's decisions under his leadership played a strategic role in molding the Constitution into an instrument of national policy. By fashioning the legal conditions for a free national market, Marshall upheld the Federalist concept of the Union during his entire tenure on the Court. He insisted that the Constitution was a product of the people rather than of the states, and by proclaiming the paramountcy of the Federal powers, the bench drew tight the "continental belt." These views were applied to the bank question in the landmark case of *McCulloch* v. *Maryland*.

Political and legal debate proved futile in resolving the issue of slavery and the power of the Federal Government to regulate it in the territories. Lawyers were called, but they could only struggle to evolve a compromise over conflicting sectional interests, perhaps to delay the inevitable. The case of *State ex rel McCready* v. *Hunt* is, in view of its source—South Carolina, the seedbed of Southern intransigence—a surprising instance of such a compromise. The court, albeit a divided one, invalidated the act requiring every officer of the military to take the oath, "I will be faithful, and true allegiance bear, to the State of South Carolina." Indeed, there were plans in the 1850's to have the whole problem of slavery settled by a decision of the Supreme Court. But there was never to be a *McCulloch* v. *Maryland* for slavery. Although the Dred Scott case can be viewed as an attempt to invoke the court's prestige, it failed. This freight was too heavy for the law to carry.

The positions of the North and South became polarized; moderate candidates were dismissed as timid compromisers. Stephen A. Douglas represents the "muddling through" tradition. His position on the extension of slavery into the territories was that the inhabitants of each area should decide for themselves in the territorial legislature whether they desired the establishment of slavery. Logically this made no sense, for it implied that a territorial legislature could do that which Congress itself, which had created the legislature, could not: prohibit the institution of slavery. From a practical point of view, however, Douglas's position can be regarded as a compromise between the extremes of Sumner and Breckenridge. But the slavery issue was so closed to compromise as to banish moderate voices and open the way for the hotspurs.

The peaceful settlement of one issue and the failure to settle another shows clearly that the bank issue simply was not as emotionally explosive as the slavery quarrel. True, the Monster Bank was a burning issue, especially during the Jacksonian period. For decades fears of the monopoly of money, and the consequent massing of power, colored national and state politics. But the "money power" never brought the nation close to civil war. This resulted in part from the ambivalence of its opponents, who viewed with fascination as well as fear the revolutionary ways of acquiring wealth through modern capitalism. The immorality of slavery was a more secure reform plank than the immorality of successful pursuit of profit, especially in a society devoted to maximizing individual opportunity. And no single class or group of classes—no matter how deeply moved by agrarian nostalgia—stood to lose so much that it would resort to extreme measures to oppose the establishment of a national bank, or to reject permanently the court's broad interpretation of the "necessary and proper" clause. So the degree of consensus which permits recourse to law materialized as to national banks; but it never materialized as to the South's peculiar institution.

1. The Nation and the State

THE NATIONAL POWER

John Marshall

Chief Justice Marshall (1755–1835) is the principal founder of the American system of constitutional law. His twin themes were that the Constitution is the act of the people of the United States, rather than of the several states, and that the Supreme Court is its authoritative expositor. These views are illustrated in the opinions following.

Stating his disapproval of Cohens v. Virginia, Thomas Jefferson wrote to his friend on the Supreme Court, Mr. Justice Johnson, "The practice of Judge Marshall of travelling out of his case to prescribe what the law would be in a moot case not before the court is very irregular and very censurable." Of this attack, Story wrote to Mason on January 10, 1822:

> *Mr. Jefferson stands at the head of the enemies of the Judiciary and I doubt not will leave behind him a numerous progeny bred in the same school. The truth is and cannot be disguised, even from vulgar observation, that the Judiciary in our country is essentially feeble, and must always be open to attack from all quarters. It will perpetually thwart the wishes and views of the demagogues, and it can have no places to give and no patronage to draw around it close defenders. Its only support is the wise and the good and the elevated in society; and these, as we all know, must ever remain in a discouraging minority in all Governments.*

Webster and Wirt were on the same side in the steamboat case, Gibbons v. Ogden, but took different courses in the argument, Webster urging the broader ground of the exclusive authority of Congress to regulate commerce on all navigable waters. In 1851, Webster wrote to Edward Everett: "I presume the argument in Gibbons v. Ogden was written by me. . . . It has been often observed that the opinion of the court delivered by Chief Justice Marshall follows closely the track of the argument. He adopts the idea which I remember struck him at the time that by the constitution, the commerce of the several states has become a unit."

THAT THE UNITED STATES form for many, and for most purposes, a single nation has yet not been denied. . . . The Constitution and laws of a State so far as they are repugnant to the Constitution and laws of the

---

Cohens v. Virginia, 6 *Wheaton* (1821), pp. 264, 413.
Gibbons v. Ogden, 9 *Wheaton* (1824), pp. 1, 222.

United States are absolutely void. The States are the constituent parts of the United States. They are members of one great empire—for some purposes sovereign, for some purposes subordinate.

POWERFUL AND INGENIOUS MINDS, taking, as postulates, that the powers expressly granted to the Government of the Union are to be contracted, by construction, into the narrowest possible compass, and that the original powers of the States are retained, if any possible construction will retain them, may by a course of well digested, but refined and metaphysical reasoning . . . explain away the Constitution of our country, and leave it a magnificent structure indeed, to look at, but totally unfit for use. They may so entangle and perplex the understanding, as to obscure principles which were before thought quite plain, and induce doubts where, if the mind were to pursue its own course, none would be perceived. In such a case, it is peculiarly necessary to recur to safe and fundamental principles.

IF CONGRESS had passed any Act which bore upon the case; any Act in execution of the power to regulate commerce, the object of which was to control State legislation over those small navigable creeks into which the tide flows, and which abound throughout the lower country of the Middle and Southern States, we should feel not much difficulty in saying that a State law coming in conflict with such Act would be void. But Congress has passed no such Act. The repugnancy of the law of Delaware to the Constitution is placed entirely on its repugnancy to the power to regulate commerce with foreign nations and among the several States; a power which has not been so exercised as to affect the question.

    We do not think that the Act empowering the Black Bird Creek Marsh Company to place a dam across the creek, can, under all the circumstances of the case, be considered as repugnant to the power to regulate commerce in its dormant state, or as being in conflict with any law passed on the subject.

THE RIGHT TO ANNUL THE CONSTITUTION

John Caldwell Calhoun

With John Caldwell Calhoun (1782–1850) was to lie the defense of the South's peculiar institution. The seeds of his defense of slavery can be seen in the following selection, though it focuses on another divisive issue.

    Wilson v. Black Bird Creek Marsh Co., 2 Pet. (1829), p. 245.
    Calhoun, Speech in Senate, February 15-16, 1833, *Speeches in Congress* (ed. Crallé, 1858), p. 197.

Calhoun had studied law in that early national school, Tapping Reeve's at Litchfield, Connecticut. He was admitted to the South Carolina bar in 1807, where "he found the pursuit uncongenial and resolved to abandon it as soon as opportunity should permit." Politics provided the opportunity. Most historians prefer to regard Calhoun as a theoretician rather than a lawyer. One nineteenth-century biographer observes that he never could have been a great lawyer, for "he was not objective enough to examine his premises with sufficient care, while he built his arguments upon them with undeviating logic"; thus, he would arrive at "shocking" conclusions with no basis other than his highly questionable original postulates. In short, Calhoun was not enthusiastic about the law and the discipline it demanded. Nevertheless, Calhoun's legal training emerges in his arduous examination of the Constitution.

Until 1828, he joined with Clay in supporting a nationalist policy of expansion. But the economic interests of the South led him into a probing analysis of the vague abstraction of national unity. After the passage of the protective tariff of 1832, Calhoun published a letter to Governor Hamilton, containing the ultimate exposition of the nullification doctrine: he stated that the Federal and state governments alike were organs of the people of the several states; that the people of a state could, by means of a convention, declare a Congressional act null and void and require the state government to prohibit enforcement within the limits of the state. This argument must be read in careful contrast to secession, which is withdrawal from the Union. Calhoun resigned the Vice-Presidency to make his argument on the floor of the Senate, against the backdrop of a South Carolina ordinance nullifying the tariff acts of 1828 and 1832. His technique, as in the following excerpt, was to submit the terms of the Constitution to microscopic scrutiny.

IT HAS BEEN SAID that South Carolina claims the right to annul the constitution and laws of the United States; and to rebut this supposed claim, the gentleman from Virginia (Mr. Rives) has gravely quoted the constitution, to prove that the constitution, and the laws made in pursuance thereof, are the supreme laws of the land—as if the State claimed the right to act contrary to this provision of the constitution. Nothing can be more erroneous: her object is not to resist laws made in pursuance of the constitution, but those made without its authority, and which encroached on her reserved powers. She claims not even the right of judging of the delegated powers, but of those that are reserved; and to resist the former, when they encroach upon the latter. . . .

Such right I hold to be essential to the existence of a division [of power]; and that, to give to either party the conclusive right of judging, not only of the share allotted to it, but of that allotted to the other, is to annul the division, and to confer the whole power on the party vested with such right.

But it is contended that the constitution has conferred on the Supreme

Court the right of judging between the States and the General Government. Those who make this objection, overlook, I conceive, an important provision of the constitution. By turning to the 10th amended article, it will be seen that the reservation of power to the States is not only against the powers, delegated to Congress, but against the United States themselves; and extends, of course, as well to the judiciary as to the other departments of the Government. The article provides, that all powers not delegated to the United States, or prohibited by it to the States, are reserved to the States respectively, or to the people. . . . The reservation of powers to the States is, as I have said, against the whole; and is as full against the judicial as it is against the executive and legislative departments of the Government. It cannot be claimed for the one without claiming it for the whole, and without, in fact, annulling this important provision of the constitution.

Against this, as it appears to me, conclusive view of the subject, it has been urged that this power is expressly conferred on the Supreme Court by that portion of the constitution which provides that the judicial power shall extend to all cases in law and equity arising under the constitution, the laws of the United States, and treaties made under their authority. I believe the assertion to be utterly destitute of any foundation. It obviously is the intention of the constitution simply to make the judicial power commensurate with the law-making and treaty-making powers; and to vest it with the right of applying the constitution, the laws, and the treaties, to the cases which might arise under them; and not to make it the judge of the constitution, the laws, and the treaties themselves. In fact, the power of applying the laws to the facts of the case, and deciding upon such application, constitutes, in truth, the judicial power. . . .

But it will be asked how the court obtained the power to pronounce a law or treaty unconstitutional, when it comes in conflict with that instrument. I do not deny that it possesses the right; but I can by no means concede that it was derived from the constitution. It had its origin in the necessity of the case. Where there are two or more rules established, one from a higher, the other from a lower authority, which may come into conflict in applying them to a particular case, the judge cannot avoid pronouncing in favor of the superior against the inferior. It is from this necessity, and this alone, that the power which is now set up to overrule the rights of the States against an express provision of the constitution was derived. It had no other origin. That I have traced it to its true source, will be manifest from the fact that it is a power which, so far from being conferred exclusively on the Supreme Court, as is insisted, belongs to every court—inferior and superior—State and General—and even to foreign courts. . . .

It is next objected, that the enforcing acts have legislated the United States out of South Carolina. I have already replied to this objection on another occasion, and will now but repeat what I then said: that they have been legislated out only to the extent that they had no right to enter. The constitution has admitted the jurisdiction of the United States within the limits of the several States only so far as the delegated powers authorize; beyond that they are intruders, and may rightfully be expelled; and that they have been efficiently expelled by the legislation of the State through her civil process, as has been acknowledged on all sides in the debate, is only a confirmation of the truth of the doctrine for which the majority in Carolina have contended.

The very point at issue between the two parties there is, whether nullification is a peaceable and efficient remedy against an unconstitutional act of the General Government, and may be asserted, as such, through the State tribunals. Both parties agree that the acts against which it is directed are unconstitutional and oppressive. The controversy is only as to the means by which our citizens may be protected against the acknowledged encroachments on their rights. This being the point at issue between the parties, and the very object of the majority being an efficient protection of the citizens through the State tribunals, the measures adopted to enforce the ordinance, of course received the most decisive character. We were not children, to act by halves. Yet for acting thus efficiently the State is denounced, and this bill reported, to overrule, by military force, the civil tribunals and civil process of the State! Sir, I consider this bill, and the arguments which have been urged on this floor in its support, as the most triumphant acknowledgment that nullification is peaceful and efficient, and so deeply intrenched in the principles of our system, that it cannot be assailed but by prostrating the constitution, and substituting the supremacy of military force in lieu of the supremacy of the laws. In fact, the advocates of this bill refute their own argument. They tell us that the ordinance is unconstitutional; that it infracts the constitution of South Carolina, although, to me, the objection appears absurd, as it was adopted by the very authority which adopted the constitution itself. They also tell us that the Supreme Court is the appointed arbiter of all controversies between a State and the General Government. Why, then, do they not leave this controversy to that tribunal? Why do they not confide to them the abrogation of the ordinance, and the laws made in pursuance of it, and the assertion of that supremacy which they claim for the laws of Congress? The State stands pledged to resist no process of the court. Why, then, confer on the President the extensive and unlimited powers provided in this bill? Why authorize him to use military force to arrest the civil process of the State? But one answer can be given: That, in a contest between the State and the General Government, if the resistance be limited on both sides to the civil process, the State, by its inherent sovereignty, standing upon its reserved powers, will prove too powerful in such a controversy, and must triumph over the Federal Government, sustained by its delegated and limited authority; and in this answer we have an acknowledgment of the truth of those great principles for which the State has so firmly and nobly contended. . . .

I know that it is not only the opinion of a large majority of our country, but it may be said to be the opinion of the age, that the very beau ideal of a perfect government is the government of a majority, acting through a representative body, without check or limitation on its power; yet, if we may test this theory by experience and reason, we shall find that, so far from being perfect, the necessary tendency of all governments, based upon the will of an absolute majority, without constitutional check or limitation of power, is to faction, corruption, anarchy, and despotism; and this, whether the will of the majority be expressed directly through an assembly of the people themselves, or by their representatives. . . . The view which considers the community as an unit, and all its parts as having a similar interest, is radically erroneous. However small the community may be, and however homogeneous its interests, the moment that government is put into operation—as soon as it begins to collect taxes and to make appropriations, the different portions of the community must, of necessity, bear different and opposing relations in reference to the action of the government. There must inevitably spring up two interests—a direction and a stockholder interest—an interest profiting by the action of the government, and interested in increasing its powers and action; and another, at whose expense the political machine is kept in motion. . . .

There is a remedy, and but one,—the effect of which, whatever may be the form, is to organize society in reference to this conflict of interests, which springs out of the action of government; and which can only be done by giving to each part the right of self-protection; which, in a word, instead of considering the community . . . a single community, having a common interest, and to be governed by the single will of an entire majority, shall upon all questions tending to bring the parts into conflict . . . take the will [of the parts],—the majority of each governing the part, and where they concur, governing the whole,—and where they disagree, arresting the action of the government. This I will call the concurring, as distinct from the absolute majority. In either way the number would be the same, whether taken as the absolute or as the concurring majority. . . . But, though the number [in the majority] is the same, the mode of counting is essentially different: the one representing the strongest interest, and the other, the entire interests of the community. The first mistake is, in supposing that the government of the absolute majority is the government of the people—that beau ideal of a perfect government which has been so enthusiastically entertained in every age by the generous and patriotic, where civilization and liberty have made the smallest progress. There can be no greater error: the government of the people is the government of the whole community— . . . the self-government of all the parts—too perfect to be reduced to practice in the present, or any past stage of human society. The government of the absolute majority, instead of being the government of the people, is but the government of the strongest interests, and, when not efficiently checked, is the most tyrannical and oppressive that can be devised. Between this ideal perfection on the one side, and despotism on the other, no other system can be devised but that which considers society in reference to its parts, as differently affected by the action of the government, and which takes the sense of each part separately, and thereby the sense of the whole, in the manner already illustrated. . . .

If we turn our attention . . . to our government and its actual operation, we shall find a practical confirmation of the truth of what has been stated, not only of the oppressive operation of the system of an absolute majority, but also a striking and beautiful illustration, in the formation of our system, of the principle of the concurring majority, as distinct from the absolute, which I have asserted to be the only means of efficiently checking the abuse of power, and, of course, the only solid foundation of constitutional liberty. That our government, for many years, has been gradually verging to consolidation; that the constitution has gradually become a dead letter; and that all restrictions upon the power of government have been virtually removed, so as practically to convert the General Government into a government of an absolute majority, without check or limitation, cannot be denied by any one who has impartially observed its operation.

It is not necessary to trace the commencement and gradual progress of the causes which have produced this change in our system; it is sufficient to state that the change has taken place within the last few years. What has been the result? Precisely that which might have been anticipated: the growth of faction, corruption, anarchy, and, if not despotism itself, its near approach, as witnessed in the provisions of this bill. And from what have these consequences sprung? We have been involved in no war. We have been at peace with all the world. We have been visited with no national calamity. Our people have been advancing in general intelligence, and, I will add, as great and alarming as has been the advance of political corruption among the mercenary corps who look to Government for support, the morals and virtue of the community at large have been advancing in improvement. What, I again repeat, is the cause? No other can be assigned but a departure from the fundamental principles of the constitution, which has converted the Government into the will of an absolute and irresponsible majority, and which, by the laws that must inevitably govern in all such majorities, has placed in conflict the great interests of the country, by a system of hostile legislation, by an oppressive and unequal imposition of taxes, by unequal and profuse appropriations, and by rendering the entire labor and capital of the weaker interest subordinate to the stronger.

This is the cause, and these the fruits, which have converted the Government into a mere instrument of taking money from one portion of the community, to be given to another; and which has rallied around it a great, a powerful, and mercenary corps of office-holders, office-seekers, and expectants, destitute of principle and patriotism, and who have no standard of morals or politics but the will of the Executive—the will of him who has the distribution of the loaves and the fishes. I hold it impossible for any one to look at the theoretical illustration of the principle of the absolute majority in the cases which I have supposed, and not be struck with the practical illustration in the actual operation of our Government. Under every circumstance, the absolute majority will ever have its American system (I mean nothing offensive to any Senator); but the real meaning of the American system is, that system of plunder which the strongest interest has ever waged, and will ever wage, against the weaker, where the latter is not armed with some efficient and constitutional check to arrest its action. Nothing but such check on the part of the weaker interest can arrest it: mere constitutional limitations are wholly insufficient. Whatever interest obtains possession of the Government, will, from the nature of things, be in favor of the powers, and against the limitations imposed by the constitution, and will resort to every device that can be imagined to remove those restraints. On the contrary, the opposite interest, that which I have designated as the stockholding interest, the tax-payers, those on whom the system operates, will resist the abuse of powers, and contend for the limitations. And it is on this point, then, that the contest between the delegated and the reserved powers will be waged; but in this contest, as the interests in possession of the Government are organized and armed by all its powers and patronage, the opposite interest, if not in like manner organized and possessed of a power to protect themselves under the provisions of the constitution, will be as inevitably crushed as would be a band of unorganized militia when opposed by a veteran and trained corps of regulars. Let it never be forgotten, that power can only be opposed by power, organization by organization; and on this theory stands our beautiful federal system of Government. No free system was ever further removed from the principle that the absolute majority, without check or limitation, ought to govern. To understand what our Government is, we must look to the constitution, which is the basis of the system. I do not intend to enter into any minute examination of the origin and the source of its powers: it is sufficient for my purpose to state, what I do fearlessly, that it derived its power from the people of the separate States, each ratifying by itself, each binding itself by its own separate majority, through its separate convention,—the concurrence of the majorities of the several States forming the constitution;— thus taking the sense of the whole by that of the several parts, representing the various interests of the entire community. It was this concurring and perfect majority which formed the constitution, and not that majority which would consider the American people as a single community, and which, instead of representing fairly and fully the interests of the whole, would but represent, as has been stated, the interests of the stronger section. No candid man can dispute that I have given a correct description of the constitution-making power: that power which created and organized the Government, which delegated to it, as a common agent, certain powers, in trust for the common good of all the States, and which imposed strict limitations and checks against abuses and usurpations. In administering the delegated powers, the constitution provides, very properly, in order to give promptitude and efficiency, that the Government shall be organized upon the principle of the absolute majority, or, rather, of two absolute majorities combined: a majority of the States considered as bodies politic, which prevails in this body; and a majority of the people of the States, estimated in federal numbers, in the other House of Congress. A combination of the two prevails in the choice of the President, and, of course, in the appointment of Judges, they being nominated by the President and confirmed by the Senate. It is thus that the concurring and the absolute majorities are combined in one complex system: the one in forming the constitution, and the other in making and executing the laws; thus beautifully blending the moderation, justice, and equity of the former, and more perfect majority, with the promptness and energy of the latter, but less perfect.

THE ABLEST VINDICATION

Daniel Webster and James Kent

Daniel Webster (1782–1852) was the greatest corporation lawyer of his day. Whatever his personal shortcomings, as a lawyer he was indomitable. It was generally rumored that he had wrestled with the Devil himself and emerged from the conflict victorious, unlike his European counterpart; it is not surprising that the Faust legend in the United States centers neither on scientist nor philosopher, but on the advocate.

As is apparent from his correspondence with Kent, Webster had long been anxious to cross swords with Calhoun over his interpretation of the Constitution.

MY DEAR SIR,—Mr. Calhoun, as you are doubtless aware, has published a labored defence of nullification, in the form of a letter, to Governor Hamilton. It is far the ablest and most plausible, and therefore the most dangerous vindication of that particular form of revolution, which has yet appeared.

In the silence of abler pens, and seeing as I think I do, that the affairs of this government are rapidly approaching a crisis, I have felt it to be my duty to answer Mr. Calhoun, and, as he adopted the form of a

---

Daniel Webster, Letter to Chancellor Kent, October 29, 1832, *Private Correspondence of Daniel Webster* (1857), p. 526.

letter, in which to put forth his opinions, I think of giving my answer a similar form. The object of this is, to ask your permission to address my letter to you. I propose to feign that I have received a letter from you calling my attention to Mr. Calhoun's publication; and then, in answer to such supposed letter, to proceed to review his whole argument at some length, not in the style of a speech, but in that of cool, constitutional, and legal discussion. If you feel no repugnance to be thus written to, I will be obliged to you for your assent; on the other hand if any reasons suggest themselves to your mind against such a form of publication, another can be readily adopted. I cannot complete the paper before the election, as I am at present a good deal pressed with professional affairs, but I hope to bring it into light in the course of the next month.

I have little to say to you, my dear Sir, upon political subjects. The whole ground is open to you. I trust you will be one of those who will have votes to give, and devoutly pray you may yet see some way of so uniting the well-disposed, as to rescue us from our peril.

I am, dear Sir, with most sincere and true regard, yours,

DANIEL WEBSTER.

DEAR SIR,—I have no objection that you should address in the form of a letter or letters to me your remarks on the Vice-President's scheme of nullification, and that you should assume it to be in answer to a letter from me relative to that subject. I shall deem it an honor to be addressed by you while engaged in the investigation of such an interesting subject. The Vice-President enclosed one of his pamphlets to me, and I read it attentively. It is ingeniously written; but such a construction of the constitution, and such principles as he deduces, are visionary and most unsound and sophistical. His repugnance to all solid constitutional principles would fix a deadly power of destruction in the very vitals of the government.

The crisis is indeed portentous and frightful. We are threatened with destruction all around us, and we seem to be fast losing our original good sense and virtue. The Democracy of this city require all their candidates to Congress to give another pledge to support all the measures of the administration. Can any thing be more degrading and monstrous? Is the proud House of Representatives and the grand inquest of the nation to be composed of such materials? . . .

If we succeed in our election, I shall take the liberty of writing you again, and ask for a free communication of sentiments. If we fail, then indeed we may hang our harps upon the willows or on the witch hazel that shades Saint Fillan's Spring!

Your speech at Worcester was admirable for its logic as well as for

---

Chancellor Kent, Letter to Daniel Webster, October 31, 1832, ibid.

its fervor and its force. If we are to be saved we shall be largely indebted to you. *"Si Pergama,"* &c.

Adieu, yours most sincerely,

JAMES KENT.

ANSWER TO CALHOUN

Daniel Webster

In Webster's response to Calhoun's masterly argument, the Constitution appears as a series of propositions upon which the logician might exercise his ingenuity. His contribution in this address, as in his earlier debate with Hayne in January, 1830, was impressive. At a public dinner given in Webster's honor Chancellor Kent summarized his achievement: "Constitutional law, by means of those senatorial discussions and the master genius that guided them, was rescued from the archives of tribunals and the libraries of lawyers, and placed under the eye, and submitted to the judgement of the American people."

THE GENTLEMAN'S SPEECH made some days ago, upon introducing his resolutions, those resolutions themselves, and parts of the speech now just concluded, may, I presume, be justly regarded as containing the whole South Carolina doctrine. That doctrine it is my purpose now to examine, and to compare it with the Constitution of the United States. I shall not consent, Sir, to make any new constitution, or to establish another form of government. I will not undertake to say what a constitution for these United States ought to be. That question the people have decided for themselves; and I shall take the instrument as they have established it, and shall endeavor to maintain it, in its plain sense and meaning, against opinions and notions which, in my judgment, threaten its subversion. . . .

The first two resolutions of the honorable member affirm these propositions, viz.:—

1. That the political system under which we live, and under which Congress is now assembled, is a *compact*, to which the people of the several States, as separate and sovereign communities, are *the parties*.

2. That these sovereign parties have a right to judge, each for itself, of any alleged violation of the Constitution by Congress; and, in case of such violation, to choose, each for itself, its own mode and measure of redress.

Daniel Webster, Speech in Senate, February 16, 1833, *Speeches in Congress* (ed. Whipple, 1879), p. 273.

It is true, Sir, that the honorable member calls this a "constitutional" compact; but still he affirms it to be a compact between sovereign States. What precise meaning, then, does he attach to the term *constitutional?* When applied to compacts between sovereign States, the term *constitutional* affixes to the word *compact* no definite idea. Were we to hear of a constitutional league or treaty between England and France, or a constitutional convention between Austria and Russia, we should not understand what could be intended by such a league, such a treaty, or such a convention. In these connections, the word is void of all meaning; and yet, Sir, it is easy, quite easy, to see why the honorable gentleman has used it in these resolutions. He cannot open the book, and look upon our written frame of government, without seeing that it is called a *constitution.* This may well be appalling to him. It threatens his whole doctrine of compact, and its darling derivatives, nullification and secession, with instant confutation. Because, if he admits our instrument of government to be a *constitution,* then, for that very reason, it is not a compact between sovereigns; a constitution of government and a compact between sovereign powers being things essentially unlike in their very natures, and incapable of ever being the same. Yet the word *constitution* is on the very front of the instrument. He cannot overlook it. He seeks, therefore, to compromise the matter, and to sink all the substantial sense of the word, while he retains a resemblance of its sound. He introduces a new word of his own, viz. *compact,* as importing the principal idea, and designed to play the principal part, and degrades *constitution* into an insignificant, idle epithet, attached to *compact.* The whole then stands as a *"constitutional compact"!* And in this way he hopes to pass off a plausible gloss, as satisfying the words of the instrument. But he will find himself disappointed. Sir, I must say to the honorable gentleman, that, in our American political grammar, CONSTITUTION is a noun substantive; it imports a distinct and clear idea of itself; and it is not to lose its importance and dignity, it is not to be turned into a poor, ambiguous, senseless, unmeaning adjective, for the purpose of accommodating any new set of political notions. Sir, we reject his new rules of syntax altogether. We will not give up our forms of political speech to the grammarians of the school of nullification. By the Constitution, we mean, not a "constitutional compact," but, simply and directly, the Constitution, the fundamental law; and if there be one word in the language which the people of the United States understand, this is that word. We know no more of a constitutional compact between sovereign powers, than we know of a *constitutional* indenture of copartnership, a *constitutional* deed of conveyance, or a *constitutional* bill of exchange. But we know what the *Constitution* is; we know what the plainly written, fundamental law is; we know what the bond of our Union and the security of our liberties is; and we mean to maintain and to defend it, in its plain sense and unsophisticated meaning. . . .

Was it Mirabeau, Mr. President, or some other master of the human passions, who has told us that words are things? They are indeed things, and things of mighty influence, not only in addresses to the passions and high-wrought feelings of mankind, but in the discussion of legal and political questions also; because a just conclusion is often avoided, or a false one reached, by the adroit substitution of one phrase, or one word, for another. Of this we have, I think, another example in the resolutions before us.

The first resolution declares that the people of the several States "*acceded*" to the Constitution, or to the constitutional compact, as it is called. This word "accede," not found either in the Constitution itself, or in the ratification of it by any one of the States, has been chosen for use here, doubtless, not without a well-considered purpose.

The natural converse of *accession* is *secession*; and, therefore, when it is stated that the people of the States acceded to the Union, it may be more plausibly argued that they may secede from it. If, in adopting the Constitution, nothing was done but acceding to a compact, nothing would seem necessary, in order to break it up, but to secede from the same compact. But the term is wholly out of place. *Accession*, as a word applied to political associations, implies coming into a league, treaty, or confederacy, by one hitherto a stranger to it; and *secession* implies departing from such league or confederacy. The people of the United States have used no such form of expression in establishing the present government. They do not say that they *accede* to a league, but they declare that they *ordain* and *establish* a Constitution. Such are the very words of the instrument itself; and in all the States, without an exception, the language used by their conventions was, that they "*ratified the Constitution*"; some of them employing the additional words "assented to" and "adopted," but all of them "ratifying."

There is more importance than may, at first sight, appear, in the introduction of this new word by the honorable mover of these resolutions. Its adoption and use are indispensable to maintain those premises, from which his main conclusion is to be afterwards drawn. But before showing that, allow me to remark, that this phraseology tends to keep out of sight the just view of a previous political history, as well as to suggest wrong ideas as to what was actually done when the present Constitution was agreed to. In 1789, and before this Constitution was adopted, the United States had already been in a union, more or less close, for fifteen years. At least as far back as the meeting of the first Congress, in 1774, they had been in some measure, and for some national purposes, united together. Before the Confederation of 1781, they had declared independence jointly, and had carried on the war jointly, both by sea and land; and this not as separate States, but as one people. When, therefore, they formed that Confederation, and adopted its articles as articles of perpetual union, they did not come together for the first time; and therefore they did not speak of the States as *acceding* to the Confederation, although it was a league, and nothing but a league, and rested on nothing but plighted faith for its performance. Yet, even then, the States were not strangers to each other; there was a bond of union already subsisting between them; they were associated, united States; and the object of the Confederation was to make a stronger and better bond of union. Their representatives deliberated together on these proposed Articles of Confederation, and, being authorized by their respective States, finally "*ratified and confirmed*" them. Inasmuch as they were already in union, they did not speak of *acceding* to the new Articles of Confederation, but of *ratifying and confirming* them; and this language was not used inadvertently, because, in the same instrument, *accession* is used in its proper sense, when applied to Canada, which was altogether a stranger to the existing union. "Canada," says the eleventh article, "*acceding* to this Confederation, and joining in the measures of the United States, shall be admitted into the Union."

Having thus used the terms *ratify* and *confirm*, even in regard to the old Confederation, it would have been strange indeed, if the people of the United States, after its formation, and when they came to establish the present Constitution, had spoken of the States, or the people of the States, as *acceding* to this Constitution. Such language would have been ill-suited to the occasion. It would have implied an existing separation or disunion among the States, such as never has existed since 1774. No such language, therefore, was used. The language actually employed is, *adopt, ratify, ordain, establish.*

Therefore, Sir, since any State, before she can prove her right to dissolve the Union, must show her authority to undo what has been done, no State is at liberty to *secede*, on the ground that she and other States have done nothing but *accede*. She must show that she has a right to *reverse* what has been *ordained*, to *unsettle* and *overthrow* what has been *established*, to *reject* what the people have *adopted*, and to *break up* what they have *ratified*; because these are the terms which express the transactions which have actually taken place. In other words, she must show her right to make a revolution. . . .

Sir, I intend to hold the gentleman to the written record. In the discussion of a constitutional question, I intend to impose upon him the restraints of constitutional language. The people have ordained a Constitution; can they reject it without revolution? They have established a form of government; can they overthrow it without revolution? These are the true questions. . . .

Sir, this is the precise object of nullification. It attempts to supersede the supreme legislative authority. It arrests the arm of the executive magistrate. It interrupts the exercise of the accustomed judicial power. Under the name of an ordinance, it declares null and void, within the State, all the revenue laws of the United States. Is not this revolutionary? Sir, so soon as this ordinance shall be carried into effect, *a revolution* will have commenced in South Carolina. She will have thrown off the authority to which her citizens have heretofore been subject. She will have declared her own opinions and her own will to be above the laws and above the power of those who are intrusted with their administration. If she makes good these declarations, she is revolutionized. As to her, it is as distinctly a change of the supreme power, as the American Revolution of 1776. That revolution did not subvert government in all its forms. It did not subvert local laws and municipal administrations. It only threw off the dominion of a power claiming to be superior, and to have a right, in many important respects, to exercise legislative authority. Thinking this authority to have been usurped or abused, the American Colonies, now the United States, bade it defiance, and freed themselves from it by means of a revolution. But that revolution left them with their own municipal laws still, and the forms of local government. If Carolina now shall effectually resist the laws of Congress; if she shall be her own judge, take her remedy into her own hands, obey the laws of the Union when she pleases and disobey them when she pleases, she will relieve herself from a paramount power as distinctly as the American Colonies did the same thing in 1776. In other words, she will achieve, as to herself, a revolution.

But, Sir, while practical nullification in South Carolina would be, as to herself, actual and distinct revolution, its necessary tendency must also be to spread revolution, and to break up the Constitution, as to all the other States. It strikes a deadly blow at the vital principle of the whole Union. To allow State resistance to the laws of Congress to be rightful and proper, to admit nullification in some States, and yet not expect to see a dismemberment of the entire government, appears to me the wildest illusion, and the most extravagant folly. The gentleman seems not conscious of the direction or the rapidity of his own course. The current of his opinions sweeps him along, he knows not whither. To begin with nullification, with the avowed intent, nevertheless, not to proceed to secession, dismemberment, and general revolution, is as if one were to take the plunge of Niagara, and cry out that he would stop half way down. In the one case, as in the other, the rash adventurer must go to the bottom of the dark abyss below, were it not that that abyss has no discovered bottom. . . .

Sir, those who espouse the doctrines of nullification reject, as it seems to me, the first great principle of all republican liberty; that is, that the majority *must* govern. In matters of common concern, the judgment of a majority *must* stand as the judgment of the whole. This is a law imposed on us by the absolute necessity of the case; and if we do not act upon it, there is no possibility of maintaining any government but despotism. We hear loud and repeated denunciations against what is called *majority government.* It is declared, with much warmth, that a majority government cannot be maintained in the United States. What, then, do gentlemen wish? Do they wish to establish a *minority* government? Do they wish to subject the will of the many to the will of the few? The honorable gentleman from South Carolina has spoken of absolute majorities and majorities concurrent; language wholly unknown to our Constitution, and to which it is not easy to affix definite ideas. As far as I understand it, it would teach us that the absolute majority may be found in Congress, but the majority concurrent must be looked for in the States; that is to say, Sir, stripping the matter of this novelty of phrase, that the dissent of one or more States, as States, renders void the decision of a majority of Congress, so far as that State is concerned. And so this doctrine, running but a short career, like other dogmas of the day, terminates in nullification.

If this vehement invective against *majorities* meant no more than that, in the construction of government, it is wise to provide checks and balances, so that there should be various limitations on the power of the mere majority, it would only mean what the Constitution of the United States has already abundantly provided. It is full of such checks and balances. In its very organization, it adopts a broad and most effective principle in restraint of the power of mere majorities. A majority of the people elects the House of Representatives, but it does not elect the Senate. The Senate is elected by the States, each State having, in this respect, an equal power. No law, therefore, can pass, without the assent of the representatives of the people, and a majority of the representatives of the States also. A majority of the representatives of the people must concur, and a majority of the States must concur, in every act of Congress; and the President is elected on a plan compounded of both these principles. But having composed one house of representatives chosen by the people in each State, according to their numbers, and the other of an equal number of members from every State, whether larger or smaller, the Constitution gives to majorities in these houses thus constituted the full and entire power of passing laws, subject always to the constitutional restrictions and to the approval of the President. To subject them to any other power is clear usurpation. The majority of one house may be controlled by the majority of the other; and both may be restrained by the President's negative. These are checks and balances provided by the Constitution, existing in the government itself, and wisely intended to secure deliberation and caution in legislative proceedings. But to resist the will of the majority in both houses, thus constitutionally exercised; to insist on the lawfulness of interposition by an extraneous power; to claim the right of defeating the will of Congress, by setting up against it the will of a single State,—is neither more nor less, as it strikes me, than a plain attempt to overthrow the government. The constituted authorities of the United States are no longer a government, if they be not masters of their own will; they are no longer a government, if an external power may arrest their proceedings; they are no longer a government, if acts passed by both houses, and approved by the President, may be nullified by State vetoes or State ordinances. Does any one suppose it could make any difference, as to the binding authority of an act of Congress, and of the duty of a State to respect it, whether it passed by a mere majority of both houses, or by three fourths of each, or the unanimous vote of each? Within the limits and restrictions of the Constitution, the government of the United States, like all other popular governments, acts by majorities. It can act no otherwise. Whoever, therefore, denounces the government of majorities, denounces the government of his own country, and denounces all free governments. And whoever would restrain these majorities, while acting within their constitutional limits, by an external power, whatever he may intend, asserts principles which, if adopted, can lead to nothing else than the destruction of the government itself.

TESTING THE OATH BY THE CONSTITUTION

Thomas Smith Grimké

Like his sisters, who were zealous anti-slavery crusaders and advocates of women's rights—"Carolina's high-souled daughters," as Whittier phrased it—Thomas Smith Grimké (1786–1834) was in constant tension with his wealthy and aristocratic environment. After graduating from Yale College in 1807, he had intended to become a minister, but under pressure from his father, a conservative judge, he studied law. Despite his espousal of unpopular causes, Grimké attained eminence at the bar and in politics. In the following extract, his argument before the court in opposition to nullification illustrates his characteristic blend of eloquence and logic. Many idealistic causes won him over: he supported movements for temperance, peace, an education which would "partake deeply and extensively of the vital spirit of American institutions," and even a reformed orthography.

WE ENTER NOW on the most important part of our argument; and propose to test the oath by the Constitution of the United States. . . .

Let us first enquire, what is the true relation subsisting between the ordinance and the Constitution of the United States? Until this be settled, we can have no satisfactory premises, from which to reason. Is the Constitution of the United States still the Constitution of South Carolina? Is the Government of the United States still the Government of South Carolina?

State ex rel. McCready *v.* Hunt, 20 *So. Car. Law.* 1 (1834), pp. 14, 36.

In point of fact, who can doubt? The people have elected their representatives, the legislature a senator—the custom-house, judiciary, and everything else, go on as before. The Ordinance of 24th November, 1832, is repealed; we have not seceded; we have not established a separate government; the relation of the State to the National Constitution is thus evidently still that of a subordinate to a superior instrument. The former is declared to be the SUPREME LAW of the land. Whilst, therefore, the Constitution of the United States shall continue to be of force in South Carolina, the State Constitution must, in point of authority, be ranked below that of the Union. Is this derogatory to the dignity of the State? Who shall venture to say that it is? when the people themselves have so ordained? The people then have declared, that the Constitution of the United States is the *supreme* Constitution of South Carolina, and the State Constitution the *subordinate* Constitution of South Carolina. *This* was the separate act of the people of the State; *that*, the joint act of the people of all the States. The people of South Carolina have no power to alter the Constitution of the United States, even as to themselves. It can only be done by a joint act. It follows, undeniably, that while the Constitution of the United States remains the Constitution of South Carolina, and can only be altered by a joint act, the people of South Carolina cannot alter even their *State* Constitution, inconsistently with that of the Union. As then the Constitution of the United States still is the supreme law of South Carolina, it is manifest, that if the ordinance had been adopted in the usual mode, as an amendment of the Constitution of South Carolina, it must be a nullity, if repugnant to the Constitution of the United States.

This conclusion leads to the question, what is the relation of the Ordinance to the State Constitution? It is superior, co-equal or subordinate in authority. If it be co-ordinate or inferior, its fate is sealed, should it not be reconcilable with the Constitution of the United States. It is then annulled by the supreme law. Is it superior? This is impossible. If so, in what sense? Was not each the act of the people? granting each convention to have been the people. If a convention be not the people, was not each, the Constitution of South Carolina and the ordinance, the act of co-equal representative assemblies? Is there any difference between the obligation to obey each? between the power to compel obedience to each? and between the means that may be employed? Is not the relation of the citizen and of the departments of the State government to each, exactly the same? If then the ordinance be consistent with the State constitution, how can it be adjudged superior when tried by those tests? If it is not consistent, and so far overrules that instrument, still what superiority has it which does not equally belong to an amendment? Is an amendment superior because it cancels and substitutes? If so, the amendment of an amendment is still further superior; and a succession of amendments would present a series of successive acts, each rising above the other in dignity and power. Who believes, who is willing to assert this? Besides, the ordinance belongs to the same branch of power as the constitution, viz: *political* as distinguished from *civil*. It stands to the Constitution of the State in the same relation that a statute or a particular subject of civil legislation bears to an entire code of civil law. The statute becomes as a matter of course, whether so declared or not, a co-equal part of the civil code. The ordinance becomes in like manner, a co-equal part of the political code. It is, in other words, a part of the constitutional, as distinguished from the statute law of the State. It is, in fact, as well as in law, if valid, a part of the Constitution of South Carolina. If this be then the true relation of the ordinance to the Constitution of South Carolina, and the Constitution of South Carolina be subordinate to the Constitution of the United States, it follows that the ordinance also must be subordinate to the Constitution of the United States. As then the Constitution of the United States is still the *supreme* Constitution of South Carolina, the ordinance must be adjudged invalid, if it be repugnant to that supreme law. . . .

When the people of South Carolina elected you as their judges, they declared to you, while the Constitution of the United States shall continue the Constitution of South Carolina, we ordain that it shall be *superior* to our *separate* will, *however the same may be declared*; we have acknowledged it to be *the supreme law of our land*; and we have solemnly agreed that "the judges in every State shall be *bound thereby*, any thing in the constitution or laws of any State to the contrary notwithstanding." We exact of you an oath to support that constitution, and we therefore empower and command you to administer it frankly and fearlessly against any *separate* act of our own will, *repugnant* to its *supremacy*. . . .

Having now established the relation of the Ordinance to the Constitution of the United States, and the authority of this Court to judge between them, we are prepared to examine and decide the question, do they conflict? On the other side, it is alleged that allegiance is indivisible, because it is asserted that it is due to sovereignty, and that sovereignty is indivisible. I shall undertake to prove that sovereignty is divisible, and that a divided allegiance actually exists in the case of every citizen of a State. I affirm, that the sovereignty originally vested in the people of the State has been divided by their own act, and that by their own acknowledgment, every citizen of the State owes allegiance to the United States as well as to the State. . . .

I proceed now to apply the doctrine I have explained to the relations of a citizen of South Carolina to the Union and the State. Let us remark that the exception in the feudal oath, both of continental Europe and England, was inserted, and became a part of the contract of the parties; because, the persons excepted, were not parties to the contract. If they had been, who will deny that without an express reservation of the superior or prior allegiance, it would have ceased forever. But as the new relation was not the act of the higher or former sovereign, he was not bound by it. Now, observe that the relation subsisting between the citizen of South Carolina and the United States, is created by the people of South Carolina, acting in their highest sovereign capacity. It is not the *separate* act of the citizen and the rest of the States; but the people of South Carolina, without any individual act of *his*, as is the case in naturalization, have created the relation. . . .

Let us next remark, that when the subject was bound not to make war against the king on behalf of his lord, it is because that very lord had acknowledged the king to be supreme over him, as long as the political constitutions which determined the relations between the king and the lord, the lord and the vassal should subsist, and have not the people of South Carolina acknowledged, that as long as the Constitution of the United States and the Constitution of South Carolina are *their* constitutions, the former shall be *supreme*, and of course, that the relation subsisting between the citizen of South Carolina and the United States, is superior to that subsisting between him and the State. The feudal constitutions styled the inferior relation that of a vassal, the superior that of a subject. But in our country vassalage has never been known, and the relation of subject ceased with the Declaration of Independence. "At the Revolution," says Ch. J. JAY, 2 Dall. p. 71, "the sovereignty devolved on the people, and they are truly the sovereigns of the country, but they are *sovereigns without subjects*." . . .

Let us look at the state of things under the new government. The constitution, according to the views presented in the first part of my argument, provides, in the obligation to support the constitution, an equivalent to, and a substitute for, an oath of allegiance, in a truly republican form. But, independently of that, the power to punish treason is the highest proof of the existence of the relation of allegiance. Treason, as a crime, is the correlative of allegiance as a duty. It is the breach of an individual, not an officer, of his duty to bear true and faithful allegiance. The Constitution of the United States, by simply recognizing the relation, acknowledges, by an irresistible implication, the power to punish; and lays but two restrictions on that power, by defining what shall constitute treason, and requiring two witnesses to the same act. These restrictions on the power admit it to be unrestricted otherwise; the admission of the power to punish admits that the crime to be punished can exist; and this provision against the crime admits the relation to exist, which it violates. What say my friends to this, seeing that the Constitution of the United States was framed by *legislative* delegates of the *States*; was laid before the people of *each* State by their *confederative* delegates in the old Congress; was adopted by the people of *each* State in *separate* State conventions; and was put into operation by the same *State* delegates, the *Confederation?* . . .

I trust, then, I may consider the position established, that allegiance is due to the United States. I have regarded it as a practical historical question, and to be treated accordingly. I have considered facts set down upon our political records, in the name, by the authority, and with a view to the good of the States and the people, as the highest manifestation of the opinion and will of the States and the people. The same proofs demonstrate the existence of a *divided* allegiance, for no one doubts that allegiance is due to the State. The only controversy is, whether any be due to the United States. I am much mistaken if this has not been put beyond all doubt, both in point of *principle*, as a question of political philosophy, and in point of *fact*, as a question of political history. . . .

But there is a still more important consideration. Grant, for the sake of the argument, that South Carolina, before the Constitution of 1789, was a perfect sovereign. Grant, also, that she was entitled to exclusive allegiance. Is it not clear that she was bound to yield a co-extensive protection? Allegiance, according to the English law, is due everywhere, at home and abroad, because protection is due from the king to the subject, *everywhere*. But South Carolina has declared, by adopting the Constitution of the United States, that she cannot, or that she will not any longer protect her citizens abroad. She has acted wisely and justly in so doing, whether we regard her or her citizens. If a citizen of South Carolina be imprisoned or oppressed in a foreign land, does he ever think of an application to the Governor or Legislature of the State? If he did apply, would they not immediately refer the matter to the President of the United States, as the proper officer marked out by *the State* itself? Suppose the governor or legislature should send a special commissioner abroad, to France or Spain or Turkey. Would he be recognized? Would he not be told, "we cannot hold any diplomatic intercourse with you; for we know not South Carolina. We know the United States as a nation and a government; and although we know South Carolina, geographically and historically, to be a part of the Union, yet we have nothing to do with her on the principles of *international* intercourse." Would not Baron Humboldt, Prince Metternich or Chancellor Brougham smile, if our envoy spoke of South Carolina as a *nation*, and of her government as a *national* government? Could an envoy worthy of such a mission be found, who would hold such language? Again, would the citizen of South Carolina, if oppressed or imprisoned abroad, apply to the consul or minister of the United States, by virtue of his title of citizen of *South Carolina?* Could he be listened to in any other capacity than as a citizen of the *United States?* He would be heard and relieved, not as a *Carolinian*, but as an *American*.

South Carolina, then, by adopting the Constitution of the United States, has substituted the States and their government, instead of herself and her government, as protector of her own citizens on the high seas and in foreign countries. If she has transferred the power and the duty to protect, must she not have transferred the correspondent allegiance? If the Emperor of Austria were to transfer such a power and duty to the King of France, as to an Austrian subject, would any feudal jurist doubt that he transferred allegiance too? The question would not be, whether he had transferred *any*, but whether he had not transferred *all?* Put the State on a footing with the Austrian emperor, as an absolute sovereign, before she adopted the Constitution of the United States; yet, after that, she cannot, like him, expect any less consequences from DIVIDED PROTECTION, than DIVIDED ALLEGIANCE. . . .

I proceed to show, that as divided allegiance was attested by the records of our political history, so is the doctrine of divided sovereignty.

Let me begin by asking the question, who *are now*, not who *were* in *former* years, the *successors* of king, lords and commons, *as to South Carolina?* It is obviously immaterial in what mode the succession came about, whether by violence, or by amicable arrangement. It is a question of fact. Now, does South Carolina possess any vestige of the great powers vested in king, lords, and commons? Cannot she be involved in a war against her will? Must she not lay down her arms, whether she wishes or not, if Congress makes peace? But why put a series of instances, when it is obvious that the practical test of powers vested in, and exercised by the United States and State, as to the people of South Carolina, demonstrates *both* to be the successors of king, lords, and commons—in other words, there are now two sovereigns, because government was divided by the division of power, and divided power is divided sovereignty.

In the 82d No. of the Federalist, it is said "we consider the State governments and the national government, as they truly are, in the light of kindred systems, and as *parts* of one *whole*." In 31 Dallas, 473, in the case of Commonwealth of Pennsylvania *v.* Cobbett, in the Supreme Court of Pennsylvania, Chief Justice M'KEAN, says: "The Government of the United States forms a part of the government of each State." "These (the State and national) form one complete government." Mr. Jefferson, in his letter to Major John Cartwright, of 5th June, 1824, (vol. 4, p. 396) says, "with respect to our State and federal governments, I do not think their relations correctly understood by foreigners. They generally suppose the former subordinate to the latter. But this is not the case. They are co-ordinate departments of one simple and integral whole. To the State governments are reserved all legislation and administration, in affairs which concern their own citizens only; and to the federal government is given whatever concerns foreigners and citizens of other States; these functions alone being made federal. The one is the domestic, the other the foreign branch of the same government—neither having control over the other, but within its own department." . . .

May I not then say, with much confidence, that I have established the doctrine of double allegiance and double citizenship, of divided government, divided power, and divided sovereignty? May I not add, that I have established them on the basis of political philosophy and political common sense, and have sustained them by testimonies the highest and clearest, derived from the political history of Europe and of our own country? After such a review of principles and authorities, may I not ask, with a just pride in the soundness and antiquity of our opinions, who is it that ventures on strange and perilous *novelties?* WHO ARE THE INNOVATORS? . . .

The next subject which we have to consider, is—what is the relative character of the allegiance due to the State and to the United States? Is either subordinate to the other, or are both equal in degree and dignity? I maintain that the allegiance due to the United States is *superior*, is *paramount*, to that which is due to the State. This also is a practical question; and I shall accordingly examine it by tests so plain and intelligible, as to come home to the common sense of every man. It has been already touched upon; and I now propose to present another view of it. . . . I hold that a superior allegiance is due to that sovereign, who possesses the *highest order of power*, precisely on the principle that a higher obligation was due to the king as the supreme lord, than any lord, intermediate between him and the vassal. I proceed now to show the great superiority of the United States over any particular State, in relation to the power yielded to the former, by the peoples of the States. My object is to speak the plain, honest truth, by showing that after all that may be said about the reserved rights of the States, the powers actually vested in the community of States, very far exceed in dignity, extent and value, any powers possessed by any particular State. These powers are, in the highest and most appropriate sense of the term, *political*—and since *allegiance* is, beyond all doubt, a *political* tie, those powers must give a decided character to the allegiance of the citizen. To illustrate—will any one deny, that the allegiance due to a *despot* is of a higher order than that due to a *limited* monarch; simply because the despot is a *more* complete sovereign than the limited monarch? Was not the allegiance due to South Carolina before she adopted the Constitution of the United States, granting her to have been then a perfect sovereign, at a higher order than that which is now due? Was it not so; because she possessed all power? If then she has lost sovereignty, with the sovereign power she has ceded; if power, i.e. sovereignty, can be divided; if divided allegiance follows divided sovereignty; if divided allegiance implies two sovereigns, the question manifestly arises, which of the sovereigns possesses the higher order of power? In other words, does the community of States possess a higher order of power, and a controlling power in relation to a single State, or does that one State possess them, in regard to that community? Can any American, who understands his country's institutions, doubt? . . .

We have now arrived at what may be regarded as the final question: —Is the ordinance inconsistent with the constitution of the Union? Independently of the clause which declares the latter to be the supreme law of the land, I could not have doubted, from the authorities adduced and the principles developed, that the Union is a superior sovereign to a State, and that the allegiance due to the former is superior to that which is due to the latter. But the Constitution of the United States leaves no doubt. If, then, I have succeeded in showing that allegiance is a political relation; that in a republic it is the relation of the citizen and the State; that the United States are a complete and perfect State and Nation; that sovereignty of the highest order, according to the surest tests that can be applied, is the attribute of this community of States; that a national allegiance is due by every citizen to that community of States; that power, and therefore sovereignty, can be divided; and so two sovereigns, one superior, one inferior, can co-exist in the same system; that allegiance, therefore, as an incident right of sovereignty, can equally be divided; that a divided allegiance is therefore due to the United States and the States; that the community of States is the supreme sovereign, the separate States the subordinate sovereigns of the system; that a superior allegiance is therefore due to the United States compared to that which is due to the State—is it possible to doubt an instant? If the ordinance attempts to elevate the allegiance due to the State above that due to the United States it is repugnant and must be declared by the authority of the *State itself*, null and void; because it attempts to set up what the people of the State have themselves declared to be their own *subordinate* constitution over that which they have declared shall be their own *supreme* constitution. . . .

The ordinance then declares that no political relation subsists between the citizen of South Carolina and the Union; that the community of States is not a sovereign, is not a nation; that sovereignty and allegiance cannot be divided; that the United States have no citizens, but only denizens; that treason in the Constitution of the United States is not a breach of any allegiance; and that the State has a right to require of every citizen and officer to swear that he owes an *exclusive* allegiance to the State, and *none* to the United States.

What is this but a denial of all that the political history of the Union establishes; of all that the States and the people have acknowledged over and over again, in various forms; and of all that facts prove, and principles sanction, and reasoning demonstrates? What is it, but denying the supremacy of the Constitution of the United States, and asserting the supremacy of the State constitution, for such the ordinance is? The ordinance, then, is utterly repugnant to the Constitution of the United States, and as already insisted on, either repeals the Constitution of the United States, and is equivalent to an act of secession, or must be declared "null and void, and no law, not binding on this state, its officers, or citizens." Such must and will be its fate. . . .

I have now discharged the duty allotted to me. Let me close this scene of anxiety and trial, with a few, a very few words more. I have felt the deep obligation to treat these questions with the simplicity and gravity of truth. I admire, I trust I have exemplified, the noble sentiment of Dexter, that in the argument of constitutional questions, he had not a right to utter what his convictions disavowed. I had resolved to speak in the spirit of a Christian, honestly as a patriot, fearlessly as an advocate, before independent judges. I felt that such a course was honorable to them and myself, to my country and my profession. I have been deeply sensible of the delicacy, as well as difficulty, of the questions, and of the unfeigned respect due to those, whose opinions I had to examine. I have come to lay my gift on the altar of God and my country; for what is an independent judiciary but my country, and what are the halls of justice but temples of the Most High? I have felt that I dared not offer my gift on such an altar, if any brother had aught against me. I have not willingly uttered a word that could, in the slightest degree, give an instant of pain; and if, by aught that has been said, I have excited a momentary unpleasantness, or have cast even a transient shade over a single countenance, may I trust to be forgiven.

2. The Executive, the Legislature, and the Courts

Controversies over the question of the separation and balance of powers among the various branches of the Federal Government arose early. Under Marshall's leadership the Supreme Court asserted the power of judicial review—which made the judiciary the ultimate arbiter of constitutionality. Jackson declared that the other two branches of the Government, the legislative and the executive, were as capable as the courts of performing that function and were equally duty-bound to do so. Underlying this position was a fear of judicial despotism, which was thought to outweigh the arguments for an independent and unprejudiced judiciary.

Distrust of a judiciary free of the pressures of popular will and control by the other branches of government has recurred. Its most violent recent manifestation, during the New Deal years, led to the proposal to "pack" the Supreme Court. The Kentucky battle and the charge of outrages by the governor of Washington are striking illustrations of this outlook, and are comparable to the contests between crown and courts in seventeenth-century England. The idea of legislative omnicompetence was strong in the Formative Era, and the unique American system of judicial review was challenged many times when judges limited the powers of the legislature both by reading natural-law concepts into the Constitution and by expounding them "independent of that instrument." Institutional guarantee against retaliation for a particular decision developed but slowly. Toward the end of the period, there was an increasing distrust of the legislature, once the repository of such high hopes, and a tendency to rely on the judiciary as a barrier against improvident action, exemplified by the invalidation of the permanent tax exemption granted to the Pennsylvania Railroad.

The power to remove judges and other officials was another bone of contention. Jackson regarded rotation in office as "a leading principle in the republican creed." The executive branch claimed plenary authority. This was opposed by the argument that the power to remove resided in the appointing power, and that the Senate therefore had virtually coequal rights. For some time the question lay dormant. Then, aroused by the widespread removals and the system of patronage established by Jackson and Van Buren, the possibility of limitations on the President's power of removal was raised among lawyers. The argument was debated with Jackson upholding the executive's unfettered power of removal, and Clay, in a long address to the Senate in 1835, arguing for limitation. In Commentaries on the Constitution, Story comes nearest to presenting both sides of the controversy. The problem was not settled until quite recent times, when the distinction *between strictly executive officers and those not within that category was established by legal decisions.*

THE ROLE OF THE JUDICIARY

North American Review

THERE IS ONE DEPARTMENT of the government which goes silently on its way, unceasing and indefatigable in its labors, neither attracting nor heeding the remarks of the multitude, though the property, the honor, the security, and even the life, of every citizen are subject to its control and protected by its power. We refer, of course, to the Judiciary. Who can estimate the sum of the influences of this portion of the social machine, or the variety of the directions in which they are exerted? Through the whole country, not a bargain is made, nor an institution founded, nor a marriage contracted, nor a death occurs, but that this powerful and almost unseen agent controls the expectations of the actors or the spectators, and decides what shall be the consequences of the act. It is this power in the state which determines, almost exclusively, the measure of the protection which government affords to all its subjects, and for which it is instituted and they are taxed. Whoever suffers a wrong, or claims a right, whatever be its nature or extent, looks to the judiciary for redress or support. In the confidence that this defence or compensation will be afforded by it, he accepts the engagements of his neighbour, relies on his promises, confides his property to other hands, walks the streets in perfect security by night as by day, and sleeps, if he chooses, with his doors unbarred, and not a weapon in his house. And how little notice is taken of the operations of this salutary agency, and how quietly it does its work! The sleepless activity of the law, the constancy with which its influence is felt, and the implicit reliance which we place in its integrity and watchfulness, seem effectually to blind us to any proper sense of its dignity and importance. We receive its benefits as we do the influences of the sun and rain, as we inhale the air, or slake our thirst from the running stream, without taking any note of the magnitude of the gift which we enjoy. Only some fearful convulsion, by loosening all the bands of social order, and violently interrupting the workings of this great machine of state, could convince men of its value by making them sensible of its loss. Ordinary political disturbances are insufficient to stay or impede its continuous operation. Even during the darkest period of our Revolution, the doors of the courts remained open, the complainant was heard, and justice was rendered.

"The Independence of the Judiciary," *North American Review* (1843), pp. 403, 411, 423.

That is but a superficial view of the subject, which regards the judiciary only as the creature of the legislature, bound merely to watch over the quiet and equal operation of the laws made for it by a superior power. Legislative action is too feeble, desultory, and short-lived, to modify to any great extent the vast body of principles and usages for the guidance of the courts, which have been silently accumulating during the lapse of ages. Slowly and painfully it introduces a few new elements into the aggregate, but the character of the whole evinces essential change only after the interval of centuries. In this country, we are even now reaping the fruits of the legislative wisdom of Edward the First, and of the acumen and wisdom of judges who occupied the bench during the reign of the Tudors. Our ancestors brought with them to these shores the great collection of unwritten maxims and customs, called *the common law*, as the most precious portion of their English birthright; and, adopted either by express enactment or quiet assumption, it has remained with us to this day, not only coloring the whole stream of our legislation, but still constituting in itself the main body of our jurisprudence. . . .

The first reason, then, why the courts are respected and upheld in their functions, is undoubtedly to be found in the nature of the subject on which they are engaged. Their office is the dispensation of *justice,*—the elucidation and enforcement of the idea of Right. They are revered from the reflected splendor and majesty of that virtue, which it is their high prerogative to unfold and maintain. . . .

However the idea of abstract justice may seem to be covered up under the complexity of laws and precedents, and the technicalities of the courts, it is still the sole object of legal proceedings. Even enactments which are merely positive, and were not founded primarily on any dictate of natural law, acquire a moral force from their long standing; they become binding on the conscience, because, having governed the previous expectations and contracts, they are properly applied to determine the respective rights, of the parties to a suit. The legislature is guided by considerations of expediency, its aim being to advance the welfare of the state by watching over its temporal interests; and if higher objects are ever promoted by it, as when it favors honesty and religion by providing for the punishment of blasphemy and fraud, it is only because these virtues are subsidiary to lower ends,—because, in the long run, even in this world, honesty is the best policy, and religion the highest gain. This task it shares with the executive, the province of which is coördinate with its own, both having the same ends in view, though different means are allotted to them for the attainment of those ends. Both are bound to the service of the state, and their rule of action is *salus reipublicæ suprema lex.* But the judiciary has a higher aim, and is governed by a nobler rule. It is bound to do justice though the heavens should fall. Thus it sometimes interferes with the action of the two other departments of government, and thwarts their best laid schemes for the public advantage, by defending the cause of Right. It bridles the legislature in the name of the constitution, and it stands between executive power and the rightful liberties of the subject. Thus the natural reverence of men for justice and the instinctive moral promptings of the heart are enlisted in favor of the courts, and hold up before the judges a shield against violence or contempt.

But the sacred character of the functions of the courts would not alone suffice to procure for them all the consideration and deference which they actually enjoy. The second, and probably the most efficient, cause of their high reputation and commanding influence is *the independence of the judiciary.* . . .

The independence of the judiciary rests upon two points,—that the judges hold office for life, except they subject themselves to impeachment, and that they receive an honorable support, which shall not be lessened during their period of service. When these points are secured, not only are all temptations to swerve from the strict path of rectitude removed as far as is practicable, but not even suspicion can be turned against them. The breath of an imputation cannot obscure the mirror of justice. And this immunity is essential to the working of the system, and to the preservation of that public confidence in the judicial tribunals, which is the surest guaranty of public order. The judges must not only *be,* but *seem,* just. . . .

We say, that all temptations are removed *as far as practicable*; for it cannot be denied that, even in this independent and honorable station, an avaricious judge may, if he chooses, "contaminate his fingers with base bribes," and sell the judgment and his own integrity. But those who lay stress upon this danger show that they have little knowledge of human nature. The gross temptation of a bribe may not allure a man to a flagrant violation of his oath, though the secret promptings of self-interest, the desire of pleasing a powerful friend, the hope of obtaining a reappointment to a lucrative office, may bias his reason by insensible degrees, and finally lead to a judgment as iniquitous, as if it had been openly purchased in court. Virtue is usually sapped and mined, not taken by storm. . . . When passion, or avarice, or ambition is tugging at the heartstrings, a man becomes a sophist to himself, and will try all the wiles of casuistry in order to varnish over the crime, and give it the poor semblance of virtue. Any one can resist Apollyon, when he comes in his proper shape, with horns and hoof, or as a grovelling snake; but the cunning devil appears as a beautiful woman or a judicious friend, and the poor dupe clasps him to his bosom and is entangled in the snare.

Now, the practice of the courts abounds with dangers of the very class which we have here described. Perplexed and difficult cases are continually rising, in which the rights of the respective parties are separated by the difference of a hair. So evenly does the matter lie between them, so doubtful is the rule of law to be applied to such an obscure and intricate question, that all the acumen of a sharp and vigorous intellect can hardly determine on which side equity and legal authority incline. Let self-interest, in the mind of the judge, put a feather into the balance, and it will turn the scale. He must be a poor sophist, in so nice a case, who cannot blind himself so far as to believe, that justice actually requires that decision which is most accordant with his own feelings and ulterior views. The constitution, therefore, wisely frees the mind of the judge from any anxiety respecting his own situation and support. He is made to feel, so far as is possible, that his post is a permanent one, not dependent on the will of a monarch, or the caprice of a party;—that he is set to be the guardian of the laws for the good of the public, and not to waste his thoughts upon his private concerns. Being thus relieved from the carking cares, which too often vex and annoy men out of their integrity, and being chosen from that class, whose talents, learning, and character are a sufficient safeguard against gross and palpable violations of right, it is not strange that the reputation of the courts has so long remained unsullied. In England, we believe, not a judge of the higher courts has been removed by address of the two houses of parliament since the independence of her judiciary was established. In this country, not one member of the national judiciary has been arraigned at the bar of the Senate on any charge affecting his honor or integrity.

It may seem superfluous to argue in defence of that constitution of the courts of law, which has been so long approved by the experience both of England and America, and by the suffrage of nearly every political or juridical writer of any note. But the advantages resulting from it are so quiet and perennial, that they easily escape the attention; and, in a free country, the mania of political innovation is so great, that without constant watchfulness, there is serious danger lest the most important institutions of society should be tampered with, till their influence is weakened or their efficiency destroyed. A theory, under a specious name, may be allowed to supplant one of those time-honored establishments, which have ever afforded the best protection to the rights of the individual, and to the highest interests of the commonwealth. There are ominous signs in this country at the present day, which lead to some apprehensions of such a fatal result. The judiciary is attacked in some of the States, not only by diminishing the salaries of the judges, where it was possible, but by doubts openly expressed whether any institution ought to exist here, which is beyond the popular control. The opinion is plainly avowed, that the will of the people, for the time being, ought to be the only law, and that all restraints upon it, of whatever nature, should be done away. So long as such opinions and doubts were confined to the electioneering harangues of a few demagogues, or to the columns of a few worthless newspapers, they could not effect much injury, and did not deserve serious notice. But when they are found embodied in official documents, when the governor of one of the "old thirteen states" gives them place in his annual message to the legislature, it behooves the friends of free government and of the reputation of the country to be on the alert, and to arrest the evil, if it be possible, ere it is too late.

We know not that this question has ever been agitated between the great political parties which divide the country. Probably it has not been, and we fervently hope that it never may be. The independence of the judiciary is no subject for the common strife of faction and interest,—no topic to be debated in the heat of contest,—no material to be hammered out into "political capital." . . .

There is a more specious argument for destroying the independence of the judiciary, which . . . is frequently urged in newspaper paragraphs and electioneering harangues, because it is better calculated than any other to make an impression on the unthinking multitude. It is founded on the doctrine that, in this country, the will of the people is, and ought to be, supreme in every respect, and no institution should be allowed to exist, which is independent of their authority. It is urged, that all our laws emanate from the people, and therefore should be referred for interpretation to the power which enacted them; that the people are as competent to decide questions of law, as to select persons who shall make the decision for them; and that a denial of this right and competency is a virtual impeachment of the constitution and the government under which we live. It is said, that the will of the people is usually made known only at stated times, and under certain forms,—as at elections, and by ballot or hand-vote upon questions regularly proposed; but that these forms and seasons are adopted only for convenience, and the same power which required the observance of them may also dispense with it; so that the popular will, however promulgated, shall form, for the time being, the supreme law, and the supreme exposition of the law.

This is all sophistry, and sophistry so gross, that one is almost ashamed to argue against it. The doctrine contained in it involves a denial of the superior advantages of society over the primitive and solitary condition of man, and a rejection of the forms and institutions by which alone the social state can be maintained. For its entire refutation, it would be necessary to go back to the theory which lies at the foundation of all government, and to show that *laws properly so called*, of supreme authority and permanent obligation, are necessary to the very existence of the social union. We propose to enter into no such discursive argument, but only to adduce a few brief considerations to show the utter inapplicability of such a theory to the form of government now existing in the United States. It will be admitted, we suppose, that the popular will cannot change the nature of right and wrong, any more than it can alter the fixed relations of quantities to each other, or change the figures in the multiplication table. It cannot make injustice, cruelty, and oppression right in the eyes of God, nor remove the stamp of his approbation from holiness and virtue. The functions of "a court of justice" are indicated by its title. Its province is to decide between man and man as to the requisitions of that law, which is not the mere creature of human enactment, but which is written in the heart, and is binding upon the conscience, of every intelligent being. Its office is to do justice, and so far from listening to the expressions of public sentiment, it is bound to disregard, if need be, in the cause of duty and integrity, the opinions, the wishes, and the interests alike of individuals and of the state.

Now, the founders of our present frame of government, whatever may have been their intentions with respect to the amount of power to be lodged directly in the hands of the people, certainly did not contemplate the establishment of a republic or a democracy, which should exist without any legal enactments whatever. On the contrary, they created a legislature, prescribed the manner in which laws should be passed, defined the subjects to which they might relate, and established the tribunal by which they were to be interpreted and enforced. A law is, from its very nature, an inflexible and universal rule, that governs the conduct, and defines the rights and duties, of all persons subject to the law-making power, during the whole period of its existence. It is not an unchangeable rule for the future, because the same power which enacted may abrogate it, and put another in its place. But it is unchangeable in its application to all cases which have grown up during its continuance. Adopt, then, the most comprehensive and unlimited theory respecting the sovereignty of the people; say that they may frame what enactments they like, on all manner of subjects, or may even annul all existing statutes, and live without law for all time to come. Still their power relates only to the present and the future. The past is fixed and irrevocable. The sovereign may enact or abrogate what rules it pleases to govern coming events and the future conduct of men; but it cannot annul the rights, the contracts, and the expectations which have grown up under the laws that did exist. In respect to these, the government covenanted with every individual, and every individual with the government, that the statute should be respected and obeyed, *on condition* that it should be fixed and universal in its obligation. The price has been paid, and the fulfilment of the contract is demanded. Men have made bargains, and contracted obligations, and regulated their conduct, in strict conformity with the law. And they now require, that those bargains should be fulfilled, those obligations respected, and their conduct declared to be innocent, and not liable to punishment. . . .

We now see the reason why the legal tribunals rightly claim to be considered as the fountains of equity, justice, and natural law, however arbitrary, impolitic, and even unjust, may be the usages and the special enactments which they are required to interpret and enforce. They are not responsible for the intrinsic merits or defects of these customs and laws; that is the business of the legislature. They only unfold and apply the great principle of natural right, or law abstractly considered; which is, that the actions of men must be judged, and their consequences determined, by a fixed law, promulgated at the time when those acts were committed, imperative and permanent in its obligation in reference to them, and definite and unchangeable in its application. To ascertain what this law is, and to apply it to the case in hand, is the high function of the courts. Public opinion cannot aid them in this task, for it is not within the province even of Omnipotence to recall the past, or to alter one jot of the eternal law of justice. The clamors of the multitude must be unheeded, for the judges are listening to a voice as awful as that which proclaimed the law in thunder from the top of Mount Sinai. It is of law thus abstractly considered, that the sublime language of Hooker hardly seems to contain an exaggeration, when he says, that "its seat is the bosom of God, and its voice is the harmony of the world."

TO ORDER A NEW TRIAL

John Bannister Gibson

IF ANYTHING IS SELF-EVIDENT in the structure of our government, it is, that the legislature has no power to order a new trial, or to direct the court to order it, either before or after judgment. The power to order new trials is judicial; but the power of the legislature is not judicial. It is limited to the making of laws; not to the exposition or execution of them. The functions of the several parts of the government are thoroughly separated, and distinctly assigned to the principal branches of it, the legislature, the executive, and the judiciary, which, within their respective departments are equal and co-ordinate. Each derives its authority, mediately and immediately, from the people; and each is responsible, mediately or immediately, to the people for the exercise of it. When either shall have usurped the powers of one or both of its fellows, then will have been effected a revolution, not in the form of the government, but in its action. Then will there be a concentration of the powers of the government in a single branch of it, which, whatever may be the form of the constitution, will be a despotism—a government of unlimited, irresponsible, and arbitrary rule. It is idle to say the authority of each branch is defined and limited in the constitution, if there be not an independent power able and willing to enforce the limitations. Experience proves that it is thoughtlessly but habitually violated; and the sacrifice of individual right is too

Braddee *v.* Brownfield, 2 *Watts & Serg. (Pa.)* (1841), p. 271.

remotely connected with the objects and contests of the masses to attract their attention. From its very position, it is apparent that the conservative power is lodged with the judiciary, which, in the exercise of its undoubted right, is bound to meet every emergency; else causes would be decided not only by the legislature, but, sometimes, without hearing or evidence. The mischief has not yet come to that, for the legislature has gone no farther than to order a rehearing on the merits; but it is not more intolerable in principle to pronounce an arbitrary judgment against a suitor, than it is injurious in practice to deprive him of a judgment, which is essentially his property, and to subject him to the vexation, risk, and expense of another contest. It has become the duty of the court to temporize no longer, but to resist, temperately, though firmly, any invasion of its province, whether great or small.

POLITICS AND JUDICIAL APPOINTMENTS

James Polk

The Polk-Buchanan dispute over an 1845 appointment to the Supreme Court indicates that the judiciary was not as insulated from political and patronage considerations as some contemporaries believed. President Polk's choice of Judge George W. Woodward of Pennsylvania was by no means entirely disinterested. Woodward's legal training and judicial experience qualified him for the position—he was eventually to become Chief Justice of the Pennsylvania Supreme Court—but his status as a prominent Democrat was equally significant. Just as clearly, in his insistence on consultation prior to judicial appointments from his native state, Secretary of State Buchanan revealed that patronage and the judiciary were not total strangers. Buchanan's choice, John M. Read of Pennsylvania, was a personal friend of his, and a loyal Democrat. Read had been recommended for the Supreme Court early in 1845 by President Tyler, but he failed to rouse enthusiasm in the Senate because of his Free Soil sympathies; Read then withdrew his name from consideration. When Buchanan failed to convince Polk that Read should have another chance to serve on the High Court, he wielded his influence to secure the Attorney Generalship of Pennsylvania for his friend. Meanwhile, President Polk's choice, Judge Woodward, also failed to receive the confirmation of the Senate.

The following extract is President Polk's account of the infighting between supporters of the rival candidates for the Court.

AFTER NIGHT Mr. Buchanan called. His manner was one of some agitation and care. He made known the object of his visit by saying he wished to

James Polk, *The Diary of a President* (ed. Nevins, 1929), pp. 39, 48, 53.

converse with me on a subject which had caused him to spend two sleep-less nights. He said that I had a right to nominate Judge Woodward to the Supreme Bench of the United States, but that I should have done so as I had done on Tuesday last without informing him of it was what he com-plained of. I promptly answered that as President of the United States I was responsible for my appointments, and that I had a perfect right to make them without consulting my cabinet, unless I desired their advice. Mr. Buchanan said it had been done by all my predecessors. I told him I did not so understand it. . . . I told him that I had not intended to mortify him by concealing the nomination from him. He said reverse the case; suppose I had been President and you Secretary of State, and I had been about to appoint a judge from Tennessee, would you not have thought you ought to have been consulted by me before I made the nomination? I told him I had once conversed with him fully, that I knew Mr. Read was his choice, that I thought Mr. Woodward the preferable man; but that perhaps it would have been better to have mentioned it to him again, but that as I knew no further conversation I could have had with him could have changed my mind, I had not thought it necessary to do so. I told him that if I supposed that he would have taken the view of it he had, I certainly should have mentioned it to him again before I made the nomination; and that I regretted that anything had occurred to give him pain. He then said that the impression was becoming general among his friends in Pennsylvania that the patronage of the government here was being wielded against him. I told him that he knew that nothing was more unfounded, and after a long conversation, in which the appointments which had been made in Pennsylvania were discussed, he expressed himself as entirely satisfied. . . .

Mr. Cameron of the Senate remained in my office after the balance of the company had retired. He said he wished to have a conversation with me. I told him I would hear him. He commenced by professing friend-ship for the administration. He said he had opposed the nomination of George W. Woodward as judge of the Supreme Court of the United States and went on to assign his reasons, which were unsatisfactory, though I did not deem it to be necessary to tell him so; indeed, I did not think they were the real reasons. . . . I told him as he had sought the conversation I would talk frankly to him. He said he desired that I should. I then told him that the public understood that there was a Democratic majority of six in the Senate, and that the effect of rejecting my principal nominations at the commencement of my administration, and especially as the Senate sat with closed doors and the public could not know the reason of the rejection, was calculated to weaken my administration, and destroy or impair my power and influence in carrying out the measures of my ad-ministration. The truth is Mr. Woodward's rejection was factious, Mr. Cameron and five other professed Democrats having united with the whole Whig party to effect it. And now those by whose votes he was rejected refuse, as the Executive Journal proves, to remove the injunction of secrecy, so that the public may know by whose votes he was rejected. I told Mr. Cameron that since the rejection it had been communicated to me that a coarse and vulgar remark had been made and applied to me, in reference to his nomination, by a professed Democrat, at which I had felt indignant, and that remark was, applying it to me for having nominated Judge Woodward, in substance: that the way to treat an ugly or stubborn negro when you first got him, was to give a d——d drubbing at the start and he would learn how to behave himself. He immediately denied that he had used such language, although I had not said that he was the person who used such language. He showed in his manner some confusion. I told him that the first use of these vulgar terms had not been attributed to him; but that afterwards they had been familiarly repeated among members of Congress and others as applied to me. I told him I had done nothing to merit such epithets of reproach; that I had exercised my constitutional power in making the nomination of Judge Woodward, and the Senate had a right to reject him, but that no man had a right to use such terms. In the after part of the conversation on this point, with a countenance and manner still confused and embarrassed, he admitted that such language had been used, but did not say by whom, but denied that it had been applied to me. . . .

Mr. Buchanan was manifestly in a bad mood, as he has been since Judge Woodward's nomination to the bench of the Supreme Court of the United States, and since he has discovered that he cannot control me in the dispensation of the public patronage. For several weeks past he has not been pleasant in his intercourse with me; has not heartily cooperated with me, but has been disposed to differ with me, as I think unnecessarily. He is, I am told, deeply mortified that I refused to appoint him judge of the Supreme Court of the United States, after Mr. Woodward's rejection by the Senate. I suspect he is seeking some public ground to break with my administration. . . . I will be careful to give him no other ground of complaint.

THE POWER OF REMOVAL

Joseph Story

§ 1537. It is observable, that the constitution makes no mention of any power of removal by the executive of any officers whatsoever. As, however, the tenure of office of no officers, except those in the judicial department,

Joseph Story, *Commentaries on the Constitution* (1851), p. 339.

is, by the constitution, provided to be during good behavior, it follows, by irresistible inference, that all others must hold their offices during pleasure, unless congress shall have given some other duration to their office. As far as congress constitutionally possess the power to regulate and delegate the appointment of "inferior officers," so far they may prescribe the term of office, the manner in which, and the persons by whom the removal, as well as the appointment to office shall be made. But two questions naturally occur upon this subject. The first is, to whom, in the absence of all such legislation, does the power of removal belong; to the appointing power, or to the executive; to the president and senate, who have concurred in the appointment, or to the president alone? The next is, if the power of removal belongs to the executive, in regard to any appointments confided by the constitution to him; whether congress can give any duration of office in such cases, not subject to the exercise of this power of removal? Hitherto the latter has remained a merely speculative question, as all our legislation, giving a limited duration to office, recognizes the executive power of removal as in full force.

§ 1538. The other is a vastly important practical question; and, in an early stage of the government, underwent a most elaborate discussion. The language of the constitution is, that the president shall "nominate, and, by and with the advice and consent of the senate, appoint," &c. The power to nominate does not naturally or necessarily include the power to remove; and if the power to appoint does include it, then the latter belongs conjointly to the executive and the senate. In short, under such circumstances, the removal takes place in virtue of the new appointment, by mere operation of law. It results, and is not separable, from the appointment itself.

§ 1539. This was the doctrine maintained with great earnestness by the Federalist; and it had a most material tendency to quiet the just alarms of the overwhelming influence, and arbitrary exercise of this prerogative of the executive, which might prove fatal to the personal independence and freedom of opinion of public officers, as well as to the public liberties of the country. . . .

§ 1540. The Federalist, while denying the existence of the power, admits by the clearest implication the full force of the argument, thus addressed to such a state of executive prerogative. Its language is: *"The consent of that body* (the senate) *would be necessary to displace, as well as to appoint.* A change of the chief magistrate, therefore, could not occasion so violent or so general a revolution in the officers of the government, as might be expected, if he were the sole disposer of offices. Where a man in any station had given satisfactory evidence of his fitness for it, a new president would be restrained from attempting a change in favor of a person more agreeable to him, by the apprehension, that a discountenance of the senate might frustrate the attempt, and bring some degree of discredit upon himself. Those, who can best estimate the value of a steady administration, will be most disposed to prize a provision, *which connects the official existence of public men with the approbation or disapprobation of that body*, which, from the greater permanency of its own composition, will, in all probability, be less subject to inconstancy than any other member of the government." No man can fail to perceive the entire safety of the power of removal, if it must thus be exercised in conjunction with the senate.

§ 1541. On the other hand, those who, after the adoption of the constitution, held the doctrine (for before that period it never appears to have been avowed by any of its friends, although it was urged by its opponents, as a reason for rejecting it) that the power of removal belonged to the president, argued, that it resulted from the nature of the power, and the convenience, and even necessity of its exercise. It was clearly in its nature a part of the executive power, and was indispensable for a due execution of the laws, and a regular administration of the public affairs. What would become of the public interests, if, during the recess of the senate, the president could not remove an unfaithful public officer? If he could not displace a corrupt ambassador, or head of department, or other officer engaged in the finances or expenditures of the government? If the executive, to prevent a non-execution of the laws, or a non-performance of his own proper functions, had a right to suspend an unworthy officer from office, this power was in no respect distinguishable from a power of removal. In fact, it is an exercise, though in a more moderated form, of the same power. Besides; it was argued that the danger that a president would remove good men from office was wholly imaginary. It was not by the splendor attached to the character of a particular president like Washington, that such an opinion was to be maintained. It was founded on the structure of the office. The man in whose favor a majority of the people of the United States would unite, to elect him to such an office, had every probability at least in favor of his principles. He must be presumed to possess integrity, independence, and high talents. It would be impossible that he should abuse the patronage of the government, or his power of removal, to the base purposes of gratifying a party, or of ministering to his own resentments, or of displacing upright and excellent officers for a mere difference of opinion. The public odium, which would inevitably attach to such conduct, would be a perfect security against it. And, in truth, removals made from such motives, or with a view to bestow the offices upon dependents, or favorites, would be an impeachable offence. One of the most distinguished framers of the constitution, on that occasion, after having expressed his opinion decidedly in favor of the existence of the power of removal in the executive, added: "In the first place, he will be impeachable by this house before the senate for such an act of mal-administration; for I contend, that the wanton removal of meritorious officers would subject him to impeachment and removal from his high trust."

§ 1542. After a most animated discussion, the vote finally taken in the house of representatives was affirmative of the power of removal in the president, without any coöperation of the senate, by the vote of thirty-four members against twenty. In the senate, the clause in the bill, affirming the power, was carried by the casting vote of the vice-president.

§ 1543. That the final decision of this question so made was greatly influenced by the exalted character of the president then in office, was asserted at the time, and has always been believed. Yet the doctrine was opposed, as well as supported, by the highest talents and patriotism of the country. The public, however, acquiesced in this decision; and it constitutes, perhaps, the most extraordinary case in the history of the government of a power, conferred by implication on the executive by the assent of a bare majority of congress, which has not been questioned on many other occasions. Even the most jealous advocates of state rights seem to have slumbered over this vast reach of authority; and have left it untouched, as the neutral ground of controversy, in which they desired to reap no harvest, and from which they retired, without leaving any protestations of title or contest. Nor is this general acquiescence and silence without a satisfactory explanation. Until a very recent period, the power had been exercised in few cases, and generally in such as led to their own vindication. During the administration of President Washington, few removals were made, and none without cause; few were made in that of the first President Adams. In that of President Jefferson the circle was greatly enlarged; but yet it was kept within narrow bounds, and with an express disclaimer of the right to remove for differences of opinion, or otherwise than for some clear public good. In the administrations of the subsequent presidents, Madison, Monroe, and J. Q. Adams, a general moderation and forbearance were exercised, with the approbation of the country, and without disturbing the harmony of the system. Since the induction into office of President Jackson an opposite course has been pursued; and a system of removals and new appointments to office has been pursued so extensively, that it has reached a very large proportion of all the offices of honor and profit in the civil departments of the country. This is a matter of fact; and beyond the statement of the fact it is not the intention of the Commentator to proceed. This extraordinary change of system has awakened general attention, and brought back the whole controversy, with regard to the executive power of removal, to a severe scrutiny. Many of the most eminent statesmen in the country have expressed a deliberate opinion, that it is utterly indefensible, and that the only sound interpretation of the constitution is that avowed upon its adoption; that is to say, that the power of removal belongs to the appointing power.

§ 1544. Whether the predictions of the original advocates of the executive power, or those of the opposers of it, are likely, in the future progress of the government, to be realized, must be left to the sober judgment of the community, and to the impartial award of time. If there has been any aberration from the true constitutional exposition of the power of removal, (which the reader must decide for himself,) it will be difficult, and perhaps impracticable, after forty years' experience, to recall the practice to the correct theory. But, at all events, it will be a consolation to those who love the union, and honor a devotion to the patriotic discharge of duty, that in regard to "inferior officers," (which appellation probably includes ninety-nine out of a hundred of the lucrative offices in the government,) the remedy for any permanent abuse is still within the power of congress, by the simple expedient of requiring the consent of the senate to removals in such cases.

BEING ABOUT TO SEPARATE

Protest of the Minority

Exacerbated by hard times, a conflict between debtors and creditors furiously divided the people of Kentucky in the early 1820's. The legislature, dominated by the debtors organized as the Relief Party, passed legislation extending the power to "replevy" (i.e., delay) the collection of judgments from three to twelve months. In addition, a bill was enacted setting up a bank for the purpose of issuing paper money which would be legal for private debts; if a creditor refused to accept such bank paper, the bill stipulated that the debtor could replevy the debt for two additional years. The creditors organized as the Anti-Relief Party and worked vainly to repeal the legislation. Finally, the Kentucky Court of Appeals declared the acts unconstitutional, in that they violated the Federal constitutional provision guaranteeing the sanctity of contracts. The issue flared anew as the Relief Party denounced the justices for acting contrary to the sovereign will of the people.

The Relief forces captured the governorship by a wide margin in 1824 and acted to remove judges of the Court of Appeals who resisted public opinion. The debtors and their allies failed, however, to obtain the two-thirds majority necessary to recall judges. As a substitute, they secured the passage of a court reorganization bill which abolished the old court and provided a new court packed with "replevin" judges. The Anti-Relief Judges refused to resign, and the issue dominated the campaign for the state legislature in 1826. Pursuing a "campaign of education," the Anti-Relief men captured the Senate and the House and promptly repealed the divisive legislation. The issue, which had threatened to erupt into civil war, gradually cooled down. After 1826, the Relief forces were largely absorbed

---

Protest of the Minority Against the Act Reorganizing the Court of Appeals (December, 1824).

into the Jacksonian following, while their opponents supported Clay and the Whigs.

The following extract, setting forth the Anti-Relief position, speaks of the rights of the minority under a democratic system of government and of the role of the judiciary as guardian of those rights.

THE UNDERSIGNED, composing the minority of the legislature, who voted against the act "reorganizing the Court of Appeals," being about to separate, perhaps never to meet on this theatre again, cannot, consistently with a sense of duty to ourselves, our constituents, and the constitution of our country, close our official duties, without uniting together, and with one voice, respectfully, but firmly and solemnly, protesting against this unprecedented act, as unconstitutional, unjust and alarming.

The constitution declares, that "the Judges of the supreme and inferior courts shall hold their offices during their good behavior, and the continuance of their respective courts." While the court continues, the judge is entitled to his office, until removed for misbehavior. If he be charged with malfeasance in office, the constitution requires that he shall be impeached; but if, for any other reasonable cause, not sufficient for an impeachment, it be proposed to remove him, it is necessary that two-thirds of both branches of the legislature should concur in an address to the Governor to remove him. The constitution tolerates no other mode of removing the judge from the office; this is denied by none. If then the court cannot be abolished or discontinued, the attempt to remove the judges by its reorganization is "palpably and obviously" unconstitutional. We insist that the Court of Appeals is created by the constitution, and therefore can only be abolished by the people, in convention.

No stronger evidence of this is necessary, than the following extracts from the constitution: "The powers of the government of the state of Kentucky shall be divided into three distinct departments, and each of them confided to a separate body of magistracy, viz: Those which are legislative, to one; those which are executive, to another; and those which are judiciary, to another." "The legislative power of this commonwealth shall be vested in two distinct branches," &c. "The judiciary powers of this commonwealth shall be vested in one supreme court," &c. Each department is created by the constitution, for wise ends—and must exist as long as the constitution endures. There must be a judiciary department, as well as legislative and executive. The ultimate powers of that department must be vested in one court of appeals. There must be an executive department. The supreme powers of that department must be vested in a chief magistrate. The Governor can only be removed from his office by two-thirds, on impeachment—the office cannot be abolished—it cannot be removed from him by any act of the legislature. The judges of the Court of Appeals can only be removed from their office by two-thirds, either by impeachment or address.

The offices cannot be removed from the judges by any act of the legislature. The court cannot be abolished; and the judges, unless removed by impeachment or address, are entitled to hold their offices during the continuance of their court. There *shall be* a Court of Appeals, and but one Court of Appeals. If the legislature can abolish, or discontinue it for a moment, there is nothing to prevent its abolition forever. But the convention who formed the constitution have not thought proper to leave to the legislature the power of creating, or destroying, or modifying, or changing the three great departments of the government; they are fixed by the constitution, and are as stable and immovable as that sacred and inviolable charter. Although the governor may die or resign, there is still an executive department, and it is the same department. And although the judges of the Court of Appeals may die or resign, there is still a Court of Appeals, and it is the same court. The officers, in each case, may change, but the office is the same—the executive still continues—the court still continues. This is the doctrine of the constitution—it is the doctrine of genuine republicanism— it was the doctrine of the republicans of 1802, with Mr. Jefferson at their head. The republican party in Congress, in 1802, acknowledged that the supreme court could not be abolished, nor the judges removed from office by an act of ordinary legislation; because the court was established by the constitution, and the judges hold their offices during good behavior, and the continuance of their court. The party were unanimous in this opinion, but insisted that inferior courts, which are established by law, may be abolished by law, whenever they become inconvenient or unnecessary.

Our constitution, like that of the nation, allows the legislature, from time to time, to establish the inferior courts; because, experience might prove the necessity of changing those courts, so as to adapt them to the condition of the country. But each constitution requires that there shall be *one* supreme court, and the language of each is substantially the same. By each, a supreme court is ordained and established. The constitution of Kentucky does not require that the inferior courts shall be circuit or quarter session courts, but it does declare and require that there should be one Court of Appeals. Our circuit courts did not exist until established by the act of 1802. But the Court of Appeals has existed from the date of the constitution. The first were created by the act of the legislature; the other was established by the paramount act of the *people* in convention. The same authority which creates, may destroy; therefore, the legislature may abolish the circuit courts—but the *people alone,* assembled in convention, can abrogate the court of appeals.

But this legislature, as if above the constitution, have arrogated the right to abolish the Court of Appeals, by its "re-organization," and to remove the incumbent judges from office, by a bare majority, whilst their "court continues"!

We consider this not only an unconstitutional and high handed measure, but one, which, if approved, will prostrate the whole fabric of constitutional liberty; *we do consider it a* REVOLUTION! We consider this unparalleled act, as an attempt, by the majority of the legislature, to consolidate their power, and perpetuate their supremacy, over the rights of the minority and the constitution, by destroying the independence and purity, and impartiality of the judiciary. And if it be countenanced by the people, we believe that our courts will be subservient to the strong party, or party in power—that we shall be governed by factions—that "liberty and equality" will be empty sounds—that the ambitious and the powerful will hold in their hands the destinies of our state—that the minority will, indeed, have "*no rights*," and will be proscribed, as we believe it has been resolved that WE shall be, during the present administration—that the freedom of speech and of conscience, and the rights of life, liberty, and property, will depend on the caprices of a fluctuating majority of the legislature; that our courts will be servile and dependent, like those of revolutionary France, under Robespierre, and those of England, under the Tudors and the Stuarts; and that the legislature of Kentucky will become practically, as omnipotent as the British parliament.

These are not the depictions of vivid fancy, or the spectres of a puerile alarm; we fear that they may become sober and solemn realities. If the people sanction this act of the majority, where is our security? Their approbation of such an act would indicate a destitution of that reverence for their constitution, which is the soul of every constitution, and without which no people ever were or ever will be free. Ours is not the language of prophecy, all of whose predictions are yet to be fulfilled—as passing scenes will prove. Although we are not initiated into the "*arcana imperii*," our eyes have seen and our ears have heard enough to enable us to understand "the signs of the times."—When we see new judges appointed to supersede the old ones, some of whom are known to have been active and clamorous in endeavors to prostrate the court; when we see, at the head of these new judges, the leader of the majority, who has been charged with exerting his influence in, and out of the legislature, in caucus and otherwise, whilst Secretary of State, to procure the passage of an act to provide offices for himself and friends; when we hear, day and night, of our chief magistrate intermeddling and endeavoring, with all his means of persuasion, to influence legislation; and when we are told that he has proscribed all, or most of those who voted against him—can we, as faithful sentinels on the people's watchtowers, tell them, "*all's well*"? We cannot, we will not; we would be faithless to ourselves and treacherous to them; we will tell them the truth, and are prepared for the consequences.

We will tell them that the new judges are virtually pledged to support the party in power; that we do believe that they are, in every essential attribute of an enlightened, independent and incorruptible bench, inferior to the old judges; that such a court, organized under such circumstances, will not, we fear, possess, or even deserve to possess, the full and unhesitating confidence of the people; that, to provide for particular men, we believe new and unnecessary offices have been created; and to consummate the object, when the people are almost sinking under embarrassment and distress, the salaries of the new judges of the Court of Appeals have been raised from four thousand five hundred dollars to eight thousand dollars.

All this we have in our places faithfully and honestly endeavored to avert, but our efforts were unavailing. The judges had been fully and constitutionally tried, and acquitted—but that which shields the felons of the country could not protect them—they are not liberated after one trial—they cannot escape. "Power" is converted into "right"—and the constitution is under the feet of a triumphant majority, who, if not checked by the people, may hereafter exercise all power, legislative, executive, and judicial; which Mr. Jefferson and other patriots of the revolution have denounced as the most intolerable despotism. Against this sort of tyranny our fathers protested in the Declaration of Independence; against this sort of tyranny they fought, and bled, and conquered and against it, those of their sons who cherish their principles, will ever PROTEST, whilst they have tongues to speak, or pens to write. And we now declare to this legislature, and to the people, that if this memorable act of a majority be submitted to, or enforced, liberty is in danger, justice is in danger, morality is in danger, religion is in danger, and every thing dear and sacred is in danger. We will have no living constitution, and against bad times and bad men there will be no security. This example will consecrate every encroachment that power can make on the rights of the poor and the humble, the persecuted and the virtuous.

The only privilege now left the minority, is to complain and remonstrate, by appealing to the people. We had thought when the fatal act passed, that we would retire from the hall of legislation, and leave the majority to act without obstacle or embarrassment; but on more mature reflection, we have deemed it most prudent to remain at our post until the last moment of the session, and to close it on our part by a united and candid expression of our unqualified opposition to a measure which, if supported, we believe, strikes the constitution of our country dead, and consigns our most cherished rights to the vortex of party strife and ambition.

Appealing, therefore, to our own consciences, and to the God of the universe, for the rectitude of our conduct and the purity of our motives, we do now, for ourselves, our constituents and our posterity, in the name of the constitution and of justice, enter on the Journal this, our solemn protest against the late memorable act of the majority, as most alarming and unconstitutional.

KIDNAPPED THE COURT

A Petition

Isaac Stevens (1818–1862) graduated first in his class in the United States Military Academy, attained the rank of major in the Mexican Civil War, and was named Governor of Washington Territory in 1853. He negotiated treaties with the Indians in order to secure more land for the growing white population, but he was not generous enough to please the Indians. A revolt broke out in early 1856 which threatened the safety of the entire territory. Indian forces defeated the regular troops at the Governor's disposal, but Stevens finally succeeded in crushing the revolt with a thousand volunteers. The interposition of the courts to shield suspected Indian sympathizers led Stevens to declare martial law, close the courts, and arrest the chief justice under the circumstances described in the following petition. Stevens resigned in 1857 to accept election to Congress as the Territory's delegate; there he proceeded to seek ratification of his Indian treaties. Although he supported Breckenridge in 1860, he opposed secession. Grudgingly, Lincoln appointed Stevens as colonel of the 79th Regiment of New York. Stevens rose to the rank of major-general before his career was terminated by a bullet in the head at the Battle of Chantilly.

The following selection examines Stevens' conduct after the suppression of the revolt and charges him with using the powers of his office to abrogate civil rights within the Territory.

IN THE LATTER PART OF THE MONTH of March, 1856, Lion A. Smith, Charles Wren, Henry Smith, John McLeod, John McField, Henry Murry and ——— Wilson, American citizens, residents of the County of Pierce, and Territory of Washington, were arrested upon their several land claims, in that county, by a detachment of volunteers under orders of Isaac I. Stevens, Governor of said Territory, without process of law, and without any complaint or affidavit being lodged against them, charging them with the commission of any offence against the law. They were taken by a guard to the town of Olympia, the capital of the Territory, detained there overnight, and then sent in custody of a guard to the U. S. Military Post at Fort Steilacoom, with a *written* request of Governor Stevens to Lieut. Col. Casey, U. S. Army, commanding that post, to retain said prisoners in *close confinement*, upon a charge of *treason*. In the early part of April, William H. Wallace and Frank Clark, attorneys at law, of counsel for said prisoners, started for Penn's Cove, Whidby's Island, a distance of a hundred miles, the residence of Hon. F. A. Chenoweth, U. S. District Judge of the Third

W. H. Wallace *et al., A Brief Notice of the Recent Outrages Committed by Isaac I. Stevens, Governor of Washington Territory* (May 17, 1856).

Judicial District of Washington Territory, to make application for the writ of *habeas corpus,* to test the legality of such imprisonment. The Governor having learned of this mission of justice and mercy, issued a proclamation, *without seal*, bearing date April 30, 1856, and in the following language:

"*Whereas*, In the prosecution of the Indian war, circumstances have existed affording such grave cause of suspicion, that certain evil disposed persons of Pierce County, have given aid and comfort to the enemy, as that they have been placed under arrest and ordered to be tried by a military commission: *And whereas*, efforts are now being made to withdraw, by civil process, these persons from purview of the said commission;

"Therefore, as the war is now being actively prosecuted throughout nearly the whole of the said county, and great injury to the public, and the plans of the campaign be frustrated, if the alleged designs of these persons be not arrested; I, Isaac I. Stephens, Governor of the Territory of Washington, do hereby proclaim MARTIAL LAW over the said county of Pierce, and do by these presents suspend for the time being, and till further notice, the functions of all civil officers in said county.

"Given under my hand at Olympia, this third day of April, eighteen hundred and fifty-six, and the year of Independence of the United States the eightieth.   Isaac I. Stevens."

On being apprised of this proclamation, Col. Casey informed the Governor, that notwithstanding its issue, were a writ of *habeas corpus* served upon him, he would feel compelled to obey its mandates; upon this, the Governor removed said prisoners again to Olympia, *out of the county*, where he pretended to hold them by the martial law he had proclaimed. In the meantime, his honor, Judge Chenoweth, had issued a writ of *habeas corpus*, and unaware of the existence of the proclamation. It is not our purpose to criticise the *intention* of the Governor, to defeat the service of a writ *after* the arrest of parties, defying, as it does, the wholesome spirit of that section of the Constitution which prohibits the enactment of *ex post facto* laws, for we have learned to our mortification, that Constitutions are nothing, law is idle, the *will* of the Governor is *supreme*. But we do boldly maintain the position that if his proclamation of martial law was based upon public necessity, urgently demanded for the public welfare, the great *writ* of *right* still stood exempt from its reach, and paramount to its operation. Truth compels us, however, to deny that the proclamation was necessary, and we need only refer to the document itself to sustain our position. The preamble to said proclamation recites that "*the suspected parties were in custody*," their evil designs, had they any, had been thwarted, and they were now in a position that they could no longer "frustrate the campaign." Nor does it appear that any effort was made to rescue the prisoners by force; nothing is alleged, save that by counsel, they attempted to secure what the national Constitution guarantees to every citizen.

The writ of *habeas corpus* issued by order of Judge Chenoweth never was served, because the prisoners had been transferred by Gov. Stevens out of Judge Chenoweth's district.

Nothing further was done until the first Monday in May, 1856, when by a law of this Territory, the term of the District Court for the County of Pierce, was to be holden. We quote from the statement made by the bar of that district, the detail of the outrages committed by the Executive during that week:

"The United States Judge, assigned to this Judicial District, being detained at home by severe illness, at the time when by law the term of the District Court was to be held, the Hon. Edward Lander, Chief Justice of this territory, who resides in the adjoining district, at the special written request of Hon. Judge Chenoweth, undertook to hold said court, and on Monday the 5th May inst., arrived at Steilacoom and opened the Court in due form. Having been informed, however, on his way to the Court by Lieut. Col. B. F. Shaw, commanding a volunteer force under authority of the Governor of this territory, that if he attempted to hold said Court, he would be forcibly prevented. Judge Lander, in order to prevent a collision between executive and judicial authority, suggested that he would simply open and adjourn the Court until Wednesday, that the Governor might be advised to withdraw his proclamation. . . .

"Governor Stevens, on the 6th inst., while declining to withdraw his proclamation, suggested that Judge Lander adjourn his court to the first Monday in June, and informed him that he had examined the law, and found no difficulty in his adjourning from any time to the next term of court.

"Upon the receipt of this information, Judge Lander having done his duty as a citizen, in endeavoring to prevent the expected collision, proceeded to fulfill those of his judicial office by opening court at the appointed time, accompanied by the Clerk, U. S. Deputy Marshal and Sheriff; he went to the court house, opened the court by proclamation in usual form, and caused the Grand Jury to be impaneled and sworn. During this time a company of volunteers, (many of them citizens of Oregon, although enrolled in this territory,) drawn from Clark County, on the Columbia river, entered the court room with loaded rifles and drew up without the bar, another company was kept in reserve without, to assist them if necessary. Judge Lander then directed the Deputy Marshal to prevent the entry of any armed men within the bar, but the commanding officer having announced that he acted under orders from Governor Stevens, directed his men to arrest the Judge and Clerk. In obedience to the order they entered the bar, the Deputy Marshal being unable to prevent it, and arrested the Judge in his seat; the Judge stating that he only succumbed to force, and declined calling upon the *posse comitatus*, because he wished to avoid bloodshed. Judge Lander and the Clerk, J. M. Chapman, were then removed by the military from the court house, and on the same day taken out of the county, and carried to Olympia. The records of the court, which were at first seized, were subsequently returned to the deputy clerk.

"During this time the citizens present, though manifesting a deep feeling of indignation at the transaction, refrained from any disorderly or violent acts. The conduct of Judge Lander was, throughout, dignified, firm and worthy of his high position, and was, we are satisfied, dictated only by a strict sense of duty."

On reaching Olympia, the Chief Justice and Clerk were not placed in confinement, though the former was not officially notified of his release till the 9th inst., and the Clerk on the 10th inst.

On Monday the 12th of May, the District Court of the Second Judicial District commenced, over which Chief Justice Lander presides, and he proceeded to the discharge of that duty.

During that day, John McLeod, Henry Smith and John McField, three of the parties arrested in Pierce County, petitioned the Judge, at Chambers, for a writ of habeas corpus to be directed to Isaac I. Stevens, Governor, &c., to bring them and their fellow prisoners before the Chief Justice, at Chambers, on Wednesday ensuing. This writ was placed in the hands of the U. S. Marshal and duly served the same day at 7, P. M. *Under cover of that night* proclamations of martial law over the County of Thurston were posted up . . .

Thursday, May 15, 1, P. M.—The Governor failing to appear and make return to the writ, on motion of petitioners' counsel, rule made absolute, and a writ of attachment issued to bring Isaac I. Stevens before the Hon. Edward Lander, Chief Justice, to answer for a contempt in refusing to make return to the writ of habeas corpus. The Governor *forcibly resisted* the service of this writ, and dispatched a company of volunteers, (*from the Territory* of Oregon,) commanded by Capt. Bluford Miller, to the house wherein Judge Lander was sitting at Chambers, and, the Marshal being ordered to keep the room clear of armed men, was compelled to lock the door. While the Marshal was engaged in making a return to the writ, and the Judge in making the order for an alias writ of attachment, Capt. Miller called upon the Judge to *surrender.* In the meantime the house was surrounded by armed men. The counsel engaged inside could distinctly hear the men cocking their rifles. The Judge in this trying moment remained firm, cool and dispassionate, and finally, the door was forced open by the soldiers, the room was filled with armed men, and the Chief Justice, together with Elwood Evans, acting clerk of the U. S. District Court, of the Second Judicial District, was seized and taken down to the executive office. In the presence of a large crowd, Chief Justice Lander was offered his liberty on condition of his "giving his honor that he would not hold any court or issue any further process, until the proclamation of martial law was revoked." This offer was made by Capt. Miller, who stated that he did it by the instruction of the Governor. Justice to Judge Lander requires that we should give his dignified and manly reply. "Tell Governor

Stevens for me, that I will not promise not to do what the law requires at my hand; say to him that I will do my whole duty, and I trust he will do his as well." On this answer he was taken into custody and carried out to camp Montgomery, out of the County of Thurston, out of his Judicial District, pending a regular term of Court—the Grand Jury being yet in session, important cases undisposed of, and much unfinished business on the docket,—making the second time which Governor Stevens has interrupted the Courts, and *kidnapped* the Court and its clerk. The clerk was then unconditionally released.

The above is a plain unvarnished statement of the facts of the case, and on them we base the following charges against Gov. Stevens, with our reasons for so doing:

I.—*He has violated his oath of office, which* INTER ALIA, *was to support the Constitution of the United States.*

1. In this, that he has attempted to suspend the writ of habeas corpus, which, by said Constitution can only be suspended by Congress, and then only in cases of invasion and rebellion, when the public safety require it.— *Vide Cons. U. S. Art.* i. *Sec.* 9.

2. In this, that he has arrested citizens, and deprived them of their liberty without process of law.—*Vide Cons. U. S. Art.* v. *Amendments.*

3. In this, that he has held persons to answer for an infamous and capital crime without any complaint or charge being preferred against them, and without a presentment or indictment of a Grand Jury being made.—*Vide Cons. of U. S. Art.* v. *Amendments.*

4. In this, that he has broken into houses of citizens without the issue of any warrant therefor, and seized persons and taken them into custody.— *Vide Cons. U. S. Art.* iv. *Amendments.*

5. In this, that he has deprived American citizens of the right of trial by jury of the district wherein the alleged crime was committed, and created a court of his own not known to or recognized by the law.—*Vide Cons. U. S. Art.* iii. *Sec.* 2; *il Art.* vi. *Amendments.*

6. In this, that he has charged men with committing *treason*, which is only cognizable by a United States Court, and ordered their trial by a tribunal of his own creation.—*Vide Cons. U. S. Art.* iii. *Sec.* 3.

7. In this, that he has defied and abrogated the supreme law of the land, rendered null and void the Constitution of the United States, and erected a military despotism with nothing to guide it but his own will.— *Vide Cons. U. S. Art.* vi.

II.—*He has acted in violation of the Organic Act creating the Territory of Washington.*

1. In this, that he has suspended the writ of habeas corpus. [See ordinance of 1787] . . .

2. In this, that he has deprived citizens of their liberty and property without process of law, and without compensation.—*Ibid.*

3. In this, that he has deprived citizens of the territory of a right of trial by jury.—*Ibid.*

III.—*He has violated and set at defiance the laws of Washington Territory.*

1. In this, that he has suspended and interrupted the terms of the District Courts of the Counties of Pierce and Thurston.—*Vide "An Act to define the judicial district of Washington Territory," Laws W. T., 1854, p.* 448.

2. In this, that he has held in custody persons not charged with any offence, and without a complaint filed.—*Vide Crim. Prac. Laws W. T., Ses. 1854, Passim.*

3. In this, that he has violated the provision of law whereby "Every person restrained of his liberty, under any pretence whatever, may prosecute a *writ* of *habeas corpus* to inquire into the causes of the restraint."—*Vide Sec.* 434 *"Of An Act to regulate the practice in civil actions," p.* 212, *Laws W. T., Ses.* 1854. . . .

Such then is the view we take of the gross outrage committed in attempting to suspend the writ of habeas corpus, and we can arrive at no other conclusion than that the Governor is a usurper, a tyrant and a despot.

The plea of ignorance in this case cannot avail him from these charges. *"Ignorantia legis neminem excusat."* We assert that it was his duty to know principles at the basis of our free institutions. A school boy could not fail to know them, and for a *Governor* to be *so ignorant*, is at once to acknowledge his unfitness for so high a position. . . .

Has eighty years growth and vigor, secured by the maintenance of the truths of that sublime instrument, taught us, the descendants of those great missionaries of civil and constitutional freedom, that the people have no rights, that absolutism and despotism are again to prevail, and every thing peculiar to American institutions at once be blotted from our national character?

In conclusion, a sense of duty we own to Chief Justice Edward Lander, who has twice been taken into that most offensive of all styles of arrest, that of being forced to yield, in the exercise of his judicial functions to an armed force, prompts us again to tender our sympathies. He has done every thing he could to maintain the supremacy of the law, and the dignity of the bench. Yielding only when overwhelmed by the soldiery of the Executive, his last judicial acts have been to order the punishment due to such outlaws, for their contempt in invading the halls of justice, to protest firmly against the despotism of a petty military tyrant, *whose day is now.* We fearlessly make the issue on this great question, and we implore the national government to redress our grievances and shield us from the despotism under which we live. Our courts are powerless, private rights are at an end, the constitution is subverted, civil process is paralyzed, to ask for process guarantied us by law, is cause for arrest, the highest judicial functionary of our territory is now a prisoner, because he dared to issue a writ of habeas corpus at the petition of five of Governor Stevens' victims.

Can this document better end than by asserting to the world, that our territory is now in such a condition, that soldiers are not needed to fight an enemy, but their leisure is devoted to interrupting courts of justice, becoming jailors to judges and clerks thereof, who but perform their legitimate public duty. Such is the "great OVERRULING PUBLIC NECESSITY" *justifying the proclamation of martial law.*

GOVERNMENT MAY NOT COMMIT
POLITICAL SUICIDE

Jeremiah Sullivan Black

Chief Justice Black wrote the decision in Mott *v.* Pennsylvania Railroad *which follows, only five years after his very different opinion in the* Sharples *case. Here he evinces the same distrust of the legislative power exemplified in 1857 by the enactment of amendments to the Pennsylvania constitution which, in reaction to* Sharples, *prohibited public credit to be pledged for corporate purposes. The* Mott *case was a herald of skepticism toward legislative action, which was to transform the attitudes of many states toward the proper sphere of government activity in economic affairs.*

Black (1810–1888) was appointed Attorney General by Buchanan in 1857. He had been Chief Justice of Pennsylvania since 1851. In the secession crises of late 1860, he was named to succeed Lewis Cass as Secretary of State, but he differed with the President over the legality of Federal coercion. His appointment to the United States Supreme Court in 1861 was not confirmed by the Senate; Republicans, Douglas Democrats, and Southern sympathizers alike could agree on this rejection—the price of his vacillation between the Federal power and the interests of the Southern states.

. . . WE NOW COME to the vital question involved in these applications. The Act of Assembly of 16th May 1857, makes provision for a public sale; and, for the purpose of inviting competition, directs that public notice of the time and place be given in one or more newspapers, of extended circu-

30 Pa. 9 (1858), **p. 25.**

lation, published in the cities of Philadelphia, Pittsburgh, Washington, Boston, New York, and in the borough of Harrisburg. It authorizes "any person or persons, or railroad or canal company now incorporated, or which may hereafter be incorporated, under the laws of this Commonwealth, to become the purchasers for any sum not less than $7,500,000." But there is a *proviso* in the 3d section, which declares that "if the Pennsylvania Railroad Company shall become the purchasers, at the said public sale, or by assignment, they shall pay, in addition to the purchase-money at which it may be struck down, the sum of 1,500,000 dollars, and *in consideration thereof*, the said railroad company and the Harrisburg, Mount Joy and Lancaster Railroad Company shall be discharged by the Commonwealth *for ever* from the payment of all taxes upon tonnage, or freight carried over said railroads; and the said Pennsylvania Railroad Company shall also be released from the payment of all other taxes or duties on its capital stock, bonds, dividends, or property, except for school, city, county, borough, or township purposes." The amount of taxes proposed to be released is beyond calculation. It can only be conjectured. It would be greatly increased by the tax, which would of course be levied on the property about to be sold to the company. Judging from the increase during the last five years, and the constant augmentation of commerce and travel along the route, it would seem reasonable to believe that in five years from this time it would be double its present amount. But conceding that the tax to be released will hereafter amount to no more, per annum, than the sum paid in 1856, the amount, according to the admissions of the railroad company itself, would be $280,739.21 per annum for ever. This sum is more than equal to the interest on $5,600,000, at 5 per cent., the rate to be charged to the purchasers. In other words, the Act of Assembly proposes to give to the railroad company a consideration equal to $5,600,000, for $1,500,000, and thus to give that company an advantage equal to $4,100,000 over every other bidder at the sale! By means of this privilege the Pennsylvania Railroad Company may drive from the field of competition all other bidders. It is essential to every fair public auction that all the bidders shall stand upon an equal footing. If the object had been to make a fair sale of this portion of the state revenue, it might have been evinced by a provision for the transfer of it to the highest bidder, without any distinction in favour of any one. But this was not done. The extraordinary *proviso* in favour of the Pennsylvania Railroad Company is partial, and entirely repugnant to the general intent of the act; and if allowed to stand, the sale under it will furnish one of the most magnificent exhibitions of a "*mock auction*" that the world has ever witnessed! We rejoice to say that the highly respectable and upright officers of the corporation disclaim, in the most solemn manner, under oath, all agency in procuring the enactment in question.

But has the constitution conferred upon the legislature the authority to extinguish *for ever*, by bargain and sale, the power to raise revenue for the support of government? All free governments are established by the people for their benefit, and the powers delegated are to be exercised for their common good, and not, under any circumstances, to be sold or destroyed, so long as the nations establishing them have the physical power to maintain their independence. Individuals cannot subsist without food. Deprive them of "the means whereby" they live, and you destroy them as certainly as if you did it by shedding their blood. The necessities of governments are as great as those of individuals. No government can exist without revenues to defray its expenses, and support its officers and agents. The revenue is the food indispensable to its existence. Deprive it of this, and you strip it of all power to perform its duties, bring it into contempt by its uselessness and helplessness, and ultimately destroy it as effectually as if it were overturned by domestic violence, or subjugated by the conquest of a foreign foe.

Government is but an aggregation of individual rights and powers. It has no more right to commit political suicide than an individual has to destroy the life given by his Creator. Contracting away the taxing power in perpetuity tends, as we have seen, inevitably to the destruction of the government. If twelve or twenty millions of taxable property may be released to-day, one hundred millions may be released to-morrow, and the principle being established, the process might go on until all power to raise revenue was gone. If this did not destroy the government, it would result in something infinitely more dangerous to the liberties of the people. It would make it the servile dependant of the wealthy corporations or individuals to whom it contracted away its means of support. Although the taxing power is but an incidental one, to be exercised only as the necessary means of performing governmental duties, it is nevertheless a branch of the legislative power which always, in its nature, implies not only the power of making laws, but of altering and repealing them, as the exigencies of the state and circumstances of the times may require: *Rutherforth's Institutes of Natural Law*, B. 3, ch. 3, § 3. If one portion of the legislative power may be sold, another may be disposed of in the same way. If the power to raise revenue may be sold to-day, the power to punish for crimes may be sold to-morrow, and the power to pass laws for the redress of civil rights, may be sold the next day. If the legislative power may be sold, the executive and judicial powers may be put in the market with equal propriety. The result to which the principle must inevitably lead, proves that the sale of any portion of governmental power is utterly inconsistent with the nature of our free institutions, and totally at variance with the object and general provisions of the constitution of the state. It may be urged that we must confide in the fidelity of the legislature, and that there is every ground for hope that they would not carry such measures to an unreasonable length. This is no answer to the argument. It is a question of constitutional authority, and not a case of confidence at all. Limitations of power, established by written constitutions, have their origin in a distrust of the infirmity of man. That distrust is fully justified by the history of the rise and fall of nations. . . .

No class of corporations stand more in need of the protection of the government, or occupy more of the time of the legislature and the courts of justice, or occasion more expense to the government, than railroad corporations. From the extensive nature of their operations, the power to take private property for the construction of their works, and their continual collision with each other's interests, and with the interests of individuals and municipal communities, they require the constant and the energetic protection of the strong arm of the government. Withdraw that protection, and they would be left to the mercy of popular outbreaks, manifesting themselves by opposition to their progress and the destruction of their works, whenever the location of their roads, or their depots, or any of their numerous and necessary operations, came in conflict with the interests of particular localities. These corporations should be the last to consent that the government should be enfeebled by the diminution of its revenues, or to ask that it should be bound to exert all its energies, and incur large and constant expenditures for their protection, while they are exempt from contributing their share.

These principles are not so infirm as to stand in need of the staff of authority for support. They are the result of that liberty and equality which was established by the revolutionary struggle of our ancestors. They are perfectly understood by every one who has capacity to comprehend the nature of our free institutions; they are deeply impressed on the hearts of the people; and they are fully recognized by the history, the objects, and the language of our state constitution.

3. Private and Public International Law

Relations between the national government and other nations was another concern of American law during this period. As a nation grows, conflicts with the interests of other sovereigns are almost inevitable; this period was one of growth both in territory and influence as the United States began to feel its strength beyond its existing borders. One of the most important statements of international policy was the Monroe Doctrine, the basis for future relations with Latin America. The tenuous legal basis for the assumption of a "big-brother" role toward Latin America is indicated by a French newspaper comment: "Mr. Monroe, who is not a sovereign, has assumed in his message the tone of a powerful monarch, whose armies and fleets are ready to march at the first signal. . . . He has prescribed to the potentates of Europe the conduct which they will observe under certain circumstances, if they do not wish to incur their own disgrace. . . . Mr. Monroe is the temporary President of a Republic situated on the east coast of North America. This republic is bounded on the south by the possessions of the King of Spain and on the north by those of the King of England. . . . By what right then would the two Americas be under its immediate sway from Hudson Bay to Cape Horn?" If not "right" it is certainly relevant to the role of the United States in international relations that it was even then ready to announce a bold doctrine.

Between 1819 when Florida was acquired from Spain, and 1867 when Alaska was purchased from Russia, the United States achieved its continental destiny and began to exert its influence far beyond its own borders. Little force was used, despite the vehemence of the exponents of expansion, and the imperialistic oratory during the 1840's when "manifest destiny" cast its spell. This was largely owing to the willingness of most American leaders to achieve their ends through diplomatic channels.

The lawyer, with his bent toward conciliation, could play an important part in the diplomacy of a period which favored negotiation. Many Secretaries of State were lawyers, Webster and Buchanan among others. This may account for what can be called a lawyerlike desire evidenced by American diplomats to put everything down in writing, following the pattern of drafting a contract between private parties.

The field of diplomacy gave the lawyer an opportunity to turn his negotiating talents to statesmanship. He did not develop a foreign policy for the country; that seemed to grow up more from the grass roots. He did, however, temper the more violent fire-eaters in society. Consistent with the prevailing temper and values of his profession, he sought to conciliate and to settle as many disputes as possible within the four corners of a document. Though he was not a professional diplomat, he could still be a talented negotiator.

INTERNATIONAL CASES OF MIXED RIGHTS

Joseph Story

As in so many other fields of law, Justice Story was the moving force behind the study of conflict of laws. For his general views, which he expressed in his Treatise on Conflict of Laws *in 1834, Story relied primarily on Continental authorities, especially the Dutchman Huber. This use of Continental developments for practical application in American law is another illustration of the resourcefulness of some leaders of the American bar.*

§ 1. THE Earth has long since been divided into distinct Nations, inhabiting different regions, speaking different languages, engaged in different pursuits, and attached to different forms of government. It is natural that, under such circumstances, there should be many variances in their institutions, customs, laws, and polity; and that these variances should result sometimes from accident, and sometimes from design, sometimes from superior skill, and knowledge of local interest, and sometimes from a choice founded in ignorance, and supported by the prejudices of imperfect civilization. Climate, and geographical position, and the physical adaptations springing from them, must at all times have had a powerful influence in the organization of each society, and have given a peculiar complexion and character to many of its arrangements. The bold, intrepid, and hardy natives of the North of Europe, whether civilized or barbarous, would scarcely desire, or tolerate, the indolent inactivity and luxurious indulgences of the Asiatics. Nations inhabiting the borders of the ocean, and accustomed to maritime intercourse with other nations, would naturally require institutions and laws, adapted to their pursuits and enterprises, which would be wholly unfit for those who should be placed in the interior of a continent, and should maintain very different relations with their neighbours, both in peace and war. Accordingly we find, that, from the earliest records of authentic history, there has been (as far at least as we can trace any,) little uniformity in the laws, usages, policy, and institutions, either of contiguous or of distant nations. The Egyptians, the Medes, the Persians, the Greeks, and the Romans, differed not more in their characters and employments from each other, than in their institutions and laws. They had little desire to learn, or to borrow, from each other; and indifference, if not contempt, was the habitual state of almost every ancient nation in regard to the internal polity of all others.

Joseph Story, *Commentaries on the Conflict of Laws* (1857), pp. 1, 18.

§ 2. Yet even under such circumstances, from their intercourse with each other, questions must sometimes have arisen, as to the operation of the laws of one nation upon the rights and remedies of parties in the domestic tribunals, especially when they were in any measure dependent upon, or connected with foreign transactions. How these questions were disposed of, we do not know; but it is most probable, that they were left to be decided by the analogies of the municipal code, or were abandoned to their fate, as belonging to that large class of imperfect rights, which rests wholly on personal confidence, and is left without any appeal to remedial justice. It is certain, that the nations of antiquity did not recognise the existence of any general or universal rights and obligations, such as among the moderns constitute, what is now emphatically called, the Law of Nations. Even among the Romans, whose jurisprudence has come down to us in a far more perfect and comprehensive shape, than that of any other nation, there cannot be traced out any distinct system of principles applicable to international cases of mixed rights. . . .

§ 4. Indeed, in the present times, without some general rules of right and obligation, recognised by civilized nations to govern their intercourse with each other, the most serious mischiefs and most injurious conflicts would arise. Commerce is now so absolutely universal among all countries; the inhabitants of all have such a free intercourse with each other; contracts, marriages, nuptial settlements, wills, and successions, are so common among persons, whose domicils are in different countries, having different and even opposite laws on the same subjects; that without some common principles adopted by all nations in this regard there would be an utter confusion of all rights and remedies; and intolerable grievances would grow up to weaken all the domestic relations, as well as to destroy the sanctity of contracts and the security of property.

§ 5. A few simple cases will sufficiently illustrate the importance of some international principles in matters of mere private right and duty. Suppose a contract, valid by the laws of the country, where it is made, is sought to be enforced in another country, where such a contract is positively prohibited by its laws; or, *vice versa,* suppose a contract, invalid by the laws of the country, where it is made, but valid by that of the country, where it is sought to be enforced; it is plain, that unless some uniform rules are adopted to govern such cases, (which are not uncommon,) the grossest inequalities will arise in the administration of justice between the subjects of the different countries in regard to such contracts. Again; by the laws of some countries marriage cannot be contracted until the parties arrive at twenty-one years of age; in other countries not until they arrive at the age of twenty-five years. Suppose a marriage to be contracted between two persons in the same country, both of whom are over twenty-one years but less than twenty-five, and one of them is a subject of the latter country. Is such a marriage valid, or not?

If valid in the country, where it is celebrated, is it valid also in the other country? Or the question may be propounded in a still more general form, Is a marriage, valid between the parties in the place, where it is solemnized, equally valid in all other countries? Or is it obligatory only as a local regulation, and to be treated every where else as a mere nullity? . . .

§ 7. It is plain, that the laws of one country can have no intrinsic force, *proprio vigore*, except within the territorial limits and jurisdiction of that country. They can bind only its own subjects, and others, who are within its jurisdictional limits; and the latter only while they remain there. No other nation, or its subjects, are bound to yield the slightest obedience to those laws. Whatever extra-territorial force they are to have, is the result, not of any original power to extend them abroad, but of that respect, which from motives of public policy other nations are disposed to yield to them, giving them effect, as the phrase is, *sub mutuæ vicissitudinis obtentu*, with a wise and liberal regard to common convenience and mutual necessities. Boullenois has laid down the same exposition as a part of his fundamental maxims. "Of strict right," says he, "all the laws made by a sovereign have no force or authority except within the limits of his domains. But the necessity of the public and general welfare has introduced some exceptions in regard to civil commerce." *De droit étroit, toutes les lois, que fait un souverain, n'ont force et autorité que dans l'étendue de sa domination; mais la nécessité du bien public et général des nations a admis quelques exceptions dans ce, qui regarde le commerce civil.*

§ 8. This is the natural principle flowing from the equality and independence of nations. It is an essential attribute of every sovereignty, that it has no admitted superior, and that it gives the supreme law within its own domains on all subjects appertaining to its sovereignty. What it yields, it is its own choice to yield; and it cannot be commanded by another to yield it as matter of right. And accordingly it is laid down by all publicists and jurists, as an incontestable rule of public law, that one may with impunity disregard the law pronounced by a magistrate beyond his territory. . . .

§ 9. The jurisprudence, then, arising from the conflict of the laws of different nations, in their actual application to modern commerce and intercourse, is a most interesting and important branch of public law. To no part of the world is it of more interest and importance than to the United States, since the union of a national government with that of twenty-four distinct, and in some respects independent states, necessarily creates very complicated relations and rights between the citizens of those states, which call for the constant administration of extra-municipal principles. This branch of public law may be fitly denominated private international law, since it is chiefly seen and felt in its application to the common business of private persons, and rarely rises to the dignity of national negotiations, or national controversies.

A TURK HAVING THREE WIVES

American Jurist

The development of private international law or conflict of laws, so important in a federal system of states, had its starting point in this era. On the theory, perhaps mistaken, that it would lead to uniformity in state and Federal court decisions, Swift v. Tyson *in 1842 construed the Judiciary Act of 1789 as obliging the Federal courts to follow only the statutory law of the states, not the substantive common law. Story's doctrine was extended to encompass a federal common law of torts, land, and conflicts of law, and was not overruled until 1938 by the strongly worded opinion of Mr. Justice Brandeis in* Erie Ry. v. Tompkins.

Often the conflicts issue arises in the "bread and butter" part of the attorney's practice. A case of breach of contract becomes far from simple if the transaction happens to have accidental contact with more than one state—because of residence of the parties, for example. Matrimonial cases with multi-state contacts are also complicated by the state's interest in marriage and the family as an institution, to say nothing of its practical interest against having to support abandoned families. Should a divorce granted in one state be valid in the state where the parties were last domiciled during the marriage? This is but one of the troublesome questions presented. Little wonder that an 1827 Louisiana opinion complains that conflict of laws raises questions which "are the most embarrassing and difficult of decisions that can occupy the attention of those who preside in Courts of Justice."

A TURK, *having three wives, to whom he was lawfully married, according to the laws of his own country, and three sons, one by each wife, comes to Philadelphia with his family, and dies, leaving his three wives and three sons alive, and also real property in this State to a large amount.*

QUERE: *Will it go to the three children equally, under the intestate law of Pennsylvania?*

It is a fixed and settled principle of the law of nations, fully recognized in this country, and particularly in Pennsylvania, that real property is regulated every where by the law of the place where it is situated, and personal property by the law of the domicil of the owner, according to the well known maxim, *"Mobilia personam Sequuntur; immobilia Situm."* *Delesbats* v. *Berquer,* 1 Binney R. 336. This principle is also laid down in Vattel, and other writers on the law of nations, to whom I need not particularly refer. The reason on which these opposite principles are founded, is easy to be understood. As to *real property,* it is essential to the commonwealth that the rules of its transmission should be clear and settled, so

"Conflict of Laws," *American Jurist* (1835), XIV, p. 275.

that a purchaser should not be obliged to have recourse to a foreign code to know whether he can acquire landed estate with safety. Personal property on the other hand, is of a transitory nature, and is frequently dispersed, (particularly in the case of merchants,) in various parts of the world. It is therefore necessary that the whole of it, wherever it may be found at the death of the owner, should be regulated by the same code, and the law of nations has fixed for that purpose on the law of his domicil, which is supposed to follow him and his property wherever he may be, and wherever his moveables or chattels may be disseminated. For in the eye of the law, they are attached to his person: though in point of fact, existing at a distance from him. . . .

But the question now is, who are in this case the lawful children, and by what law is this question to be determined? I answer without hesitation, by the law of the country where the parents were married, and where the children were born. It is evident that if the intestate, instead of being a Turk, was a Frenchman, and had left an only son, born before marriage, although that son, if born here, would be a bastard, yet being born in France, where such children are held legitimate, he would also be held legitimate either here or in England, and if he could otherwise inherit, though an alien, would inherit as such. For such is the law of nations, as it is clearly laid down by Lord Ellenborough, in the case of *Poffer* v. *Brown,* 5 East. 131, where he says: "We *always* import, together with their persons, the existing relations of foreigners, as between themselves, according to the laws of their respective countries, except where those laws clash with the rights of our own subjects here,"—an exception which is clearly just in itself, and cannot, I think, be controverted. But this exception is not applicable to the present case.

I am then of opinion, according to these principles, that the three children of our Turk in the case stated, having all been born out of our country, would be entitled to take the estate of their intestate father as tenants in common.

Nor does this militate against the doctrine above laid down, that descents are to be regulated by the law of the country where the land lies; because this law operates by description, by directing the property to go to certain persons whom it designates, as widow, children, brothers, sisters, &c.; but the question whether individuals do or do not stand in these relations to each other is quite a different one, and belongs entirely to the law of their own country. . . .

But the most difficult question now comes, that of the three Turkish widows; for such they certainly are, according to the laws of their country. The Act of Assembly gives one-third of the estate for life to the intestate's widow, and has made no provision for more than one. Are our Turkish ladies to take that one-third between them? or is one of them alone entitled to it? in short, are any of them to have any share of this estate, and what share?

These questions appear susceptible of different decisions, according to different circumstances. Leaving out of the question, the circumstance of the Turk's having come to this country with his three wives and three children, and supposing that he had remained with them at home, and purchased there real property lying in this State,—in that case I am satisfied that neither of the three wives would take any thing. I shall now state my reasons for this opinion.

It must be observed in the first place, that by the 13th Section of the Act of Assembly above cited, (Purd. 291,) it is enacted: "That the share of the estate of the intestate, directed to be allowed to the widow, shall be in lieu and satisfaction of her dower at common law."

This share, therefore, thus given to the widow by this Act of Assembly, is in nature of dower, or perhaps, it may better be considered as a statutory jointure given to her in lieu and bar of dower.

Now let us consider what is dower,—It is an estate which the law gives to the wife for her sustenance, and the nurture and education of her younger children. 2 Blac. Com. 129. The first thing that strikes us here is, that this object is purely municipal, for the law of England does not care, and is not bound to care for the maintenance of foreign widows, nor the support of foreign children. Farther, Lord Coke tells us, that it is a reward for the sacrifice of the wife's pudicity. *Doti ejus parcatur quia præmium pudoris est.* Co. Lit. 31 a. And indeed, Blackstone goes further, and tells us that in Bracton's time, the criterion of a proper age for a wife to be entitled to dower, which is now fixed at nine years, was *Si uxor possit dotem promereri et virum sustinere.* 2 Black. Com. 130. To be entitled to her dower, she must have been capable of *earning* it in a manner that needs not be further explained.

Dower then, in England, arises from an implied contract which the law creates between the husband and the wife, and takes effect from the moment they are married. But the law of England, or the law of Pennsylvania, creates no such contracts between aliens who intermarry with each other in foreign countries. Dower is not ordered by the law of nature as the succession of children to their father's estates. It is the mere offspring of municipal law. An alien wife, therefore, who abroad marries an alien husband, or a husband who marries an alien wife, submits to no implied contract created by the laws of a foreign country; and the mere act of buying lands in a country where dower exists, cannot create such a contract between them. The alien wife, therefore, in such a case, is not entitled to dower of her husband's lands in England or in Pennsylvania, even putting the disability of aliens to hold lands out of the question; much less can she claim a jointure or estate in nature thereof given in lieu of dower. It must be presumed, (as is in fact the case every where,) that either the law of her own country, or a special contract made before marriage, has provided for her maintenance in case of her husband's dying before her, and she cannot, in common justice, have the benefit of the additional advantage of dower out of the lands which her husband purchases abroad. She has her remedy against his heirs for whatever her country's laws, or her marriage articles have stipulated in her favor; but I think that on no account whatever can she claim dower out of his lands here.

This I take to be the law, in case our Turk and his wives had remained abroad; the same I consider it to be if they had been cast on our shores by shipwreck, or had come hither only as travellers or passengers, without intending to fix their residence in our country.

But the case would be different if the Turk and his family, after coming here, had fixed their domicil in Pennsylvania. In that case, I consider, that they would immediately become subject to our laws, which would recognize only the first wife, and consider the others in the light of concubines. What penalty the Turk would incur if he continued to cohabit with all three, we need not consider. It could not be, perhaps, bigamy, as the marriages were all contracted abroad, but it certainly would be an indictable offense.

As to the widow, in case of his death, I mean only the first wife, I am inclined to believe that she might avail herself of the *lex domicilii,* and claim her third out of her husband's lands, but in that case she would, in my opinion, forfeit her claims under the laws of her own country, which otherwise I think she could recover as a creditor out of her husband's estate. If she had married under articles, she might claim under them, but not under an Act of Assembly at the same time.

As to the two other wives, I have said they could not be entitled to their widow's share under our Act of Assembly, or dower at common law, yet I think they might sue the children or their husband's executors, on their marriage articles, if they had any; for their consent in coming over to this country could not be presumed.

THE AMERICAN CITIZENS CAPTURED

AT SANTA FÉ

───────

Daniel Webster

When it came to describing his personality, Webster's contemporaries, as Carl Schurz said, borrowed their similes "from kings, cathedrals, and mountain peaks." But his brief tenure as Secretary of State was the only office which allowed him full scope for his ambitions and talents. Harrison

───────

The Diplomatic and Official Papers of Daniel Webster (1848), pp. 321, 327.

appointed him to the office, and he continued on under Tyler, although his fellow Whigs resigned on the succession.

George Wilkins Kendall, the subject of Webster's letter, was born in New Hampshire in 1809. In 1837 Kendall established the New Orleans Picayune, *and became renowned as a humorist and satirist. He was always an adventurer, and joined the Santa Fé Trading Expedition in 1841. As a result of interference with Mexican rule of the city, Kendall's group was imprisoned. Kendall endured horrible prison conditions—including confinement with lepers. Friends secured his release in 1843 on payment of ransom, and his* Narrative of the Santa Fé Expedition, *published in 1844, received widespread acclamation. In the* Picayune, *Kendall urged war with Mexico, and after the outbreak of hostilities he joined General Taylor and accompanied the troops on almost all the major campaigns. Since he sent war reports back via a self-created pony-express he is generally called the first war correspondent.*

Then as now, the status of noncombatants during time of war was a major problem of international law. In Webster's letter protesting Mexico's capture and harsh treatment of American noncombatants, the same views are expressed as those which the United States has recently taken with regard to the imprisonment of civilians by Communist nations.

Washington, April 15, 1842

Sir,—I have to address you upon the subject of those citizens of the United States who were captured with the Texan expedition to Santa Fé, and who, as is believed, were not parties to that expedition, so far as it was military and hostile to Mexico, if, in fact, a hostile invasion of Mexico was among its purposes, but accompanied it only as traders, tourists, travellers, men of letters, or in other characters and capacities showing them to be *non-combatants*; but who, nevertheless, were taken and held as prisoners, compelled to undergo incredible hardships in a winter's march of two thousand miles, and at its end subjected to almost every conceivable degree of indignity and suffering.

By the law and practice of civilized nations, enemies' subjects taken in arms may be made prisoners of war; but every person found in the train of an army is not to be considered as therefore a belligerent or an enemy. . . . If, therefore, individuals armed only according to the custom of the country, but having no hostile purposes of their own, and free from all military authority or employment, fall in with or follow the march of troops proceeding toward a point of attack, these individuals are not *combatants,* and not subject to be taken and treated as prisoners. These considerations may be applied to those citizens of the United States for whose release from imprisonment the interposition of this government has been requested. . . .

It does not very satisfactorily appear, from any correspondence or information now in this department, in what light Mexico looks upon those persons made prisoners at Santa Fé, whom she has a right to consider as engaged in the service of Texas, and therefore as her enemies. We must presume that she means to regard them as prisoners of war. There is a possibility, however, that a different mode of considering them may be adopted, and that they may be thought to be amenable to the municipal laws of Mexico. Any proceeding founded on this idea would undoubtedly be attended with the most serious consequences. It is now several years since the independence of Texas, as a separate government, has been acknowledged by the United States, and she has since been recognized in that character by several of the most considerable powers of Europe. The war between her and Mexico, which has continued so long, and with such success, that for a long time there has been no hostile foot in Texas, is a public war, and as such it has been and will be regarded by this government. It is not now an outbreak of rebellion, a fresh insurrection, the parties to which may be treated as rebels. The contest, supposed, indeed, to have been substantially ended, has at least advanced far beyond that point. It is a public war, and persons captured in the course of it, who are to be detained at all, are to be detained as prisoners of war, and not otherwise.

It is true that the independence of Texas has not been recognized by Mexico. It is equally true that the independence of Mexico has only been recently recognized by Spain; but the United States having acknowledged both the independence of Mexico before Spain acknowledged it, and the independence of Texas although Mexico has not yet acknowledged it, stands in the same relation toward both those governments, and is as much bound to protect its citizens in a proper intercourse with Texas against injuries by the government of Mexico, as it would have been to protect such citizens in a like intercourse with Mexico against injuries by Spain. The period which has elapsed since Texas threw off the authority of Mexico is nearly as long as the whole duration of the Revolutionary war of the United States. No effort for the subjugation of Texas has been made by Mexico, from the time of the battle of San Jacinto, on the 21st day of April, 1836, until the commencement of the present year, and during all this period Texas has maintained an independent government, carried on commerce, and made treaties with nations in both hemispheres, and kept aloof all attempts at invading her territory. If, under these circumstances, any citizen of the United States, in whose behalf this government has a right on any account or to any extent to interfere, should, on a charge of having been found with an armed Texan force acting in hostility to Mexico, be brought to trial and punished as for a violation of the municipal laws of Mexico, or as being her subject engaged in rebellion, after his release has been demanded by this government, consequences of the most serious character would certainly ensue. You will, therefore, not fail, should any indication render it necessary, to point out distinctly to the government of Mexico the dangers, should the war between her and Texas continue, of considering it, so far as citizens of the United States may be concerned, in any other light than that of a public national war, in the events and progress of which prisoners may be made on both sides, and to whose condition the law and usages of nations respecting prisoners of war are justly applicable.

And this makes it proper that I should draw your particular attention to the manner in which the persons taken near Santa Fé have been treated, as we are informed. . . . Having been carried to Santa Fé from the place of capture, [they] were there deprived of their arms. To this there can be no objection, if we consider them as prisoners of war, because prisoners of war may be lawfully disarmed by the captor; but they were also despoiled, not only of every article of value about their persons, but of their clothing also, their coats, their hats, their shoes, things indispensable to the long march before them. If these facts be not disproved, they constitute an outrage by the local authorities of Mexico for which there can be no apology. The privations and indignities to which they were subjected, during their march of two thousand miles to the city of Mexico, at the most inclement season of the year, were horrible, and, if they were not well authenticated, it would have been incredible that they should have been inflicted in this age, and in a country calling itself Christian and civilized. During many days they had no food, and on others only two ears of corn were distributed to each man. To sustain life, therefore, they were compelled to sell, on the way, the few remnants of clothing which their captors had left them; but by seeking thus to appease their hunger, they increased the misery which they already endured from exposure to the cold. Most dreadful of all, however, several of them, disabled by sickness and suffering from keeping up with the others, were deliberately shot, without any provocation. Those who survived to their journey's end were, many of them, afflicted with loathsome disease; and those whose health was not broken down have been treated, not as the public law requires, but in a manner harsh and vindictive, and with a degree of severity equal, at least, to that usually inflicted by the municipal codes of most civilized and Christian states upon the basest felons. Indeed, they appear to have been ranked with these; being thrust into the same dungeons with Mexican malefactors, chained to them in pairs, and, when allowed to see the light and breathe the air of heaven, required, as a compensation therefor, to labor, beneath the lash of a task-master, upon roads and public works of that country.

The government of the United States has no inclination to interfere in the war between Mexico and Texas, for the benefit or protection of individuals, any further than its clear duties require. But if citizens of the United States who have not renounced, nor intended to renounce, their allegiance to their own government, nor have entered into the military service of any other government, have nevertheless been found so connected with armed enemies of Mexico as that they may be lawfully captured and detained as prisoners of war, it is still the duty of this government to take so far a concern in their welfare, as to see that, as prisoners of war, they are treated according to the usage of modern times and civilized states.

Indeed, although the rights or the safety of none of their own citizens were concerned, yet, if, in a war waged between two neighboring states, the killing, enslaving, or cruelly treating of prisoners should be indulged, the United States would feel it to be their duty, as well as their right, to remonstrate and to interfere against such a departure from the principles of humanity and civilization. These principles are common principles, essential alike to the welfare of all nations, and in the preservation of which all nations have, therefore, rights and interests. But their duty to interfere becomes imperative in cases affecting their own citizens.

It is therefore that the government of the United States protests against the hardships and cruelties to which the Santa Fé prisoners have been subjected. It protests against this treatment in the name of humanity and the law of nations; in the name of all Christian states; in the name of civilization and the spirit of the age; in the name of all republics; in the name of Liberty herself, enfeebled and dishonored by all cruelty and all excess; in the name of, and for the honor of, this whole hemisphere. It protests emphatically and earnestly against practices belonging only to barbarous people in barbarous times.

By the well-established rules of national law, prisoners of war are not to be treated harshly, unless personally guilty toward him who has them in his power; for he should remember that they are men, and unfortunate.

When an enemy is conquered, and submits, a great soul forgets all resentment, and is entirely filled with compassion for him. This is the humane language of the law of nations; and this is the sentiment of high honor among men. The law of war forbids the wounding, killing, impressment into the troops of the country, or the enslaving or otherwise maltreating of *prisoners of war*, unless they have been guilty of some grave crime; and from the obligation of this law no civilized state can discharge itself.

Every nation, on being received, at her own request, into the circle of civilized governments, must understand that she not only attains rights of sovereignty and the dignity of national character, but that she binds herself also to the strict and faithful observance of all those principles, laws, and usages which have obtained currency among civilized states, and which have for their object the mitigation of the miseries of war.

No community can be allowed to enjoy the benefit of national character, in modern times, without submitting to all the duties which that character imposes. A Christian people, who exercise sovereign power, who make treaties, maintain diplomatic relations with other states, and who should yet refuse to conduct their military operations according to the usages universally observed by such states, would present a character singularly inconsistent and anomalous.

This government will not hastily suppose that the Mexican republic will assume such a character. . . .

In conclusion, I am directed by the President of the United States now to instruct you, that, on the receipt of this despatch, you inquire carefully and minutely into the circumstances of all those persons who, having been taken near Santa Fé, and having claimed the interposition of this government, are still held as prisoners in Mexico; and you will demand of the Mexican government the release of such of them as appear to have been innocent traders, travellers, invalids, men of letters, or for any other reason justly esteemed non-combatants, being citizens of the United States. To this end it may be proper to direct the consul to proceed to the places where any of them may be confined, and to take their statements under oath, as also the statements of other persons to whom they may respectively refer. If the Mexican government deny facts upon which any of the parties claim their release, and desire time for further investigation of their respective cases, or any of them, proper and suitable time must be allowed; but if any of the persons described in the next preceding paragraph, and for whose release you will have made a demand, shall still be detained, for the purpose of further inquiry or otherwise, you will then explicitly demand of the Mexican government that they be treated henceforward with all the lenity which, in the most favorable cases, belongs to the rights of prisoners of war; that they be not confined in loathsome dungeons, with malefactors and persons diseased; that they be not chained or subjected to ignominy, or to any particular rigor in their detention; that they be not obliged to labor on the public works, or put to any other hardship. You will state to the Mexican government that the government of the United States entertains a conviction that these persons ought to be set at liberty without delay; that it will feel great dissatisfaction if it shall still learn that Mr. Kendall, whose case has already been made the subject of an express demand, and others of equal claims to liberation, be not set at liberty at the time when you receive this despatch; but that, if the government of Mexico insists upon detaining any of them for further inquiry, it is due to the government of the United States, to its desire to preserve peace and harmony with Mexico, and to justice and humanity, that, while detained, these persons should enjoy to the fullest extent the rights of prisoners of war; and that it expects that a demand so just and reasonable, a demand respectfully made by one friendly state to another, will meet with immediate compliance. Having made this demand, you will wait for an answer; and if within ten days you shall not receive assurances that all the persons above mentioned, who may still be detained, will be thenceforward treated in the same manner which has now been insisted upon, you will hold no further official intercourse with the government of Mexico until you shall receive further directions from your own government. You will thereupon communicate with this department, detaining for that purpose the messenger who carries this. In your communication you will state, as fully and as accurately as possible, the circumstances of each man's case, as they may appear by all the evidence which at that time may be possessed by the legation. In making your demand for the better treatment of the prisoners, you will take especial care not to abandon or weaken the claim for their release, nothing more being intended in that respect than that proper time should be allowed to the government of Mexico to make such further inquiries as may be necessary.

Your predecessor has already been directed, that, if any of the persons suffer for the want of the common necessaries of life, he should provide for such wants until otherwise supplied; a direction which you will also observe.

THE CANADIAN–AMERICAN PIRATES

Daniel Webster

The case of Alexander McLeod also illustrates a perennial problem. McLeod, a British soldier, was brought to trial by the state of New York for the killing of an American during an invasion by Canadians into American waters. The issue—a soldier's individual responsibility for acts committed under orders—is the same as that raised in the war crime trials following World War II. McLeod was acquitted in order to prevent an international incident. His story provides an excellent example of the impact that a federal system, with separate, independent state judiciaries, can have on the conduct of international relations.

MR. FOX informs the government of the United States, that he is instructed to make known to it that the government of her Majesty entirely approve the course pursued by him in his correspondence with Mr. Forsyth in December last, and the language adopted by him on that occasion; and that that government have instructed him "again to demand from the government of the United States, formally, in the name of the British government, the immediate release of Mr. Alexander McLeod";

The Diplomatic and Official Papers of Daniel Webster (1848), p. 123.

that "the grounds upon which the British government make this demand upon the government of the United States are these: that the transaction on account of which Mr. McLeod has been arrested, and is to be put upon his trial, was a transaction of a public character, planned and executed by persons duly empowered by her Majesty's colonial authorities to take any steps and to do any acts which might be necessary for the defence of her Majesty's territories, and for the protection of her Majesty's subjects; and that, consequently, those subjects of her Majesty who engaged in that transaction were performing an act of public duty, for which they cannot be made personally and individually answerable to the laws and tribunals of any foreign country."

The President is not certain that he understands precisely the meaning intended by her Majesty's government to be conveyed by the foregoing instruction.

This doubt has occasioned with the President some hesitation; but he inclines to take it for granted that the main purpose of the instruction was, to cause it to be signified to the government of the United States that the attack on the steamboat "Caroline" was an act of public force, done by the British colonial authorities, and fully recognized by the Queen's government at home; and that, consequently, no individual concerned in that transaction can, according to the just principles of the laws of nations, be held personally answerable in the ordinary courts of law, as for a private offence; and that upon this avowal of her Majesty's government, Alexander McLeod, now imprisoned on an indictment for murder alleged to have been committed in that attack, ought to be released by such proceedings as are usual and are suitable to the case.

The President adopts the conclusion, that nothing more than this could have been intended to be expressed, from the consideration that her Majesty's government must be fully aware that in the United States, as in England, persons confined under judicial process can be released from that confinement only by judicial process. . . . Even in the case of ambassadors, and other public ministers whose right of exemption from arrest is personal, requiring no fact to be ascertained but the mere fact of diplomatic character, and to arrest whom is sometimes made a highly penal offence, if the arrest be actually made, it can only be discharged by application to the courts of law. . . . If, therefore, any course different from such as have been now mentioned was in contemplation of her Majesty's government, something would seem to have been expected from the government of the United States as little conformable to the laws and usages of the English government as to those of the United States, and to which this government cannot accede.

The government of the United States, therefore, acting upon the presumption, which it readily adopted, that nothing extraordinary or unusual was expected or requested of it, decided, on the reception of Mr.

Fox's note, to take such measures as the occasion and its own duty appeared to require. . . .

The government of the United States entertains no doubt, that, after this avowal of the transaction as a public transaction, authorized and undertaken by the British authorities, individuals concerned in it ought not, by the principles of public law and the general usage of civilized states, to be holden personally responsible in the ordinary tribunals of law for their participation in it. And the President presumes that it can hardly be necessary to say that the American people, not distrustful of their ability to redress public wrongs by public means, cannot desire the punishment of individuals when the act complained of is declared to have been an act of the government itself. . . .

The indictment against McLeod is pending in a State court; but his rights, whatever they may be, are no less safe, it is to be presumed, than if he were holden to answer in one of the courts of this government.

He demands immunity from personal responsibility by virtue of the law of nations, and that law in civilized states is to be respected in all courts. None is either so high or so low as to escape from its authority in cases to which its rules and principles apply.

This department has been regularly informed by his Excellency, the Governor of the State of New York, that the Chief Justice of that State was assigned to preside at the hearing and trial of McLeod's case, but that, owing to some error or mistake in the process of summoning the jury, the hearing was necessarily deferred. The President regrets this occurrence, as he has a desire for a speedy disposition of the subject. The counsel for McLeod have requested authentic evidence of the avowal by the British government of the attack on and the destruction of the "Caroline," as acts done under its authority, and such evidence will be furnished to them by this department.

It is understood that the indictment has been removed into the Supreme Court of the State by the proper proceeding for that purpose, and that it is now competent for McLeod, by the ordinary process of *habeas corpus,* to bring his case for hearing before that tribunal.

The undersigned hardly needs to assure Mr. Fox, that a tribunal so eminently distinguished for ability and learning as the Supreme Court of the State of New York may be safely relied upon for the just and impartial administration of the law in this as well as in other cases; and the undersigned repeats the expression of the desire of this government, that no delay may be suffered to take place in these proceedings which can be avoided. . . .

The undersigned has now to signify to Mr. Fox, that the government of the United States has not changed the opinion which it has heretofore expressed to her Majesty's government of the character of the act of destroying the "Caroline."

It does not think that that transaction can be justified by any reasonable application or construction of the right of self-defence under the laws of nations. It is admitted that a just right of self-defence attaches always to nations as well as to individuals, and is equally necessary for the preservation of both. But the extent of this right is a question to be judged of by the circumstances of each particular case; and when its alleged exercise has led to the commission of hostile acts within the territory of a power at peace, nothing less than a clear and absolute necessity can afford ground of justification. . . .

Her Majesty's government are pleased, also, to speak of those American citizens who took part with persons in Canada, engaged in an insurrection against the British government, as "American pirates." The undersigned does not admit the propriety or justice of this designation. If citizens of the United States fitted out, or were engaged in fitting out, a military expedition from the United States, intended to act against the British government in Canada, they were clearly violating the laws of their own country, and exposing themselves to the just consequences which might be inflicted on them, if taken within the British dominions. . . .

It is well known to Mr. Fox, that authorities of the highest eminence in England, living and dead, have maintained that the general law of nations does not forbid the citizens or subjects of one government from taking part in the civil commotions of another. There is some reason, indeed, to think that such may be the opinion of her Majesty's government at the present moment. . . .

All will see that, if such things be allowed to occur, they must lead to bloody and exasperated war. And when an individual comes into the United States from Canada, and to the very place on which this drama was performed, and there chooses to make public and vainglorious boast of the part he acted in it, it is hardly wonderful that great excitement should be created, and some degree of commotion arise.

This republic does not wish to disturb the tranquillity of the world. Its object is peace, its policy peace. It seeks no aggrandizement by foreign conquest, because it knows that no foreign acquisitions could augment its power and importance so rapidly as they are already advancing by its own natural growth, under the propitious circumstances of its situation. But it cannot admit that its government has not both the will and the power to preserve its own neutrality, and to enforce the observance of its own laws upon its own citizens. It is jealous of its rights, and among others, and most especially, of the right of the absolute immunity of its territory against aggression from abroad; and these rights it is the duty and determination of this government fully and at all times to maintain, while it will at the same time as scrupulously refrain from infringing on the rights of others.

The President instructs the undersigned to say, in conclusion, that he confidently trusts that this and all other questions of difference between the two governments will be treated by both in the full exercise of such a spirit of candor, justice, and mutual respect as shall give assurance of the long continuance of peace between the two countries.

A COMMONWEALTH OF NATIONS

Charles Sumner

A recurrent concern of international law is analyzed in strangely contemporary terms in the following speech by Charles Sumner. The topic of the speech on Boston's Independence Day in 1845 that marked the turning point of Sumner's career had been the same. His theme, "Can there be in our age any peace that is not honorable, any war that is not dishonorable?" was taken as a personal insult by the many military and naval guests in the audience, but cheered by the others.

AND, FIRST, of *War and the War System in the Commonwealth of Nations*. By the Commonwealth of Nations I understand the Fraternity of Christian Nations recognizing a Common Law in their relations with each other, usually called the Law of Nations. This law, being established by the consent of nations, is not necessarily the law of all nations, but only of such as recognize it. The Europeans and the Orientals often differ with regard to its provisions; nor would it be proper to say, that, at this time, the Ottomans, or the Mahometans in general, or the Chinese, have become parties to it. The prevailing elements of this law are the Law of Nature, the truths of Christianity, the usages of nations, the opinions of publicists, and the written texts or enactments found in diplomatic acts or treaties. In origin and growth it is not unlike the various systems of municipal jurisprudence, all of which are referred to kindred sources. . . .

The Law of Nations is, then, the Supreme Law of the Commonwealth of Nations, governing their relations with each other, determining their reciprocal rights, and sanctioning all remedies for the violation of these rights. To the Commonwealth of Nations this law is what the Constitution and Municipal Law of Massachusetts are to the associate towns and counties composing the State, or what, by apter illustration, the National Constitution of our Union is to the thirty several States which now recognize it as the supreme law.

Charles Sumner, *War System of the Commonwealth of Nations* (1849), pp. 186, 258.

But the Law of Nations,—and here is a point of infinite importance to the clear understanding of the subject,—while anticipating and providing for controversies between nations, recognizes and establishes War as final Arbiter. It distinctly says to nations, "If you cannot agree together, then stake your cause upon *Trial by Battle*." The mode of trial thus recognized and established has its own procedure, with rules and regulations, under the name of Laws of War, constituting a branch of International Law. . . .

Provisions of the Municipal Law of Massachusetts, and of the National Constitution, are not vain words. To all familiar with our courts it is well known that suits between towns, and likewise between counties, are often entertained and satisfactorily adjudicated. The records of the Supreme Court of the United States show also that States of the Union habitually refer important controversies to this tribunal. Before this high court is now pending an action of the State of Missouri against the State of Iowa, founded on a question of boundary, where the former claims a section of territory—larger than many German principalities—extending along the whole northern border of Missouri, with several miles of breadth, and comprising more than two thousand square miles. Within a short period this same tribunal has decided a similar question between our own State of Massachusetts and our neighbor, Rhode Island,—the latter pertinaciously claiming a section of territory, about three miles broad, on a portion of our southern frontier.

Suppose that in these different cases between towns, counties, states, War had been *established* by the supreme law as arbiter; imagine the disastrous consequences; picture the imperfect justice which must have been the end and fruit of such a contest; and while rejoicing that in these cases we are happily relieved from an alternative so wretched and deplorable, reflect that on a larger theatre, where grander interests are staked, in the relations between nations, under the solemn sanction of the Law of Nations, War is *established* as Arbiter of Justice. Reflect also that a complex and subtile code, known as Laws of War, is established to regulate the resort to this arbiter. . . .

1. The most complete and permanent substitute would be a Congress of Nations, with a High Court of Judicature. Such a system, while admitted on all sides to promise excellent results, is opposed on two grounds. *First,* because, as regards the smaller states, it would be a tremendous engine of oppression, subversive of their political independence. Surely, it could not be so oppressive as the War System. But the experience of the smaller, States in the German Confederation and in the American Union, nay, the experience of Belgium and Holland by the side of the overtopping power of France, and the experience of Denmark and Sweden in the very nightshade of Russia, all show the futility of this objection. *Secondly,* because

the decrees of such a court could not be carried into effect. Even if they were enforced by the combined power of the associate nations, the sword, as the executive arm of the high tribunal, would be only the melancholy instrument of Justice, not the Arbiter of Justice, and therefore not condemned by the conclusive reasons against international appeals to the sword. From the experience of history, and particularly from the experience of the thirty States of our Union, we learn that the occasion for any executive arm will be rare. The State of Rhode Island, in its recent controversy with Massachusetts, submitted with much indifference to the adverse decree of the Supreme Court; and I doubt not that Missouri and Iowa will submit with equal contentment to any determination of their present controversy by the same tribunal. The same submission would attend the decrees of any Court of Judicature established by the Commonwealth of Nations. There is a growing sense of justice, combined with a growing might of public opinion, too little known to the soldier, that would maintain the judgments of the august tribunal assembled in the face of the Nations, better than the swords of all the marshals of France, better than the bloody terrors of Austerlitz or Waterloo. . . .

2. There is still another substitute for War, which is not exposed even to the shallow objections launched against a Congress of Nations. By formal treaties between two or more nations, Arbitration may be established as the mode of determining controversies between them. In every respect this is a contrast to War. It is rational, humane, and cheap. Above all, it is consistent with the teachings of Christianity. . . .

The complete overthrow of the War System, involving the disarming of the Nations, would follow the establishment of a Congress of Nations, or any general system of Arbitration. Then at last our aims would be accomplished; then at last Peace would be organized among the Nations. Then might Christians repeat the fitful boast of the generous Mohawk: "We have thrown the hatchet so high into the air, and beyond the skies, that no arm on earth can reach to bring it down." Incalculable sums, now devoted to armaments and the destructive industry of War, would be turned to the productive industry of Art and to offices of Beneficence. As in the dead and rotten carcass of the lion which roared against the strong man of Israel, after a time, were a swarm of bees and honey, so would the enormous carcass of War, dead and rotten, be filled with crowds of useful laborers and all good works, and the riddle of Samson be once more interpreted: "Out of the eater came forth meat, and out of the strong came forth sweetness."

Put together the products of all the mines in the world,—the glistening ore of California, the accumulated treasures of Mexico and Peru, with the diamonds of Golconda,—and the whole shining heap will be less than the means thus diverted from War to Peace. Under the influence of such a change, civilization will be quickened anew. Then will happy Labor find its reward, and the whole land be filled with its increase. There is no aspiration of Knowledge, no vision of Charity, no venture of Enterprise, no fancy of Art, which may not then be fulfilled. The great unsolved problem of Pauperism will be solved at last. There will be no paupers, when there are no soldiers. The social struggles, so fearfully disturbing European nations, will die away in the happiness of unarmed Peace, no longer incumbered by the oppressive system of War; nor can there be well-founded hope that these struggles will permanently cease, so long as this system endures. The people ought not to rest, they cannot rest, while this system endures. . . .

Such is our cause. In transcendent influence, it embraces human beneficence in all its forms. It is the comprehensive charity, enfolding all the charities of all. None so vast as to be above its protection, none so lowly as not to feel its care. Religion, Knowledge, Freedom, Virtue, Happiness, in all their manifold forms, depend upon Peace. Sustained by Peace, they lean upon the Everlasting Arm. And this is not all. Law, Order, Government, derive from Peace new sanctions. Nor can they attain to that complete dominion which is our truest safeguard, until, by the over- throw of the War System, they comprehend the Commonwealth of Nations,—

> "And Sovereign LAW, *the* WORLD's *collected will,*
> O'er thrones and globes elate,
> Sits empress, crowning good, repressing ill."

Part III

LAW
AND
REFORM

Introduction

The formative era of American law was both creator and product of a far-reaching reform movement which drastically altered the nation's social structure. In 1841 Emerson could write: "In the history of the world the doctrine of reform has never seen such scope as at the present hour. . . . The demon of reform has a secret door into the heart of every lawmaker, of every inhabitant of every city." He was summarizing the proliferation of idealistic programs and radical political movements which shook the foundations of the law.

Modern analytic historians have dissected the movements for change in religion, political parties, education, and morals that so transformed the United States, but by and large have made a usual omission: scant attention is paid by students of intellectual history to reforms in the law. It is difficult to account for this neglect, as many of the heated social controversies are couched in legal and constitutional terms. If problems of the present are best viewed through the historical prism, then past legal debates should provide rich insights into current issues.

One reason why the historian has bypassed the social testimony of the law may be that he is unable to penetrate the technical layer which insulates law from the layman. And in this period much of the force for legal improvement was directed against this technical machinery—the forms of pleading, joinder of parties, and competence of forums. Procedural law had originated largely as a result of historical accident or out of a particular state of society; it contained a mass of technicalities developed by ingenious medieval logic and then overrefined by the eighteenth century. Many of the original reasons for niceties of pleadings had ceased to exist, and often they were not even remembered; yet the rules which they had engendered, rules grown outrageously rigid and formal, continued to trap the unwary. A principal object of legal reform was the elimination or modernization of those archaic rules which seemed to defeat rather than to ensure justice. In his 1847 report to the New York Legislature, David Dudley Field recommended sweeping away "the needless distinctions, the scholastic subtleties and the dead forms which have disfigured and encumbered our jurisprudence."

A great deal was achieved in this area of law. Although they may continue to influence us from the grave, the forms of action were formally interred. The parties were required to state their pleadings in simple, concise language. Defenses previously available only in a court of equity could now be interposed in an action at law. Amendments of pleadings

were made easier; variance between allegation and proof was no longer
fatal. The system of proof was liberalized, and interest no longer necessarily disqualified witnesses. Equitable jurisdiction was hammered out and
conflicts with common-law courts were limited, so that substantial rights
should not be lost because of a mistake in the choice of forum. Legal
remedies were made more available and their scope was broadened. The
Code of Procedure adopted by New York in 1848, and destined to become
a model for some thirty states, was described in 1863 as "the greatest
innovation upon the common law which was ever effected by a single
statute." Roscoe Pound ranks Edward Livingston and David Dudley Field
with Bentham himself as "leaders in the legislative law-making in the
English-speaking world."

But this type of procedural reform is "lawyer's law." Its somewhat
abstruse topics never were and never will be of great interest to others.
The average non-lawyer was apt to remain indifferent as to whether a
remedy should be in law or in equity or whether, as the reformers contended, the difference should be eliminated altogether by their merger. He
regarded it as a dull controversy between specialists, and even processes
which profoundly shaped everyday life—the problems of delay in meting
out justice and whether to maintain trial by jury—were muffled by the same
legal garb. The average citizen was content to leave all such questions to
the lawyers because, as he mistakenly thought, they alone were affected.

In sharp contrast is the attitude toward codification, another major
objective of law reform at this time. Despite its obviously technical nature
the codification movement aroused intense feelings, even engaging the
minds of men who could know little of its implications. It represented an
act of faith in Jacksonian democracy: laws should be simple, clear, and
easily ascertained—available within the four corners of a code to Everyman.
Intermixed was a feeling that the new democracy required immediate
modification of the law, and that this could only be achieved by the legislative knife, not by cumbersome *ad hoc* judicial proceedings.

The common or customary law had come down undeclared, even
unwritten, except for chance, judicial opinion applying it now to this, now
to that set of facts. To its defenders it represented the distillation of the
wisdom and experience of centuries; to its opponents it was an unwieldy
mass of cases, abounding with contradictory precedents. While only a trickle
compared with the thousands of cases now reported annually, the more
than two hundred volumes of reports seemed like the camel's load of cases
believed to have been necessary to gain a point of law during the decline
of the Roman Empire. The American Benthamites claimed that this mass
of individual cases could be reduced to form and system; that the code
would make man's rights and obligations known and accessible; that
simplicity and certainty were to be the touchstones.

Some disputants argued the issue in terms of the inherent differences in the way of thinking of the legislative and the judicial branches. Traditional lawyers pitted the merits of the flexible decisional doctrines emerging from case-by-case adjudication "coeval with the world," against the legislative game of blindman's buff which addresses rigid directives to situations still hidden in the more or less impenetrable future. Fenimore Cooper's Dunscomb, "emphatically a common-law lawyer," was not alone in preferring "the perfection of human reason" manifested by the unwritten law, to a patchwork code which remained the unstable plaything of successive legislatures. Phrased in that way, who would not?

Attitudes toward the wisdom of adopting codes of law were evidently colored by the question of whether confidence was to be reposed in judicial finding or legislative declaration of law, which were in growing competition. Otherwise, the emotion churned up by the codification movement is difficult to explain. Robert Rantoul, in his Oration at Scituate in 1854, charged that judge-made law was special legislation, and that "the discretion of a good man is often nothing better than caprice, . . . while the discretion of a bad man is an odious and irresponsible tyranny." On the other hand, the source of the law-finding was the key factor in the thinking of many lawyers opposing codification. To them legislatures represented the most debased elements of the Republic and were reckless and demagogic, unaware of what kept a society together, while judges, intellectual, elegant and constrained, were trustworthy and safe, insurers of life, liberty, and property.

During the years there was increased recognition of individual rights, both in statutes and judicial decisions. Safeguards were thrown around infants, the insane, and criminals—in *People* v. *Freeman* (1847), William Seward established his legal reputation by his argument presenting insanity as a defense in criminal law. The legal emancipation of women was effected. Imprisonment for debt was abolished. Prison reforms were instituted. Lawyers worked busily to show, depending on their bias, that the Constitution of the United States was a pro- or anti-slavery document—with portentous results. The Supreme Court decision that the legal status of a slave who returned to a slave state after having left it was determinable by the courts of that state alone, might seem merely to settle a ticklish point of law, but it helped to precipitate the Civil War. Arguments relating to the rights of Negroes—including, in one interesting forerunner of contemporary litigation, their segregation in the public school system—were put to rest in the courtroom. A social reform like the Federal bill "praying for an appropriation of land for the relief of the indigent insane"—the culmination of twelve years of campaigning by Dorothea Dix—met a legal death; it was vetoed on constitutional grounds by President Pierce, an attorney. Even temperance movements, aimed at saving men from the consequences of dissipation, ended by being embodied in statutes and ulti-

mately passed under the scrutiny of judges. By 1856, fifteen states had
enacted prohibition laws, of which five had been declared invalid, at least
in part, in state supreme courts, which interpreted constitutional checks as
incorporating common-law limitations upon change.

Pleas for social programs were often cloaked in legal language, even
for presentation to a nonprofessional audience. Several extra-legal reform
battles pivoted about issues of law, often turning into struggles over the
use and interpretation of legal language. Taney's opinion in the Dred Scott
case was published by Southerners; the minority views of McLean and
Curtis were circulated as campaign documents by the Republicans. Legal
terminology was borrowed freely. Many a political leader with a legal background chose to continue "talking like a lawyer" even though he had ceased
to practice. Lincoln himself phrased his Cooper Union Speech as if he were
drafting a set of pleadings: "You say we are sectional. We deny it. That
makes an issue; and the burden of proof is upon you."

The bewildering array of reforms offered for legislation or court determination in this period seems to demand that two questions be asked: First,
was American society peculiarly prone to rely upon the passage of a law for
the resolution of social issues? Second, was it too ready to move to the
coercive power of the state on matters which would have been better left
to private accommodation? "The people appear to advocate the passing
of a law," the contemporary English observer William Harroh reported,
"that they may have the pleasure of breaking it."

To a considerable extent resort to law was inevitable. It was sometimes necessary to ensure that everyone would be subject to the same sanction, and this could only be done by passage of an inclusive law. Thus, the
proponents of abstinence turned to the legislature for help, because the only
way to secure their ends was to prohibit the manufacture or sale of hard
liquor. Similarly, land reformers had to push a Homestead Act through
Congress. But law was not invoked merely when it was unavoidable. Other
factors in the United States caused a positive impulse toward legislation.

The vehicle of change in any society is often the revision of its law.
A legal pronouncement imposes form on the chaos of ideas and events. It
legitimizes change by defining a new right and the procedure for securing
it. In view of the legal orientation of American society, belief in law as a
means of legislative and judicial innovation was not surprising. During
the first years of independence men realized that they could meet the needs
for change through legal vehicles: law provided a means for getting things
done and getting things done quickly. This self-reinforcing process led them
to rely increasingly on legal solutions to social problems. This is the more
favorable aspect of the emphasis on legalism. Radical as the reform movement could be—burning the Constitution, nullifying measures of Congress,
licensing the acts of Lovejoy and Brown—there were no barriers tossed up

in the streets, no toppling of the government by force. In a society with a written constitution and concern that power should not be abused, extreme actions to foster reform—for example, the demolition of saloons by ardent prohibitionists—became an issue of civil liberties which ultimately landed in court.

The attitudes of the nation, as well as those of legal theorists, toward the potential and value of concerted effort affected the frequency of resort to law. Men such as Livingston—the eminent Louisiana codifier, "the Montesquieu of Jackson's Cabinet"—believed that life could be changed by conscious juristic effort. They believed in action, seeing man as by nature a maker and a doer. Thus, since they could rely upon its ability to translate aims into achievements, the legal act was frequently invoked.

Two ideas are paramount in applying law to social reform. One is the belief that human institutions are not self-explanatory, but must be called before the bar of disinterested thinking and required to justify themselves. This implies the second: that through human reason, human life can be improved. "Let but a vigorous effort of will be made, and we shall witness a glorious triumph of common sense over arbitrary forms—of reason over technicality," trumpeted the champion of a bill for procedural reform in Ohio. And Charles Sumner, filled with the enthusiasm of his first year at the Harvard Law School, expressed exuberant faith in man's reason and capacity: "And again, hear Burke: 'There is nothing in the world really beneficial that does not lie within the reach of an informed understanding and a well-directed pursuit. There is nothing that God has judged good for us that He has not given us the means to accomplish, both in the natural and moral world!' What a sentiment! How rich in expression, how richer in truth!" Sumner's career, which touched the nerve center of the country's political and social matrix, appears to have added fuel to his euphoric fire. "Wherever we turn," he told the Phi Beta Kappa Society of Union College toward the end of his life, "is Progress—in science, in literature, in knowledge of the earth, in knowledge of the skies, in intercourse among men, in the spread of liberty, in words of beneficence, in the recognition of Human Brotherhood. Thrones where Authority seemed to sit secure, with the sanction of centuries, are shaken, and new-made constitutions come to restrain the aberrations of unlimited power. Men everywhere, breaking away from the Past, are pressing on to the things that are before."

This faith in the power of reason and in the perfectibility of man was an imported ideology. In 1830, Livingston wrote thanking Bentham for what he had learned from the Englishman:

> [I] take pleasure in acknowledging, that although strongly impressed with the defects of our actual system of penal law, yet the perusal of your works first gave method to my ideas, and taught me to consider legislation as a science governed by certain principles applicable to all its different branches, instead of an occasional exer-

cise of powers called forth only on particular occasions, without relation to, or connection with, each other.

In both countries, the possibility of a science of law was an exciting idea.
Law came to be regarded as a symmetrical structure of neatly dovetailed
logic. There was a definite right or wrong answer to a legal question; and
the bricks of correct doctrine could be laid by the processes of reasoning.

The concurrent movement for law reform in England was a comfort
and support. Even, for example, in so technical a field as the competency
of parties to act as witnesses in their own case, the British Practice Act of
1851 had wide influence in Vermont, Ohio, Minnesota, and New York. As
sometimes happens with contemporary legal borrowing, the recipient regarded the doctrine as more inviolate than did the originator. England was
ready to change its institution of rigid pleadings before Americans could
bring themselves to revise their imported counterpart, which lent substance
to the reformers' charge that they were more conservative than the English.
And at the same time as providing borrowings, the difference between the
two societies could be turned into an apologia for reform: it was easy to
argue that an English rule was unsuited to a pioneer country and thus
demanded revision.

The most powerful stimulus to progress in American legal ideas came
from the country's abundant resources and apparently boundless opportunities. Growth seemed natural, inevitable, in an unopened continent. The
lawyers regarded their experience in the youthful America—indeed their
own advancement in a fluid society unmatched by any in Europe—as both
proof and product of progress.

Natural law became embedded in the movements for social reform.
Although not the special province of the lawyer it was, in a sense, his
commodity. He applied natural law: what ought to be, against positive law:
what is. The concept was rapidly adopted by the reformer. The Bible and
the Declaration of Independence were his favorite yardsticks with which
to measure conduct and existing legal precepts, and the banner on his ideological equipage was woven of Reason and the "nature" of law. Whether
he was attacking the complex procedure of lawyer's law or a general evil
of society, the reformer's language was strikingly similar. There was a
rhetoric held in common by such men as Pennington, denouncing the form
of judicial proceeding as "an evil incompatible with liberty—in discord
with the spirit of our free institutions"; by Thoreau and Paulding, one arguing that "the Law of God" is on the side of abolitionism, the other, that it
is on the side of slavery; by Raymond, demanding that property rights
should be limited to a life interest because a fee simple interest "is a falsehood and an absurdity, because it is contrary to a self-evident principle of
natural law, or law of God." Legal and social reformers alike claimed to be
meeting the demand for an ideal system of law, sometimes to an extreme,

as when Seward characterized it "a higher law than the Constitution." The music of natural-law doctrines sounded loudest in the symphony of reform.

The legal profession, while being regarded as the instrument to work reform upon others, has itself been a prime object for reform ever since the days of Jeremy Bentham. The suggestions made by the reformers met with various degrees of compromise on the part of lawyers. They were surely not the only group who opposed change, but they in particular provided an excellent target for the opposition. Concerted attacks must have hardened their resistance; constant reiterations of the need to chase them from the temple were hardly likely to win plaudits from a profession both sensitive and well imbued with self-esteem. The emotional charges of would-be reformers were met by a reaction equally stubborn in many lawyers: the legal system of the country was the embodiment of all that was proper; if any imperfection existed—for human institutions were all liable to imperfection—it would soon fade away. This irrefutable argument effectively prevented useful discussion.

Misunderstanding was accentuated by the fact that so much of law is highly technical. It would not have been surprising if the profession as a whole had participated actively and deliberately in the reform of lawyer's law, since they alone could understand how to achieve it. The evidence of contemporary materials, however, indicates that this was not so, except for a short time at the very end of the period. The final report of the New York Practice Commission was made in 1850, but the Code of Criminal Procedure it proposed was not adopted until 1882, and the complete Code of Civil Procedure was never enacted. A vested interest in specialized knowledge caused considerable reluctance in lawyers to embrace reforms in an institution which they had studied as law clerks and taught as attorneys. In 1835, Timothy Walker, editor of the *Western Law Journal* and professor of law, commented:

> If legal reform be called for, the people must bring it about. If opposition come from any quarter, we anticipate it from lawyers. And the reason is natural. They are the most directly interested in keeping things as they are. The more abstruse and recondite you make the law, the more indispensable will be their professional services. Those of them who have attained a commanding eminence, by years of laborious study, can hardly be expected to recommend measures which would render half their learning useless. Nor would interest be their sole motive of opposition. They have acquired an attachment, bordering upon reverence, for those time-hallowed mysteries, which it has cost them so many years to explore.

With heavy irony another commentator observed:

> A movement towards a radical change in the practice of law courts in a neighborhood state has recently startled the Bar of New

England. The powerful hand of progress has been prying under the pedestal of the most time-honored institutions of law. Edifices, built with the granite of Littleton, the cement of Coke, the trowell of Blackstone, the masonic genius of a hundred chief justiciaries, have been set swaying as if they were fresh and flexible, instead of being covered with the moss of many generations. The doctrine of perfectibility, gradually elaborated out of change—the most omnipotent doctrine of modern times—has at last penetrated a sphere which has been held almost sacred, hitherto, against the novelties of advancement, and is working like a resistless leaven throughout the system. The venerable seer of jurisprudence . . . shudders to see the gray hairs of the worshipful head of the law rapidly dropping off, and her children trampling them under their feet.

Many lawyers considered the criticism of reformers something to be ignored as the raving of the misinformed. To frame a system of pleadings "suited to the capacities of ignorance and imbecility," growled a veteran lawyer, "is an impossibility." Accuracy requires complexity and shading. And a reformer's "interminable delay" may be a lawyer's "breathing spell," just as a "burdensome expense" may be redefined as a "fair recompense." Seward wrote:

> [I] believe you know that I *defend* slander and libel suits always by delay as far as practicable. There is nothing for a plaintiff, in such cases, like haste; nor is there any advantage for a defendant like time; that diminishes the grievance complained of.

The behavior of lawyers as a whole, however, was not uniform. According to the *North American Review*, "even from the profession we do not hear an undivided voice." Field, who suffered the trials of all trailblazers, in his article "What Shall Be Done with the Profession?" may only have been putting on a bold front, but he did express the belief that a majority of the profession was "for change of some sort."

The codification movement stands somewhere between the reform of lawyer's law and social reform in the degree to which the profession accepted it. Although faith in the common law seems to have been the stronger, lawyers seemed genuinely uncertain whether laws were better announced by legislative statute or by judicial opinion. The arguments for and against a codified system were spelled out well, fervently, and at great length. The *Report of the Massachusetts Commission* remains an outstanding exposition of the merits of both enacted and decisional law and of the ways in which they supplement, not compete with, each other.

With respect to social reform in general, there are indications that both the bench and bar dragged their feet. Many were quick with easy rationalizations of social evils. In cases involving segregation, as in insanity, women's rights, and prohibition, reforms were often found to violate fundamental legal principles, although sound legal arguments could have been advanced just as well to sustain them.

Some historians have attempted to attribute the rise of reform movements in the United States to the fact that people were not burdened by the weight of tradition as in other countries, and that the transplanted European was in rebellion against conditions of the Old World. Insofar as these were the causes, it is not hard to see how they applied less to lawyers than to others. Also, many lawers were comfortable and not anxious to upset the equilibrium. The lawyer, first by training, and perhaps later by instinct, is tied to the past; accustomed to dealing with precedents, expectations, and past transactions, he changes slowly, case by case.

Those lawyers who did become involved in the substantive reform movements of the period can be found not only in one crusade, but in many. There was a virtual interlocking directorate of reformers. Sumner was not only in the forefront of abolitionism; he was also a leader in agitating for international tribunals. Bigelow worked for temperance and education; and Phillips for female suffrage and improvements in labor conditions. Many of these lawyers became professional reformers, interested in change and in championing the causes of the underprivileged no matter what the expertise required to evaluate the issues.

Such, at least, would have been the judgment of those members of the profession who concentrated on the reform of lawyer's law. They seldom explored other social problems; they did not participate in humanitarian movements; yet the two kinds of reform often intertwined. Consider the work performed by attorneys for the New York Prison Association, or the Louisiana Act of 1820 which called for a code of criminal law to be

> founded on one principle, viz, the prevention of crime; that all offences should be clearly and explicitly defined, in language generally understood; that punishment should be proportioned to offences; that the rules of evidence should be ascertained as applicable to each offence; that the mode of procedure should be simple, and the duty of magistrates, execution officers and individuals assisting them, should be pointed out by law.

When lawyers were stirred to reform, most of their energies, even on the side of opposition, went into subjects most in keeping with their immediate competence and sympathies. The focus of their reform energies tended to be on the question of procedure—how to get things done—rather than on the results they were trying to achieve. The lawyer who specialized in legal apparatus let his duties to his fellow man be measured by the needs of the profession. Perhaps this was a wise allocation of limited energies; probably it was also a manifestation of skepticism toward the notion that so many social ends could be achieved at once. Rather than diffusing his energy by attempting to secure social perfection on all fronts, the lawyer was content with improvements in the administration of justice—no small matter when the achievements of any society are evaluated. Although his attitude toward other social reforms was not obstructionist, he had little sympathy for the zealots leading the endlessly sprouting causes, those "terrible simplifiers," in Jacob Burckhardt's phrase. His was the voice of moderation, rather than of indifference. Choate unrealistically urged that "the further agitation of the subject of slavery be excluded from and forbidden in national politics." Shaw railed against those who sought "to destroy the respect of the community for the law and its administration, without which the dearest rights of humanity would be without protection." A proposed merger of law and equity evoked a characteristically temporizing comment:

> It ought, however, to be remembered that all progress, which truly tends to improvement, ever has been, and ever must be gradual, silent and noiseless, as the reformations of time and the revolutions of the heavenly spheres. True wisdom is never a babbler, never a boaster; is never heard vaunting amid the noise and shoutings of the multitude; it is modest, mistrustful of itself, seeking rather to obviate known evils and inconveniences, than by sweeping changes, to create these of which we can know nothing of their number or extent.

Here is the Polonius role of law. Lawyers lent respectability and a professional tone to many social reform movements. They were sincere in their efforts to make tribunals accessible to Everyman, with less delay and cost; to eliminate technicalities in pleadings; and to permit state litigation to supersede private controversy. But, for the most part, they contented themselves with efforts to cope with change only where a clear community consensus had emerged, or deeper experience with the subject revealed the likely consequences of modification. Pope, whose iambics were the literary companion of Chief Justice Marshall, was their poet laureate, not Swift.

The verdict of time differs from that of the players in assessing the attainments of the legal reform movements. In their professional activity, lawyer-reformers attained a considerable measure of success on questions of concern to the practicing lawyer. Technicalities and finer procedural points were abolished, notwithstanding objections from those who claimed that reforms were "ruining the science of pleading." Revisions were made in the different forms of action at law and suits in equity, the need to choose the proper action at the litigant's peril, and the rigid terminology of statements of causes and defenses. The creation of a speedy and effective system of justice was adopted as a proper end for the legal profession— an explicit promise which still haunts its complacency. "Law Reform," William Cory said primly in 1834, "is a most appropriate and elevated range for the professional mind." Whether pushed from behind by the rhetoric of the Democrats or pulled along by a few of the more inventive lawyers, the fact is that the bar did recognize and, to a considerable degree, did respond to the challenge. Procedure was the point on which the law was conspicuously in need of reform and, as technicians who had grasped the intricacies of the machinery, they alone had sufficient know-how to devise improvements. Inevitably a great deal remained to be done to simplify and systematize principles and practice; but this should not minimize their positive attainments in this area of reform.

The codification movement fared somewhat differently. "The commission failed entirely," was Field's appraisal, "and it failed because the men appointed to it had no faith in the codification of the common law. They thought only of a new revision of the statutes. We wanted no revision. We wanted codification." The focus of agitation, codification, has left few traces, but procedural reform took hold. Whether the scattered adoption of codes in isolated fields of law was due to the opposition of the bar, to some wisdom attributed to a case-by-case method, or to an unwillingness to discard all ties with the English heritage is hard to say. To some, codification smacked too much of the professor and undervalued the teachings of actual experience; to others it bore the stigma of monarchical or despotic states. Perhaps the vigors of an untamed legal order would not yield to the tidiness relished by civilian academics. Peter Du Ponceau, the one prominent lawyer actually nurtured in the civil law, felt that abolishing the common law would be a futile act: "We should still recur to it for principles and illustrations, and it would rise triumphant above its own ruins, deriding and defying its impotent enemies." The reception of English common law through the filter of the courts was destined to be the way of development for American law. Perhaps it can be ascribed to legal immaturity; the case-law system was functioning well. "A code in the common law states of nineteenth century America," writes Dean Pound, "would have required far longer to develop into a workable body of American law than it took under the leadership of our great doctrinal writers to make such a body of law from the traditional materials." Emotive terms, like "maturity," are hardly likely to pierce the shell of history's obscurity. Nevertheless, this era's swirling movements for full-blown codification on the French model went far toward sharpening the law's awareness of itself and developing that maturity. Basic areas of the law were reduced to statutory form, but its development lay primarily with the judiciary and its bold innovations. "Revision" and "consolidation" of statutes, which reduced the bulk of law to an orderly arrangement, did become an accepted pattern in many states. So codification arrived through the back door.

Outside the confines of their specialty—the internal housekeeping—pursuit of wealth and immersion in politics still left important lawyers time to deal with the broader questions of social justice. The cleavages in the country did not spare the legal profession. After they became pronounced

Free Soilers, Dana and Sumner were no longer admitted to proper Boston homes and their legal business was seriously impaired. Similarly, at the opposite pole, the appointment as Lecturer in Law at Harvard of Judge Loring, who had decided in favor of returning the fugitive slave Burns to his master, raised such a storm that the Board of Overseers refused to confirm his appointment.

A special characteristic of American law was developed in that the society agreed to use the law as a tool for evolutionary growth. The role of the courts as overseers of proposed revisions gave confidence even to those adversely affected in the process of change. The vigorous humanitarian movements found lawyers actively engaged—on both sides of the issues. They were, in a special sense, intellectuals arguing about and dealing with the broad trends of the society. In debates on some issues, such as the Constitution's toleration of slavery and the liberty of the individual to get drunk, positive law arguments predominated; in debates over other aspects of reform, ranging from treatment of criminals to mass education, the arguments had recourse to natural law. Both types of debate suggest the pervasiveness of the legal discourse. Though the lawyers did not speak with one voice, they were deeply involved; for it was primarily through change in the law and the development of legal agencies that most of the great movements for social reform were able to respond to the demands of the age.

1. Lawyer's Law

ATTITUDES TOWARD PROCEDURAL REFORM

In his report to the Legislature of Georgia in 1850, Judge Lumpkin presented what might be called the lawyer's traditional attitude toward reform: "Let well enough alone," as he put it, and change only where unavoidable. This attitude was echoed in the Western Law Journal *two years later, which held that change must be justified by "some pressing acknowledged certainty."*

Opposed to Revolution

JOSEPH H. LUMPKIN

Joseph Henry Lumpkin was born in Oglethorpe County, Georgia. He was graduated from the College of New Jersey (later Princeton) in 1819, and returned to Georgia to study law. He was renowned for his well-reasoned and scholarly arguments and was elected to the legislature in 1824. He assisted in the framing of the Georgia Penal Code in 1833.

Up to 1845, Georgia had clung to a unique system of jurisprudence. Each judge of the superior (circuit) court was the final arbiter of all litigation in his circuit, not bound by the decisions of his predecessors or colleagues and often not even by his own previous decisions. Lumpkin approved of this system, but a popular mandate for change was acknowledged in 1845 when the Georgia Supreme Court was created and empowered with the right of judicial review. Lumpkin was elected to the new court for a six-year term. His associates promptly elected him Chief Justice, and he remained on the bench for four terms, easing the transition from the old to the new system. He died in office in 1867.

IN OBEDIENCE to the resolution of the Legislature, passed in 1847, that the Judges of the Supreme Court be requested to make a report to the present Assembly, stating any existing defect in the laws of Georgia, and suggesting a remedy for the same; and to give their opinion on the expediency and

---

Joseph H. Lumpkin, "Report to the Legislature of Georgia," *Western Law Journal* (December, 1850), VII, p. 383.

practicability of so condensing and simplifying the laws, as will place them more within the knowledge of the citizens of the State generally, thereby securing the more speedy and certain attainment of the ends of justice; the undersigned begs leave to submit for *himself*, respectfully, the following Report premising simply that the want of time from the pressure of official duties has, he regrets to say, prevented that careful and extensive examination of the subject, which its importance demands.

I would remark in the outset, that I have taken occasion, frequently in my place from the Bench, as my published opinions will show, to express my unqualified admiration of the far-reaching wisdom, as well as the liberal and enlarged views of the authors and founders of our judicial system. No history of Georgia will be complete, nor worthy of its subject, which omits to search out and hold forth prominently to the veneration of posterity, the names of those worthies who were evidently in advance of the age in which they lived, and who evinced such a profound knowledge, both of the law as it then stood, and the reforms which it required. The memory of such men should be cherished, as constituting no small portion of the rich inheritance of our people. Lord Brougham, and those associated with him, in re-modeling the English Law, received the most extravagant praise, for recommending to the British Parliament things, as *new*, which had been in successful practice in this State for thirty years. And even New-York, which is supposed to have gone a whole bar's-length and more beyond any other State in the Union, in the work of progress and reform, is content to end pretty much where Georgia started, half a century ago; still our laws partake of the frailty and imperfection of every thing human. There are not only inherent defects, which experience has revealed, but principles and rules of practice, which were proper enough when adopted, which by lapse of time and change of circumstances require repeal or modification. It was the opinion of Mr. Jefferson, that every political constitution should be revised and amended every twenty-five years. The law cannot claim exemption any more than *forms* of government, from the spirit of change, so strikingly characteristic of the present age.

We are decidedly opposed, however, to *revolution*. Prudence would dictate, that a system which has been long established, should not be materially altered, on account of frivolous objections or slight inconveniences. *Let well enough alone* is a sound maxim in legislation, as in everything else. All we propose, therefore, is adopting, or rather *retaining,* the present code, civil and criminal, in its fundamental features; to lop off only its excrescences, to winnow away the rottenness which the mildew of time has produced, and engraft on the main stock such new provisions as will accommodate the whole to the present state of society and of the world, and to an epoch distinguished above all others for sound thought, self-judgment, and vigorous common sense—one which, obstinately refusing obedience to *mere* authority, demands a reason for its credence, and which rejects with infidel scorn and derision whatever is false and heretical in law, ethics, and government.

Need to Justify Change

WESTERN LAW JOURNAL

LAW REFORM in Ohio has ceased to be a question of mere speculation; the new constitution has imparted to it the character of the highest practical importance. The commission, therein provided for, must now be raised; and when raised, it must do something; and the great danger is that it will do altogether too much. Pride of character and of opinion will be apt to lead the commissioners into this rather than into the opposite error. The task and labor of merely supplying the defects, which time and human progress show to exist in the present system, will appear too humble for men appointed under such a clause as this in the new constitution. This seems to look to great and sweeping changes; changes looking like revolution. Besides, the spirit of the hour is a spirit of radicalism; a spirit of self-sufficiency, which regards the wisdom and experience of the past as mere dry dust, wholly without vitality, unadapted to the circumstances of the present, and unfitted for the wonderful progress and developments, of which the future promises to be so fruitful. Hence the past, with all its experiences and like long results of time, is regarded as worthless, undeserving of notice; deserving only to be abolished and to give way to the new creations of this nineteenth century. . . .

Improvement can only be secured by retaining our hold upon the past; it must have its roots there, and grow out of it. To cut loose from the past, is to introduce anarchy, whether in government or law. Improvement implies *order*, and order can only be preserved by allying the future to the past through the present.

This principle is no less applicable to judicial reform than to government and law. Lord Mansfield said, in 1787, near the close of his long and splendid judicial career, that "great alterations in the course of the administration of justice ought to be sparingly made, and by degrees, and rather by the court than by legislature." 2 Campbell Lives, C. J.'s, 420. Lord Mansfield himself was the greatest law reformer that ever presided in a court of justice; and hence his opinion is entitled to the more weight. Reforms, made by the court, are made understandingly, made to obviate a felt evil; and, therefore, its effect and operation are known; and no confusion and uncertainty result therefrom. Whereas the destruction of an old and tried system, and the creation of a new and untried one, imply years of judicial anarchy; years of confusion and uncertainty, during which the learned and the unlearned are alike ignorant of what may or may not be law. Nor can this knowledge be obtained until after the courts shall have discussed and expounded, and construed, and applied practically the new system to the infinite and multiplied relations of life and its business. This conflict and uncertainty and confusion can only be obviated by ingrafting all changes and reforms upon existing law and principles, just as time and experience show the defects and evils; and then these changes should be limited to supplying these defects; to a removal of these evils. By such reform, confusion and uncertainty will be avoided. And the history of law and its administration show, along the line of its progress, many and important changes, large and wholesome reforms, rendered expedient by the perpetual fluctuations in the business and relations of human life. But these changes have never partaken of the nature of revolution. Old forms and practice, and laws, to which society had become accustomed, and with the working of which it had become as familiar as with household words, have not been rashly displaced to make way for some new theory; nor merely because some other plan might have been preferable, as more symmetrical. Every change had to justify itself, not by some fine-drawn speculation, but by some pressing acknowledged necessity.

Extremes is ever a bad counsellor—whether he hold on to the past with a death-grasp, or would repudiate it for his own fine-spun theories. There are two classes of mind here symbolized; the one sees nothing but perfection in the past, the other nothing but imperfection; the one would never make a change, the other would change every thing; but out of the conflict of these extremes issues all salutary reforms; reforms which embody the truth of both, uniting what is good in the past with whatever of improvement is inclosed in the future.

Government and law, and the administration of justice, were no *invention* of man. They are the products of society itself, originating in its wants and necessities. Society has there as much as the individual; and the individual might as well do without food and clothing as society without government and law, and the administration of justice. It is by these alone that order is secured, without which society can not exist. Hence has government and law, and the administration of justice grown up noiselessly; no one knowing how, just as the wants of society required, assuming just such forms as were best fitted to meet these wants. Hence, whoever would ignore the past, sets up his own weak reason against the instincts of society; instincts as unerring as those which guide the wild fowls in their annual migrations, and teaches the little wren, and swallow, and robin, how and when to build their nests. . . .

It would also be well for us in Ohio to recollect that most of the abuses, complained of in England and New York, never did exist here. We reformed all these in our very first practice act. We there adopted the principles of the common law code of procedure, without the formalities and forms which had become absolute in England, and were wholly inapplicable here. And yet the literature of law reform ignores all this, and discourses on as though we in Ohio were buried beneath the whole mass of obsolete forms and practical absurdities, which a few years since continued to disgrace the administration of justice in England, and to some extent in New York.

Shall It Be Wholly Reformed?

DAVID DUDLEY FIELD

As the fugue evokes the name of Bach so the code in the United States is associated with David Dudley Field. His driving purpose was to put the whole body of law, substantive and procedural, into a written code. Through his agitations, provisions were added to the New York State Constitution of 1846 for a general code, a single court having jurisdiction in both law and equity, and the appointment of "commissioners to revise, reform, simplify and abridge the rules of practice, pleadings, forms and proceedings of the Courts of Record." Field dominated the commission, from which he had been omitted at first as too radical. A Code of Civil Procedure went into effect in 1848; it has been estimated that, by the turn of the century, more than thirty jurisdictions had adopted it. Between 1860 and 1865 complete codes were reported, but Field's efforts were never fully successful: of the substantive law codes only the penal code was adopted, and that not until 1881. The struggle was a battle royal in New York for generations. Greater success was attained in four other states, which adopted all five of the "Field codes."

THE CONSTITUTION OF THIS STATE, which goes into effect to-day, will render great changes necessary in our system of legal procedure. . . .

Important modifications of the equity practice are . . . made indispensable, in order to adapt it to the new mode of taking testimony. But I think that the Convention intended, and that the people expect, much greater changes than these. We know that radical reform in legal proceedings, has long been demanded by no inconsiderable number of the people; that a more determined agitation of the subject has been postponed by its friends, till such time as there should be a reorganization of the judicial

David Dudley Field, *"What Shall Be Done with the Practice of the Courts?"* (1847), p. 5.

establishment, upon the idea that a new system of procedure and a new system of courts ought to come in together; that it was a prominent topic in the Convention itself, where its friends were in an undoubted majority; and that the manifestations of public sentiment out of doors, were no less clear, than were the sentiments of that body. Indeed, if now, after all that has been done within the last five years, there should be made only such changes as the Constitution absolutely commands, there will be great and general disappointment.

The profession stands at this time in a position in which it has not before been placed. Shall it set itself in opposition to the demand of a radical reform; shall it be indifferent to it; or shall it unite heartily in its prosecution? None can reform so well as we, as none would be benefited so much. We cannot remain motionless. We must either take part in the changes, or set ourselves in opposition to them, and then, as I think, be overwhelmed by them. Even if it were originally a matter of indifference whether they should be made, or it were certain that any change was undesirable, it is no longer possible to resist the current, which sets so strongly in that direction.

But it really never was a matter of indifference to the best part of the legal profession, whether there should be a reform in legal proceedings. A certain portion of them, undoubtedly, were opposed to all change; but there were others who were true reformers; and a majority of the body were for change of some sort. I will not say that they were agreed in respect to the extent of the changes required. Some were for a radical reform; others thought moderate amendments sufficient; it was a feeble minority which denied the need of any.

If it had depended upon the Bar alone, I believe that many important amendments would have been made, which we are now without. Various causes have contributed to prevent their doing as much as they would otherwise have done, the principal of which is, the jealousy with which concert of action on their part was regarded by others. It is a mistake to suppose that our present legal machinery has been regarded by them with much favor. On the contrary, I think they have disliked it generally. They would choose something better to drive over our modern ways, than this cumbrous thing—three hundred years old and more—ill adapted to our present circumstances, unequal to our present wants, and so altered and mended, that scarce any two parts seem of a piece. Possibly I mistake the opinions and the inclinations of the majority of my profession. The part they take in their present circumstances will show what their opinions and inclinations really are.

Every consideration, as it seems to me, makes it expedient for us all now to enter heartily upon the work of amendment. Those of us, who have long been laboring for a radical reformation of the law, and those who have felt less inclination for it, should find this an occasion to act together in the common pursuit of thorough and wise reforms. We feel the inconvenience of the present state of things. We know that the technicality and the drudgery of legal proceedings are discreditable to our profession. Justice is entangled in the net of forms.

There are, undoubtedly, some inconveniences attending every change. To accommodate one's self to a new mode of transacting business, after he has long been habituated to an old one, requires an effort. The chains of habit are always strong, and perhaps the nature of legal studies, which inculcate adherence to precedents, makes them lie stronger on lawyers than on any other class of persons. . . .

For all reasons, therefore, it appears to me the wiser and the safer plan, when we are about it, to make a radical reform; in short, to go back to first principles, break up the present system, and reconstruct a simple and natural scheme of legal procedure. The adoption of such a scheme would be one of the most beneficent reforms of this age.

Believing, therefore, that great changes are inevitable in any event, and that this is a period favorable to the adoption of all the reforms which are really required, I wish it were possible to engage every member of the legal profession, in the promotion of a wise, safe, and radical reform. Radical reform will come sooner or later, with us or without us. Shall we co-operate to make it at the same time wise and safe?

Such a reform, I am persuaded, should have in view nothing less than a uniform course of proceeding, in all cases, legal and equitable.

I am not to be understood as making war upon the profession. I honor it for its virtue, for its great liberality in the cause of universal philanthropy. I honor it for the greatness of the talents of the many who "gladden the social circle with their presence," who adorn the Bar and the Bench, and reflect credit upon society and the world. I condemn it for its subserviency to forms, that have no sensible meaning; that violate every rule of common sense,—that are stumbling-blocks in the road to justice. I for one will adhere to them no longer. I am for that reform which will make the administration of justice the most economical, speedy, and certain. Such a reform no honest man will find fault with; and every lawyer especially should give it his influence. Such is the intention, and I hesitate not to say will be the effect, of the passage of this bill. True it is, it wipes out, at one sweep, what some are pleased to call the hoarded wisdom of a thousand years; but what are in truth the unmitigated evils of more than that length of time.

True it is, it unceremoniously dissolves partnership, as well as fellowship, with those distinguished names of John Doe and Richard Roe. True it is, that trespass, *quære clausum fregit, vi et armis, contra pacem,* trover, case, with its *omnium gatherum,* replevin, detinue, ejectment, with its incomprehensible fictions,—debt, assumpsit, and covenant, with the solemnity of its seal, will all pass among the "things that were," and among the things that never ought to have been. What a great blessing to get rid of such jargon. . . .

Its great virtue, as I comprehend it, is the dispensing entirely with all the present forms of proceeding, and introducing in their stead one plain form for the commencement of all suits. The second section of the bill is explicit, and easily understood. It is the *facts* of every client's case that should be spread upon the record, and that in the simplest and shortest manner; for it is upon the adjudication of those facts, that the result of his case depends; and the less technical he is, in his pleadings, the more certainty there is that justice will be done him. The present system of pleading gives him whose cause is dubious, many chances to wind in and wind out, so that it is sometimes difficult to tell whether you are going forwards, or coming backwards.

If fictions and technicalities are *necessary* in the *administration* of justice, they are just as necessary to be introduced and followed in the every day transactions of life. In our contracts and dealings with our fellow men, it is the substance, clothed in the plainest and most definite language, that most recommends itself to our favorable consideration. In all the out-door business of life, so to speak, fiction is dispensed with—men look to the reality, and not to the shadow of things. The moment you employ a lawyer to collect your claim, enforce your contract, defend your character, &c., &c.—the order of things is materially changed. From the time he writes his precipe, to the entering up of the judgment, he is met at every step, with oftentimes the merest technicality, purposely interposed, to delay and prevent the fair administration of justice. His client neither understands or comprehends the course pursued. It is all Greek to him. One thing he finds out in the conclusion, that injustice has been done him, and he has the satisfaction too of knowing, that he has been lawing at his own expense. The man who has thus been treated, whose rights and interests have thus been sacrificed, goes away from the Court with a feeling of disgust, yea, contempt, for the law and its ministers. It is idle to expect the people to venerate such laws. As well ask the man in chains to respect the tyrant that has forged his fetters. . . .

By a continuation of the present system, an opportunity is given for unjust advantages; by an adoption of the plan proposed, no such opportunities will be afforded. No wonder the people despise and repudiate forms which have so many loop-holes of escape—forms condemned by dear-bought experience, through time "whereof the memory of man runneth not to the contrary"—forms repudiated, I am proud to say, by the enlightened wisdom and judicial experience of the first State in America —forms, condemned as worse than useless; as stupendous evils, by the best legal minds of our own State. Sir, this system of legal proceedings, like that of African slavery, will not be much longer *countenanced* or *endured*. If the cruel tyrant does not *soon* relieve the poor, oppressed slave from the yoke of his bondage, he will, I trust in God, relieve himself. If the lawyers, and legislators, do not *soon* wipe out this reproach upon the administration of public justice, the people will soon come to these halls and do it themselves.

Their deep strong cry, and one that will be felt is, give us legal reform.

Abolish your fictions and ruinous technicalities; mock and insult us no longer, by a farcical administration of the law. The law was made for the protection of the citizen, in his rights, his person, his reputation, and his property.

Sir, I have done discussing its provisions. It needs no discussion. It recommends itself to the consideration of all those who desire to build up a plain and practical system for the adjudication of all cases, that any one sees proper to bring into a court of justice. If it does not *now* become a law, the time is rapidly approaching when it *will*. Legal Reform is unmistakeably written in legible characters, and will progress to its consummation. Lawyers must part with their ancient gods of fiction, their idols of technicality, for the people will no longer tolerate them.

THE SYSTEM OF PLEADING

A Byword and a Jest

JOHN BANNISTER GIBSON

Thirty-seven years of continuous service on the Supreme Court of Pennsylvania was the record of John Bannister Gibson (1780–1853). After years at the bar distinguished chiefly by practice on the violin, he came to life on the bench. Over six thousand cases came before him; and his twelve hundred written opinions profoundly influenced the jurisprudence of the state.

IN PENNSYLVANIA, it is true, agreements of parties or counsel have been recognized as the law of the case so far as regards question of right; and they have had an influence even in overturning forms of law and making a Pennsylvania record, when sent into another state, a by-word and a jest. We have heard of one sort of action being turned into another, and money counts being filed in trespass or trover; but, though such a practice is simply barbarous, it supposes the existence of a proper form of action,

---

Gibson, C. J., Bellas *v.* Dewart, *17 Pa.* (1851), pp. 85, 88.

with pleadings to admit the merits of the case. It is [to] the facilities afforded by these agreements, encouraging as they do laziness and inattention, that our exuberant ignorance of the principles of an action, and of practice, is to be ascribed, together with the teasing and profitless litigation which it produces.

Double Pleadings

AMERICAN JURIST

TAKE AN EXAMPLE that recently occurred. An action was brought on a promissory note, and the declaration consisted of three counts; 1st. on the note; 2d. money had and received; 3d. money paid. The defendant pleaded to all the counts; 1st. the general issue; 2d. that the defendant did not promise within six years; 3d. that the action did not accrue within six years. The plaintiff joined the general issue; 2d, replied that the defendant did promise within six years; 3d, that he was out of the state when the action accrued, and did not return until within six years of the time of commencing the action. 1st. The defendant joined issue of the promise within six years; and rejoined, upon the strength of a provision in the law of Massachusetts; 2d, that the defendant left goods in the state which might have been attached, and issue was taken upon the fact of goods of the defendant being so left in the commonwealth. Here were, then, three issues: 1st, the general issue, 2d, on the defendant's having promised within six years, and 3d, on his having left goods in the commonwealth liable to attachment.

As it happened, both the parties were under precisely the same embarrassment with this rule against double replying and rejoining. The plaintiff depended upon proving that the defendant was not in the state at the time when the note became due, or that he had made a new promise within six years, and the choice between these two grounds was so difficult, that he was unwilling to make an election. The two special pleas of the defendant, however, gave him the opportunity to make replication of the two reasons why the statute of limitations ought not, as he supposed, to apply to his case. So we see in this case, that the very difficulty proposed to be avoided by this rule, namely, the plurality of issues, if it really be any difficulty, does now actually occur, provided the pleas are sufficiently numerous, and the subsequent pleadings are so conducted, as, in each stage, to leave an adequate number of points exposed, on which to engraft duplicity.

"Double Pleadings," *American Jurist* (April, 1831), V, p. 280.

A Lawyer's Story

NEBRASKA ADVENTURER

TOM STRIKES Dick over the shoulders with a rattan as big as your little finger. A lawyer, in his indictment, would tell you the story as follows: "And whereas the said Thomas, at the said place, on the day and year aforesaid, in and upon the body of the said Richard, against the peace of the people of the State of New Hampshire, and *their dignity*, did make a most violent assault, and inflicted a great many and divers blows, kicks, cuffs, thumps, bumps, contusions, gashes, hurts, wounds, damages, and injuries, in and upon the head, neck, breast, stomach, hips, knees, shins, and heels of said Richard, with divers sticks, canes, poles, clubs, logs of wood, stones, daggers, dirks, swords, pistols, cutlasses, bludgeons, blunderbusses, and boarding pikes, then and there held in the hands, fists, claws and clutches of him the said Thomas."

The Proceedings Were Always Simple

LAW REPORTER

THE PROCEEDINGS of the Courts of this Commonwealth were always simple when compared with those of the English Common Law Courts, from which those proceedings were mainly derived. But we borrowed, among other things, special pleading. No one can have understood this system without a profound admiration of it as a work of human genius, nor without perceiving that it is capable of accomplishing perfectly, those objects of first-rate importance where facts are to be tried by a jury, the separation of the law from the fact, and the production of simple and exact issues, to be submitted to their appropriate tribunals.

It certainly was not to be wondered at, that special pleading, which had been considered an integral part of the common law, and which had so many excellencies to recommend it, should have been imported with that law and introduced into use here. But it was found that it had great defects as a practical system. In perfectly skilful and cautious hands it worked admirably, but, unfortunately, perfect knowledge of so complicated

Nebraska Adventurer (July 5, 1856), p. 1.
"Reform in Pleading," *Law Reporter* (1851), XIII, p. 602.

and subtle a system, and extreme vigilance in the use of it, are things not to be reckoned on in practice; and accordingly this sharp and powerful machine inflicted many wounds on the ignorant and unwary. This was seen to be wrong, but instead of looking for the defects in the system, and amending them, if capable of amendment, and, if not, changing it for another, a course of legislation was begun, which has ended in having no system at all.

Thus, as early as 1783, (*Stat.* 1783, *Ch.* 38, *Sec.* 8,) it was enacted that executors, administrators and guardians should not be compelled to plead specially, but might give any defence in evidence under the general issue; as if it were a hardship, not to be inflicted on these classes of persons, but which must still be endured by suitors generally. Similar favors, as it would seem they were considered, were from time to time granted to all persons sued before justices of the peace, except in cases where title in trespass was to be pleaded, (than which few things are more difficult to do rightly,) to persons sued on penal statutes, to civil officers and persons acting by their commands, insurance companies and dog-killers; and, finally, by Statute 1836, ch. 273, all special pleas in bar were abolished, the general issue, general demurrers, pleas in abatement, (to which a general demurrer operates as special,) motions in arrest of judgment, writs of error and declarations according to the old system being still retained. So that he who now surveys what remains sees every plaintiff left to inhabit the old building, while all others are turned out of doors. We seem to be walking for a short distance in the ancient but strongly built streets of an old town, and all at once to step out into the open fields, having here and there a piece of sunken fence and a half-filled up ditch, and some ruins of broken walls, which afford excellent lurking places for concealment and surprise, but no open highway for the honest traveller.

The evils of this state of things may not readily occur to the mind, but they are very great. They are felt, in preparation for, during, and after the trial. Neither party has any legal means of knowing what questions of fact or law are to be tried. Each must therefore conjecture, as well as he can, all reasonable possibilities, and prepare for them. This not only occasions much needless labor of the party and his counsel, but the expense of witnesses to prove facts which on the trial are found to be immaterial, or are not admitted. This last consequence, by no means exhausts itself in the needless fees of witnesses. In this industrious community it is to most persons an inconvenience and cause of loss to attend the Courts as witnesses; this inconvenience and loss are, not seldom, very considerable; and the onerous duty should be imposed on as few persons as possible.

Both parties coming to the trial with no certain knowledge of the points of the case, or the course which the trial is to take, each must feel his way as he goes; the Court and jury must do the same, and it often happens that it is not till the concluding arguments of the counsel are made, that the jury can get any clear idea of what is to be tried by them; the case on neither side having been opened, because neither side knew what the case was. The immediate effects are, very dilatory conduct of the trial, and the consumption of much time in beating over ground, which is found, at last, to lie quite outside of the case. The remote effects are, to induce a loose habit of preparation for the trial, to compel the Court to rule on questions without any general view of the case, and to find out the matters to be tried, often, near the close of the trial; to cause a *nisi prius* trial to be a kind of preliminary inquiry to get the case into shape, instead of a trial of it; to render verdicts less important; and, as a consequence of the operation of all these causes, to make it almost a general rule that cases of considerable importance go before the whole Court upon exceptions or motions for new trials. The commissioners have carefully endeavored not to overstate the effects of the present condition of our law of procedure, and they know that the opinions of many experienced persons, both judges and lawyers, concur with their own on this subject.

Looking back over the course which has been pursued, and seeing the end at which we have arrived, the commissioners submit that the principles of legislation on this subject have been erroneous. They do so with the highest respect for former Legislatures, and with diffidence as to their own conclusions. But they feel it to be their duty to state those conclusions frankly, and to submit, for the consideration of the Legislature, the reasons on which they are founded.

The course of legislation clearly shows that former Legislatures, feeling the evils resulting from special demurrers, motions in arrest of judgment, and the other machinery by which the rules of special pleading have been enforced, and seeing the hardships and frequent failures of justice to suitors which they have occasioned, instead of keeping in view the great objects of pleading, and the substantial means of attaining those objects, and endeavoring to diminish the number of technical rules, and to restrict the limits within which objections should be allowed to be taken, have swept away from time to time the essential with the useless, the substantial with the formal, without regard to any differences between them; and have done this by a series of acts which have rested on no principle, but have been occasional, fragmentary, and partial. Even the last sweeping act, while it prohibits defendants from pleading specially, relieves the plaintiff from no technical rule which could be taken advantage of by general demurrer, or motion in arrest of judgment, or writ of error.

The question for us is, What should be done? The answer to this question must depend upon the choice which is made of one of several general modes of procedure. One is, to have all the proceedings, after the parties are summoned, conducted orally. Under this, the parties come before the tribunal with their witnesses, and talk out their case. Neither party has any legal means of knowing, beforehand, what the other will say or prove. There are no limits for the debate, nor certainty nor definiteness concerning the subject of dispute, nor record of what has been done. It is obvious that this would not answer our wants. In a rude state of society, whose manners are simple, and whose affairs are easy of comprehension, it is probably the best of all modes. No man can suppose it fitted for this rich, populous and refined Commonwealth. The oral plan, probably all will agree, must be rejected, and we must have written allegations. These are demanded for four purposes; 1st. That each party may be under the most effectual influences, which the nature of the case admits of, so far as he admits or denies any thing, *to tell the truth*. 2d. That each party may have notice of what is to be tried, so that he may come prepared with the necessary proof, and may save the expense and trouble of what is not necessary. 3d. That the Court may know what the subject-matter of the dispute is, and what is asserted or denied concerning it, so that it may restrict the debate within just limits, and discern what rules of law are applicable. 4th. That it may ever after appear what subject-matter was then adjudicated, so that no further or other dispute should be permitted to arise concerning it. . . .

Now, if the trial has been had, if all parties and the Court have treated the allegations as sufficient, it is extremely difficult to see why, in our practice, they should not be deemed so. A trial is not like a lesson, or a work of discipline or instruction, to be gone over again because it was not perfectly done the first time. Counts in contract and tort are not to be joined, because it may be inconvenient to try them together. But if they have been tried together, and the inconvenience suffered, or found in that particular case not to exist, it would seem to be a strange way to attempt to lessen the inconvenience by setting aside all that was done, and doing the work over again. Allegations are made, that the parties may have notice. But if both parties were content to act upon what they had, why should either be allowed to complain afterwards? The verdict ought to conform to the allegations, so that it may be known that the jury have passed on the actual subject of dispute. But if the losing party makes no objection to it, and suffers a judgment to be rendered in conformity with it, why should he be allowed afterwards to say, that the real dispute has not been settled? How do we know it has not? He may answer, "Because the allegations show it." He should have said that earlier. Suppose he were to say, "I made a mistake in my allegations, and *they* do not present the actual case, and so the jury have not passed on the real right of the matter." The ready answer would be, "You should have shown that before verdict." Why should he not show the other before judgment? In short, why should any rule of proceeding be enforced in a particular case, after the practical object of that rule has either been attained, or waived by the parties, so that its attainment is no longer possible? The rule, *for that case,* should be deemed to have answered its purpose, and be no more spoken of. . . .

Acting upon this principle, the commissioners have retained the declarations known to the common law, but have reduced the forms of action to three,—*contract, tort* and *replevin.* They recommend the verification of pleadings, by oath or affirmation, at every stage. They have provided the most stringent rules for effecting the speedy settlement of actions. They have secured to each party the right to resort to the knowledge of the other. They have materially altered the powers of forcible entry and detainer. They have removed the rules of exclusion as to witnesses, entirely abolishing the test of interest and infamy, preserving, nevertheless, the sacredness of that confidence which should exist between husband and wife, and providing that in no cases shall they be witnesses for or against each other, and exempting parties to a suit from an oral examination, although they are required to answer . . .

[What the law] requires, will make it necessary—if we may be permitted to state it in their own homely language—for every country lawyer to drive an express wagon to the clerk's office once a fortnight, to look after his cases. In fine, it is stated that the requirements of this law will certainly destroy the practice of those lawyers who are mere writ-makers. If such be the operation of it, perhaps the public will not complain. But whether it be so or not, we are sure that no one will dare to complain of us for saying, that the system of legal procedure in this Commonwealth should be arranged for the convenience and security of all its citizens, and that it is not a matter which lawyers, as a class, have an exclusive right to control. We regret, extremely, to learn that such an opposition has been started, and we cannot think that it extends widely. There is no reason to fear that this report is the result of a rash and ill-judged thirst for reform. The known conservative tendencies, and high professional pride of all the gentlemen on the commission, afford ample reason for confidence in the spirit of the movement.

There is one thing more to be considered. The desire for legal reform has now become so strong among all classes in this country, that it cannot be checked. This is proved by the course which has been adopted in New York and other States, and the firmness with which any attempt at a retrograde movement has been resisted. It is idle to contend against it, especially when all admit that there are so many sound reasons which warrant such a feeling. It therefore eminently becomes the profession, to allow the movement to go on, especially when it can be conducted under the guidance of the most distinguished and respected of their own members.

How Procedural Reform Was Accepted

LAW REFORM TRACTS

IT WAS TO BE EXPECTED that a change, so radical as that made by the New York Code of Procedure, would encounter a good deal of opposition in professional quarters, and especially among the judiciary. The judges are usually advanced beyond the middle period of life; trained from their majority in habits of subservience to precedent; reposing on other men's studies; thinking the thoughts of their predecessors; looking only at the past, with their backs to the future; it is the most natural thing in the world, that they should recoil from change, as that which disturbs their rest, multiplies their labors, and perplexes their understandings. There are, of course, exceptions, and those not few; men of earnest and patient thought, who, not content with walking in the tracks of others, look to the right and left, willing to find a better way for themselves; who regard the law and its administration, not as ends, but as means to the great ends of justice; and who receive with favor every attempt to render these means easier to be found, and more rapid and certain in their results. These are noble examples of great magistrates, magnifying their office; but the majority is not of this character, and a reforming judge must still be regarded as an exception to a general rule.

We propose, in these pages, to inquire how far the judges of New York have acted in correspondence with the general tendency. They are divisible into three classes; the first, friends of the code, and desirous to forward whatever scheme promises a better administration of justice; the second, unfriendly in feeling, but not ready to thwart the legislative will, and disposed fairly to administer the laws as they find them; and the third, hostile in feeling and hostile in purpose, throwing such impediments as they dare, in the way of the new law, and sometimes venturing even to pervert an opinion upon its construction into a lecture upon its policy. The first class, comprising some of the most eminent names in the state, we need not here consider, reserving to another time that duty, more pleasing than the one we have now before us. The second class, also, we pass over for the present, remarking only that there are most estimable judges, who, disinclined, by reason of the character of their minds, and their fixed habits, to receive any change favorably, are yet scrupulously faithful to their oaths, receiving the law respectfully from the legislature, and administering it with purity and singleness of purpose. It is the third class only, to which we purpose now to ask attention.

"The Administration of the Code," *Law Reform Tracts* #1 (1852).

That such a class should exist, is a grave reproach. It is essential to all free government, and especially to our republican form, that the three great departments should be kept distinct,—legislative, executive, and judicial,—each working in its own sphere, and all conducing to the common good. This distinction ought to exist in fact, as well as in name. Each department must content itself with its own province, neither intermeddling, nor seeking to intermeddle, with that of another. If the executive may execute a law, or not, at its pleasure; if it may execute, what it conceives to be good, and leave what it supposes a bad law unexecuted, the legislature may be thwarted by the executive. If the judiciary may construe one law liberally and another law strictly, as it pleases; if it may misconstrue here, and explain away there, interpolating in one part, and striking out in another; if it may embarrass the operation of what the legislature has enacted; if, in pronouncing its judgments, it may inveigh against the law; then it may thwart the legislature, more effectually even than an unfaithful and hostile executive.

The judiciary has no concern with the policy or impolicy of a statute. If its interference in the law-making department had been desired, the people would have provided for it by the constitution. In theory, it has neither sympathy nor passion; its only attribute is judgment. It receives the law from the law-giver, and it administers it as it receives it, and the executive executes its judgments. The executive has the same right to revise the judgment, as the judiciary to revise the law. Each must restrict itself to its own department, content with that and faithful in that, or it will not only check the machine of the state, but destroy at last the foundations of its own power.

A great anomaly in our institutions is the existence of an unwritten law, of which the judiciary is the only repository, and therefore both maker and expounder. Time will remove this anomaly, for our people will yet perceive that there is the same reason in a republican government for a written law, as for a written constitution. The present existence of the unwritten law makes it, however, the more necessary, that the small portion which is written should be guarded against the revision of the judiciary, and that the habits, which their constant remodeling of the unwritten law begets, should not be carried into the department of the statutes.

When the code was first promulgated, it was received by the class to which we refer, not only with aversion, but with a disposition and determination, to do every thing possible to obstruct it, procure its repeal, and return to the old state of things. Every person who understands our judicial system, and the unreasonable power that the large body of unwritten law gives to the judiciary, will readily perceive the immense resources which hostile judges had at their disposal, to effect their object. Every question raised before them was an opportunity to misconstrue and

to pervert. Language cannot be so framed, as not to be frequently susceptible of different interpretations. If the more rational one be looked for,
the most consistent with the spirit and design of the whole law, the difficulty is soon surmounted; but if a hidden meaning be sought, a construction at war with the general scope of the instrument, and more
inconvenient to the suitor, it can be found. A slight play upon words, a
little twisting and interchange of sentences, and an abundant draught upon
the old common law, will suffice for the accomplishment of the design.

The first year was a year of fiery trial. Hostile judges confounding,
misconstruing, and denouncing; hostile lawyers imputing their own mistakes to the law, magnifying every difficulty which they found, and seeking
others where there were none; all that these could do to overthrow the
code, was done. But they were defeated; and though they have hitherto
prevented the legislature from completing the work then begun, they have
found a return to the old system impossible, and have abandoned it as
hopeless. Indeed, some of the fiercest opponents of the new system are
now among the most clamorous for its completion. The great struggle
for the principles of the code is thus ended; and whatever contest may
henceforth arise, will arise upon the question of its being finished, as it
was proposed.

It may perhaps seem ungracious in the friends of the code, after this
defeat of their adversaries, to dwell upon their mistakes or their misconduct. But we think these ought not to be forgotten. They should be
put into a form of more general circulation than reports upon practice,
that the public may understand what agents were at work to baffle the
will of the legislature, and prevent a reform of the law. A good deal remains to be done, to finish the work, thus begun, and we shall do well
to know who are to oppose us, and whom we have to overcome.

The unfairness with which this class of judges has treated the code,
is a matter of such general notoriety, as scarcely to be disputable. We have
heard, many times, from the lips of professional men not friendly to the
system, the expression of their disgust at the treatment it has received.
"Whatever they may think of it," is a common form of expression, "the
judges have no right to attack it from the bench. They have nothing to do
with its policy; they are bound to administer it honestly, and give it a fair
trial." We will venture the opinion, that there is not a lawyer in this state,
enjoying any degree of consideration, whatever may be his sympathies
or his tastes, who does not think that the conduct of these judges has been
in the highest degree improper. In other states, we are sure the same
opinion prevails. We have at this moment before us a letter from one of
the most eminent lawyers of the western states, containing the following
passage: "I have been reading cases in the Code Reporter, and am satisfied that no language or words can render the meaning so plain, as to prevent obscurity and doubt. But this has not annoyed me so much, as the

manifest bad faith with which your code has been treated by some of your judges. And there is no remedy for such conduct on the part of judges. It may contain all kinds of rules, requiring a liberal construction, but if the judge is not inclined so to construe, he will evade or trample upon such rules." We think there is a remedy for such conduct, though it be not prompt and direct. There is, first, the responsibility of the elected judge to his constituents, a responsibility likely to be enforced, as he comes before them for reëlection, and certain to defeat him, whenever there prevails an impression of such official misconduct, as is implied in an attempt to defeat or embarrass the operation of a law. There is, next, that responsibility to the legislature, which may be enforced by removal from office, a remedy justly to be applied to a willful perversion of the law, or neglect to study and apply it. And, last and best of all, there is that responsibility to the opinion, both of the profession and the public, which is, in our time, the greatest safeguard against the abuse of the judicial office. Give to the acts of the judges the most complete publicity, subject them to criticism, fair but severely just, place the judgment seat in a clear light before the public eye, and the most delinquent judge who ever dishonored the bench, will be either driven from it by the heat of public censure, or softened into an inoffensive man.

Unintelligible to the Great Mass of People

KENTUCKY CONSTITUTIONAL CONVENTION

Popular disapproval of the organization and phrasing of Kentucky laws was evident as early as 1805, when the frequent use of abbreviations, Latin and French phrases, and vague wording was criticized by a Kentucky attorney. Interpretations varied with each change on the bench, and were left "very much to be supplied by the decision of the judges." The fact that Kentucky judges were appointed rather than elected seemed to lead to abuse of this wide discretionary privilege. Movements to amend the Kentucky Constitution of 1799 met with repeated failure in the first decades of the nineteenth century largely as a result of conservative pressure against expanding popular rule. By 1848, however, popular anger over certain features of the Constitution dovetailed with a movement for legal codification, and finally resulted in the Kentucky Constitutional Convention of 1849. Changes were made in the election and tenure of the legislature and the governor, and the election period was reduced from three days to one in order to discourage election manipulation. Concern-

Report of the Debates and Proceedings of the Convention for the Revision of the Constitution of the State of Kentucky (1849), p. 903.

ing the codification question, a resolution was offered which pledged the legislature to appoint a commission within five years of the conclusion of the convention to codify, revise, and clarify the law. In a practical sense the problem was eased by the elimination of appointive judges; all judges were to be elected by the people for a fixed number of years. Even county clerks, attorneys, and coroners were made elective. The reform constitution was approved by popular vote in 1850.

Responding to the currents of reform in the nation at large, the convention members acted to remove barriers toward popular sovereignty with the hope for "wisdom and moderation by the freemen of Kentucky." Conservative Kentuckians denounced the convention as one which had thrown "everything pell mell into the ballot box."

MR. GHOLSON. What possible objection can there be to a provision like this? I appeal to the farmers of this body, who know the necessity of a codification of the laws, to sustain it. I appeal to the magnanimity of the lawyers of this house to sustain a provision which is clearly for the benefit of the commonwealth. When I charged it upon the gentleman from Nelson (Mr. Hardin) the other day, that with all his ability he could not find many of the Statutes of this Commonwealth, he did not deny it then, nor will he do it now. How then can the farmers and common plain citizens be expected to do that which an eminent lawyer admits his inability to do? With respect to the expense to be incurred . . . I desire to say that I am willing to pay a proper compensation for the work that may be performed, and so I doubt not are my constituents. It cannot cost a tythe of what the gentleman supposes: but if it does cost it all, sir, there is nothing that my constituents will more readily pay for than laws which they can find, and understand when found. And even if the Legislature shall, as it is intimated they may, reject the digest that may be prepared, under this provision, we shall have the confidence of our fellow citizens for the attempt we may have made to make the laws plain and intelligible.

I protest against any alteration of this provision. I hope that all foreign and heathenish words will be dispensed with, and that the English language alone will be used. I wish also that every law shall relate but to one subject. Our code of laws will then be readily referred to, and easily understood, and justice may be dealt out equally to all. If it is the desire of gentlemen here that the laws shall be simplified, I trust they will sustain this section. I admit that the retention of this section may militate against the interests of lawyers, but it will enable the plain, unlettered men of the Commonwealth to know what are the laws under which they live. Besides this, it will aid the administrator of justice, inasmuch as it will be the means of removing the difficulties under which Justices of the Peace, and even the Judges on the bench, labor in consequence of the many conflicting laws and decisions which now perplex and annoy them, and render justice so uncertain.

Mr. NUTTALL. Chitty I believe is the best writer on pleadings, and if he has not been able to lay down clear, intelligible and useful rules, I shall despair of obtaining them from any commission that we may appoint. Eminent as many of our lawyers are, the task will be a herculean one to whoever may undertake it. As to the use of certain Latin words, I am of opinion that they have become so common and so well understood, and are from their use so very expressive, that we had better not interfere with them, and create confusion by the change. . . .

The gentleman has made some remarks about special pleading. If he supposes that lawyers are more in favor of special pleading than other men, he is greatly mistaken. The great object that all lawyers have in view, is to come at the truth. How are you to do it? Can you do it better by the Civil code? If you can, take the plan of Mr. Livingston and adopt the Civil code.

I will now tell the house what can be done at a very small expense. I would suggest a modification of the clause now under consideration, and do away with the difference between Chancery and Common law proceedings. Take now the simplest kind of action—that of assumpsit, and you have an action that can be got through with in three or four months. For example, A files in Court a claim against B for the sum of $500 for goods and merchandise. He calls upon B to say, "did you buy all the property named in that account, and at what price? If you did not buy it all, how much, and what articles did you buy? If you did not buy it at the price therein stated, then at what price did you buy it? If you did not buy it at any specified price, did you buy it with the understanding to pay what it is worth, and, if so, how much is it worth?"

Now, B acknowledges that he bought all the articles, but without a fixed price on all. Very well; take a judgment for that. He acknowledges that he bought all except a pair of boots, which are charged seven dollars, for which he only agreed to pay five. Then you take a judgment so far. Now what would be the result of such a course as this? Why, you save a vast amount of time and expense, and you narrow down the question in dispute to the mere matter of two dollars. I only give this as a sample of the method by which our pleadings might be improved. . . .

Now, if I understand the gentleman correctly, he complains not that the ends of justice are not attained, but that they are attained in a manner unintelligible by the great mass of the people. But, sir, the gentleman will certainly admit that it is better they should be thus attained than not attained at all. If you strike out one plan, give us another, that will be equally as intelligible, and more simple; otherwise you gain nothing by the change. Give us a plan that will answer the purposes of justice, and be more simple than that now in use, and I will go for it, provided that while you simplify the rules of practice, you render them equally certain in their operation. Certainty is more necessary than simplicity; in point of fact, Mr. President, the special pleading of the present day, is done as much as anything for the purpose of saving expense to the litigants, and the time of Courts. What do you mean by special pleading? If you take an issue upon a fact, you must set it forth so that a Court and Jury, and the plaintiff and defendant, may understand what fact is to be tried—how much is admitted, and how much is denied. No man will deny that that end ought to be attained; all admit that it is attained by special pleading. Let the gentleman then take a plain, straight-forward course, and leave this matter in the hands of the Legislature, whose proper business it is to attend to such a matter as this. I stated when I was on my feet before, that I voted against the second section, because I was afraid that, like the State of Louisiana, the Legislature might go to great expense in this matter, which I think is altogether unnecessary.

Mr. TURNER. This is a matter which will never interest me much as a lawyer, as my days of practice are pretty much over; but I do regard this proposition as one of the most mischievous that has yet been brought under the consideration of this Convention. The gentleman declaims against Latin phrases which are common to law books; but I would ask him, has not every art and profession its peculiar technicalities? Does not the doctor label his medicines in a language known only to [himself]? Does not the house carpenter and the ship builder each use terms peculiar to his vocation, which he alone, as a general rule at least, understands? If the gentleman will read the Bridgewater Treatises, he will find in the various branches of science that he must study the technicalities peculiar to each, and he must understand them too, or he cannot understand the science to which they apply.

Something has been said, sir, about revising the code, and putting all law phrases in plain English. The people of New York undertook to do this, and how did they define a writ of *ne exeat?* Why, sir, they said it was a writ of "no go"; (laughter,) and no man understands what "no go" means any better than he understood a *"ne exeat."*

Language, sir, is in a great measure arbitrary, and we may as well learn the meaning of one word as of another. But I would ask, why should we go down into this little business, which the Legislature have never descended to? Are we, the great Constitution makers of the State of Kentucky, to spend our time here in determining how a man's boots shall be blacked, or in what manner his house should be swept? Sir, if we pass this resolution, we have not the power to carry it into effect. The Legislature have all power to do this, and it appears to me that this interference is useless and unnecessary. If ever we are to finish the business of this session, it is time that we refrained from dwelling on these little matters, and set ourselves seriously to work to embody the general principles of the Constitution which we are sent here to make.

Mr. STEVENSON. So far from regarding this as a matter of small importance, I think, sir, it is a question demanding our serious consideration. We have met to put the ship of State upon a new tack. We have said that the Legislature shall meet but once in every two years, and we have confined their duties to the passing only of general laws. We have made great alterations already in the jurisprudence of the State, and I think it is but wise that the question now before us should have the calm consideration of this body, and that with our new Courts and new Judges, we should have a new code and a new system of practice. One argument that has been used here in opposition to this course, is that it will involve the State in too much expense; but sir, in my opinion, it will not involve half so much expense as the present mode, besides obviating much delay and disappointment. There is a case reported in the papers to-day, which may serve to illustrate this assertion—the case of *Graves* v. *Graves*. The case is something like this: The man died, leaving a will by which he disposed of his property; the wife renounced the will, and demanded that the executors should set apart a portion of the property for her benefit. Now, here are lawyers feed at high rates; the cost of witnesses and jury, and all for what? Simply to decide what the rule of law is in such cases. Now, how many hundreds of dollars are often spent in deciding this simple question; and how often do we find the very best judges and lawyers in the land differing most widely on the simple question as to whether one statute has the effect of repealing another. . . .

I merely mention this to show that in the multiplication of statutes there is great difficulty in determining what the law really is, and hence the necessity of having some competent persons to arrange and classify, and digest our statutes. This is what I understand by the proposition of my friend; and I think there could not be a more appropriate time than the present to take this subject into our serious consideration, engaged as we now are in making a new Constitution. . . .

Mr. GHOLSON. When I introduced this proposition I heard no objection to it. It was so undeniably right, that I did not say a word in its support. I did not expect this stern opposition to it even now. Why, the Parliament of Great Britain, that country from which all our laws have come, has recently caused the laws of that country to be codified, for which purpose ten Judges were appointed, and they are now practising under their new code, while we adhere to that which is regarded as outlandish, and is discarded in the land of its birth. . . .

The codification, sir, of the law, is no new thing. It has been done in many parts of the world, and the advancing wealth and population of countries, and the mutations of civilization, will always render it periodically necessary. Lord Bacon tells us that when laws accumulate so as to render it necessary to revise them and collect their spirit into a new and intelligible system, that those who accomplish it are among the benefactors of mankind. In the profession of law there are two classes. One seeking to make the rules of justice exalted, and their application simple, and the other seeking to involve it in a labyrinth of perplexities. We know that when the laws of Rome became so immensely voluminous that justice was lost in its vast extent of rules, Justinian directed the compilation of that code, which did more than any other single work to restore Europe from the darkness of the middle ages, and shed abroad the illumination of legal science, and which still forms the basis of European jurisprudence.

Napoleon, when he ruled the destinies of France, ordered that the laws should be codified and digested . . . The progress of law reform did not stop here. Lord Brougham, the most renowned orator, and one of the most accomplished jurists and statesmen of England, within the last ten years, undertook to procure in the House of Lords a similar reform. England has found the old and cumbrous forms of administering justice, transmitted from the darkness of the feudal ages, unsuited to the present progress of society, and within that time her code of practice and pleading has been revised, and simplified, and we in Kentucky, at this hour, cling with fondness to a system tinged with feudal barbarism, after it has been exploded in the mother country. Statutory enactments and judicial decisions have done something to give it form and symmetry, and adapt it to our wants, but it still retains most of the crude features and barbarous characteristics of its origin.

Louisiana, which adopted the Civil law as the basis of its jurisprudence, with great wisdom secured the services of Edward Livingston, in the arrangement of her laws, and what has been the effect? The minds of the jurists of America are gradually turning to the Civil law, and they begin to give it the preference to the Common law. . . .

In the State of New York, in the year 1846, a feature similar to the one now under consideration was engrafted on its Constitution, appointing a commission to report to the Legislature such reforms as were necessary in the law. Those gentlemen, who rank among the first jurists in the nation, executed that order. The result of their labors has been adopted by the Legislature, and the people have derived the most solid benefits from it. They removed many of the old inconveniences, destroyed many of the old obstructions which clogged the avenues of justice, and have substituted reforms which the people of that State will never relinquish. I have looked at that report, in which the whole present code of procedure and practice does not occupy more than a fourth of the space occupied by one of our volumes of the Statutes, and it contains many great and wise alterations; but those alterations are now generally approved, both by the people and the profession. . . .

In Ohio, this subject has been urged with great zeal, ability, and perseverance, by Judge Walker, an eminent jurist, through the columns of the Western Law Journal. And the attention of the legal profession in the West has been urgently and eloquently invoked, for codification and reform, resulting from the necessity which day after day presses itself upon the consideration of the public; and I venture to predict that it will, at no distant day, be carried out in most of the States of the confederacy.

I have said thus much, Mr. President, to describe the progress of law reform in other countries and in the United States, and to show that by the adoption of a provision such as that under consideration, we may attain some of those benefits which other governments have secured. I do not anticipate, however, by such a provision to obtain a panacea for legal difficulties, or strip the law of those technicalities which have prevailed, and will ever prevail in a science so complex. But that is no reason why we should not do all in our power to revise, arrange, and simplify it, to make it as accessible as possible to the common understandings of men, and to make the administration of justice as plain as we can. It is desirable to remove the rubbish and set the house in order, though it is scarcely to be expected that it will always remain so. It is for these reasons that I advocate the commission, and believe in its utility. . . . But Mr. President, although I know I am not an interesting speaker, (and few farmers are,) yet I do not feel disposed to remain silent, whether I am the sole guardian of the farmers or not, and let this important measure be mutilated or defeated. The remarks of the gentlemen of the bar, show whence this opposition in reality springs. It is not the expense alone. No sir, this is the ostensible, but not the real cause; no sir, far from it. It is the effect, (as shown by the remarks of honorable gentlemen,) which they see this is to have upon that darling pet of the profession, "special pleading." It is I fear, because it seeks the abolition of that fruitful source of profit to the lawyers, and intolerable expense to all other classes of society, that causes it to be so violently opposed here by most of that class of the delegates. . . .

From this it will be seen most clearly, that the laws only, and not both laws and pleadings are to be in "plain English." I knew full well, sir, that it would not do to ask the lawyers in this body to do their pleadings in a plain, common sense, truthful English style. I knew they would not give up their fictions, falsehoods, and to all but themselves, unintelligible lingo. Hence all that I asked for was that the laws should be in "plain English."

I ask, sir, who can object to this that does not intend to keep the people in ignorance of what the laws really are? I ask, emphatically ask, gentlemen who propose to strike out this provision, why they do it? Why it is that they will present to the common farmer or mechanic, a law which, as an officer, he must be called upon to administer, in a language which he does not, cannot understand? The thing is unjust and unreasonable, and can have no other effect (and for this it is intended,) but to produce erroneous decisions which lawyers will get fees to reverse. It is the interest of all others but lawyers, that the laws should be plain and easily understood; that justice shall in all cases be done in the first instance. It is their interest that justice be not done, that litigation be multiplied and increased, that the laws shall be doubtful, dark, mysterious, and uncertain; this sir, is their meat and their drink; from this source it is that they amass their princely fortunes. But, sir, the day of retribution is at hand; a spirit of reform is abroad in the land. Some of our sister States have wiped these foul blots from their Statute books, and God speed the day when Kentucky—my glorious old mother Commonwealth—shall rise in her majesty, shake off the iron shackles which were forged in the dark days of feudalism and are now imposed by lawyer craft, and take her own true, proud, and republican stand along side of New York and Missouri. Sir, I have said it elsewhere and I repeat it here, that the object and inevitable effect of the present mode of pleading, and the rules of evidence, is to narrow down the case and prevent justice from being done. From the moment a case is docketed in Court, the whole object of the lawyers on both sides, is to get the advantage in pleading, narrow down the case, exclude testimony, and prevent justice being done. So uncertain are the distinctive lines that mark the difference between trespass, and trespass on the case, and between Common law and Chancery suits, that the best lawyers in the land are often at a loss, and bring their suits wrong. This is notorious, it is undeniably true, sir, and yet honorable gentlemen, sensible men, oppose "legal reform." Again, sir, a plaintiff's own witness, when showing as clear a case of wrong as words can show, often drives him out of Court with all the bill of costs to pay; and for what, sir? Not because he has not been wronged, not because justice is not on his side, but because some old British form had not been complied with, or because an ignorant or inattentive lawyer had misapplied one of the various outlandish phrases by which suits at law are designated. And do these things need no reform, sir? How long are we to bear these impositions? For one, sir, in the name of the sixteen hundred freemen who sent me here, against their longer continuance I solemnly protest. These various forms of actions, these metaphysical distinctions between those forms, together with the various arbitrary and senseless rules of evidence, stand like driftwood in the channel of what should be the pure stream of justice. They pollute its limpid waters. They obstruct its current; nay, sir, they often turn it back and cause it to flow the wrong way. These things, sir, destroy the confidence of the people in the Courts of the country. To the common citizen, when he enters a Circuit Court all is as dark as the gloom of midnight; he neither does nor can comprehend what is going on before him. Ask for a reformation of these things, and what is the reply? It is, touch not the wisdom of a thousand years. Yes, sir, 'tis the wisdom of a thousand years devoted to the up-building of lawyer craft; to the manufacture of hair splitting and undefinable legal distinctions that have no common sense in them, that never was intended to, never did, never will, nor never can promote and facilitate the administration of justice.

THE MACHINERY OF JUSTICE

The Judicial Function

THEODORE SEDGWICK

Theodore Sedgwick (1811–1859) wrote extensively on legal and judicial problems. He conceived of himself as a Jacksonian, a strong sympathizer with the laborers and antagonist of "monopolies," and he edited the political writings of William Leggett. But certain aspects of the movement, which touched him professionally—such as the popular election of judges—could never be acceptable to him.

AMONG OTHER SIGNS of the attention paid in England to this subject, is the recent establishment of *"The Society for promoting the Amendment of the Law,"* composed of their first lawyers, and promulgating its opinions through *The Law Review*. From this magazine we take the following rules for the formation of a Judiciary. It may not be amiss to examine them with reference to our own system. . . .

The first rule requires a sufficient number of Judges. In this respect we are grossly and glaringly deficient. The judicial force, under the Constitution of 1821, never was sufficient for its business since the day of its creation. The upper judiciary are worked like slaves, and are immensely in arrears. The Court of Chancery, the Supreme Court and this Circuit, present a condition of things disgraceful to the State, most pernicious to the suitor, and ruinous to the Bar; for it is not to be forgotten, that however severe the pressure of delay on each particular litigant, all the combined and accumulated evils press with ten-fold force on the head of the profession. Indeed, the mischief is so great, that all the trouble and expense of a Convention will be as nothing, if it simply secures the prompt trial and decision of cases.

The present state of things can be remedied by the power to make temporary appointments of Commissioners, to clear the calendars, and it probably can be remedied in no other way.

It is very doubtful whether, with our parsimonious notions of economy, we shall ever be willing to pay for a sufficient regular judicial system. But the gradual accumulation of business can always be kept under, if there exists any where the power to appoint temporary Commissioners. In fact, if such a power now existed, as far as the judiciary is concerned, no Convention would be needed.

Theodore Sedgwick, "Law Reform," *Western Law Journal* (January, 1846), III, p. 145.

The introduction of such a principle would have every way the happiest effects. It would remedy the evils resulting from the impossibility of anticipating or keeping pace with the growth of our population. It would hold out a stimulus to professional ambition, and at the same time serve as an excellent test of professional merit.

The second rule requires justice to be locally administered. As far as *trials* are concerned, our system is not very defective. As to *arguments,* it is intolerably burdensome. Every motion, however trivial, has to be made either at New York, Albany, Utica, Rochester, or Saratoga, and the amount of delay and expense to which this leads is unimaginable.

The third rule is sufficiently adhered to in the Court of Chancery, inasmuch as the whole power is vested in a single individual. But in the Supreme Court, the Judges are carefully sequestered from all contact with the people. They are denied all personal knowledge of the suitor, the witnesses or the jurors, and withdrawn from the public gaze; unseen by and unknown to the masses whom they govern, they promulgate their great decrees. There is no individual responsibility whatever.

The fifth rule respects the tenure of the judicial office, and fixes it for life. . . .

The total absence of responsibility in the judicial officer (for impeachment is practically a nullity) would undoubtedly be an anomaly in our system. We have introduced a check of a very absurd character. The limitation of sixty years secures short tenure of service, but it puts an end to the judicial career just at a time when it may, in many cases, be the most useful. This applies to the Supreme Court and Chancellor. The Judges of the Court of Error are even less permanent. Elected only for four years—elected as politicians—nothing, certainly, can be less stable.

The election of Judges directly by the people, as Judges, and for judicial service alone, for tenures of reasonable length, with an indefinite capacity for re-election, would, unquestionably, with all its objectionable features, give more permanence to the judiciary than it now possesses. We are speaking now of permanence alone, and in a relative point of view. . . .

The sixth rule forbids promotion. We have no such principle, nor does it seem desirable. To declare a human being in the first place irresponsible, and in the second place to remove all motive of emulation, seems at first sight to be a pretty good receipt for making a tyrant and a drone. Promotion on the Bench may undoubtedly result from party considerations; but after all, we have not the creative power: we must take man as we find him, and endeavor, by checking his evil propensities, and stimulating his good ones, to get all we can out of him. It is not the way to begin this process by enacting that his best efforts shall be crowned by no reward.

The seventh rule forbids fees. The execrable system is in full force in some of our Courts, and banished from others; and perhaps no difference is more strongly marked than that produced by the absence or presence of this corrupting mode of judicial remuneration. One long shout of satisfaction would rise from the whole Bar, if judicial fees were abolished, and the benefit would not rest here. Professional fees would follow; and the lawyer, like any other laborer, be forced to make his own arrangement with his client.

The eighth rule excludes judicial patronage, and is in general force here, with the exception of the Clerks of their own Courts, whom it seems proper enough to place in this way under their control.

The ninth rule forbids any connection between the judicial and political character, and is carried out among us.

The tenth rule, which declares the judicial and legislative functions incompatible, is grossly violated in the Court of Errors.

The eleventh rule, in regard to the compensation of the Judiciary, is almost entirely disregarded among us. A very large portion of the expenses of the system is thrown in the shape of fees directly on the suitors, thus making a very unequal and unjust system of taxation.

The twelfth rule provides for Courts of Appeal, and is again entirely disregarded in our Court of Errors, which is a very bad copy of the worst portion of the English law system—the House of Lords.

The thirteenth, so far as it contemplates the exclusion of party or personal influence, is most desirable, and most impracticable. No such state of things ever has existed, nor this side of the millennium can it exist. Judges will, as a general rule, always be selected from the party in power; and as to personal influence, there is no particular reason to believe it less potent with Presidents and Governors than, on the other side of the water, with the crowned vice-gerents of Heaven. The rule thus far is purely Utopian.

The fourteenth provides for the publicity of judicial proceedings, with the exception of those cases, however, where it is supposed that public decency, or the peace of families, requires secrecy.

It may be well doubted, if any such exceptions should be tolerated in this country. Where *family* is a thing known to the law, it may be otherwise. We make, or intend to make, but one set of rules for "High Life above Stairs," and for "High Life below Stairs." One of the very greatest checks of crime is public exposure, and it would be no little incentive to evil in the wealthier classes, if they were made certain that their delinquencies would be shrouded from the public eye, in the recesses of a secret tribunal. The absolute publicity of our Argus-Briareus press, with all its inconveniences and mischiefs, has great counterbalancing benefits.

We have thus rapidly run over these rules, laid down by high foreign authority, as the test and criterion of a good judiciary. And one thing should be borne in mind, that it is far more important deeply to impress on our minds the principles which should govern the matter, than to

attempt to work out any entire and complete system. What is desirable
is, to settle in our minds the principles on which the judiciary should be
based. That done, their application is comparatively an easy matter.

Which is preferable—the circuit, or the nisi-prius system? Shall the
Court of last resort possess legislative as well as judicial functions? What
shall be the tenure of the judicial office—elective, or by appointment?
Shall the Courts of Law and of Equity be kept distinct, or their powers
blended in the same tribunal? These questions, and questions of this kind,
require in each man's mind clear and distinct answers. When that is done,
the rest is easy.

It should also be kept in view that the Convention cannot act upon
matters of detail. They can organize a judiciary—they cannot cure the
evils which deform our practice and pleading. These things are matters
which require reform at once, careful and extensive; and the Convention
could do nothing better than to organize a Commission for the express
purpose of making such alterations as the progress of the rest of our
jurisprudence requires. Our real law has undergone a complete modification: our commercial law is based upon reason; but we are practising in
the nineteenth century, with all the formulas, forms, and fuss of the
seventeenth.

Such a commission, in the hands of men conversant with the working
of the present system—not too young to be unacquainted with all the
details of practice, nor too old to be indifferent to the importance of
change, would, of itself, produce immense good.

Unsuitability of Juries

JAMES FENIMORE COOPER

*Over the years taste has changed, and Cooper is now read more for his
social criticism than for his adventure stories. Although he was not a
Federalist of the old school, Cooper was, in both a social and a legal sense,
extremely affected by tradition and conservative principles. The basis of his
ideal republic is "traditional common sense": the individual's rights are protected by the natural social order, and common rights are protected by
careful constitutional balance. He frequently shows a distrust of mass
democracy and of mass law—especially its underestimation of tradition.
He feels that law should reflect the "natural" social values—and that a
social hierarchy is both natural and desirable. These ideas are reflected
in his characters Aristabulus Bragg and Steadfast Dodge, and even more
clearly in his support of the landlords during the Anti-Rent riots in New
York. Such acts violated the contract clause of the Constitution. But it
was more significant to Cooper that the riots were in opposition to precisely the group whose values and class-consciousness he so admired.*

James Fenimore Cooper, *The Ways of the Hour* (1850), p. v.

THE OBJECT OF THIS BOOK is to draw the attention of the reader to some of the social evils that beset us; more particularly in connection with the administration of criminal justice. So long a time has intervened since the thought occurred, and so many interruptions have delayed the progress of the work, that it is felt the subject has been very imperfectly treated; but it is hoped that enough has been done to cause a few to reflect on a matter of vital importance; one that to them may possess the interest of novelty.

A strange indifference exists as to the composition of the juries. In our view, the institution itself, so admirable in a monarchy, is totally unsuited to a democracy. The very principle that renders it so safe where there is a great central power to resist, renders it unsafe in a state of society in which few have sufficient resolution to attempt even to resist popular impulses.

A hundred instances might be given in which the juries of this country are an evil; one or two of which we will point out. In trials between railroad companies and those who dwell along their lines, prejudice is usually so strong against the former, that justice for them is nearly hopeless. In certain parts of the country, the juries are made the instrument of defeating the claims of creditors who dwell at a distance, and are believed to have interests opposed to the particular community where the debtor resides. This is a most crying evil, and has been the source of many and grievous wrongs. Whenever there is a motive for creating a simulated public opinion, by the united action of several journals, justice is next to hopeless; such combinations rarely, if ever, occurring in its behalf. In cases that are connected with the workings of political schemes, and not unfrequently in those in which political men are parties to the suits, it is often found that the general prejudices or partialities of the out-door factions enter the jury-box. This is a most serious evil too; for, even when the feeling does not produce a direct and flagrant wrong, it is very apt so far to temper the right as to deprive it of much of its virtue. In a country like this, in which party penetrates to the very bottom of society, the extent of this evil can be known only to those who are brought into close contact with the ordinary workings of the institution.

In a democracy, proper selections in the material that are necessary to render juries safe, become nearly impossible. Then, the tendency is to the accumulation of power in bodies of men; and in a state of society like our own, the juries get to be much too independent of the opinion of the court. It is precisely in that condition of things in which the influence and authority of the judge guide the juror, and the investigation and substantial power of the juror react on the proceedings of the court, that the greatest benefits have been found to accrue from this institution. The reverse of this state of things will be very likely to produce the greatest amount of evil.

It is certain that the juries are falling into disrepute throughout the length and breadth of the land. The difficulty is to find a substitute. As they are bodies holding the lives, property and character of every member of the community, more or less, in their power, it is not to be supposed that the masses will surrender this important means of exercising their authority voluntarily, or with good will. Time alone can bring reform through the extent of the abuses.

The writer has not the vanity to suppose that anything contained in this book will produce a very serious impression on the popularity of the jury. Such is not its design. All that is anticipated is to cause a portion of his readers to reflect on the subject; persons who probably have never yet given it a moment of thought.

There is a tendency, at the present time, to court change for its own sake. This is erroneously termed a love of reform. Something very like a revolution is going on in our midst, while there is much reason to apprehend that few real grievances are abated; the spurious too exclusively occupying the popular mind, to render easy a just distinction between them. When an American prates about aristocracy, it is pretty safe to set him down as knavish or ignorant. It is purely cant; and the declaimers would be puzzled to point to a single element of the little understood and much-decried institution, the country being absolutely without any, unless the enjoyment of the ordinary rights of property can be so considered. But the demagogue must have his war-cry, as well as the Indian; and it is probable he will continue to whoop as long as the country contains minds weak enough to furnish him with dupes.

Unanimity in the Jury Verdict

KNICKERBOCKER MAGAZINE

Jury trial, then as now, was a focus of dispute. English jurists, notably Lord Devlin, have recently extolled the virtues of obviating the delays and uncertainties of jury trials in civil cases. In 1841 the traveler John Henry Vessey reflected Fenimore Cooper's view: "Such is the go-ahead character of these people that they try a man by public opinion beforehand and when they are summoned on a jury to try him on the evidence, they swear they are now unbiased, having expressed an opinion. . . . I wish that some Englishmen sighing at home for more liberty than would do them good would come out here, and see how democratic institutions work in this country."

Lawyers complained that pleadings and issues to the jury were so obscure that special instructions and, in many instances, a redraft of verdicts was necessary. The susceptibility of juries was underlined in an

"The Trial by Jury," *Knickerbocker Magazine* (June, 1840), XV, p. 478.

anecdote told about Jeremiah Mason. "Oh, Mr. Webster is much the greatest," stated a jury member. "And yet Mr. Mason's clients won all the verdicts." Came the reply: "That was because Mr. Mason always happened to be on the right side."

IT IS NOT OUR WONT to quarrel with antiquity, or to feel favor for modern innovation, in any shape. The "march of improvement" is too rapid altogether, to suit either our tastes or our habitudes; and as a lawyer, loving the profession to which we were bred, it must be a very glaring defect in the common law principles and practices of the science, which could lead *us*, at any rate, into the desire, or even the willingness, to see them superseded by any change of form, or novelty of administration. We shall claim, therefore, at least the merit of sincerity in the remarks we make, and we hope at the same time so to conduct the discussion, as to convince the reader that our propositions have been well considered.

Our present business is with the principle, or rather desecration of principle, which requires UNANIMITY IN THE VERDICT. *That* principle has been rotten, from its first adoption, and is abundantly more so now than ever. The very reasons that might have been urged in its favor some half a dozen centuries since, are among the strongest that could be adduced against it in the present state of society, and under the meliorated and "more enlightened" ideas of modern times.

While government was arbitrary, and while the prince and his minions were in constant warfare with the people; when regal power, and regal power alone, made up the main spring of authority; it was undoubtedly of great consequence to the subject to hold this barrier between himself and the royal prerogative. It was a protection of potent force. He could not be punished for crime, real or imaginary, against the crown, but by the unanimous decision of his peers; and of course the chances of unjust conviction were very much diminished by the requirement that the *whole* panel of twelve men should pronounce upon his case, instead of a majority. In such times, it is conceded that the system was favorable to liberty, and the circumstance may in some measure justify the eulogium bestowed upon this mode of trial; especially when it is contrasted with the absurdities of other modes in vogue during the darker ages of English jurisprudence. Compared, for instance with the "wager of battle," with the "fire and water ordeal," by which Queen Emma singed her slippers; compared with the *peine forte et dure*, in which the prisoner was pressed to death, upon the presumption that he was guilty because he chose to stand mute under the accusation against him, the trial by jury may very well have been claimed as a "palladium"; under whatever form of absurdity it may have been framed or conducted. It is our object, however, to prove that the principle has no possible application to *our* state of civilization, and our modifications of legal polity; and in carrying out our views on this subject, we shall confine ourselves strictly to two points.

FIRST, that there is no magic in the number *twelve*; but that a jury composed of nine, eleven, thirteen, or fifteen, would be abundantly preferable; and,

SECONDLY, that the requirement of unanimity in making up a verdict, is alike at war with common sense, common justice, and with the well known operations of human nature; involving a profound absurdity upon its very face, and calling upon mankind for the performance of a moral impossibility. . . .

In the first place, such a requirement is directly in the teeth of human nature itself. No twelve—no three men, were ever yet congregated upon the globe, whose minds coincided. They may chance to agree upon an isolated point; they may come together on a given proposition; but no plurality of mere men can interchange opinions during half an hour, with an *honest* concurrence in each others' views; and however courtesy and good feeling may seem to assimilate them, they differ; deferentially, perhaps, but still they differ. To suppose that a dozen men may come to the same conclusion on the clearest case that may be submitted to their judgment, is to look for a mental phenomenon which the law exhibits very little wisdom in calling for. . . .

But, these are abstractions; let us look at the subject in a less general view. What is the practical operation of our jury system?

We hesitate not to say that it is equally militant with the republicanism which we profess so much to reverence, and with all the ends of substantial justice; alike repugnant to the general spirit of our institutions, and to the wholesome dispensation of equal laws. What *is* the character of this system? How *does* it work in practice? Is the verdict of the jury the judgment of the twelve "peers" who compose the panel, or is it the major voice of those men? It is neither the one nor the other, except by the merest accident; and it rarely speaks, even nominally, the opinion of the whole body, without the exercise of a gambling resort to chance, or a fraudulent compromise with conscience. Wretches sometimes

"hang, that jurymen may dine."

In other words, juries are urged into unanimity by their appetites, and agree to think alike, lest their dinner should get cold. . . .

It were strong language to use, we acknowledge, but, it is a settled opinion with us, that *as much felony is committed* WITHIN *the jury boxes, as is brought before them for trial!* At any rate, more *perjury* is there perpetrated, than is ever put regularly on trial before courts of justice; and most of this is brought about by the obstinacy or stupidity of the minor number. It is not often that the *jury* decides the case. It is perhaps a single one of the number!

A single juror cannot, to be sure, give a substantive verdict against the opinions of his eleven compeers, but he can always, and very often *does* perform acts that amount to the same thing. He can prevent the administration of justice; he can nullify the honest efforts of his brethren, and render of no avail all their disposition to do right; he can save from the gallows or the penitentiary the criminal whose punishment is essential to the well-being of society; in short, he can, by his own stupid *sic volo,* set aside not only all the interests of the community, but he can abrogate all the laws of the land. He not only holds a veto on the entire criminal code, but he has in his hands the power of perverting the course of justice in all its channels. Every contract between man and man, every issue on which depend the rights of individuals, is at his mercy. An Englishman or an American has very little reason for the boast that he finds safety and protection in the juries of his country. He finds no such thing. Juries, *as juries,* are utterly powerless in the premises; for eleven of the number are completely controlled by any duodecimal fraction that may choose to make itself of more arithmetical consequence than the *whole number.* . . .

Our jury system is out of all analogy with the genius of the government. It recognizes a principle utterly at war with the primal considerations upon which that government was founded, and breaks in wantonly upon the symmetry of its proportions. If there be any one feature more to be admired, and more sedulously to be cherished, than another, in the frame-work of this government, it is the principle that we are under the guidance of majorities; that we have here provided for that most rational, the *only* rational *régime,* in civil government, *the preponderance of the major opinion*; the doctrine that the few shall submit to the many. In other words, we have come to the conclusion in this country, that the balance of equity is rather likelier to be found in the majority than in the minority. At all events, it is a principle pervading every department of our polity, (save the one under consideration,) that it is somewhat safer to confide power to ten men, than to one. So at least we understand the genius of our institutions; such we believe to be its scope and tendency; and so we *know* are they recorded in the written evidences of the popular will; so do they stand in the constitution of the United States, of the several states of the union, in the respective statute-books of the states and of the nation; and in every other muniment which the people have thrown around their political household for the defence of their rights and their liberties. Do they see any sense in placing the juridical jurisdiction on a different footing? Are they of opinion that the *lesser voice* is safest in a court of justice, while every where else it is only looked upon as wrong, because it *is* the lesser voice? Is there so much magic in a jury-box, that men actually change their natures as soon as they enter? Is it the opinion that one man there is worth a dozen?

We are aware that some of the foregoing remarks may appear to prove too much. It may seem, or "seem to seem," to the caviller, for instance, that it is undermining the main proposition, to say, as we have said, that it is next to impossible to get any three men to agree on a given subject, and that *therefore* we ourselves reason against a fundamental element of our own argument; since if *that* number can never be brought to exact coincidence of opinion, it is preposterous to suppose that *seven* out of twelve men can do so. Softly and soothly, Monsieur Sophist, if it is perfectly convenient for you! You, instead of ourselves, are probably upon an "erroneous scent."

It strikes us that *seven* men are rather more likely to agree, than twelve; at any rate, less likely to "agree to disagree," by reason of the utter impossibility of agreeing, when even a single individual of the number holds full control over the entire panel. So long as it is understood that any number, no matter how much short of the whole, hold the verdict in their own hands, there is of course no hope, no inducement, for that matter, to modify opinion, or concede sentiment. Eleven jurors may in vain have done their best to reconcile minor discordances of view, if the twelfth man has made up his mind to decide the case according to his own arbitrary (perhaps corrupt) determination. If he chooses to do so, there is no power on earth to prevent him. *He* is the "palladium of liberty," not the jury! It is idle to prate of "twelve peers"; it is *one* "peer" who sits in judgment. The trial *per pais*, or by the country, of which we boast so much, is simply a trial by a single individual blockhead; or at best a trial in which the law gives to a few boobies the power of overruling a majority of sensible men. . . .

If any number less than the largest, in a given body, is to govern, it were as well at once to acknowledge ourselves monarchists, and discard the doctrines which we profess to cherish. Let us say, honestly and aboveboard, that the *sic jubeo* of Russia and of Turkey is preferable to the democratic principle of our own government. Let us elect our law-givers, our presidents, governors, and all subordinate magistrates, on that blessed plan; declaring every candidate who is lucky enough to receive the least number of votes, duly chosen to office. Having *secured* a minority, the presumption is clearly in favor of his fitness!

The Daughter and Servant

JOHNSON V. NOBLE

Johnson v. Noble *represents a legislative alternative to judicial trials. It adumbrated the time when a vast body of disputes would be taken away from the courts and vested in other agencies for the sake of speed and efficiency—though at the price of other values.*

13 *New Hamp.* (1842), p. 286.

CASE AGAINST THE DEFENDANT, for debauching one L. M. Johnson, the daughter and servant of the plaintiff, *per quod servitium amisit,* &c.

The action was commenced May 1, 1839, and made returnable at the then next September term of the court of common pleas in this county, at which term, by an agreement of the parties, it was referred under a rule of court to the decision of certain persons as referees. At the hearing before the referees, the deposition of said L. M. Johnson was read in evidence, in which she testified to the fact of promises of the defendant to marry her, made both before and after the alleged injury. She also testified that at the time of the alleged injury she resided in the family of one Waldron, as a domestic; that during her stay at Waldron's she made and considered her mother's house her home; was in the habit of affording assistance to her mother, the plaintiff, by giving her money from time to time, and of going to her mother's and assisting her by her personal labor a fortnight at a time, as often as once a year, and sometimes more frequently. She further testified, on cross examination, that she was twenty-four years old in July, 1838, and had lived at Waldron's nearly four years prior to March, 1838—the period of the injury complained of.

The referees made a report, awarding damages and costs of reference in favor of the plaintiff. . . .

WOODS, J. The objections made by the defendant, and specifically stated in the case, are not sustained by the decisions of the English courts, and of the courts of this country, and cannot therefore prevail against the report.

They resolve themselves substantially into this—that the referees have not acted in conformity with their authority, inasmuch as, according to the view of the defendant, they were bound to decide the cause upon legal and competent evidence, and according to the strict rules of law; whereas, as it is alleged, they have not so decided, but have decided the matter submitted, upon incompetent evidence and in disregard of the law; and the evidence which was admitted of the breach of promise of marriage was incompetent to prove any fact properly in issue upon the case before the referees; and the proofs laid before them showed, that no such relation of master and servant existed between the plaintiff and her daughter, as would in point of law give a right of action, and warrant a finding in favor of the plaintiff.

Assuming the positions relied upon to be true in point of fact; that is, assuming that evidence not admissible upon a trial at law was laid before the referees, and that upon the facts proved their decision was not according to strict principles of law; nevertheless, we are all of the opinion that the decision was well authorized, and that those circumstances furnish no ground for setting aside the report.

It is unquestionably among the fundamental and well established rules upon the subject of arbitrament, that the action of the referees must conform to the submission. Their whole authority, indeed, whether the submission be under a rule of court or otherwise, springs from the act of the parties in making the submission; and, as a necessary and legitimate consequence, any exercise of power by them, in making a decision, not in conformity with the intention of the parties as indicated in the submission, is wholly unauthorized.

And, on the other hand, it has long been a familiar practice, for parties having subjects of difference, to establish tribunals of their own choice, for the determination of their controversies, pending in court or otherwise; and the judgments of those tribunals, made fairly within the scope of the authority conferred, have long been regarded, sanctioned and enforced in courts of law and equity, by each according to its authority and legitimate mode of proceeding, as the results of proceedings well authorized by law, and binding upon the parties.

And certain it is, that in no point of view can such agreements be regarded as against sound policy,—as being inconvenient or detrimental to those who choose to resort to them, or to others; and there would seem to be no reason why such agreements and the awards fairly made in pursuance of them, should not be sustained. In fact, the policy of the law is most decidedly in favor of settlements by arbitrators, and their awards should be sustained whenever it can be done consistently with the rules of law. And it seems accordingly to be well settled, that it is competent for parties to submit their matters in difference, as well in relation to the law as the fact, to the decision of arbitrators or referees, and to bind themselves by their judgments thereon. . . .

Under a general submission, therefore—by which I mean a submission containing no express reservation or limitation upon the authority conferred—both the law and fact are submitted to the judgment of the arbitrators, or referees, for their consideration and decision. And it is very well settled, that in such case arbitrators are not restricted by the submission to decide according to strict principles of law, but their decision will be in conformity with the submission, although it be made in disregard of the law, and contrary thereto. They are not bound to decide upon "mere dry principles of law," but may decide upon principles of equity and good conscience, and may make their award *"ex aequo et bono."* . . .

In the case under consideration, the submission was general and unrestricted as to the power conferred, and the mode of the exercise of that power. The report is silent as to the principles and grounds of the decision; and no aid of the court is asked by the report, either in the determination of the law or facts of the case; either in express terms, or by implication. The referees have exercised the power conferred upon them, as rightfully they might, in the determination of both the law and the facts of the case, without such aid, and it falls not within the proper exercise of the authority of the court to set aside, or in any other way disturb the report made under such circumstances.

2. Common Law or Code?

THE BENEFITS PROPOSED

Massachusetts Commissioners

The Massachusetts Commissioners, whose report had nationwide effects, were headed by Mr. Justice Story. He described the appointment: "Much against my will I was placed at the head of the commission. We shall report favorably to the codification of some branches of the commercial law. But the report will be very qualified and limited in its objects. We have not yet become votaries to the notions of Jeremy Bentham." Though their recommendations moved the legislature to the appointment of a commission to codify the civil law, the code it recommended in 1844 was rejected.

THE THREE LEADING QUESTIONS presented for the consideration of the Commissioners are:

1. The practicability of reducing to a written and systematic code the common law of Massachusetts, or any part thereof.

2. The expediency of such a reduction, if practicable.

3. The plan or plans, by which the same can be best accomplished, if expedient. . .

I. The Commissioners are, in the first place, of opinion, that it is not expedient to attempt the reduction to a Code of the entire body of the common law of Massachusetts, either in its general principles, or in the deductions from or the applications of those principles, so far as they have been ascertained by judicial decisions, or are incontrovertibly established.

II. The Commissioners are, in the next place, of opinion that it is expedient to reduce to a Code those principles and details of the common law of Massachusetts, in civil cases, which are of daily use and familiar application to the common business of life and the present state of property and personal rights and contracts, and which are now so far ascertained and established as to admit of a scientific form and arrangement, and are capable of being announced in distinct and determinate propositions. What portions of the common law properly fall under this predicament will be in some measure considered hereafter.

III. The Commissioners are, in the next place, of opinion, that it is

---

Report of Commissioners to the Governor of the Commonwealth of Massachusetts, *Story's Miscellaneous Writings* (1852), pp. 698, 715.

expedient to reduce to a Code the common law, as to the definition, trial and punishment of crimes, and the incidents thereto.

IV. The Commissioners are, in the next place, of opinion, that the law of evidence, as applicable both to civil and criminal proceedings, should be reduced to a Code.

And, in order to guard against any objections founded upon a misconception of the nature, objects, and effects of such a codification, the Commissioners propose to insert in such a Code, the following fundamental rules for its interpretation and application.

I. The Code is to be interpreted and applied to future cases, as a Code of the common law of Massachusetts, and not as a Code of mere positive or statute law. It is to be deemed an affirmance of what the common law now is, and not as containing provisions in derogation of that law, and therefore subject to a strict construction.

II. Consequently, it is to furnish the rules for decisions in courts of justice, not only in cases directly (*ex directo*) within its terms, but indirectly, and by analogy, in cases where, as a part of the common law, it would and ought to be applied by courts of justice, in like manner.

III. In all cases not provided for by the Code, or governed by the analogies therein contained, the common law of Massachusetts, as now existing, is to furnish the rules for decision, unless so far as it is repugnant to the common law affirmed in the Code, or to the statute law of the State.

Such is the basis of the Code proposed by the Commissioners, and such the principles, by which they propose, that those who shall be called upon to perform the duty of codification, should be guided.

The Commissioners are aware, that there are many objections, which have been and may be urged, not only against any codification of the common law, in the broadest sense of the terms, but also against any codification whatever, even of the limited nature and extent which they have ventured to recommend. These objections have been urged not only at home, but abroad; not only in countries governed by the common law, but in countries governed by the civil law, and by their own customary law; not only in public debates, but in elaborate treatises by jurists of distinguished reputation and ability. A proper respect, therefore, for the opinions thus promulgated, requires them to take notice of some of the most prominent objections, and to submit such answers as have occurred to them touching the subject.

One of the most general objections urged against the establishment of a Code is, the utter impossibility of making it perfect, or applicable to all future changes in the condition, rights, and property of a nation. It has been said, that no system of laws can remain for a great length of time unchanged; for the progress, or even the regress of civil society, must constantly call for new modifications of the existing laws; and that one of the peculiar excellencies of the common law consists in its adaptation to all circumstances, and, in a general sense, to all the exigencies which civil society may present. It is not necessary to controvert the general truth of this remark. On the contrary, it may be fully admitted and yet in no degree impair the reasoning in favor of a Code. The fact that no system of human laws can be made so perfect as not to require future revisions, modifications, amendments, and even partial repeals, in the new changes of society, furnishes no just objection to the adoption of some positive laws, providing for the ordinary concerns of a nation. It would be deemed little short of an absurdity to declare, that, because no perfect laws can be made, therefore no laws should be made. Even the common law does not pretend, in the slightest degree, to be a perfect system. On the contrary, it has undergone and is constantly undergoing changes, to meet the new exigencies of society; and the aid of Legislature is constantly invoked to cure its defects, and improve its remedial justice. If the common law had the theoretical perfection and excellence attributed to it in the objection (which can be admitted only with many qualifications and exceptions), still, it is not perceived how this perfection and excellence are impaired by putting into a positive text, what is supposed, by the objection itself, to be clear and determinate, and to make it rest, not upon disputable deductions, but upon the positive sanctions of the Legislature, declaring it to be the common law. In truth, the objection, though in its form general, seems principally addressed to a case where a nation should establish a particular Code of laws, and abolish all other laws not provided for in that Code. In such a case, it may be admitted, that the unavoidable imperfections of the Code would often produce very great mischief and injustice, and require incessant enactments by the Legislature to overcome them. In this view the objection has no application to codification, as proposed by the Commissioners; for every thing not governed by the Code is to be left precisely as it now is. Courts of justice are to be at full liberty to apply the existing common law to non-enumerated cases, exactly as they now do. And, from the materials thus furnished by judicial decisions, improvements and additions may, from time to time, be engrafted by the Legislature on the Code itself. It will thus become, what it ought to be, a perpetual index to the known law, gradually refining, enlarging and qualifying its doctrines, and, at the same time, bringing them together in a concise and positive form for public use.

Another objection, which has been urged by distinguished jurists of continental Europe, is, that the jurisprudence of a country (in their sense of the phrase) is perpetually changing its form and character with every succeeding age; and any attempt to give it permanency in its principles or its applications must make it inflexible, and unfit for the purposes of social justice. Thus, for example, it is asserted, that the customary law of some of the continental nations is in a perpetual though gradual state of change; and that this is a state most useful and salutary to be preserved; for otherwise the jurisprudence of one age would become obligatory upon another, and prevent the improvements in it which might be best adapted to its prosperity and social advancement. This objection, whatever may be its force or value when applied to the state of the customary law in some of the countries of continental Europe, vanishes when it is attempted to be applied to our common law. In America and in England, the common law is not, in the sense of the objection, of such a changeable nature. When once a doctrine is fully recognized as a part of the common law, it for ever remains a part of the system, until it is altered by the Legislature. A doctrine of the common law settled three hundred years ago is just as conclusive now, in a case which falls within it, as it was then. No court of justice can disregard it, or dispense with it; and nothing short of legislative power can abrogate it. With us the notion that courts of justice ought to be at liberty from time to time to change established doctrines to suit their own views of convenience or policy, would be treated as a most alarming dogma, subversive of some of the best rights of a free people, and especially of the right to have justice administered upon certain fixed and known principles. Our ancestors adopted in its fullest meaning the maxim, that it is a wretched servitude, where the law is vague and uncertain. Hence it is, that precedents in our courts of justice are of very high authority, and, with rare exceptions, conclusive as to the principles which they decide and establish; and subsequent judges are not at liberty to depart from them, when they have once become a rule of rights or of property. The whole of the judicial institutions in England and America rest upon this doctrine as their only solid foundation. But upon the Continent of Europe, or at least in some parts of it, the case is very different. The decisions of courts of justice (technically called jurisprudence) go no further than to decide the merits of the particular case. They furnish no determinate rule for other cases of a like nature. Precedents are not of absolute authority, or, in a general sense, of any cogent obligation. The doctrines of the judges of one age may be, and are disregarded by those of another. And it is quite competent for an advocate to insist upon principles and reasoning which are adverse to a long train of decisions, and entirely subversive of their authority. The objection, therefore, so far as it can apply to America and England, is an objection, not to a Code, but to the common law itself; for the common law has this very inflexibility of character, and permanence of doctrine, of which the objection complains. With us in Massachusetts, the common law is now just as much of general obligation, and of general fixedness in its doctrines, and as binding upon courts of justice, as it would be if reduced to a Code, and no more. When new cases arise, they are governed (as we have seen) by such analogies to those which have already been decided, or by such principles of natural justice, as are properly applicable to them. When old cases arise, the established doctrines furnish the sole rule, by which they are decided.

But though this last objection is principally, if not exclusively, confined to the jurists of continental Europe, there is one of a kindred nature, which is sometimes pressed by the opponents of codification on both sides of the Atlantic. It is, that the moment that the common law shall become the text of a positive code, it will cease to be common law; it will be inflexible in its applications, and subject to none of those implied and reasonable exceptions and modifications, which now constitute its peculiar character. This objection would certainly have much weight, if it were a necessary result that the codification of the common law would thus destroy its flexibility, and reduce it to a hard and unyielding positive text. But the Commissioners are of opinion that no such result would or ought to follow. On the contrary, they propose, (as has been already suggested) that the reduction of the common law to a text should not be held to change the nature or character of the interpretation or application of its doctrines.

An objection of a different character, and which, indeed, is that which in one shape or another is found afloat through the community, is, that every Code of the common law must necessarily be imperfect, and leave much still to be explained by very imperfect lights; that so far as the principles and details of the common law are capable of codification, they are, or are supposed to be, now well known, and a Code is not necessary to ascertain or promulgate them; that the benefits of a Code must, therefore, be slight and unimportant, since it can provide for comparatively few cases of real doubt, and may even lead to mischievous errors in reasoning or application of the text.

This objection may perhaps be best answered by a consideration of the benefits, which may be derived from a codification of the common law. It has been already admitted, that every such codification must, from the nature of things, be imperfect; for it never can embrace all the past, present, and future changes in society, which may require new rules to govern them. But this is an objection, in its general form, founded upon the absolute infirmity of human nature for every purpose of perfect action, and is not limited to codification. It by no means follows, that because legislation cannot do every thing, or foresee every thing, therefore no legislation should exist, either to remedy evils, to ascertain rights, or to secure property. The benefits proposed by a Code may be summed up in the following propositions.

I. In the first place, certainty, clearness, and facility of reference are of great importance in all matters of law, which concern the public generally. It is desirable, in every community, that the laws, which govern the rights, duties, relations, and business of the people, should, as far as practicable, be accessible to them for daily use or consultation. No one, indeed, is so rash as to suppose, that, with the very different occupations, means of education, and opportunities of leisure, of the mass of the people, it is possible for them fully or accurately to understand all the laws in their full force and extent. This must, under all circumstances, require thorough study, laborious diligence, and a great variety of accessary knowledge. But it does not follow, that, because all cannot be attained, therefore the more general and useful rules may not be brought under the notice of the people, and, according to their attainments and leisure, be made the means of guarding them from gross mistakes in business, or gross violations of the rights of others. Now, certainly, if a rule or doctrine of the common law exists in a determinate form or with a determinate certainty, it is capable of being so expressed in the text of a Code. If so capable, then it is not easy to perceive why it should not be so expressed that it may furnish a guide for inquirers, to clear away a private doubt, or to satisfy a hesitating judgment.

But this is not all. At present the known rules and doctrines of the common law are spread over many ponderous volumes. They are nowhere collected together in a concise and systematic form, having a positive legislative sanction. They are to be gathered from treatises upon distinct and independent subjects, of very different merit and accuracy; from digests and abridgments; from books of practice and from professional practice; and above all, from books of reports of adjudged cases, many hundreds of which now exist, and which require to be painfully and laboriously consulted in order to ascertain them. These rules and doctrines may be well known and well understood by eminent lawyers and judges, by profound students, who possess an ample library of law books, and by others, who devote their whole leisure to the purpose. And yet men less eminent, less studious, or with less means to provide a library, or to consult it, may be unable to arrive at the same certainty, and may even be misled by their partial examinations, into serious errors and mistakes. A leading rule may have some exceptions, which have escaped the researches of the party and yet be as well established as the rule itself. Many lawsuits are now founded upon errors and mistakes of this sort, which the mere imperfection of the means within the reach of the interested party, or of his counsel, has unavoidably produced. A single line of a Code, properly and accurately prepared upon such a subject, might at once have dissipated every doubt and uncertainty, as to the nature, extent and operation of the existing rule.

II. And this leads the Commissioners to remark, in the next place, that one great use of a Code of the common law, in its principal branches, will be the abridgment of professional as well as of private labor, in ascertaining and advising upon a rule or doctrine of that law. A vast deal of time is now necessarily consumed, if not wasted, in ascertaining the precise bearing and result of various cases, which have been decided touching a particular topic. If the result is at all contested by the adverse party, no counselor would feel safe without a thorough examination of all the leading cases (even though they should spread over centuries), lest he should be surprised at the argument by a loose dictum, a questionable authority, or an ambiguous statement, either distinguishing or controlling the case before him. Hence it is, that lawyers in the fullest practice are compelled to the most severe studies upon points upon which they do not entertain much if any doubt, lest, in the long array of cases which may be cited upon any disputed or undisputed point, there should be some intimation which might injuriously affect their clients' rights or remedy. And yet, it is not too much to say, that often a single page of a Code would contain, in a clear and explicit statement, all that the researches of a week, or even of a month, would scarcely justify them in affirming with an unfaltering confidence.

One great advantage, therefore, of a Code, an advantage which in a practical view can scarcely be over estimated, is, that it supersedes the necessity, in ordinary cases at least, of very elaborate researches into other books; and, indeed, it often supersedes, in all cases but those of rare and extraordinary occurrence, the necessity of consulting an immense mass of learned collections and digests of antecedent decisions.

This has accordingly been found to be one of the ordinary results of codification, whenever it has been successfully accomplished. Thus, we are informed, that the Codes of Justinian superseded for ordinary use some camels' loads of written Commentaries on the law. And it is notorious that the civil Code of France (commonly called the Napoleon Code), has, in like manner, thrown out of the daily consultation of jurists a voluminous bulk of treatises upon the customary and provincial law of that country. There are cases, indeed, in which now those voluminous collections must still be consulted. But the occasions are, probably, not one in a hundred of what they were before that Code was promulgated. In like manner, it may be unhesitatingly affirmed, that the maritime and commercial Ordinances of Louis XIV., of 1673 and 1681, not only put an end to a vast extent of litigation in the different maritime provinces of that kingdom, but also furnished rules so clear and so equitable, as to have been adopted as the basis of much of the maritime law of other countries, and especially of that of England.

III. In the next place, it may be stated, in connection with the preceding head, and as illustrative of it, that there are in the common law many points, which, though on the whole now established by a considerable weight of judicial authority, are not absolutely beyond the reach of forensic controversy, if learned counsel should choose to stir them. There are, for example, many questions, which have given rise to litigation in different ages, and upon which there may be found in the reports, not only occasional diversities of judicial opinion, but many nice distinctions and differences, and many incidental dicta, which serve greatly to perplex the inquiries of the ablest lawyers. Where authorities are to be found on each side of a point; where the circumstances of cases, very nearly resembling each other in most respects, are yet distinguishable from each other by nice shades of difference, or have been so distinguished, thus furnishing grounds for reasoning and controversy as to the precise extent of a principle, no judges would feel at liberty to stop the argument, although in their judgment, the weight of authority should be clearly against the suggested distinction or difference. Much of the time of courts of justice is consumed in arguments of this sort, where there are numerous cases, with some slight differences of circumstances, bearing on the same general rule, all of which may be required to be examined and distinguished. It was said by an eminent Judge (Lord Eldon), upon one occasion, where some question of artificial or technical law was under discussion before him, that there were upwards of three hundred cases bearing on that question, which had already been decided. To master them, with all their minute distinctions of circumstances, would of itself be a vast labor. And yet it is not perhaps too much to say, that four or five lines of text in a Code, stating the true general rule, deducible from the best of them, would at once have put aside the necessity of any further consideration of most of these cases.

There are, besides, numerous points, upon which there are now to be found conflicting decisions, or dicta of courts of justice, which shake the authority of certain doctrines. In cases of this sort, it seems desirable to establish which of these decisions constitutes the true rule, or at least to give a positive affirmance of the true rule, when it can be fairly ascertained what that is. And perhaps also in some instances of daily practical importance, where there is a real doubt what the true rule of the common law is, it may not be without use to fix it in a like positive form.

The Commissioners do not indulge the rash expectation, that any Code of the known existing common law will dry up all the common sources of litigation. New cases must arise, which no Code can provide for, or even ascertain. These must necessarily be left to be disposed of by courts of justice, as they shall occur in future. But the Commissioners are of opinion, that a Code which shall contain the clearly established principles of the common law, will be attended with great benefits to the public, for the reasons already stated. It will show what the existing law is, as far as it goes, in a clear and intelligible manner. It will have a tendency to suppress useless and expensive litigation. It will greatly abridge the labors of judges, as well as of the profession, by furnishing a starting point for future discussions, instead of imposing the necessity of constant researches through all the past annals of the law.

UNWRITTEN LAW

Timothy Walker

The following debate between Timothy Walker and Washington Van Hamm in the pages of the Western Law Journal *brings out the divisive issues implicit in the question of common law or code.*

Timothy Walker, "Codification," *Western Law Journal* (June, 1844), I, p. 434.

THE PROPOSITION is to supersede the common, or unwritten law, by enlarging the boundaries of written law. Now, the common law comes down to us with letters of commendation from remote antiquity. Sage after sage, through a long lapse of time, has paid it the tribute of lofty panegyric. It has not only been said to embody "the hoarded wisdom of a thousand years," but also to be in reality, "the perfection of reason." Americans are called upon especially to revere it, as the parent of modern liberty. Because it withstood, with genuine Saxon obstinacy, the early encroachments of Norman power, we are required to believe that it breathes throughout the very soul of indomitable freedom; and that, for this reason, our ancestors brought it over to this country, and cherished it as their most precious birthright. But to all such suggestions, it is sufficient here to reply, that if hoary antiquity and unbounded encomium had been permitted to preclude scrutiny, the philosophy of Aristotle would still enslave the human mind. We set out, therefore, with the protestation, that neither the antiquity of the common law, nor its present wide supremacy, prove anything, one way or the other, as to its comparative excellence. Let the two systems be examined, as if both were till now unheard of.

What then is meant by *written law*? By written law we understand the formal and solemn enactments of Legislation. It comprehends both *constitutions, treaties,* and *statutes*; but is chiefly made up of the last. Now as we elect and compensate a body of men, for the exclusive purpose of providing us with laws, it would seem, at first glance, as if we need have no other laws than those which some time or other had passed through the regular forms of enactment by the Legislature. But the truth is, that not one fiftieth part of the laws by which our rights are regulated, have ever been promulgated from a legislative hall, so as to come within the definition of written law.

What then is meant by *unwritten law,* and whence does it derive its authority? The common law is called unwritten, because there is no record of its formal enactment by any legislative body. The theory sometimes maintained, is, that its principles must once have been enacted in due form, but that the record of such enactment has been lost. This, however, is mere theory. The fact is that the whole body of common law is the vast work of *Judicial Legislation.* In other words, it has been made from first to last by *Judges*; and the only record of it is to be found in the *Reports* of their decisions. The system has grown up to its present enormous bulk, by gradual accretions, from the earliest periods of English history down to the present moment. The *Reports* of decisions in England and America, together with *Indexes, Digests,* and *Abridgments,* all of which go to make up the records of the common law, already amount to a *thousand volumes*; and the number is increasing every year more rapidly than before. To illustrate the formation of the system, let us suppose that a question arose in times far back, concerning which the written laws contained no provision. In such a case, if the judge could find a reported decision in point, he was governed by it. If not, he sought for cases analogous, and moulded his decision according to their principles. If neither of these, then, rather than let a wrong go unredressed, he threw himself upon his best discretion, and made a law to suit the case. In this way every principle of the common law has been adjudicated, and each adjudication forms a *precedent* for subsequent cases. Accordingly it may happen that the rights of an American citizen, in the nineteenth century, will depend upon the opinion of a British judge, pronounced in the tenth century. For if a question now arises, concerning which our written law is silent, we go to the *Reports*. If those of our state contain nothing in point, we ransack the other American reports. If none of these settle the question, we consult the English reports, searching back to the earliest times. Nay we even have recourse to the laws of Justinian, or to wheresoever else we can obtain light; and in this way, a decision is finally made.

It will be seen from this description, that in the theory of the common law, precedents when once established, are *absolutely binding,* and that consequently *judicial discretion* is limited to new cases. But this is far from being practically true. Judges feel at liberty, on what appears to them good reason, not only to *overrule* the decisions of other courts, but even their own prior decisions. The number of reported cases already overruled, cannot be less than *two thousand.* And this wide liberty is taken for the purpose of avoiding an evil inherent in the system. It results from the very nature of things, that many of the doctrines established centuries ago, in states of society altogether different from the present, must be totally unsuitable to our condition. Yet upon the strict theory before mentioned, these decisions would be absolutely imperative, until superseded by Legislation. Now in such cases, where a rigid adherence to precedents would induce a decision at war with present fitness and propriety, the judge assumes the province of a legislator, and overrules the ancient authority. In fact, the Supreme Court of this state has laid down, upon this subject, the broad position, that it will be governed by what we call the common law, only so far as it is adapted to our circumstances. So that the question, what is the law of Ohio, can only be answered by saying, that it is what our judges please to determine.

Having thus ascertained the difference between the two kinds of law, we are prepared to answer the first question propounded by the resolution; namely, is it practicable to make such a code as is contemplated?

On this point we do not entertain a doubt. The whole body of law, in whatever form it exists, must be composed of a series of principles, and surely it cannot be impossible to collect these principles together, arrange them into a system, and give them a legislative sanction. This is all the resolution contemplates.

No doubt it would be a work of vast labor, requiring the highest order of intellect. It might task, for years, the highest powers of the Marshalls, the Websters, and the Storys of our land. But there is a wide difference between difficulty and impossibility. It is not pretended that ordinary legislators would be equal to such an undertaking. But they are capable of designating commissioners who would be competent; and the people are able to compensate them. In preparing the code proposed, the framers would only have to do for the law, what has been done for every other art and science; that is, to arrange principles into a system. All the principles of the common law which are worthy of being retained, would be ready at their hands, to be incorporated with such additions and modifications, as wisdom and experience should suggest. And when a code should be thus elaborated and matured, it would only remain for the legislature to add its formal sanction; and the Herculean work would be accomplished.

But we are not left to conjecture on this point. The thing has been done, over and over again. It was done in Greece, by the memorable codes of Lycurgus and of Solon—in Rome, by the mighty work of Justinian—in Prussia, by the code of Frederick the Great—and in France, by the code of Napoleon, the noblest work of all. The achievement of this great enterprise was one of the few remembrances, that cheered the fallen Emperor on his lonely rock. "I shall go down to posterity"—said he—"with that code in my hand." Nor are we wholly without examples in this country. The name of Livingston is rendered immortal by his code. Nay, this is not all. To say nothing of our constitutional law, which is all written—while what is called the British constitution, still remains a mere collection of precedents; we have succeeded in dispensing altogether with the common law with regard to *crimes*. On a few pages of our statute book, may be found all the crimes which our courts can punish—and the same is true of the criminal law of the United States. Now if this has been done in *criminal* matters, why may it not be done in *civil* matters? But the question of *practicability* requires no further enforcement. What man has done, man can do again.

We turn, then, to the question of *expediency*—and here we are met at once by the chilling assertion, that it would be impossible to render a code *complete*, and therefore we had better retain the common law. Let us examine this position. Is the common law complete? Does it contain well settled principles enough to meet every future case? If so, the objection vanishes at once; for we have shown that all these principles might be incorporated into the code. But the truth is, that in the nature of things no system, whether of written or unwritten law, can be, in this sense, complete. Take away from the common law the *judicial discretion,* which makes the law for new cases, as fast as they arise, and its manifold deficiencies would soon be felt. Now what is there to hinder this same judicial discretion from supplying, in the same way, the deficiencies of a code? That the most elaborate code would be deficient, we may safely admit; since no human sagacity could anticipate all future cases. In the ever multiplying relations of human affairs, the imagination cannot run forward to the time when new cases will not present themselves. But are these now provided for by the common law? Certainly not. So far, then, as respects *new cases*, the imperfection of our nature creates the same necessity for judicial discretion, whether we have a code or not. But the advantage of a code would be, that judicial discretion would then be confined to new cases only, which is not the case now. We have seen that judicial precedents have not the binding authority of legislative acts. Now, although it may be generally true, that when a precedent has been overruled, the principle substituted is abstractly better than that which is abrogated, yet every such instance must be attended with the evil of a *retroactive law*. It takes the world by surprise. What men have considered settled, they suddenly find unsettled; and they begin to lose confidence in the stability of their rights. But under a code, limiting judicial discretion to new cases, no such consequence could result. In fact, there would be nothing to apprehend, from a discretion thus guarded. To be convinced of this, we need only to consider the manner in which new cases are now decided. The issue is made up by opposing parties, who present the question in all possible aspects, and explore the whole universe of argument, to maintain their respective grounds. When, therefore, the judge makes up his opinion, he does it with every conceivable means of being right. And his motives are as powerful, as his means of information are ample. If he belong to an inferior court, he knows that his opinion is liable to be reviewed by a superior tribunal. If not, it is to be reported, for the scrutiny of the whole profession. And finally, if with all these probabilities to the contrary, his opinion should prove to be wrong, the very next legislature could rectify it, by an addition to the code. The objection, therefore, of *incompleteness*, vanishes upon examination; and this is the only serious objection we have heard stated.

Let us now glance at some of the positive advantages. And first, instead of searching, as we now must, through a thousand volumes, to ascertain what our rights are, we should find them perhaps in eight or ten volumes. Now, if it be important that men should have the means of knowing the laws by which their actions are to be regulated, this is a benefit not to be overestimated. Two references, however, will help us to appreciate it. The first is to the written constitutions of our country—who would willingly exchange conditions with England, and live under an unwritten constitution—a constitution of common law—a patchwork of precedents? No wonder Reform is there the perpetual cry. The other reference is to our criminal code. What citizen would willingly exchange it for the criminal common law? Now, by running over a few pages, we can ascertain, with absolute certainty, what actions will expose us to punishment.— Without this code, though we might have searched through a hundred volumes, we still could not be sure, that a long forgotten precedent might not be raked up from some musty volume of black-letter reports, to authorise a blow from the arm of the law.

A second advantage would be, increased *certainty* as to what the law is. Now, as we have seen, all is doubtful. Two thousand cases may arise, in which authorities can be found on both sides. In fact, the common law may be truly said to lie hidden in the breast of the judge. It is usual to rail at that fundamental proposition of the Justinian code, which declares, that the Prince's pleasure has the force of law. But under the wide latitude assumed in Ohio, as to the common law, you have but to substitute *judge* in the place of *prince*, to make the proposition a maxim here. Now, the code proposed, would do away with this uncertainty—and instead of wasting a long life in unavailing efforts to be able to declare with certainty what the law is, we might turn at once to the very page and section.

The third advantage would be, that, by leaving out of the code, all that portion of the common law, which, because it was well adapted to the age of barbarism in which it originated, is, for that very reason, totally unfit for us, we should have a system of laws in harmony with each other, and with the general spirit of our institutions. . . .

We would not, however, be understood as saying that the common law has no good features. We speak of it as a system considered with reference to this age and country. We are not surprised that the first emigrants prized it so highly. It was not only the rule under which they had been reared, but it was infinitely better than no rule at all. They were not prepared at once to frame a code for themselves; and did well to take that which was ready furnished to their hands. But we are surprised that two centuries have been suffered to elapse, with so little effort to improve our legal condition. We can only account for the fact, by reflecting that the mass of the community wait for lawyers to take the lead in legal reform, and that lawyers have reason to be well contented with the system as it is. A clear, concise, and well arranged code, to which all who can read might have access, would not, to say the least, tend to increase their business; and perhaps it would be asking too much of their patriotism, to require them to take the lead in legislating bread out of their own mouths. If the reform is to be effected, the first move must be made out of the pale of the profession.

We shall advert to but one further argument. The prevalence of laws never enacted by legislators, is inconsistent with the theory of our social compact. The people, in their primary, free, and sovereign capacity, have organized themselves into a body politic, upon certain fundamental principles, declared in their constitution. One of these principles is, that a body of men, representing the people, and speaking in their name, shall, in the mode pointed out, frame laws for their government. The constitution recognizes no other legislative power, and no other mode of making laws. It supposes that laws derive their authority from the fact of being enacted in due form by the body constituted for that purpose. Now all we ask is to have this principle carried out universally into practice. Let us have a code of laws emanating from this authority, so comprehensive that we shall have no occasion to resort to the feudal ages for rules of conduct. Let us have the means of knowing with certainty what laws have a just claim upon our obedience, by reference to the rolls of state. Let no citizen be able to say, even with the appearance of plausibility, that he is not bound to submit to a given law, because it has never been enacted by the legislative power, and therefore he has no evidence that it is a law.

In conclusion, we remark, that, should any believe it impossible to supersede altogether the unwritten law, codification does not contemplate this; but only to circumscribe its limits as much as possible. If therefore we cannot have a complete code, let us have one as nearly complete as possible.

The work proposed is certainly an arduous one; but its successful execution would be the greatest benefaction that legislation could confer. They who shall be instrumental in achieving it will deserve well of their generation. And it wants but the resolute determination. Let proper men be commissioned for the task, and due provision made for compensating them, and we shall have a code which will very soon save, in the expense of litigation, more than the cost of making it; and what is still more important, we shall fully redeem the great republican pledge, as yet but partially redeemed, of *establishing* justice.

IN ANSWER TO JUDGE WALKER

Washington Van Hamm

Washington Van Hamm was a practicing lawyer in Hamilton County, Cincinnati, Ohio, in 1852. He had been a member of the Bench and Bar of Cincinnati, an informal group, since 1831.

IT IS VERY DIFFICULT, in an old, settled community, like our own, to undo all the customs and habits of the people, and introduce among them an entirely new order of things. For such would be the case if a regular code of law were adopted. . . .

For if the code consisted simply of a collection of our present laws, and an adoption of the present decisions of our Courts, I would ask, of what benefit could it be? It would be merely a republication of what we already have in a sufficiently convenient form. I take it, that by *codification* is meant, not merely a collection of all our present laws into one or more

Washington Van Hamm, "Codification—Its Practicability and Expediency," *Western Law Journal* (September, 1844), I, p. 229.

volumes, but an enlargement of our present laws, whether legislative or judicial, so as to include within the system a remedy for every injury, whether public or private. A scheme like this, if it were practicable to bring it about, would be of inestimable importance to our people. But how can it be done? . . .

Now let us suppose that the Legislature, in their wisdom, should select three or five of the most learned members of the bar, for the purpose of "so enlarging and systematizing the written law, as to reduce it to a regular code." And let us suppose further, that these learned gentlemen should so well succeed in the accomplishment of the object proposed, as to send forth to the good people of Ohio, under legislative sanction, eight or ten volumes, containing the whole civil and criminal law of the State, and receive therefor the plaudits of the whole population, learned and unlearned. . . .

Now let us look calmly at this state of things, and see whether "the glorious uncertainty of the law" would no longer exist. . . . Fortunately or unfortunately, for us, we are prone to differ in our views of the plainest things; we are not disposed to think alike, talk alike, or to construe codes and statutes alike; nor is it possible for the people of Ohio, with all their energy, enthusiasm of character, and industry, to remain even for a single year in the same condition. We are moving forward with telegraphic speed to greatness and glory. Nothing, save war, pestilence, or famine, can stay the march of this wonderful people.

To show in the clearest light, that no additional certainty would arise from the establishment of a code, I will take the liberty of offering the following illustration. Upon the very day of the publication and taking effect of this supposed code, Mr. John Doe, a plain, unlettered man, reads in plain letters from a plain paragraph, a single section of this new and untried code, and puts, as he supposes, a plain, common sense construction upon it, and thereupon concludes, that he has a remedy for an injury sustained. He directs his steps towards the office of a learned counsellor, who puts precisely the same interpretation upon this same section that his client has done before him. Suit is accordingly commenced, and every thing goes on swimmingly until the attorney of the defendant, Mr. Richard Roe, files his demurrer or plea, and argues before the Court, on the trial of the case, that the construction put upon the code is entirely erroneous. The Court, upon mature deliberation, taking into consideration the circumstances under which the code was enacted, and the probable intention of the Legislature, are of opinion, that the law is with the defendant, and adjudge costs against the plaintiff. This decision of this honorable Court is reported to the people of the State, in another volume, as explanatory of a single section of the new code. Henceforward, not only plain, unlettered men, but learned counsellors and jurists, are compelled to look up a volume of reports, containing judicial constructions put on this new code. Thus it will be with almost every section of the new code. Judicial constructions of the new code must be hunted up to know exactly the meaning of the Legislature. I put this case to the judgment of any man, whether learned or unlearned, as a fair instance of the condition of the law, immediately after the taking effect of this new code. And if such be the case immediately afterwards, how many volumes of reports, construing this new code, would we have in Ohio, in the course of ten years? Again: in the course of a year, owing to the change of the circumstances and condition of our people, an injury arises for which no remedy is to be found in the code. What is to be done? Either the judge is to go beyond the pale of written law and make a remedy for the particular case, or the injured party must go unredressed. And who, I would respectfully ask, can foresee the many hundreds and thousands of cases which may arise, and which are not provided for in the code? . . .

Indeed, in my apprehension, there is no mode so well calculated to produce litigation, as the placing of law books in the hands of those who have never made the science of law their particular study. It is like placing a medical work in the hands of one who knows nothing of the science of medicine. The patient reads and prescribes for himself, and in ninety-nine cases out of a hundred, he is compelled to employ a physician to undo the mischief done by his own rash prescriptions. As an apt illustration of the injury done by placing law books in the hands of those who are unacquainted with the science, I would respectfully refer the reader to Swan's Treatise—and I do so without disrespect to the learned author, for whom as a man and as a judge I have the highest regard—but it does seem to me, that this book, gotten up for the very purpose of enabling every man to be his own lawyer, has been productive of more trouble and litigation and costs to the people, than all the hidden mysteries of the law prior to its publication. Individuals who were previously in the habit of applying to lawyers for advice, after the publication of Swan's Treatise, immediately flew to its pages as a sovereign remedy for all their troubles; and being unable to put a proper construction upon the law, as laid down in that excellent work, they get into the very midst of litigation, and then are compelled to apply to a lawyer for his assistance in getting them out. Just so it is with professional men, when they attempt to take upon themselves mechanical and agricultural employments. Knowing but little, practically at least, without the sphere of their own professions, they make poor farmers, and poor mechanics. A *jack-at-all-trades* is generally esteemed a good-for-nothing-sort of man. Let each individual in society attend strictly to his own profession or trade, without attempting to take upon himself the duties of all professions and trades, and men will be more prosperous and happy. It is said, and wisely said, that a man can be great in only one thing. If he attempt to be great in every thing, he is very apt to fail in all things.

I regret exceedingly, that Judge Walker, in his report, has seen proper to say so many harsh things of the profession of which he is a member. If these hard remarks had come from one who is not a lawyer, I should not have been surprised at any thing that might be said derogatory to the character of the profession; but coming, as they do, from an eminent member of the bar, I feel called upon, in this connection, to say a few words in vindication of the profession. Judge Walker's main charge against the profession is opposition to *legal reform.* This is a very serious charge. And, it seems to me, that it is a charge unfounded in fact. If true, one might readily "impute to the members of that honorable profession, narrow and unworthy motives." The members of the profession are, as a matter of course, better acquainted with the law, its perfections and imperfections, than any other class of people. It is their daily and hourly study. While others see but the surface, the profession itself, or a portion at least of the profession, see and know its depths. Such being the case, if they are opposed to *legal reform*, not only may "narrow and unworthy motives" be imputed to them, but also dishonorable and dishonest conduct. Further, says Judge Walker, "They, (the lawyers), are most directly interested in keeping things as they are." Again, he says, "it would be asking too much of their (the lawyers') patriotism, to require them, (the lawyers), to take the lead in legislating bread out of their own mouths." This, the reason given for opposition on the part of lawyers to legal reform, is the severest thrust of all. What does it amount to? Why, that lawyers are opposed to legal reform, because their pecuniary interests would suffer thereby. If this charge be true, lawyers must be, not only wicked men, but dangerous men; and it is high time for the people, the whole people, to whom Judge Walker most eloquently and forcibly appeals, to rise in the majesty of their strength, and hunt down these men, who prey on the very vitals of society. But are not these charges mere vapor, without substance? What is legal reform? It is very easy to cry aloud from the house-tops, Reform, Reform, but it is a very different thing to answer the query, "What is legal Reform?"

I have attempted to show, in the preceding remarks, that codification would not be legal reform; that it is impracticable, and, of course, inexpedient; and that the very objections, that are now made in this report to our present judicial system, would, in a very short time, apply to the new code, together with various other objections not incident to our present system. Now, before this wholesale charge of opposition to legal reform is made against the legal profession, it would be well for those who make it to declare, unequivocally, what their standard of legal reform is, so that in the examination of the question of opposition on the part of members of the profession to legal reform, honest minds may be able to decide, satisfactorily to themselves and others, whether there be truth in the charge. It will not do to say, because a lawyer is opposed to codification, that, therefore, he is opposed to legal reform, because, in the very words of the author of the report, "The project of framing a systematic code of written law, has found ardent advocates and *opponents* among the most intelligent and philanthropic minds of the age." Hence *codification* and *legal reform,* in the apprehension of some of the "most intelligent and philanthropic minds of the age," are very different things. . . .

Then I would again ask, "What is legal reform?" The best answer that can be given to this question is; it is a correction of all errors and abuses in an existing system of law. This question being answered, another equally important arises, and that is, who is to discover and correct these errors and abuses? The only answer, I imagine, that can be given to this query, under our republican form of government, is, the people, through their representatives. But the difficulty, suggested before in these remarks, here arises; that the people, and their representatives also, differ as to the true meaning of legal reform. So that I cannot conceive of any better method of bringing about legal reform than the one we have now in practice.—As soon as the representatives of the people discover any defects in the existing system, let them, at once, apply the remedy. By doing a little at a time, as defects and imperfections are discovered, the law will be more apt to approach perfection, than by hewing down all old established institutions, and erecting in their stead new and untried schemes. . . .

I cannot agree with Judge Walker, that "neither the antiquity of the common law, nor its present wide supremacy, prove any thing, one way or the other, as to its comparative excellence." Without looking to the antiquity of the common law, or its wide supremacy in other countries of the globe, the mere fact, that it has been supreme in our own happy country for more than a half century, and that the people of the United States are still happy and prosperous, goes far, very far, to show the excellence of the common law. And as it must be admitted by all, that a system of law has much to do with the happiness of a people, would it be right and proper, without the most positive assurance of bettering our condition, to make so great a change in our judicial system, as to uproot our dear old common law and plant in its stead a tree whose branches would require incessant pruning, and whose fruit would fall to the ground, sickly and withered, by reason of the want of cultivation, depth of soil, and moisture.

Another position taken in the report is, that we should be governed only by laws enacted by our own legislature, that we compensate legislative bodies for the very purpose of making laws for us, and that we ought to have need only for such laws as are enacted by our legislature; that all unwritten law is judicial legislation, and the record of it is only to be found in reports of the judges. In the commencement of our career as a nation, it may possibly have been well to have so determined and to have acted accordingly. If our forefathers, with all the lights before them, men of great wisdom and knowledge as they are acknowledged by all to have been, had so constructed our general and state constitutions, probably we may have been better off at the present day; but they saw before them this good old body of common law, which had been thoroughly tested by the scrutiny of the great minds of all ages, and which was, in great part, applicable to the condition of our own people, and they saw proper to adopt it as part and parcel of our own form of government. And now at this late day, after our whole system of government has worked well, and at a time when the common law is incorporated into the very system itself, it is proposed to pluck it out and establish a *regular code.* I should be pleased to know, from any gentleman learned in the law, how the new code would be more *regular* than the old system, composed as it is of written and unwritten law. I will venture the prediction, that not only lawyers, but the great mass of the people of this country, are now better acquainted with the unwritten or common law than with the statute law of our State. Every man knows just as well, that he is bound by his contract, and will be compelled to respond thereto in damages, if he fail in complying with its terms, as he does, that if he steals his neighbor's property he will have to suffer the penalty attached to the crime of larceny. Every judge knows from experience, that it is just as difficult to put a true construction upon a statute, as upon a contract. In both cases the intention of the framers is to be hunted out. . . .

The author of the report, in aid of his plan of codification, cites his readers to the "memorable codes of Lycurgus and Solon," to "the mighty work of Justinian," to "the code of Frederick the Great," and to "the code of Napoleon, the noblest work of all." These, says he, prove the practicability as well as expediency of codification. In answer to this mode of argument, it may be well to inquire into the comparative happiness and prosperity of the people of Greece, Rome, Prussia, and France, and the people of the United States. The best system of laws promotes the greatest good of the greatest number.—Where do we find a people, either in ancient or modern times, so prosperous and happy as the American people? Where else, but in the United States, have life, liberty, and property been thoroughly and entirely protected by law? In France, notwithstanding the wonderful *code Napoleon,* bloodshed and ruin have been the common property of Frenchmen; and notwithstanding their many attempts to establish a republican form of government, despots, tyrants, and monarchs have always got the better of the people. Greece and Rome were once mighty republics, but are so no longer. But in our own country, under the blessings of the common law, governed and controlled by our free and republican constitutions, all is happiness and prosperity. No man complains, that his life, liberty, or property is in danger, by reason of the want of sufficient laws for their protection. . . .

The second advantage mentioned in the report is "increased *certainty* as to what the law is." I think I have sufficiently shown, that with the best code there would still remain "the glorious uncertainty of the law." And I think I have also clearly shown, that there is a wide difference between the "prince's pleasure" and the "judge's pleasure." The prince is limited by no constitutions and laws, whereas the judge is limited by both. The prince may overrule a previous decision, in the very face of right and justice;

and still the "king can do no wrong." But a judge in Ohio, is bound by the Constitution of the United States, by the Constitution of his own State, by the statute law, and by precedent when it is in conformity with right and justice.

The third advantage mentioned is, that all those parts of the common law adapted to an age of barbarism, and not suited to our own condition, would be left out of the code; and that our laws would be in harmony with each other. This objection, it seems to me, is of no validity; because only those parts of the common law applicable to our condition are in force in our State. Nor do the "incongruities and technicalities" of "the common and statute law, taken together," render it necessary for us to adopt a code of law. These incongruities, and these technicalities, may be gotten rid of by the Legislature, by special enactments at any session. Some of these technicalities were disposed of by our last Legislature in an act relating to the practice of our Courts, which act has already been in-dorsed by the Western Law Journal; and with but little difficulty, compared with the enormous labor of codification, may others be disposed of by succeeding Legislatures.

For my part, although I am willing to admit there is much justice in the remarks of Judge Walker upon this point, I am fearful, if law is not now a science, with all its incongruities, and technicalities, and fictions, and abuses, that it never will be entitled to that appellation, although code upon code should be established from this time to the latest generation.

The last argument is, that the common or unwritten law "is inconsistent with the theory of our social compact." If so, I have only to remark, that it is very strange that the great men of our country, the Washingtons, the Hamiltons, the Madisons, the Marshalls, the Livingstons, the Storys, the Pinckneys, and the Taneys, have never discovered, that in carrying out the great principles of the common law, they have been acting in the very face of the Constitutions of our country.

NO ONE NEED BE IGNORANT

Edward Livingston

Edward Livingston (1764–1836), a member of the distinguished New York family, was elected to Congress and later appointed mayor of New York. During his term one of his agents absconded with federal funds, and Livingston assumed full responsibility, an undertaking which left him with a constant struggle for money. He moved to New Orleans, was elected to

Edward Livingston, *A System of Penal Law* (1833), p. 3.

the legislature, and prepared a Code of Crimes and Punishments, Code of Procedure, Code of Evidence, and Code of Reform and Prison Discipline. He was the prime technician and publicist of codes until Field. He became a United States senator and in 1831 held the office of Secretary of State under Jackson.

No ACT OF LEGISLATION can be or ought to be immutable. Changes are required by the alteration of circumstances; amendments, by the imperfection of all human institutions; but laws ought never to be changed without great deliberation, and a due consideration as well of the reasons on which they were founded, as of the circumstances under which they were enacted. It is therefore proper, in the formation of new laws, to state clearly the motives for making them, and the principles by which the framers were governed in their enactment. Without a knowledge of these, future legislatures cannot perform the task of amendment, and there can be neither consistency in legislation, nor uniformity in the interpretation of laws.

For these reasons, the general assembly of the state of Louisiana declare that their objects in establishing the following code, are—

To remove doubts relative to the authority of any parts of the penal law of the different nations by which this state, before its independence, was governed.

To embody into one law, and to arrange into system, such of the various prohibitions enacted by different statues as are proper to be retained in the penal code.

To include in the class of offences, acts injurious to the state and its inhabitants, which are not now forbidden by law.

To abrogate the reference, which now exists, to a foreign law, for the definition of offences and the mode of prosecuting them.

To organize a connected system for the prevention as well as for the prosecution and punishment of offences.

To collect into written codes, and to express in plain language, all the rules which it may be necessary to establish for the protection of the government of the country, and the person, property, condition and reputation of individuals; the penalties and punishments attached to a breach of those rules; the legal means of preventing offences, and the forms of prosecuting them when committed; the rules of evidence, by which the truth of accusations are to be tested; and the duties of executive and judicial officers, jurors, and individuals, in preventing, prosecuting, and punishing offences: to the end that no one need be ignorant of any branch of criminal jurisprudence, which it concerns all to know.

Charles Schultz.

3. Social Reform

SLAVERY AND NEGRO RIGHTS

The Pretensions of Slavery

LYSANDER SPOONER

Lysander Spooner (1808–1887) was a major spokesman for the constitutionalists who protested the Fugitive Slave Law. His literal-minded approach to the Constitution resulted in an odd individualism. He was dissatisfied with the postal service from Boston to New York and successfully opened his own private agency, the American Letter Mail Company, in competition with the Federal Government. Eventually prosecution forced him to suspend operations. His The Unconstitutionality of the Laws of Congress Prohibiting Private Mails *argued that the constitutional power was permissive, not exclusive. He was an inexorable logician; his pamphlets and other writings offered ingenious constructions to lawyers on the anti-slavery side, as can be seen in the following excerpt.*

WE EXAMINED in a former article the pretensions of slavery, as it existed in the British North American colonies prior to the revolution which converted those colonies into the United States of America—to rest upon a legal basis. We found in most of the colonies statutes of the colonial assemblies of an earlier or later date, and in all of them a practice, assuming to legalize the slavery of negroes, Indians, and the mixed race; to make that slavery hereditary wherever the mother was a slave, and in all claims of freedom to throw the burden of proof on the claimant. But we also found that this practice, and all the statutes attempting to legalize it, were in direct conflict with great and perfectly well settled principles of the law of England, which was also the supreme law of the colonies; principles which the colonial legislatures and the colonial courts had no authority to set aside or to contradict; and thence we concluded that American slavery, prior to the Revolution, had no legal basis, but existed as it had done in England for some two centuries or more prior to Somerset's case; a mere usurpation on the part of the masters, and a mere wrong as respected those alleged to be slaves. . . .

Lysander Spooner, "Has Slavery in the United States a Legal Basis?" *Massachusetts Quarterly Review* (June, 1848), I, pp. 273, 292.

Let us begin with the commonwealth of Virginia. The convention of delegates and representatives from the several counties and corporations which assumed the responsibility of framing a new government for that state, very properly prefaced their labors by setting forth a Declaration of Rights, as its "basis and foundation." This Declaration of Rights, bearing date June 12, 1776, announced among other things, "that all men are by nature equally free and independent, and have certain inherent rights, of which, when they enter into a state of society, they cannot by any compact deprive or divest their posterity; namely, the enjoyment of life and liberty, with the means of acquiring and possessing property, and pursuing and obtaining happiness and safety." Upon "the basis and foundation" of this Declaration of Rights, the convention proceeded to erect a "constitution, or form of government," in which it was provided that the "common law of England," and all statutes of parliament not local in their character, made in aid of the common law prior to the settlement of Virginia, "together with the several acts of the General Assembly of this colony *now in force,* so far as the same may consist with the several ordinances, *declarations*, and resolutions of the general convention, shall be considered as in full force until the same shall be altered by the legislative power of this colony." But this provision could give no validity to the colonial acts for the establishment of slavery; in the first place, because those acts, legally speaking, were not *in force,* and never had been, being void from the beginning, enacted in defiance of great principles of the English law, by which the powers of the colonial assembly were restricted; and in the second place, because they did not and could not consist with that "declaration of the convention," above quoted, laid down by the convention itself as "the basis and foundation" of the new government. . . .

The convention of Maryland, (which upon the breaking out of hostilities with the mother country had displaced the proprietary government,) following in the footsteps of Virginia, adopted, on the 3d of November, 1776, a Declaration of Rights, the introductory part of a new constitution, in which they declared, "that all government of right originates from the people; is founded in compact only, and is constituted solely for the good of the whole"; and "that the *inhabitants* of Maryland are entitled to the common law of England; to all English statutes applicable to their situation, passed before the settlement of Maryland, and introduced and practised on in the colony; and also to all acts of the old colonial assembly 'in force' on the first of June, 1774." But the acts of assembly sanctioning and legalizing slavery were not "in force" on the first of June, 1774, nor at any other time. They never had been in force; they were contrary to the law of England, to a correspondency with which the colonial assembly was specially limited by charter. Yet it is on these void acts that the supposed legality of slavery in Maryland still continues to rest.

The constitution of North Carolina, formed Dec. 17th, 1776, contains not one single word respecting slavery. That institution did not receive even the semblance of support derived in Virginia and Maryland from the continuation in force of the colonial acts; for no act of the colonial assembly of North Carolina had ever attempted to define who were or might be slaves. Nor was any such attempt made by the newly established assembly. Slavery remained in the state of North Carolina what it had been in the colony,—a mere custom, a sheer usurpation, not sustained by even the semblance of law. . . .

Let it be remembered, however,—and this consideration, though frequently overlooked or disregarded, is absolutely essential to a correct understanding of the case,—that the Federal convention did not assemble to revise the laws or institutions of the states, nor to determine or enforce the political or social rights appertaining to the inhabitants of the states, as such. . . . The business of the Federal convention was, so to amend the articles of confederation as to carry into effect the objects at which that confederation aimed; namely, the enabling the states to act as one nation in their foreign affairs; and securing the several states and their individual inhabitants against injustice, oppression, or injury, on the part of other states or their individual inhabitants.

It might indeed become necessary, for the accomplishment of these objects, to interfere to some extent with some of the existing laws and institutions of the states, or at least to reserve to the authorities to be created by the new constitution, the power of doing so; and under the plan adopted, of submitting that constitution to be separately ratified by each of the states, any alterations so made or authorized would rest on the same basis of popular consent with the state constitutions themselves. But this interference with state constitutions or state laws, any interference in any shape with the internal affairs of the states, was a power to be very daintily exercised, especially in its application to particular cases; otherwise, any constitution which the convention might form, would be sure of being rejected by the states.

It was from this view of the case that the convention omitted to prefix to the Federal constitution any general Bill of Rights;—an omission much complained of by those who opposed its adoption. It was not in their character as individuals about to enter into a primary political organization, but in their character as inhabitants of certain states already constituted and organized, that the Federal constitution had to do with the people of America. Their rights as inhabitants of each particular state, it belonged to the state governments to settle: the Federal constitution had only to declare what should be their additional and supplementary rights as citizens and inhabitants of the confederacy.

Under this view of the subject, slavery in the states was a matter with which the convention was not called upon directly to interfere, and which, indeed, could not be directly interfered with, without exposing the proposed constitution to certain rejection. It did, however, come before the convention incidentally; and the question which we now have to consider is, Whether, in dealing with it thus incidentally, the Federal constitution has acknowledged the *legal* existence of slavery, in any of the states, so as to bind the confederacy, and to impart to that institution in the states, that legal character which the laws of the states themselves have failed to give to it.

The article in the Federal constitution principally relied upon by those who maintain the affirmative on this point, is that which determines the ratio of representation in the House of Representatives. That article is frequently spoken of as though it were the great compromise; the fundamental concession upon which the constitution was based. This was not so. The great difficulty that occurred at the outset was to reconcile the pretensions of the larger and the smaller states. . . .

The question is, whether the use of the phrase *three fifths of all other persons,* recognizes the validity of the slave laws of any particular state, and affords a sufficient basis for those laws to stand upon, notwithstanding their original defects already pointed out? The first thing to be observed is, that the validity of those laws was not of the least consequence in settling the point under consideration, to wit, the productiveness of the industry of the several states. Whether the negroes of Virginia, for instance, were held in slavery by law or against law, made in this point of view no difference at all. Suppose, for example, (as we hold,) that they were illegally deprived of their liberty; the illegality of their servitude would not increase their industry, or the wealth of the state, so as to entitle her whole population to be counted, in determining her representation. What the constitution had to deal with, in settling this distribution of representation, was a question of external fact, not a question of law or right. The question of the individual rights of the inhabitants of the states was one over which this article required the assumption of no control. Their condition in fact, not their condition in law, was the real point according to which the distribution was to be regulated.

Even in referring to the matter of fact great caution was used. "The question of slavery in the states," said Gerry, in reference to another point to be presently considered, "ought not to be touched, but we ought to be careful not to give it any sanction." Madison thought it wrong to admit into the constitution "the idea that there could be property in men";—and the whole phraseology of the instrument was carefully settled in accordance with this view.

It is fair enough to conclude that the "other persons," referred to in this article, were those held as slaves in the several states. But the constitution takes care not to commit itself by calling them slaves, or by using any term that would seem to pass a judgment on the legal character on particular legal incidents of their condition. That remains what it was; this article does not affect it in any way; and if the laws of the states fail, as we maintain, to give any legal authority to those who claim to be masters, surely they will look for it in vain in this article of the Federal constitution.

When the Federal convention, in the course of its labors, arrived at the clauses investing Congress with the power to regulate navigation and foreign commerce, a new occasion for compromise arose. Ten states out of the thirteen had already prohibited the importation of slaves from abroad, and if the Federal government were invested with unlimited control over the intercourse with foreign countries, it was plain enough that one of its first acts would be the prohibition of the African slave-trade.

For this, Georgia and the Carolinas were not prepared; and the opinion was very warmly and confidently expressed by the delegates of those states, that such an unlimited power conferred upon Congress, would insure in those states the rejection of the constitution. To avoid this result, a provision was inserted, "that the emigration or importation of such persons as any of the states now existing shall think proper to admit, shall not be prohibited by Congress, prior to the year 1808; but a tax or duty may be imposed on such importation, not exceeding ten dollars for each person."

We observe in this clause the same cautious phraseology as in that which we have already discussed. As to the legal character or condition of the persons so to be admitted, nothing whatever is said. There is not the slightest implication that the constitution assented in any way that any of the persons so introduced into the states should be held in a state of slavery. If that was done, it could only be on the responsibility of those who did it, and of the states that allowed it. The constitution did not assent to it, and by the power which it reserved to itself,—all the power which was possible under the circumstances,—it secured the right, after the lapse of twenty years, of preventing the possibility of such an occurrence. But for this right thus reserved to the Federal government, there is every reason to believe that in all the states south of Virginia the foreign slave-trade would be now vigorously prosecuted. The concession made to Georgia and the Carolinas was temporary and limited; the point carried was of a permanent character.

There still remains one other clause of the constitution, relied upon as sanctioning slavery in the states. "No person held to service or labor in one state, under the laws thereof, escaping into another, shall, in consequence of any law or regulation therein, be discharged from such service or labor; but shall be delivered up on claim of the party to whom such service or labor may be due." It may be worth while to mention in this connection, that in the original draft of the apportionment clause, the phrase "bound to servitude" was used, following in this respect the proposed amendment to the articles of confederation from which the idea of the federal ratio was derived. But "servitude" was struck out, and "service" substituted, as Madison informs us, because "servitude" seemed to be only appropriate to express the condition of slavery. Yet in the article now under consideration, the term "service" is employed;—"no person held to service or labor." But without dwelling on this distinction, it is sufficient for our purpose to refer to the pointed difference between this and the apportionment clause, in the express reference which this clause makes to law. Practice, usage, fact merely, is not sufficient, but law is required. "No person held to service or labor in one state, *under the laws thereof*," &c. The question, then, whether this clause stipulates for the return of fugitive slaves, is entirely dependent on the previous question whether there is any lawful slavery in any of the states;—a question upon which this clause expresses no opinion, and throws not the slightest light whatever. If there is any such slavery, it must exist by virtue of state laws, laws complete and authoritative in themselves; for whatever might have been the intention, or whatever the legal effect of this clause, it neither intended to give, nor has it any effect to give, a legal or rightful character to claims of service not previously rightful and legal.

The three clauses of the Federal constitution above considered, are the only portions of that instrument which have ever been set up as giving any sanction to the slave system of the states. So far from finding in these clauses any such sanction, we find, on the contrary, evidence of a fixed determination in the constitution not to yield it. They contain no endorsement of the slave laws of the states, no recognition even of slavery as a state institution, entitled to the favorable regard of the Federal government. General Pinckney of South Carolina, in the course of the debates of the convention, more than once insisted on some such guaranty for slave property; but, so far from yielding to this demand, the greatest care was taken not to admit into the constitution the idea that there could be property in men; that is to say, the very fundamental idea upon which the whole slave system rests. It was impossible for the Federal constitution, by its own proper vigor, to abolish slavery, or to make its abolition one of the conditions of the federal compact; for on such conditions no constitution could be formed; but on the other hand, the greatest care was taken not to give any sanction to a practice or a principle so inconsistent with those natural rights upon which all the American constitutions professed to be founded.

This view of the Federal constitution corresponds very nearly with the view taken of it, both north and south, for many years subsequent to its adoption. It is only within a very recent period that the idea has been set up, that the "compromises of the constitution" include the recognition of slavery as an institution of the states, or some of them, entitled to protection and support. Not only does the Federal constitution, so far from recognizing slavery in that character, take the greatest pains to avoid doing so; but in point of fact, as we maintain, slavery is not even a state institution, legally speaking, but a mere usurpation, unsupported by law, and in that character certainly not entitled to support or countenance from the Federal government, or any other.

It needs, as we believe, only this free discussion, to show that even the technical legality behind which slavery claims to entrench itself, cannot be maintained. This point has hitherto been conceded to the slaveholders, hastily, without examination, and, as we believe, without reason. The fact seems to be, that although the people of the southern states were willing to allow slavery to continue among them as a matter of fact, they left its legality to rest upon the enactments and practice of the colonial times, without undertaking by any fundamental act of sovereignty on their part to confer any new or additional legality upon it. The legality of slavery rests, then, upon a colonial usage,—a usage not only unsustained by the English law, but in several most important points, directly contradictory to it; a usage totally incapable of furnishing any legal foundation for any claim of right; a usage upon which neither the state constitutions nor the Federal constitution undertake to confer a legal character.

An Appraisal of Spooner's Argument

WENDELL PHILLIPS

Attacking Spooner is Wendell Phillips (1811–1884), the legal spokesman of the Garrisonians, who argued that the Constitution affirmed the right to slavery and had therefore made—in the phrase from Isaiah—"a covenant with death and an agreement with hell." Phillips, a famous orator— he spoke more than two thousand times on "The Lost Arts"—inherited wealth and social standing, and is a prime example of patrician turned reformer, lending his legal talents to the most radical movements of the age.

TWO YEARS AGO, LYSANDER SPOONER, Esq. published an essay on the Unconstitutionality of Slavery. We shall but fulfill an old promise in reviewing the argument it contains. Events beyond our control have delayed us till now, which we regret only as it seems to have led some of Mr. Spooner's admirers to imagine that the delay proceeded from an unwilling-

Wendell Phillips, "Review of Lysander Spooner's Article on Unconstitutionality of Slavery," *Massachusetts Quarterly Review* (1851), IV, p. 3.

ness, on our part, to measure lances with so skillful an adversary. We exhort them, on the contrary, to believe that we have no innate antipathy to the idea of an Anti-Slavery Constitution;—that so far from being obstinately wedded to our own opinion, Mr. Spooner, or any one else, shall find in us a most ready, willing, and easy convert to a doctrine, which will restore to us the power of voting,—a right we much covet,—and a direct share in the Government of the country, a privilege we appreciate as highly as any one can. Only *convince* us fairly and we will outdo Alvan Stewart himself in glowing eulogy of this new-found virtue of the American Constitution. Indeed, if merely *believing* the Constitution to be Anti-Slavery would really make it so, we would be the last to stir the question. If the beautiful theories of some of our friends could oust from its place the ugly reality of a pro-slavery administration, we would sit quiet, and let Spooner and Goodell convert the nation at their leisure. But alas, the ostrich does not get rid of her enemy by hiding her head in the sand. Slavery is not abolished, although we have persuaded ourselves that it has no right to exist. The pro-slavery clauses of the National Compact still stand there in full operation, notwithstanding our logic. The Constitution will never be amended by persuading men that it does not need amendment. National evils are only cured by holding men's eyes open, and forcing them to gaze on the hideous reality. To be able to meet a crisis men must understand and appreciate it.

All that we have to do, *as Abolitionists,* with Mr. Spooner's argument is to consider its influence on the Anti-Slavery cause. He maintains that the *Judges of the United States Courts have the right to declare Slavery illegal,* and he proposes that they should be made to do so. We believe that, in part, he mistakes fancy for argument; in part, he bases his conclusions on a forced interpretation of legal maxims, and that the rest of his reasoning, where not logically absurd and self-contradictory, is subversive of all sound principles of Government and of public faith. Any movement or party, therefore, founded on his plan, would, so soon as it grew considerable enough to attract public attention, be met by the contempt and disapprobation of every enlightened and honest man. To trust our cause with such a leader is to insure its shipwreck. To keep, therefore, so far as our influence extends, the Anti-Slavery movement in its legitimate channel, to base it on such principles as shall deserve and command the assent of every candid man, to hold up constantly before the nation the mirror of its own deformity, we undertake the distasteful task of proving the Constitution hostile to us and the slave. . . .

Before we touch on the argument of Mr. Spooner's Essay, we wish to call attention to two points:

1st. Allowing, for the moment, as he claims, that the Constitution contains no guarantee or recognition of Slavery . . . we go on to ask, (of Abolitionists, not of Mr. Spooner,) how comes it that, as he all along confesses, Courts, Congress, and the people have uniformly warped and twisted the whole instrument aside and awry to serve and sustain Slavery? that the whole *Administration* of the Government, from its very commencement, has been pro-slavery? If the Constitution be guiltless of any blame in this matter, then surely there must be some powerful element at work in the Union itself, which renders it impossible for this to be an Anti-Slavery *nation*, even when blessed with an *Anti-Slavery* Constitution; and thus the experience of fifty years proves *Union* itself under *any form*, to be impossible without guilt. In such circumstances, no matter what the Constitution is, whether good or bad, it is the duty of every honest man to join in the war-cry of the American Anti-Slavery Society, *"no Union with Slaveholders."* For if we could not escape the infamy and the sin of such a pro-slavery *administration* as ours has always been, under a Constitution pure as Mr. Spooner describes this to be, then, as we never can have a better, we ought to give up the experiment.

2d. As far as we can understand him, Mr. Spooner does not deny the universal Northern doctrine, that the Executive officers of the Government are bound, while they retain their situations, to obey and execute the laws in that manner and sense which the Supreme Court decide and enjoin. . . . Of course no one has ever denied that the Supreme Court now construes the Constitution in a pro-slavery sense. This, then, is the law of the land until altered. Here again the position of the American Anti-Slavery Society is untouched. For whatever be the real character of the Constitution, if those who *now swear* to support that instrument are bound to support it in the sense which the Courts give it, then, surely, no Abolitionist can consistently take such an oath or ask another person to do so.

With neither of these points has Mr. Spooner himself anything to do. He, we believe, does not profess to be an Abolitionist; at least, in this essay he considers the question simply as a lawyer, without entering into its further bearings. We suggest them for the benefit of those Abolitionists who try to hide themselves behind him, and make a use of his argument which he never intended, and probably would not sanction.

Mr. Spooner's first chapter is employed in answering the question, "What is law?" . . .

His conclusion is, "that law is simply the rule, principle, obligation, or requirement of natural justice." . . .

And finally he maintains: . . . "It follows that government can have no powers except such as individuals may *rightfully* delegate to it; that no law, inconsistent with men's natural rights, can arise out of any contract or compact of government: *that constitutional law, under any form of government, consists only of those principles of the written Constitution, that are consistent with natural law, and man's natural rights*; and that any other principles, that may be expressed by the letter of any constitution, are void and not law, and all judicial tribunals are bound to declare them so." . . .

Surely, mankind cannot be presumed to have so universally mistaken what they were about, as to have *uniformly* set up Governments, that were not *legal* in their own sense of the term! And as surely words must be interpreted according to the sense mankind choose to put upon them, and not according to the caprice of an individual. Mr. Spooner is at liberty to say, that much of what the world *calls* law is not obligatory, because it is not just in the eye of God; and there all good men will agree with him. But to assert that because a thing is not right it is not *law*, as that term is commonly and rightfully used, is entering into the question of what constitutes the basis of government among men; and according to a man's theory of Government, will be his denial or assent to the proposition. Does Mr. Spooner mean to say merely, that a nation in making its laws has no right, in the eye of God, to perpetrate injustice? We agree with him. It is a doctrine certainly as old as Cicero, and may be traced through Grotius and Locke, and all writers on the subject, down to Jefferson and Channing. Nations are bound by the same rule of right and wrong, as individuals: agreed. Or does he mean to say that in settling what shall be *the rule* of civil conduct, the voice of the majority is not final and conclusive, on its own officers, in *all the departments of government?* Then we differ from him entirely, and assert, that, on his plan, Government is impossible. An individual may, and ought to resign his office, rather than assist in a law he deems unjust. But while he retains, under the majority, one of *their* offices, he retains it on *their conditions,* which are, to obey and enforce *their* decrees. There can be no more self-evident proposition, than that, in every Government, the majority must rule, and their will be *uniformly* obeyed. Now, if the majority enact a wicked law, and the Judge refuses to enforce it, which is to yield, the Judge, or the majority? Of course, the first. On any other supposition, Government is impossible. Indeed, Mr. Spooner's idea is practical no-governmentism. It leaves every one to do "what is right in his own eyes." After all, Messrs. Goodell and Spooner, with the few who borrow this idea of them, are the real no-government men; and it is singular, how much more consistent and sound are the notions of Non-resistants on this point, —the men who are generally considered, though erroneously, to be no-government men. . . .

"Only that which is just, is law, and all judicial tribunals are bound so to declare." This is Mr. Spooner's proposition. Grant, for the purpose of this argument, that only what is just is law. We allow that no laws in support of Slavery are *morally* binding. Possibly Mr. Spooner means the same thing, only expresses it more strongly. The only important point at issue is—*when Governments enact such laws, what is the proper remedy?*

This question has been answered in three ways.

1st. Old-fashioned patriotism replies, with Algernon Sydney: "Resistance to tyrants is obedience to God." Mr. Spooner states that "the only duties any one owes a wicked Constitution, are disobedience, resistance, destruction."

2d. Next comes the Christian rule, that too sanctioned by Locke, and by Plato—the course of the Quakers—the motto of the American Anti-Slavery Society—"SUBMIT to every ordinance of man"—but suffer any penalty rather than JOIN in doing a wrong act; meanwhile, let your loud protest prepare a speedy and quiet revolution.

3d. Thirdly comes Mr. Spooner's plan:

"If the majority, however large, of the people of a country enter into a contract of government, called a constitution, by which they agree to aid, abet, or accomplish any kind of injustice, this contract of government is unlawful and void—and for the same reason that a contract of the same nature between two individuals, is unlawful and void. Such a contract of government confers no rightful authority upon those appointed to administer it. . . . Judicial tribunals, sitting under the authority of this unlawful contract or constitution, are bound, equally with other men, to declare it, and all unjust enactments passed by the Government in pursuance of it, unlawful and void. These judicial tribunals cannot, by accepting office under a Government, rid themselves of that paramount obligation, that all men are under, to declare, if they declare anything, that justice is law; that Government can have no lawful powers, except those with which it has been invested by lawful contract; and that an unlawful contract for the establishment of Government, is as unlawful and void as any other contract to do injustice. . . . No oaths, which judicial or other officers may take to carry out and support an unlawful contract or Constitution of Government, are of any moral obligation." . . .

And here begins the real and only important dispute between us. The reader may forget, if he pleases, all we have said. Mr. Spooner's differences and our own, up to this point, are mere questions of theory. It matters little which side be adopted. His position now is:

That laws and constitutions which violate justice, are void. They are as little binding in the eye of the law, as in the eye of God. They are *legally* as well as morally void.

So far we agree with him, or differ so slightly, that here we care not to dispute the matter. He goes on:

A Judge *holding office under such Constitutions* is authorized and bound to treat them as *void*, and to decide cases, not according to them, but as his sense "of natural justice" dictates.

Here we differ from him, maintaining that the position of the officers of such a Government differs from that of the private individual; their duty is to resign their posts whenever unwilling to fulfill the conditions on which they receive them, and then, AS MEN, treat the laws as void.

This question is not to be confounded with one somewhat similar to it, and which has been sometimes discussed, especially in England, whether a Judge there may disregard an unjust statute? Our present question is different, for it should be remembered that in England, there is no written Constitution. Even if a Judge had such powers there, WHICH HE HAS NOT, it would by no means follow, that he had the same under our form of Government. There the Judge swears, simply to bear true allegiance to the King. It might, therefore, with some plausibility, be argued, that having no test to which to bring acts of Parliament, except the rules of natural justice, Judges were authorized to declare them void when inconsistent with those rules. Such a doctrine, however, is repudiated by the almost unanimous voice of the English law.

But however it may be in England, here the case is different. Our Government is founded on contract. See, Pream, Mass. Cons.: J. Q. Adams's Oration at Quincy, p. 17: Jay, C. J., 2 Dall. 471. So agrees Mr. Spooner. . . .

Under our Constitution, then, the people and the office-holder make a contract together. They grant him certain specified powers, and demand of him certain specified duties. He deliberately looks over the catalogue (that is, the Constitution,)—assents to it,—swears that he agrees to it, and will perform his part,—and so takes office and acquires power. *That power,* Mr. Spooner thinks, he may retain while he refuses to perform the conditions on which he received it; and *that power,* granted him expressly, and only for the support of the Constitution, he is *bound* to use for the destruction of that instrument! Mr. Spooner's ground is that, "immoral contracts are void." Granted; but if they are absolute nullities, then the Governments supposed to spring from them, do not exist, since they have nothing to spring from. Accordingly, the supposed Judge is *no Judge,* and has no authority to *declare or decide anything.* As Mr. Spooner says, . . . "Such a contract of Government confers *no rightful authority* upon those appointed to administer it." Of course he would not have a Judge use a *wrongful* authority, for any purpose.

"Immoral contracts are not binding." Agreed. But are men at liberty to enter into agreements which they know at the time are immoral? Of course not. Is not the mere fact that men swear to support the Constitution sufficient proof to the nation that *they* do not consider the clauses of that instrument immoral, but feel at liberty, and really intend, to carry them out? What higher evidence or pledge can a man give that he considers a contract moral, than taking an oath to execute and support it?

Again, "immoral contracts are not binding." True. But if I receive a sum of money, on my promise to commit murder, and afterward, my moral sense awakens, and I refuse to do the deed, does that authorize me to retain the money? Such a moral sense would be a most accommodating one! and such godliness might well be "accounted gain"!

The rule plainly is that, if power is put into our hands on certain conditions, and we become, *from any cause*, unable or unwilling to fulfill those conditions, we ought to surrender back the power to those who granted it. If, therefore, the Constitution is pro-slavery, (as Mr. Spooner and ourselves are now supposing it to be,) the Judges have agreed to do certain pro-slavery acts, and they must perform their whole contract, or yield up the power they received on that condition. Judges are the people's servants, employed to do certain acts. If they cannot *do those acts,* let them "be no longer stewards."

Is Virtue Constitutional?

HENRY DAVID THOREAU

Influenced by the Jeffersonian concept of government as an imperfect human creation, Thoreau insisted on the maintenance of the individual will in the face of laws adopted by a mass democracy. He argued that mass law and mass government ignored the individual's moral decision, which was largely a matter of intuition. He felt that Nature, rather than man, should be the teacher, and that majority opinion could hardly be considered an acceptable substitute. In short, Thoreau refused to acknowledge any laws which failed to "establish justice in the world." Laws could be wrong, he insisted, and said that it was more desirable to cultivate respect for right than respect for law. Thoreau chose civil disobedience as his method of protest and spent time in jail for refusing to pay taxes to be used for a war (the Mexican War) he considered unjust. But it is essential to realize that Thoreau resisted the role of the reformer. He simply insisted upon the right of the individual to follow his own moral conscience. This point of view led inevitably to Thoreau's opposition to the Fugitive Slave Act of 1850. "I cannot for an instant recognize that political organization as my *government which is the* slave's *government also," he declared. Duty required disobedience to an unjust law. Thoreau's belief in the power of "passive resistance" is shared to this day by movements for social and legal change, as any reading of current newspaper headlines will reveal.*

THE LAW will never make men free; it is men who have got to make the law free. They are the lovers of law and other who observe the law when the government breaks it. . . . I would remind my countrymen that they are to be men first, and Americans only at a late and convenient hour. . . .

I am sorry to say that I doubt if there is a judge in Massachusetts who is prepared to resign his office, and get his living innocently, whenever it is required of him to pass sentence under a law which is merely

Henry David Thoreau, *Slavery in Massachusetts* (1854), p. 181.

contrary to the law of God. I am compelled to see that they put themselves, or rather are by character, in this respect, exactly on a level with the marine who discharges his musket in any direction he is ordered to. They are just as much tools, and as little men. Certainly, they are not the more to be respected, because their master enslaves their understandings and consciences, instead of their bodies.

The judges and lawyers,—simply as such, I mean,—and all men of expediency, try this case by a very low and incompetent standard. They consider, not whether the Fugitive Slave Law is right, but whether it is what they call *constitutional*. Is virtue constitutional, or vice? Is equity constitutional, or iniquity? In important moral and vital questions, like this, it is just as impertinent to ask whether a law is constitutional or not, as to ask whether it is profitable or not. They persist in being the servants of the worst of men, and not the servants of humanity. The question is, not whether you or your grandfather, seventy years ago, did not enter into an agreement to serve the Devil, and that service is not accordingly now due; but whether you will not now, for once and at last, serve God,—in spite of your own past recreancy, or that of your ancestor,—by obeying that eternal and only just CONSTITUTION, which He, and not any Jefferson or Adams, has written in your being.

The amount of it is, if the majority vote the Devil to be God, the minority will live and behave accordingly,—and obey the successful candidate, trusting that, some time or other, by some Speaker's casting-vote, perhaps, they may reinstate God. This is the highest principle I can get out or invent for my neighbors. These men act as if they believed that they could safely slide down a hill a little way,—or a good way,—and would surely come to a place, by and by, where they could begin to slide up again. This is expediency, or choosing that course which offers the slightest obstacles to the feet, that is, a downhill one. But there is no such thing as accomplishing a righteous reform by the use of "expediency." There is no such thing as sliding up hill. In morals the only sliders are backsliders.

Thus we steadily worship Mammon, both school and state and church, and on the seventh day curse God with a tintamar from one end of the Union to the other.

Will mankind never learn that policy is not morality,—that it never secures any moral right, but considers merely what is expedient? chooses the available candidate,—who is invariably the Devil,—and what right have his constituents to be surprised, because the Devil does not behave like an angel of light? What is wanted is men, not of policy, but of probity, —who recognize a higher law than the Constitution, or the decision of the majority. The fate of the country does not depend on how you vote at the polls,—the worst man is as strong as the best at that game; it does not depend on what kind of paper you drop into the ballot-box once a year, but on what kind of man you drop from your chamber into the street every morning.

What should concern Massachusetts is not the Nebraska Bill, nor the Fugitive Slave Bill, but her own slaveholding and servility. Let the State dissolve her union with the slaveholder. She may wriggle and hesitate, and ask leave to read the Constitution once more; but she can find no respectable law or precedent which sanctions the continuance of such a union for an instant.

Let each inhabitant of the State dissolve his union with her, as long as she delays to do her duty.

The events of the past month teach me to distrust Fame. I see that she does not finely discriminate, but coarsely hurrahs. She considers not the simple heroism of an action, but only as it is connected with its apparent consequences. She praises till she is hoarse the easy exploit of the Boston tea party, but will be comparatively silent about the braver and more disinterestedly heroic attack on the Boston Court-House, simply because it was unsuccessful!

Covered with disgrace, the State has sat down coolly to try for their lives and liberties the men who attempted to do its duty for it. And this is called *justice!* They who have shown that they can behave particularly well may perchance be put under bonds for *their good behavior.* They whom truth requires at present to plead guilty are, of all the inhabitants of the State, preëminently innocent. While the Governor, and the Mayor, and countless officers of the Commonwealth are at large, the champions of liberty are imprisoned.

Only they are guiltless who commit the crime of contempt of such a court. It behooves every man to see that his influence is on the side of justice, and let the courts make their own characters. My sympathies in this case are wholly with the accused, and wholly against their accusers and judges. Justice is sweet and musical; but injustice is harsh and discordant. The judge still sits grinding at his organ, but it yields no music, and we hear only the sound of the handle. He believes that all the music resides in the handle, and the crowd toss him their coppers the same as before.

Do you suppose that that Massachusetts which is now doing these things,—which hesitates to crown these men, some of whose lawyers, and even judges, perchance, may be driven to take refuge in some poor quibble, that they may not wholly outrage their instinctive sense of justice,—do you suppose that she is anything but base and servile? that she is the champion of liberty?

Show me a free state, and a court truly of justice, and I will fight for them, if need be; but show me Massachusetts, and I refuse her my allegiance, and express contempt for her courts. . . .

I have lived for the last month—and I think that every man in Massachusetts capable of the sentiment of patriotism must have had a similar experience—with the sense of having suffered a vast and indefinite loss. I did not know at first what ailed me. At last it occurred to me that what I had lost was a country. I had never respected the government near to which I lived, but I had foolishly thought that I might manage to live here, minding my private affairs, and forget it. For my part, my old and worthiest pursuits have lost I cannot say how much of their attraction, and I feel that my investment in life here is worth many per cent. less since Massachusetts last deliberately sent back an innocent man, Anthony Burns, to slavery. I dwelt before, perhaps, in the illusion that my life passed somewhere only *between* heaven and hell, but now I cannot persuade myself that I do not dwell *wholly within* hell. The site of that political organization called Massachusetts is to me morally covered with volcanic scoriæ and cinders, such as Milton describes in the infernal regions. If there is any hell more unprincipled than our rulers, and we, the ruled, I feel curious to see it. . . .

But it chanced the other day that I scented a white water-lily, and a season I had waited for had arrived. It is the emblem of purity. It bursts up so pure and fair to the eye, and so sweet to the scent, as if to show us what purity and sweetness reside in, and can be extracted from, the slime and muck of earth. I think I have plucked the first one that has opened for a mile. What confirmation of our hopes is in the fragrance of this flower! I shall not so soon despair of the world for it, notwithstanding slavery, and the cowardice and want of principle of Northern men. It suggests what kind of laws have prevailed longest and widest, and still prevail, and that the time may come when man's deeds will smell as sweet. Such is the odor which the plant emits. If Nature can compound this fragrance still annually, I shall believe her still young and full of vigor, her integrity and genius unimpaired, and that there is virtue even in man, too, who is fitted to perceive and love it. It reminds me that Nature has been partner to no Missouri Compromise. I scent no compromise in the fragrance of the water-lily. It is not a *Nymphæa* DOUGLASSII. In it, the sweet, and pure, and innocent are wholly sundered from the obscene and baleful. I do not scent in this the time-serving irresolution of a Massachusetts Governor, nor of a Boston Mayor. So behave that the odor of your actions may enhance the general sweetness of the atmosphere, that when we behold or scent a flower, we may not be reminded how inconsistent your deeds are with it; for all odor is but one form of advertisement of a moral quality, and if fair actions had not been performed, the lily would not smell sweet. The foul slime stands for the sloth and vice of man, the decay of humanity; the fragrant flower that springs from it, for the purity and courage which are immortal.

Slavery and servility have produced no sweet-scented flower annually, to charm the senses of men, for they have no real life: they are merely a decaying and a death, offensive to all healthy nostrils. We do not complain that they *live*, but that they do not *get buried*. Let the living bury them; even they are good for manure.

Equality Before the Law

CHARLES SUMNER

Throughout his many years in the Senate, Sumner's goal was "absolute human equality, secured, assured, and invulnerable." His eloquent pleas failed to move Chief Justice Shaw, whose opinion remained law until the repudiation of the separate but equal doctrine in 1954. Shaw ruled that prejudice was "not created by law, and probably cannot be changed by law," and refused to interfere with the discretion of the school committee.

MAY IT PLEASE YOUR HONORS:—
Can any discrimination on account of race or color be made among children entitled to the benefit of our Common Schools under the Constitution and Laws of Massachusetts? This is the question which the Court is now to hear, to consider, and to decide.

Or, stating the question with more detail, and with more particular application to the facts of the present case, are the Committee having superintendence of the Common Schools of Boston intrusted with *power*, under the Constitution and Laws of Massachusetts, to exclude colored children from the schools, and compel them to find education at separate schools, set apart for colored children only, at distances from their homes less convenient than schools open to white children?

This important question arises in an action by a colored child only five years old, who, *by her next friend*, sues the city of Boston for damages on account of a refusal to receive her into one of the Common Schools.

It would be difficult to imagine any case appealing more strongly to your best judgment, whether you regard the parties or the subject. On the one side is the City of Boston, strong in wealth, influence, character; on the other side is a little child, of degraded color, of humble parents, and still within the period of natural infancy, but strong from her very weakness, and from the irrepressible sympathies of good men, which, by a divine compensation, come to succor the weak. This little child asks at your hands her *personal rights*. So doing, she calls upon you to decide a question which concerns the personal rights of other colored children,— which concerns the Constitution and Laws of the Commonwealth,—which concerns that *peculiar institution* of New England, the Common Schools,— which concerns the fundamental principles of human rights,—which concerns the Christian character of this community. Such parties and such interests justly challenge your earnest attention.

Charles Sumner, Argument in Roberts *v.* City of Boston, 5 *Cush. (Mass.)* (1849), p. 198.

Though this discussion is now for the first time brought before a judicial tribunal, it is no stranger to the public. In the School Committee of Boston for five years it has been the occasion of discord. No less than four different reports, two majority and two minority, forming pamphlets, of solid dimensions, devoted to this question, have been made to this Committee, and afterwards published. The opinions of learned counsel have been enlisted. The controversy, leaving these regular channels, overflowed the newspaper press, and numerous articles appeared, espousing opposite sides. At last it has reached this tribunal. It is in your power to make it subside forever.

The Question Stated.

Forgetting many of the topics and all of the heats heretofore mingling with the controversy, I shall strive to present the question in its juridical light, as becomes the habits of this tribunal. It is a question of jurisprudence on which you are to give judgment. But I cannot forget that the principles of morals and of natural justice lie at the foundation of all jurisprudence. Nor can any reference to these be inappropriate in a discussion before this Court.

Of Equality I shall speak, not only as a sentiment, but as a principle embodied in the Constitution of Massachusetts, and obligatory upon court and citizen. It will be my duty to show that this principle, after finding its way into our State Constitution, was recognized in legislation and judicial decisions. Considering next the circumstances of this case, it will be easy to show how completely they violate Constitution, legislation, and judicial proceedings,—*first*, by subjecting colored children to inconvenience inconsistent with the requirements of Equality, and, *secondly,* by eestablishing a system of Caste odious as that of the Hindoos,—leading to the conclusion that the School Committee have no such power as they have exercised, and that it is the duty of the Court to set aside their unjust by-law. In the course of this discussion I shall exhibit the true idea of our Common Schools, and the fallacy of the pretension that any exclusion or discrimination founded on race or color can be consistent with Equal Rights.

In opening this argument, I begin naturally with the fundamental proposition which, when once established, renders the conclusion irresistible. According to the Constitution of Massachusetts, *all men, without distinction of race or color, are equal before the law.* In the statement of this proposition I use language which, though new in our country, has the advantage of precision.

Equality Before The Law: Its Meaning.

I might, perhaps, leave this proposition without one word of comment. The equality of men will not be directly denied on this occasion; and yet it is so often assailed of late, that I shall not seem to occupy your time superfluously, I trust, while endeavoring to show what is understood by this term, when used in laws, constitutions, or other political instruments. Here I encounter a prevailing misapprehension. Lord Brougham, in his recent work on Political Philosophy, announces, with something of pungency, that "the notion of Equality, or anything approaching to Equality, among the different members of any community, is altogether wild and fantastic." Mr. Calhoun, in the Senate of the United States, assails both the principle and the form of its statement. He does not hesitate to say that the claim in the Declaration of Independence is "the most false and dangerous of all political errors,"—that it "has done more to retard the cause of liberty and civilization, and is doing more at present, than all other causes combined,"—that "for a long time it lay dormant, but in the process of time it began to germinate and produce its poisonous fruits." Had these two distinguished authorities chosen to comprehend the extent and application of the term thus employed, something, if not all, of their objection would have disappeared. That we may better appreciate its meaning and limitation, I am induced to exhibit the origin and growth of the sentiment, which, finally ripening into a formula of civil and political right, was embodied in the Constitution of Massachusetts.

Equality as a sentiment was early cherished by generous souls. It showed itself in dreams of ancient philosophy, and was declared by Seneca, when, in a letter of consolation on death, he said, *Prima enim pars Æquitatis est Æqualitas*: "The chief part of Equity is Equality." But not till the truths of the Christian Religion was it enunciated with persuasive force. Here we learn that God is no respecter of persons,—that he is the Father of all,—and that we are all his children, and brethren to each other. When the Saviour gave us the Lord's Prayer, he taught the sublime doctrine of Human Brotherhood, enfolding the equality of men. . . .

Hooker and Locke saw the equality of men in a state of Nature; but their utterances found more acceptance across the Channel than in England.

It is to France that we must pass for the earliest development of this idea, its amplest illustration, and its most complete, accurate, and logical expression. In the middle of the last century appeared the renowned *Encyclopédie*, edited by Diderot and D'Alembert. This remarkable production, where science, religion, and government are discussed with revolutionary freedom, contains an article on Equality, first published in 1755. Here we find the boldest expression of this sentiment down to that time. "Natural Equality," says this authority, "is that which exists between all men by the constitution of their nature only. This Equality is the principle and the foundation of Liberty. Natural or moral equality is, then, founded upon the constitution of human nature common to all men, who are born, grow, subsist, and die in the same manner. . . ."

The civilization of the age joins in this appeal. I need not remind you that this prejudice of color is peculiar to our country. You may remember that two youths of African blood only recently gained the highest honors in a college at Paris, and on the same day dined with the King of the French, the descendant of St. Louis, at the Palace of the Tuileries. And let me add, if I may refer to my own experience, that at the School of Law in Paris I have sat for weeks on the same benches with colored pupils, listening, like myself, to the learned lectures of Degerando and Rossi; nor do I remember, in the throng of sensitive young men, any feeling toward them except of companionship and respect. In Italy, at the Convent of Palazzuolo, on the shores of the Alban Lake, amidst a scene of natural beauty enhanced by historical association, where I was once a guest, I have, for days, seen a native of Abyssinia, recently from his torrid home, and ignorant of the language spoken about him, mingling, in delightful and affectionate familiarity, with the Franciscan friars, whose visitor and scholar he was. Do I err in saying that the Christian spirit shines in these examples?

The Christian spirit, then, I again invoke. Where this prevails, there is neither Jew nor Gentile, Greek nor Barbarian, bond nor free, but all are alike. From this we derive new and solemn assurance of the Equality of Men, as an ordinance of God. Human bodies may be unequal in beauty or strength; these mortal cloaks of flesh may differ, as do these worldly garments; these intellectual faculties may vary, as do opportunities of action and advantages of position; but amid all unessential differences there is essential agreement and equality. Dives and Lazarus are equal in the sight of God: they must be equal in the sight of all human institutions.

This is not all. The vaunted superiority of the white race imposes corresponding duties. The faculties with which they are endowed, and the advantages they possess, must be exercised for the good of all. If the colored people are ignorant, degraded, and unhappy, then should they be especial objects of care. From the abundance of our possessions must we seek to remedy their lot. And this Court, which is parent to all the unfortunate children of the Commonwealth, will show itself most truly parental, when it reaches down, and, with the strong arm of Law, elevates, encourages, and protects our colored fellow-citizens.

The Politics of Judicial Opinion-Writing

ROBERT C. GRIER

Dealing not with the free Negro but the slave was the famous Dred Scott case. The case was in the courts for over ten years and had been before the Supreme Court since 1854. Though it was apparently ready for de-

---

Mr. Justice Grier, Letter to James Buchanan, Feb. 23, 1857, Charles Warren, *The Supreme Court in United States History*, II (1926), p. 295.

cision in 1856, it was further deferred in order not to influence the Presidential election. Had the decision been released on schedule, it might have caused the election of Frémont rather than Buchanan. The following letter from Mr. Justice Grier to the President-elect is a surprisingly frank discussion of the situation.

YOUR LETTER came to hand this morning. I have taken the liberty to show it, in confidence, to our mutual friends, Judge Wayne and the Chief Justice [Roger B. Taney].

We fully appreciate and concur in your views as to the desirableness at this time of having an expression of the opinion of the Court on this troublesome question. With their concurrence, I will give you in confidence the history of the case before us, with the probable result. Owing to the sickness and absence of a member of the Court, the case was not taken up in conference till lately. The first question which presented itself was the right of a negro to sue in the Courts of the United States. A majority of the Court were of the opinion that the question did not arise on the pleadings and that we were compelled to give an opinion on the merits. After much discussion it was finally agreed that the merits of the case might be satisfactorily decided without giving an opinion on the question of the Missouri Compromise; and the case was committed to Judge Nelson to write the opinion of the Court affirming the judgment of the Court below, but leaving these difficult questions untouched. But it appeared that our brothers who dissented from the majority, especially Justice McLean, were determined to come out with a long and labored dissent, including their opinions and arguments on both the troublesome points, although not necessary to a decision of the case. In our opinion both the points are *in* the case and may be legitimately considered. Those who hold a different opinion from Messrs. McLean and Curtis on the power of Congress and the validity of the Compromise Act feel compelled to express their opinions on the subject, Nelson and myself refusing to commit ourselves. A majority including all the Judges south of Mason and Dixon's line agreeing in the result, but not in their reasons,—as the question will be thus forced upon us, I am anxious that it should not appear that the line of latitude should mark the line of division in the Court. I feel also that the opinion of the majority will fail of much of its effect if founded on clashing and inconsistent arguments. On conversation with the Chief Justice, I have agreed to concur with him. Brother Wayne and myself will also use our endeavors to get brothers Daniel and Campbell and Catron to do the same. So that if the question must be met, there will be an opinion of the Court upon it, if possible, without the contradictory views which would weaken its force. But I fear some rather extreme views may be thrown out by some of our southern brethren. There will therefore be six, if not seven (perhaps Nelson will remain neutral) who will decide the Compromise law of 1820 to be of *non-effect*. But the opinions will not be delivered before Friday the 6th of March. We will not let any others of our brethren know anything about *the cause of our anxiety* to produce this result, and though contrary to our usual practice, we have thought it due to you to state to you in candor and confidence the real state of the matter.

Rights of a Citizen

DRED SCOTT V. SANDFORD

THE WORDS "people of the United States" and "citizens" are synonymous terms, and mean the same thing. They both describe the political body who, according to our republican institutions, form the sovereignty, and who hold the power and conduct the Government through their representatives. They are what we familiarly call the "sovereign people," and every citizen is one of this people, and a constituent member of this sovereignty. The question before us is, whether the class of persons described in the plea in abatement compose a portion of this people, and are constituent members of this sovereignty? We think they are not, and that they are not included, and were not intended to be included, under the word "citizens" in the Constitution, and can therefore claim none of the rights and privileges which that instrument provides for and secures to citizens of the United States. On the contrary, they were at that time considered as a subordinate and inferior class of beings, who had been subjugated by the dominant race, and, whether emancipated or not, yet remained subject to their authority, and had no rights or privileges but such as those who held the power and the Government might choose to grant them.

It is not the province of the court to decide upon the justice or injustice, the policy or impolicy, of these laws. The decision of that question belonged to the political or law-making power; to those who formed the sovereignty and framed the Constitution. The duty of the court is, to interpret the instrument they have framed, with the best lights we can obtain on the subject, and to administer it as we find it, according to its true intent and meaning when it was adopted.

In discussing this question, we must not confound the rights of citizenship which a State may confer within its own limits, and the rights of citizenship as a member of the Union. It does not by any means follow, because he has all the rights and privileges of a citizen of a State, that he must be a citizen of the United States. He may have all of the rights and privileges of the citizen of a State, and yet not be entitled to the rights and privileges of a citizen in any other State. For, previous to the adoption of

19 *Howards* (1856), p. 404.

the Constitution of the United States, every State had the undoubted right to confer on whomsoever it pleased the character of citizen, and to endow him with all its rights. But this character of course was confined to the boundaries of the State, and gave him no rights or privileges in other States beyond those secured to him by the laws of nations and the comity of States. Nor have the several States surrendered the power of conferring these rights and privileges by adopting the Constitution of the United States. Each State may still confer them upon an alien, or any one it thinks proper, or upon any class or description of persons; yet he would not be a citizen in the sense in which that word is used in the Constitution of the United States, nor entitled to sue as such in one of its courts, nor to the privileges and immunities of a citizen in the other States. The rights which he would acquire would be restricted to the State which gave them. The Constitution has conferred on Congress the right to establish an uniform rule of naturalization, and this right is evidently exclusive, and has always been held by this court to be so. Consequently, no State, since the adoption of the Constitution, can by naturalizing an alien invest him with the rights and privileges secured to a citizen of a State under the Federal Government, although, so far as the State alone was concerned, he would undoubtedly be entitled to the rights of a citizen, and clothed with all the rights and immunities which the Constitution and laws of the State attached to that character. . . .

The question then arises, whether the provisions of the Constitution, in relation to the personal rights and privileges to which the citizen of a State should be entitled, embraced the negro African race, at that time in this country, or who might afterwards be imported, who had then or should afterwards be made free in any State; and to put it in the power of a single State to make him a citizen of the United States, and endue him with the full rights of citizenship in every other State without their consent? Does the Constitution of the United States act upon him whenever he shall be made free under the laws of a State, and raised there to the rank of a citizen, and immediately clothe him with all the privileges of a citizen in every other State, and in its own courts?

The court think the affirmative of these propositions cannot be maintained. And if it cannot, the plaintiff in error could not be a citizen of the State of Missouri, within the meaning of the Constitution of the United States, and, consequently, was not entitled to sue in its courts.

It is true, every person, and every class and description of persons, who were at the time of the adoption of the Constitution recognised as citizens in the several States, became also citizens of this new political body; but none other; it was formed by them, and for them and their posterity, but for no one else. And the personal rights and privileges guarantied to citizens of this new sovereignty were intended to embrace those only who were then members of the several State communities, or who should afterwards by birthright or otherwise become members, according to the provisions of the Constitution and the principles on which it was founded. It was the union of those who were at that time members of distinct and separate political communities into one political family, whose power, for certain specified purposes, was to extend over the whole territory of the United States. And it gave to each citizen rights and privileges outside of his State which he did not before possess, and placed him in every other State upon a perfect equality with its own citizens as to rights of person and rights of property; it made him a citizen of the United States.

It becomes necessary, therefore, to determine who were citizens of the several States when the Constitution was adopted. And in order to do this, we must recur to the Governments and institutions of the thirteen colonies, when they separated from Great Britain and formed new sovereignties, and took their places in the family of independent nations. We must inquire who, at that time, were recognised as the people or citizens of a State, whose rights and liberties had been outraged by the English Government; and who declared their independence, and assumed the powers of Government to defend their rights by force of arms.

In the opinion of the court, the legislation and histories of the times, and the language used in the Declaration of Independence, show, that neither the class of persons who had been imported as slaves, nor their descendants, whether they had become free or not, were then acknowledged as a part of the people, nor intended to be included in the general words used in that memorable instrument.

It is difficult at this day to realize the state of public opinion in relation to that unfortunate race, which prevailed in the civilized and enlightened portions of the world at the time of the Declaration of Independence, and when the Constitution of the United States was framed and adopted. But the public history of every European nation displays it in a manner too plain to be mistaken.

They had for more than a century before been regarded as beings of an inferior order, and altogether unfit to associate with the white race, either in social or political relations; and so far inferior, that they had no rights which the while man was bound to respect; and that the negro might justly and lawfully be reduced to slavery for his benefit. He was bought and sold, and treated as an ordinary article of merchandise and traffic, whenever a profit could be made by it. This opinion was at that time fixed and universal in the civilized portion of the white race. It was regarded as an axiom in morals as well as in politics, which no one thought of disputing, or supposed to be open to dispute; and men in every grade and position in society daily and habitually acted upon it in their private pursuits, as well as in matters of public concern, without doubting for a moment the correctness of this opinion.

And in no nation was this opinion more firmly fixed or more uniformly acted upon than by the English Government and English people. They not only seized them on the coast of Africa, and sold them or held them in slavery for their own use; but they took them as ordinary articles of merchandise to every country where they could make a profit on them, and were far more extensively engaged in this commerce than any other nation in the world.

The opinion thus entertained and acted upon in England was naturally impressed upon the colonies they founded on this side of the Atlantic. And, accordingly, a negro of the African race was regarded by them as an article of property, and held, and bought and sold as such, in every one of the thirteen colonies which united in the Declaration of Independence, and afterwards formed the Constitution of the United States. The slaves were more or less numerous in the different colonies, as slave labor was found more or less profitable. But no one seems to have doubted the correctness of the prevailing opinion of the time. . . .

The general words [of the Declaration of Independence] above quoted would seem to embrace the whole human family, and if they were used in a similar instrument at this day would be so understood. But it is too clear for dispute, that the enslaved African race were not intended to be included, and formed no part of the people who framed and adopted this declaration; for if the language, as understood in that day, would embrace them, the conduct of the distinguished men who framed the Declaration of Independence would have been utterly and flagrantly inconsistent with the principles they asserted; and instead of the sympathy of mankind, to which they so confidently appealed, they would have deserved and received universal rebuke and reprobation.

Yet the men who framed this declaration were great men—high in literary acquirements—high in their sense of honor, and incapable of asserting principles inconsistent with those on which they were acting. They perfectly understood the meaning of the language they used, and how it would be understood by others; and they knew that it would not in any part of the civilized world be supposed to embrace the negro race, which, by common consent, had been excluded from civilized Governments and the family of nations, and doomed to slavery. They spoke and acted according to the then established doctrines and principles, and in the ordinary language of the day, and no one misunderstood them. The unhappy black race were separated from the white by indelible marks, and laws long before established, and were never thought of or spoken of except as property, and when the claims of the owner or the profit of the trader were supposed to need protection.

This state of public opinion had undergone no change when the Constitution was adopted, as is equally evident from its provisions and language.

Debate on Slavery

ABRAHAM LINCOLN and STEPHEN A. DOUGLAS

Mr. Chief Justice Taney could have returned Dred Scott to slavery from Minnesota on the ground of no standing, but he went on to declare the Missouri Compromise unconstitutional and did away with squatter sovereignty. This raised the basic issue with which the Lincoln-Douglas debates were concerned, as to the acceptance of the Supreme Court's determination. The free-soil North refused to accept the decision, much as the South was soon to refuse to accept the results of a Presidential election. Defiance of positive law—most eloquently voiced by Thoreau—was no longer the sign of the crackpot.

Abraham Lincoln

THE SECOND INTERROGATORY that I propounded to [Judge Douglas] was this:

Can the people of a United States Territory, in any lawful way, against the wish of any citizen of the United States, exclude slavery from its limits prior to the formation of a State Constitution?

To this Judge Douglas answered that they can lawfully exclude slavery from the Territory prior to the formation of a constitution. He goes on to tell us how it can be done. As I understand him, he holds that it can be done by the Territorial Legislature refusing to make any enactments for the protection of slavery in the Territory, and especially by adopting unfriendly legislation to it. . . .

If I rightly understand him, I wish to ask your attention for a while to his position.

In the first place, the Supreme Court of the United States has decided that any Congressional prohibition of slavery in the Territories is unconstitutional—that they have reached this proposition as a conclusion from their former proposition that the Constitution of the United States expressly recognizes property in slaves, and from that other constitutional provision that no person shall be deprived of property without due process of law. Hence they reach the conclusion that as the Constitution of the United States expressly recognizes property in slaves, and prohibits any person from being deprived of property without due process of law, to pass an act of Congress by which a man who owned a slave on one side of a line would be deprived of him if he took him on the other side, is depriving him of that property without due process of law. That I understand to be the decision of the Supreme Court. I understand also that Judge Douglas adheres most firmly to that decision; and the difficulty is, how is it possible

Abraham Lincoln, *Collected Works*, III (1953), pp. 128, 142, 400.

for any power to exclude slavery from the Territory unless in violation of that decision? That is the difficulty.

In the Senate of the United States, in 1856, Judge Trumbull in a speech, substantially if not directly, put the same interrogatory to Judge Douglas, as to whether the people of a Territory had the lawful power to exclude slavery prior to the formation of a constitution? Judge Douglas then answered at considerable length, and his answer will be found in the *Congressional Globe*, under date of June 9th, 1856. The Judge said that whether the people could exclude slavery prior to the formation of a constitution or not *was a question to be decided by the Supreme Court*. He put that proposition, as will be seen by the *Congressional Globe*, in a variety of forms, all running to the same thing in substance—that it was a question for the Supreme Court. I maintain that when he says, after the Supreme Court have decided the question, that the people may yet exclude slavery by any means whatever, he does virtually say, that it is *not* a question for the Supreme Court [Applause.] He shifts his ground. . . . He did not stop then to tell us that whatever the Supreme Court decides the people can by withholding necessary "police regulations" keep slavery out. . . .

I hold that the history of this country shows that the institution of slavery was originally planted upon this continent *without* these "police regulations" which the Judge now thinks necessary for the actual establishment of it. Not only so, but is there not another fact—how came this Dred Scott decision to be made? It was made upon the case of a negro being taken and actually held in slavery in Minnesota Territory, claiming his freedom because the act of Congress prohibited his being so held there. *Will the Judge pretend that Dred Scott was not held there without police regulations?* There is at least one matter of record as to his having been held in slavery in the Territory, not only without police regulations, but in the teeth of Congressional legislation supposed to be valid at the time. This shows that there is vigor enough in Slavery to plant itself in a new country even against unfriendly legislation. It takes not only law but the *enforcement* of law to keep it out. That is the history of this country upon the subject.

I wish to ask one other question. It being understood that the Constitution of the United States guarantees property in slaves in the Territories, if there is any infringement of the right of that property, would not the United States Courts, organized for the government of the Territory, apply such remedy as might be necessary in that case? It is a maxim held by the Courts, that there is no wrong without its remedy; and the Courts have a remedy for whatever is acknowledged and treated as a wrong.

Again: I will ask you my friends, if you were elected members of the Legislature, what would be the first thing you would have to do before entering upon your duties? *Swear to support the Constitution of the United States.* Suppose you believe, as Judge Douglas does, that the Constitution of the United States guarantees to your neighbor the right to hold slaves in that Territory—that they are his property—how can you clear your oaths unless you give him such legislation as is necessary to enable him to enjoy that property? What do you understand by supporting the Constitution of a State or of the United States? Is it not to give such constitutional helps to the rights established by that Constitution as may be practically needed? Can you, if you swear to support the Constitution, and believe that the Constitution establishes a right, clear your oath, without giving it support? Do you support the Constitution if, knowing or believing there is a right established under it which needs specific legislation, you withhold that legislation? Do you not violate and disregard your oath? I can conceive of nothing plainer in the world. There can be nothing in the words "support the Constitution," if you may run counter to it by refusing support to any right established under the Constitution. And what I say here will hold with still more force against the Judge's doctrine of "unfriendly legislation." How could you, having sworn to support the Constitution, and believing it guaranteed the right to hold slaves in the Territories, assist in legislation *intended to defeat that right*? That would be violating your own view of the Constitution. Not only so, but if you were to do so, how long would it take the courts to hold your votes unconstitutional and void? Not a moment.

Lastly I would ask—is not Congress, itself, under obligation to give legislative support to any right that is established under the United States Constitution? I repeat the question—is not Congress, itself, bound to give legislative support to any right that is established in the United States Constitution? A member of Congress swears to support the Constitution of the United States, and if he sees a right established by that Constitution which needs specific legislative protection, can he clear his oath without giving that protection? Let me ask you why many of us who are opposed to slavery upon principle give our acquiescence to a fugitive slave law? Why do we hold ourselves under obligations to pass such a law, and abide by it when it is passed? Because the Constitution makes provision that the owners of slaves shall have the right to reclaim them. It gives the right to reclaim slaves, and that right is, as Judge Douglas says, a barren right, unless there is legislation that will enforce it.

The mere declaration "No person held to service or labor in one State under the laws thereof, escaping into another, shall in consequence of any law or regulation therein be discharged from such service or labor, but shall be delivered up on claim of the party to whom such service or labor may be due" is powerless without specific legislation to enforce it. Now on what ground would a member of Congress who is opposed to slavery in the abstract vote for a fugitive law, as I would deem it my duty to do? Because there is a Constitutional right which needs legislation to enforce it. And although it is distasteful to me, I have sworn to support the Constitution, and having so sworn I cannot conceive that I do support it if I withheld from that right any necessary legislation to make it practical. And if that is true in regard to a fugitive slave law, is the right to have fugitive slaves reclaimed any better fixed in the Constitution than the right to hold slaves in the Territories? For this decision is a just exposition of the Constitution as Judge Douglas thinks. Is the one right any better than the other? Is there any man who while a member of Congress would give support to the one any more than the other? If I wished to refuse to give legislative support to slave property in the Territories, if a member of Congress, I could not do it holding the view that the Constitution establishes that right. If I did it at all, it would be because I deny that this decision properly construes the Constitution. But if I acknowledge with Judge Douglas that this decision properly construes the Constitution, I cannot conceive that I would be less than a perjured man if I should refuse in Congress to give such protection to that property as in its nature it needed. . . .

Stephen A. Douglas

If the decision of the Supreme Court, the tribunal created by the Constitution to decide the question, is final and binding, is he not bound by it just as strongly as if he was for it instead of against it originally. Is every man in this land allowed to resist decisions he does not like, and only support those that meet his approval? What are important courts worth unless their decisions are binding on all good citizens? It is the fundamental principles of the judiciary that its decisions are final. It is created for that purpose so that when you cannot agree among yourselves on a disputed point you appeal to the judicial tribunal which steps in and decides for you, and that decision is then binding on every good citizen. It is the law of the land just as much with Mr. Lincoln against it as for it. And yet he says that if that decision is binding he is a perjured man if he does not vote for a slave code in the different territories of this Union. Well, if you (turning to Mr. Lincoln) are not going to resist the decision, if you obey it, and do not intend to array mob law against the constituted authorities, then, according to your own statement, you will be a perjured man if you do not vote to establish slavery in these territories. My doctrine is, that even taking Mr. Lincoln's view that the decision recognizes the right of a man to carry his slaves into the territories of the United States, if he pleases, yet after he gets there he needs affirmative law to make that right of any value. . . .

Abraham Lincoln

[Judge Douglas] denounces all who question the correctness of that decision, as offering violent resistance to it. But who resists it? Who has, in spite of the decision, declared Dred Scott free, and resisted the authority of his master over him?

Judicial decisions have two uses—first, to absolutely determine the case decided, and secondly, to indicate to the public how other similar cases will be decided when they arise. For the latter use, they are called "precedents" and "authorities."

We believe, as much as Judge Douglas, (perhaps more) in obedience to, and respect for the judicial department of government. We think its decisions on Constitutional questions, when fully settled, should control, not only the particular cases decided, but the general policy of the country, subject to be disturbed only by amendments of the Constitution as provided in that instrument itself. More than this would be revolution. But we think the Dred Scott decision is erroneous. We know the court that made it, has often over-ruled its own decisions, and we shall do what we can to have it to over-rule this. We offer no *resistance* to it.

Judicial decisions are of greater or less authority as precedents, according to circumstances. That this should be so, accords both with common sense, and the customary understanding of the legal profession.

If this important decision had been made by the unanimous concurrence of the judges, and without any apparent partisan bias, and in accordance with legal public expectation, and with the steady practice of the departments throughout our history, and had been in no part, based on assumed historical facts which are not really true; or, if wanting in some of these, it had been before the court more than once, and had there been affirmed and re-affirmed through a course of years, it then might be, perhaps would be, factious, nay, even revolutionary, to not acquiesce in it as a precedent.

But when, as it is true we find it wanting in all these claims to the public confidence, it is not resistance, it is not factious, it is not even disrespectful, to treat it as not having yet quite established a settled doctrine for the country.

CRIMINAL LAW

Abolition of Capital Punishment

EDWARD LIVINGSTON

I APPROACHED the inquiry into the nature and effect of this punishment with the awe becoming a man who felt, most deeply, his liability to err, and the necessity of forming a correct opinion on a point so interesting to

Edward Livingston, *Report on the Project of a New Penal Code* (1824), pp. 35, 57.

the justice of the country, the life of its citizens, and the character of its laws. I strove to clear my understanding from all prejudices which education, or early impressions might have created, and to produce a frame of mind fitted for the investigation of truth, and the impartial examination of the arguments on this great question. For this purpose, I not only consulted such writers on the subject as were within my reach, but endeavoured to procure a knowledge of the practical effect of this punishment on different crimes in the several countries where it is inflicted. In my situation, however, I could draw but a very limited advantage from either of these sources: very few books on penal law, even those most commonly referred to, are to be found in the scanty collections of this place, and my failure in procuring information from the other states, is more to be regretted on this than any other topic on which it was requested. With these inadequate means, but after the best use that my faculties would enable me to make of them; after long reflection, and not until I had canvassed every argument that could suggest itself to my mind, I came to the conclusion, that the punishment of death should find no place in the code which you have directed me to present. In offering this result, I feel a diffidence, which arises, not from any doubt of its correctness; I entertain none; but from the fear of being thought presumptuous in going beyond the point of penal reform, at which the wisdom of the other states has hitherto thought proper to stop; and from a reluctance to offer my opinions in opposition to those (certainly more entitled to respect than my own) which still support the propriety of this punishment for certain offences. On a mere speculative question, I should yield to this authority; but here I could not justify the confidence you have reposed in me, were I to give you the opinions of others, no matter how respectable they may be, instead of those which my best judgment assured me were right.

The example of the other states is certainly entitled to great respect; the greater, because all, without exception, still retain this punishment; but this example loses some of its force when we reflect on the slow progress of all improvement, and on the stubborn principles of the common law, which have particularly retarded its advance in jurisprudence.

In England, their parliament had been debating for near a century before they would take off capital punishment from two or three cases, in which every body allowed it was manifestly cruel and absurd: they have retained it in at least an hundred others of the same description; and when we reflect on these facts, and observe the influence which the prevailing opinions of that country have always had on the literature and jurisprudence of ours, we may account for the several states having stopped short in the reform of their penal law, without supposing them to have arrived at the point of perfection, beyond which it would be both unwise and presumptuous to pass. As to the authority of great names, it loses much of its force since the mass of the people have begun to think for themselves;

and since legislation is no longer considered as a trade, which none can practise with success, but those who have been educated to understand the mystery; the plain matter of fact, practical manner, in which that business is conducted with us, refers more to experience of facts than theory of reasoning: more to ideas of utility drawn from the state of society, than from the opinions of authors on the subject. If the argument were to be carried by the authority of names, that of Beccaria, were there no other, would ensure the victory. But reason alone, not precedent nor authority, must justify me in proposing to the general assembly this important change; reason alone can persuade them to adopt it. I proceed therefore to develope the considerations which carried conviction to my mind, but which being perhaps now more feebly urged than they were then felt, may fail in producing the same effect upon others. A great part of my task is rendered unnecessary, by the general acknowledgment, universal, I may say, in the United States, that this punishment ought to be abolished in all cases, excepting those of treason, murder and rape. In some states arson is included; and lately, since so large a portion of our influential citizens have become bankers, brokers, and dealers in exchange, a strong inclination has been discovered to extend it to forgery, and uttering false bills of exchange. As it is acknowledged then to be an inadequate remedy for minor offences, the argument will be restricted to an inquiry, whether there is any probability that it will be more efficient in cases of greater importance. Let us have constantly before us, when we reason on this subject, the great principle, that the end of punishment is the prevention of crime. Death, indeed, operates this end most effectually, as respects the delinquent; but the great object of inflicting it is the force of the example on others. If this spectacle of horror is insufficient to deter men from the commission of slight offences, what good reason can be given to persuade us that it will have this operation where the crime is more atrocious? . . .

The fear of death, therefore, will rarely deter from the commission of great crimes. It is, on the contrary, a remedy peculiarly inapplicable to those offences. Ambition, which usually inspires the crime of treason, soars above the fear of death; avarice, which whispers the secret murder, creeps below it; and the brutal debasement of the passion that prompts the only other crime, thus punished by our law, is proverbially blind to consequences, and regardless of obtacles that impede its gratification—threats of death will never deter men who are actuated by these passions; many of them affront it in the very commission of the offence, and therefore readily incur the lesser risk of suffering it, in what they think the impossible event of detection. But present other consequences more directly opposed to the enjoyments which were anticipated in the commission of the crime, make those consequences permanent and certain, and then, although milder, they will be less readily risked than the momentary pang attending the loss of life; study the passions which first suggested the offence, and apply your punishment to mortify and counteract them. The ambitious man cannot bear the ordinary restraints of government—subject him to those of a prison; he could not endure the superiority of the most dignified magistrate—force him to submit to the lowest officer of executive justice; he sought, by his crimes, a superiority above all that was most respectable in society—reduce him in his punishment to a level with the most vile and abject of mankind. If avarice suggested the murder—separate the wretch for ever from his hoard; realize the fable of antiquity; sentence him, from his place of penitence and punishment, to see his heirs rioting on his spoils; and the corroding reflection that others are innocently enjoying the fruits of his crime, will be as appropriate a punishment in practical as it was feigned to be in poetical justice. The rapacious spendthrift robs to support his extravagance, and murders to avoid detection; he exposes his life that he may either pass it in idleness, debauchery and sensual enjoyment, or lose it by a momentary pang—disappoint his profligate calculation; force him to live, but to live under those privations which he fears more than death; let him be reduced to the coarse diet, the hard lodging, and the incessant labour of a penitentiary.

Substitute these privations, which all such offenders fear, which they have all risked their lives to avoid; substitute these, to that death which has little terror for men whose passions or depravity have forced them to plunge in guilt, and you establish a fitness in the punishment to the crime; instead of a momentary spectacle, you exhibit a lesson, that is every day renewed; and you make the very passions which caused the offence the engines to punish it, and prevent its repetition.

Reformation is lost sight of in adopting this punishment, but ought it to be totally discarded? May not even great crimes be committed by persons whose minds are not so corrupted as to preclude the hope of this effect? They are, sometimes, produced by a single error—often are the consequences of a concatenation of circumstances never likely again to occur, and are very frequently the effect of a momentary hallucination, which, though not sufficient to excuse, ought sometimes to palliate the guilt; yet the operation of these several causes, the evident gradation in the degrees of guilt which they establish, are levelled before this destructive punishment. The man who, urged by an irresistible impulse of nature, sacrifices the base seducer who has destroyed his domestic happiness; he who having been calumniated, insulted, and dishonoured, at the risk of his own life, takes that of the slanderer; are, in the eye of this harsh law, equally deserving of death with the vile assassin who murders for hire, or poisons for revenge; and the youth, whose weakness in the commission of a first offence has yielded to the artful insinuations or overbearing influence of a veteran in vice, must perish on the same scaffold with the hardened and irreclaimable instigator of his crime. It may be said, that the pardoning power is the proper remedy for this evil; but the pardoning power, in capital cases, must be exercised, if at all, without loss of time; without that insight into character which the penitentiary system affords. It is, therefore, necessarily liable to abuse; and there is this further objection to its exercise, that it leaves no alternative between death and entire exemption from punishment; but in every degree of crime, some punishment is necessary; the novice, if subject to no reclaiming discipline, will soon become a professor in guilt: but let the corrective be judiciously applied, and its progress will discover whether he may be again trusted in society, or whether his depravity is so rooted as to require continued confinement.

In coming to a resolution on this solemn subject, we must not forget another principle we have established, and I think on the soundest reasons, that other things being equal, that punishment should be preferred, which gives us the means of correcting any false judgment, to which passion, indifference, false testimony, or deceiving appearances, may have given rise. Error from these, or other causes, is sometimes inevitable, its operation is instantaneous, and its fatal effects in the punishment of death, follow without delay; but time is required for its correction; we retrace our steps with difficulty; it is mortifying to acknowledge that we have been unjust, and during the time requisite for the discovery of the truth, for its operation on our unwilling minds, for the interposition of that power, which alone can stop the execution of the law, its stroke falls, and the innocent victim dies. What would not then the jurors who convicted; the judges who condemned; the mistaken witness who testified to his guilt; what would not the whole community who saw his dying agonies, who heard, at that solemn moment, his fruitless asseverations of innocence; what would they not all give to have yet within their reach the means of repairing the wrongs they had witnessed or inflicted?

Instances of this kind are not unfrequent; many of them are on record; several have taken place in our own day, and a very remarkable example which was given but a few years since, in one of the northern states, shows, in a striking manner, the danger of those punishments which cannot be recalled or compensated, even though the innocence of the sufferer is rendered clear to demonstration. A few such instances, even in a century, are sufficient to counteract the best effects that could be derived from example. There is no spectacle that takes such hold on the feelings as that of an innocent man suffering by an unjust sentence; one such example is remembered, when twenty of merited punishment are forgotten; the best passions take part against the laws, and arraign their operation as iniquitous and inhuman. This consideration alone, then, if there were no others, would be a most powerful argument for the abolition of capital punishments; but there are others no less cogent.

To see a human being in the full enjoyment of all the faculties of his mind, and all the energies of his body; his vital powers attacked by no disease; injured by no accident; the pulse beating high with youth and health; to see him doomed by the cool calculation of his fellow-men to certain destruction, which no courage can repel, no art or persuasion avert; to see a mortal distribute the most awful dispensation of the Deity, usurp his attributes and fix, by his own decree, an inevitable limit to that existence which Almighty power alone can give, and which its sentence alone should destroy; must give rise to solemn reflections, which the imposing spectacle of a human sacrifice naturally produces, until its frequent recurrence renders the mind insensible to the impression. But in a country where the punishment of death is rarely inflicted, this sensation operates in all its force; the people are always strongly excited by every trial for a capital offence; they neglect their business, and crowd round the court; the accused, the witnesses, the counsel, everything connected with the investigation becomes a matter of interest and curiosity; when the public mind is screwed up to this pitch, it will take a tone from the circumstances of the case, which will rarely be found to accord with the impartiality acquired by justice.

If the accused excite an interest from his youth, his good character, his connections, or even his countenance and appearance, the dreadful consequences of conviction, and that, too, in the case of great crimes as well as minor offences, lead prosecutors to relax their severity, witnesses to appear with reluctance, jurors to acquit against evidence, and the pardoning power improperly to interpose. If the public excitement take another turn, the consequences are worse; indignation against the crime is created into a ferocious thirst of vengeance; and if the real culprit cannot be found, the innocent suffers on the slightest presumption of guilt; when public zeal requires a victim, the innocent lamb is laid on the altar, while the scape-goat is suffered to fly to the mountain. This savage disposition increases with the severity and the frequency of capital inflictions, so that in atrocious as well as in lighter offences, this species of punishment leads sometimes to the escape of the guilty, often to the conviction of the innocent.

Whoever has at all observed the course of criminal proceedings, must have witnessed what I have just endeavoured to describe; undeserved indulgence, unjust severity; opposite effects proceeding from the same cause; the unnecessary harshness of the punishment.

But when no such fatal consequences are to be the result, the course of justice is rarely influenced by passion or prejudice. The evidence is produced without difficulty, and given without reluctance; it has its due effect on the minds of jurors, who are under no terrors of pronouncing an irremediable sentence: and pardons need not be granted, unless innocence is ascertained, or reformation becomes unequivocal.

Another consequence of the infliction of death is, that if frequent it loses its effect; the people become too much familiarized with it to consider it as an example; it is changed into a spectacle, which must frequently be repeated to satisfy the ferocious taste it has formed. It would be extremely useful in legislation, if the true cause could be discovered of this atrocious passion for witnessing human agonies and beholding the slaughter of human beings. It has disgraced the history of all nations; . . . the history of our own country, young as it is, is not free from this stain. The judicial murder of the wizards and witches of New England, and of a great number of poor wretches, during what was called the negro-plot at New York, furnish us with domestic lessons on this subject. . . .

But if this punishment be kept for great occasions, and the people are seldom treated with the gratification of seeing one of their fellow-creatures expire by the sentence of the law; a most singular effect is produced; the sufferer, whatever be his crime, becomes a hero or a saint; he is the object of public attention, curiosity, admiration, and pity. . . . His prison becomes a place of pilgrimage, its tenant, a saint awaiting the crown of martyrdom; his last looks are watched, with affectionate solicitude; his last words are carefully remembered and recorded; his last agonies are beheld with affliction and despair; and after suffering the ignominious sentence of the law, the body of the culprit whose death was infamy, and whose life was crime, is attended respectfully and mournfully to the grave, by a train that would not have disgraced the obsequies of a patriot or a hero. This sketch, though highly coloured, is drawn from life: the inhabitants of one of the most refined and wealthy of our state capitals, sat for the picture, and although such exalted feelings are not always excited, or are prudently repressed, yet they are found in nature, and in whatever degree they exist, it cannot be doubted, that in the same proportion, they counteract every good effect that punishment is intended to produce. . . .

Thus the end of the law is defeated, the force of example is totally lost, and the place of execution is converted into a scene of triumph for the sufferer, whose crime is wholly forgotten, while his courage, resignation, or piety, mark him as the martyr, not the guilty victim, of the laws.

Where laws are so directly at war with the feelings of the people whom they govern, as this and many other instances prove them to be, these laws can never be wise or operative, and they ought to be abolished. . . .

The . . . argument I have heard urged, is . . . the danger to be apprehended from innovation. I confess, I always listen to this objection with some degree of suspicion. That men who owe their ranks, their privileges, their emoluments, to abuses and impositions, originating in the darkness of antiquity, and consecrated by time; that such men should preach the danger of innovations, I can well conceive; the wonder is, that they can find others weak and credulous enough to believe them. But in a country where these abuses do not exist; in a country whose admirable system of government is founded wholly on innovation, where there is no antiquity to create a false veneration for abuses, and no apparent interest to perpetuate them;

in such a country, this argument will have little force against the strong reasons which assail it. Let those, however, who honestly entertain this doubt, reflect that, most fortunately for themselves and for their posterity, they live in an age of advancement: not an art, not a science, that has not in our day made rapid progress towards perfection. The one of which we now speak has received, and is daily acquiring, improvement; how long is it since torture was abolished? Since judges were made independent? Since personal liberty was secured, and religious persecution forbidden? All these were, in their time, innovations as bold at least as the one now proposed. The true use of this objection, and there I confess it has force, is to prevent any hazardous experiment, or the introduction of any change that is not strongly recommended by reason. I desire no other test for the one that is now under discussion, but I respectfully urge that it would be unwise to reject it, merely because it is untried, if we are convinced it will be beneficial. Should our expectations be disappointed, no extensive evil can be done; the remedy is always in our power. Although an experiment, it is not a hazardous one, and the only inquiry seems to be, whether the arguments and facts stated in its favour are sufficiently strong to justify us in making it. Indeed, it appears to me that the reasoning might, with some propriety, be retorted against those who use it, by saying, "All punishments are but experiments to discover what will best prevent crimes; your favourite one of death has been fully tried. By your own account, all nations, since the first institution of society, have practised it, but you yourselves must acknowledge, without success. All we ask, then, is that you abandon an experiment which has for five or six thousand years been progressing under all the variety of forms which cruel ingenuity could invent; and which in all ages, under all governments, has been found wanting. You have been obliged reluctantly to confess that it is inefficient, and to abandon it in minor offences; what charm has it then which makes you cling to it in those of a graver cast? You have made your experiment; it was attended in its operation with an incalculable waste of human life, a deplorable degradation of human intellect; it was found often fatal to the innocent, and it very frequently permitted the guilty to escape. Nor can you complain of any unseasonable interference with your plan that may account for its failure: during the centuries that your system has been in operation, humanity and justice have never interrupted its course; you went on in the work of destruction, always seeing an increase of crime, and always supposing that increased severity was the only remedy to suppress it: the mere forfeiture of life was too mild; tortures were superadded, which nothing but the intelligence of a fiend could invent, to prolong its duration and increase its torments; yet there was no diminution of crime; and it never occurred to you, that mildness might accomplish that which could not be effected by severity." This great truth revealed itself to philosophers, who imparted it to the people; the strength of popular opinion at length forced it upon kings, and the work of reformation, in spite of the cry against novelty, began. It has been progressive. Why should it stop, when every argument, every fact, promises its complete success? We could not concur in the early stages of this reformation; perhaps the credit may be reserved to us of completing it; and I therefore make no apology to the general assembly for having so long occupied them with this discussion. In imposing so important a change, it was necessary to state the prominent reasons which induced me to think it necessary; many more have weighed upon my mind, and on reviewing these, I feel with humility and regret how feebly they are urged. The nature of the subject alone will, however, create an interest sufficient to promote inquiry, and humanity will suggest arguments which I have not had sagacity to discover or the talent to enforce.

For the Sake of the Prisoner

PRISON ASSOCIATION OF NEW YORK

The New York City Prison Association was incorporated by the state legislature in 1846. The Association was empowered to appoint committees with the power to visit and examine all prisons in the state, and was to report annually to the legislature on their findings with any recommendations for the improvement of the prison system. Such committees had the legal right to question prison officials under oath and, in addition, could converse with prisoners without the presence of prison officials. An 1849 bill to abolish these rights of inspection and examination passed the Senate but was defeated in the Assembly. The organization continued well into the twentieth century. By 1895, after fifty years of service, the Association had visited and counseled a hundred and twenty thousand prisoners and had investigated more than thirty thousand complaints.

To THE HONORABLE, the Assembly of the State of New-York. The Memorial of the Executive Committee of the Prison Association of the city of New-York respectfully shows,

That your memorialists deem it their duty to submit to your honorable body a few observations concerning the bill from the Senate, now pending before you for the modification of the Charter of our Association.

In respect to county jails, this bill, as we are informed, proposes to take from the Association the power of *examining* any prisoner, by which,

---

Prison Association of New York, Memorial, March 8, 1849, *New York State Assembly #243.*

we presume, it is intended to deny to us the permission given by the general law to inspectors of county prisons, and extended to our body by its Charter, of *conversing* with the prisoners "without the presence of the keepers"; such being the only power of this nature which is possessed, or has been exercised, by us. But in respect to the state prisons, the bill entirely takes away from the Association all authority to inspect them.

We should be obliged to regard the passage of a bill making such alterations in our charter, as a formal legislative condemnation either of the plans and objects of our Association, or of the measures by which we attempted to carry them into effect. As to the former, we will not do the Legislature the injusice to suppose, that they can disapprove of any well meant effort for the improvement of prison discipline, and reformation of prisoners, or the decrease of crime, the great objects for which our Association has been formed. As to the latter, while we are conscious that our views are liable to mistake; that our labors are quite imperfect; and that in both we fall far behind the calls of humanity and of duty; we have the satisfaction of knowing, that some of them have been productive of good, and we are sure, that all have been prompted by a sincere and earnest wish to promote the interests of law, humanity and virtue.

We respectfully submit that the powers of inspection which the Legislature have given us, are vitally important to the ascertainment of facts, the detection of abuses, the suggestion of improvements, and the discovery of the remedies that ought to be applied. These powers, the Legislature will bear in mind, are simply those of inquiry. No control is given to us over the prison authorities. We cannot order that a blow less or more shall be struck; that food shall be changed, increased or diminished, that anything shall be added to or taken from the time of labor assigned to convicts. We cannot separate in our county prisons the male from the female, the young from the old, the mere vagrant from the hardened criminal. In regard to the state prisons our powers are equally limited.

The object of the Legislature in bestowing upon us these guarded powers of inquiry and inspection, your honorable body will perceive, by reference to our charter, was to enable the Legislature, by our aid, "to perfect the government and discipline of our prisons, by bringing to their knowledge the facts necessary for their just and intelligent action."

Pursuant to their charter, your memorialists have already presented to the Legislature the history of their proceedings for the past year; and they appeal with confidence to this report, for evidence, that intentionally they have neither perverted their trust, nor been neglectful of their duties.

By the proposed modification of our charter, our capacity for usefulness will be essentially impaired. We can do but little for the detained; we shall be injuriously limited in our investigations for improving the discipline of our prisons; and we shall be almost entirely dependent on the representations and statements of keepers in our endeavors to aid the discharged convict on his return to society, and thus be deprived of that personal knowledge which is necessary to the wise administration of this duty. . . .

Your memorialists, therefore, respectfully submit to the honorable Assembly, that the proposed modification of the charter of the Prison Association is not called for by the public interest; and that, on the contrary, the public good will be best promoted by leaving the charter for the present at least, unaltered. They submit, that the nature and result of their past labors, at least, entitle them to the benefit of further trial.

Your memorialists and their associates have no private ends to gain by the continuance of their present powers; they desire such continuance for the sake of the prisoner whom they would reclaim from his sins, and relieve from his sufferings.

They desire it for the sake of society, whose interests they seek to protect, by the restoration to uprightness and honesty of those of its members who have gone astray.

They desire it for the sake of our common humanity. Philanthropists in other states, and in distant lands, have hailed the establishment of this Association, as an omen of good to mankind. They have praised our labors far beyond their deserts; and this praise necessarily extends to the authority which gave us a legal existence and invested us with powers of extensive usefulness. Other states and kingdoms are calling to their aid the wise and the good in their endeavors to raise the fallen and elevate everywhere the character and influence of their public institutions. And we cannot believe that our own State is prepared to retrace steps and abandon the measures that it has hitherto taken in the same noble career.

ON THE VETO OF THE INSANE LAND BILL

William H. Seward

William Henry Seward (1801–1872) studied law after graduating from Union College in 1820 and was admitted to the New York bar in 1822. He is claimed (with some justification) to be one of the founders of the Cravath firm in the history of that partnership by Robert T. Swaine. A lifelong reformer, he was a leader of the anti-slavery faction during his two terms in the United States Senate; he served as Secretary of State under both Lincoln and Johnson and was active also in pressing for educational reforms and for better treatment for immigrants. Seward's reform tend-

William H. Seward, Speech, June 19, 1854, *Appendix to Congressional Globe,* p. 959.

*encies led him to support the 1854 bill (backed by Dorothea Dix) to offer
public lands for the benefit of the indigent insane. Seward shepherded the
bill through the Senate, but it was vetoed by President Pierce. The following excerpt is Seward's rebuttal. Seward's interest in the problem of insanity goes back at least to 1846, when he defended William Freeman,
an insane twenty-three-year-old Negro who had murdered almost an entire
family. The incident raised a storm of hate and prejudice in which it
appeared that no one would dare to defend the accused. Seward, at the
risk of sacrificing his career, defended Freeman in a plea for understanding
the plight of the insane. Freeman was found guilty and sentenced to death,
but he died soon after; and an autopsy revealed that his brain had been in
a state of rapid decay.*

CONGRESS HAS PASSED A BILL by which ten millions of acres of the public
domain are granted to the several States, with unquestioned equality, on
condition that they shall accept the same, and sell the lands at not less
than one dollar per acre, and safely invest the gross proceeds, and forever
apply the interest thereon to the maintenance of their indigent insane
inhabitants. This bill is a contribution to the States, made from a peculiar
national resource, at a time when the Treasury is overflowing. It is made
at the suggestion, and it is not stating the case too strongly to say, through
the unaided, unpaid, and purely disinterested influence of an American
woman, (Miss Dix) who, while all other members of society have been
seeking how to advance their own fortunes and happiness, or the prosperity and greatness of their country, has consecrated her life to the
relief of the most pitiable form in which the Divine Ruler afflicts our
common humanity.

The purpose of the bill has commended it to our warmest and most
active sympathies. Not a voice has censured it, in either House of Congress.
It is the one only purpose of legislation, sufficiently great to arrest attention, that has met with universal approbation throughout the country,
during the present session. It seems as if some sad fatality attends our
public action, when this measure is singled out from among all others, to
be baffled and defeated by an Executive veto. Such, however, is the fact.
The bill has been returned by the President with objections which it is now
our constitutional duty to consider. . . .

In considering the President's message, we are struck with the fact
that it is desultory, illogical, and confused. While commending the purpose
of the bill, the President denies the expediency of the measure, and
denies also the power of Congress to adopt it. It is impossible, however, to
separate the argument directed against the expediency of the measure from
the argument directed against the power. So the argument against the
expediency rests chiefly on an assumption that the measure is a usurpation
of power, while the argument against the power reposes chiefly on the
inexpediency of its exercise.

This criticism is important, because the confusion I have described impairs the force of the argument, and because, moreover, Congress may well confide in their own conclusions as to the *expediency* of a measure, while they are bound to pay extraordinary respect to Executive suggestions impugning its constitutionality. I do not stop to demonstrate the correctness of this criticism. Every Senator who has discussed the message, on either side, has betrayed, I think, an embarrassment resulting from it.

In the second place, the message seems to me, I do not say disingenuous, but singularly unfair and unjust in the statement of the question.

The bill confines itself to a single purpose, viz: that of aiding the States in enabling them to maintain one peculiar class of destitute persons, by an appropriation of equal and just parts of the public domain, leaving all other objects and all other sources of public wealth out of view, and abstaining altogether from interference with the States in the performance of even that one duty.

But the President is not content to state the question thus. He approaches it by an induction. He says:

"It cannot be questioned that if Congress have power to make provision for the indigent insane without the limits of this District, it has the same power to provide for the indigent who are not insane, and thus to transfer to the Federal Government the charge of all the poor in all the States."

After amplification of this proposition, without argument, the President arrives at the statement of the question before him, and announces it in these words:

"The question presented, therefore, clearly is upon the constitutionality and propriety of the Federal Government assuming to enter into a novel and vast field of legislation, namely, that of providing for the care and support of all those among the people of the United States who by any form of calamity become fit objects of public philanthropy."

You need not only place this statement of the case by the side of the President's own statement of the provisions of the bill, to enable you to see that it is flagrantly erroneous and unjust. But I will illustrate it directly. Congress does, in unquestioned conformity with the Constitution, exercise some powers in the States which are concurrent with similar powers enjoyed by the States themselves. Thus Congress establishes here and there, throughout the States, hospitals for sick and disabled seamen. Is that equivalent to assuming the support and care of all the poor, on land as well as sea, belonging to the States? Congress establishes lighthouses and constructs harbors of refuge within the States, and provides regulation for the construction and management of steamboats and ships on navigable waters within the States. Is that equivalent to usurpation of the entire control over commerce and navigation within the States? Congress distributes seeds and treatises on agriculture. Is that equivalent to usurpation of jurisdiction over agriculture throughout the States? Congress discriminates by bounties, drawbacks, and duties, so as to favor agriculture, the fisheries, and manufactures. Is that equivalent to assumption of supreme and exclusive power over all those great national interests? Congress prescribes regulations of the militia, and furnishes to the States arms, ammunition, and ordinance, for the equipment and exercise of the militia. Is that equivalent to usurpation of the entire support, control, and direction of the armed police of the States?

I call your attention, next, sir, to the fact that this message presents unfairly the relative structures and characters of the Federal Union and of the States. The President says:

"Are we not too prone to forget that the Federal Union is the creation of the States, and not they of the Federal Union? . . ."

Thereby implying that the States are still entirely sovereign, while the Federal Government is a mere Confederation, and not equally sovereign within its sphere. Now, no one ever thought that the States were creatures of the Federal Union; but it is equally true, in my judgment, that the Federal Union is not the creature of the States. Both are States connected with and yet independent of each other. Each of them was established directly by the people—the several State governments by the people of the States, respectively, and the Federal Union by the people of all the States. Each is shorn of some attributes of sovereignty, and each is supreme within its sphere. . . .

While, therefore, the President's expositions of that subject may serve to raise prejudices against the bill, it is quite certain that they are altogether foreign from a consideration of its merits.

If it shall seem to you, Mr. President, that the criticisms I have offered might have been spared, I hope it will be a sufficient defense to say that these criticisms dispose of two thirds of the entire message of the President, and leave only two or three points in the whole case to be examined. In the manner I have described, the President reaches at last the principal question, viz: whether Congress has power to pass this bill by virtue of the third section of the fourth article of the Constitution, which is as follows:

"The Congress shall have power to dispose of, and make all needful rules and regulations respecting the territory or other property belonging to the United States; and nothing in this Constitution shall be so construed as to prejudice any claims of the United States, or of any particular State."

The President denies that this section contains the power claimed by Congress. Now, it is apparent, first, that the land appropriated by the bill is a part of "the territory or other property of the United States"; and, secondly, that the term "to dispose of" includes any way and every way by which Congress can divest the United States of those lands, whether by sales to States or individuals, or by gifts to States or individuals.

The bill apportions and bestows the lands among and upon the States, and is therefore constitutional, unless it can be shown that the absolute power contained in that section is limited by some other provision of the Constitution, which inhibits the proposed disposal of them. . . .

We know historically, and from the commentators in the Federalist, that there was, at the time of the adoption of the Constitution, much uncertainty about the boundary lines between the States, and of course about their respective titles to, or interest in, the unoccupied domain which was ceded by the several States to the United States, and also that all of the States interested in the said domain had not executed deeds of cession at the time the Constitution was framed by the convention; and we know, from the same evidence, that the clause relied upon by the President was designed merely to save any rights or titles which had not been and should not be ceded to the United States, and also at the same time to save just claims which the United States had, by or independent of such deeds of cession. Now, it is absurd to say that the bill before us prejudices any claim of the United States; for it assumes that the property disposed of is exclusively the property of the United States. It is equally absurd to say that it prejudices the claim of any particular State; for no State has laid any claim, or can lay any claim, to the lands in question. This disposes of the supposed limitation in the third section of the fourth article.

The sixth article manifestly has no relation to the public domain. It is in these words:

"All debts contracted and engagements entered into before the adoption of this Constitution, shall be as valid against the United States under this Constitution as under the Confederation."

It is satisfied by applying it to the then existing public debt, and to then existing treaties. We learn from the Federalist that it was so understood by the framers of the Constitution.

Mr. Madison recites it in the forty-third number of the Federalist, with this remark:

"This can only be considered as a declaratory proposition, and may have been inserted, among other reasons, for the satisfaction of the foreign creditors of the United States, who cannot be strangers to the pretended doctrine, that a change in the political form of society has the magical effect of dissolving its moral obligations."

There is, then, no limitation or qualification of the absolute power of Congress to dispose of the domain contained in the Constitution itself. . . .

But the President argues that the public domain, or the proceeds resulting from sales of it, and not expended, cannot be apportioned among the States, but must remain a common fund, which, as it has been pledged heretofore, and is now pledged, so hereafter it may again be pledged for public debts. But this argument proves too much. It would invalidate all grants of bounty lands, in consideration of past services in the Army and Navy of the United States. And it would equally invalidate all grants for the construction of canals and railroads, neither of which modes of disposing of the public lands has the President condemned. . . .

The President expresses deep concern lest this contribution by the Federal Government to the States should impair their vigor and independence. But it is not easy to see how a contribution which they are at liberty to reject, and which they are to apply to a necessary and to a proper purpose of government, in entire independence of the Federal Government, can wound their self-respect, or deprive them of any of their attributes of sovereignty.

The President is, moreover, deeply disturbed by an apprehension that if the policy of this bill should be pursued, its noble purposes would be defeated, and the fountains of charity within the States would be dried up. The President must not needlessly afflict himself in this wise, on the score of humanity. Experience is against his fears. Congress has never manifested a disposition of profuse liberality towards the States. Every community that has received from the Federal territory or property military bounties or pensions, is at least as brave and patriotic as it was before. Every community that has received from the same sources contributions for the purposes of internal improvement is more enterprising than before. Every community that has received aid for its schools of learning has been rendered more zealous and more munificent in the cause of education.

Thus, sir, I have reviewed the President's objections. In conclusion, it remains for me to express the opinion that, as in the early days of the Republic, there was a school of latitudinarian construction of the Constitution, which school was quite erroneous, so, also, there was a school whose maxim was strict construction of the Constitution, and this school has accumulated precedents and traditions equally calculated to extinguish the spirit of the Constitution. Circumstances have altogether changed since that school was founded. The States were then rich and strong; the Union was poor and powerless. Virginia lent to the United States $100,000 to build their Capitol. But the States could not enlarge themselves. They possessed respectively either no public lands at all, or very small domains, and to such domains they have added nothing by purchase or conquest. Charged with the expenses of municipal administration, including the relief of the indigent, the cure of the diseased, the education of the people, and the removal of natural obstructions to trade and intercourse, they reserved, nevertheless, only the power to raise revenues by direct taxation, one which always was, and always will be, regarded with jealousy and dislike, and is therefore never one that can be freely exercised.

The Union, on the contrary, by conquest and purchase, has quadrupled its domain, and is in possession of superabundant revenues derived from that domain and from imposts upon foreign commerce, while it also enjoys the power of direct taxation. Contrast the meager salaries of the officers of the States with the liberal ones enjoyed by the agents of the Union. Contrast the ancient narrow and cheerless Capitols of Annapolis, Harrisburg, and Albany, with this magnificent edifice, amplifying itself to the north and the south, while it is surrounded by gardens traversed by spacious avenues and embellished with fountains and statuary, and you see at once that the order of things has been reversed, and that it tends now not merely to concentration, but to consolidation. I know not how others may be affected by this tendency, but I confess that it moves me to do all that I can, by a fair construction of the Constitution, not to abate the Federal strength, and diminish the majesty of the Union, but to invigorate and aggrandize the States, and to enable them to maintain their just equilibrium in our grand but exquisitely contrived political system.

THE LEGAL CONDITION OF WOMEN

Timothy Walker

IN THIS ESSAY, I shall first consider the *political rights* of women, and secondly, their *legal rights*.

I. Their Political Rights.

By political rights, I understand those which appertain to the formation and administration of government. Of these, woman has absolutely none. When our Declaration of Independence asserts that all *men* are created equal, and that they are entitled to life, liberty, and happiness, as natural and unalienable rights, there is no doubt that *women* are intended to be included. We should blush to promulgate a political creed, which professedly excluded half of the human race from the transcendent birthright of liberty. We could find nothing in nature or revelation to justify us in proclaiming woman to be a slave. But, although woman is theoretically free, she is practically disfranchised. You could frame no definition of *merely political slavery*, which would not include her case. Even where universal suffrage prevails, she is neither allowed to vote nor to be voted for. She can hold no office of honor, trust, or profit, under government. She is thus made amenable to laws which she can have no

Timothy Walker, "The Legal Condition of Women," *Western Law Journal* (1849), I, p. 145.

voice in making. The right of suffrage constitutes so clearly the very foundation of freedom, that without it man would consider himself a slave. But from this right woman has ever been excluded. In Ohio this exclusion is emblazoned upon the Constitution itself, which confines the right of suffrage, in so many words, to *"white male inhabitants."* Mark the import of these words, and you will find a standard by which to estimate woman's political privileges. Women and negroes are united in the exclusion.

I make this statement because truth requires it, and not to express censure or excite discontent. I do not apprehend, and surely would not recommend a female revolution. But I must add, that precisely the same cause, which produced the Revolution of these colonies, exists in the case of women—namely, *taxation without representation.* If that sex *can* have an interest different from ours, which I trust is not the case, that interest is utterly unrepresented in our government; and yet that sex are taxed for their property to precisely the same extent as the other. In a word, we require them to *support* and *obey* government as much as if they were men; but we allow them no share in its administration.

That women do not regard their case in the same light, is evident from their patient acquiescence. I presume they feel it to be a privilege, rather than a grievance. I speak of the great majority. Doubtless there are some female bosoms in which the flame of political ambition burns; but I know they are few. Where is the lady, who, if there were no Constitutional exclusion, would not exclude herself? The noise, the glare, the turmoil, the corruption, attendant upon elections, form no congenial element for female sensitiveness, diffidence, and delicacy. On the contrary, the very characteristics which glorify woman, and make her a "ministering angel" at home, utterly unfit her for these coarse and turbulent scenes. In short, the general participation of that sex in political affairs, could have no other effect than to transform them into a race of Amazons. Hence that woman who best understands her true interest and glory, will probably be most thankful for her political disfranchisement.

II. *Their Legal Rights.*

Having seen that woman has no voice in making laws, let us see in what light the laws regard her. This will depend upon her condition, whether *single* or *married.*

1. *Single Women.* So long as a woman is content to remain single, her legal rights and capabilities are, for the most part, in this country, precisely the same as those of the other sex. I say in this country; for in England, by their arbitrary law of inheritance, males were most unrighteously preferred to females. When a parent died, however affluent, the son took every thing, and the daughter nothing. The injustice of this rule is so palpable and outrageous, that we can hardly call it a merit to have it done away.

If either is to be preferred, it certainly ought to be the female; because she is the least able to make her way in poverty through a cold and unfeeling world. But our law stops at the point of perfect equality, and leaves neither party to complain. Women inherit here precisely as men; and in every other respect, so far as property is concerned, single women stand on the same footing as men. They can make all the contracts, and do all the legal acts which men can. The general rule is, that the legal competency of a single woman is the same as that of a man. The only exceptions which I recollect, are in favor of woman. These are, *First*, as to the time of becoming of age. The age of legal sufficiency is generally the same for both sexes—namely, twenty-one. But in this State the female is of age at eighteen; and there are some other differences. She can choose a guardian at *twelve*, the male not until *fourteen*. She can marry at *fourteen*, the male not until *eighteen*. She can only be bound out until *eighteen*, the male until *twenty-one*. In short, the law considers a woman to arrive at maturity three or four years sooner than a man; and all experience proves this to be true. *Secondly*, as to arrests. By a commendable exhibition of gallantry in our legislators, no female can be arrested in this State for debt. In this exemption, women are named in connection with the officers and soldiers of the Revolution. But observe, that the privilege is confined to arrests for *civil* matters only. As to *crimes*, their sex is no apology. When a woman becomes a felon, she is treated with no delicacy, because she deserves none. The gaol, the penitentiary, and the scaffold, are alike the destination of both sexes. And even in regard to debts, you will not understand me as saying that a female is not liable for them. She is only exempted from *arrest*; but her property may be proceeded against in the same manner as that of a man. Her exemption is, that her person cannot be taken and incarcerated. Thus much for the single state of woman. Where she is not equal to man, she has the advantage.

2. *Married Women.* A change now comes over the dream of woman's liberty. The merging of her name in that of her husband, is but an emblem of the fate of all her legal rights. The torch of Hymen lights up the funeral pile on which those rights are sacrificed. The legal doctrine is, that a husband and wife become but one person, and that person is the husband. He is the substantive, she the mere adjective—he the significant figure, she the cipher. Her legal existence is merged in his. There is scarcely a legal act of any description which she is competent to perform. In the eye of the law, he is every thing, and she nothing. This leading idea tinctures even the legal phraseology on this subject. From time immemorial, *Baron and Feme* have been the technical names for husband and wife. Now *Baron* means *Lord*, in plain English; and the old law writers, when they condescended to speak in English, often used the ungallant word *Lord* instead of husband. I know of no language which more exactly portrays the subordination in which the law places the wife, than that which Milton makes Eve address to Adam:

"My author and disposer, what thou bid'st,
Unargued I obey: so God ordains.
God is thy law, thou mine: to know no more,
Is woman's happiest knowledge and her praise."

The reason usually assigned for giving the legal pre-eminence of the husband, is to establish an indissoluble unity of interest between the parties. This is to say, lest the wife should be tempted to assert rights in opposition to her husband, she is humanely declared to have no separate rights. The argument commonly used is briefly this: The husband being the stronger of the two, policy requires that his dominion should be admitted by the law, for in his hands, the power supports itself without any external interference. Give but the legal authority to the wife, and every moment would produce a revolt on the part of the husband. They, who, from some ill defined notion of justice or generosity, would extend to women an absolute equality, only hold out to them a dangerous snare. Let the law, by conferring equality on wives, once release them from that necessity of pleasing, which is at present imposed on them, and it would in fact only subvert the empire they now enjoy. Man forgets his self-love, while secure of his prerogative. Substitute a jealousy of rival power, and his wounded pride would soon rouse up in him a dangerous antagonist. As it is, he bears rule over his wife's person and conduct: she bears rule over his inclinations. He governs by law, she by persuasion.

I am merely stating the argument. It is not my province to vindicate it. . . .

If, on the whole, that sex should think themselves unreasonably restricted, I should agree with them. I can see neither policy, justice, nor humanity, in many of the legal doctrines respecting married women. They bear every mark of a barbarous origin. There is nothing but their *antiquity* in their favor. They admit only of the miserable apology, that they were established a thousand years ago, when woman was little more than a slave to man.

Were society now to be re-organized, no doubt there would be a mighty change in this respect. Woman would not be made the helpless thing she now is. It would never enter the mind of a legislator, to place her so entirely at the mercy of man. The man who should broach such an idea for the first time, in the nineteenth century, would be branded as a savage. The press would assail him with its million tongues. He would be fain to fly from the execrations of Christians, and herd with Turks, who are said

"To hold that woman is but dust,
A soulless toy for tyrants' lust."

Yet, reprehensible as the law now is in this respect, it has been vastly improved. Had I time to trace its history, I could show that when Blackstone declared the female sex to be decided favorites of the English law, their condition was almost infinitely worse than it is in this country. Let them be consoled, therefore, by the fact, that public opinion has been constantly laboring in their favor. The progress is slow, but sure. Nothing is so hard to reform as laws. It is easier to level a mountain, than to overthrow a time-hallowed usage. Public opinion is the opinion of millions. This is the power which creates a usage, and the only power which can overthrow it. Before the laws which enslave woman can be changed, you must change the minds of millions. And this change is now going on. One after another, as we have seen, female disabilities have been done away. Almost every year some fetter is broken, and thus giving promise that the wife will one day be disenthralled. Power will be given her to save at least her own property from being squandered by a wasteful husband. But until this takes place, I would impress upon all who read this, the importance of so settling property upon women, as to obviate the injustice of the law. This always can be done, and always ought to be done. Such an arrangement can never do any harm, and may do immeasurable good. It provides a haven against a storm: and the probability that the storm may not come, is no excuse for neglecting to provide for it.

In regard to political rights, I know not that there is any tendency towards the placing of woman on a level with man, even should such be her desire. On this point, the sex will probably have to rest satisfied with their indirect influence. They must expect to legislate only through their influence over legislators. I mean their influence as wives, mothers, sisters, instructors, authors, and companions; an influence which is every day increasing with each advance in civilization. In this way only can woman hope to be a law-giver; and here her sphere is boundless. No constitutions can limit her power, for its foundation is laid in our nature. How often have women actually governed empires through the instrumentality of men. No human being had such power over the iron-hearted Napoleon as the inimitable Josephine. Catherine of Russia is another example. Peter the Great was inexorable to all but her. But she could sway his proud soul at her pleasure. These are but two examples out of thousands. But space will not permit me to enlarge.

THE TEMPERANCE MOVEMENT

Closely related to the anti-slavery crusade was the temperance movement. The fight against liquor was the one instance where the splinter groups could coalesce: each reformer believed temperance to be necessary to advance his special concern. By 1834 it was estimated that as many as five thousand societies had pledged one million people to temperance. The

Maine Law of 1851 took the next step and inaugurated a short-lived prohibition movement, providing that no person should manufacture or sell, directly or indirectly, any intoxicating liquor. The prohibition move- ment raised serious questions about government power from a legal point of view. Mr. Justice Curtis, smarting under attacks in the License Cases, wrote: "I had no doubt, when the opinion was given, it would be attacked, not by reasoning, for that I did not fear, but by abuse, which I feared as little. . . . Neither Mr. Greeley nor anyone can overthrow the opinion pronounced in this case; and if their articles can even temporarily influence any portion of the public mind, it is only because there is not enough knowledge to judge, and not enough deference to suspend their opinions." In Fisher v. McGirr, *Shaw employed a lawyer's stress on procedure; im- perfections in the selected means here voided an end, no matter how laudable. Shortly afterward, the legislature enacted a new prohibition statute, complying with the standards laid down in the case.*

Confiscation and Seizure

THE MAINE LAW

DOES NOT the chief power of the law lie in the seizure and confiscation of intoxicating liquors?

Neal Dow, Esq. Confiscation and seizure are the great things, with the speed and certainty with which penalties follow; no evasion will succeed. — *Rev. F. Yates.* Unquestionably. This removes all deception. The rum-casks *cannot lie,* and they are the only witnesses to be trusted. Another important feature of the law is the removal of all discretion from the courts. This has been a great difficulty heretofore. — *Prof. Stowe.* Exactly. To attack the liquor itself, rather than the drinker or seller, is the true policy. If there is *no rum* the drinker cannot drink nor the dealer agitate. — *Dr. C. Jordan.* The chief power of any temperance law lies in its penalties and its certainty. It has been demonstrated in this State, that no law of *uncertain penalties* will have any influence. — *J. E. God- frey, Esq.* The chief power of the law lies in the seizure of liquors, the imprisonment of the offender, and, if I may coin a word, the *unpropertying* of liquors. — *Rev. C. Palfrey.* By no means. The penalty for the third offense is imprisonment. And perhaps the most effective provision of the statute is that no liquor debt can be enforced by law. — *Rev. J. B. Weston.* Seizure and confiscation are *the power* of the law. These, and the speed and facility with which they are effected, make it impossible to evade the

The Maine Law: Its Constituency, Successful Operation and Legal Acceptance (1851).

law to any great extent. — *James M. Lincoln, Esq.* No doubt the chief power of the law lies in the seizure and confiscation of liquors, but it also has force in this particular, that it leaves no discretion to the courts; the duty assigned the magistrates cannot be evaded; if there is responsibility he throws it on the law; his course is marked out for him, and he cannot depart from it. — *Dr. Rust.* Seizure and confiscation form one element of the power of the law. Another is the penalties affixed to second and third violations, and the obstacles in the way of appeal. Another is the case of obtaining evidence against violators and the impossibility of their escaping when once arraigned. — *Joshua Nye, Jr.* The whole power of the law lies in this; and with this provision no man, even if he is worth millions, can for any time resist the law. Dealers will admit that the attempt is useless. — *A. P. Higgins, Esq.* In this lies our only hope. Leave this out, and farewell to the suppression of the traffic. — *Nathaniel Wilson.* I cannot designate any single power. It is the *combination* that makes it what it is. — *M. Davis, Esq., of Belfast.* Better have no law at all, at present, unless you can get one making spiritous liquors contraband, and *exposing them to destruction.* All laws without this will only fail. No law against the sale merely, however stringent, can be effectual. Our law of 1846 was every thing that such a law could be. As prosecuting attorney for a county league, I carried through some three hundred prosecutions under it. This checked the business, and in a few towns broke it up. But in large places it produced no effect, and was finally dropped. And I am fully convinced, *from six years of unceasing effort in this business,* that the only way to stop the traffic in spiritous liquors is to make them contraband, give the right to search and destroy them where found.

Part IV

A
LEGAL
FRAMEWORK
FOR
ECONOMIC
DEVELOPMENT

A Lincoln

Introduction

For at least two generations the United States has been regarded as the most highly developed and by far the richest nation in the world in terms of economic growth. The evidence is everywhere and incontrovertible. It is, nevertheless, a surprisingly recent condition. In the 1830's the United States was the prime example of an "undeveloped country"—as the losses of credulous English investors in state, canal, and railroad bonds attested. Fortunately the country was generously endowed with natural resources: coal, mineral ores, lumber, vast fertile lands crisscrossed by navigable rivers and lakes, and a climate favorable to agriculture. And if it did not possess a skilled labor force from the outset, it soon acquired one by providing a haven for the oppressed of the older nations who were industrially more advanced. But raw materials and technical know-how, important—indeed indispensable—as they are, are not enough to put the transition into high gear. Before a country can embark on an economic "takeoff," to borrow Professor Rostow's expression, it must have the institutional apparatus to organize a complex economy.

Many of the essential institutions emerged during this period. Legal developments were conducive to stability and order, which, in turn, assured investor confidence. By granting a considerable measure of autonomy to private decision-makers, law encouraged businessmen to undertake long-range planning. The legal order supported the establishment of interstate economic institutions and instruments, which permitted a flow of national capital through what became a national economic market. "Commercial jurisprudence," as Story called it, shaped the corporate form of enterprise, which fostered the pooling of capital and managerial skill, and was destined to be the chief vehicle of the remarkable American economic growth.

Lawyers were no more unanimous in their private views toward the issues raised by industrialization than they were with respect to politics or the other stirring issues of the time. But this did not prevent their forging, as a profession, the institutional framework which was their contribution to the industrial explosion. When the law did not keep in step with the nation's expanding business, demands for changes ensued. So the steady development of law between 1820 and 1860 has a direct relationship with the rise of the new merchant, banking, and entrepreneurial classes. The aspirations of the people were so linked with national enrichment that questions probing the ends of the good society were rarely a barrier to legal accommodation.

In certain issues affecting business the United States began to break new legal ground. Foremost among these was the law governing that artificial creature, the corporation. True, the corporate form itself was not an American invention. Municipal corporations had been known to English law for centuries before the colonization of the New World; and the conceptual ancestor of the modern corporation is generally traced to the "juristic person" in the Rome of the Caesars. The modern business corporation, however, dates from the pre–Civil War period. Though only a few existed in 1820, corporations thereafter increased rapidly in number and complexity as the corporate privilege was sought and obtained in all phases of economic activity. The corporate device permitted agglomerations of capital far beyond the means of any single group of investors, and achievements proportionately great: without it railroad construction, which knit the economy of the states together, would have been impossible.

But like every new product of any complexity, the corporation had problems which became apparent only with experience. These centered around minority stockholders' rights, proxy voting, dividends, financial reporting procedures, pre-emptive rights, and shareholder derivative suits. New bodies outgrew ancient precedents; novel patterns developed. The first edition of Angell and Ame's *Corporations*, brought out in 1832, discusses approximately four hundred and fifty American decisions; by 1861, in the seventh edition, twenty-four hundred were cited, indicating not only that the case law of corporations had grown, but that its principles were mainly indigenous.

As a counterpoint to the steadily mounting volume of its promotional activities in chartering business corporations, the state had a regulatory role. Checks on economic power paralleled constitutional limitations on governmental power. The duration, alteration, and repeal of corporate charters became lively political issues. The task of striking the balance between encouraging business initiative and preventing or remedying its abuses devolved on the legal profession.

Immunity from individual liability for the debts of the enterprise, today considered the chief advantage of a corporation, was hotly contested. The controversy evoked moral as well as pragmatic overtones. Professor Louis Hartz has shown that in Pennsylvania the anti-charter dogma "thrived by virtue of an ideological rationale largely independent of policy considerations." Corporate privilege was attacked as contrary to the natural-law doctrine of the Revolution. Small entrepreneurs added that it was unjust to expect them to compete with incorporated firms possessing the advantage of limited liability; "the danger of associated wealth, with special privilege, and without personal liability" was used by New Jersey Democrats as an election platform plank. In 1835 Robert Rantoul argued in the Massachusetts Legislature that the "people will stand up against Corporations. They will say, 'We will see whether the citizens of the Commonwealth are to govern themselves or are to be governed by Corporations!' " Until 1830 Massachusetts followed a policy of granting corporate charters in large numbers, but burdening them with shareholder liability. Between 1809 and 1853 at least eight state legislatures enacted statutes making shareholders individually liable for their corporations' debts.

But the economic pressure was overwhelming. As the factory system developed, competition forced a change in this vacillating policy. Shipowners and merchants began to invest their fortunes in domestic manufacture and their opposition to the corporate form and limited liability waned. Realistic fears that industry would not be attracted into the state overcame anticorporation arguments. Views like those of Governor Levi Lincoln prevailed. He argued that unlimited liability, by making shares in most Massachusetts textile companies nearly worthless, was bringing financial ruin to many families; unless the law were changed "the manufacturing interest, to a great extent, must be abandoned in Massachusetts."

The stimulus of economic forces toward a general acceptance of corporations was reinforced by legal developments which eliminated the basis for charges of monopoly. The need to secure special legislation had been onerous and time-consuming for the businessman; it also afforded opportunities for legislative logrolling and corruption. Naturally, great resentment had been aroused when any one appeared to be singled out for special favors. Legislative adaptation took the form of a drastic reduction in the number of special acts by which the privilege of forming a corporation might be individually conferred. After 1830, states began to adopt general incorporation acts. In 1848 New York enacted the broadest general corporation act in the country, which satisfied egalitarian values by authorizing incorporation as a routine matter. By further limiting monopoly possibilities, judicial decisions did much to allay the fears impeding general public acceptance of the new addition to the business community.

Two paradoxical cases altered the course of American business history, one on the side of state regulation, and one on the side of business expansion. *Dartmouth College* held that state legislation amending the school's charter was invalid under the impairment-of-contracts clause of the United States Constitution. It might be assumed that the rule of law thus established stimulated corporate growth; management could draw up a plan and individuals could underwrite it secure in the knowledge that it could not be frustrated by the state's subsequent curtailment of powers. But the matter did not rest there. State legislatures countered the increased freedom of corporations by including time-limit provisions in charters, and by making every charter subject to alteration, amendment, or repeal. Since the legislatures were moved to impose restriction in order to allay new fears of corporate abuse, a decision which could have enlarged the scope of business initiative may in fact have narrowed it.

In contrast, other decisions, which initially seemed restrictive, promoted business expansion. The *Charles River Bridge* decision, one of the landmarks in American legal history, held that the legislature had not impaired the rights of a bridge company under its charter by a subsequent grant to another company for a second bridge in the immediate vicinity. The heightened prospect of competition allowed by this decision hardly seems calculated to whet the enthusiasm of potential investors: had time priority been protected, the risk of the investment would have been reduced. But this decision had a paradoxical element. Its net effect was to encourage corporate growth. Now that monopoly restrictions would not hamper them, investors would risk their money in new, competitive enterprises—canals, turnpikes, railroads. Because, as Taney pointed out:

> If this court should establish the principles now contended for, what is to become of the numerous railroads established on the same line of travel with turnpike companies; and which have rendered the franchises of the turnpike corporations of no value? . . . The millions of property which have been invested in railroads and canals, upon lines of travel which had been before occupied by turnpike corporations, will be put in jeopardy. We shall be thrown back to the improvements of the last century, and obliged to stand still, until the claims of the old turnpike corporations shall be satisfied, and they shall consent to permit these States to avail themselves of the lights of modern science, and to partake of the benefit of those improvements which are now adding to the wealth and prosperity, and the convenience and comfort of every other part of the civilized world.

By its strict construction of the rights attaching to a corporate charter, the Taney court helped to remove the stigma of monopoly from the corporate form, and also encourage competition in business enterprises which offered greater consumer satisfactions. The irrevocable commitment of particular areas of power and development into private hands had contributed greatly to the general feelings of hostility against corporations. Its elimination smoothed the way toward the growing legislative preference for a release-of-energy policy. And it was Taney who wrote *Bank of Augusta* v. *Earle* in 1839, which held that a corporation had the power to sue on a contract signed outside the state in which it was chartered. The contrary opinion in the Circuit Court "had frightened half the lawyers and all the corporations of the country out of their properties," Story wrote Sumner. Taney also authored *Louisville R.R.* v. *Letson* (1844) which granted corporations access to the Federal courts by regarding them as citizens of the state for purposes of suit.

The corollary issue of state-business relations—the spheres of public and private decision-making—was also delineated in this period. An example of the extreme is the *Mott* case, a vigorous affirmation of the power and responsibility of the state to supervise the corporation closely, which was to be challenged and whittled down in the post–Civil War rush toward industrial empire. But the more enduring result of this period was the legal foundation for corporate dominance of American economic activity, largely free of government control. Abuses—speculation in stock, misuse of other people's money, and the diversion of ownership from control— occurred sporadically, but not often enough to evoke cries for government regulation.

In addition to the hostility generally faced by corporations, banks encountered special difficulties. The power they wielded might not alone have sufficed to set them apart, but the period was haunted by a scarcity of capital. While Western states either prohibited banks altogether or permitted the establishment of a limited number only, Jackson argued vigorously against the national bank's constitutionality. His veto message, composed with the aid of Taney, wove together the social philosophy of the Jacksonian movement so boldly that Biddle described it as "a manifesto of anarchy, such as Marat and Robespierre might have issued to the mob."

In time hostility toward banking corporations faded. The federal system under which each state served as its own laboratory, and the general lack of experience with this newly emerging economic force, led to a wide variety of techniques and methods. But continued experimentation with bank reforms and credit laws led to a crystallization toward the end of the period; greater uniformity emerged out of common experience. While states expressed different degrees of liberality on other matters in their legislation, by 1860 all but Oregon and Texas had enacted "free banking" statutes, or general laws of incorporation for banking institutions. From a single national bank (and a sprinkling of state banks) banking had become a major business throughout the nation.

The concept of delegating sovereignty to private decision-makers dominated the period's philosophy of economic enterprise, even though those seeking historical precedents for public action place great emphasis on the regulatory measures which also occurred. Apart from those sectors of public investment where government entered dramatically on the scene, its intervention was primarily in the Adam Smith tradition of curing the frictions of the market rather than of substituting government power for private enterprise. Short of polar cases, the market was not excluded from economic affairs; the premise was a qualified market economy rather than an administered one with price and production functions assumed by a central authority. This is borne out, for example, by the regulation of the new business insurance companies in the 1850's by state-established administrative commissions.

In *The Law of Contracts* (1855), Theophilus Parsons emphasized as "the very first rule" the need for construing contracts "by distinct principles," for "the rectitude, consistency, and uniformity of all construction enables all parties to do justice to themselves." By establishing certainty of law, the major work of bargaining and drafting the terms of an agreement could be left to the private sovereigns of the society themselves. Individuals could contract for themselves "free" of any protection by government edict. Usury laws are an outstanding example. In attempting to implement the theory of letting capital seek its own level, there was much agitation, a good deal of it successful, for the abolition of interference with the interest rates set by private enterprise. Money was treated like any other commodity and was to be controlled only by the laws of free trade.

Moralists can make much of the fact that the expansion of the United States credit system was paralleled by an expansion in the bankruptcy system. Whether or not the two were causally related, both were undoubtedly tied to the rapid, perhaps overrapid, growth of the business economy. The modern system of bankruptcy began in this period: a system for administering the estate not only of the businessman, but of any insolvent, voluntary or involuntary, of whatever calling. Imprisonment for debt was abolished. These developments vividly reflect that philosophy of the "second chance," so typical of a fast-moving commercial economy. The sharp fluctuations of the business cycle which characterized the period helped to propagate the belief that economic misfortune was not necessarily the result of laziness or a defect of character, but was an integral part of capitalism. Debtors might be salvaged as venturers who could again contribute productively to society. Such developments could not have been made by men thinking only in terms of "vested rights"; they show a growth from "title to contract, and a bit beyond."

Although the basis for industrialization was laid primarily through legislation, the courts could not preserve an attitude of detached superiority. Their struggle to provide a law favorable to railroads was directly influenced by their belief that such a course would aid trade and commerce. For a time public opinion held that what was good for the railroads was good for the United States, and the courts concurred. Decisions manifested a bias toward dynamic as contrasted with static capital. The high degree of flexibility which characterized American judicial decisions permitted the courts to adapt the law to changing economic conditions by reinterpreting precedents. This was not done without a wrench. *Murray* v. *S. C. Railroad Co.* is a fascinating instance of a lingering ambivalence which permitted the master to escape liability for injury caused by a fellow servant, despite growing awareness of the inevitability of accident in industrial enterprises. Tradition could be invoked, for ancient tort doctrines were permeated with fault concepts: no recovery unless a breach of moral obligation could be shown. But the courts were also inhibited by the belief that the imposition of liability for such damage might cripple a young and struggling enterprise, the railroad, even though the alternative decision inflicted a burden on a class little able to bear it. Free, individual self-assertion was to be a mainspring of legal development.

Industrialization brought the beginning of the population concentration that was to transform the United States from a rural to an urban society, and alter the nation's traditional psychology radically. The farmer was supplanted by the city dweller, thousands of workers were drawn into the new manufacturing cities, and the legal implementation of community planning had its beginnings. Deterioration of cities, the prevalence of slums, and the need for adequate sanitation and water supply created an unrest which led the state to exert its power. Housing shortages resulted in rudimentary legislation which foreshadowed the Federal Housing Acts of 1949 and 1954. Other dislocations caused by the industrial revolution are revealed in the *Commonwealth* v. *Hunt* case. Its recognition of the legality of the common objectives of trade unions is the starting point of modern labor law.

This is not to suggest that the lawyer of the 1830's singlehandedly, or even deliberately, paved the way for economic expansion, even though he helped to devise the fundamental working arrangements of the industrial society. When he participated with full engagement in the expansion it was because his only choice was to adjust himself to the new era. There was nothing very philosophical about such a decision. If he wanted to prosper, he had to come to terms with emergent capitalism. Thus when that rising force encountered obstacles left over from eighteenth-century institutions, it was in the lawyer's interest to clear them away. In many ways he was unaware of the implications of his actions. He had not studied economic theory, and what he knew of the "dismal science" had probably been derived from his own experience in business. In this very lack of awareness lay some of his strength: as the frontiersman has been more generally praised for the craftsmanship of his axe than for his literary ability, so the lawyer of this era is renowned for his pragmatic quality. He was not an Olympian observer, standing outside the business process, predicting its course and moralizing about its significance, nor was he an idealist, hampered by theories or lost in refinement and abstraction: he was a practical man concerned with making a living.

While becoming closely associated with business he did not regard himself as the promoter of a corporate economy. There was, in fact, no national business community with common aims and unified organizations. Business associations existed only locally and it was within the framework of these groups that the lawyer operated. Piece by piece, day by day, through a dynamic series of adjustments, he organized the basis for the great industrial machine. By his counseling, drafting, and regulations in individual cases, he incidentally translated economic theories into a workable language for a growing business.

The image of the corporation as a monopoly or a device for the promotion of mercantilist policy was out of place in a society where widespread distribution of capital had enabled a great number of men to strike out on their own. If there were many groups capable of building a bridge over a river, and no single group could claim to represent the interests of the commonwealth in any special way, then there was no sense in giving one of them a monopoly. Hence a new legal concept was introduced, that of general incorporation. No sublime theory of democratic egalitarianism was needed; it was a matter of common sense. And the lawyer, practical as he was, cooperated by putting into legal terminology the dicta of experience. Practicality decided a potential conflict of interest which arose from the collision of two phases of capitalism, the old and the new methods of transportation, in 1856. Metaphor springs to life as, on the Mississippi, the steamboat "Effie Afton" collides with the first railroad bridge over the river. Lincoln—who had represented them both earlier—resolved the potential conflict in ethics by taking the side of the first retainer. Practicality permitted the flow of commerce across state lines by a general private commercial law, which had a striking similarity among the several states. Dealings in paper rights to property, mortgages, stocks, bonds, and other securities, foreshadowed the displacement of landed wealth by monetary wealth. The states were becoming truly united by economic ties. In his *Commentaries on the Law of Bills of Exchange*, Story observed: "America received from the parent country the materials, out of which she has constructed her own system of Commercial Jurisprudence, and her labors have, as we trust, added to the common stock some valuable illustrations and some solid doctrines."

Hard-working and ambitious, lawyers were absorbed by a profitable present. They aided businessmen over legal hurdles in the overhaul of the patent-law system in 1836, and the establishment of the Patent Office under a Commissioner of Patents. Again, there was no profound ideology behind the move; it was a practical adjustment to an actual situation. On other public questions, such as limited stockholder liability, there was more conscious selection. In their arguments to the legislature and courts, as in the molding of public opinion and action, lawyers sharpened issues and marshalled arguments in presenting alternatives. Their awareness in making a rational selection from competing values and means made the decisions taken on behalf of private clients, matters of public importance.

The lawyer's interest in constitutionalism fostered the assurance necessary for economic growth by creating a favorable climate for investors, both foreign and domestic. But the amount of certainty can be overstated. Law always has the opposing clarion call of flexibility; and in periods of expanding economy, the common law tends to favor open investment opportunities as opposed to security. Similar to the *Charles River* paradox was the *O'Reilly* v. *Morse* case, which limited the extent of the Morse patent on telegraphy. On the one hand, investors cannot be assured of a perpetual monopoly; on the other, the financial backers of fresh discoveries can go forward without express fears of being sued for infringement of earlier inventions. It was not that the decisions both helped and impeded commercialism, but that elements of both certainty and change were in constant tension, and that in this period the freedom to grow and expand received the judicial nod. Opportunity—witness the railroad cases —was favored rather than security, but the belief was that industrialists could still be harnessed to social welfare. Business expansion was to be encouraged by the law, but there were also attempts to enforce new restraints and to avoid the victimization caused by this expansion. Thus the balance between big business and concern for individual protection was better adjusted than it was to be in the years immediately after the Civil War.

The need for new legal instrumentalities and fresh concepts to give the entrepreneur the organization and discipline he required was recognized—despite a generation of Jacksonian polemic. Basic legal ideas of contract, property, bankruptcy, torts, negotiable instruments, and other parts of economic law were molded for use by the new industrialism. Providing the institutional framework for the expansion of production and markets was a major accomplishment that can be credited to the legal order of this period.

1. The Corporations

LIMITED LIABILITY

_____

Isaac Parker

NOTHING could show more conclusively the public opinion, that individuals were not answerable by the principles of common law than the legislature's reluctance to establish shareholder liability by statute.*

The Legislature have thought fit, and we think wisely, to subject the property of all members of these [manufacturing] corporations to a liability for the debts of the company. . . . The interest of the community seems to require that the individuals whose property, thus put into a common mass, enables them to obtain credit universally, should not shelter themselves from a responsibility, to which they would be liable as members of a private association.†

CORPORATE POWER

_____

American Jurist

IN THIS COUNTRY, a corporation is a community of men, possessing, in conformity to constitutional or legislative provision, certain property, income, or rights, and subject to certain burdens, distinct from other men.

The objects in the creation of corporations, were to perpetuate succession, without submitting to the embarrassing forms of administration and guardianship, on the decease of incorporators, and to enable numerous bodies of men, acting under a charter, as municipal, pecuniary, or other associations, to negotiate as an individual. . . .

In England, corporations are divided into aggregate and sole, the latter of which, they claim the merit of having invented. The incidents to a

_____

* Spear v. Grant, 16 Mass. (1819), pp. 9, 14.
† Marcy v. Clark, 17 Mass. (1821), pp. 266, 269.
"Corporations," American Jurist (October, 1830), IV, p. 298.

sole corporation are of such a character, that the honor of the invention will probably never be disputed. This division is of little value in the United States. Few sole corporations exist here, and are of trifling importance. . . .

Thus freed from the embarrassment of variety in these respects, it might be supposed, that the laws on the subject were simple. It is far otherwise. The doctrine is now better understood than formerly, and legislative and judicial correction has been usefully applied to qualify the extravagant consequences resulting from the application of corporate powers as formerly understood. But still the system is defective, and requires for its correction, the best efforts of the jurist. In England, trading and stock-holding corporations, are not of ancient origin. It was not till recently, that they became numerous there. In our republics, they are still more numerous, and it is difficult to set bounds to the general desire to increase them. This desire naturally grows from the genius of our institutions; for our governments, political and municipal, are founded on corporate principles. In Massachusetts alone, the chartered capital of banks and insurance offices, amounts to about $30,000,000. And the various manufacturing companies have charters to hold a still greater amount. In addition to these, are the various turnpikes, bridges, canals,—and many other corporations, created for the mere purpose of holding and managing wharves, public houses, and other estates. These already embrace a large portion of the property of the state, and some of them are of such an accumulating character, that unless restrained by legislative enactment, judicial construction, or the good sense and discretion of the stockholders, they will absorb the greatest part of the substance of the commonwealth.

The extent of the wealth and power of corporations among us, demands that plain and clear laws should be declared for their regulation and restraint; for without a salutary and strict control over them, every one may be compelled to adopt the fears of the Roman Emperor, who, when requested to institute a fire company of one hundred and fifty men, on an assurance that they should not extend their powers beyond the objects of the association, refused the grant, observing that associations had greatly disturbed the peace of cities, and whatever name he gave them, they would not fail to be mischievous. 2 Kent Com. 217.

The doctrine of corporations, in this country, on account of their extent, as well as the defective state of their existence and operation, presents a most interesting field of inquiry to American jurists, and demands that their best energies should be applied to the subject, that corporations may be protected and wisely directed in effecting the great public and private good, of which they are capable, and restrained from inflicting the public and private evils within their power, and to which they are often tempted by their own views of interest. . . .

The quaint language of Lord Coke, and other venerable ancient luminaries of the law, describing corporations as having no souls or consciences, as mere capacities to sue and be sued, has been productive of much mischief, and led to many judicial decisions, which the enlightened reason of this age cannot but deplore. From such doctrines, the managers of corporations have sometimes been led to forget that *they* had souls and moral responsibility; and in the performance of what they deemed their duty, in the corporate name, they have done such things as, on their individual responsibility, they would never have ventured to do. . . .

Experience and the wisdom of modern times have demonstrated the necessity of regulating the rights and liabilities of corporations, so far as the condition of their being permitted, by the same principles of law that govern individuals. To effect this the judicial tribunals of our age have labored with an honest and not unfruitful zeal. The barriers of irresponsibility, by which corporations were formerly surrounded, have been successfully invaded, and partially broken down; but much yet remains to be done to secure to the public all the benefits that these bodies are calculated to give, and protect individuals from the evils which they have the power to inflict. The boldest and most effectual step in this career of improvement, was the judicial decision that corporations are liable in indebitatus assumpsit.

It is now the settled law in this country, established by the Supreme Court of the United States, and by the highest judicial tribunals in many of the states, that corporations can establish rights and incur liabilities by implication.

This principle was fully settled in the case of the United States Bank *v.* Dandridge, which was ably argued, and is reported in 12 Wheaton, 64. In this case, which was decided in 1827, Chief Justice Marshall dissented from the court and gave his opinion at length. As was natural to expect, when the decision of the court was opposed by so great an authority, the whole strength on both sides was put forth. Every authority and argument, for and against the position, are there presented; and few more elaborate and satisfactory reports can be found.

Chief Justice Marshall said he believed that his opinion, which had been declared in the court below, gave general surprise to the profession, and was generally condemned; still he adhered to it. The case is now before the nation, and Judge Marshall, great as the authority of his opinion is, will have increasing cause to find that in this case he is disapproved. . . .

Although now corporations are more subject than formerly, to the laws that govern individuals, and thereby much of their irresponsibleness is taken away; yet they have advantages over individuals, in the great capitals with which they usually operate, and the enduring quality of their being; which enable them to persevere in their objects for ages with a steady aim, and undiminished capital, free from the paralyzing effects of inexperienced youth, or superannuated age, and the distribution of estates, which occur in the succession of generations, and frequently check individual operations both by want of capacity and capital.

It is the opinion of many that individuals without more protection cannot maintain a fair competition with corporations, if here they have all the English common law incidents attached to them. And in England and some of the states they have been subjected to various restraints.

In England, corporations, unless it is expressly otherwise provided by the charter, are now limited and rendered incapable of taking lands without the king's license. This has been effected by a series of statutes, called the statutes of mortmain. They were at first designed to restrain the accumulations of ecclesiastical corporations. But the statute, 15 Rich. 2. 65, declared that civil or lay corporations were within the mischief, and it brought them within the prohibition. The common law capacity of taking and holding lands by corporations is now, in that country, wholly taken away by statute.

The statutes of mortmain are in force in Pennsylvania; and there, they hold all deeds and devises of lands to corporations void, unless sanctioned by their charters. 3 Binney, 626. In New York the statutes of mortmain are not in force, but there they hold, that by force of their statutes, no religious corporation can sell without an order from the chancellor. The evils felt by the power and growing number of corporations in New York, induced them, on the amendment of their constitution, made in 1821, to provide that in future no corporation should be created or renewed, without the consent of two thirds of the members elected to each branch of the legislature. By their general statute of wills, now in force, they withhold from corporations, the power to become devisees of real estate, and in their grants of charters for private benefit they now usually insert a clause empowering the legislature to alter, modify, or repeal the charter at pleasure. And yet, with all these guards against the power and multiplication of corporations, the ablest jurists in New York, speak of them as growing evils. 2 Kent Com. 219.

In Massachusetts, where probably there is a greater propensity to multiply corporations than any where else, they have all the incidental powers, unrestrained by statutes of mortmain or wills; and generally they are granted without a clause, reserving to the legislature, the power to repeal or modify them. We can look for restrictions only to the charters, or the general statutes regulating and prescribing the powers and duties of particular classes of corporations, which are referred to in the particular charters, and made a part of them. And it has been determined in that state that a corporation can take devises and bequests in trust for pious and charitable uses. . . .

With these broad powers existing in the great and rapidly increasing numbers of corporations, this branch of jurisprudence assumes an importance in Massachusetts, and a few other states, greater than it possesses elsewhere; and the Union may look to the profession in this part of the republic, for a just exposition of the rise, progress, power, liability, decline, and dissolution of corporations. . . .

It is difficult to discover the reason why the common law clothed corporations on the moment of their springing into being with so many important rights. It vested equal power in all, though the objects for which they were created were almost as various as human operations, some being extremely limited in their objects, and affecting the interests of but few individuals, and others operating on the most valuable rights of large communities. These cannot require prerogatives and privileges of equal extent; and in this respect the common law seems to have failed of its usual excellence in its adaptation to the wants of society.

A sounder rule seems to be that every corporation should be considered as invested with all the powers necessary to effect the legal purposes for which it was created, and no more. Whether the establishment of such a rule requires legislative provision, or may be achieved by judicial construction, depends on the question, whether the English common law relative to corporations has been adopted in its full extent in the several states, or whether it remains unsanctioned, or has become obsolete. In many parts of the country the common law doctrine has been questioned, and in some distinctly denied. The author of the Commentaries on American Law says, that the modern doctrine is to consider corporations as possessing only such powers as are specifically granted in the act of incorporation, or are necessary for carrying into effect the powers expressly granted. . . . The courts in Massachusetts have made many decisions, from which it must be inferred that they favor the doctrine, and are inclined to adopt it, that corporations have no powers but such as are plainly granted in their charters, or are clearly necessary to effect the useful purposes for which they were created. Such rules of construction can hardly yet be considered as established any where in their full extent. In the courts above referred to, the common law incidents to corporations are sometimes cited with approbation, and in other state courts they are generally referred to without qualification. The evident utility of the new construction will probably soon recommend it to general adoption.

When such becomes the declared law of the states, and when it shall become the law that corporations are generally liable for the acts of their authorized agents; for contracts by implication; for all wrongs and injuries that they are capable of inflicting; and for all injurious omissions to perform their duties, there will be no longer need of statutes of mortmain and wills; or constitutional impediments or restraints to the multiplication of corporate charters. It might still, however, be wise for legislatures to reserve more direct control over corporations of future creation than they are accustomed to do in most of the states. The enjoyment of a corporate franchise is not of common right. It is the grant of the whole people of certain powers to a few individuals, to enable them to effect some specific benefit, or promote the general good. When the corporation fails to produce the expected benefit, and far more when its charter is perverted to injurious purposes, the whole people ought to have the power to control the operations, and even to revoke the charter.

When these doctrines shall become fully established, and legislatures grow careful to reserve visitatorial powers in granting charters for civil corporations, the fear and apprehension of corporations now existing, and too justly forced by experience into the public mind, will probably subside. Such fears have induced the legislatures in some of the states to adopt measures, which should, and to a great extent do, deter the public from encountering the perils resulting from the ownership of the corporate stocks.

The making of every corporator liable in all events for every debt of the company, may tend to protect the individuals, who deal with them, from danger of loss, but it will rob the public of many of the benefits that should result from the exercise of corporate charters. Prudent men will not take stock, if thereby they must become general copartners with all the other stockholders, who may become their associates without their consent, and in defiance of their opposition to such fellowship. Such a provision has heretofore been introduced in the grant of charters for manufacturing purposes in Massachusetts. The effect has been to drive millions of capital into the neighboring states for investment. And there it will remain. It is questionable whether the recent alleviating act is an adequate remedy. True policy requires that charters of corporations should be well guarded, carefully adapted to their objects, and kept under wholesome legislative and judicial control. But they should be made entirely free from onerous and appalling liabilities, the tendency of which is to drive prudent men from them, and to leave them in the hands of desperate speculators.

Another quality ascribed in the ancient books to aggregate corporations is immortality. And on this incident many curious and whimsical theories have been built. This position is as false as it is absurd. The most striking practical comment on it is, that a large proportion of those that have been created in Europe, and many in this country, have ceased to exist; their immortality notwithstanding. It is only true to this extent: that when their duration is not limited in the grant, they are capable of being made to endure indefinitely, provided from time to time the necessary measures are taken to continue their succession, and provided they continue to effect the objects for which they were made, and refrain from violating the laws. They may be dissolved in various ways, as by the limitation of time contained in the acts establishing them, by surrendering their charters, by the death of all the members, and by forfeiture of charter, through negligence or abuse of its franchises.

Since so great a portion of our national wealth is held and managed by corporations, the laws applicable to them ought to be very diligently studied by American lawyers. The growing importance of the subject demands, and it is hoped it may ere long receive, increased attention.

MUNICIPALITY AS STOCKHOLDER

Jeremiah Sullivan Black

The flexibility of the corporate device is marked clearly in the Pennsylvania mixed corporation upheld in the Sharples *opinion which follows. It is yet another refutation of the idea that government regulation of the economy is a New Deal invention.*

The attorneys who attacked the constitutionality of the act appealed to the higher-law theories of Coke, Blackstone, Kent, Vattel, Locke, and Marshall: "natural justice . . . the great God of Nature . . . public liberty . . . eternal justice . . . universal law . . . Magna Carta . . . higher matters . . . rights inherent, inalienable, indefeasible . . . natural right . . . divine law . . . private right . . . the law of laws." The issue was not one for the precedent-splitting "subtlety of the criminal lawyers," but was for "statesmen." The retort of the railroad attorneys: "This is all very well in the theories of politics, but it can maintain no standing among the exact rules of legal science."

THE OPINION OF Black, C. J., was as follows:

On the 6th of March, 1852, an act was passed by the legislature, authorizing the corporate authorities of Philadelphia city to subscribe for shares in the stock of the Philadelphia, Easton, and Water-Gap Railroad Company, and to raise the money necessary to pay for such stock by a loan on the credit of the city. On the 9th of May, 1852, a similar act was passed for a similar subscription to the stock of the Hempfield Railroad Company. In pursuance of these acts, the Select and Common Councils required the Mayor, as the executive magistrate of the city, to subscribe for ten thousand shares in the Hempfield Company forthwith, and for the same number in the Water-Gap Company, upon certain conditions. The Mayor has made one subscription accordingly, and intends to make the other as soon as the condition of the ordinance is complied with.

The plaintiffs are residents of the city, owners of property therein, and tax payers. They complain that these subscriptions will add another million of dollars to the already heavy debt of the city, impair the public credit thereof, and greatly augment the taxes of the people. The object of the bill is to restrain the Mayor from carrying the ordinances into effect. The whole subject has been argued on the motion for a special injunction. Our decision now will terminate the controversy, and have all the effect of a final decree.

Sharples *v.* Mayor of Philadelphia, 21 *Pa.* (1853), pp. 147, 158.

None of the facts are disputed. No question of construction is raised on the Act of Assembly, or on the ordinances. It is not pretended that anything has been done, or is likely to be done by the authorities of the city, except what the legislature meant to authorize. But the plaintiffs assert that the laws are unconstitutional and void. Whether the legislature can pass a valid act giving to a municipal corporation the power of subscribing to the stock of a railroad company, is the sole question before us.

This is, beyond all comparison, the most important cause that has ever been in this Court since the formation of the government. The fate of many most important public improvements hangs on our decision. If all municipal subscriptions are void, railroads, which are necessary to give the state those advantages to which everything else entitles her, must stand unfinished for years to come, and large sums, already expended on them, must be lost. Not less than fourteen millions of these stocks have been taken by boroughs, counties, and cities within this Commonwealth. They have uniformly been paid for, either with bonds handed over directly to the railroad companies, or else with the proceeds of similar bonds sold to individuals who have advanced the money. It may well be supposed that a large amount of them are in the hands of innocent holders, who have paid for them in good faith. We cannot award the injunction asked for, without declaring that all such bonds are as destitute of legal validity as so much blank parchment. Besides the deadly blow it would give to our improvements, and the disastrous effect of it on the private fortunes of many honest men, at home and abroad, it would seriously wound the credit and character of the state, and do much to lessen the influence of our institutions on the public mind of the world.

The reverse of this picture is not less appalling. It is even more so, as some view it. If the power exists, it will continue to be exerted, and generally it will be used under the influence of those who are personally interested, and who do not see or care for the ultimate injury it may bring upon the people at large. Men feel acutely what affects themselves as individuals, and are but slightly influenced by public considerations. What each person wins by his enterprise, is all his own; the public losses are shared by thousands. The selfish passion is intensified by the prospect of immediate gain; private speculation becomes ardent, energetic, and daring, while public spirit—cold and timid at the best—grows feebler still when the danger is remote. Under these circumstances it is easy to see where this ultra-enterprising spirit will end. It carried the state to the verge of financial ruin; it has produced revulsions of trade and currency in every commercial country; it is tending now, and here, to the bankruptcy of cities and counties. In England, no investments have been more disastrous than railway stocks, unless those of the South Sea bubble be an exception. In this country they have not generally been profitable. The dividends of the largest works in the neighboring states, north and south of us, have disappointed the stockholders. Not one of the completed railroads in this state has uniformly paid interest on its cost. If only a few of the roads projected in Pennsylvania should be as unfortunate as all the finished ones, such a burden would be imposed on certain parts of the state, as the industry of no people has ever endured without being crushed. Still, this plan of improving the country, if unchecked by this Court, will probably go on until it results in some startling calamity, to rouse the masses of the people.

But all these considerations are entitled to no influence here. We are to deal with this strictly as a judicial question. However clear our convictions may be, that the system is pernicious and dangerous, we cannot put it down by usurping authority which does not belong to us. That would be to commit a greater wrong than any which we could possibly repair by it. So on the other hand, the loss to the bond-holders—the ruin of the railroad companies—the injury to the commerce, and even the stain on the character of the state, are considerations which cannot be weighed for a moment, in any scale of ours, against the constitutional rights of the parties before us. We will therefore address ourselves to the serious business of ascertaining whether the laws in question do violate the constitution or not.

It is important, first of all, to settle the rule of interpretation. This can be best done by a slight reference to the origin of our political system. . . . To me, it is plain that the General Assembly may exercise all powers which are properly legislative, and which are not taken away by our own, or by the federal constitution, as it is that the people have all the rights which are expressly reserved.

We are urged, however, to go further than this, and to hold that a law, though not prohibited, is void if it violates the spirit of our institutions, or impairs any of those rights which it is the object of a free government to protect, and to declare it unconstitutional if it be wrong and unjust. But we cannot do this. It would be assuming a right to change the constitution, to supply what we might conceive to be its defects, to fill up every *casus omissus*, and to interpolate into it whatever in our opinion ought to have been put there by its framers. The constitution has given us a list of the things which the legislature may not do. If we extend that list, we alter the instrument, we become ourselves the aggressors, and violate both the letter and spirit of the organic law as grossly as the legislature possibly could. If we can add to the reserved rights of the people, we can take them away; if we can mend, we can mar; if we can remove the landmarks which we find established, we can obliterate them; if we can change the constitution in any particular, there is nothing but our own will to prevent us from demolishing it entirely. . . .

There is nothing more easy than to imagine a thousand tyrannical things which the legislature may do, if its members forget all their duties, disregard utterly the obligations they owe to their constituents, and recklessly determine to trample upon right and justice. But to take away the power from the legislature because they may abuse it, and give to the judges the right of controlling it, would not be advancing a single step, since the judges can be *imagined* to be as corrupt and as wicked as legislators. It has been said of the ablest judge that ever sat on this bench, and one whose purity of character was as perfect as any who has ever lived or ever will live, that his opinions on such subjects are not to be relied on. If this be so, then transferring the seat of authority from the legislature to the Courts, would be putting our interests in the hands of a set of very fallible men, instead of the respectable body which now holds it. What is worse still, the judges are almost entirely irresponsible, and heretofore they have been altogether so, while the members of the legislature, who would do the imaginary things referred to, "would be scourged into retirement by their indignant masters."

I am thoroughly convinced that the words of the constitution furnish the only test to determine the validity of a statute, and that all arguments, based on general principles outside of the constitution, must be addressed to the people, and not to us.

A proposition which results as plainly as this does, from the reason of the thing, can scarcely need the aid of authority; for it must be admitted that such measures cannot be sustained on principles of moral justice and propriety. But, if the doctrine I am denying could be allowed to prevail, it would decide this case in favor of the plaintiffs, without looking into the constitution at all. This consideration, together with the great ability and earnestness with which it was pressed upon us by the counsel, entitles it to the fullest refutation we can give. . . .

A tax for a private purpose is unconstitutional, though it pass through the hands of public officers; and the people may be taxed for a public work, although it be under the direction of an individual or private corporation. The question then, is, whether the building of a railroad is a public or a private affair. If it be public it makes no difference that the corporation which has it in charge is private.

A railroad is a public highway for the public benefit, and the right of a corporation to exact a uniform, reasonable, stipulated toll from those who pass over it, does not make its main use a private one. The public has an interest in such a road, when it belongs to a corporation, as clearly as they would have if it were free, or as if the tolls were payable to the state, because travel and transportation are cheapened by it to a degree far exceeding all the tolls and charges of every kind, and this advantage the public has over and above those of rapidity, comfort, convenience, increase of trade, opening of markets, and other means of rewarding labor and promoting wealth. In Bonaparte *v.* The Camden and Amboy Railroad Company (1 *Baldwin* 223), although the charter of the defendants had more features in it of a close monopoly for the mere private emolument of the stockholders, than any other similar company in the country, yet the road was held to be a public work, and the plaintiff's land, taken to build it on, was decided to have been taken for public use.

It is a grave error to suppose that the duty of a state stops with the establishment of those institutions which are necessary to the existence of government; such as those for the administration of justice, the preservation of the peace, and the protection of the country from foreign enemies; schools, colleges, and institutions, for the promotion of the arts and sciences, which are not absolutely necessary, but highly useful, are also entitled to a public patronage enforced by law. To aid, encourage, and stimulate commerce, domestic and foreign, is a duty of the sovereign, as plain and as universally recognised as any other. It is on this principle that the mint and post-office are in the hands of the government; for they are but aids to commerce. For the same reason we maintain a navy to keep open the highway of nations. It was a commercial restriction which caused the revolution, and injuries to our trade which produced the subsequent war against England, with all its expense of money and blood. Canals, bridges, roads, and other artificial means of passage and transportation from one part of the country to the other, have been made by the sovereign power, and at the public expense, in every civilized state of ancient and modern times. I need not say how much of this has been done in Pennsylvania; but if the works erected by the Commonwealth for the promotion of her commerce, are not public improvements, then every law relating to them is void; every citizen may repudiate his share of the state debt, if he pleases, and defend his property by force against a collector of state taxes.

It being the duty of the state to make such public improvements, if she happen to be unable or unwilling to perform it herself to the full extent desired, she may accept the voluntary assistance of an individual, or a number of individuals associated together and incorporated into a company. The company may be private, but the work they are to do is a public duty; and along with the public duty there is delegated a sufficient share of the sovereign power to perform it. The right of eminent domain is always given to such corporations. But the right of eminent domain cannot be used for private purposes; and therefore if a railroad, canal, or turnpike, when made by a corporation, is a mere private enterprise, like the building of a tavern, store, mill, or blacksmith's shop, there never was a constitutional charter given to an improvement company, and every taking of land or materials under any of them, was a flagrant trespass.

If the making of a railroad is a public duty, which the state may either do entirely at the public expense, or cause to be done entirely by a private corporation, it follows that such a work may be made partly by the state, and partly by a corporation, and the people may be taxed for a share of it, as rightfully as for the whole. The corporation may be aided by an exertion of the taxing power, as well as with the right of eminent domain. Accordingly we find that from the earliest times the Commonwealth has subscribed to the stock of such corporations, and paid over the money to them in pursuance of laws which no one ever doubted to be constitutional. Many millions of the state debt have been created in that way.

Now, if the legislature may create a debt and lay taxes on the whole people to pay for such subscriptions, may they not, with more justice and greater propriety, and with as clear a constitutional right, allow a particular portion of the people to tax themselves to promote in a similar manner a public work, in which they have a special interest? I think this question cannot be answered in the negative. It will surely not be pretended that all taxes are unconstitutional, which are not laid by the state directly, which are not general, or which do not go into the state treasury. If this could be maintained it would make our general road law unconstitutional from beginning to end. Counties and townships have always had the right given to them, and the duty cast upon them, of erecting their own public buildings, and making their own roads. Local taxes for local purposes, and general taxes only for purposes which concern the whole state, are a vital principle of our political system, and there is no feature in it which has attracted more unqualified admiration from those who understand it best. Its justice is too obvious to need explanation. I cannot conceive of a reason for doubting that what the state may do in aid of a work of general utility, may be done by a county, or a city, for a similar work which is especially useful to such county or city, provided the state refuses to do it herself, and permits it to be done by the local authorities.

The city's charter was granted by the legislature. It may be enlarged. The same power which gave them the privileges which they have, may give them others. It cannot be so enlarged as to enable the corporate authorities to embark the city in a private business, or to make the people pay for a thing in which they have no interest. But within these limits there is nothing to prevent an indefinite extension of their corporate powers.

But it is insisted that the right of a city or county to aid in the construction of public works, must be confined to those works which are within the locality whose people are to be taxed for them. The Water-Gap Company stops its road north of Vine street, outside of the city limits, and the Hempfield road has its eastern terminus at Greensburg, three hundred and forty-six miles west of Philadelphia. I have already said that it is the *interest* of the city which determines the right to tax her people. That interest does not necessarily depend on the mere location of the road. Therefore the location cannot be an infallible criterion. If the city cannot have an interest in a road which stops in the Northern Liberties, then Dock Ward can have no interest in one which terminates in Upper Delaware Ward, and all the subdivisions of the city, which it does not actually enter, may be exempted on the same score. A railroad may run through a county without doing its inhabitants the least service. May such a county assist to make it, while a city which it supplies with bread and whose trade is doubled by it must not do so, merely because it ends outside of an imaginary line that limits the corporate jurisdiction? It seems very plain that a city may have exactly the same interest in a road which terminates outside of her borders, as if the depot were within them, and a great deal more than if it passed quite through. If she has an interest in any part, she has probably an equal interest in every part. Railroads are generally made to connect important trading points with each other. The want of a link at one place breaks the desired connexion as much as at another. Philadelphia has now a road to Greensburg. The Hempfield Company proposes to carry it on to Wheeling. I do not see that the city is not as much interested in the Hempfield road as she would be in making an independent road, starting at the corner of Schuylkill Fifth and Market streets, and running by way of Greensburg the whole distance to Wheeling.

But it is not our business to determine what amount of interest Philadelphia has in either of these improvements. That has been settled by her own officers, and by the legislature. For us it is enough to know that the city may have a public interest in them, and that there is not a palpable and clear absence of all possible interest perceptible by every mind at the first blush. All beyond that is a question of expediency, not of law, much less of constitutional law. We would certainly be exercising a novel jurisdiction, if we would listen to an appeal from the councils on a point of local policy, and we would be giving a novel judgment, too, if we would decide a statute to be unconstitutional, because the corporate authorities of a city, in acting under it, mistook the true interest of their constituents.

We must take it for granted that the councils and the Mayor have fairly represented the majority of their constituents. It may operate with great hardship on the minority, but in this country it is private affairs alone, and not public, that are exempt from the domination of majorities. It may be conceded that the power of piling up these enormous public burdens, either on the whole people, or on a portion of them, ought not to exist in any department of a free government; and if our fathers had foreseen the fatal degeneracy of their sons, it can scarcely be doubted that some restriction on it would have been imposed. But we, the judges, cannot supply the omission. . . .

If the judgment we are about to give should be wrong, it will be our fault, for we have been well assisted. Three causes, involving the same question, were heard in immediate succession, and were argued with an ability fully proportioned to the immense magnitude of the interests, public and private, which were at stake. I do not propose to shift any part of the responsibility upon our predecessors, or upon the judges in other states, who have heretofore decided the question, and therefore I have examined it as if it were a case of the first impression; but it would be wrong to close without saying that the conclusion here reached is sustained by the highest tribunals in Virginia, (8 *Leigh* 120); New York, (24 *Wendell* 75); Connecticut, (15 *Conn.* 75); Tennessee, (9 *Humph.* 152); Kentucky, (9 *B. Monroe* 256); Illinois, (5 *Gilman* 405); and Ohio (unreported). These cases are entitled to our highest respect. In most of them, and especially the later ones, the subject is very ably discussed, and they are a manifest triumph of reason and law over a strong conviction in the minds of the judges that the system they sustain was impolitic, dangerous, and immoral. Besides these, we have a case in our own books, (1 *Jones* 61), which cannot be distinguished from this, and which ought to have something more than respect. We owe it the deference due to a declaration of the law, made by ourselves, on the faith of which the people in this and other states have invested millions of money.

I am of opinion that the motion for a special injunction ought to be refused.

JUDICIAL RESTRAINT

John Bannister Gibson

THESE ARE NOT THE DAYS to encourage individuals, or the masses, to snatch the reins from the constituted organs of the government. . . .

[A] work of human hands is never perfect; but it is better to bear the ills we have than fly to those we know not of. The legal presumption is, that an officer will do his duty; or that if he do not, the representatives of the people will impeach him, and the senators convict him. The American who denies it, denies a political aphorism, that public virtue is the basis of a republic, and one that is a postulate of his own government. If the presumption is false, it was the business of the convention which framed the constitution on that basis without providing counterchecks to the disturbing forces of party conflict, or of the legislature which framed the statute before us, to dispose of the fallacy. It is our business not to dislocate the joints and articulations of the government, to correct errors of legislation, whether immediately by the people or by their representatives; but to pronounce the law as we find it.

Commonwealth *v.* Burrell, 7 *Pa.* (1847), pp. 34, 40.

THEY CANNOT BIND THE STATE

BY CONTRACT

Roger Taney

Taney's 1833 opinion, written during his tenure as Attorney General in Jackson's cabinet, concerned a law passed by the New Jersey Legislature under which the Camden and Amboy Railroad and the Delaware and Raritan Canal Company obtained a monopoly of a transportation route. It is worth noting that the attorneys for the old bridge company in the famous Charles River Bridge *case were in possession of this opinion; they were aware of the issues it raised and attempted to answer them in their brief and oral arguments—especially since the author was by then Chief Justice. Taney's views in both cases reflect the Jacksonian animus against vested interests and the desire to re-establish effective competition.*

SIR:—I proceed to state my opinion on the questions you have proposed to me at the instance of the Trenton and New Brunswick Turnpike Company.

It is now too well settled to be disputed, that a charter granted by a state to a company incorporated to make a road or canal, where the funds for the work are provided by individuals, is a contract on the part of the state, and the public cannot by subsequent legislation without the consent of the corporation alter the terms of the charter.

The second section of the act of March 2d, 1832, passed by the legislature of New Jersey, contains a stipulation that the state shall not for a specified time incorporate any company, (except such as are therein mentioned) for the purpose of making a rail road to be used for the transportation of passengers or merchandise between the cities of Philadelphia and New York, or to compete in business with the Camden and Amboy road without the consent of the united Camden and Rail Road Companies.

This pledge on behalf of the state, is not given in express and direct terms, but it may be finally implied from the words of the law. And assuming this to be the interpretation of the act of March 2d, 1832, the question arises whether the legislature had the power to enter into such a contract with the Canal and Road Companies, and thereby to bind the state and all future legislative bodies of the state to adhere to its conditions.

R. B. Taney, Opinion, 1833, *Note Book of Simon Greenleaf,* Treasure Room, Harvard Law School, p. 1.

As the legislature exercises only a delegated power, it is quite clear that they cannot bind the state by contract or otherwise, beyond the scope of the authority granted to them by their constituents. The legislative body is not the depository of the entire sovereignty of the state and capable of binding the people by its acts in all cases whatsoever. It is the agent of the sovereign power, appointed for the purpose of executing certain trusts, and when it steps beyond the limits of its authority, its acts are void and do not bind the people by whom it was chosen. Like all other cases of delegated power, the constituent is not bound further than the agent is authorized to act for him. . . .

It will I presume be admitted on all hands, that the legislature of New Jersey exercises a limited authority, and that it does not represent the entire power of the people of the state. Their constitution provides for the election of the members of the legislature every year, and does not specifically enumerate the powers which the legislative department shall exercise but the authority of that branch of government, is in some respects expressly restrained by the constitution, and there are obviously other limitations necessarily to be implied from the nature of our institutions and the principles of free representative government. Frequent elections which have been considered one of the great safe guards of the people would lose much of their value, if a single legislature might disarm their successors of the most important legislative powers, and bind the people of the state and their descendants forever. . . .

The question is, have the people of New Jersey delegated to the legislative body the power to make such contract, and to deprive them for the time specified of the power of prosecuting such works of internal improvement as they may deem necessary to advance their interests and promote the prosperity of the state? . . .

It must be acknowledged that there would appear to be high authority for regarding this power as an incident to the power of legislation—in the act of Congress incorporating the Bank of the United States, there is an agreement on the part of the United States not to authorize any bank out of the District of Columbia, during the existence of that charter; and similar pledges may be found in similar cases, in the legislation of different States, where the Constitution has not expressly conferred on the legislature the power to make them.

But with every respect for the distinguished men who have sanctioned such legislation in the General Government, or in the States, I cannot think that a legislative body, holding a limited authority under a written Constitution, can by contract or otherwise, limit the legislative power of their successors. The power which the Constitution gives to the legislative body, must always exist in that body until it is altered by the People, and cannot be restricted by a mere legislative act. If they can deprive their successors of the power of chartering companies of a particular description or in particular places, it is obvious that upon the same principle, they might deprive them of the power of chartering any corporations for any purpose whatever; and if they might by contract, or otherwise, deprive their successors of this legislative power, they could surrender any other legislative power whatever in the same manner, and bind the State forever to submit to it. The existence of such power in a representative body has no foundation in reason, or in public convenience, and is inconsistent with the principles upon which all our political institutions are founded. For if a legislative body may thus restrict the power of its successors, a single improvident act of legislation may entail lasting and incurable evil on the people of a state. It may compel them to forego the advantages which their local situation affords, and prevent them from using the means necessary to promote the prosperity and happiness of the community. It is unnecessary to state cases in which evils of the most serious character might arise from such a power in the Legislature. They will readily suggest themselves to any one who reflects on the subject. . . .

The charter for a Rail Road from Trenton to New Brunswick would not be inconsistent with the capacities and franchises granted to the present united Canal and Rail Road Companies. They would still exercise and enjoy them, though they would prove less profitable. And if the state cannot now authorize the Turnpike Company or any other Company to make a Rail Road from Trenton to New Brunswick, it is not because it would be inconsistent with the capacities, franchises or privileges with which the present companies have been clothed; but because the Legislature of 1832 have not only exercised the power of creating Corporations, but have restricted the legislative power of their successors on the same subject. *If they may restrict it in this particular, where is the power of restriction to end?* It is not given in express terms by the Constitution of New Jersey, and its existence appears to me to be inconsistent with the spirit of our institutions, and dangerous to the best interests of the community. It cannot be regarded as an ordinary legislative power in a representative Government, when the power of the agent is not unlimited over the rights of the constituents.

In my opinion, therefore, the agreement contained in the act of March 2d, 1832, is not binding on the state of New Jersey, so far as it proposes to restrain future legislative bodies of that state from authorizing the construction of a rail road within the limits mentioned in the act assembly. And . . . the legislature may now lawfully grant the power to make such a road to any company already incorporated or hereafter to be incorporated. And such a grant would be a valid one, and the execution of it could not be prevented by the united Rail Road and Canal Companies herein before mentioned.

The remaining question is, what would be the rights of the Company who relied on such a pledge? May a subsequent Legislature entirely disregard it? This question assumes that the Legislature had no right to make such a contract and that the state is not bound by it.

As a matter of law the answer would be obvious. Every one is so far presumed to know the law, that in ordinary cases civil and criminal, he is bound as if he did know it. The corporations therefore ought not to have relied on a pledge which they are bound to know the legislature had not the constitutional power to give: If they have done so they must abide the consequences.

But the principles of moral justice would undoubtedly in many cases require that the state should indemnify a party who had confided in the public agents and had mistaken their power. And if the Legislature of New Jersey should determine to disregard the restrictions imposed in these charters on Legislative power, it would be for them to decide what amount of compensation, if any, was due to the united companies; and whether any ought to be given, and how much, are questions upon which it would hardly be proper for me to express an opinion.

I have the honour to be very respectfully,

Your obedient Servant,
R. B. TANEY

2. Industrial Society: Banking, Credit, and Bankruptcy

Central banking is now taken for granted. But its establishment was a matter of great controversy and, in this period, of constitutional law. The Second Bank of the United States was a privately managed corporation with a charter from the Federal Government, which owned one-fifth of the stock. Serving as the Federal Government's fiscal agent, its powers were also used to regulate state commercial bankers. Clay, Webster, and other advisors urged Nicholas Biddle, its president after 1823, to apply for a recharter in 1832, four years ahead of the expiration date. Jackson's veto, delivered with "all the fury of a chained panther, biting the bars of his cage," became the paramount issue of the coming Presidential campaign. Jackson was decisively re-elected over Clay, and the Bank's charter was not renewed.

THE BANK OF THE UNITED STATES

Constitutionality of the Bank: Necessary and Proper

JOHN MARSHALL

MR. CHIEF JUSTICE Marshall delivered the opinion of the Court.

In the case now to be determined, the defendant, a sovereign State, denies the obligation of a law enacted by the legislature of the Union, and the plaintiff, on his part, contests the validity of an act which has been passed by the legislature of that State. The constitution of our country, in its most interesting and vital parts, is to be considered; the conflicting powers of the government of the Union and of its members, as marked in that constitution, are to be discussed; and an opinion given, which may essentially influence the great operations of the government. No tribunal can approach such a question without a deep sense of its importance, and of the awful responsibility involved in its decision. But it must be decided peacefully, or remain a source of hostile legislation, perhaps of hostility of a still more serious nature; and if it is to be so decided, by this tribunal

McCulloch *v.* State of Maryland, 4 *Wheaton* (1819), p. 400.

alone can the decision be made. On the Supreme Court of the United States has the constitution of our country devolved this important duty.

The first question made in the cause is, has Congress power to incorporate a bank?

It has been truly said, that this can scarcely be considered as an open question, entirely unprejudiced by the former proceedings of the nation respecting it. The principle now contested was introduced at a very early period of our history, has been recognised by many successive legislatures, and has been acted upon by the judicial department, in cases of peculiar delicacy, as a law of undoubted obligation.

It will not be denied, that a bold and daring usurpation might be resisted, after an acquiescence still longer and more complete than this. But it is conceived that a doubtful question, one on which human reason may pause, and the human judgment be suspended, in the decision of which the great principles of liberty are not concerned, but the respective powers of those who are equally the representatives of the people, are to be adjusted; if not put at rest by the practice of the government, ought to receive a considerable impression from that practice. An exposition of the constitution, deliberately established by legislative acts, on the faith of which an immense property has been advanced, ought not to be lightly disregarded. . . .

This government is acknowledged by all to be one of enumerated powers. . . . But the question respecting the extent of the powers actually granted, is perpetually arising, and will probably continue to arise, as long as our system shall exist. . . . A constitution, to contain an accurate detail of all the subdivisions of which its great powers will admit, and of all the means by which they may be carried into execution, would partake of the prolixity of a legal code, and could scarcely be embraced by the human mind. It would probably never be understood by the public. Its nature, therefore, requires, that only its great outlines should be marked, its important objects designated, and the minor ingredients which compose those objects be deduced from the nature of the objects themselves. . . . In considering this question, then, we must never forget, that it is *a constitution* we are expounding.

Although, among the enumerated powers of government, we do not find the word "bank" or "incorporation," we find the great powers to lay and collect taxes; to borrow money; to regulate commerce; to declare and conduct a war; and to raise and support armies and navies. The sword and the purse, all the external relations, and no inconsiderable portion of the industry of the nation, are entrusted to its government. It can never be pretended that these vast powers draw after them others of inferior importance, merely because they are inferior. Such an idea can never be advanced. But it may with great reason be contended, that a government, entrusted with such ample powers, on the due execution of which the happiness and prosperity of the nation so vitally depends, must also be entrusted with ample means for their execution. The power being given, it is the interest of the nation to facilitate its execution. It can never be their interest, and cannot be presumed to have been their intention, to clog and embarrass its execution by withholding the most appropriate means. . . .

The constitution of the United States has not left the right of Congress to employ the necessary means, for the execution of the powers conferred on the government, to general reasoning. To its enumeration of powers is added that of making "all laws which shall be necessary and proper, for carrying into execution the foregoing powers, and all other powers vested by this constitution, in the government of the United States, or in any department thereof." . . .

But the argument on which most reliance is placed, is drawn from the peculiar language of this clause. Congress is not empowered by it to make all laws, which may have relation to the powers conferred on the government, but such only as may be *"necessary and proper"* for carrying them into execution. The word *"necessary,"* is considered as controlling the whole sentence, and as limiting the right to pass laws for the execution of the granted powers, to such as are indispensable, and without which the power would be nugatory. That it excludes the choice of means, and leaves to Congress, in each case, that only which is most direct and simple.

Is it true, that this is the sense in which the word "necessary" is always used? Does it always import an absolute physical necessity, so strong, that one thing, to which another may be termed necessary, cannot exist without that other? We think it does not. If reference be had to its use, in the common affairs of the world, or in approved authors, we find that it frequently imports no more than that one thing is convenient, or useful, or essential to another. To employ the means necessary to an end, is generally understood as employing any means calculated to produce the end, and not as being confined to those single means, without which the end would be entirely unattainable. . . .

This comment on the word is well illustrated, by the passage cited at the bar, from the 10th section of the 1st article of the constitution. It is, we think, impossible to compare the sentence which prohibits a State from laying "imposts, or duties on imports or exports, except what may be *absolutely* necessary for executing its inspection laws," with that which authorizes Congress "to make all laws which shall be necessary and proper for carrying into execution" the powers of the general government, without feeling a conviction that the convention understood itself to change materially the meaning of the word "necessary," by prefixing the word "absolutely." This word, then, like others, is used in various senses; and, in its construction, the subject, the context, the intention of the person using them, are all to be taken into view.

Let this be done in the case under consideration. The subject is the execution of those great powers on which the welfare of a nation essentially depends. It must have been the intention of those who gave these powers, to insure, as far as human prudence could insure, their beneficial execution. This could not be done by confiding the choice of means to such narrow limits as not to leave it in the power of Congress to adopt any which might be appropriate, and which were conducive to the end. This provision is made in a constitution intended to endure for ages to come, and, consequently, to be adapted to the various *crises* of human affairs. To have prescribed the means by which government should, in all future time, execute its powers, would have been to change, entirely, the character of the instrument, and give it the properties of a legal code. It would have been an unwise attempt to provide, by immutable rules, for exigencies which, if foreseen at all, must have been seen dimly, and which can be best provided for as they occur. To have declared that the best means shall not be used, but those alone without which the power given would be nugatory, would have been to deprive the legislature of the capacity to avail itself of experience, to exercise its reason, and to accommodate its legislation to circumstances. . . .

The result of the most careful and attentive consideration bestowed upon this clause is, that if it does not enlarge, it cannot be construed to restrain the powers of Congress, or to impair the right of the legislature to exercise its best judgment in the selection of measures to carry into execution the constitutional powers of the government. If no other motive for its insertion can be suggested, a sufficient one is found in the desire to remove all doubts respecting the right to legislate on that vast mass of incidental powers which must be involved in the constitution, if that instrument be not a splendid bauble.

We admit, as all must admit, that the powers of the government are limited, and that its limits are not to be transcended. But we think the sound construction of the constitution must allow to the national legislature that discretion, with respect to the means by which the powers it confers are to be carried into execution, which will enable that body to perform the high duties assigned to it, in the manner most beneficial to the people. Let the end be legitimate, let it be within the scope of the constitution, and all means which are appropriate, which are plainly adapted to that end, which are not prohibited, but consist with the letter and spirit of the constitution, are constitutional. . . .

If a corporation may be employed indiscriminately with other means to carry into execution the powers of the government, no particular reason can be assigned for excluding the use of a bank, if required for its fiscal operations. To use one, must be within the discretion of Congress, if it be an appropriate mode of executing the powers of government. That it is a convenient, a useful, and essential instrument in the prosecution of its fiscal operations, is not now a subject of controversy. All those who have been concerned in the administration of our finances, have concurred in representing its importance and necessity; and so strongly have they been felt, that statesmen of the first class, whose previous opinions against it had been confirmed by every circumstance which can fix the human judgment, have yielded those opinions to the exigencies of the nation. Under the confederation, Congress, justifying the measure by its necessity, transcended perhaps its powers to obtain the advantage of a bank; and our own legislation attests the universal conviction of the utility of this measure. The time has passed away when it can be necessary to enter into any discussion in order to prove the importance of this instrument, as a means to effect the legitimate objects of the government.

But, were its necessity less apparent, none can deny its being an appropriate measure; and if it is, the degree of its necessity, as has been very justly observed, is to be discussed in another place. Should Congress, in the execution of its powers, adopt measures which are prohibited by the constitution; or should Congress, under the pretext of executing its powers, pass laws for the accomplishment of objects not entrusted to the government; it would become the painful duty of this tribunal, should a case requiring such a decision come before it, to say that such an act was not the law of the land. But where the law is not prohibited, and is really calculated to effect any of the objects entrusted to the government, to undertake here to inquire into the degree of its necessity, would be to pass the line which circumscribes the judicial department, and to tread on legislative ground. This court disclaims all pretensions to such a power. . . .

The choice of means implies a right to choose a national bank in preference to State banks, and Congress alone can make the election. . . .

The branches, proceeding from the same stock, and being conducive to the complete accomplishment of the object, are equally constitutional. It would have been unwise to locate them in the charter, and it would be unnecessarily inconvenient to employ the legislative power in making those subordinate arrangements. The great duties of the bank are prescribed; those duties require branches; and the bank itself may, we think, be safely trusted with the selection of places where those branches shall be fixed; reserving always to the government the right to require that a branch shall be located where it may be deemed necessary.

It being the opinion of the Court, that the act incorporating the bank is constitutional; and that the power of establishing a branch in the State of Maryland might be properly exercised by the bank itself, we proceed to inquire—

2. Whether the State of Maryland may, without violating the constitution, tax that branch? . . .

If we measure the power of taxation residing in a State, by the extent of sovereignty which the people of a single State possess, and can confer on its government, we have an intelligible standard, applicable to every case to which the power may be applied. We have a principle which leaves the power of taxing the people and property of a State unimpaired; which leaves to a State the command of all its resources, and which places beyond its reach, all those powers which are conferred by the people of the United States on the government of the Union, and all those means which are given for the purpose of carrying those powers into execution. We have a principle which is safe for the States, and safe for the Union. We are relieved, as we ought to be, from clashing sovereignty; from interfering powers; from a repugnancy between a right in one government to pull down what there is an acknowledged right in another to build up; from the incompatibility of a right in one government to destroy what there is a right in another to preserve. We are not driven to the perplexing inquiry, so unfit for the judicial department, what degree of taxation is the legitimate use, and what degree may amount to the abuse of the power. . . .

That the power to tax involves the power to destroy; that the power to destroy may defeat and render useless the power to create; that there is a plain repugnance, in conferring on one government a power to control the constitutional measures of another, which other, with respect to those very measures, is declared to be supreme over that which exerts the control, are propositions not to be denied. But all inconsistencies are to be reconciled by the magic of the word CONFIDENCE. Taxation, it is said, does not necessarily and unavoidably destroy. To carry it to the excess of destruction would be an abuse, to presume which, would banish that confidence which is essential to all government.

But is this a case of confidence? Would the people of any one State trust those of another with a power to control the most insignificant operations of their State government? We know they would not. Why, then, should we suppose that the people of any one State should be willing to trust those of another with a power to control the operations of a government to which they have confided their most important and most valuable interests? In the legislature of the Union alone, are all represented. The legislature of the Union alone, therefore, can be trusted by the people with the power of controlling measures which concern all, in the confidence that it will not be abused. This, then, is not a case of confidence, and we must consider it as it really is.

If we apply the principle for which the State of Maryland contends, to the constitution generally, we shall find it capable of changing totally the character of that instrument. We shall find it capable of arresting all the measures of the government, and of prostrating it at the foot of the States. The American people have declared their constitution, and the laws made in pursuance thereof, to be supreme; but this principle would transfer the supremacy, in fact, to the States.

If the States may tax one instrument, employed by the government in the execution of its powers, they may tax any and every other instrument. They may tax the mail; they may tax the mint; they may tax patent rights; they may tax the papers of the custom-house; they may tax judicial process; they may tax all the means employed by the government, to an excess which would defeat all the ends of government. This was not intended by the American people. They did not design to make their government dependent on the States.

Gentlemen say, they do not claim the right to extend State taxation to these objects. They limit their pretensions to property. But on what principle is this distinction made? Those who make it have furnished no reason for it, and the principle for which they contend denies it. They contend that the power of taxation has no other limit than is found in the 10th section of the 1st article of the constitution; that, with respect to every thing else, the power of the States is supreme, and admits of no control. If this be true, the distinction between property and other subjects to which the power of taxation is applicable, is merely arbitrary, and can never be sustained. This is not all. If the controlling power of the States be established; if their supremacy as to taxation be acknowledged; what is to restrain their exercising this control in any shape they may please to give it? Their sovereignty is not confined to taxation. That is not the only mode in which it might be displayed. The question is, in truth, a question of supremacy; and if the right of the States to tax the means employed by the general government be conceded, the declaration that the constitution, and the laws made in pursuance thereof, shall be the supreme law of the land, is empty and unmeaning declamation. . . .

The Court has bestowed on this subject its most deliberate consideration. The result is a conviction that the States have no power, by taxation or otherwise, to retard, impede, burden, or in any manner control, the operations of the constitutional laws enacted by Congress to carry into execution the powers vested in the general government. This is, we think, the unavoidable consequence of that supremacy which the constitution has declared.

We are unanimously of opinion, that the law passed by the legislature of Maryland, imposing a tax on the Bank of the United States, is unconstitutional and void.

This opinion does not deprive the States of any resources which they originally possessed. It does not extend to a tax paid by the real property of the bank, in common with the other real property within the State, nor to a tax imposed on the interest which the citizens of Maryland may hold in this institution, in common with other property of the same description throughout the State. But this is a tax on the operations of the bank, and is, consequently, a tax on the operation of an instrument employed by the government of the Union to carry its powers into execution. Such a tax must be unconstitutional.

A Deadly Blow

NILES REGISTER

A DEADLY BLOW has been struck at the Sovereignty of the States, and from a quarter so far removed from the people as to be hardly accessible to public opinion. . . . Nothing but the tongue of an angel can convince us of its compatibility with the Constitution. . . . Far be it from us to be thought as speaking disrespectfully of the Supreme Court, or to subject ourselves to the suspicion of a contempt of it. We do not impute corruption to the Judges, nor intimate that they have been influenced by improper feelings,—they are great and learned men; but still, only men. . . . We are awfully impressed with a conviction that the welfare of the Union has received a more dangerous wound than fifty Hartford Conventions, hateful as that assemblage was, could inflict,—reaching so close to the vitals as seemingly to draw the heart's blood of liberty and safety, and which may be wielded to destroy the whole revenues, and so do away the sovereignties of the States. . . . The principles established . . . are far more dangerous to the Union and happiness of the people of the United States than anything else that we ever had to fear from foreign invasion. A judicial decision which threatens to annihilate the sovereignties of the States; which will sanction any species of monopoly and make the productive many subservient to the unproductive few,—it creates a most disgusting monopoly. The reasoning of the opinion exhibits a catching at words, and an establishment of facts by implication, with a Sibylline mystery thrown over things hitherto supposed to be very comprehensible, embellished too with a lawyer-like pleading that we wish had been dispensed with.

The Opinion Continues to Be Denounced

JOHN MARSHALL

THE OPINION in the Bank case continues to be denounced by the democracy in Virginia. An effort is certainly making to induce the Legislature which will meet in December to take up the subject and to pass resolutions

Niles Register, March 13, 1819, in Charles Warren, *The Supreme Court in United States History,* I (1937), p. 522.

John Marshall, Letter, May 27, 1819, *Massachusetts Historical Society Proceedings, 2d Series* (1900–01), p. 325.

not very unlike those which were called forth by the Alien and Sedition Laws in 1799. Whether the effort will be successful or not may perhaps depend in some measure on the sentiments of our sister States. To excite this ferment, the opinion has been grossly misrepresented; and where its argument has been truly stated, it has been met by principles one would think too palpably absurd for intelligent men. But prejudice will swallow anything. If the principles which have been advanced on this occasion were to prevail, the Constitution would be converted into the old Confederation.

It Cannot Be "Necessary" or "Proper"

ANDREW JACKSON

TO THE SENATE:

The bill "to modify and continue" the act entitled "An act to incorporate the subscribers to the Bank of the United States," was presented to me on the 4th July instant. Having considered it with that solemn regard to the principles of the constitution which the day was calculated to inspire, and come to the conclusion that it ought not to become a law, I herewith return it to the Senate, in which it originated, with my objections.

A Bank of the United States is, in many respects, convenient for the Government, and useful to the people. Entertaining this opinion, and deeply impressed with the belief that some of the powers and privileges possessed by the existing bank are unauthorized by the constitution, subversive of the rights of the States, and dangerous to the liberties of the people, I felt it my duty, at an early period of my administration, to call the attention of Congress to the practicability of organizing an institution combining all its advantages, and obviating these objections. I sincerely regret, that, in the act before me, I can perceive none of those modifications of the bank charter which are necessary, in my opinion, to make it compatible with justice, with sound policy, or with the constitution of our country. . . .

It has been urged as an argument in favor of rechartering the present bank, that the calling in its loans will produce great embarrassment and distress. The time allowed to close its concerns is ample; and if it has been well managed, its pressure will be light, and heavy only in case its management has been bad. If, therefore, it shall produce distress, the fault will be its own; and it would furnish a reason against renewing a power which has been so obviously abused. But will there ever be a time

---

Andrew Jackson, Veto Message, July 10, 1832, Richardson, *Messages of the Presidents* (1896), p. 576.

when this reason will be less powerful? To acknowledge its force, is to admit that the bank ought to be perpetual, and, as a consequence, the present stockholders, and those inheriting their rights as successors, be established a privileged order, clothed both with great political power, and enjoying immense pecuniary advantages, from their connection with the Government. . . .

The fourth section . . . secures to the State banks a legal privilege in the Bank of the United States, which is withheld from all private citizens. If a State bank in Philadelphia owe the Bank of the United States, and have notes issued by the St. Louis branch, it can pay the debt with those notes; but if a merchant, mechanic, or other private citizen be in like circumstances, he cannot, by law, pay his debt with those notes; but must sell them at a discount, or send them to St. Louis to be cashed. This boon conceded to the State banks, though not unjust in itself, is most odious; because it does not measure out equal justice to the high and the low, the rich and the poor. To the extent of its practical effect, it is a bond of union among the banking establishments of the nation, erecting them into an interest separate from that of the people: and its necessary tendency is to unite the Bank of the United States and the State banks in any measure which may be thought conducive to their common interest.

The ninth section of the act recognizes principles of worse tendency than any provision of the present charter.

It enacts that "the cashier of the bank shall annually report to the Secretary of the Treasury the names of all stockholders who are not resident citizens of the United States; and, on the application of the Treasurer of any State, shall make out and transmit to such Treasurer a list of stockholders residing in, or citizens of such State, with the amount of stock owned by each." Although this provision, taken in connection with a decision of the Supreme Court, surrenders, by its silence, the right of the States to tax the banking institutions created by this corporation, under the name of branches, throughout the Union, it is evidently intended to be construed as a concession of their right to tax that portion of the stock which may be held by their own citizens and residents. In this light, if the act becomes a law, it will be understood by the States, who will probably proceed to levy a tax equal to that paid upon the stock of banks incorporated by themselves. In some States that tax is now one per cent., either on the capital or on the shares, and that may be assumed as the amount which all citizen or resident stockholders would be taxed under the operation of this act. As it is only the stock *held* in the States, and not that *employed* between them, which would be subject to taxation, and as the names of foreign stockholders are not to be reported to the Treasurers of the States, it is obvious that the stock held by them will be exempt from this burden. Their annual profits will, therefore, be one per cent. more than the citizen stockholders; and, as the annual dividends of the bank may be safely estimated at seven per cent., the stock will be worth ten or fifteen per cent. more to foreigners than to citizens of the United States.

The amount of stock held in the nine western and south-western States, is $140,200, and in the four southern States, is $5,623,100, and in the middle and eastern States, is about $13,522,000. The profits of the bank in 1831, as shown in a statement to Congress, were about $3,455,598: of this there accrued, in the nine western States, about $1,640,048; in the four southern States, about $352,507; and in the middle and eastern States, about $1,463,041. As little stock is held in the west, it is obvious that the debt of the people, in that section, to the bank, is principally a debt to the eastern and foreign stockholders; that the interest they pay upon it, is carried into the eastern States and into Europe; and that it is a burden upon their industry, and a drain of their currency, which no country can bear without inconvenience and occasional distress. . . .

In another of its bearings this provision is fraught with danger. Of the twenty-five directors of this bank, five are chosen by the Government, and twenty by the citizen stockholders. From all voice in these elections, the foreign stockholders are excluded by the charter. In proportion, there-fore, as the stock is transferred to foreign holders, the extent of suffrage in the choice of directors is curtailed. Already is almost a third of the stock in foreign hands, and not represented in elections. It is constantly passing out of the country; and this act will accelerate its departure. The entire control of the institution would necessarily fall into the hands of a few citizen stockholders; and the ease with which the object would be accomplished, would be a temptation to designing men to secure that control in their own hands, by monopolizing the remaining stock. There is danger that a president and directors would then be able to elect them-selves from year to year, and, without responsibility or control, manage the whole concerns of the bank during the existence of its charter. It is easy to conceive that great evils to our country and its institutions might flow from such a concentration of power in the hands of a few men, irresponsible to the people.

Is there no danger to our liberty and independence in a bank, that, in its nature, has so little to bind it to our country? The President of the bank has told us that most of the State banks exist by its forbearance. Should its influence become concentrated, as it may under the operation of such an act as this, in the hands of a self elected directory, whose interests are identified with those of the foreign stockholder, will there not be cause to tremble for the purity of our elections in peace, and for the independence of our country in war? . . .

If we must have a bank with private stockholders, every consideration of sound policy, and every impulse of American feeling, admonishes that it should be *purely American*. . . .

It is maintained by the advocates of the bank that its constitutionality in all its features ought to be considered as settled by precedent, and by the decision of the Supreme Court. To this conclusion I cannot assent. Mere precedent is a dangerous source of authority, and should not be regarded as deciding questions of constitutional power, except where the acquiescence of the people and the States can be considered as well settled. So far from this being the case on this subject, an argument against the bank might be based on precedent. One Congress, in 1791, decided in favor of a bank; another, in 1811, decided against it. One Congress, in 1815, decided against a bank; another, in 1816, decided in its favor. Prior to the present Congress, therefore, the precedents drawn from that source were equal. If we resort to the States, the expressions of legislative, judicial, and executive opinions against the bank, have been, probably, to those in its favor as four to one. There is nothing in precedent, therefore, which, if its authority were admitted, ought to weigh in favor of the act before me.

If the opinion of the Supreme Court covered the whole ground of this act, it ought not to control the co-ordinate authorities of this Government. . . .

The principle here affirmed is, that the "degree of its necessity," involving all the details of a banking institution, is a question exclusively for legislative consideration. . . . Under the decision of the Supreme Court, therefore, it is the exclusive province of Congress and the President to decide whether the particular features of this act are *necessary* and *proper* in order to enable the bank to perform conveniently and efficiently the public duties assigned to it as a fiscal agent, and therefore constitutional; or *unnecessary* and *improper*, and therefore unconstitutional. Without commenting on the general principle affirmed by the Supreme Court, let us examine the details of this act in accordance with the rule of legislative action which they have laid down. It will be found that many of the powers and privileges conferred on it cannot be supposed necessary for the purpose for which it is proposed to be created, and are not, therefore, means necessary to attain the end in view, and consequently not justified by the Constitution.

If Congress possessed the power to establish one bank, they had power to establish more than one, if, in their opinion, two or more banks had been "necessary" to facilitate the execution of the powers delegated to them in the constitution. . . . It was possessed by one Congress as well as another, and by all Congresses alike, and alike at every session. But the Congress of 1816 have taken it away from their successors for twenty years, and the Congress of 1832 proposes to abolish it for fifteen years more. It cannot be *"necessary"* or *"proper"* for Congress to barter away, or divest themselves of any of the powers vested in them by the constitution to be exercised for the public good. It is not *"necessary"* to the efficiency of the bank, nor is it *"proper"* in relation to themselves and their successors. They may *properly* use the discretion vested in them; but they may not limit the discretion of their successors. This restriction on themselves, and grant of a monopoly to the bank, is, therefore, unconstitutional. . . .

On two subjects only does the constitution recognize in Congress the power to grant exclusive privileges or monopolies. . . .

Out of this express delegation of power, have grown our laws of patents and copy-rights. As the constitution expressly delegates to Congress the power to grant exclusive privileges, in these cases, as the means of executing the substantive power "to promote the progress of science and useful arts," it is consistent with the fair rules of construction, to conclude that such a power was not intended to be granted as a means of accomplishing any other end. On every other subject which comes within the scope of Congressional power, there is an ever living discretion in the use of proper means, which cannot be restricted or abolished without an amendment of the constitution. Every act of Congress, therefore, which attempts, by grants of monopolies, or sale of exclusive privileges for a limited time, or a time without limit, to restrict or extinguish its own discretion in the choice of means to execute its delegated powers, is equivalent to a legislative amendment of the constitution, and palpably unconstitutional.

This act authorizes and encourages transfers of its stock to foreigners, and grants them an exemption from all State and national taxation. So far from being *"necessary and proper"* that the bank should possess this power to make it a safe and efficient agent of the Government in its fiscal operations, it is calculated to convert the Bank of the United States into a foreign bank, to impoverish our people in time of peace, to disseminate a foreign influence through every section of the Republic, and, in war, to endanger our independence.

The several States reserved the power, at the formation of the constitution, to regulate and control titles and transfers of real property; and most, if not all of them, have laws disqualifying aliens from acquiring or holding lands within their limits. But this act, in disregard of the undoubted right of the States to prescribe such disqualifications, gives to aliens, stockholders in this bank, an interest and title, as members of the corporation, to all the real property it may acquire within any of the States of this Union. This privilege granted to aliens is not *"necessary"* to enable the bank to perform its public duties, nor in any sense *"proper,"* because it is vitally subversive of the rights of the States.

The Government of the United States have no constitutional power to purchase lands within the States, except "for the erection of forts, magazines, arsenals, dock-yards and other needful buildings"; and even for these objects only "by the consent of the Legislature of the State in which the same shall be." By making themselves stockholders in the bank, and granting to the corporation the power to purchase lands for other purposes, they assume a power not granted in the constitution, and grant to others what they do not themselves possess. It is not *necessary* to the receiving, safe keeping, or transmission of the funds of the Government, that the bank should possess this power; and it is not *proper* that Congress should thus enlarge the powers delegated to them in the constitution. . . .

The Government is the only *"proper"* judge where its agents should reside and keep their offices, because it best knows where their presence will be *"necessary."* It cannot, therefore, be *"necessary"* or *"proper"* to authorize the bank to locate branches where it pleases to perform the public service, without consulting the Government, and contrary to its will. The principle laid down by the Supreme Court concedes that Congress cannot establish a bank for purposes of private speculation and gain, but only as a means of executing the delegated powers of the General Government. By the same principle, a branch bank cannot constitutionally be established for other than public purposes. The power which this act gives to establish two branches in any State, without the injunction or request of the Government, and for other than public purposes, is not *"necessary"* to the due *execution* of the powers delegated to Congress. . . .

It is maintained by some that the bank is a means of executing the constitutional power "to coin money, and regulate the value thereof." Congress have established a Mint to coin money, and passed laws to regulate the value thereof. The money so coined, with its value so regulated, and such foreign coins as Congress may adopt, are the only currency known to the constitution. But if they have other power to regulate the currency, it was conferred to be exercised by themselves, and not to be transferred to a corporation. If the bank be established for that purpose, with a charter unalterable without its consent, Congress have parted with their power for a term of years, during which the constitution is a dead letter. It is neither necessary nor proper to transfer its legislative power to such a bank, and therefore unconstitutional.

By its silence, considered in connection with the decision of the Supreme Court in the case of McCulloch against the State of Maryland, this act takes from the States the power to tax a portion of the banking business carried on within their limits, in subversion of one of the strongest barriers which secured them against federal encroachments. Banking, like farming, manufacturing, or any other occupation or profession, is *a business*, the right to follow which is not originally derived from the laws. Every citizen, and every company of citizens, in all of our States, possessed the right, until the State Legislatures deemed it good policy to prohibit private banking, by law. If the prohibitory State laws were now repealed, every citizen would again possess the right. The State banks are a qualified restoration of the right which has been taken away by the laws against banking, guarded by such provisions and limitations as, in the opinion of the State Legislatures, the public interest requires. These corporations, unless there be an exemption in their charter, are, like private bankers and banking companies, subject to State taxation. The manner in which these taxes shall be laid, depends wholly on legislative discretion. It may be upon the bank, upon the stock, upon the profits, or in any other mode which the sovereign power shall will.

Upon the formation of the constitution, the States guarded their taxing power with peculiar jealousy. They surrendered it only as it regards imports and exports. . . .

The principle is conceded that the States cannot rightfully tax the operations of the General Government. They cannot tax the money of the Government deposited in the State banks, nor the agency of those banks in remitting it; but will any man maintain, that their mere selection to perform this public service for the General Government would exempt the State banks, and their ordinary business, from State taxation? . . . Upon what principle, then, are the banking establishments of the Bank of the United States, and their usual banking operations to be exempted from taxation? . . . There is no more appropriate subject of taxation than banks, banking, and bank stocks, and none to which the States ought more pertinaciously to cling. . . .

If our power over means is so absolute that the Supreme Court will not call in question the constitutionality of an act of Congress, the subject of which "is not prohibited, and is really calculated to effect any of the objects entrusted to the Government," although, as in the case before me, it takes away powers expressly granted to Congress, and rights scrupulously reserved to the States, it becomes us to proceed in our legislation with the utmost caution. Though not directly, our own powers and the rights of the States may be indirectly legislated away in the use of means to execute substantive powers. We may not enact that Congress shall not have the power of exclusive legislation over the District of Columbia, but we may pledge the faith of the United States, that, as a means of executing other powers, it shall not be exercised for twenty years or forever. We may not pass an act prohibiting the States to tax the banking business carried on within their limits, but we may, as a means of executing our powers over other objects, place that business in the hands of our agents, and then declare it exempt from State taxation in their hands. Thus may our own powers and the rights of the States, which we cannot directly curtail or invade, be frittered away and extinguished in the use of means employed by us to execute other powers. That a Bank of the United States, competent to all the duties which may be required by the Government, might be so organized as not to infringe on our own delegated powers, or the reserved rights of the States, I do not entertain a doubt. Had the Executive been called upon to furnish the project of such an institution, the duty would have been cheerfully performed. In the absence of such a call, it is obviously proper that he should confine himself to pointing out those prominent features in the act presented, which, in his opinion, make it incompatible with the constitution and sound policy. A general discussion will now take place, eliciting new light, and settling important principles; and a new Congress, elected in the midst of such discussion, and furnishing an equal representation of the people according to the last census, will bear to the Capitol the verdict of public opinion, and, I doubt not bring this important question to a satisfactory result.

THE PRICE OF CAPITAL

Demands for financing, which were raised on all sides in a vigorous and expanding nation with a capital shortage, met head-on the Biblical admonition against the taking of interest. Despite vague feelings of discomfort, a "gentleman of New York" managed to justify a repeal of legislative ceilings upon the permissible rate.

The following petition, attacking the Massachusetts laws which forbade interest rates exceeding 6 per cent, was presented to the state senate in March, 1834. After consideration of the petition, a committee reported that it had been favorably impressed by the arguments of the more than two hundred "intelligent and responsible citizens of Boston." Though the committee agreed that usury laws as they then stood were "inexpedient" and invited evasion and fraud, they were reluctant to make a radical change in the law. A repeal of the usury laws concerning promissory notes and bills of exchange payable within specific dates was recommended. With this step, the committee felt, it appeared "expedient to begin the reform." A law containing the committee's suggestions was enacted before the end of the 1834 session.

As If the Law Could Oblige

A NEW YORK GENTLEMAN

THE ACCOMPANYING REMARKS are strictly what they profess to be—extracted from the correspondence of a gentleman of this city, whose son while pursuing his studies at a distance from home, had requested some explanations of the banking system and monetary concerns of the country. They are given to the public in their original shape as appearing in this

Familiar View of the Operation and Tendency of Usury Laws, *The Correspondence of a Gentleman of New York, with His Son* (1837), pp. 2, 60.

way best adapted to the perusal of those, who are not altogether familiar with the subject.

The coincidence of this correspondence with the efforts now making in the legislature of this state for the repeal, or modification, of the *usury law*; and the apparent expediency of replying without loss of time to some of the objections made to this repeal, especially those urged in the essay of the *Rhode Islander*, have induced the writer to commit his remarks to the press, and must furnish his apology for doing this with less preparation than it would otherwise have been his duty to bestow, upon a subject of so much importance. . . .

There is another subject closely connected with that of our banking system, which it is important for you to understand—I mean the operation of the *usury laws*, as they are called: That is, the laws limiting the rate at which money is to be borrowed or loaned.

I am the more desirous to give you my views on this subject, because as a *law student* you may easily be influenced in your opinions in this particular, by gentlemen of that profession—and I have never met with a lawyer who did not advocate the restrictive side of the question; and indeed I may caution you that the habits of thinking peculiar to the practice of the law are too apt to favour the multiplication of legal enactments. . . .

Since my remarks on this subject have been written, the bill before the legislature of this state, for a repeal of the usury law, has been laid on the table; and this, it appears, under an apprehension that such a repeal would occasion the calling in of a large portion of the existing loans on mortgage throughout the state.

This apprehension, it must be perceived, is founded upon some of the mistaken views with which I have been combating.

It is taken for granted, that the loans now made at or under seven per cent, are so made because the law will not permit a higher rate of interest. As if the law could oblige money lenders to loan at the rate prescribed, when they could employ their money more advantageously otherwise; and as if the legal rate of interest in all other transactions were the actual rate. And it is consequently taken for granted, too, that if there should be no legal rate, the actual rate would be, under equal circumstances, increased.

I believe the operation would be very different from this. If there are not other circumstances besides the repeal of the statute to change the money market, the interest would be the same; and it would appear that lenders placed their money in loans on bond and mortgage at seven per cent, not because the law obliged them to do so, but because they were contented with this rate of interest.

If, on the contrary, there should be a change from other causes in the demand for money, such as would make the lenders desirous of with-drawing these loans, in order to do better with their capital, there will then be this important difference—that the statute being repealed, they will allow their loans to continue at an increased rate of interest, say from eight to ten per cent per annum, instead of seven; whereas, if the statute be not repealed, they will refuse to continue their loans altogether; they will insist upon *foreclosing* their mortgages, and thus bring a ruinous distress upon those who would otherwise be obliged to pay only a little additional interest. . . .

Let us suppose the case of an honest industrious farmer, in middling circumstances. He has a homestead which cost him $1500; of this amount $1000 remain on mortgage. After years of toil he has brought his ground into the highest state of cultivation. Besides paying his yearly interest of seventy dollars, it affords, with his labour, a support for himself and his family, and perhaps a small sum to spare. The bond, however, has now become due; money is more in demand than it was when he first borrowed. The holder of the mortgage tells him, that, being able to do better with his capital, and the law not permitting him to receive more than seven per cent in the old way, he must have his money. The farmer tries to borrow elsewhere—he is told, "the law will not allow us to receive more than seven per cent on bond and mortgage, and we can do better in other ways, therefore we cannot lend you at all." The farmer proposes giving a premium, or something in addition to the interest. He is told, "we cannot accept of such an offer, for if you were afterwards to make it a proof of usury, we should lose the whole, and we cannot take that risk." The poor man must then go home to his family with a heavy heart, announcing to his wife and children, that every thing must be sold to satisfy the mortgage. Suppose at this moment a friend should inform him that the usury law was repealed; and that he might now borrow the money at the rate of nine per cent per annum, although he could not do it before for seven.—What joy would not such an annunciation afford him and his family! Instead of being turned houseless upon the world, as they expected to be; and of being driven, perhaps, with the small remains of their little property, to seek a footing in the wilderness, by the purchase of a few acres of un-settled land, they are able still to enjoy the fruits of their years of toil, and still to remain in possession of their beloved home, without other inconvenience than that of paying yearly twenty dollars additional interest.

The melancholy portion of this picture is not merely a *fancy sketch*— I have heard of such cases, and have no doubt its reality may be found in the numberless instances of those whom we see yearly removing westward, and westward, even to the Rocky Mountains. They have sold their little farms to satisfy mortgages, because they could no longer borrow within the precise limit prescribed by law.

It is for the landholders of our state then, as well as for the farmer, to consider how far such legal restrictions are incompatible with the agricultural as well as with the commercial and manufacturing interests of the country.

Inconvenience Arising from Usury Laws

A PETITION

THE UNDERSIGNED, citizens of Boston, having long experienced the inconveniences arising from the existing Usury Laws of Massachusetts and being persuaded that the Honorable Legislature will, whenever the subject is properly brought before them, provide an adequate remedy for the evils complained of, have deemed it suitable and proper to appear as petitioners before that honorable body, setting forth in their petition the inconveniences to which the present laws give rise and praying such a modification of those laws as will, in their opinion remove the evil.

We, your petitioners would therefore respectfully represent—that, in our judgement, the existing Usury Laws, so far as they limit the rate of interest, are founded on erroneous principles, and are at variance with the commercial spirit of the age. We think that every article of human traffic, whether money or any other thing, is alike subject to fluctuations of value, and that consequently, the market price of them all, is constantly liable to change. We think that the price of money or more properly speaking, the price of its use, not less than the price of lumber, corn, tobacco, cotton, or any other great commercial staple is and must be regulated by the extent of the demand in the market and that every attempt to fix the value and render the price of either of these articles invariable is not only vain but wholly unjust; and that it is, in the case of all these commodities, an equal infringement of private rights. . . .

We are also of opinion that while the present restrictions were intended to favor the interests of borrowers, they are even more injurious to borrowers than to lenders. But before demonstrating this proposition we beg leave respectfully to express our convictions that any attempt of the law to favor one particular class of citizens to the injury of any other class, is unjust, unconstitutional, and contrary to the spirit of freedom and equal rights; and although in this case the attempt is wholly unsuccessful, yet we cannot regard it, on that account, as less contrary to sound principles; and, both as borrowers and as lenders, we are equally hostile to the laws which sustain the attempt.

Petition for the Repeal of the Usury Laws, March 4, 1834, *Massachusetts Senate No. 66.*

We will now endeavor to show that, in their practical effect, these laws are injurious to borrowers of money. Whenever the demand for money is such in the market as to render it worth more than the established rate of interest, the borrower, however pressing his want, however strong his necessity, cannot raise the requisite loan; for the money owner is not compelled to part with his money at less than its worth; and he will not be so foolish as to lend when he can find more profitable modes of investment;—and the borrower, although willing to pay any premium for relief, must suffer all the pressure of his emergency without the possibility of obtaining assistance. Cases of this sort we have all experienced and observed very frequently; and we know them to form the most serious obstructions to successful enterprise. So also we are aware that many instances occur in which the personal character of the borrower is such as to render the owner of money reluctant to venture on his credit at the usual rate;—while, did the law allow, the applicant would be glad to pay a premium proportioned to the risk. In this manner, borrowers experience a compound evil, being unable to pay for the desired article according to its market value or their own necessities; and many a man is ruined who, if he could have been allowed to offer seven or eight, or more per cent. would have realized a fortune. Can any reason be assigned why the privilege of charging interest proportioned to the risk, allowed on bottomry loans should not be extended to every other species of loan?

The inconvenience experienced by money lenders, under the laws, though great, is yet less than that felt by borrowers, although these laws were intended for the borrowers' advantage. For, if the holders of money cannot lend at an interest equivalent to the value of the capital, they can invest that capital in those more profitable modes of traffic which create the money demand. Thus to them only one avenue of business is closed, while to the borrower, every resource is cut off. But it is certainly worthy of legislative attention that, even in a single particular, the process of business is impeded; and legislators, as such, in our opinion, are to be held responsible for the losses that the community may suffer in the person of its citizens, from this impediment.

The law is manifestly wrong in supposing that, if left unrestricted, money lenders would acquire an overgrown influence and exercise an oppressive power. Nothing of this sort can be reasonably feared, while we have such a host of banks and other monied corporations in addition to individual lenders, all in the market, and all engaged in active competition. No inconvenience of this kind is ever complained of in the case of bottomry loans, where the lenders are not restricted by any statute. No evil is found to exist in the matter of insurance premiums, where the risk is uniformly the measure of the rate. Competition, as much in the pecuniary facilities required by business men, as in the facilities of travel by land and sea, determines the price of those facilities. And is there not as much probability that the public will be burdened with exorbitant stage and steamboat fares, as with extortionous charges for the use of money? We are firm in the opinion that all money transactions should be regulated, like those in other articles of trade, only by this spirit of competition; and that no greater evils would or could, in the present age arise from the traffic in money being thus unrestricted, than are now felt from the perfect freedom allowed to traffic in other commodities. And it passes our understanding to see why that, whether money, or goods, which is made the instrument of profit to him who uses it, should not in all cases, be sold at its real value.

The evils that grow out of our laws are enhanced by the fact that the rate of interest in a neighboring state is one per cent per annum higher than in Massachusetts. In consequence of this difference, by which a constant drain is produced from our market, a vast amount of capital, which, if they were fettered by no law, would remain in circulation amongst our fellow citizens, is drawn into the New York market, and totally lost to our borrowers whose embarrassments are thereby increased. This evil is constantly and severely felt. But at particular times as in the present pressure on the money market, its burden is especially heavy and causes the greatest distress, particularly to those who are least able to sustain it, viz. business young men whose capital is small and of whom credit is the support. Were the present laws repealed, our own capital would remain in our own use, and the capital of the neighboring states would flow in upon us in such a manner that our business would be greatly extended and increased.

We would respectfully direct the attention of the Legislature to the numerous modes that have been devised for evading the laws; modes of transacting business, which, besides being circuitous and inconvenient, and besides taking away the sanction and protection of the law from those who engage in them, leaving no security but what is termed honor, thus increasing the risk, and of course the premium paid—besides these evils, which are loss of time, money, comfort and security—produce a fearful disregard of the laws, and establish a precedent of the utmost danger, while they tend to throw pecuniary negotiations in the hands of unprincipled and dangerous men. We need not specify the various methods by which the law is now evaded, and by which interest above six per cent is taken, in defiance of law, under the various names of "premium," "exchange," and "commission"; for these are matters of notoriety, and need only be alluded to in order to secure the attention of the Legislature. So long as our laws remain unchanged, it is vain to hope for a better state of things.

Such being the opinion of your petitioners they respectfully pray that the Usury Laws may be so modified as to leave the rate of interest, like the rate of premiums on insurances, perfectly open to contract,—providing, however, that in all cases where interest accrues, and the particular rate has not been expressly agreed upon between the parties, the present shall remain the legal rate.

A UNIFORM SYSTEM OF BANKRUPTCY

In an acquisitive age, there was a sense that failure was an individual responsibility, due to defect in character or, perhaps, a shirking of hard work. However, as the economic world became more volatile and the number of business failures increased, tolerance emerged for the bankrupt —but only on the theory that the sinner would return and try once more.

The Fault Is Not in the Constitution

DANIEL WEBSTER

Webster was not without personal involvement on the points he argued so eloquently in the following debate. Despite his high fees—$13,400 in 1834, $15,183 in 1835, $21,793 in 1836 (the largest fee he ever received was $15,000 in the Goodyear Rubber case, which established the validity of that company's patents, argued when he was Secretary of State and over seventy years old)—carelessness in personal investments left him at the mercy of his clients. Financial worries always pressed on him; at times he wished he "had been born a miser."

I FEEL A DEEP and anxious concern for the success of this bill, and, in rising to address the Senate, my only motive is a sincere desire to answer objections which have been made to it, so far as I may be able, and to urge the necessity and importance of its passage. Fortunately, it is a subject which does not connect itself with any of the party contests of the day; and although it would not become me to admonish others, yet I have prescribed it as a rule to myself, that, in attempting to forward the measure, and to bring it to a successful termination, I shall seek no party ends, no party influence, no party advancement. The subject, so far as I am concerned, shall be sacred from the intrusion of all such objects and purposes. I wish to treat this occasion, and this highly important question, as a

Daniel Webster, Speech, May 18, 1840, *Speeches and Orations of Daniel Webster* (ed. Whipple, 1879), p. 471.

green spot in the midst of the fiery deserts of party strife, on which all may meet harmoniously and amicably, and hold common counsel for the common good.

The power of Congress over the subject of bankruptcies, the most useful mode of exercising the power under the present circumstances of the country, and the duty of exercising it, are the points to which attention is naturally called by every one who addresses the Senate.

In the first place, as to the power. It is fortunately not an inferred or constructive power, but one of the express grants of the Constitution. "Congress shall have power to establish uniform laws on the subject of bankruptcies throughout the United States." These are the words of the grant; there may be questions about the extent of the power, but there can be none of its existence.

The bill which has been reported by the committee provides for voluntary bankruptcies only. It contains no provisions by which creditors, on an alleged act of bankruptcy, may proceed against their debtors, with a view to subject them and their property to the operation of the law. It looks to no coercion by a creditor to make his debtor a subject of the law against his will. This is the first characteristic of the bill, and in this respect it certainly differs from the former bankrupt laws of the United States, and from the English bankrupt laws.

The bill, too, extends its provisions, not only to those who, either in fact or in contemplation of law, are traders, but to all persons who declare themselves insolvent, or unable to pay their debts and meet their engagements, and who desire to assign their property for the benefit of their creditors. In this respect, also, it differs from the former law, and from the law of England.

The questions, then, are two: 1st. Can Congress constitutionally pass a bankrupt law which shall include other persons besides traders? 2d. Can it pass a law providing for voluntary cases only, that is, cases in which the proceedings originate only with the debtor himself? . . .

Bankruptcies, in the general use and acceptation of the term, mean no more than failures. A bankruptcy is a fact. . . . Whenever a man's means are insufficient to meet his engagements and pay his debts, the fact of bankruptcy has taken place; a case of bankruptcy has arisen, whether there be a law providing for it or not. . . . Over the whole subject of these bankruptcies, or these failures, the power of Congress, as it stands on the face of the Constitution, is full and complete.

And now, let us see how it is that this broad and general power is, or can be, limited by a supposed reference to the English system. . . . Let it be admitted that the framers of the Constitution looked to England for a general example; they must be supposed, nevertheless, to have looked to the power of Parliament, and not to the particular mode in which that power had been exercised, or the particular law then actually existing. The true analogy is, as it seems to me, between power and power; the power of Parliament and the power of Congress; and not between the power of Congress and any actually existing British statute, which might be, perhaps, in many respects, quite unsuitable to our condition. . . .

I think, then, that Congress may pass a law which shall include persons not traders, and which shall include voluntary cases only. And I think, further, that the amendment proposed by the honorable member from New Jersey is, in effect, exactly against his own argument. I think it admits all that he contends against. In the first place, he admits voluntary bankruptcies, and there were none such in England in 1789. This is clear. And in the next place, he admits any one who will say that he has been concerned in trade; and he maintains, and has asserted, that in this country any body may say that. . . .

The gentleman's real object is, not to confine the bill to traders, but to embrace every body; and yet he deems it necessary for every person applying to state, and to swear, that he has been engaged in trade. This seems to me to be both superfluous and objectionable; superfluous, because, if we have a right to bring in persons under one name, we may bring in the same persons under another name, or by a general description; objectionable, because it requires men to state what may very much resemble a falsehood, and to make oath to it. Suppose a farmer or mechanic to fail; can he take an oath that he has been engaged in trade? If the objection to bring in others than traders is well founded in the Constitution, surely mere form cannot remove it. Words cannot alter things. The Constitution says nothing about traders. Yet the honorable gentleman's amendment requires all applicants to declare themselves traders; and if they will but say so, and swear so, it shall be so received, and nobody shall contradict it. In other words, a fiction, not very innocent, shall be allowed to overcome an unconstitutional objection. The gentleman has been misled by a false analogy. He has adopted an example which does not apply to the case, and which he yet does not follow out. The British statutes are confined to traders. But then they contain a long list of persons who, it is declared, shall be deemed and taken to be traders within the acts. This list they extend, from time to time; and whenever any one included within the list becomes a voluntary bankrupt, he avers, in substance, that he is a trader, within the act of Parliament. . . .

But now, Sir, I come to a very important inquiry. The Constitution requires us to establish *uniform* laws on the subject of bankruptcy, if we establish any. What is this uniformity, or in what is it to consist? The honorable gentleman says that the meaning is, that the law must give a coercive power to creditors, as well as a voluntary power to debtors; that this is the constitutional uniformity. I deny this altogether. No idea of uniformity arises from any such consideration. The uniformity which the Constitution requires is merely a uniformity throughout all the States. It is a local uniformity, and nothing more. The words are perfectly plain, and the sense cannot be doubted. The authority is, to establish uniform laws on the subject of bankruptcies throughout the United States. Can any thing be clearer? To be uniform is to have one shape, one fashion, one form; and our bankrupt laws, if we pass them, are to have one shape, one fashion, and one form in every State. If this be not so, what is the sense of the concluding words of the clause, "throughout the United States"? My honorable friend from Kentucky has disposed of this whole question, if there ever could be a question about it, by asking the honorable gentleman from New Jersey what *uniform* means, in the very same clause of the Constitution, where the word is applied to rules of naturalization; and what it means in a previous clause, where it declares that all duties of impost shall be *uniform* throughout the United States. . . .

Leaving this very important part of the case, another question arises upon the proposed amendment. Shall the bankruptcy act, in its application to individuals, be voluntary only, or both voluntary and compulsory? It is well known that I prefer that it should be both. I think all insolvent and failing persons should have power to come in under its provisions, and be voluntary bankrupts; and I think, too, that, as to those who are strictly merchants and traders, creditors ought to have a right to proceed against them, on the commission of the usual acts of bankruptcy, and subject them to the provisions of the act. But the committee think otherwise. They find many objections to this from many parts of the country, and especially from the West. In a country so extensive, with a people so various, with such different ideas and habits in regard to punctuality in commercial dealings, great opposition is anticipated to any measure so strict and so penal as a coercive bankruptcy. I content myself, therefore, with what I can get. I content myself with the voluntary bankruptcy. I am free to confess my leading object to be, to relieve those who are at present bankrupts, hopeless bankrupts, and who cannot be discharged or set free but by a bankrupt act passed by Congress. I confess that their case forms the great motive of my conduct. It is their case which has created the general cry for the measure. Not that their interest is opposed to the interest of creditors; still less that it is opposed to the general good of the country. On the contrary, I believe that the interest of creditors would be greatly benefited even by a system of voluntary bankruptcy alone, and I am quite confident that the public good would be eminently promoted. In my judgment, all interests concur; and it is the duty of providing for these unfortunate insolvents, in a manner thus favorable to all interests, which I feel urging me forward on this occasion.

And now, Sir, whence does this duty arise which appears to me so pressing and imperative? How has it become so incumbent upon us? What are the considerations, what the reasons, which have so covered our tables with petitions from all classes and all quarters, and which have loaded the air with such loud and unanimous invocations to Congress to pass a bankrupt law?

Let me remind you, then, in the first place, Sir, that, commercial as the country is, and having experienced as it has done, and experiencing as it now does, great vicissitudes of trade and business, it is almost forty years since any law has been in force by which any honest man, failing in business, could be effectually discharged from debt by surrendering his property. The former bankrupt law was repealed on the 19th of December, 1803. From that day to this, the condition of an insolvent, however honest and worthy, has been utterly hopeless, so far as he depended on any legal mode of relief. This state of things has arisen from the peculiar provisions of the Constitution of the United States, and from the omission by Congress to exercise this branch of its constitutional power. By the Constitution, the States are prohibited from passing laws impairing the obligation of contracts. Bankrupt laws impair the obligation of contracts, if they discharge the bankrupt from his debts without payment. The States, therefore, cannot pass such laws. The power, then, is taken from the States, and placed in our hands. It is true that it has been decided, that, in regard to contracts entered into after the passage of any State bankrupt law, between the citizens of the State having such law, and sued in the State courts, a State discharge may prevail. So far, effect has been given to State laws. I have great respect, habitually, for judicial decisions; but it has, nevertheless, I must say, always appeared to me that the distinctions on which these decisions are founded are slender, and that they evade, without answering, the objections founded on the great political and commercial objects intended to be secured by this part of the Constitution. But these decisions, whether right or wrong, afford no effectual relief. The qualifications and limitations which I have stated render them useless, as to the purpose of a general discharge. So much of the concerns of every man of business is with citizens of other States than his own, and with foreigners, that the partial extent to which the validity of State discharges reaches is of little benefit.

The States, then, cannot pass effectual bankrupt laws; that is, effectual for the discharge of the debtor. There is no doubt that most, if not all, the States would now pass such laws, if they had the power; although their legislation would be various, interfering, and full of all the evils which the Constitution of the United States intended to provide against. But they have not the power; Congress, which has the power, does not exercise it. This is the peculiarity of our condition. The States would pass bankrupt laws, but they cannot; we can, but we will not. And between this want of power in the States and want of will in Congress, unfortunate insolvents are left to hopeless bondage. There are probably one or two hundred thousand debtors, honest, sober, and industrious, who drag out lives useless to themselves, useless to their families, and useless to their country, for no reason but that they cannot be legally discharged from debts in which misfortunes have involved them, and which there is no possibility of their ever paying. I repeat, again, that these cases have now been accumulating for a whole generation.

It is true they are not imprisoned; but there may be, and there are, restraint and bondage outside the walls of the jail, as well as in. Their power of earning is, in truth, taken away; their faculty of useful employment is paralyzed, and hope itself become extinguished. Creditors, generally, are not inhuman or unkind; but there will be found some who hold on, and the more a debtor struggles to free himself, the more they feel encouraged to hold on. The mode of reasoning is, that, the more honest the debtor may be, the more industrious, the more disposed to struggle and bear up against his misfortunes, the greater the chance is, that, in the end, especially if the humanity of others shall have led them to release him, their own debts may be finally recovered.

Now, in this state of our constitutional powers and duties, in this state of our laws, and with this actually existing condition of so many insolvents before us, it is not too serious to ask every member of the Senate to put it to his own conscience to say, whether we are not bound to exercise our constitutional duty. Can we abstain from exercising it? The States give to their own laws all the effect they can. This shows that they desire the power to be exercised. Several States have, in the most solemn manner, made known their earnest wishes to Congress. If we still refuse, what is to be done? Many of these insolvent persons are young men with young families. Like other men, they have capacities both for action and enjoyment. Are we to stifle all these for ever? Are we to suffer all these persons, many of them meritorious and respectable, to be pressed to the earth for ever, by a load of hopeless debt? The existing diversities and contradictions of State laws on the subject admirably illustrate the objects of this part of the Constitution, as stated by Mr. Madison; and they form that precise case for which the clause was inserted. The very evil intended to be provided against is before us, and around us, and pressing us on all sides. How can we, how dare we, make a perfect dead letter of this part of the Constitution, which we have sworn to support? The insolvent persons have not the power of locomotion. They cannot travel from State to State. They are prisoners. To my certain knowledge, there are many who cannot even come here to the seat of government to present their petitions to Congress, so great is their fear that some creditor will dog their heels, and arrest them in some intervening State, or in this District, in the hope that friends will appear to save them, by payment of the debt, from imprisonment. These are truths; not creditable to the country, but they are truths. I am sorry for their existence. Sir, there is one crime, quite too common, which the laws of man do not punish, but which cannot escape the justice of God; and that is, the arrest and confinement of a debtor by his creditor, with no motive on earth but the hope that some friend, or some relative, perhaps almost as poor as himself, his mother it may be, or his sisters, or his daughters, will give up all their own little pittance, and make beggars of themselves, to save him from the horrors of a loathsome jail. Human retribution cannot reach this guilt; human feeling may not penetrate the flinty heart that perpetrates it; but an hour is surely coming, with more than human retribution on its wings, when that flint shall be melted, either by the power of penitence and grace, or in the fires of remorse.

Sir, I verily believe that the power of perpetuating debts against debtors, for no substantial good to the creditor himself, and the power of imprisonment for debt, at least as it existed in this country ten years ago, have imposed more restraint on personal liberty than the law of debtor and creditor imposes in any other Christian and commercial country. If any public good were attained, any high political object answered, by such laws, there might be some reason for counselling submission and sufferance to individuals. But the result is bad, every way. It is bad to the public and to the country, which loses the efforts and the industry of so many useful and capable citizens. It is bad to creditors, because there is no security against preferences, no principle of equality, and no encouragement for honest, fair, and seasonable assignments of effects. As to the debtor, however good his intentions or earnest his endeavors, it subdues his spirit, and degrades him in his own esteem; and if he attempts any thing for the purpose of obtaining food and clothing for his family, he is driven to unworthy shifts and disguises, to the use of other persons' names, to the adoption of the character of agent, and various other contrivances, to keep the little earnings of the day from the reach of his creditors. Fathers act in the name of their sons, sons act in the name of their fathers; all constantly exposed to the greatest temptation to misrepresent facts and to evade the law, if creditors should strike. All this is evil, unmixed evil. And what is it all for? Of what benefit to any body? Who likes it? Who wishes it? What class of creditors desire it? What consideration of public good demands it?

Sir, we talk much, and talk warmly, of political liberty; and well we may, for it is among the chief of public blessings. But who can enjoy political liberty if he is deprived, permanently, of personal liberty, and the exercise of his own industry and his own faculties? To those unfortunate individuals, doomed to the everlasting bondage of debt, what is it that we have free institutions of government? What is it that we have public and popular assemblies? What is even this Constitution itself to them, in its actual operation, and as we now administer it? What is its aspect to them, but an aspect of stern, implacable severity? an aspect of refusal, denial, and frowning rebuke? nay, more than that, an aspect not only of austerity and rebuke, but, as they must think it, of plain injustice also, since it will not relieve them, nor suffer others to give them relief? What love can they feel towards the Constitution of their country, which has taken the power of striking off their bonds from their own paternal State governments, and yet, inexorable to all the cries of justice and of mercy, holds it unexercised in its own fast and unrelenting grasp? They find themselves bondsmen, because we will not execute the commands of the Constitution; bondsmen to debts they cannot pay, and which all know they cannot pay, and which take away the power of supporting themselves. Other slaves have masters, charged with the duty of support and protection; but their masters neither clothe, nor feed, nor shelter; they only bind.

But, Sir, the fault is not in the Constitution. The Constitution is beneficient as well as wise in all its provisions on this subject. The fault, I must be allowed to say, is in us, who have suffered ourselves quite too long to neglect the duty incumbent upon us. The time will come, Sir, when we shall look back and wonder at the long delay of this just and salutary measure. We shall then feel as we now feel when we reflect on that progress of opinion which has already done so much on another connected subject; I mean the abolition of imprisonment for debt. What should we say at this day, if it were proposed to reëstablish arrest and imprisonment for debt, as it existed in most of the States even so late as twenty years ago? I mean for debt alone, for mere, pure debt, without charge or suspicion of fraud or falsehood.

Against a National Bankruptcy Law

THEOPHILUS PARSONS

TO THE WIDE PREVALENCE of actual insolvency, was due the law which was passed in 1841, after an earnest but unsuccessful endeavor in the year previous.

If the amount or number of applications for the law is a true measure of its need or its utility, this law was not passed too soon. In Massachusetts, for example, there were 3,389 applicants for relief, and the creditors numbered 99,619, more than a third of the adult male population of the State, and the amount of their claims exceeded thirty millions of dollars, averaging about three hundred and fifty dollars to a creditor.

This law was repealed March 3, 1843, one year six months and fourteen days after it was enacted; and in this short period it affected more property, and gave rise to more numerous and more difficult questions, than any other law has ever done, in the same period. It was repealed because it had done its work. The people demanded it, that it might settle claims and remove encumbrances and liens and sweep away an indebted-

Theophilus Parsons, *The Laws of Business for Business Men* (1857), p. 235.

ness that lay as an intolerable burden on the community. When it had done this, it began, or was thought to have begun, to favor the payment of debt by insolvency too much, and the people demanded its repeal.

We have no national bankrupt law now. We shall probably never have one until another similar national emergency shall arise; and perhaps not then, because the State insolvent laws are now so well constructed and systematized, that they effect, though not quite so well, nearly all the purposes of a national law.

Death of a Poor Debtor

GEORGE GREENVILLE

In the prison dark and dreary,
    Lay a wasting, dying man,
Heart-sick, home-sick, worn and weary,
    With life's journey almost ran;
With no friendly voice to cheer him,
    With no loved one by his side,
Fast death's shadows gathered near him,
    Deepened, darkened, till he died.

Oh! who shall know the anguish
    Of that sick and lonely one,
Forced within those walls to languish,
    Till the pulse of life was gone;
For what crime of nameless horror,
    For what deadly, damning sin,
Was he doomed in woe and sorrow,
    Thus to die a cell within.

None; except the crime of being
    Poor, and wasting with disease,
That was hasting fast to free him
    From life's troubles, toils and cares:
Yet men stern and iron hearted,
    Could *in jail* a brother hold,
Till the breath of life departed,
    For a paltry sum of gold!

George Greenville, *Death of a Poor Debtor in Boston Jail* (1851).

Ye who sit in legislation—
  Can ye see and not abhor
Such things in this *Christian* nation?
  Why uphold them by your law?
In the name of God eternal,
  He whose throne is Love and Light,
Blot a statute so infernal
  From your books of boasted Right.

3. Railroads

"The first puff of the engine on the iron road," wrote Judge Thomas of the Massachusetts Supreme Judicial Court, "announced a revolution in the law of bailments and of common carriers."

In many ways, transportation to bind the separate economic areas, rather than production, was the prerequisite for the rapid expansion of industrialism. From 1830 to 1848, five thousand and twenty-five miles of railroads were built. By 1850, railroad securities dominated transactions on the New York Stock Exchange. Between 1850 and the depression of 1857, twenty-three hundred miles of track were constructed each year at an average cost of sixty million dollars; by 1860, the tracks cost more than a billion and a half dollars and constituted the greatest investment in the country.

Law could not remain static when faced by such changes. The "few broad and comprehensive principles" of the common law were developed to organize the daily business of the railroads. The first lawbook treating of railroads came out in 1849—Angell on Carriers. One of the vexing issues was that of liability for loss of goods. Originally, as Shaw states in Commonwealth v. Fitchburg R.R. *(1858), "the railroad contemplated by our earliest legislation . . . was but an iron turnpike, the use of which was to be paid for by tolls collected of persons travelling upon it." But soon the companies became themselves the carriers of goods and passengers. As a common carrier, the railroad's liability was that of an insurer, which was deemed by most state courts too heavy a burden for the new enterprise to support.* Illinois Central Railroad Co. v. Morrison, *which follows, indicates the way out taken by some courts.*

The same concern that growing enterprises might be strangled by costs underlies the case of Murray v. S. C. Railroad Co. *The majority holding that a worker, injured through no fault of his own but through the negligence of a fellow servant, could not sue the common employer, was cemented into law by the famous Shaw opinion in* Farewell v. Boston and Worcester R.R. *(1842). The harsh conclusion of the South Carolina Court, that the burden of industrial accidents was to be cast on the workers themselves, is tested in the accompanying three dissents.*

SPECIAL CONTRACTS

Sidney Breese

BREESE, J. The question presented in this case is one of importance to the business public, and to the railroad interests, and has received due attention from the court.

Illinois Central Railroad Company *v.* Morrison and Crabtree, *19 Illinois* (1857), pp. 136, 139.

That railroad companies are common carriers cannot be disputed, and, being so, they are bound and controlled, as a general principle, by all the common law rules applicable to such a position—they becoming, in fact, insurers.

Until the establishment and use of railroads for the conveyance of property, it was not generally considered that common carriers could, by special contract, limit their liability, or take themselves out of the severe rules which governed such business.

At this time, railroads have acquired much of the carrying trade of the country, and reversing the former order of things, now carry the very animals which propelled the old machines used for that purpose. It was quite an era in trade and transportation, when speedy means were devised by railroads for carrying live stock from one extreme of the country to the other, and, on its origination, new rules were found necessary, or modifications of old ones, as applicable to this new system, which, whilst protecting these magnificent and costly enterprizes, should be so guarded that no injury to the public should flow from them.

Transportation of live stock in railroad cars, in their rapid motion, is attended with great hazard, against which, if the companies owning them had no power of protection, irretrievable ruin to them might be the necessary consequence. Accordingly, we see that the courts in England, where the railroad system, though yet perhaps in its infancy even there, has been brought to great perfection, and in most of the older and well regulated, and highly commercial States of our Union, have declared that these companies may protect themselves from their general liability as common carriers, by special contracts. . . .

A portion of these cattle, it appears, were left at Onarga, a station north of Urbana, and another car obtained there, in which they (36 head,) were placed, and a similar release executed, on the 12th November, in the name of D. A. Morrison, by his son, without any authority, as he testifies, from his father. And, on the 15th, ninety-one head were shipped, and a similar release executed by James Crabtree in the name of D. A. Morrison, but, as he testifies, without any authority from Morrison. These two last releases were excluded from the jury.

The parol agreement, made by Morrison in person, in the view we have taken of the case, attaches to the whole transaction, to the extent, at least, of four hundred head of cattle, no matter whose they were, whether owned by Morrison alone, or jointly with others. The agreement made, was for the transportation of four hundred head, and they were delivered at different times. . . .

The declaration is in case, and sets out nothing more than the general and ordinary duties of defendants as common carriers, with a count in trover added.

In such case, the defendants have a right to defend themselves by the special contract.

The defendants have paid a valuable consideration for the risks assumed by the plaintiffs, by accepting reduced rates, and the plaintiffs have had the full benefit of the reduction. It would be great injustice to require the company to pay for escaping risks, and then burden them with the losses against which, by fair contract, they have purchased exemption.

The whole case shows, merely, a hiring of cars and motive power—there being no complete delivery of the cattle to the defendants, as the owners, or their agents, or some one of them accompanied them and had them in their own charge. They could not be stowed away, like inanimate matter, and had the power of locomotion, and were exposed to various accidents, the risk of all which the company paid the plaintiffs to assume.

We think the rule a good one, as established in England and in this country, that railroad companies have a right to restrict their liability as common carriers, by such contracts as may be agreed upon specially, they still remaining liable for gross negligence or willful misfeasance, against which good morals and public policy forbid that they should be permitted to stipulate. . . .

As the Circuit Court seemed to have entertained views of the law different from those here expressed, the judgment is reversed, and the cause remanded for further proceedings not inconsistent with this opinion.

THE FELLOW-SERVANT RULE

Supreme Court of South Carolina

THIS WAS AN ACTION on the case, against the defendants, for an injury sustained in their service.

The plaintiff is a tailor by trade. He resided at Aiken, and applied to Capt. Robertson, the agent of the company, for employment. He declined employing him, on account of his intemperate habits and consequent rashness. He, however, went on to Charleston, and was employed as a second fireman, on the 18th May. He selected the engine and engineer to which he was to be attached and under whom he was to serve. William E. Perry was the engineer. About the 27th of May, 1837, the plaintiff's second or third trip, as the engine was ascending the road from Charleston, near the Four Hole Swamp, just before entering an excavation, and within about three hundred yards of it, one of the witnesses (Johnson, the first fireman,) said he saw a horse standing near the commencement of the excavation, within ten steps of the road, feeding slowly towards it: he

Murray *v.* Railroad Company, 1 *McMull (So. Car.)* (1841), p. 385.

touched the engineer on the back, and asked him if he saw the horse: he
made no reply: the engine ran on: the plaintiff said to the engineer,
"Stop, we are in danger": the engine still proceeded, until within fifty or
sixty yards of the horse: this witness said he then put his hand on the
"escape steam valve," and told the engineer again to stop, for there was
danger of running over the horse, and pointed towards him: he, the
engineer, then shut off the steam: by this time the horse stepped upon the
road, and there stood: the engine, with the steam shut off, ran within six
or eight feet of the horse: the engineer gave her all the steam she could
carry, to carry her as quick as possible, and with the least danger, over
the horse. At this moment, this witness took hold of the awning post, and
swung himself outside the engine, for the purpose of jumping off on the
left hand side of it: in this position he could see under the engine, which
struck and ran over the horse: as it left the road on the right hand side, the
witness jumped off on the left. His post was on the left, and the plaintiff's
on the right, of the engine: the brake to stop the engine was on the right,
and nearer the plaintiff than the witness: when the engineer shut off the
steam, the brake was not let down: (he said he was too much agitated by
fear to think of the brake:) had it been let down, the engine might have
been stopped. As the engine left the road, the plaintiff's leg dropped between the foot board of the engine and tender, and as these two came
violently together, when the engine stopped, his leg was crushed, and his
thigh was afterwards amputated midway. This witness gave it as his
opinion, very distinctly, that the accident might have been avoided, and
resulted from the carelessness of the engineer, in not stopping the engine
as soon as cautioned: he thought that as the engine was running only at
the rate of ten or twelve miles per hour, it might have been stopped before
they reached the horse. He said it was not the fireman's duty to let down
the brake, unless ordered by the engineer. Meredith, the conductor of the
train, said, just as they emerged from an excavation, he saw the horse
about fifteen yards from the road, moving from behind some bushes, and
running in an oblique direction towards the road, and in the direction the
engine was pursuing; he ran thus about twenty yards, when he leaped
upon the road between the rails, just at the entrance of another excavation:
as he did so, the engine struck him, and passed over him, and was thrown
off the track. The engine was running from sixteen to twenty miles an hour.
From the time this witness saw the horse, he said that he thought the only
way to avoid him was to outrun him. He said, that to stop the engine, it
is the duty of the engineer to shut off the steam, and the firemen to let
down the "brake": it is, however, the engineer's duty to order the fireman
to let down the brake. Perry was proved to be a skilful professional engineer. The witnesses, Robertson and Ross, concurred in saying, that it
was the duty of the engineer to shut off the steam, and the fireman to let
down the brake, (and that was the particular duty of the second fireman)
whether ordered by the engineer or not, to stop the engine, and prevent

any accident. About 300 feet is as short a space as within which the engine can be stopped, when running at the average rate of fifteen miles an hour.

The jury were instructed, that the plaintiff's service subjected him to all the ordinary risks and perils of the employment. Each officer of the company, as to strangers and inferiors, was to be considered as the company; and every command or act given or done by him, must be regarded as given or done by the company themselves. If a superior officer had given an order to an inferior, to do an act not necessary to be done, and not within the duty of the inferior, and in doing it, injury resulted to the inferior, then the company would be responsible. If, in running the road, a superior officer (the engineer) did his duty so carelessly as to subject a servant of the company to unnecessary danger, and which the servant could not avoid, then the company would be liable. But if the peril, from which the injury resulted, was unavoidable, or if the engineer did every thing ordinary prudence suggested, to avoid it—and, notwithstanding, a servant sustained injury, it would be one of the risks to which his contract of service subjected him, and he could not recover. So, too, if the servant, (the second fireman) did not do his duty, and to its neglect (as not letting down the brake) the injury might be fairly ascribed, then, in that case, his injury would be attributable to himself, and he could have no redress against the company. . . . [The jury awarded $1,500 to the plaintiff.]

Curia, per EVANS, J. In the consideration of the question involved in this case, I shall assume that the verdict establishes the fact that the plaintiff's injury was the effect of the negligence of the engineer, and then the question arises whether the rail road company is liable to one servant for an injury arising from the negligence of another servant. The business of the company is the transportation of goods and passengers. Its liability in these respects, is, in general, well defined and understood by the profession; and if the plaintiff's case came within any of the principles applicable to these cases, we should have no difficulty in deciding it. The application of steam power to transportation on rail roads, is of recent origin, but the principle by which the liability of a carrier is fixed and ascertained, is as old as the law itself. There is nothing in the fact, that the defendant is a corporation, except that of necessity it must act altogether by agents. The liability is precisely the same as if the defendant was an individual acting by the agency of others. The principle is the same, whether you apply it to a rail road, a steam boat, a wagon, a stage coach, or a ship. If this plaintiff is entitled to recover, I can see no reason why the owner of any of the above modes of conveyance, should not be liable under the same circumstances. If the owner of a wagon should employ two men, one to drive and the other to load, and either of them should so negligently perform his work as to injure the other, the owner of the wagon would be liable. The principle will extend to all the vocations of life wherein more than one person is employed to effect a single object; and a new class of liabilities would arise, which I do not think has ever heretofore been supposed to exist. It is admitted, no case like the present has been found, nor is there any precedent suited to the plaintiff's case, unless he stands in the relation of a passenger to the company. In this point of view, his counsel has chosen to regard him, for I understand the declaration alleges he was a passenger. Now, a passenger is every where spoken of, as one who pays for transportation. In all the operations necessary for this, he is passive. The moment he becomes an operator, for then his character is changed, he becomes the servant of the company, and not its passenger. It would be a confusion of terms so to regard him. He is no more a passenger than a sailor or a stage driver. There is nothing in the definition of bailment, or the classification of the different kinds of liability growing out of that relation, which applies to the plaintiff's case, and if he is entitled to recover, it must be on principles which apply equally to all operations of life in which agents are employed. There is no question that, in general, the principal is liable for the acts of the agent, performed in the execution of his agency, or in and about the business of his principal. Thus, the owners of a rail road would be liable to passengers for an injury sustained by the negligence of any of its servants, superior or subordinate, because it is implied in the undertaking to carry, not only that the road and cars are good, but that the servants employed are competent and will perform their duty. For the loss of goods, the law annexes a still greater responsibility. So, also, if one employ an agent to execute any work whereby an injury may result to a stranger, the law requires it to be done with care, and if a stranger sustain an injury, his principal is liable, as was decided in *O'Connell* vs. *Strong*, (Dud. Rep. 265.) But the plaintiff is neither a passenger nor a stranger, and if he can recover, it must be in his hermaphrodite character as a passenger fireman. In the cases above enumerated, the principal is represented by the agent, and unless he be liable, the great operations of life can not be carried on— no man would have adequate security for his person or his property. The owner of goods would not trust them on a rail road, or a steam boat, if his only security was the liability of the mere servants employed. No passenger would commit his safety to a rail road, steam boat, or stage coach, if, in case of injury, he could look to none but the agents usually employed about these modes of transportation. So, also, no man would have any guarantee for the security of his property, if his only remedy for negligence was the irresponsible or insolvent agents which another might employ. In all these, and similar cases, the reasons of the liability of the principal are clear, and the law books are full of cases or precedents which apply to them; but it is not so with the plaintiff's case; there is neither authority nor precedent for it.

It was said, in the argument, that if the engineer had been the owner of the road, he would have been liable. Of this I apprehend there would have been no doubt, but then his liability would have arisen, not from his being the owner, but because the injury arose from his own act. That he is now liable, seems to me to admit of no doubt. But it by no means follows as a consequence, that because he is liable, those who employ him are liable also. One acting as agent may subject himself to liability in a variety of cases, for which his principal would not be liable; and this may be as well in cases of contract as in cases of tort. The extent of the liability of the principal, for the acts of the agent, can, in general, be readily ascertained from the object of the contract, and the relative position of the parties. A passenger desires to be transported from one place to another; the carrier undertakes to do this, and is liable if he fails. It is wholly immaterial by whose default the injury resulted. There has been a breach of the contract, and he has a right to look to him with whom his contract was made. With the plaintiff, the defendants contracted to pay hire for his services. Is it incident to this contract that the company should guarantee him against the negligence of his co-servants? It is admitted he takes upon himself the ordinary risks of his vocation; why not the extraordinary ones? Neither are within his contract—and I can see no reason for adding this to the already known and acknowledged liability of a carrier, without a single case or precedent to sustain it. The engineer no more represents the company than the plaintiff. Each in his several department represents his principal. The regular movement of the train of cars to its destination, is the result of the ordinary performance, by each, of his several duties. If the fireman neglects his part, the engine stands still for want of steam; if the engineer neglects his, every thing runs to riot and disaster. It seems to me, it is, on the part of the several agents, a joint undertaking, where each one stipulates for the performance of his several part. They are not liable to the company for the conduct of each other, nor is the company liable to one for the misconduct of another; and, as a general rule, I would say, that where there was no fault in the owner, he would be liable only for wages to his servants; and so far has this doctrine been carried, that in the case of seamen, even wages are forfeited if the vessel be lost, and no freight earned.

In the above observations, I have endeavored to confine myself strictly to the case before the Court. It is not intended to prejudge other questions, which may arise between the company and its servants; nor do I mean to say, that a case may not occur, where the owner, whether an individual or company, will be liable for the acts of one agent to another; but then it must be in such cases as where the owner employs unfit and improper persons as agents, by whose ignorance or folly another is injured. Upon such a case, it will be time enough to express an opinion when it arises. The present is not such a case. The engineer, according to the evidence, was competent, though he may have been rash in the particular instance in which the plaintiff's injury was sustained. He was known to the plaintiff as well as to the company, for it appears by the report that he selected the engineer under whom he was willing or prepared to serve. It seems to me the plaintiff is not, therefore, entitled to retain his verdict, and a motion for a new trial is granted. . . .

JOHNSON, Chancellor. I concur in this opinion, and will only add a word in illustration of my own views of the question.

The foundation of all legal liability, is the omission to do some act which the law commands, the commission of some act which the law prohibits, or the violation of some contract, by which the party is injured. There is no law regulating the relative duties of the owners of a steam car, and the persons employed by them to conduct it. The liability, if any attaches, must therefore arise out of contract. What was the contract between these parties? The plaintiff, in consideration that the defendants would pay him so much money, undertook to perform the service of fire-man on the train. This is all that is expressed. Is there any thing more implied? Assuming that the injury done, was in consequence of the negligence of the engineer, the defendants would not be liable, unless they undertook to answer for his diligence and skill. Is that implied? I think not. The law never implies an obligation in relation to a matter about which the parties are or may, with proper diligence, be equally informed. No one will ever be presumed to undertake for that which a common observer would at once know was not true. The common case of the warranty of the soundness of a horse, notoriously blind, may be put in illustration. The warranty does not extend to the goodness of the eyes, because the purchaser knew, or might have known, with proper care, that they were defective.

Now, the plaintiff knew that he was not to conduct the train alone. He knew that he was to be placed under the control of the engineer. He knew that the employment in which he was engaged was perilous, and that its success was dependant on the common efforts of all the hands; and, with proper diligence and prudence, he might have been as well, and it does not follow that he might not have been better, informed than the defendants, about the fitness and security of all the appointments connected with the train. If he was not, it was his own want of prudence, for which defendants are not responsible. If he was, he will be presumed to have undertaken to meet all the perils incident to the employment.

There is not the least analogy between this case and that of common carriers of goods or transporters of persons. They are liable in respect to the price paid. Not so here. The plaintiff paid nothing for his transportation; on the contrary, he was to be paid for his labor, and for the perils to which he was exposed, as incident to his employment. No prudent man would engage in any perilous employment, unless seduced by greater wages than he could earn in a pursuit unattended by any unusual danger.

O'NEALL, J., dissenting. This case was tried by myself, and although, had I been on the jury, I should have found for the defendants, yet there were certainly facts in the evidence, which might have led another to a different conclusion; and, therefore, I am not disposed to disturb the verdict. This makes it necessary to consider the legal doctrine which I laid down to the jury.

In substance, I held, that if the injury to the plaintiff resulted from the negligence of the engineer, then the plaintiff was entitled to recover. This doctrine, a large majority of my brethren think erroneous, and however much deference is due to their opinions, yet, as I consider them to be wrong, I think it my duty to state my own views.

This case is one of the first arising out of the conveyance of human beings by locomotives on Rail Roads. It goes beyond the ordinary case of a passenger, and presents a claim on the part of a hired servant, against his employers, for an injury sustained in their service. If it arose out of any of the old fashioned modes of conveyance, managed by the defendants themselves, could there be a doubt that they would be liable, if the injury resulted from negligence? Take the case of a stage coach, driven by the owner, and let it be supposed that the plaintiff was hired as a guard, and that he was injured in that employment, by the careless driving of the defendant, who would hesitate to say that he was entitled to recover? No one who had a proper regard to legal principles.

Is there any distinction in law as to the effect, which the employment of the plaintiff is to have, in the different kinds of service in which he may engage? I think there is none. If Mr. Tupper, the able and efficient officer of the company, had, in person, managed the engine, and the plaintiff had been injured by his carelessness, I would most respectfully ask, how could it be pretended that the company was not liable?

I admit here, once and for all, that the plaintiff, like any other servant, took, as consequence of his contract, the usual and ordinary risks of his employment. What is meant by this? No more than that he could not claim for an injury, against which the ordinary prudence of his employers, their agents or himself, could provide. Whenever negligence is made out as the cause of injury, it does not result from the ordinary risks of employment.

How far are the defendants liable for the acts of the engineer? In the language used in Bacon's Abridgement, Tit. Master and Servant, letter R., "it is highly reasonable that they should answer for such substitute, at least *civiliter*; and that his acts, being pursuant to the authority given him, should be deemed the acts of the master." Now, to this authority, it will not do to say the defendants did not authorize the engineer to run his engine so carelessly as to injure the plaintiff. They put him in command of it, and authorized him with it to run the road. If, in the doing of this act, which is according to their authority, he acts negligently, then they are liable for the consequences, for they result from the doing of their business, by one then employed by them. . . . In ordinary cases, this would not be questioned. But it is supposed that this case is not governed by the ordinary rules applicable to cases of liability, arising out of the relation of master and servant. I am at a loss to conceive any just reason for this notion. The law, it seems to me, is to be regarded as a general science, applicable to every case coming within the letter or the reason of the rule. . . .

In the cases of *Drayton* ads. *Moore,* and *Parker & Co.* vs. *Gordon,* (Dud. Rep. 272,) it was said, "when a master employs slaves in any public employment or trust, such as tradesmen, ferrymen, wagoners, patroons of boats, or masters of vessels in the coasting or river navigation, he undertakes, not only for their skill, and faithfulness to all who may employ them, but also, for their general skill and faithfulness to the whole community." This rule stated as to slaves, applies more forcibly to hired servants, and my brother Johnson, who then resisted the rule as to slaves, admitted it in its fullest extent as to hired servants. Taking this as settled law, how stood the plaintiff in his contract with the defendants in relation to the engineer? Had he not the right, according to law, to regard the defendants as contracting both for his skillfulness and faithfulness? It seems to me, there can be no doubt about it. Well, this being so, if the engineer was negligent, the defendants' undertaking for his faithfulness was broken, and they are most clearly liable.

It is, however, urged (and that is, as I understand, the ground on which the Court of Errors decides the case) that this case is one of novel impression, and not to be decided by the ordinary rules of the law of bailment. Conveyance by locomotives on railways is supposed to be more analogous to shipping than any thing else; and hence, unless a sailor could recover for an injury arising from the neglect of the master, it is supposed that a fireman cannot, for an injury arising from the neglect of the engineer. Before I discuss the case in this new aspect, I deny that any mode of conveyance on land is to be put on a footing with the navigation of the ocean in ships. That is governed by principles of law coeval with society, and in many respects common to every civilized nation of the earth. Conveyances on land are also regulated by a very ancient and well settled law, wholly distinct from the other. It will, however, be sufficient to shew by one plain view, that the law applicable to mariners cannot affect this case. Unless a vessel earns freight, the mariner is entitled to no wages. Suppose a locomotive running from Charleston to Aiken should burn up the entire train, and thus earn no freight, would not all the hands hired by the defendants to manage her, be entitled to their wages? There could be no more doubt that they would, than that a man hired to drive my wagon to

Charleston, who, by some unforeseen accident should lose his load, would still be entitled to his wages. This shews that in the very beginning there is such a difference in the law of a ship and that of a locomotive, that it is impossible the law of the former can decide the right of a servant employed in the latter, to recover for an injury arising from the neglect of the engineer.

But if it were otherwise, and this case depended upon maritime law, still I am inclined to think the plaintiff ought to recover. No exactly analogous case can be found. In Phillips on Ins. 463, Judge Story is represented as saying, in the case of the Saratoga, "It appears to me, that upon the established doctrine of our law, where the freight is lost by *inevitable accident*, the seamen cannot recover wages, as such, from the ship owner." I concede that this dictum is the true law regulating a mariner's right to wages. If the freight was lost by the master's neglect, it could not then be ascribed to *inevitable accident*; and then, I think, the seaman would be entitled to recover. If this is true in relation to wages, the same rule must hold as to the mariner's right to recover for any injury arising from the negligence of the master.

But, it is said, it would be impolitic to make the defendants liable for any injury accruing to a fireman, from the neglect of the engineer. This would be worth inquiring into with great care in the Legislature; but, in a Court, I think we have nothing to do with the policy of a case; the law of it is our guide. But if we are to look to the policy, then I should argue that the more liability imposed on the rail road company, the more care and prudence would be thereby elicited. This result is what the community desires. For it secures life and property, committed to their care.

I think the motion ought to be dismissed. . . .

J. JOHNSTON, Ch., also dissenting. It may not diminish the force of the observations made by Mr. Justice O'Neall, if I state very briefly the reasons which induce me to concur in his dissent.

It is admitted that the duties and liabilities between masters and hired servants, result only from the nature and terms of the contract which forms the relation; and that neither party is allowed to extend or abridge the contract. That the master cannot exact other services than those stipulated for; nor, by any indirection, subject the servant to any other than the ordinary perils incident to the employment; and that if he does, by any agency whatever, or by any means, whether of design or negligence, accumulate upon the servant, while in the performance of his duty, any dangers beyond these inherent in the service itself, they fall upon the latter, not as a servant, (for his contract does not bind him to endure them,) but as a man, and the law entitles him to redress.

It is also admitted that these principles are not confined to cases where one servant only is employed, but prevail when a plurality are at the same time engaged by the same master. Their application, however, in cases of the latter description, depends upon the terms of the contract. If several jointly contract to perform a specified duty, the master is not liable to either of them for injuries resulting from the faithlessness or negligence of his coadjutor; all of them being, substantially, agents for each other, to perform their joint undertaking. But when their engagements are several, each undertaking for himself, to perform distinct offices, in a matter susceptible of a division of labor, each stands to the master in the same relation, and is entitled to the same rights, as if he was the only servant employed. The master is responsible to him, as he would be to a stranger, for the misconduct of the others, who are exclusively his, the master's, agents. . . .

I give no opinion upon the evidence. I take the verdict for the facts; and, according to the finding of the jury, the plaintiff faithfully performed his particular duty, and, while performing it, was injured by the faithlessness or negligence with which the company, acting in the person of another agent, executed a duty incumbent upon them. Ought the plaintiff's remedy to be doubtful?

The elements of the contract between him and the defendants, are these: on their part, so far as they were to contribute to the propelling of the cars, that they would carry him safely; and, on his part, that on the trip he would perform certain offices. With respect to the last, he was their servant; with regard to the first, he was their passenger; and as their passenger, they have crippled him. The distinction is plain, and the propriety of applying it would be as plain, if instead of being stationed where he was, he had only been a clerk, hired by the company, to travel up and down in the cars, and take a minute of their operations. Yet, on principle, no discrimination can be drawn against him on account of his being a fireman, and not travelling clerk; because he had as little connection with, or control over, the department from which his injury sprang, or the agent to whom it was exclusively committed by the defendants, as if he had been assigned any imaginable duty in the remotest part of the train.

SPEECH TO THE JURY IN THE

ROCK ISLAND BRIDGE CASE

Abraham Lincoln

The Rock Island Bridge argument is the longest Lincoln address to a jury of which we have a record. Herndon, his law partner, described Lincoln, the jury lawyer:

Abraham Lincoln, *Collected Works* (1953), p. 415.

In this state, and especially about the center of it we have no tables, boxes, stands, behind which we address and speak either to jurors or to crowds. It is open before us and we speak from the level floor where we address the jury and about on a level with them. Sometimes the jurors are raised a little, the back seat being higher than the front, so that those behind can see and hear. . . .

Lincoln's voice was, when he first began speaking, shrill, squeaking, piping, unpleasant; his general look, his form, his pose, the color of his flesh, wrinkled and dry, his sensitiveness and his momentary diffidence, everything seemed to be against him, but he soon recovered. I can see him now, in my mind distinct. On rising to address the jury or the crowd he quite generally placed his hands behind him, the back part of his left hand resting on the palm of his right hand. As he proceeded and grew warmer, he moved his hands to the front of his person, generally interlocking his fingers and running one thumb around the other. Sometimes his hands, for a short while, would hang by his side. In still growing warmer, as he proceeded in his address, he used his hands—especially and generally his right hand—in his gestures; he used his head a great deal in speaking, throwing or jerking or moving it now here and now there, now in this position and now in that, in order to be more emphatic, to drive the idea home. . . .

As Mr. Lincoln proceeded further along with his oration, if time, place, subject, and occasion admitted of it, he gently and gradually warmed up; his shrill, squeaking, piping voice became harmonious, melodious, musical, if you please, with face somewhat aglow; his form dilated, swelled out, and he rose up a splendid form, erect, straight, and dignified; he stood square on his feet with both legs up and down, toe even with toe—that is, he did not put one foot before another; he kept his feet parallel and close to and not far from each other. . . . He frequently took hold with his left hand, his thumb erect, of the left lapel of his coat, keeping his right hand free to gesture in order to drive home and to clinch an idea. In his greatest inspiration he held both of his hands out above his head at an angle of about fifty degrees, hands open or clenched according to his feelings and his ideas.

MR. A. LINCOLN addressed the jury: He said he did not purpose to assail anybody, that he expected to grow earnest as he proceeded, but not ill-natured. There is some conflict of testimony in the case, but one quarter of such a number of witnesses, seldom agree, and even if all had been on one side some discrepancy might have been expected. We are to try and reconcile them, and to believe that they are not intentionally erroneous, as long as we can. He had no prejudice against steamboats or steamboatmen, nor any against St. Louis, for he supposed they went about as other people would do in their situation. St. Louis as a commercial place, may desire that this bridge should not stand, as it is adverse to her commerce, diverting a portion of it from the river; and it might be that she supposed that the additional cost of railroad transportation upon the productions of Iowa, would force them to go to St. Louis if this bridge was removed. The meetings in St. Louis were connected with this case, only as some witnesses were in it and thus had some prejudice [to] add color to their testimony.

The last thing that would be pleasing to him would be, to have one of these great channels, extending almost from where it never freezes to where it never thaws, blocked up. But there is a travel from East to West, whose demands are not less important than that of the river. It is growing larger and larger, building up new countries with a rapidity never before seen in the history of the world. He alluded to the astonishing growth of Illinois, having grown within his memory to a population of a million and a half, to Iowa and the other young and rising communities of the Northwest.

This current of travel has its rights, as well as that north and south. If the river had not the advantage in priority and legislation, we could enter into free competition with it and we would surpass it. This particular line has a great importance, and the statement of its business during little less than a year shows this importance. It is in evidence that from September 8, 1856, to August 8, 1857, 12,586 freight cars and 74,179 passengers passed over this bridge. Navigation was closed four days short of four months last year, and during this time, while the river was of no use, this road and bridge were equally valuable. There is, too, a considerable portion of time, when floating or thin ice makes the river useless, while the bridge is as useful as ever. This shows that this bridge must be treated with respect in this court and is not to be kicked about with contempt.

The other day Judge Wead alluded to the stripe [strife?] of the contending interests, and even a dissolution of the Union. Mr. Lincoln thought the proper mood for all parties in this affair, is to "live and let live," and then we will find a cessation of this trouble about the bridge. What mood were the steamboat men in when this bridge was burned? Why there was a shouting, a ringing of bells and whistling on all the boats as it fell. It was a jubilee, a greater celebration than follows an excited election.

The first thing I will proceed to is the record of Mr. Gurney and the complaint of Judge Wead, that it did not extend back over all the time from the completion of the bridge. The principal part of the navigation after the bridge was burned passed through the span. When the bridge was repaired and the boats were a second time confined to the draw, it was provided that this record should be kept. That is the simple history of that book.

From April 19, 1856, to May 6—17 days—there were 20 accidents, and all the time since then, there has been but 20 hits, including 7 accidents; so that the dangers of this place are tapering off, and, as the boatmen get cool, the accidents get less. We may soon expect, if this ratio is kept up, that there will be no accidents at all. . . .

If we are allowed by the Legislature to build a bridge, which will require them to do more than before, when a pilot comes along, it is unreasonable for him to dash on, heedless of this structure, which has been *legally put there*. The Afton came there on the 5th, and lay at Rock Island until next morning. When the boat lies up, the pilot has a holiday, and would not any of these jurors have then gone around there, and got acquainted with the place? Parker has shown here that he does not understand the draw. I heard him say that the fall from the head to the foot of that pier was four feet! He needs information. He could have gone there that day and have seen there was no such fall. He should have discarded passion, and the chances are that he would have had no disaster at all. He was bound to make himself acquainted with it.

McCammon says that "the current and the swell coming from the long pier, drove her against the long pier." Drove her towards the very pier from which the current came! It is an absurdity, an impossibility. The only reconciliation I can find for this contradiction, is in a current which White says strikes out from the long pier, and then, like a ram's horn, turns back, and this might have acted somehow in this manner.

It is agreed by all that the plaintiffs' boat was destroyed; that it was destroyed upon the head of the short pier; that she moved from the channel, where she was, with her bow above the head of the long pier, till she struck the short one, swung around under the bridge, and there was crowded under the bridge and destroyed.

I shall try to prove that the average velocity of the current through the draw with the boat in it, should be five and a half miles an hour; that it is slowest at the head of the pier,—swiftest at the foot of the pier. Their lowest estimate, in evidence, is six miles an hour, their highest twelve miles. This was the testimony of men who had made no experiment—only conjecture. We have adopted the most exact means. The water runs swiftest in high water, and we have taken the point of nine feet above low water. The water, when the Afton was lost, was seven feet above low water, or at least a foot lower than our time. Brayton and his assistants timed the instruments—the best known instruments for measuring currents. They timed them under various circumstances, and they found the current five miles an hour, and no more. They found that the water, at the upper end, ran slower than five miles; that below it was swifter than five miles, but that the average was five miles. Shall men, who have taken no care, who conjecture, some of whom speak of twenty miles an hour be believed, against those who have had such a favorable and well-improved opportunity? They should not even *qualify* the result. Several men have given their opinions as to the distance of the Carson, and I suppose if *one* should go and *measure* that distance, you would believe him in preference to all of them.

These measurements were made when the boat was not in the draw. It has been ascertained what is the area of the cross-section of the stream, and the area of the face of the piers, and the engineers say, that the piers being put there will increase the current proportionably as the space is decreased. So with the boat in the draw. The depth of the channel was 22 feet, the width 116 feet—multiply these and you have the square feet across the water of the draw, viz.: 2,552 feet. The Afton was 35 feet wide and drew five feet, making a fourteenth of the sum. Now one-fourteenth of five miles is five-fourteenths of one mile—about one third of a mile— the increase of the current. We will call the current 5½ miles per hour.

The next thing I will try to prove is that the plaintiffs' boat had power to run six miles an hour in that current. It has been testified that she was a strong, swift boat, able to run eight miles an hour up stream in a current of four miles an hour, and fifteen miles down stream. Strike the average and you will find what is her average—about 11½ miles. Take the 5½ miles, which is the speed of the current in the draw, and it leaves the power of the boat in that draw at six miles an hour, 528 feet per minute, and 8⅘ feet to the second.

Next I propose to show that there are no cross currents. I know their witnesses say that there are cross currents—that, as one witness says, there are three cross currents and two eddies. So far as mere statement without experiment, and mingled with mistakes can go, they have proved. But can these men's testimony be compared with the nice, exact, thorough experiments of our witnesses. Can you believe that these floats go across the currents? It is inconceivable that they could not have discovered every possible current. How do boats find currents that floats cannot discover? We assume the position then that those cross currents are not there. My next proposition is that the Afton passed between the S. B. Carson and Iowa shore. That is undisputed.

Next I shall show that she struck first the short pier, then the long pier, then the short one again and there she stopped. Mr. Lincoln cited the testimony of eighteen witnesses on this point. How did the boat strike Baker when she went in? Here is an endless variety of opinion. But ten of them say what pier she struck; three of them testify that she struck first the short, then the long, then the short pier for the last time. None of the rest substantially contradict this. I assume that these men have got the truth, because I believe it an established fact.

My next proposition is that after she struck the short and long pier and before she got back to the short pier the boat got right with her bow out. So says the Pilot Parker—that he "got her through until her starboard wheel passed the short pier." This would make her head about even with the head of the long pier. He says her head was as high or higher than the head of the long pier. Other witnesses confirm this one. The final stroke was in the splash door, aft the wheel. Witnesses differ but the majority say that she struck thus.

Court adjourned.

Mr. A. Lincoln resumed. He said he should conclude as soon as possible. He said the colored map of the plaintiffs, which was brought in during the advanced stages of the trial, showed itself that the cross currents alleged did not exist; that the current as represented would drive an ascending boat to the long pier, but not to the short pier as they urged. He explained from a model of a boat where the splash door is, just behind the wheel. The boat struck on the lower shoulder of the short pier, as she swung round, in the splash door, then as she went on round she struck the point or end of the pier, where she rested. Her engineers say the starboard wheel then was rushing round rapidly. Then the boat must have struck the upper point of the pier so far back as not to disturb the wheel. It is forty feet from the stern of the Afton to the splash door, and thus it appears that she had but forty feet to go to clear the pier.

How was it that the Afton, with all her power, flanked over from the channel to the short pier without moving one inch ahead? Suppose she was in the middle of the draw, her wheel would have been 31 feet from the short pier. The reason she went over thus is, her starboard wheel was not working. I shall try to establish the fact that that wheel was not running, and, that after she struck, she went ahead strong on this same wheel. Upon the last point the witnesses agree—that the starboard wheel was running after she struck—and no witnesses say that it was running while she was out in the draw flanking over. Mr. Lincoln read from the testimony of various witnesses to prove that the starboard wheel was not working while she was out in the stream. Other witnesses show that the captain said something of the machinery of the wheel, and the inference is that he knew the wheel was not working. The fact is undisputed, that she did not move one inch ahead, while she was moving this 31 feet sideways. There is evidence proving that the current there is only five miles an hour, and the only explanation is that her power was not all used—that only one wheel was working. The pilot says he ordered the engineers to back her out. The engineers differ from him and say that they kept one going ahead. The bow was so swung that the current pressed it over; the pilot pressed the stern over with the rudder, though not so fast but that the bow gained on it, and, only one wheel being in motion, the boat merely stood still so far as motion up and down is concerned, and thus she was thrown upon this pier.

The Afton came into the draw after she had just passed the Carson, and, as the Carson no doubt kept the true course, the Afton going around her, got out of the proper way, got across the current, into the eddy which is west of a straight line drawn down from the long pier, was compelled to resort to these changes of wheels, which she did not do with sufficient adroitness to save her. Was it not her own fault that she entered wrong? so far wrong that she never got right. Is the defence to blame for that?

For several days we were entertained with depositions about boats "smelling a bar." Why did the Afton then, after she had come up smelling so close to the long pier sheer off so strangely? When she got to the centre of the very nose she was smelling, she seems suddenly to have lost her sense of smell and flanks over to the short pier.

Mr. Lincoln said there was no practicability in the project of building a tunnel under the river, for there is not a tunnel that is a successful project, in the world. A suspension bridge cannot be built so high, but that the chimneys of the boats will grow up till they cannot pass. The steamboatmen will take pains to make them grow. The cars of a railroad, cannot, without immense expense, rise high enough to get even with a suspension bridge, or go low enough to get down through a tunnel. Such expense is unreasonable.

The plaintiffs have to establish that the bridge is a material obstruction, and that they managed their boat with reasonable care and skill. As to the last point, high winds have nothing to do with it, for it was not a windy day. They must show "due skill and care." Difficulties going down stream, will not do, for they were going up stream. Difficulties with barges in tow, have nothing to do with it, for they had no barge. He said he had much more to say, many things he could suggest to the jury, but he would close to save time.

4. The Beginnings of Urbanism

With the increase and concentration of populations and investments, law begins to reflect problems of city life. The more complex patterns of organized life are apparent in the street-widening cases, with the attendant problem of drawing the line where compensation must be paid for the restriction of property rights. Fire laws, building codes, and safety measures were passed. Lawyers still focused largely on the common-law doctrines of nuisance, all unaware they were laying the precedents for modern zoning power, subdivision control, and urban renewal.

Thomas v. Winchester—Mrs. Thomas's medicine was labeled dandelion instead of belladonna—is a good example of the many areas of law altered by urbanism. While the court could not face up to the repeal of the ancient privity requirement, it did recognize the archaic nature of the face-to-face requirement for liability, in view of the new distribution systems and the many intermediaries now existing between the producer and the ultimate consumer. Proceeding by way of marginal increment rather than big leaps, the court made a marked inroad into business immunity through the dangerous instrumentality exception it began to engraft on the common law.

Industry was not yet entirely concentrated in the factory system, but the trend was strong. Immigrants flocked to the city's trades and industries. Commonwealth v. Hunt reshaped the rule of the English common law that associations of workingmen to raise prices or wages were illegal per se.

POPULATION INCREASE

Western Law Journal

THE GREAT INCREASE of population and development of the vast resources of the United States, have given an impetus to the growth of American cities which has no parallel in history. Civic communities, as distinguished from rural, already constitute an important feature of American civilization; and it is our duty to look to the effects which they are likely to produce upon our social and political institutions. Controlled chiefly by laws emanating immediately from the local authorities, the inhabitants of cities feel little interest in the legislation of the State or national govern-

---

"Juvenile Reform Schools," *Western Law Journal* (1852), IX, p. 75.

ment, and their social sympathies rarely extending beyond the limits of the corporation within which they reside, it is not to be expected that they will cherish that deep interest in the general welfare of the nation, which animates the inhabitants of rural districts. Besides, from the nature of civic pursuits a considerable portion of the population of all great cities must be employed as menial servants and day laborers—conditions calculated to degrade men in their own estimation, and render them an easy prey to the temptations of vice. Ignorant, destitute of property and uninfluenced by public opinion, there is but one step from useful employment to the alms-house or to the commission of crime; whilst their offspring, growing up in the midst of vice, without precept or examples of virtue, become knaves and vagabonds by profession. Who can contemplate the fact, that in one year in a single city of the United States 21,299 individuals have been committed to prison for crimes and misdemeanors, without being startled at the thought that a large portion of the number were voters, whose suffrages could be bought for a trifle or influenced by the prospect of plunder to be obtained by war?

In monarchical governments this class of population can exercise no influence over the policy of the nation; but not so under republican institutions, where every freeman has a voice, either directly or indirectly in making the laws, and in giving direction to State and national policy. Already the influence of the disorganizing rabble of our great cities is beginning to be felt throughout the land, admonishing the friends of order and republican institutions, that the time has come when measures should be devised and adopted to guard against the dangers to be apprehended from the vices incident to populous cities.

But it is not in a political view, merely, that the existence of this degraded class of city population is to be deprecated: they disturb the repose and affect the individual interests of all around them; and, while they subsist upon the fruits of honest men's labor, like a pestilence, they contaminate the moral atmosphere, and bring affliction to many worthy parents, by decoying their offspring into the paths of vice.

Moreover, the degraded population of large cities is antagonistic to our republican institutions, more dangerous and more to be feared than all the nations of the earth. It is, therefore, the duty of the Government to guard against the dangers to be apprehended from this source with as much vigilance, and with as little regard to the cost, as against the encroachments of foreign powers.

As a consequence of these views, we hold that it would be a just and wise policy on the part of the general government to donate a reasonable quantity of the public lands to all the States to be appropriated to the special object of establishing "Juvenile Reform Schools" in or near the principal cities. We can imagine no use to which a portion of the public domain can be applied that would, in our opinion, tend so much to the conservation of the principles upon which our institutions are based, or, in a higher degree promote individual and social happiness.

LAND FOR STREETS

Opening of New Avenues

THE STATUTE was not passed for private, but for public purposes. The landowner was not so much as mentioned, and although his just rights were not disregarded, it would be derogatory to the legislature of 1816 to suppose that they looked exclusively to the advantage of a few individuals. Although the anticipations of that day have been more than realized the legislature evidently looked forward to the period when Brooklyn was to be a great and flourishing town; and they provided for the opening of new avenues, as the public interests might require, without imposing any unnecessary burden either upon individuals or the town. The owner of land then used for agricultural purposes was advised on the one hand where to place his buildings, and how to lay out and sell his village lots, so as to derive all the advantages of a new street in prospect; and on the other, he was admonished that if he occupied the designated site of the street with his buildings, he was doing a wrong to others for which he should not be compensated in damages when the time arrived for opening the new thoroughfare.

The Power to Plan

BUT IT HAS BEEN OBJECTED in this case that it was not competent for the legislature to pass an Act in anticipation of a future increase of the population of the city, with a view to accommodate such increased population by laying off a district of the country, or lands adjacent to the city, and directing a survey and location of streets, lanes, alleys, and public squares, to be made in it, so that if the population should increase in such degree as to render it expedient to make it a part of the city at some distant day, it should be added thereto as such. It would be matter of great regret, I think, if it were the case, that the legislature could not exercise such a power. But it is clear that they are not limited by the constitution in this respect; and it is equally clear that the public might, and indeed frequently would

Matter of Furman Street, 17 *Wend. (N.Y.)* (1836), p. 649.
Musser *v.* Hyde, 2 *Watts & Serg. (Pa.)* (1841), p. 320.

be subjected to great inconvenience, if such a power did not exist, and could not be exercised by them in prospect of the rapidly progressive and increasing improvement and population of the state, so as to accommodate and meet the exigencies of the public at a future day.

Just Compensation

WHILE IT IS CLEAR that the sovereign power has the right to impose a tax in such amount as to it may seem meet, and also to appropriate private property to public uses, yet it cannot do the latter without making just compensation for it. The sacredness of the rights of property, is everywhere recognized by the spirit of the common law, Magna Charta, and our Bill of Rights. Under our present Constitution . . . there would be no question, for it distinctly provides . . . that compensation shall be made before the property is taken. Although the language of the Bill of Rights of 1776 is not so distinct, its spirit is equally as comprehensive so far as the right to idemnification is involved. We hold, therefore, that it was not competent for the legislature to confiscate the property of the citizen, and we regard the provision of the Act of 1817, which denies to the proprietor the use of his land, as nothing short of an act of confiscation. . . . We hold that a person owning a lot lying on the bed of the street which is taken for the public use, is entitled to be compensated for it precisely as if no street was opened over it.

CONSTITUTIONAL POWER TO TAKE

PRIVATE PROPERTY

Timothy Walker

I HAVE RECEIVED the following letter, which, though much occupied with other matters, I have concluded to answer at once. My readers will understand that I do it in haste.

Columbus, Ind., April 9, 1844.
T. WALKER, ESQ., ED. LAW JOURNAL,
Sir—The members of the bar, here, are very desirous to know the rule of decision which has obtained in those States where Rail Roads and Canals have been made by corporations, in regard to the

Moale *v*. Mayor of Baltimore, 5 *Md.* (1854), p. 314.
Western Law Journal (1844), I, pp. 371, 374.

constitutional right of the legislature to invest such corporations with power to take private property for such improvements.

We have a Rail Road in progress here, under an act of incorporation conferring, in the broadest terms, *the power to force the right of way*, by paying an assessment made exclusively by the corporation. We are generally inclined to question the constitutionality of the law, and the scarcity of reports here deprives us of adequate means to satisfy ourselves fully.

In consultation with all the gentlemen of the profession, residing here, it was agreed that it might not be improper, for a subscriber to your journal, to request of you to notice this subject in your next number. An abbreviated notice of the current of decisions, or a short editorial embracing the subject—or in such other manner as may be dictated by your better judgment, would be useful and instructive to us, here, and would be acknowledged as a courtesy.

I am, with much respect, your obedient servant,

GEO. E. TINGLE. . . .

These declarations and decisions assert two great principles. First, the private right of an individual must yield to the *eminent domain* of government, whenever the public good requires it. And this is well, for otherwise it would be in the power of one obstinate owner to prevent the execution of any of those great public improvements, which contribute so much to the general convenience and happiness. Secondly, to equalize the burthen, and avoid all hardship, the owner of the property so taken is to receive a compensation, which shall be full, and just. Any law, therefore, which should condemn private property for any other than a public use, or which should not provide for such a compensation, would be unconstitutional. One question which has arisen under these provisions, is, whether the compensation must be paid before the property is taken? The answer is, that if a law authorising property to be taken provide an equitable mode of ascertaining compensation, and direct it to be paid, the law is valid; but in any given case, if the owner of the property can make it appear, that his compensation would be doubtful, or improbable, he may obtain an injunction against taking the property, until compensation has been secured. Another question is, whether benefits are to be taken into view in fixing the amount of compensation? Upon this question there has been much contrariety of opinion. There is an obvious distinction to be made between paying for property already taken, and paying for consequential injury, where property is not taken. To the latter case the constitutional provisions do not apply. It is a mere question of damages; and as there can be no actual damages where the benefit exceeds the injury, there is no doubt, that benefits may be properly offset against consequential injuries. But can benefits be offset against the value of property actually taken? In this State, where the compensation must be *"in money,"* the answer must undoubtedly be in the negative; for the benefits derived from the vicinity of a public improvement, however great, are not literally money. But how is it, where the compensation is only required to be "just" or "full," without specifying money? Can benefits then be offset against property? It would seem they cannot; for while many share in the benefits of any great public work, besides those whose property is taken for its construction, this rule would make the burden fall wholly on the latter class, which would be *unjust*. It may be said, however, that where a man is not made absolutely poorer, by taking part of his property, no injury is done to him. But the answer is, that comparatively he is made poorer by so much as the property is worth, because his neighbors, whose property is not taken, share equally in the benefits. On the whole then, the rule would seem to be, that property actually taken for public benefits must be paid for, without reference to benefits, which can only be offset against consequential damages. Still another question is, whether the amount of compensation must be determined by a jury of twelve persons? It has been decided, that any fair and equitable mode will be sufficient, as by disinterested appraisers or commissioners. As to what are public uses, it has been held, that canals, turnpikes, rail roads, toll bridges, supplies of water for a town, and the like are public uses; and that the legislature may exercise its right of appropriating private property for such uses through private corporations.

SLUMS: A COMMON NUISANCE

John Savage

THIS WAS AN ACTION on the case tried at the Albany circuit in March, 1833, before the Hon. James Vanderpoel, one of the circuit judges.

The declaration charged the defendant with pulling down five dwelling houses. On the trial it appeared that the dwelling houses consisted of one building, originally erected as a *tan-house*, 70 feet long, 12 feet high, which was divided into five apartments. These apartments, during the summer of 1832, while the *Asiatic cholera* prevailed in Albany, were inhabited, as one witness stated, by between 40 and 50, and as another stated, by between 60 and 80 Irish emigrants, each apartment containing two or three families. The premises were extremely filthy; under the floors were 20 *tan vats*, most of which were filled with putrid stagnant water, which oozed through the floors on walking over them; some of the inmates were sick, and two, a woman and a child, laying dead in the house.

Meeker *v.* Van Rensselaer, 15 *Wend. (N.Y.)* (1836), p. 397.

The premises were situate in the fifth ward of the city, in which ward the defendant, being at the time an *alderman*, resided. The inmates of the dwelling were requested to remove to temporary buildings erected by the corporation, in a healthy part of the city, and were told that their luggage would be taken there free of expense. They refused, and the defendant directed the buildings to be torn down, which was done accordingly. Several witnesses testified that the premises were a nuisance, which could be abated in no other way than that resorted to. The defendant proved that the *board of health* of the city had directed the nuisance to be abated; to this proof the plaintiff objected, insisting that the *minutes* of the board or *written evidence* of their orders should be produced: the objection was overruled, and *parol evidence* was received. The plaintiff also objected to the proof given of the *request* to the inmates of the building to remove; which objection was overruled. The plaintiff inquired of a witness whether there were not many other buildings in the city, similarly situated with those destroyed, in which the cellars had been drained and other measures resorted to for their purification, and whether any other buildings had been torn down. To this inquiry the defendant objected, and the objection was sustained. The judge charged the jury, if they should find that the building torn down was a nuisance, and that the defendant resided in the neighborhood and had done no more than what was necessary to abate it, that they ought to find a verdict in his favor; but if they should find that the building was not a nuisance, then the defendant was liable to damages. The jury found a verdict for the defendant. The plaintiff asked for a new trial. . . .

By the Court, Savage, C. J. It was not denied upon the trial that the building torn down was a common nuisance, nor was it upon the argument. It may not be improper, however, to refer to the cases collected in *Bacon's Abr. tit. Nuisance*, to see what has been adjudged a nuisance. It may be proper to remark that a nuisance is an annoyance; any thing that worketh hurt, inconvenience or damage. *Jacob's Law Dict.* It is a common nuisance indictable to divide a house in a town for poor people to inhabit in, by reason whereof it will be more dangerous in the time of sickness and infection of the plague. 2 *Rolle's Abr.* 139. So manufactures, lawful in themselves, may become nuisances, if erected in parts of towns where they cannot but greatly incommode the inhabitants and destroy their health. Whether the houses of the plaintiff were of that description, was fairly left to the jury by the judge in his charge. A more offensive nuisance cannot be imagined than the buildings described by the witnesses in this case.

The first exception taken on the trial was, that the witness should not have been asked whether the inhabitants were not requested to leave the buildings before they were pulled down. The object of the inquiry no doubt was, to show that the conduct of the defendant was not wanton, but that he was influenced by considerations of the public good, and not of private injury to the plaintiff. The question was proper and unexceptionable.

It was objected that parol evidence should not have been received of the orders of the *board of health*. This objection was well taken. The board of health is a tribunal created by statute, clothed with large discretionary powers; and being a public body, its acts should be proved by the highest and best evidence which the nature of the case admits of. Every proceeding of a judicial character must be in writing. It is not to be presumed that minutes of their proceedings are not kept by such a body, and that determinations which seriously affect the property of individuals, were not reduced to writing, but rest in parol. In the case of *Wormer* v. *The City of Albany, ante* 262, the minutes of the proceedings of the board were incorporated with the proceedings of the corporation, of which the board of health were members, and were proved by a witness a member of both boards. Here the proof was defective; but in my judgment it is not material, because the defendant did not need any authority from the board of health. As a citizen of the 5th ward, who desired to preserve the public health, and especially as an alderman, he was fully justified in every act done by him.

It was also objected that proof should have been received of other modes of abating nuisances, than by pulling down houses. Such proof would have been wholly irrelevant. The proof in this case, from the plaintiff's own witness, was, that there was no other way to correct the evil but by pulling down the building. Had it been proved that in the case of other nuisances draining or filling up had been resorted to, such proof would not have contradicted the testimony in this cause. In my opinion a new trial should be refused.

New trial denied.

THE DANGEROUS INSTRUMENTALITY

EXCEPTION

Charles H. Ruggles

RUGGLES, CH. J. delivered the opinion of the court. This is an action brought to recover damages from the defendant for negligently putting up, labeling and selling as and for the extract of *dandelion*, which is a simple and harmless medicine, a jar of the extract of *belladonna*, which is a deadly poison; by means of which the plaintiff Mary Ann Thomas, to

---

Thomas *v.* Winchester, 2 *Seld.* (1852), p. 397.

whom, being sick, a dose of dandelion was prescribed by a physician, and a portion of the contents of the jar, was administered as and for the extract of dandelion, was greatly injured, &c.

The facts proved were briefly these: Mrs. Thomas being in ill health, her physician prescribed for her a dose of dandelion. Her husband purchased what was believed to be the medicine prescribed, at the store of Dr. Foord, a physician and druggist in Cazenovia, Madison county, where the plaintiffs reside.

A small quantity of the medicine thus purchased was administered to Mrs. Thomas, on whom it produced very alarming effects; such as coldness of the surface and extremities, feebleness of circulation, spasms of the muscles, giddiness of the head, dilation of the pupils of the eyes, and derangement of mind. She recovered however, after some time, from its effects, although for a short time her life was thought to be in great danger. The medicine administered was *belladonna, and not dandelion*. The jar from which it was taken was labeled "½ *lb. dandelion, prepared by A. Gilbert, No.* 108, *John-street, N. Y. Jar* 8 *oz.*" It was sold for and believed by Dr. Foord to be the extract of dandelion as labeled. Dr. Foord purchased the article as the extract of dandelion from Jas. S. Aspinwall, a druggist at New-York. Aspinwall bought it of the defendant as extract of dandelion, believing it to be such. The defendant was engaged at No. 108 John-street, New-York, in the manufacture and sale of certain vegetable extracts for medicinal purposes, and in the purchase and sale of others. The extracts manufactured by him were put up in jars for sale, and those which he purchased were put up by him in like manner. The jars containing extracts manufactured by himself and those containing extracts purchased by him from others, were labeled alike. Both were labeled like the jar in question, as "prepared by A. Gilbert." Gilbert was a person employed by the defendant at a salary, as an assistant in his business. The jars were labeled in Gilbert's name because he had been previously engaged in the same business on his own account at No. 108 John-street, and probably because Gilbert's labels rendered the articles more salable. The extract contained in the jar sold to Aspinwall, and by him to Foord, was not manufactured by the defendant, but was purchased by him from another manufacturer or dealer. The extract of dandelion and the extract of belladonna resemble each other in color, consistence, smell and taste; but may on careful examination be distinguished the one from the other by those who are well acquainted with these articles. Gilbert's labels were paid for by Winchester and used in his business with his knowledge and assent. . . .

The case depends on the first point taken by the defendant on his motion for a nonsuit; and the question is, whether the defendant, being a remote vendor of the medicine, and there being no privity or connection between him and the plaintiffs, the action can be maintained.

If, in labeling a poisonous drug with the name of a harmless medicine, for public market, no duty was violated by the defendant, excepting that which he owed to Aspinwall, his immediate vendee, in virtue of his contract of sale, this action cannot be maintained. . . .

This was the ground on which the case of *Winterbottom* v. *Wright*, (10 *Mees. & Welsb.* 109,) was decided. A. contracted with the postmaster general to provide a coach to convey the mail bags along a certain line of road, and B. and others, also contracted to horse the coach along the same line. B. and his co-contractors hired C., who was the plaintiff, to drive the coach. The coach, in consequence of some latent defect, broke down; the plaintiff was thrown from his seat and lamed. It was held that C. could not maintain an action against A. for the injury thus sustained. The reason of the decision is best stated by Baron Rolfe. A.'s duty to keep the coach in good condition, was a duty to the postmaster general, with whom he made his contract, and not a duty to the driver employed by the owners of the horses.

But the case in hand stands on a different ground. The defendant was a dealer in poisonous drugs. Gilbert was his agent in preparing them for market. The death or great bodily harm of some person was the natural and almost inevitable consequence of the sale of belladonna by means of the false label. . . .

In respect to the wrongful and criminal character of the negligence complained of, this case differs widely from those put by the defendant's counsel. No such imminent danger existed in those cases. In the present case the sale of the poisonous article was made to a dealer in drugs, and not to a consumer. The injury therefore was not likely to fall on him, or on his vendee who was also a dealer; but much more likely to be visited on a remote purchaser, as actually happened. The defendant's negligence put human life in imminent danger. Can it be said that there was no duty on the part of the defendant, to avoid the creation of that danger by the exercise of greater caution? or that the exercise of that caution was a duty only to his immediate vendee, whose life was not endangered? The defendant's duty arose out of the nature of his business and the danger to others incident to its mismanagement. Nothing but mischief like that which actually happened could have been expected from sending the poison falsely labeled into the market; and the defendant is justly responsible for the probable consequences of the act. The duty of exercising caution in this respect did not arise out of the defendant's contract of sale to Aspinwall. The wrong done by the defendant was in putting the poison, mislabeled, into the hands of Aspinwall as an article of merchandise to be sold and afterwards used as the extract of dandelion, by some person then unknown. The owner of a horse and cart who leaves them unattended in the street is liable for any damage which may result from his negligence. (*Lynch* v. *Nurdin*, 1 *Ad. & Ellis, N. S.* 29; *Illidge* v. *Goodwin*, 5 *Car. & Payne*, 190.)

The owner of a loaded gun who puts it into the hands of a child by whose indiscretion it is discharged, is liable for the damage occasioned by the discharge. (5 *Maule & Sel.* 198.) The defendant's contract of sale to Aspinwall does not excuse the wrong done to the plaintiffs. It was a part of the means by which the wrong was effected. The plaintiffs' injury and their remedy would have stood on the same principle, if the defendant had given the belladonna to Dr. Foord without price, or if he had put it in his shop without his knowledge, under circumstances which would probably have led to its sale on the faith of the label.

In *Longmeid* v. *Holliday*, (6 *Law and Eq. Rep.* 562,) the distinction is recognized between an act of negligence imminently dangerous to the lives of others, and one that is not so. In the former case, the party guilty of the negligence is liable to the party injured, whether there be a contract between them or not; in the latter, the negligent party is liable only to the party with whom he contracted, and on the ground that negligence is a breach of the contract.

The defendant, on the trial, insisted that Aspinwall and Foord were guilty of negligence in selling the article in question for what it was represented to be in the label; and that the suit, if it could be sustained at all, should have been brought against Foord. The judge charged the jury that if they, or either of them, were guilty of negligence in selling the belladonna for dandelion, the verdict must be for the defendant; and left the question of their negligence to the jury who found on that point for the plaintiff. If the case really depended on the point thus raised, the question was properly left to the jury. But I think it did not. The defendant, by affixing the label to the jar, represented its contents to be dandelion; and to have been "prepared" by his agent Gilbert. The word 'prepared' on the label, must be understood to mean that the article was manufactured by him, or that it had passed through some process under his hands, which would give him personal knowledge of its true name and quality. Whether Foord was justified in selling the article upon the faith of the defendant's label, would have been an open question in an action by the plaintiffs against him, and I wish to be understood as giving no opinion on that point. But it seems to me to be clear that the defendant cannot, in this case, set up as a defense, that Foord sold the contents of the jar as and for what the defendant represented it to be. The label conveyed the idea distinctly to Foord that the contents of the jar was the extract of dandelion; and that the defendant knew it to be such. So far as the defendant is concerned, Foord was under no obligation to test the truth of the representation. The charge of the judge in submitting to the jury the question in relation to the negligence of Foord and Aspinwall, cannot be complained of by the defendant.

GARDINER, J. concurred in affirming the judgment, on the ground that selling the belladonna without a label indicating that it was a *poison*, was declared a misdemeanor by statute; (2 *R. S.* 694, § 23;) but expressed no opinion upon the question whether, independent of the statute, the defendant would have been liable to these plaintiffs.

UNIONIZATION IS NOT CRIMINAL CONSPIRACY

Lemuel Shaw

The vague crime of conspiracy, especially as defined in the Philadelphia Shoemakers' Case of 1806, was used to suppress the efforts of unions to improve conditions of employment. This fitted the prevailing legal philosophy: collective bargaining infringed the liberty of contract of both employers and employees. It matched the prevailing economic philosophy: collective bargaining interfered with the natural pricing operations of the free market.

Against this background and precedent, and in view of his generally conservative position, it is remarkable that Shaw found the flexibility to support the position of the trade unions in the following decision. Some argue that the judgment in fact represents a "conservative" victory in that it warded off a radical movement which might have jeopardized the protective tariff on textiles. In a sense, too, it disarmed the codification movement, whose representative, Robert Rantoul, was the defense attorney in the Hunt *case; he addressed the jury for two days, not forgetting in the course of it to compare the labor union to the closed-shop aspects of the Boston bar, and including parts of his Scituate oration. Surely it was difficult to argue after the decision, as Rantoul had earlier done on many occasions, that the common law was "subversive of the fundamental principles of free government." But Shaw's motive nevertheless remains inscrutable.*

THIS WAS AN INDICTMENT against the defendants, (seven in number,) for a conspiracy. The first count alleged that the defendants, together with divers other persons unknown to the grand jurors, "on the first Monday of September 1840, at Boston, being workmen and journeymen in the art and manual occupation of boot-makers, unlawfully, perniciously and deceitfully designing and intending to continue, keep up, form, and unite themselves into an unlawful club, society and combination, and make unlawful by-laws, rules and orders among themselves, and thereby govern themselves and other workmen in said art, and unlawfully and unjustly to extort

---

Commonwealth *v.* Hunt, 4 *Metc. (Mass.)* (1842), p. 111.

great sums of money by means thereof, did unlawfully assemble and meet together, and, being so assembled, did then and there unjustly and corruptly combine, confederate and agree together, that none of them should thereafter, and that none of them would, work for any master or person whatsoever, in the said art, mystery or occupation, who should employ any workman or journeyman, or other person, in the said art, who was not a member of said club, society or combination, after notice given him to discharge such workman from the employ of such master; to the great damage and oppression, not only of their said masters employing them in said art and occupation, but also of divers other workmen and journeymen in the said art, mystery and occupation; to the evil example of all others in like case offending, and against the peace and dignity of the Commonwealth."

The second count charged that the defendants, and others unknown, at the time and place mentioned in the first count, "did unlawfully assemble, meet, conspire, confederate and agree together, not to work for any master or person who should employ any workman not being a member of a club, society or combination, called the Boston Journeymen Bootmakers' Society in Boston, in Massachusetts, or who should break any of their by-laws, unless such workman should pay to said club and society such sum as should be agreed upon as a penalty for the breach of such unlawful rules, orders and by-laws; and by means of said conspiracy, they did compel one Isaac B. Wait, a master cordwainer in said Boston, to turn out of his employ one Jeremiah Horne, a journeyman boot-maker, because said Horne would not pay a sum of money to said society for an alleged penalty of some of said unjust rules, orders and by-laws."

The third count averred that the defendants and others unknown, "wickedly and unjustly intending unlawfully, and by indirect means, to impoverish one Jeremiah Horne, a journeyman boot-maker, and hinder him from following his trade, did" (at the time and place mentioned in the former counts) "unlawfully conspire, combine, confederate and agree together, by wrongful and indirect means to impoverish said Horne, and to deprive and hinder him from following his said art and trade of a journeyman boot-maker, and from getting his livelihood and support thereby; and in pursuance of said conspiracy, they did wrongfully, unlawfully and indirectly prevent him, the said Horne, from following his said art, occupation, trade and business, and did greatly impoverish him." . . .

The defendants were found guilty, at the October term, 1840, of the municipal court. . . .

SHAW, C. J. Considerable time has elapsed since the argument of this case. It has been retained long under advisement, partly because we were desirous of examining, with some attention, the great number of cases cited at the argument, and others which have presented themselves in course, and partly because we considered it a question of great importance to the Commonwealth, and one which had been much examined and considered by the learned judge of the municipal court.

We have no doubt, that by the operation of the constitution of this Commonwealth, the general rules of the common law, making conspiracy an indictable offence, are in force here, and that this is included in the description of laws which had, before the adoption of the constitution, been used and approved in the Province, Colony, or State of Massachusetts Bay, and usually practised in the courts of law. Const. of Mass. *c.* VI. § 6. . . .

But the great difficulty is, in framing any definition or description, to be drawn from the decided cases, which shall specifically identify this offence—a description broad enough to include all cases punishable under this description, without including acts which are not punishable. Without attempting to review and reconcile all the cases, we are of opinion, that as a general description, though perhaps not a precise and accurate definition, a conspiracy must be a combination of two or more persons, by some concerted action, to accomplish some criminal or unlawful purpose, or to accomplish some purpose, not in itself criminal or unlawful, by criminal or unlawful means. We use the terms criminal or unlawful, because it is manifest that many acts are unlawful, which are not punishable by indictment or other public prosecution; and yet there is no doubt, we think, that a combination by numbers to do them would be an unlawful conspiracy, and punishable by indictment. . . .

Several rules upon the subject seem to be well established, to wit, that the unlawful agreement constitutes the gist of the offence, and therefore that it is not necessary to charge the execution of the unlawful agreement. *Commonwealth* v. *Judd*, 2 Mass. 337. And when such execution is charged, it is to be regarded as proof of the intent, or as an aggravation of the criminality of the unlawful combination.

Another rule is a necessary consequence of the former, which is, that the crime is consummate and complete by the fact of unlawful combination, and, therefore, that if the execution of the unlawful purpose is averred, it is by way of aggravation, and proof of it is not necessary to conviction; and therefore the jury may find the conspiracy, and negative the execution, and it will be a good conviction.

And it follows, as another necessary legal consequence, from the same principle, that the indictment must—by averring the unlawful purpose of the conspiracy, or the unlawful means by which it is contemplated and agreed to accomplish a lawful purpose, or a purpose not of itself criminally punishable—set out an offence complete in itself, without the aid of any averment of illegal acts done in pursuance of such an agreement; and that an illegal combination, imperfectly and insufficiently set out in the indictment, will not be aided by averments of acts done in pursuance of it.

From this view of the law respecting conspiracy, we think it an offence which especially demands the application of that wise and humane rule of the common law, that an indictment shall state, with as much certainty as the nature of the case will admit, the facts which constitute the crime intended to be charged. This is required, to enable the defendant to meet the charge and prepare for his defence, and, in case of acquittal or conviction, to show by the record the identity of the charge, so that he may not be indicted a second time for the same offence. It is also necessary, in order that a person, charged by the grand jury for one offence, may not substantially be convicted, on his trial, of another. This fundamental rule is confirmed by the Declaration of Rights, which declares that no subject shall be held to answer for any crime or offence, until the same is fully and plainly, substantially and formally described to him.

From these views of the rules of criminal pleading, it appears to us to follow, as a necessary legal conclusion, that when the criminality of a conspiracy consists in an unlawful agreement of two or more persons to compass or promote some criminal or illegal purpose, that purpose must be fully and clearly stated in the indictment; and if the criminality of the offence, which is intended to be charged, consists in the agreement to compass or promote some purpose, not of itself criminal or unlawful, by the use of fraud, force, falsehood, or other criminal or unlawful means, such intended use of fraud, force, falsehood, or other criminal or unlawful means, must be set out in the indictment. . . .

With these general views of the law, it becomes necessary to consider the circumstances of the present case, as they appear from the indictment itself, and from the bill of exceptions filed and allowed. . . .

Stripped then of these introductory recitals and alleged injurious consequences, and of the qualifying epithets attached to the facts, the averment is this; that the defendants and others formed themselves into a society, and agreed not to work for any person, who should employ any journeyman or other person, not a member of such society, after notice given him to discharge such workman.

The manifest intent of the association is, to induce all those engaged in the same occupation to become members of it. Such a purpose is not unlawful. It would give them a power which might be exerted for useful and honorable purposes, or for dangerous and pernicious ones. If the latter were the real and actual object, and susceptible of proof, it should have been specially charged. . . . An association may be formed, the declared objects of which are innocent and laudable, and yet they may have secret articles, or an agreement communicated only to the members, by which they are banded together for purposes injurious to the peace of society or the rights of its members. Such would undoubtedly be a criminal conspiracy, on proof of the fact, however meritorious and praiseworthy the declared objects might be. The law is not to be hoodwinked by colorable pretences. It looks at truth and reality, through whatever disguise it may assume. But to make such an association, ostensibly innocent, the subject of prosecution as a criminal conspiracy, the secret agreement, which makes it so, is to be averred and proved as the gist of the offence. But when an association is formed for purposes actually innocent, and afterwards its powers are abused, by those who have the control and management of it, to purposes of oppression and injustice, it will be criminal in those who thus misuse it, or give consent thereto, but not in the other members of the association. In this case, no such secret agreement, varying the objects of the association from those avowed, is set forth in this count of the indictment.

Nor can we perceive that the objects of this association, whatever they may have been, were to be attained by criminal means. The means which they proposed to employ, as averred in this count, and which, as we are now to presume, were established by the proof, were, that they would not work for a person, who, after due notice, should employ a journeyman not a member of their society. Supposing the object of the association to be laudable and lawful, or at least not unlawful, are these means criminal? The case supposes that these persons are not bound by contract, but free to work for whom they please, or not to work, if they so prefer. In this state of things, we cannot perceive, that it is criminal for men to agree together to exercise their own acknowledged rights, in such a manner as best to subserve their own interests. One way to test this is, to consider the effect of such an agreement, where the object of the association is acknowledged on all hands to be a laudable one. Suppose a class of workmen, impressed with the manifold evils of intemperance, should agree with each other not to work in a shop in which ardent spirit was furnished, or not to work in a shop with any one who used it, or not to work for an employer, who should, after notice, employ a journeyman who habitually used it. The consequences might be the same. A workman, who should still persist in the use of ardent spirit, would find it more difficult to get employment; a master employing such an one might, at times, experience inconvenience in his work, in losing the services of a skilful but intemperate workman. Still it seems to us, that as the object would be lawful, and the means not unlawful, such an agreement could not be pronounced a criminal conspiracy.

From this count in the indictment, we do not understand that the agreement was, that the defendants would refuse to work for an employer, to whom they were bound by contract for a certain time, in violation of that contract; nor that they would insist that an employer should discharge a workman engaged by contract for a certain time, in violation of such contract. It is perfectly consistent with every thing stated in this count, that the effect of the agreement was, that when they were free to act, they would not engage with an employer, or continue in his employment, if such employer, when free to act, should engage with a workman, or continue a workman in his employment, not a member of the association. If a large number of men, engaged for a certain time, should combine together to violate their contract, and quit their employment together, it would present a very different question. Suppose a farmer, employing a large number of men, engaged for the year, at fair monthly wages, and suppose that just at the moment that his crops were ready to harvest, they should all combine to quit his service, unless he would advance their wages, at a time when other laborers could not be obtained. It would surely be a conspiracy to do an unlawful act, though of such a character, that if done by an individual, it would lay the foundation of a civil action only, and not of a criminal prosecution. It would be a case very different from that stated in this count. . . .

But further; if this is to be considered as a substantive charge, it would depend altogether upon the force of the word "compel," which may be used in the sense of coercion, or duress, by force or fraud. It would therefore depend upon the context and the connexion with other words, to determine the sense in which it was used in the indictment. If, for instance, the indictment had averred a conspiracy, by the defendants, to compel Wait to turn Horne out of his employment, and to accomplish that object by the use of force or fraud, it would have been a very different case; especially if it might be fairly construed, as perhaps in that case it might have been, that Wait was under obligation, by contract, for an unexpired term of time, to employ and pay Horne. As before remarked, it would have been a conspiracy to do an unlawful, though not a criminal act, to induce Wait to violate his engagement, to the actual injury of Horne. . . . But whatever might be the force of the word "compel," unexplained by its connexion, it is disarmed and rendered harmless by the precise statement of the means, by which such compulsion was to be effected. It was the agreement not to work for him, by which they compelled Wait to decline employing Horne longer. On both of these grounds, we are of opinion that the statement made in this second count, that the unlawful agreement was carried into execution, makes no essential difference between this and the first count.

The third count, reciting a wicked and unlawful intent to impoverish one Jeremiah Horne, and hinder him from following his trade as a bootmaker, charges the defendants, with others unknown, with an unlawful conspiracy, by wrongful and indirect means, to impoverish said Horne and to deprive and hinder him, from his said art and trade and getting his support thereby, and that, in pursuance of said unlawful combination, they did unlawfully and indirectly hinder and prevent, &c. and greatly impoverish him.

If the fact of depriving Jeremiah Horne of the profits of his business, by whatever means it might be done, would be unlawful and criminal, a combination to compass that object would be an unlawful conspiracy, and it would be unnecessary to state the means. Such seems to have been the view of the court in *The King* v. *Eccles*, 3 Doug. 337, though the case is so briefly reported, that the reasons, on which it rests, are not very obvious. . . .

Suppose a baker in a small village had the exclusive custom of his neighborhood, and was making large profits by the sale of his bread. Supposing a number of those neighbors, believing the price of his bread too high, should propose to him to reduce his prices, or if he did not, that they would introduce another baker; and on his refusal, such other baker should, under their encouragement, set up a rival establishment, and sell his bread at lower prices; the effect would be to diminish the profit of the former baker, and to the same extent to impoverish him. And it might be said and proved, that the purpose of the associates was to diminish his profits, and thus impoverish him, though the ultimate and laudable object of the combination was to reduce the cost of bread to themselves and their neighbors. The same thing may be said of all competition in every branch of trade and industry; and yet it is through that competition, that the best interests of trade and industry are promoted. It is scarcely necessary to allude to the familiar instances of opposition lines of conveyance, rival hotels, and the thousand other instances, where each strives to gain custom to himself, by ingenious improvements, by increased industry, and by all the means by which he may lessen the price of commodities, and thereby diminish the profits of others.

We think, therefore, that associations may be entered into, the object of which is to adopt measures that may have a tendency to impoverish another, that is, to diminish his gains and profits, and yet so far from being criminal or unlawful, the object may be highly meritorious and public spirited. The legality of such an association will therefore depend upon the means to be used for its accomplishment. If it is to be carried into effect by fair or honorable and lawful means, it is, to say the least, innocent; if by falsehood or force, it may be stamped with the character of conspiracy. It follows as a necessary consequence, that if criminal and indictable, it is so by reason of the criminal means intended to be employed for its accomplishment; and as a further legal consequence, that as the criminality will depend on the means, those means must be stated in the indictment. If the same rule were to prevail in criminal, which holds in civil proceedings—that a case defectively stated may be aided by a verdict—then a court might presume, after verdict, that the indictment was supported by proof of criminal or unlawful means to effect the object. But it is an established rule in criminal cases, that the indictment must state a complete indictable offence, and cannot be aided by the proof offered at the trial. . . .

It appears by the bill of exceptions, that it was contended on the part of the defendants, that this indictment did not set forth any agreement to do a criminal act, or to do any lawful act by criminal means, and that the agreement therein set forth did not constitute a conspiracy indictable by the law of this State, and that the court was requested so to instruct the jury. This the court declined doing, but instructed the jury that the indictment did describe a confederacy among the defendants to do an unlawful act, and to effect the same by unlawful means—that the society, organized and associated for the purposes described in the indictment, was an unlawful conspiracy against the laws of this State, and that if the jury believed, from the evidence, that the defendants or any of them had engaged in such confederacy, they were bound to find such of them guilty.

In this opinion of the learned judge, this court, for the reasons stated, cannot concur. Whatever illegal purpose can be found in the constitution of the Bootmakers' Society, it not being clearly set forth in the indictment, cannot be relied upon to support this conviction. So if any facts were disclosed at the trial, which, if properly averred, would have given a different character to the indictment, they do not appear in the bill of exceptions, nor could they, after verdict, aid the indictment. But looking solely at the indictment, disregarding the qualifying epithets, recitals and immaterial allegations, and confining ourselves to facts so averred as to be capable of being traversed and put in issue, we cannot perceive that it charges a criminal conspiracy punishable by law. The exceptions must, therefore, be sustained, and the judgment arrested.

Part V

THE
SEARCH
FOR
LEGAL
IDENTITY

Introduction

Between 1820 and 1860, developments in American legal institutions were hailed by their proponents as unparalleled progress toward a higher civilization. In evaluating these claims it is only fair to throw on the scales the fact that the appraisers were interested parties because they were the creators of the various undertakings, or at least intellectual subscribers. Moreover, the appraisal was often made in the first full flush of enthusiasm. A new nation, especially one rising from the flames of revolt, tends to pride itself on its indigenous institutions and ways of life. Garbed in its institutions of the judiciary, jury, legislature, administrative agencies and the like, law is peculiarly a microcosm of the society which is developing national traits and rejoicing in their real or fancied uniqueness.

At the distance of a hundred-odd years these developments in law can be viewed with greater detachment. Now that they are not so potently symbolic of a nation's growth it is possible to see which were indeed unique, and perhaps to explain why.

There were two opposing forces at work in the law of the Formative Era: there was the old and the given: the accepted law, English traditions, settled business relations, and privilege through wealth and status; and there was the new: universal suffrage, anti-monopoly, anti-professionalism, a Bill of Rights, and an animosity to corporations. The law's job was to mediate between these two forces and to maintain the status quo until a general consensus could be reached and conflicts resolved. This function made the law of the period unique.

The common law fitted into the category of the old and conservative. The role of the Loyalist judges in the Revolution emphasized this identification. Evolved in England, its origins clearly labeled, this legal system seemed an anomaly to many for that very reason; the public was naturally hostile to all that smacked of its pre-Revolutionary masters. Popular sentiment demanded a drastic break with the law of the past. The Philadelphia lawyer Charles Jared Ingersoll was not alone in his legal nationalism when he complained that English adjudications ". . . are received with a respect too much bordering on submission." "Must we tread always in their steps, go where they go, be what they are, do what they do, and say what they say?" queried William Sampson, the Irish barrister who had been forcibly deported by the Tory British government, only to emerge as a leader of the New York bar. These were attitudes shared by other members of the bar and undoubtedly strengthened the arguments advanced in the codification movement that the common law was too easy a vehicle for the exercise of excessive judicial power.

A countervailing pressure was exerted by many Eastern intellectuals. Imbued with a sense of the need and the duty to preserve continuity with the past, they argued that the common law had evolved a pattern of rational symmetry out of concrete experiences. The vast erudition and even greater claims asserted by Kent and Story were marshaled to subdue native suspicion.

The course which American law actually followed was not wholly in accord with either philosophy and owed something to both. Independence did not bring about the return of the borrowed law; nor did it establish a cut-off date for borrowing from it. The United States was to remain deeply indebted to England for the basic orientation of its law. The courts began the process of having the common law accepted. Their starting point was the set of principles evolved under the case system; but the common law was accepted only insofar as court scrutiny of the special American environment and practices found it suitable. The influential treatises of Kent, Greenleaf, and Story were avowedly adaptations of the common law to the new American environment. Like American lawyers generally, those authors chose to start with the common-law heritage and apply to it a mixture of reason, ideology, and empirical observation to elaborate fresh principles. This meant that they weighed precedent carefully, but were free from an undeviating acceptance of any prior law which would render the legal system over-rigid. Because the country was so new, it was a feasible method, which did not imperil vested rights or crystallized expectations.

Borrowing became reciprocal. The former colonies proved such apt and adaptive pupils that in 1835 Professor Amos wrote to John Pickering: "In America, jurisprudence has reached a much higher state of perfection than in the Old World, perhaps because circumstances have rendered you less subservient to the thralldom of antiquated principles and hereditary prejudices; perhaps also because a republican government is more congenial to improvements dependent on the free exercise of human thought. . . . England," he added, "may hope to march more quickly and more safely in this career if assisted by the liberal spirit of your American jurists."

The interplay of development in the two common-law countries can be seen especially in their respective movements for legal reform. Each country's reformers drew support from the other. Codification is a good example of this process. The codification movement of the period, Professor Perry Miller claims, was native to America in the sense that it was produced by, and was part of, an effort to ascertain the meaning of an independent America. But while codification may have reflected a nationalistic desire to assert a separate identity, the underlying motive of the lawyer, legislator, executive, and judge was not to find an identity as such, but to reach working solutions for pressing problems. In England, too, there were strong movements for codification as their legal system grew more complex. Putting expediency before nationalism, the United States lawyers were perfectly willing to draw heavily upon English experience. Even though the patriotic editor of the *Law Register* could find scarcely one important case in a bale of English reports, most American lawyers looked to that same bale for precedents and models, for general concepts of reform and for specific changes. But—and this is the process which generated genuinely independent assessments—each legal ruling so furnished was accepted, adapted, or rejected only after its merits in relation to the United States had been determined. Crucial decisions, such as the place of religion in national affairs, were debated along these lines—and if the Tudor notion of a State religion was unrealistic in nineteenth-century America, so too was the English feudal law of real property.

Several themes of American law developed in the process of sifting and selecting the portions of English law to be accepted or rejected, and in determining what new elements were to be infused either by judicial decision or by a statute. Others arose from the intellectual puzzle of reconciling state laws with each other and with national law. As new commonwealths were established by successive waves of westward expansion, the role of law as the cement of a politically unified nation became crucial.

The United States has always been an experiment in the practice of democracy on a larger geographical scale than the city-state; and its very size, creating the need to develop a workable relationship between a central body and local governments, led to a unique contribution of the American legal system: federalism. But as Dicey wrote: "A federal system can flourish only among communities imbued with a legal spirit and trained to reverence the law." Tension between the cult of local law and those fearing an intolerable legal diversity therefore became a key issue of the Formative Era.

Diversity in the substantive law of the states is a pronounced characteristic of the American legal system; it is also a condition that shaped its development. The existence of multiple "sovereign" states, each having its own laws, led in this period's outstanding treatises to unusual breadth of treatment—studies of the law of other nations, comparison of laws and first principles of jurisprudence. Kent and Story were truly cosmopolitan in their jurisprudence; their familiarity with the writings of the civilians and their reliance upon them to fill the gaps of the common law, as well as to provide starting points for reasoning, has not been matched since that time. Such an approach had many consequences. It led to a competition, so to speak, in the wise guidance of affairs: each state tested legal solutions for itself, learned from the experience of the others, and looked to them for new solutions and helpful examples. It also helped to work out the political compromises necessary for this particular society. The balance in each state could be set according to local conditions and such local talents and resources as were available. Indeed, it embodied the essential assumption of a pragmatic law system: that there need not be one answer to a difficult problem, and that out of a multiplicity of responses progress can be made toward feasible and workable solutions.

Another factor, which by its very nature propelled American law toward individuality, was the geography of the country. It was new, vast, and had an abundance of western lands. It is probable that this would have affected legal institutions even had the lawyers failed to perceive its significance; but that they were very much aware made it inevitable that natural conditions should play a large part in directing the development of the legal system. The needs and ideas of men who were opening up a continent could not be served adequately by the law of a feudally organized society. Pioneer society was impatient of form, eager to cut through red tape. Legal doctrines originating in a small island off the coast of Europe had to be transformed by judicial or legislative alchemy. The vast public domains called for legislation which would allow them to be used as a resource for immigrant settlement. Land was a prize, and the attitudes it engendered were important. It set the framework for American views toward private decision-making and regulation by state power in other spheres as well.

Various decisions illustrate the influence of the physical setting. Much of pre–Civil War law—homestead rights, water laws, even rules of descent —developed in direct response to the existence of practically untouched natural resources, coupled with a democratic faith that all should have the opportunity to share in the generous endowment. Details of litigation should be viewed in relation to this theme, which still survives culturally in the television programs and Western movies glorifying the conflict between cattle ranchers and farmers. It is the basis for the transformation of Eastern law (which had been earlier adapted from English law) by the even newer America: the West.

One instance of the way the moving frontier adapted the law to its geographic condition is the West's development of its own system in water law, prior appropriation, to meet arid conditions and water scarcities. To Mr. Justice Cardozo, writing at a much later period, this innovation was "a conscious departure from a known rule, and the deliberate adoption of a new one, in obedience to the projecting of a social need so obvious and so insistent as to overrun the accepted channel and cut a new one for itself." The element of romanticism in this explanation stands as a warning against overgeneralization; with respect to the same situation that prompted Cardozo's statement, Mr. Justice Miller commented less poetically, if perhaps more accurately, that the Western judges "did not know enough to do the wrong thing, so they did the right things."

Wilderness often meant the absence of duly established authority. This, too, had a profound effect on the nature of American law. Ishmael's hanging of his brother-in-law in Cooper's *The Prairie* is a vivid example of frontier justice: "when the law of the land is weak, it is right the law of nature should be strong." The touch of violence was never far away. Meeting the need for peace and order, or even for a more equitable distribution of riches, meant on occasion taking law out of the hands of the legal profession, even assuming its members were physically present, and putting it into *ad hoc* committees which would, temporarily at least, assuage the sense of injustice. But apparently the values of these people impelled them to varnish extra-legal acts with a patina of legality. The vigilance committees, "settlers' clubs," and "claimants' unions" formed to adjudicate boundary and title disputes all claimed to be legitimately organized and duly constituted—by right of natural law, if not the law of the land.

Resorting to natural law, though justified by Westerners because of their special circumstances, was by no means confined to them. It pervaded the law of this era. Even old, long-settled New York was a frontier. It was a frontier of an emerging class, one which was emerging throughout the entire nation. In New York, too, demands which could not be met by ordinary principles of law found expression in direct appeal to the extra-legal means of anti-rent associations. Working outside the law entailed a defiance of institutional settlements which shook the foundation of the social order—even though it was described by its proponents as an attempt to purify those very institutions. At times, the extra-legal organizations of the day went so far as to take over the most traditional functions of securing justice in organized societies, to the extent of gathering evidence, holding trials, and inflicting punishments.

Whether to support change within the present legal mold or to rationalize extra-legal action, East and West alike looked to natural law. Nor was the ideology of natural law a tool only of the innovator or the dissident; it aided the conservative as well. He used it to block change. Since it meant all things to all men, natural law became a wonderful means of adapting, innovating, or stabilizing legal institutions. Its brooding omnipresence was not unlike the literary symbol that dominated the period: Moby Dick. You know it is near, you feel its import, but at any given moment it is difficult to pierce its meaning and trace its exact effects.

Natural law was teamed up with another unique characteristic, the primacy of judicial review, to enable the weakest branch of the government to annul the measures of the strongest. Judicial opinions relied heavily on the doctrine of natural law. It lent a universal, timeless validity to their decisions. Judges of the Formative Era injected natural-law propositions into their opinions by means of evocative phrases: "fundamental principles of right and justice," "character and genius of our government," "rule of reason," "vested right," "eternal principles of justice which no government has a right to disregard."

Concepts of natural law punctuated the arguments raging over slavery. As Professor B. F. Wright has pointed out, "Not all of the arguments on either side of the slavery controversy were based upon the theory of a law superior to those of man's making, but it is certainly true that if the argument for natural law were taken from the theories advanced by either party comparatively little would be left." Perhaps the most famous attack against slavery, couched in the language of natural law, is found in Thoreau's writings. In *Slavery in Massachusetts* he rebukes judges and lawyers who "consider, not whether the fugitive law is right, but whether it is what they call *constitutional.*" *Civil Disobedience* tested the very existence of government by this law of God.

Freedom from great disparities of wealth and artificial class distinctions loomed large in political slogans of the era, based on a belief in natural law. That men are entitled to a free choice in the conduct of their lives and affairs, became the hallmark of American life; and these convictions left their mark on American law. Contemporaries seemed never to tire of the saying that legal doctrines should be judged by conformity to "the virtue of free American institutions." Few subjects escaped this basic referent. Even technical changes in the law of real property (crowned by the New York Law Revision Commission of 1828) received this rationale. It was used to justify giving married women control of their property. Again, a series of articles in the *American Law Register* dealing with the "Rights and Liabilities of Parents in Respect of Their Minor Children" returned to a free people's law: "Where the people are the supreme rulers education is the main pillar of the political fibre, and may require laws rendering it obligatory upon parents to provide education." It was even used to champion litigiousness: "A multitude and a variety of suits must ever spring up spontaneously and prodigally, in the soil of free institutions, free thoughts, and free actions: where rights are valued on principles as the noblest property and this is counted as worthless, except as the fruits of those," said Frederick Robinson in his oration on "Law and the Judiciary" in 1834. And almost automatically in the codification debates, civil law was equated with feudal aristocracy, and natural law with free government.

Legal circles tended to interpret natural law as a guarantee of the right to satisfy natural acquisitive instincts. The major thrust of the law during this period was to encourage private persons to define for themselves the details of their undertakings; much of the American legal system concerned itself with the affirmative release of private energies. A large proportion of both the judicial decisions and the statutes took delegation of sovereign power to private groups for granted—a legal parallel to the classic liberalism of the Adam Smith economic market. But this ideology was often warped when it came to action. Frequent resort was made to regulation of individual activities, even though under the guise of removing impediments to the "natural" course of development. Furthermore, owing to the New World environment, there were legal struggles to provide social capital in the form of roads, canals, and ports— expenditures beyond the means of private investors—in order to strengthen national expansion. The idealism of the Puritan tradition was mingled with the pragmatism of the Yankee peddler—legal opinions, political contro- versies, and reform movements abounded with expressions of divine law and intense spirituality, counter-balanced, in almost the same breath, by a "get-things-done" philosophy, a bent for practicality and self-help.

But underlying the language of disagreement there was over-all a re- markable consensus on the final goals of society, and, as always when the spectrum of political conflict is relatively narrow, the machinery of the law was geared to accommodation and compromise rather than to radical change. It sought solutions to problems in a balance between conflicting interests, dehydrated of moral overtones. Thus, on the political level, en- ergies were concentrated on creating an equilibrium between federal and state sovereignties, as well as on making the judiciary an offset to arbitrary power. In the economic sphere legislatures and courts undertook consider- able regulation of business, curbing the evils caused by the new commer- cialism and industrialization, even as they aided the creation of corporations and greater freedom for enterprise.

American society, at this precise moment in history, with this interest in compromise and balance, provided a unique setting for the special quali- ties of the common-law case-by-case decision method. The common-law system avoids making sweeping changes. Proceeding slowly, according to each set of facts as they emerge, it advances at one point, holds back at the next, and goes forward again at a third. The stop-and-go technique by which the law evolves, far from deserving the epithet "obstruction to progress" hurled by some commentators, is a method by which society holds together. It offers a breathing period for gathering a consensus, and a time for passions to cool. It maintains counter-vailing tensions between the old and the new.

So perfectly suited were social conditions and the common-law method that it would be hard to decide which was the mirror and which the reflection. The affinity between the two helps explain the growing pro- fessionalism of legal activity throughout the era, as represented in educa- tion, texts, and reporting of judicial opinions. At a time of radical social upheaval the aspirations of those seeking a place in the sun make the con- servative and monopolistic position of any professional an uncomfortable one; when the rules are abandoned no honor accrues to the man who can recite them. The lawyer is particularly vulnerable, for when there is no spirit in society for accommodation, there is equally no time or need for the professional accommodator. An issue like slavery (when, interestingly enough, all efforts at compromise were branded as "legalistic" settlements) reveals the limitations of law once the ends of society diverge sharply. But where the social structure admits of compromise it demands specialists in the art. The professional, client-oriented outlook was natural in a diverse society—no narrow social philosophy could survive a caseload which included old burghers, new industrialists, planters, Jacksonian woodsmen, and immigrants from every nation of Europe. In representing now the corporation, now the stockholder, the lawyer became adept in expressing the claims of new social groups in terms of those stout American values generally accepted, and thus in making tolerable the changes that inevitably came when these groups were absorbed by society.

It might be felt that, as opposed to those lawyer-statesmen and lawyer-judges who dealt with the fundamentals of sovereign or corporate power, those whose energies were given to accommodating change, and even taming it, must have been a pedestrian group. But rebellion against the established order is not the only form of creativity. Identification with the manifest destiny of the country still left room for the rewards of professional craft. Even at some distance from the dramatic issues of political and social settlement, leeway remained for legal inventiveness; the very newness of America posed novel questions for the legal order. It was confronted with the task of reshaping, liberalizing, and supplementing a traditional body of legal materials. And even where the basic mold was already cast the legal mind enjoyed, as it still enjoys, a sense of achievement in working out themes of consistency and coherence. "Our greatest satisfactions derive from craftsmanship," Learned Hand has reminded the profession. Indeed, the satisfactions derived from the intricacy and special techniques of legal reasoning can at times be so great as to distort the basic purpose of the exercise.

At his best, the pre-Civil War lawyer exhibited subtle balances in temperament: a respect for authority, but a willingness to revise; a respect for the English common law, but only as suitable to American circumstances; moral fervor, yet a hardheaded acceptance of reality. Abraham Lincoln, qua lawyer, typifies in his practice and in his public professions these contradictory yet complementary strands. Not only did the lawyer reflect the special mood of United States culture, but he was rewarded for his efforts by being recognized as indispensable to its survival. It was this sense of participation in the mainstream of American life, of acting at the center of power, which gave the legal profession its self-confidence and optimism throughout the period.

The American legal tradition—with one notable exception, the Civil War—has been remarkably successful in growing without revolutionary violence by adapting its institutions to meet the day's demands. In himself the American lawyer embodied the compromises which American society worked out—public service and involvement in national affairs, but as part of personal fulfillment and material enrichment. The sober lawyer rarely questioned the aspirations of the middle class then coming to power. He was too much a prime exemplar of that group. Nor were many of the profession fierce enough in championing the underprivileged. Yet it was a legal order which successfully assimilated change. A society, law-dominated, here laid the foundations for democratic participation in economic and political development; law affirmatively advanced the larger purposes of the society, as it, in turn, was shaped to society's needs and visions.

Common Law and
American Circumstances

RECEPTION BY THE JUDICIARY

So Far As It Is Applicable to Our Circumstances

JAMES KENT

THE COMMON LAW, so far as it is applicable to our situation and government, has been recognized and adopted, as one entire system, by the
constitutions of Massachusetts, New York, New Jersey, and Maryland. It
has been assumed by the courts of justice, or declared by statute, with the
like modifications, as the law of the land in every state. It was imported by
our colonial ancestors, as far as it was applicable, and was sanctioned by
royal charters and colonial statutes. It is also the established doctrine,
that English statutes, passed before the emigration of our ancestors, and
applicable to our situation, and in amendment of the law, constitute a part
of the common law of this country.

The best evidence of the common law is to be found in the decisions
of the courts of justice, contained in numerous volumes of reports, and in
the treatises and digests of learned men, which have been multiplying
from the earliest periods of the English history down to the present time.
The reports of judicial decisions contain the most certain evidence, and
the most authoritative and precise application of the rules of the common
law. Adjudged cases become precedents for future cases resting upon
analogous facts, and brought within the same reason; and the diligence
of counsel, and the labor of judges, are constantly required, in the study
of the reports, in order to understand accurately their import, and the
principles they establish. But to attain a competent knowledge of the
common law in all its branches has now become a very serious under-

James Kent, 1 *Commentaries* (1836), p. 472.

taking, and it requires steady and lasting perseverance, in consequence of the number of books which beset and encumber the path of the student.

A Total Rejection of Many Rules

JOHN BANNISTER GIBSON

A POSITION HAS BEEN TAKEN by counsel, which, in its full extent, I think no one will concede: that on the arrival of our ancestors in the province, the whole common law of England was cast on them, as an inheritance is cast on the heir, without power on their part to prevent its descending on them; the whole or particular parts to be entered on and occupied in actual use, as occasion might from time to time require. It is undoubtedly true as a general rule, subject however to exceptions, that the first settlers of a colony carry with them the laws and usages of the mother country. . . . But to a greater or less extent, there necessarily exists in every country a species of legislation by the people themselves, which in England and in this country is the foundation of the common law itself, or in other words general custom obtaining by common consent; and this sort of legislation will be more freely used in the infancy of a colony, where an abrupt change of the circumstances and condition of the colonists must require a correspondent alteration of the laws and usages of the mother country to fit them to actual use, than in a country whose jurisprudence has been the gradual product of time and experience. In the infancy of this colony it produced not only a modification of some of the rules of the common law, but a total rejection of many of the rest. . . . It is said by Judge Yeates, whose personal experience extended half a century back and who was well skilled in the earlier traditions of the province, that the uniform idea had been that only such parts of the common law as were applicable to the local situation of the colonists were received by them. . . . I do not say that nonuser alone ought to be considered as conclusive evidence of universal assent . . . ; but where to a clear and unqualified nonuser for more than half a century, we find subjoined positive acts of the whole community evincing a disclaimer of the existence of a particular law, it ought to be conclusive; for it is not to be credited that a law can be in force, and its existence, at the same time, be a secret to every member of the community, whether lettered or layman.

Lyle *v.* Richards, 9 *Serg. & Rawle (Pa.)* (1813), p. 322.

Common Law Versus Civil Law

WILLIAM HARPER

WITH RESPECT TO THE CIVIL LAW, however enlightened and admirable a system of jurisprudence it may be, it is not our law, nor have our courts any authority to declare it so. Our legislature has adopted another system of laws. Where our law is obscure or doubtful, it is frequently of great utility in explaining or determining it, more especially as a great portion of our law was derived from that source. But if the common law be clear, we are not authorized to depart from it because the provisions of another system may be better and more suited to our circumstances; nor if it be defective, are Courts authorized to supply the deficiency by drawing from a foreign source.

The Law Merchant

TITUS HUTCHINSON

WE ARE DRIVEN, then, to the question, will the court here adopt the rules of the law merchant, touching the necessity of demand upon the maker, and notice back to the indorser, in order to charge him, as the same are known in England? The court see no reason why they should not, where the circumstances of the parties do not render them inapplicable. Where the law in England requires notice to be given back on the same day, if the facilities of demand and notice back are the same here, there is no reason why the rule should not be the same. The law merchant is a part of the common law of England, and as such is adopted by statute here, so far as it is applicable to our local situation and circumstances, and is not repugnant to the constitution, or any act of the legislature of this state. And so far the courts of this state are bound to recognize it.

Fable v. Brown, 2 Hill. Eq. (S.C.) (1835), p. 390.
Nash v. Harrington, 2 Aiken (Vt.) (1826), p. 9.

SPRUNG FROM THE DARK AGES

Robert Rantoul

Robert Rantoul (1805–1852), the foremost Democratic member of the Massachusetts bar, is best remembered as a selfless crusader for liberal causes. After graduating from Harvard in 1826, he set up practice as a lawyer first in Salem, the hometown of Joseph Story, and then in Boston.

One of the most brilliant orators of the day, he worked for the abolition of slavery and the death penalty, and for the promotion of tax-supported public schools, the temperance movement, free trade, and labor unions. Predictably he opposed corporations and monopolies, even attacking the right of his own college to exclusive control of transport across the Charles River Bridge. Equally predictably he opposes everything Story stands for in the following argument against the "ambiguous, purblind, perishable Common Law." In the law as thoroughly a rationalist as Story, his opposition was therefore all the more significant.

Rantoul was elected to the United States Senate in 1851 to fill Webster's unexpired term, but died a year later before he could fulfill the promise of his talents.

TRUE INDEPENDENCE requires us to forbear from longer aping foreign manners, when inconsistent with republican simplicity. It requires the corrupt portion of the population of our great cities, to be kept in check by our sound, substantial yeomanry, our intelligent mechanics, and our hardy tars. These, we may safely trust, are uncontaminated.

Our legislation, also, should be of indigenous growth. The laws should be intelligible to all, equal in their operation; and should provide prompt and cheap remedies for their violation. . . .

The common law sprung from the dark ages; the fountain of justice is the throne of the Deity. The common law is but the glimmering taper by which men groped their way through the palpable midnight in which learning, wit, and reason were almost extinguished; justice shines with the splendor of that fulness of light which beams from the Ineffable Presence. The common law had its beginning in time, and in the time of ignorance; justice is eternal, even with the eternity of the allwise and just Lawgiver and Judge. The common law had its origin in folly, barbarism, and feudality; justice is the irradiance of divine wisdom, divine truth, and the

Luther Hamilton, *Memoirs of Robert Rantoul, Jr.* (1854), pp. 277, 279.

government of infinite benevolence. While the common law sheds no light, but rather darkness visible, that serves but to discover sights of woe, —justice rises, like the Sun of Righteousness, with healing on his wings, scatters the doubts that torture without end, dispels the mists of scholastic subtilty, and illuminates with the light that lighteth every man that cometh into the world. Older, nobler, clearer, and more glorious, then, is ever-lasting justice, than ambiguous, base-born, purblind, perishable common law. That which is older than the creation may indeed be extolled for its venerable age; but among created things, the argument from antiquity is a false criterion of worth. Sin and death are older than the common law; are they, therefore, to be preferred to it? The mortal transgression of Cain was anterior to the common law: does it therefore furnish a better precedent?

Judge-made law is *ex post facto* law, and therefore unjust. An act is not forbidden by the statute law, but it becomes by judicial decision a crime. A contract is intended and supposed to be valid, but it becomes void by judicial construction. The legislature could not effect this, for the Constitution forbids it. The judiciary shall not usurp legislative power, says the Bill of Rights: yet it not only usurps, but runs riot beyond the confines of legislative power.

Judge-made law is special legislation. The judge is human, and feels the bias which the coloring of the particular case gives. If he wishes to decide the next case differently, he has only to *distinguish*, and thereby make a new law. The legislature must act on general views, and prescribe at once for a whole class of cases.

No man can tell what the common law is; therefore it is not law: for a law is a rule of action; but a rule which is unknown can govern no man's conduct. Notwithstanding this, it has been called the perfection of human reason.

The common law is the perfection of human reason,—just as alcohol is the perfection of sugar. The subtle spirit of the common law is reason double distilled, till what was wholesome and nutritive becomes rank poison. Reason is sweet and pleasant to the unsophisticated intellect; but this sublimated perversion of reason bewilders, and perplexes, and plunges its victims into mazes of error. . . .

It is said, that where a chain of precedents is found running back to a remote antiquity, it may be presumed that they originated in a statute which, through lapse of time, has perished. Unparalleled presumption this! To suppose the legislation of a barbarous age richer and more comprehensive than our own. It was without doubt a thousand times more barren. But what if there were such statutes? The specimens which have survived do not impress us with a favorable opinion of those that may have been lost. Crudely conceived, savage in their spirit, vague, indeterminate, and unlimited in their terms, and incoherent when regarded as parts of a system, the remains of ancient legislation are of little use at present, and what is lost was probably still more worthless. If such laws were now to be found in our statute book, they would be repealed at once; the innumerable judicial constructions which they might have received would not save them. Why then should supposed statutes, which probably never had any but an imaginary existence, which if they ever existed were the rude work of barbarians, which cannot now be ascertained, and if they could be, would be despised and rejected as bad in themselves, and worse for our situation and circumstances,—why should such supposed statutes govern, in the nineteenth century, the civilized and intelligent free-men of Massachusetts?

These objections to the common law have a peculiar force in America, because the rapidly advancing state of our country is continually present-ing new cases for the decision of the judges; and by determining these as they arise, the bench takes for its share more than half of our legislation, notwithstanding the express provisions of the Constitution that the judiciary shall not usurp the functions of the legislature. If a common law system could be tolerable anywhere, it is only where every thing is stationary. With us, it is subversive of the fundamental principles of a free govern-ment, because it deposits in the same hands the power of first making the general laws, and then applying them to individual cases; powers distinct in their nature, and which ought to be jealously separated.

But even in England, common law is only a part of a system, which, as a whole, would be incomplete without *equity*. We strive to make the part supply the place of the whole. Equity is the correction of that wherein the law by reason of its generality is deficient; yet we have taken the law, deficient as it confessedly is, without the correction, except in certain cases, where by degrees, and almost without the knowledge of the people, equity powers have been given to the courts. A court of chancery would not be tolerated here, for reasons which I have not time to enter upon; and without that adjunct, the common law system would not be tolerated in England. The remedy is to fuse both into one mass, adopting such principles of equity as are really necessary, simplifying the whole, enacting the result in the form of statutes, and, from time to time, supplying defects and omissions, as they are discovered. It is hardly necessary to observe, that in doing this, opportunity should be taken to reform and remodel the great body of the law, which stands in need of such a revision more than any other science. Some immense advances, it is true, have been made within the last two years, of which the total abolition of special pleading is not the least remarkable. But instead of being satisfied with what has been gained, it should only encourage us to step forward more boldly in what remains to do. All American law must be statute law.

CESSANTE RATIONE LEGIS, CESSAT IPSA LEX

Greene C. Bronson

MR. JUSTICE BRONSON DISSENTING, delivered the following opinion: . . .

Navigable rivers belong to the public. Other streams may be owned by individuals. This doctrine is founded on principles of public policy, so obviously just and wise, that it is no matter of astonishment to find it prevailing all over Europe, and, so far as I know, all over the civilized world. Indeed it would be strange, if any enlightened people had failed to perceive the importance of declaring all navigable waters public property.

In England a rule of evidence has been adopted, which although it recognizes the doctrine, does not always give it complete practical effect. By the common law, the flow and reflow of the tide is the criterion for determining what rivers are public. This rule is open to the double objection, that it includes some streams which are not in fact navigable, and which consequently might well be the subject of individual ownership; and it excludes other streams which are in fact navigable, and which in every well regulated state should belong to the public.

Although the ebb and flow of the tide furnishes an imperfect standard for determining what rivers are navigable, it nevertheless approximates the truth, and may answer very well in the island of Great Britain, for which the rule was made. But such a standard is quite wide of the mark when applied to the great fresh water rivers of this continent; and would never have been thought of here, if we had not found the rule ready made to our hands. Now, I think no doctrine better settled, than that such portions of the law of England as are not adapted to our condition form no part of the law of this state. This exception includes not only such laws as are inconsistent with the spirit of our institutions, but such as were framed with special reference to the physical condition of a country differing widely from our own. It is contrary to the spirit of the common law itself, to apply a rule founded on a particular reason, to a case, where that reason utterly fails. *Cessante ratione legis, cessat ipsa lex.*

The doctrine of the common law in relation to the ownership of fresh rivers has never been distinctly acted upon in this state when the river was in fact navigable, except in a single instance, and the judgment rendered on that occasion has since been reversed for error.

Starr v. Child, 20 *Wend. (N.Y.)* (1838), p. 158.

MARRIAGE AND DIVORCE

Joel Prentiss Bishop

Joel Prentiss Bishop was born in Oswego County, New York, in 1814. A good part of his youth was spent working on a farm, and he received an irregular education at Oneida Institute and Stockbridge Academy. In 1830 he taught in public school, and after 1835 became the editor of The Friend of Man, *organ of the New York State Anti-Slavery Society. Bishop moved to Boston in the early 1840's and entered a law office. In 1844, he was admitted to the bar and in 1852 published* Commentaries on the Law of Marriage and Divorce, *which gained immediate recognition for his "individual view and fresh treatment." Thereupon, he retired from legal practice to devote all his energies to legal scholarship.* Commentaries on Criminal Law *(1856) secured his reputation. From 1856 to 1896, he published almost a dozen works on subjects ranging from* Statutory Crimes *(1873) to* Law of Contracts *(1887). His contemporaries respected his work but often complained of his enormous vanity; one observer declared that Bishop had more pride than any "other man of distinction since the death of Cicero."*

In the following excerpt, Bishop illustrates some of the problems involved in adapting the body of English common law to a new set of judicial institutions in America.

The succeeding excerpt (Boston and Worcester R.R. v. Dana) shows an American court delving into the origins of an English rule of law to see if the rule ought to be carried over into the jurisprudence of the New World.

§ 16. From what we have seen of the English ecclesiastical law, there would appear to be no room for doubt, that so far as it undertakes to regulate the civil affairs of men, it forms, substantially, a part of the common law of this country. But there is some evident confusion in the authorities upon this point, and in some of the cases there is a manifest unexpressed hesitancy in the minds of the judges. It will be desirable, therefore, to consider this question a little in detail, and in the light of principle, as well as of authority. . . .

§ 21. Now we have never had ecclesiastical judicial tribunals in any of the States of the Union, either during colonial times, or since the revolution. And though the power to settle the estates of deceased persons, and perhaps some other judicial powers which in England, are vested in the ecclesiastical courts, were early committed to other tribunals here, yet judicial divorces, even from bed and board, are comparatively of modern origin among us. All jurisdiction in these cases is conferred by express statutes wherein specific causes of divorce are assigned, and the court is designated to which the injured party is to apply. Yet it follows, from the principles already stated, that a tribunal thus invested with the jurisdiction, must, in the exercise of it, employ the same rules of law which the ecclesiastical courts do, except in so far as they may be found unsuited to the new tribunal, or in conflict with specific constitutional or statutory provisions, or the general spirit of the laws. . . .

§ 22. Of the cases apparently adverse to this view, that of Burtis *v.* Burtis, decided by Chancellor Sandford in New York, is an admirable illustration of one of the principles we have stated, namely, that a jurisdiction must be conferred, directly or indirectly, by statute, before the particular law can be practically administered. This was a bill in equity to annul a marriage on the ground of physical impotence in the defendant. At the time it was filed the statute had not been enacted, authorizing the courts of equity to grant divorces for that cause; but it was contended that the right existed under the laws which our forefathers imported from England, and that the court of chancery was the proper one to exercise the jurisdiction. It was held, however, that this being a matrimonial question of which the English ecclesiastical tribunals have exclusive cognizance, the New York chancery was not competent to afford relief, notwithstanding it was authorized to grant divorces in certain other specific cases. But the learned Chancellor, in pronouncing this judgment, took occasion to assert, apparently, still broader ground, and to hold that the statutes of the State, authorizing divorces, are original provisions, and that no part of the English ecclesiastical law had been adopted in New York. . . .

§ 25. So Chancellor Kent had long before laid down the broad principle that, "the general rules of English jurisprudence on this subject, must be considered as applicable, under the regulation of the statute, to this newly-acquired branch of equity jurisdiction," and that the legislature, in granting the power of divorce, "intended that those settled principles of law and equity on this subject, which may be considered as a branch of the common law, should be here adopted and applied."

§ 26. This question has been ably discussed by the Supreme Court of Georgia. In that State no court had authority to hear causes of divorce, until the constitution of 1798 was adopted, or perhaps until the passage of the act of 1802, four years after, to carry into effect an article of the constitution upon the subject. That article limited divorces to *"legal principles,"* which the court construed to mean the law of the State at the time of the adoption of the constitution. And the court held that as there had been no previous colonial or State legislation on the subject "that branch of the common law known and distinguished as the ecclesiastical law" was then the law of the State, and so by force of the words of the constitution became stereotyped as a part of that instrument. True there had been in 1784 a general act adopting the common law, with the usual qualification, but this seems not to have much influenced the decision. Indeed it could not, for it was merely declaratory of the common law rule.

§ 27. There is another authority which may be deemed stronger than any single direct decision. It is the universal fact, running through all the cases, that everywhere in this country, the English decisions on questions of marriage and divorce, are referred to with precisely the same apparent deference as is shown to the decisions of the courts of common law and of equity, upon other subjects. And from this fact, from the reason of the thing, and from the cases already cited, we may conclude that they are entitled to the same weight. Nor, as we contemplate the learning and practical wisdom which usually pervade the judgments delivered at Doctors' Commons, can we fail to concur with Chancellor Kent in the opinion that this "supplemental part of the common law, seems to be a brief, chaste and rational code. It forms, in some respects, a contrast to the unwieldy compilations which constitute the canon law of the Roman Catholic countries, and which contain very circumstantial and many unprofitable regulations on the subject of marriage and divorce."

§ 28. To avoid misapprehension, it may be well to observe that the practice of all courts is a matter which, to a considerable extent, is within their own control. Besides, there is some reason for the suggestion that when the legislature commits to a court of law or of equity, jurisdiction over a particular cause of divorce, it cannot be presumed to intend that the court shall administer the remedy according to forms of procedure so entirely alien to those employed in other cases in the same court, as are the forms in use in the English ecclesiastical tribunals. Yet, on the other hand, it is noticeable that when courts of law have been invested with equity jurisdiction, they have followed the practice of courts of equity. Perhaps this may be accounted for in part by the fact that equity remedies could not be administered in common law forms. But, either in consequence of some course of reasoning which none of the cases explain, or in consequence of the fact that until latterly the practice of the ecclesiastical courts was not understood even in England, beyond the walls of Doctors' Commons, none of the American tribunals have, to any minute extent, copied the English practice, though in some particulars they have done so, and we cannot, therefore, consider it as binding in this country. The precise line between practice and law, as applied to this question, has been nowhere drawn, and it must be left to good sense and further judicial inquiry. The consideration of this topic does not enter into the plan of the present volume.*

TO FOLLOW THE ENGLISH?

George T. Bigelow

THE DOCTRINE, that all civil remedies in favor of a party injured by a felon are, as it is said in the earlier authorities, merged in a higher offence against society and public justice, or, according to more recent cases, suspended until after the termination of a criminal prosecution against the offender, is the well settled rule of law in England at this day, and seems to have had its origin there at a period long anterior to the settlement of this country by our English ancestors. . . .

But although thus recognized and established as a rule of law in the parent country, it does not appear to have been, in the language of our constitution, "adopted, used, and approved in the province, colony, or State of Massachusetts Bay, and usually practised on in the courts of law." The only recorded trace of its recognition in this commonwealth is found in a note to the case of *Higgins* v. *Butcher*, Yelverton, (American ed.) 90 *a*, note 2, by which it appears to have been adopted in a case at *nisi prius* by the late Chief Justice Sewall. The opinion of that learned judge, thus expressed, would certainly be entitled to very great weight, if it were not for the opinion of this court in *Boardman* v. *Gore*, 15 Massachusetts, 338, in which it is strongly intimated, though not distinctly decided, that the rule had never been recognized in this State, and had no solid foundation, under our laws, in wisdom or sound policy. Under these circumstances, we feel at liberty to regard its adoption or rejection as an open

* It may be well to observe, here, that there are no American cases in which the subject-matter of this section has been much discoursed. The statement in it, is the general result of my own reflections, after having read all the reported American decisions relating to divorce, with a familiarity with the principles of the English practice which, though not equal to that possessed by the proctors and advocates of the ecclesiastical courts, was acquired only at the expense of a good deal of labor. We frequently in this country see the allegation of faculties; and the libel for divorce in many of the States has some little resemblance to the English libel; but I have never met with an instance in which the other pleadings have followed the English method, nor in which the testimony has been taken in the way it is there, to say nothing to the numerous minor peculiarities which stand as thick as forest trees along the course of a suit in the ecclesiastical courts. Nor has the rule of evidence, which always requires the testimony of two witnesses, or of one with corroborating circumstances, been adopted in this country.

Boston and Worcester Railroad Corporation v. Dana, 1 *Gray (Mass.)* (1854), p. 96.

question, to be determined, not so much by authority, as by a consideration of the origin of the rule, the reasons on which it is founded, and its adaptation to our system of jurisprudence.

The source, whence the doctrine took its rise in England, is well known. By the ancient common law, felony was punished by the death of the criminal, and the forfeiture of all his lands and goods to the crown. Inasmuch as an action at law against a person, whose body could not be taken in execution and whose property and effects belong to the king, would be a useless and fruitless remedy, it was held to be merged in the public offence. Besides, no such remedy in favor of the citizen could be allowed without a direct interference with the royal prerogative. Therefore a party injured by a felony could originally obtain no recompense out of the estate of a felon, nor even the restitution of his own property, except after a conviction of the offender, by a proceeding called an appeal of felony, which was long disused, and wholly abolished by statute 59 George 3, ch. 46; or under statute 21 Henry 8, ch. 11, by which the judges were empowered to grant writs of restitution, if the felon was convicted on the evidence of the party injured, or of others by his procurement. 2 Carrington & Payne, 43, note. But these incidents of felony, if they ever existed in this state, were discontinued at a very early period in our colonial history. Forfeiture of lands or goods, on conviction of crime, was rarely, if ever, exacted here; and in many cases, deemed in England to be felonies and punishable with death, a much milder penalty was inflicted by our laws. Consequently the remedies, to which a party injured was entitled in cases of felony, were never introduced into our jurisprudence. No one has ever heard of an appeal of felony, or a writ of restitution under *St.* 21 H. 8, *c.* 11, in our courts. So far therefore as we know the origin of the rule and the reasons on which it was founded, it would seem very clear that it was never adopted here as part of our common law.

Without regard however to the causes which originated the doctrine, it has been urged with great force and by high authority, that the rule now rests on public policy; 12 East, 413, 414; that the interests of society require, in order to secure the effectual prosecutions of offenders by persons injured, that they should not be permitted to redress their private wrongs, until public justice has been first satisfied by the conviction of felons; that in this way a strong incentive is furnished to the individual to discharge a public duty, by bringing his private interest in aid of its performance, which would be wholly lost, if he were allowed to pursue his remedy before the prosecution and termination of a criminal proceeding. This argument is doubtless entitled to great weight in England, where the mode of prosecuting criminal offences is very different from that adopted with us. It is there the especial duty of every one, against whose person or property a crime has been committed, to trace out the offender, and prosecute him to conviction. In the discharge of this duty, he is often compelled to employ counsel; procure an indictment to be drawn and laid before the grand jury, with the evidence in its support; and if a bill is found, to see that the case on the part of the prosecution is properly conducted before the jury of trials. All this is to be done by the prosecutor at his own cost, unless the court, after the trial, shall deem reimbursement reasonable. . . .

The whole system of the administration of criminal justice in England is thus made to depend very much upon the vigilance and efforts of private individuals. There is no public officer, appointed by law in each county, as in this commonwealth, to act in behalf of the government in such cases, and take charge of the prosecution, trial, and conviction of offenders against the laws. It is quite obvious that, to render such a system efficacious, it is essential to use means to secure the aid and coöperation of those injured by the commission of crimes, which are not requisite with us. It is to this cause, that the rule in question, as well as many other legal enactments, designed to enforce upon individuals the duty of prosecuting offences, owes its existence in England. But it is hardly possible, under our laws, that any grave offence of the class designated as felonies can escape detection and punishment. The officers of the law, whose province it is to prosecute criminals, require no assistance from persons injured, other than that which a sense of duty, unaided by private interest, would naturally prompt. On the other hand, in the absence of any reasons, founded on public policy, requiring the recognition of the rule, the expediency of its adoption may well be doubted. If a party is compelled to await the determination of a criminal prosecution before he is permitted to seek his private redress, he certainly has a strong motive to stifle the prosecution and compound with the felon. Nor can it contribute to the purity of the administration of justice, or tend to promote private morality, to suffer a party to set up and maintain in a court of law, a defence founded solely upon his own criminal act. The right of every citizen under our constitution, to obtain justice promptly and without delay, requires that no one should be delayed in obtaining a remedy for a private injury, except in a case of the plainest public necessity. There being no such necessity calling for the adoption of the rule under consideration, we are of opinion that it ought not to be ingrafted into our jurisprudence.

DEPARTURES IN THE LAW OF PROPERTY

Resistance toward the legal system grew steadily in New York State during the early 1820's. The law was too largely "judge-made" and too vaguely defined. In 1825, a plan was presented to the legislature to revise the law under five general headings: 1) law relating to government; 2) domestic and property and contract law; 3) law relating to the judiciary and procedure in civil cases; 4) law of crime and punishment; and 5) local law. Under the leadership of three energetic lawyers—John Duer, a leading member of the bar and a man of "quickness and fertility of intellect"; John C. Spencer, a former district attorney, congressman, and at that time state senator; and Benjamin F. Butler, prominent attorney and former law partner of Martin Van Buren—the reform group finally succeeded in goading the legislature into a revision and codification of statutes in 1828. Critics, such as Chancellor Kent, denounced "the extent of demolition," but the new code undeniably simplified the descent of real property, clarified questions of transfer of property, and generally made the rules of the law amenable to common sense. The revised statutes went into effect on January 1, 1830.

In the following excerpt, the New York Law Revision Commission justifies its proposed reforms of the law of real property, arguing that the old system was suited only to "a barbarous age" and that reform was needed "if a nation were to advance at all in civilization and freedom."

The second excerpt, Coster v. Lorillard, points up the cultural differences which underlay American law's departure from its English antecedents.

Not an Alarming Innovation

NEW YORK LAW REVISION COMMISSION

THE MODIFIED ABOLITION of uses and trusts, which is proposed in this Article, is doubtless an extensive, and may perhaps be viewed by some, as an alarming innovation. The Revisers will therefore be pardoned for saying, that their opinions on this subject, the slow result of much examination and reflection, have settled in the conviction, that every plan to reform and simplify the law of real property, which shall not contain substantially the change now recommended, will be found imperfect, and in a great measure ineffectual. . . .

It is justly remarked by Mr. Cruise, in the preface to his admirable digest, that "the law of real property is the most extensive and abstruse branch of English jurisprudence." That law has undergone many salutary changes in this state; yet the observation of Mr. Cruise is still true, even when applied to the system as adopted and modified by ourselves. Such indeed are its extent and intricacy, that even in the legal profession, it is very imperfectly understood by any, who have not made it an object of peculiar study and attention; and so remote are its principles and maxims from ordinary apprehension, that to the mass of the community, they seem to be shrouded in impenetrable mystery. It is surely needless to add, that in the same proportion as the law is complex and obscure, is litigation

3 Report, *New York Law Revision Commission* (1828), pp. 35, 39.

frequent, expensive and uncertain. Ignorance of the law is the parent of controversy; and that ignorance must always continue, whilst the avenues to knowledge are difficult to all, and to most inaccessible. Under such circumstances, it is plainly a duty to inquire into the source of these evils, the means of their removal, or the necessity of their continuance. If the defects of the system spring unavoidably from the nature of the subject which it is framed to regulate, we must submit to their continuance; but if they are accidental and factitious, we ought diligently to seek, and firmly to apply, the necessary remedies.

The first inquiry, therefore, is, considering the nature of the subject, is there any necessity that the laws of real property should be, in a peculiar degree, extensive and abstruse?

If we direct our attention to the laws of other nations and countries, we shall find, perhaps to our surprise, that so far as they relate to real property, they are in a great measure free from the objections to which our own system is liable. In the civil law, the regulations concerning the enjoyment, alienation and transmission of real estate, comparatively speaking, are neither numerous, nor difficult to be understood, and in the Code Napoleon, they form a very small and perfectly intelligible portion of that immortal work. It is not extravagant to say, that the French law of real estate, may be sufficiently understood, by a few days of diligent study.

If we look to the objects which laws in relation to real property are meant to attain, they do not seem to present any intrinsic difficulties, that should prevent us from framing a simple and intelligible system. The owner is to be protected in the enjoyment of his property; his power of disposition is to be defined; the transmission of his estate to his descendants or relatives, is to be regulated; its mode of alienation is to be prescribed; its liability to the claims of creditors must be secured, and to purchasers, the means of investigating the ownership must be afforded. The proper rules on these various subjects would seem derivable, from a few principles of clear and general utility, level to the comprehension of all whose rights are to be affected by their application.—We have no difficulty in believing, that every man of common sense may be enabled, as an owner of real property, to know the extent of his rights, and the mode of their exercise; and as a purchaser, to judge, with some assurance, of the safety of the title he is desirous to acquire.

It appears a necessary conclusion, from these remarks, that if our law of real estate is voluminous and obscure, in a peculiar degree, it is to peculiar causes that these defects are owing, and this conclusion is amply justified, when we advert to the history of this law, and the character of its provisions.

It is not an uniform and consistent system, complex only from the multitude of its rules, and the variety of its details; but it embraces two sets of distinct and opposite maxims, different in origin, and hostile in principle. We have first, the rules of the common law, connected throughout with the doctrine of tenures, and meant and adapted to maintain the feudal system, in all its rigor; and we have next, an elaborate system of expedients, very artificial and ingenious, devised in the course of ages, by courts and lawyers, with some aid from the legislature, for the express purpose of evading the rules of the common law, both in respect to the qualities and the alienation of estates, and to introduce modifications of property before prohibited or unknown. It is the conflict continued through centuries between these hostile systems, that has generated that infinity of subtleties and refinements, with which this branch of our jurisprudence is overloaded.

It is this conflict which seems to have involved the law of real property in inextricable doubt, whilst nearly in every case, as it arises, the uncertainty is, whether the strict rules of ancient law, or the doctrines of modern liberality, are to prevail; whether effect is to be given to the intention, or a technical and arbitrary construction is to triumph over reason and common sense.

The truth of these observations is illustrated in a striking manner, by the history and progress of the law of uses and trusts.

The severe burthens and numerous restrictions which the feudal law imposed on real property, are generally known. It was a system that could flourish only in a barbarous age, and under a despotic government.

It consulted solely the interests of the monarch, and a landed aristocracy; and to maintain their power, the real owners and cultivators of the soil were to be held in military bondage. If a nation was to advance at all in civilization and freedom, it was quite impossible such a system could be perpetuated, and it was to relieve those who were groaning under its oppression, yet had not the means or power of procuring its direct repeal, that uses were first invented. . . .

To uses, even as they now exist, there are strong, and as they seem to us, unanswerable objections:

1. They render conveyances far more complex, verbose and expensive, than is at all requisite, and they perpetuate in deeds, the use of a technical language, which, although intelligible to lawyers, is to the rest of the community a mysterious jargon.

2. Where a conveyance to uses contains limitations intended to take effect at a future day, they may be entirely defeated by what is technically called a disturbance of the seisin, in other words, by a forfeiture or change of the estate of the person seized to the use.

3. It is frequently very difficult to determine, whether the uses in a conveyance are so created as to be executed by the statute, and whether a particular limitation is to take effect as an executed use, as an estate at common law, or as a trust. These difficulties are, and must continue, whilst uses are preserved, a constant source of litigation.

It is to remove these serious inconveniences, (and others not of trifling import might be added,) that the Revisers propose the entire abolition of uses, whilst by the new provisions which they have suggested, all the benefits admitted to flow from the present system, are retained and increased. By making a grant without the actual delivery of possession or livery of seisin, effectual to pass every estate and interest in lands, (as is proposed in a subsequent article,) the utility of conveyances deriving their effect from the statute of uses, is superseded, and a cheap, intelligible and universal form of transferring titles is substituted in their place. The new modifications of property which uses have sanctioned, are preserved by repealing the rules of the common law, by which they were prohibited, and permitting every estate to be created by grant, which can be created by devise. And this is the effect of the provisions in relation to expectant estates, contained in the first Article of this Title. . . .

The Revisers will not conceal that they attach much importance to the provisions of this Chapter, and feel a serious anxiety that they may be adopted by the legislature. That anxiety they would fain hope, does not arise from any selfish motives, but springs from the sincere belief, that these provisions, if adopted, will sweep away an immense mass of useless refinement and distinctions; will relieve the law of real property, to a great extent, from its abstruseness and uncertainty, and render it, as a system, intelligible and consistent: that the security of creditors and purchasers will be increased; the investigation of titles much facilitated; the means of alienation be rendered far more simple and less expensive; and finally, that numerous sources of vexatious litigation, will be perpetually closed.

Property, Power, and Pride

COSTER V. LORILLARD

ARE THE DIFFICULTIES and applications with which this cause from the beginning has been shrouded, intrinsic or artificial? Do they result from a conflict between the common law and the statute; from the impossibility of defining the respective boundaries of each, of ascertaining where the one terminates and the other commences its operation? These are questions which naturally force themselves upon the mind. In an English court of common law, the will under consideration would present very little, if any, difficulty. All its provisions would receive a judicial sanction. In the examination which I have given to this cause, I have come to the conclusion that its decision must be wholly controlled by the Revised Statutes; that the common law, in reference to real property, to its tenure and transmission, with all their incidents, is wholly abolished. To elucidate the opinion

14 *Wend. (N.Y.)* (1835), p. 369.

I have formed, some preliminary observations respecting the old law, the mischief and the remedy, will be necessary. It is highly proper, in such a cause, to advert to first principles. The rules of the common law in respect to real property are exceedingly difficult and complex. They are deeply imbued with the mystified ignorance of the scholastic ages. The doctrines of uses and trusts, of remainders and executory devises, are beyond the comprehension of any mind which has not been long drilled and disciplined in the school of legal science. Indeed many of these doctrines have been elaborated to such a degree of metaphysical refinement, that they sometimes elude the grasp of the most profound and discriminating lawyer. "These rules," say the revisers in their notes, "are in a great measure arbitrary and technical, and, in the language of Blackstone, it were endless to attempt to enter into the particular subtleties and refinements into which, in the course of centuries, they have been spun out and subdivided. . . . Hence have arisen the evils of which the nation is now complaining, and which their wisest statesmen are seeking to redress; the complexity of their titles, the great hazard and expense of alienation, and the frequent and ruinous litigation in which estates are involved. . . ."

The rules of the common law also authorize the exclusion of real property from alienation, for a much longer period than is consistent with the interests of society. The absolute ownership in property, of him who uses or possesses it, is indispensable to secure the greatest degree of care in its preservation and improvement. If, for instance, all the real property in this state, was in the occupancy of individuals who were merely to collect and enjoy the rents and profits for twelve lives in being, and then to surrender it to others, such an arrangement would impede the accumulation of wealth, obstruct the current of improvement, and blight the public prosperity. Modern science has clearly developed the important and fundamental truth, that the welfare and happiness of states and nations is materially dependent on the increase and proper distribution of wealth. Every rule of law, therefore, which impedes or discourages the acquisition or alienation of property, is a subtraction from the elements of public prosperity. The desire to accumulate, which is both the cause and effect of civilization, should be unfettered, and permitted to exercise its influence freely upon all; for it is only when the incentives to amass by industry and frugality are equally operative upon all, that the greatest and most beneficial results will be attained. If a portion of those who are to occupy the theatre of life fifty or one hundred years hence, were to be born and educated with the knowledge that, on attaining the age of twenty-one, they were to come into possession of great wealth, that they were freed from the necessity of labor and industry, that they were a privileged class, *nati consumere fruges*, and exempted from the ordinary wants and contingencies of human life—what more effectual means could be adopted to paralyze their industry and poison their morals; and the contagious example of idleness, extravagance and dissipation upon the rest of the community would tend to the most pernicious consequences. To appreciate the result of such a state of things, we have only to turn our eyes to the land of the common law, where property, power and pride are transmissible to the eldest born, from generation to generation, and where those who are thus shielded from the common wants and necessities of mankind are also exempt from those virtues and sympathies which are ordinary concomitants of man's nature. *Haud ignara mali, miseris succurrere disco.*

The progress of knowledge and civilization is however greatly in advance of the institutions of that country; and it is perhaps safe to predict that ten years more will see the feudal tenures entirely abolished. The ruggedness of their ancient features has been from time to time relaxed; but it has always been a striking characteristic of the common law, that, encumbered with its ponderous train of complicated machinery, it has constantly lagged behind the intelligence of each successive age. Every branch of the common law, (and there are many,) which has been moulded to the form and structure of the British government, is at war with the simplicity of our republican institutions. The aggregation of wealth in the hands of an aristocracy, its exclusion from alienation in perpetuity or for long periods of years, by remainders, trusts, uses and powers, to gratify the vanity of the possessor and the pride of the recipient, are regulations diametrically opposed to those principles of equality upon which our government is founded. At common law, when a man dies intestate, his real property descends to his eldest son in entire exclusion of all his other children. The male who happens first to come into existence, without any reference to his personal merit, may thus be thrown into the possession of immense wealth, whilst all his brothers and sisters are reduced to beggary. This is the unfeeling and barbarous rule in the feudal ages—a rule which has been adopted by the common law, but against which the humanity and civilization of modern times is carrying on a vigorous warfare. Many years ago, a device was adopted to bar an entailment by fine and recovery; and estates might be thus partially unfettered, and subjected to alienation by deed or devise. When the iron chain of the law was thus broken, a testator might by will divide his property among his children or relations, in pursuance of the natural sympathies of the human heart; and the most enlightened and human judges of England, instinctively impelled by the laws of nature, have struggled to elude the heartless disposition of the common law, by resorting to a most liberal interpretation of wills; by implying meaning and sometimes words, and by giving to words employed in these instruments a much more extensive and efficacious import than they gave to the same words when used in deeds. They have gone even beyond this. In furtherance of the dictates of humanity, they have resorted to what is called the doctrine of *cy pres,* by which, in certain cases, if they could not give entire effect to the intention of the testator, they approximated *as near,* or (more literally) *so near* to that point as the strong barriers of the law would permit. Under the common law, the lands of an intestate who leaves no lineal or collateral relations, escheats to the king, although the father or mother of the intestate, or both, may be living; and the reason assigned for this outrage upon nature affords a characteristic example of scholastic logic. Reduced to syllogism, it is literally as follows: "Lands must ascend in order to pass from a child to a parent. Now, no heavy body can go upwards. And lands, being heavy, cannot therefore ascend." This is a fair specimen of ancient ratiocination. It regards the estate, instead of the right to its possession, and substitutes the laws of gravitation for filial affection and the ties of blood. The Revised Statutes, when carefully examined, will be found to have remedied these mischiefs, and to have provided every requisite rule and regulation with respect to the acquisition, the enjoyment, and the transmission of property, real and personal; and to simplify this important subject, so that it might be understood by the community, every common law rule and regulation is abrogated. Part 2d, ch. 1st, tit. 1st, sec. 3d, vol. 1st, p. 718, establishes an allodial tenure, which is wholly unknown to the common law: "and all feudal tenures, of every description, with all their incidents, are abolished." The language of this section is too clear and explicit to admit of doubt. It creates a new tenure, which invests the owner of real property with the primordial right; it bestows upon him that unqualified ownership which was bestowed upon Adam; it establishes the most simple and the most natural rule; and it sweeps away the whole catalogue of feudal tenures, with all the incidents that have been engrafted upon them by the common law; not only rents and services, but remainders, trusts, uses and powers. If there can be any doubt whether the words "with all their incidents," which are used in this section, were intended to embrace trusts, uses and powers, that doubt is wholly removed by subsequent sections. In section 45, p. 727, it is provided, that "uses and trusts, except as authorized and modified in this article, are abolished." All the uses and trusts of the common law are thus abrogated; and none whatever can be tolerated in this state, except those which are specially authorized, defined and modified by the statute. The language of the statute in relation to powers is equally explicit. Section 73, p. 732, is as follows: "Powers, as they now exist by law, are abolished; and from the time this chapter shall be in force, the creation, construction and execution of powers shall be governed by the provisions of this article." The language of these several sections tends to one simple object—the entire abrogation, the utter repeal of all common law tenures, with all their complicated incidents and appurtenances; and the substitution in their stead of a new tenure, and new trusts, uses and powers adapted to the simplicity of our institutions. The constitution of this state authorizes the abrogation of the common law; and unless this ancient, complicated and barbarous system exercises a power and a thraldom over us, superior to the constitution and laws, it is entirely abrogated in relation to the tenure, the acquisition, the enjoyment and the transmission of property, both real and personal. It is a matter of curious history, to trace the successive inroads upon the common law, which have been made during the last half century, by more than fifty prominent acts of the legislature. Shortly after the revolution, primogeniture and entailments were abolished, and rules of descent were established, imperfect however, compared to the regulations of the existing laws. Uses, trusts, tenancies, dower, and other branches of the law relating to real property, underwent various and repeated modifications. Legislation acquired confidence by practice, and wisdom by experience. At the time of the revision, the monarchical machinery of landed tenures had been much simplified; and every one will recollect that it was the boast of that period, that our whole code of laws was to be remodelled, divided and concentrated into appropriate titles and subdivisions, and rendered so plain and simple that every citizen who would read might understand his rights and duties. But if we are not yet emancipated; if we are still afloat on the fathomless abyss of metaphysical subtleties; if we must steer our devious track among springing and secondary uses, resulting trusts, executory devises and cross-remainders; if the statute is subordinate only, and must be subjected to the ordeal, to the red hot ploughshares of the common law, we are then in a situation infinitely worse than before the revision. For if the statute is to be construed as in any way subordinate to the old system, there will then be a double conflict of technicalities, the statute warring against the common law, and the common law against the statute; "confusion will be worse confounded," and every cause involving principles like the present will be an insoluble enigma.

One of the Roman tyrants has excited the detestation of mankind, for having caused the laws to be written in such small characters, and placed so high upon pillars that they were not legible; nor is a milder censure due to the revisers and the legislature, if they have subjected us to the double complication of statutory and common law regulations; for there is no difference in principle, whether, laws are incapable of being read, or, when read, of being understood by the mass of mankind, for whose benefit laws should be enacted. But this is not the case. One of the leading objects of the revision was to disenthral the community from the common law, in relation to every rule respecting the tenure and transmission of property. These rules favored trusts and uses, which were incompatible with our institutions. They authorized testamentary accumulations of property, without any other obvious design than to gratify human vanity; they sanctioned trusts for longer periods of years, so that the rich man could throw over posterity the dark shadow of his accumulated wealth. They permitted any amount of the great capital of the community (which is composed of the aggregate wealth of all) to be diverted from the business purposes of life—to be dragged from the prolific stream of alienation, and lashed to sterile rocks upon the shore. These were the evils of the old system, which it was the object of the legislature to remedy; and if the obvious intent of the statute is not perverted, the remedy will be found to be complete.

2. The Western Frontier

THE LAW SITTING TOO TIGHT UPON ME

James Fenimore Cooper

"I HAVE COME, old man, into these districts, because I found the law sitting too tight upon me, and am not over fond of neighbors who can't settle a dispute without troubling a justice and twelve men; but I didn't come to be robbed of my plunder, and then to say thankee to the man who did it!"

"He who ventures far into the prairie, must abide by the ways of its owners."

"Owners!" echoed the squatter, "I am as rightful an owner of the land I stand on, as any governor of the States! Can you tell me, stranger, where the law or the reason is to be found, which says that one man shall have a section, or a town, or perhaps a county to his use, and another have to beg for earth to make his grave in? This is not nature, and I deny that it is law. That is, your legal law."

"I cannot say that you are wrong," returned the trapper, whose opinions on this important topic, though drawn from very different premises, were in singular accordance with those of his companion, "and I have often thought and said as much, when and where I have believed my voice could be heard."

COMMON LAW IN THE WILDERNESS

Joseph Story

THE COMMON LAW OF ENGLAND is not to be taken in all respects to be that of America. Our ancestors brought with them its general principles, and claimed it as their birthright: but they brought with them and adopted only that portion which was applicable to their situation. There could be

---

James Fenimore Cooper, *The Prairie* (1827), p. 64.
Story, J., Van Ness *v.* Pacard, 2 *Pet.* (1829), p. 137.

little or no reason for doubting that the general doctrine as to things annexed to the freehold, so far as it respects heirs and executors, was adopted by them. The question could arise only between different claimants under the same ancestor, and no general policy could be subserved by withdrawing from the heir those things which his ancestor had chosen to leave annexed to the inheritance. But between landlord and tenant it is not so clear that the rigid rule of the common law, at least as it is expounded in 3 East, 38, was so applicable to their situation as to give rise to necessary presumption in its favor. The country was a wilderness, and the universal policy was to procure its cultivation and improvement. The owner of the soil as well as the public had every motive to encourage the tenant to devote himself to agriculture and to favor any erection which should aid this result; yet, in the comparative poverty of the country, what tenant could afford to erect fixtures of much expense or value, if he was to lose his whole interest therein by the very act of erection? His cabin or log hut, however necessary for any improvement of the soil, would cease to be his the moment it was finished. It might, therefore, deserve consideration whether, in case the doctrine were not previously adopted in a state by some authoritative practice or adjudication, it ought to be assumed by this court as a part of the jurisprudence of such state, upon the mere footing of its existence in the common law.

THE PUBLIC LANDS

An Immense Source of Power

WESTERN LAW JOURNAL

THE PUBLIC DOMAIN of the United States may be regarded as an immense source of moral and political power; and if managed with wisdom, this power may be preserved and enlarged for the benefit of the nation throughout an indefinite period of time. Let a portion of it be applied to the construction of great lines of railways, calculated to bring the inhabitants of the Atlantic coast in speedy communication with the dwellers on the shores of the broad Pacific; and others that will bring the people of the South in close communion with those of the extreme North; and along these iron bonds, as the electric fluid along the wires of the telegraph, a current of human sympathy will continually flow in every direction throughout the

"The Public Domain—Homestead Bill," *The Western Journal and Civilian* (October, 1852), IX, p. 9.

land, harmonizing the hearts as well as the interests of those most distant from each other. Then, let another portion be appropriated for the indigent Insane, as already proposed in Congress. But above all let us appropriate an amount to the purposes of education which shall be sufficient to ensure a reasonable degree of instruction to all the indigent of the respective States, to the end of time. The public domain is quite sufficient for the accomplishment of all these objects,—national attainments which would make the American people the marvel of the earth, and the means of improving the condition of all other nations.

With such glorious objects in view, and possessing ample means for their attainment, the nation will stultify itself and disappoint the just expectations of mankind, if, like an inexperienced youth,—a spendthrift,—it should squander its rich inheritance upon transient objects, and divest itself of the power bestowed upon it by a benevolent Providence for the benefit of future generations. . . .

By adopting this policy, and refusing grants to individuals, even for public services, a salutary check would be put to the popular desire for conquest, and there would be less danger of getting into wars with other nations.

Right of Ownership

GUSTAF UNONIUS

THIS SPOT was one of the prettiest one could ever hope to see. The lake, about two miles long, and branching off into a number of bays and coves, was surrounded almost everywhere by dry, high shores. Only in a couple of places was the ground low and swampy. . . . Now, we insisted firmly, it was no use to go any farther, especially as the land, in addition to being incredibly beautiful, seemed also to be excellent in every other respect. . . .

Since we did not want any of the thousands of prospective settlers roaming about the country looking for homesites to get ahead of us, we decided to return to Milwaukee at once and announce at the Land Office that we each wanted to take under pre-emption a quarter section of land. Pearmain informed us, however, that the section in question, as well as others in the same township, could not be purchased at the Land Office or be occupied under pre-emption right. The situation was that a company had been organized some years earlier for the purpose of constructing a canal from Milwaukee to the Mississippi. To this company Congress had

"A Pioneer in Northwest America 1841–1858," *The Memoirs of Gustaf Unonius* (1950), pp. 159, 325, 328.

ceded, on certain conditions, all odd-numbered sections along the proposed canal route, and to such a section the piece of land on which we wanted to settle belonged. However, a certain time had been set in which the canal was to be completed, and of that time only two or three years still remained. The work, which had hardly been begun, had stopped long ago, and it seemed almost impossible that the company should ever be able to carry out its contract. Hence it was fairly certain that when the time specified in the contract had expired, these canal lands would revert to the United States and be offered for sale in the regular way. Nevertheless, until that time had expired, the land could not be purchased at the Land Office. As far as the canal company was concerned, no one ever bothered to make any payments to it for this land, since it was regarded as certain that the land would revert to the Government and then be offered at half the price demanded by the canal company. We might therefore take it for granted that we should not have to pay for land thus occupied for a couple of years. Considering our financial status, this was welcome news, although we realized that there would be some uncertainty about our right of ownership, inasmuch as the canal company still had the legal right to sell these sections. Suppose that we, without regarding the company, were to take possession of a piece of land, cultivate it, and build our home on it as though it were our own, what was to prevent some other person after a few months from purchasing it? In this case, would there be anything for us to do but leave our homestead without even being able to claim remuneration for the work we had put into it? Pearmain maintained, however, that we need not fear this eventuality. Many before us had taken possession of land in just this way. In their right of ownership they were protected by what he termed club law, the law, that is, which the people themselves in remote regions had established because of the peculiar conditions under which they were living. According to this law Judge Lynch makes all judicial decisions. No one could prevent the canal company from selling the land, but it was quite possible effectively to prevent the land's being sold to anyone but its present occupant, who had spent time and money making it habitable. All the settlers, whether on land held by Congress or by the canal company, had made a compact to stand by and protect one another against such trespassing. And woe betide anyone who sought to appropriate another man's land! He would do well before taking possession of his purchased ground to obtain the highest possible insurance on his house and life; otherwise neither would be worth much. I know of only one instance where such a thing was attempted, but I shall have more to say of this later on.

There may be divergent views on such a law of terror, but there is much that may be said in its defense. Nobody was the loser by it. Not the Government, for when the privilege of the canal company expired, the land would have to be paid for, and then club law would not protect the settler from having to do his duty. Nor was the canal company the loser, for it had to all practical intents and purposes already lost its rights and would be compelled, when it found itself unable to carry out its agreements, to return to the Government the property tentatively given to it. On the other hand, the rights of the poor settler were protected. He was saved from having to pay double the price of other land without getting any additional privileges. At the same time the community profited, for in this way the land was settled and tilled earlier than otherwise would have been the case.

Inasmuch as others did not fear to settle on this kind of land, we thought we might risk it, all the more because in this way we might count on two or three years of suspended payment, in our circumstances a great privilege. Our capital had been melting away so fast that the combined cash supply of Carl and me was reduced to about four hundred dollars. From this amount we still had to purchase land, build our home, buy at least one team of oxen, a cow, a few pigs, and some essential household articles. In addition, we had to provide food for at least the first winter. How this small amount was to see us through was hard for us or anybody else to see. Here there was no opportunity to borrow money. Notwithstanding all this, we were of good courage, though I cannot deny that with my poetic dreams of a "cottage and a hearth" were mingled in realistic moments some very doubtful intermezzos.

Under these conditions we were happy indeed to cross off from our calculation, at least for the time being, the two hundred dollars—exactly one-half of our present cash—that we had hitherto expected to pay for a quarter section of congressional land. For though we had planned to use our pre-emption rights, these would not have allowed us more than a year to pay, and it was not likely that we should find it any easier in twelve months than now. On the other hand, we might well hope to have improved our finances enough in two or three years to be able to pay for our land. We had at least during this time some harvests to expect, which naturally we could not look for the first year. . . .

We needed to take no steps to insure our claim except to inform our neighbors that we were planning to make our home here, and as a sign of our intention, start some improvement to indicate that this part of the section had been occupied. Pearmain, as an experienced settler prepared for any eventualities, had brought his axe. As Columbus on first landing in the new world had raised the Castilian flag inscribed with *F & I*, the initials of his sovereigns, so we chopped down a few trees, and into the bark of a couple of others cut a big *C*, signifying "Claimed," a sign that we in our own name had taken possession of the W½ of Section 33, Township 8, Range 18, *in hac altera mundi parte* [in this other part of the world], with full and complete legal right of possession, to be inhabited, settled, and held by us and our descendants forever. . . .

Now it happened that an American who apparently had more money than most newcomers had moved here from one of the eastern states and had bought a quarter section that had not up to that time been settled, and paid the price demanded by the canal company. To this no one had any objection since he was encroaching on nobody's rights. We merely laughed at him for wasting good money. But when he also after a time bought eighty acres adjoining his quarter on which a poor immigrant shortly before had settled under the protection of the club law and on which he was just building a cabin, that was quite another story.

Owing to this development and the dispute arising from it, a call went out to all the settlers in the township to meet in the schoolhouse. Almost all of us Swedes were there at the appointed time. The gathering was large, and in the weatherbeaten faces of some of the backwoodsmen there was an expression of wrath and determination that suggested they had already made up their minds in a way boding no good to the culprit. Others, apparently quite calm, had seated themselves close to the red-hot stove, and the low room was soon filled with stifling heat and the smell of burnt leather. Some Americans are accustomed, when it is cold, to putting their feet almost into the fire. Enter a hotel or some other public place in the wintertime and you will find them rocking in their chairs, as many as possible crowding around the stove, their feet resting upon it. The snow underneath the soles of their shoes will melt and sizzle on the hot sheet iron, and from the singed boots rises one pillar of smoke beside another, making a sweet smell at least for the cobbler, if not for anyone else. . . .

After greeting the chairman with the customary "Mr. President and Gentlemen," he developed in a coherent, orderly address, presented with natural ease and fluency, the subject of the canal lands. He sought to show that the canal company had never done anything but cheat both Congress, which had voted public funds for performing work the company was evidently neither able nor willing to carry through, and the individual settlers, who in the hope of corresponding advantages had paid a higher price for that land than the law provided; that under these conditions it was nothing less than a fraud for the Government to continue to demand a higher price for this land than for any other; that the people had a perfect right to oppose such a proceeding; but that the land in the meantime ought not to be left idle and unpopulated when daily new crowds of immigrants, "a respectable class of native citizens and foreigners," were arriving to build for themselves happy homes and in a few years lift this "glorious territory to one of the greatest and most important states in the union."

He next developed each settler's legal and moral right to the claim he had chosen with intent and purpose to make on it his home, calling it "the greatest piece of rascality" that ever could be perpetrated that anybody should secretly proceed to buy the same; and he sincerely hoped that now that such an unjust deed had been done, they all might stick together as one man and establish an example of stern justice so that they might for the future be protected from such encroachments. . . .

He proposed another punishment. Though stern and corrective, it involved no violence, and once inflicted on the culprit, could not lead to countersteps by the real representatives of the law or give occasion to a suit against those who had imposed it. He suggested that the accused be placed under a kind of interdict: that no one was to speak to him, have any intercourse with him, or visit him in his house, and if he came to the threshold of any other man's, he was not to be admitted. No one was to buy from him or sell anything to him. In short, he was to be regarded as an excommunicated man, avoided and shunned by all, till he had atoned for his error and deeded the land in question to the man to whom it really belonged. For this he was to be paid the legal price when the dispute concerning the canal lands finally had been settled.

His suggestion won the approval of the meeting. It contained an element of novelty; it could even be published in the papers as a warning to other claim jumpers; it would lend a kind of respectability to the entire community. Petterson was complimented as a clever, just, and wise judge under the lynch law. To be sure, the proposal did not please the Irishman and his friends. Fire and violence would have agreed far better with their volatile and fiery spirits, and tarring and feathering would to them have been as exciting a spectacle as a bullfight to a Spaniard. For once, though, they had to forego the pleasure. Petterson's proposal was adopted and recorded in the minutes as unanimously approved, with the amendment that whosoever might be found breaking the agreement and entering into any kind of intercourse whatsoever with the interdicted man was to be regarded as guilty along with him and to be visited with the same punishment.

The decision of the meeting was carried out, with the result that the wrongdoer soon found it advisable to give the opposite party full restitution for the loss he had suffered.

Circular to the Tenants of the Manor of Blenheim

JOHN A. KING

John A. King, eldest son of Rufus King, spent most of his youth in England where his father was United States Minister. After returning to the United States, he studied law and was admitted to the bar. Cultivation of his Long Island farm and New York politics were his primary concerns after 1815. He was elected to the state legislature in 1818, 1832, 1838, and 1840.

Circular Addressed by John A. King to the Tenants of the Manor of Blenheim, *New York State Assembly #222* (April 8, 1845), p. 16.

He became affiliated with the National Republicans and later with the Whigs. In 1848 he was elected to Congress on a Whig ticket, but in Congress he opposed Clay's compromises and the Fugitive Slave Act of 1850. His anti-slavery feelings finally led him to the Republican party, on whose ticket he was elected to the governorship of New York by a large majority in 1856. He retired after an uneventful term.

This rather charming circular, which has the flavor of a medieval pope addressing an erring king, or the Czar his subjects, is in sharp contrast with the tone of the preceding Unonius extract.

The Anti-rent riots enveloped New York between 1839 and 1846. They resulted from popular hatred of a feudal leasehold system by which landlords exacted yearly fees in produce, labor, or money. In 1839, when the Rensselaer heirs demanded the payment of more than a third of a million dollars in back rent, riots broke out. Officials attempting to serve writs of ejection were beaten, and Governor Seward called out the militia. Anti-rent societies replaced rioters and between 1842 and 1847 elected more than an eighth of the state legislature. Anti-renters controlled the New York Constitutional Convention of 1846, which abolished feudal tenures and prohibited the establishment of land leases which ran for more than twelve years. Most leases were eventually transformed into fee simple ownership.

JAMAICA, L. I. July, 1844.

SIR—Early in April last, I was informed of your fixed purpose to refuse and resist the payment of rent to me; and soon afterwards of your having met in large numbers, in different parts of the patent of Blenheim, for the purpose of forming yourselves into an anti-rent society; and as the most effective mode of carrying out your deliberate intentions in this respect, that you had proceeded to pass resolutions denying the validity of my title; refusing to pay any more rent; raising money to defray all expenses and costs, to which, as a consequence of such determination you might be subjected; and requiring also, that a certain number of your members should disguise themselves as indians, who, by threats of personal violence, should prevent my agent, or the officers of the law, from collecting the rent respectively due from you. Whatever grievance, if any, others may have—whatever grounds of complaint, well or ill-founded, may exist as to the tenure by which others hold lease-land—certain I am, you, at least, have none. Since this property came into my possession on which you live, and from whose soil is drawn, not only your own support, but the small rent stipulated to be paid by you for the use and occupation of the same, you have been treated with a liberality and fairness, which should rather have strengthened the relations which exist between us, than have furnished the ground for the denial of my title, and the state of feeling and excitement, and the refusal to pay, which now so extensively prevails among you. I neither know, nor do I care to know, who, and what they are, that have thus caused you to swerve from your free and self-incurred obligations to pay rent for the lands you have leased of me—lands, which have been in my possession, and in the possession of those from whom I derive my title, since the year 1788—lands, which when they became mine, about the year 1830, for a full and valuable consideration, were greatly in arrears for rent, were, in many instances, subject to a wheat rent, and that payable in Albany, at a great distance from the residence of you all. I came among you as soon as these lands were mine; I saw you, heard your story, settled with each of you, upon terms and conditions which you admitted were liberal and satisfactory. From time to time for many years, I have been among you; and never, without those feelings of pride and confidence which was the result of the relations which existed between us. My great aim and desire were, to render you contented and happy, and I thought I had done so. Nor was this all; as churches were established among you, I gave to each denomination annually a contribution towards its support. And when you complained that it was hard to carry the wheat to Albany, in payment of your rent, and that it could no longer be raised in Blenheim; I agreed to commute that payment in kind at Albany, for a money rent payable in Blenheim; and also to receive a certain sum in cash per acre as a commutation for the wheat rent; and for ever after 15 cents an acre in lieu of it. I offered, also, when you were all agreed to purchase the right of soil, to sell to you at fair prices—thus removing all ground of objection to the payment of rent under a durable lease. In short, in all ways, and upon every occasion when we have met together, and through my agent, who has lived among you for many years, and has always possessed your and my entire confidence, I have ever made it my duty to consult, so far as I could, the welfare, convenience and ability of you all. You may judge then, of the extreme surprise and regret with which I received the intelligence of your determination to withhold the payment of your rents, and of your combination to resist the collection of the same at all hazards. The first great principle of the moral law is, to do as you would be done by. Now, suppose the case reversed, and you the owner of the land, and I, by voluntary agreement, the lessee of the same, bound to pay rent, for its use and occupation; your means of supporting your family and assisting your children, dependent upon, and derived from this property, lawfully yours; what would you think, or how would you act, if seduced from my duty and my engagements, by the counsel of evil friends and advisers, I should first deny your title, and then, as a natural consequence, refuse to pay rent to you; your honest due; your lawful demand; what would be your course under such circumstances, for the protection of your property, for the collection of your rents? If I had dealt harshly with you; if I had exacted the last farthing; if I had shown, by my conduct and actions, that there was nothing in common between us, there might, perhaps, have been some reasons for your listening to the advice of evil counsellors, to the influences and examples of wrong-doers on other patents. Such a state of things you know, and I know, has never existed between us. Hence then,

I repeat, you may judge of my surprise and regret, on hearing of the proceedings in which you have been engaged; and I now, after having left you full time for reflection, and a safe and quiet return to your obligations, make this appeal to you as men, as citizens bound by every legal and moral tie, to fulfil your agreements—to cast off the evil counsellors, the interested leaders, who have drawn you from the quiet path of duty, and of voluntary contract, to enter upon that of contention, violence and ultimate defeat and submission; choose you then, while it is yet time, between him who has ever so far proved himself your friend, and those, who, in an evil moment, and for interested and selfish purposes, have wrought upon your feelings by false statements to do what you have already done and still propose to accomplish. I desire you to reflect upon what I have stated; to be assured that there is no ground, not the slightest, for the charge that my title is defective, and which you, at least, are prevented from questioning. I have forborne, and may yet for a while forbear, to enforce the collection of my rents by law, and if need be, by the power of the county. Yet, you must remember, that forbearance has its limits; and that if you persist in your refusal to fulfil your obligations, I shall be compelled to appeal to the law, for the vindication of my rights and the enjoyment of my property. I must defend and protect my interest in Blenheim, purchased for a large sum of money. Your denial of my title, and refusal to pay rent, leave me no other course; and when that appeal is once made, the law, it alone, must be the umpire between us. The decision of this question rests with you; should it still continue to be adverse to my rights, I shall as surely and as firmly rely upon a jury of my countrymen, as I have heretofore reposed confidence upon your good will and fidelity to your engagements. If you wish to see me, I am ready to come among you, whenever you shall inform my agent that you are prepared to receive me. In the mean time, ponder well, and reflect calmly upon the state of things which now exists between us, which cannot last; tread back your steps; comply with your contracts; be just to me; be just to yourselves.

Miners' Claims

ORASMUS COLE

COLE, J. It appears that the respondents, in the spring of 1837, were engaged in mining upon a quarter section of land in La Fayette county, and had purchased, before that time, of one Jamison, for the sum of $2,500, a lot upon said quarter section, known as the "Jamison lot," and were

Smith v. Wood, 12 *Wis.* (1860), p. 382.

mining and taking out from said tract of land large quantities of mineral or lead ore, when the appellant Wood, and one Carlin, entered forty acres of the said quarter section, at the United States land office, and obtained a receiver's receipt of entry. The respondents, on being informed of the entry by Wood and Carlin, procured affidavits establishing the fact of their occupancy and mining upon the land, and went to Wood and Carlin and made claim to the land entered by them, representing that their diggings and the "Jamison lot," were included within such entry, when Wood and Carlin executed a bond, in the penal sum of five hundred dollars, to convey to the respondents the forty acres, providing it should appear that the "Jamison lot" was upon said tract, and they should obtain a patent for the land from the United States. The respondents continued personally to work upon the land, and to lease it for mining purposes, until 1854, when they learned that a patent had issued to Wood and Carlin. In the meantime Carlin had died, leaving a widow and adult and minor children, and Wood refused to convey his interest in the land. It appears that Wood, in fact, had sold and conveyed his interest in the land to one Burrell; but if he had not, under the case made out by the bill, a court of equity would not compel him to execute the bond voluntarily entered into.

The United States lead mines, on the upper Mississippi, were early reserved from sale, and, in pursuance of an act of congress, were leased for limited terms, by agents acting under the direction of the President. There was great opposition to the system among the miners, and many never applied for or received any leases from the general government, but went on to the public lands, made claims, worked upon them and sold the mineral discovered and taken from their diggings. These claims were generally respected by the miners, even in cases where there was no lease, and were a subject of bargain and sale among them. We infer that the respondents purchased one of these claims, paying therefor a large sum of money. But it seems this claim, or mineral lot, was embraced within a forty acre tract, which had not been reserved as mineral land, and therefore was subject to entry. Every one at all acquainted with the early history of the lead district of the territory of Wisconsin, well knows that many lands containing rich veins of mineral, were entered. These entries were valid, unless the general government saw fit to vacate them, and the purchaser acquired an absolute title. So there can be no doubt that Wood and Carlin obtained a good title to the tract entered by them. What obligation were they under to recognize any claim upon the land thus entered? What legal or equitable right had the respondents to call upon them for a conveyance of this land? We cannot perceive that they had any whatever. And although Wood and Carlin gave a bond for a conveyance, yet as this was without consideration, why should a court of equity now enforce a specific performance of it? It is a voluntary agreement, and, although under seal, ought not to be enforced.

Acquiring Water Rights

HUGH C. MURRAY

MURRAY, C. J., delivered the opinion of the Court:

The only question involved in this case is, whether a party who locates upon and appropriates public lands belonging to the United States, is entitled to the use of streams and water-courses naturally flowing through such lands, as against persons subsequently appropriating and using the waters of said streams. By the common law, the proprietor of lands upon the banks of a water-course owns to the middle of the stream, and the proprietor of the lands through which the stream flows is held to be the owner of the bed of the stream, and entitled to the use of the water which flows over his land.

The property in the water, by reason of riparian ownership, is in the nature of a usufruct, and consists in general not so much in the fluid as in the advantage of its impetus. This, however, must depend in a great measure upon the natural as well as the artificial wants of each particular country. The rule is well settled that water flows in its natural channels, and should be permitted thus to flow, so that all through whose lands it passes may enjoy the privilege of using it. A riparian proprietor, while he has the undoubted right to use the water flowing over his land, must so use it as to do the least possible harm to other riparian proprietors.

The uses to which water may be appropriated are: 1st, To supply natural wants, such as to quench thirst, to water cattle, for household or culinary purposes, and, in some countries, for the purposes of irrigation. These must be first supplied, before the water can be applied to the satisfaction of artificial wants, such as mills, manufactories, and the like, which are not indispensable to man's existence. Water is regarded as an incident to the soil, the use of which passes with the ownership thereof. As a general rule, a property in water cannot be acquired by appropriation, but only by grant or prescription.

Having thus stated the fundamental principles upon which this right is founded, it is evident that the only difficulty in this case arises, first, from the fact that the defendant is not the owner in fee of the land, but that the title to it is in the government of the United States; and second, the necessity of laying down some rule consistent with our former decisions, and the policy of the State, which has been to protect mining interests and improvements as far as possible.

In Irwin *v.* Phillips, which is the leading case upon the subject of

---

Crandall *v.* Woods, *8 Cal.* (1857), p. 136.

the appropriation of water, it was admitted that the lands upon which the mining-claims were situated, and through which the water ditch was located, were government lands, and that the mining-claims were located after the water had been appropriated.

In delivering the opinion of the Court, Mr. Justice Heydenfeldt remarks: "It is insisted by the appellants that, in this case, the common law doctrine must be invoked, which prescribes that a water-course must be allowed to flow in its natural channel. But upon an examination of the authorities which support that doctrine, it will be found to rest upon the fact of the individual rights of landed proprietors upon the stream, the principle being, both at the civil and common law, that the owner of lands on the banks of a water-course owns to the middle of the stream, and has the right, in virtue of his proprietorship, to the use of the water in its pure and natural condition. In this case, the lands are the property either of the State or of the United States, and it is not necessary to decide to which they belong for the purposes of this case. It is certain that, at the common law, the diversion of water-courses could only be complained of by riparian owners, who were deprived of the use, or those claiming directly under them. Can the appellants assert their present claim as tenants-at-will? To solve this question it must be kept in mind that their tenancy is of their own creation, their tenements of their own selection, and subsequent, in point of time, to the diversion of the stream. They had the right to mine where they pleased throughout an extensive region, and they selected the bank of a stream from which the water had been already turned for the purpose of supplying the mines at another point."

Since this decision, a special property has been recognized in water, not in the sense in which the word property is ordinarily used; but the Courts have held, that a right to water as a usufruct, may be acquired by appropriation, as against a subsequent appropriator, who shows no title to the soil; and that by the appropriation of water, and the construction of a canal, the party acquires an easement or franchise, which he may enjoy and protect. If this is an innovation upon the old rules of law upon this subject, it is such a one as the peculiar circumstances of the country, and the immense importance of our mining interest, will justify.

In the case of Starr v. Child, 20 Wend., Judge Bronson, in speaking of the obligations of American Courts to follow the rules of common law, as laid down by the Courts of England, uses the following strong language:

"Although the ebb and flow of the tide furnishes an imperfect standard for determining what rivers are navigable, it nevertheless approximates to the truth, and may answer very well in the island of Great Britain, for which the rule was made. But such a standard is quite wide of the mark when applied to the great fresh-water rivers of this continent, and would never have been thought of here if we had not found the rule ready made to our hands. Now, I think no doctrine better settled, than that such portions of the law of England as are not adapted to our condition, form no part of the law of this State. This exception includes not only such laws as are inconsistent with the spirit of our institutions, but such as are framed with special reference to the physical condition of a country differing widely from our own. It is contrary to the spirit of the common law itself, to apply a rule founded on a particular reason, to a case where that reason utterly fails. *Cessante ratione legis, cessat ipsa lex.*"

To proceed, however, with the case before us. If the rule laid down in Irwin *v.* Phillips, is correct as to the location of mining-claims and water-ditches, for mining purposes, and *priority* is to determine the rights of the respective parties, it is difficult to see why the rule should not apply to all other cases where land or water had been appropriated. The simple question was, that as between persons appropriating the same land, or land and water both, as the case might be, that the subsequent appropriator takes, subject to the rights of the former.

But an appropriation of land carries with it the water on the land, or a usufruct in the water, for in such cases the party does not appropriate the water, but the land covered with water. If the owners of the mining-claim, in the case of Irwin *v.* Phillips, had first located along the bed of the stream, they would have been entitled, as riparian proprietors, to the free and uninterrupted use of the water, without any other or direct act of appropriation of the water, as contra-distinguished from the soil. If such is the case, why would not the defendant, who has appropriated land over which a natural stream flowed, be held to have appropriated the water of such stream, as an incident to the soil, as against those who subsequently attempt to divert it from its natural channels for their own purposes.

One who locates upon public lands with a view of appropriating them to his own use, becomes the absolute owner thereof as against every one but the government, and is entitled to all the privileges and incidents which appertain to the soil, subject to the single exception of rights antecedently acquired. He may admit that he is not the owner in fee, but his possession will be sufficient to protect him as against trespassers. If he admits, however, that he is not the owner of the soil, and that the fact is established that he acquired his rights subsequent to those of others, then, as both rest alike for their foundation upon appropriation, the subsequent locator must take subject to the rights of the former, and the rule, *qui prior est in tempore, potior est in jure,* must apply. . . .

It is understood, that the location of land carries with it all the incidents belonging to the soil. Those who construct water-ditches will do so with reference to the appropriations of the public domain that have been previously made, and the rights that have been already acquired, with a full knowledge of their own rights as against subsequent locators.

In the case before us, the plaintiffs are not the proprietors of a ditch constructed for mining purposes, (although we have endeavored to show that this would make no difference.) They claim that they purchased the privilege of the water from one Woods, and conducted the same by means of pipes, etc., to the town of Grass Valley, for the use of the inhabitants. The water in dispute had its source in natural springs rising upon the ranch or farm of Woods, who located the land in 1850. In 1851, the ranch of the defendant which was contiguous to that of Woods, was located, and the water flowed by natural channels upon it. Woods sold the privilege of diverting the water to the Union Water Co., in 1852. At the time of this sale the rights of the defendants had accrued. Woods had no power of disposition over the water; he could use it for the purpose of supplying the wants of himself and his stock; and if there was sufficient, might, without interfering with the rights of those below him, have used a portion for the purposes of irrigation; but he had no right to divert it from its natural channel, or prevent it from flowing upon the lands of the defendants. Evans *v.* Merriweather, 3 Scam.; and Arnold *v.* Foot, 12 Wend.

It does not appear, from the evidence in this case, that the water would have flowed through the town of Grass Valley, or that it was the only water which could be obtained for the purpose of supplying the town; neither does it appear that the amount used by defendant for irrigation was so large as to materially diminish the quantity, or render the supply inadequate to the wants of the inhabitants of the town.

The plaintiffs declare as a company, and count upon their appropriation, and not upon their rights as riparian proprietors. This relieves the case of the question, whether granting the defendant had a right to use the water to supply his natural wants, he could use it for the purpose of irrigating his land.

Judgment reversed, and cause remanded.

NEVER THE TWAIN SHALL MEET

American Law, *a Review*

SOUTHWESTERN LAW JOURNAL

A WRITER in an Eastern journal has recently said, that the Western decisions and reports are of but little value. And this sort of summary notice of the bench and the bar of the Mississippi valley, though highly unjust

---

Review of Timothy Walker's *Introduction to American Law,* in *Southwestern Law Journal* (1844), I, p. 112.

and invidious, is in a great measure the result of the tributary position which the profession in the West has voluntarily assumed. Whatever crosses the mountains stamped with the seal of Eastern paternity is sure to meet with a cordial reception. This, no doubt, is according to the natural order of things, for it has not been many ages, since the Institutes of the Roman Emperors gave color and complexion to the jurisprudence of England; nor but a few years since even our Eastern brethren could find no decisions and works of respectable authority, which did not come from the precincts of Westminster Hall, and under the sanction of British authority. A briefless barrister, who, while dragging out his years of probation, may have given variety to the usual monotony of his existence by preparing a treatise on law, was then sometimes of equal authority with our most respectable tribunals. But now that our Story, our Greenleaf, our Kent and our Dane, have added new stores to the mass of legal learning and have found their way even into Westminster Hall, as authority, it is but natural, perhaps, that our Eastern friends should regard us in the West as provincials, justly tributary to them, and that we should look only to those points which have been enlightened by these great luminaries of the law, for authoritative decisions and reports. . . .

These remarks are made in no unkind spirit towards the East; but they are made because they are mere naked facts; not as a matter to be deplored or regretted, nor as a cause of mortification. It is natural that it should be so. The great Valley of the Mississippi now contains one third of the entire population of the United States, and these 7,000,000 of the Western population are the growth of but a few years. Theirs has been a life of active toil, of adventurous enterprise, and has dealt with nature and not with books; it has been one of actions and not of words; of practice and labor and not of speculation. But the time is coming and will soon come, when the great West will take her place in the ranks of literary and scientific enterprise. Slowly but with certainty, she will also take her stand in legal learning, in the fields of jurisprudence, not yet fully explored; and she will build up, with her millions of population, a system of jurisprudence capable of expanding with her growth and embracing the immense variety of her resources and her wants. It is true, little has yet been done by Western lawyers in giving form and shape to their labors. But any one who will take the trouble to examine the 200 volumes of Western Reports, some of which we noticed in the first number of this Journal, cannot but be impressed with the great amount of litigation in the West and South-West, as well as the energy, learning and research of the Bench and the Bar. It is true, aside from the discussion of the questions which have actually arisen in the Courts, and from the learning and research called for in the investigation of these questions, neither the Bar nor the Bench seem to have desired to push their speculations. But this gives value and importance to what has been done; and it would not be saying too much to assert that the world has not in the same time, in any age, produced a greater number of adjudications upon great and important points of law, having a bearing upon the rights and interests of an equal number of human beings, than has been produced in the great Valley of the West. They are, it is true, to some extent covered up with rubbish and "without form and void," requiring the hand of some master spirit to embody them into one great system. In the West, hitherto, there have been but few able and learned lawyers, whose professional duties, in actual litigation, have not been too arduous to afford them leisure to enter into this unoccupied field. Amongst them there has been but little leisure from actual litigation and from the prevailing spirit of the times, in the general rush for wealth and political distinction, to allow them to turn their attention to the more quiet and unobtrusive fields of jurisprudence. Amongst them there has as yet been little of the *"otium cum dignitate"* which is so congenial to the pursuits of the jurist; and they have generally sought that fame which brings with it its present rewards, in preference to that which looks only to coming years for the recompense of its toils.

Yet even in the West a spirit which is less selfish and which looks less to emolument and the applause of the multitude, is growing up in the profession. The learned gentlemen who have charge of the *law schools* at Lexington and Cincinnati, have been gradually infusing a more liberal spirit into the ranks of the Bar, and we expect in a few years to witness great and decided improvements in the true devotion of the lawyers to their profession. We will find them mingling less in the political strifes of the day and partaking less of the spirit of *speculation,* which looks upon wealth and money as the true standard of respectability.

The able and learned work of Mr. Walker, whose title has been placed at the head of this article, needs no commendation from us. But being, as its title imports, an *Introduction to American Law,* designed for students, and purporting to embody the first principles of American Law, and a Western book, emanating from the professor of a Western Law School, we may justly regard it as the first of those works which may be expected hereafter to be given to the world, as an embodiment of the scattered learning of our Western reports. The learned author says, "The American Blackstone is yet to be desired." "Why has not some distinguished lawyer, after retiring from the more active labors of his profession, added one more laurel to his brilliant wreath, by embodying, for the instruction of those who are to come after him, the matured results of wisdom and experience?"

As a guide-book to young men who are just beginning the study of the law, Mr. Walker's work is invaluable; and it is of such a general character, that it might be well introduced into every gentleman's library, as well as made a text-book in all our schools and colleges. But it was not in this connection that we designed to notice the work; for having been seven years before the public, it has received, so far as we have seen, the unqualified approbation of the most learned men of the country. It was in reference to its station as one, amongst the first Western books of an elementary and general character, adapted to the wants of the profession, that we desired to notice it. Mr. Walker, if he should write no more, would by this work have secured "a liquidation of that debt which every man owes to his profession."

Long Since Ceased to Sentimentalize

OLE MUNCH RAEDER

Ole Munch Raeder was an astute young jurist who had received an impressive legal education in his native Norway, as well as in France and Germany. Raeder was appointed by the Norwegian government to study the legal and jury systems in the United States, England, and Canada. His investigations, published in three volumes, later provided the basis for the adoption of the jury system in Norway. Raeder's fame also rests upon the letters he published concerning American social institutions while traveling in America during the 1840's. These letters are notable for their detailed, accurate, and incisive observations of the frontier.

JANESVILLE, October 4, 1847

I BELIEVE I told you in my last letter that I planned to go with Judge Irvin on a circuit-tour, and now I have done so. First I spent a week at Jefferson, then two weeks at Elkhorn, and we arrived here in Rock County day before yesterday. You may well believe, there is a stir in a little town like Janesville when the court and its followers come to town. These little county seats are still as a rule so small that the houses are packed when the thirty-six petit jurors, sixteen grand jurors, a score or two of lawyers, and a whole company of witnesses take possession. The one or two hotels in the town are so full of people that there is no great comfort in staying there. They have the annoying practice here as also, to some extent, in the East, of making the single rooms so small that it is almost literally impossible to turn around in them. I have had great difficulty in finding space for my trunk in my room here, and I have to push it to one side in order to get over to the wash-stand. . . . If one dislikes the small single rooms he may stay in one of the larger rooms, but here he must keep company with a crowd of Yankees. . . .

This Mr. Irvin is a Locofoco and a negro-hater, but we get along very amicably nevertheless. He is a Virginian of the old school,—that of the time when Virginia ranked very high on this continent in intellectual achievement and when about fifty of her sons were members of

Ole Munch Raeder, *America in the Forties* (ed. Malmin, 1929), pp. 112, 152.

Congress as representatives from all parts of the country. Mr. Irvin came out here fifteen years ago when there were only a few settlements at Green Bay and in the mining district, dating mostly from the time of French occupation. The interior was Indian country, and on his circuit-tours he generally had to sleep out in the open after his rifle had supplied him with food. Court was held in little log cabins in those days, and they were always packed, of course. Once he decided to hold court under a large tree, like an Indian council, but a heavy rainstorm prevented him from carrying out this romantic plan. On one occasion the sheriff was greatly puzzled as to what to do; the law reads that the grand jury is to deliberate behind closed doors, but in the hut where the sessions were being held there was only one room. The result was that the court had to go outside and explore the country. The hut was on the banks of the Mississippi and there was a cave near by, hollowed out by the water which had later receded; here the grand jury was assembled.

One might think that the judge would take great interest in the rapid changes that have been taking place in his district, right before his very eyes, so to speak, so that he could see great changes every time he went out on his trips. But he takes it all very coolly; he tells how the country has little by little assumed its present appearance and has been dotted here and there with pleasant little villages, while large courthouses with domes and columns testify to the great truth that a country must be built under the law. I asked him once if it did not give him a certain thrill to view all this development, in which he himself had played such a considerable part. He answered that he had long since ceased to sentimentalize. To him these flourishing farms merely speak of greater possibilities for cases of trespassing; the woods are more likely to be molested now than before; and there are more and more horse thieves. On his first trips two lawyers went with him and took all the cases they found in the various localities. Now as many as two hundred lawyers are kept busy in the territory, at least half of them within his district; there are three such districts in all. There are more lawyers every year. In the two counties where I have been, I have seen at least a dozen of them take oath; most of them were from Ohio and some from New York. The rule is that if they have been admitted to the bar elsewhere, they need merely a recommendation from one of the attorneys here; if not, they have to be quizzed by a committee appointed by the court. There is no legal restriction as to their number. . . .

Here, in this section of America especially, there are many of the lawyers who do not particularly command one's respect, either for their natural abilities or for their culture and training. When a lawyer in the East finds the competition too sharp for him he generally goes west. The same is true of many young men who hesitate to begin their careers too close to their home communities, where every one knows them. I have spoken with some lawyers of this kind, who knew so little about European conditions even in their own special field that they thought the English common law was in force in Norway. One of them was greatly surprised when I told him that we not only had our own laws but our own government as well; he had the impression that we were subjects of Queen Victoria! The lawyers out here do have their merits, however. They certainly are kind and obliging to strangers. Furthermore, many of them play trumpets, trombones, flutes, or other musical instruments; these come together and organize bands which enliven things very considerably as the court visits the different towns. One of my good friends is an excellent piccolo player.

AN EYE FOR AN EYE

Although the people of the United States generally live in respect for law, there was then, as there is now, a strand of impatience with law which often discharged into violence. "Our nation," President Kennedy declared when he dispatched Federal troops to the University of Mississippi to guard the legal rights of one Negro student, "is founded on the principle that observance of the law is the eternal safeguard of liberty and defiance of the law is the surest road to tyranny." But all too often a part of the community considers direct action more apt for the solution of a problem than the irksome processes of law. In many ways between 1820 and 1860 society seems to have been law-dominated to an extraordinary degree, and its very omnipresence produced periodic rebellions against the constraints. On the frontier particularly, people were used to the direct elimination of irritants; indeed, the limits imposed by more civilized areas, of which law was a considerable part, frequently had been the very impetus to Western migration. As a result, a small but significant minority came to treat a bullet as the ultimate argument—a roughhewn version of natural law.

Oh, He Was Murdered

FRANCES TROLLOPE

THEIR UNEQUALLED FREEDOM, I think, I understand better. Their code of common law is built upon ours; and the difference between us is this, in England the laws are acted upon, in America they are not.

I do not speak of the police of the Atlantic cities; I believe it is well

---

Frances Trollope, *Domestic Manners of the Americans* (1832), p. 136.

arranged: in New York it is celebrated for being so; but out of the range of their influence, the contempt of law is greater than I can venture to state, with any hope of being believed. Trespass, assault, robbery, nay, even murder, are often committed without the slightest attempt at legal interference.

During the summer that we passed most delightfully in Maryland, our rambles were often restrained in various directions by the advice of our kind friends, who knew the manners and morals of the country. When we asked the cause, we were told, "There is a public-house on that road, and it will not be safe to pass it."

The line of the Chesapeake and Ohio canal passed within a few miles of Mrs. S***'s residence. It twice happened during our stay with her, that dead bodies were found partially concealed near it. The circumstance was related as a sort of half-hour's wonder; and when I asked particulars of those who, on one occasion, brought the tale, the reply was, "Oh, he was murdered, I expect; or may-be he died of the canal fever; but they say he had marks of being throttled." No inquest was summoned; and certainly no more sensation was produced by the occurrence than if a sheep had been found in the same predicament.

Respect Paid to the Law

FRANCIS LIEBER

Francis Lieber (1800–1872) emigrated to America at the age of twenty-seven after taking part in the campaign of Waterloo and the Greek War of Liberation. A scholar of political science with numerous books to his credit, he founded the Encyclopaedia Americana, *and was ultimately appointed Professor of Law at Columbia. Academic life could not dampen his romanticism, for like Fabrizio in* The Charterhouse of Parma *he had been lastingly impressed by his encounter with the forces of Napoleon Bonaparte.*

. . . HERE, ON THE OTHER HAND, as soon as the election is over the contest is settled, and the citizen obeys the law. "Keep to the right, as the law directs," you will often find on signboards on bridges in this country. It expresses the authority which the law here possesses. I doubt very much whether the Romans, noted for their obedience to the law, held it in higher respect than the Americans.

A traveller who goes from the European continent to England is

Letters to a Gentleman in Germany (ed. Francis Lieber, Philadelphia, 1834), p. 34.

struck with the respect paid to the law in that country. I conversed once with an English stage-coachman on a certain law, which I thought very oppressive: "Yes," said he, "but such is the law of the land." You might travel all over Austria and Prussia before a postillion would give you such an answer. He would say, in a similar case, "Yes, but they take good care that you do not get round them." If you go from England to the United States, you find that there the law is held in still higher respect. But to see the whole truth, to feel the full weight of what I say, it is necessary to see the law administered on minor occasions, to see riots quelled by citizens themselves sworn in for the occasion, to see banks and mints without sentinels, to travel thousands of miles and never meet with a uniform; and farther, to observe that what the law requires is here held honorable. No man looks upon a district attorney as upon a tool of government because he prosecutes in the name of the United States.

The Punishment of Abiram

JAMES FENIMORE COOPER

Abiram was guilty of the death of his nephew, the oldest son of Ishmael and Esther. Now Ishmael decides on the punishment to be meted out:

"HAVE YOU THAT BOOK at hand, woman? it may happen to advise in such a dreary business."

Esther fumbled in her pocket, and was not long in producing the fragment of a Bible which had been thumbed and smoke-dried till the print was nearly illegible. . . .

"There are many awful passages in these pages, Ishmael," she said, when the volume was opened, and the leaves were slowly turning under her finger, "and some there ar' that teach the rules of punishment."

Her husband made a gesture for her to find one of those brief rules of conduct which have been received among all Christian nations as the direct mandates of the Creator, and which have been found so just, that even they who deny their high authority, admit their wisdom. Ishmael listened with grave attention as his companion read all those verses which her memory suggested, and which were thought applicable to the situation in which they found themselves. He made her show him the words, which he regarded with a sort of strange reverence. A resolution once taken was usually irrevocable in one who was moved with so much difficulty. He put his hand upon the book and closed the pages himself, as much as to

James Fenimore Cooper, *The Prairie* (1827), pp. 424-434.

apprise his wife that he was satisfied. Esther, who so well knew his character, trembled at the action, and casting a glance at his steady eye, she said,—

"And yet, Ishmael, my blood and the blood of my children is in his veins! cannot mercy be shown?"

"Woman," he answered, sternly, "when we believed that miserable old trapper had done this deed, nothing was said of mercy!"

Esther made no reply, but folding her arms upon her breast she sat silent and thoughtful for many minutes. Then she once more turned her anxious gaze upon the countenance of her husband, where she found all passion and care apparently buried in the coldest apathy. Satisfied now that the fate of her brother was sealed, and possibly conscious how well he merited the punishment that was meditated, she no longer thought of mediation. No more words passed between them. Their eyes met for an instant, and then both arose and walked in profound silence towards the encampment.

The squatter found his children expecting his return in the usual listless manner with which they awaited all coming events. The cattle were already herded, and the horses in their gears in readiness to proceed, so soon as he should indicate that such was his pleasure. The children were already in their proper vehicle, and, in short, nothing delayed the departure but the absence of the parents of the wild brood.

"Abner," said the father, with the deliberation with which all his proceedings were characterized, "take the brother of your mother from the wagon, and let him stand on the 'arth."

Abiram issued from his place of concealment, trembling, it is true, but far from destitute of hopes as to his final success in appeasing the just resentment of his kinsman. After throwing a glance around him with the vain wish of finding a single countenance in which he might detect a solitary gleam of sympathy, he endeavored to smother those apprehensions that were by this time reviving in their original violence, by forcing a sort of friendly communication between himself and the squatter:—

"The beasts are getting jaded, brother," he said; "and as we have made so good a march already, is it not time to camp? To my eye you may go far before a better place than this is found to pass the night in."

" 'Tis well you like it. Your tarry here ar' likely to be long. My sons, draw nigh and listen. Abiram White," he added, lifting his cap, and speaking with a solemnity and steadiness that rendered even his dull mien imposing, "you have slain my first-born, and according to the laws of God and man must you die!"

The kidnapper started at this terrible and sudden sentence, with the terror that one would exhibit who unexpectedly found himself in the grasp of a monster from whose power there was no retreat. Although filled with the most serious forebodings of what might be his lot, his courage had not been equal to look his danger in the face, and with the deceitful consolation with which timid tempers are apt to conceal their desperate condition from themselves, he had rather courted a treacherous relief in his cunning, than prepared himself for the worst.

"Die!" he repeated, in a voice that scarcely issued from his chest; "a man is surely safe among his kinsmen?"

"So thought my boy," returned the squatter, motioning for the team that contained his wife and the girls to proceed, as he very coolly examined the priming of his piece. "By the rifle did you destroy my son; it is fit and just that you meet your end by the same weapon."

Abiram stared about him with a gaze that bespoke an unsettled reason. He even laughed, as if he would not only persuade himself but others that what he heard was some pleasantry intended to try his nerves. But nowhere did his frightful merriment meet with an answering echo. All around was solemn and still. The visages of his nephews were excited, but cold towards him, and that of his former confederate frightfully determined. This very steadiness of mien was a thousand times more alarming and hopeless than any violence could have proved. The latter might possibly have touched his spirit and awakened resistance, but the former threw him entirely on the feeble resources of himself.

"Brother," he said, in a hurried, unnatural whisper, "did I hear you?"

"My words are plain, Abiram White: thou has done murder, and for the same must thou die!"

"Esther! sister, sister, will you leave me! O! sister! do you hear my call?"

"I hear one speak from the grave!" returned the husky tones of Esther, as the wagon passed the spot where the criminal stood. "It is the voice of my first-born, calling aloud for justice! God have mercy, God have mercy on your soul!"

The team slowly pursued its route, and the deserted Abiram now found himself deprived of the smallest vestige of hope. Still he could not summon fortitude to meet his death, and had not his limbs refused to aid him he would yet have attempted to fly. Then, by a sudden revolution from hope to utter despair, he fell upon his knees, and commenced a prayer in which cries for mercy to God and to his kinsman were wildly and blasphemously mingled. The sons of Ishmael turned away in horror at the disgusting spectacle, and even the stern nature of the squatter began to bend before so abject misery.

"May that which you ask of Him be granted," he said, "but a father can never forget a murdered child."

He was answered by the most humble appeals for time. A week, a day, an hour, were each implored with an earnestness commensurate to the value they receive when a whole life is compressed into their short duration. The squatter was troubled, and at length he yielded in part to the petitions of the criminal. His final purpose was not altered, though he changed the means. "Abner," he said, "mount the rock and look on every side that we may be sure none are nigh."

While his nephew was obeying this order, gleams of reviving hope were seen shooting across the quivering features of the kidnapper. The report was favorable, nothing having life, the retiring teams excepted, was to be seen. A messenger was, however, coming from the latter in great apparent haste. Ishmael awaited its arrival. He received from the hands of one of his wondering and frighted girls a fragment of that book which Esther had preserved with so much care. The squatter beckoned the child away, and placed the leaves in the hands of the criminal.

"Esther has sent you this," he said, "that in your last moments you may remember God."

"Bless her, bless her! a good and kind sister has she been to me! But time must be given that I may read; time, my brother, time!"

"Time shall not be wanting. You shall be your own executioner, and this miserable office shall pass away from my hands."

Ishmael proceeded to put his new resolution in force. The immediate apprehensions of the kidnapper were quieted by an assurance that he might yet live for days, though his punishment was inevitable. A reprieve to one abject and wretched as Abiram, temporarily produced the same effects as a pardon. He was even foremost in assisting the appalling arrangements, and of all the actors in that solemn tragedy, his voice alone was facetious and jocular.

A thin shelf of the rock projected beneath one of the ragged arms of the willow. It was many feet from the ground, and admirably adapted to the purpose which, in fact, its appearance had suggested. On this little platform the criminal was placed, his arms bound at the elbows behind his back, beyond the possibility of liberation, with a proper cord leading from his neck to the limb of the tree. The latter was so placed, that when suspended the body could find no foot-hold. The fragment of the Bible was placed in his hands, and he was left to seek his consolation as he might from its pages.

"And now, Abiram White," said the squatter, when his sons had descended from completing this arrangement, "I give you a last and solemn asking. Death is before you in two shapes. With this rifle can your misery be cut short, or by that cord, sooner or later, must you meet your end."

"Let me yet live! O, Ishmael, you know not how sweet life is when the last moment draws so nigh!"

" 'Tis done," said the squatter, motioning for his assistants to follow the herds and teams. "And now, miserable man, that it may prove a consolation to your end, I forgive you my wrongs and leave you to your God."

Ishmael turned and pursued his way across the plain at his ordinary sluggish and ponderous gait. Though his head was bent a little towards the earth, his inactive mind did not prompt him to cast a look behind. Once, indeed, he thought he heard his name called in tones that were a little smothered, but they failed to make him pause. . . .

Life in Louisiana

DION BOUCICAULT

Dion Boucicault was born in Dublin, Ireland. He came to New York in 1853 and quickly became a dominant influence on the American theater. Boucicault wrote or adapted over one hundred and twenty plays, including dramatizations of such English novels as Nicholas Nickleby *and* The Heart of the Midlothian. The Octoroon, *from which the following scene is taken, was first performed in New York in 1859.*

SOLON. We got him!

SCUD. Who?

SOLON. The Injiun!

SCUD. Wahnotee? Where is he? D'ye call running away from a fellow catching him?

RATTS. Here he comes.

OMNES. Where? Where?

(Enter Wahnotee. They are all about to rush on him.)

SCUD. Hold on! stan' round thar! no violence—the critter don't know what we mean.

JACKSON. Let him answer for the boy then.

M'CLOSKY. Down with him—lynch him.

OMNES. Lynch him! (Exit Lafouche.)

SCUD. Stan' back, I say! I'll nip the first that lays a finger on him. Pete, speak to the red-skin.

PETE. Whar's Paul, Wahnotee? What's come ob de child?

WAHNOTEE. Paul wunce—Paul pangeuk.

PETE. Pangeuk—dead!

WAHNOTEE. Mort!

M'CLOSKY. And you killed him?

(They approach him.)

SCUD. Hold on!

PETE. Um, Paul reste?

Dion Boucicault, *Life in Louisiana* (1859), p. 38.

WAHNOTEE. Hugh vieu. (Goes.) Paul reste ci!

SCUD. Here, stay! (Examining the ground.) The earth has been stirred here lately.

WAHNOTEE. Weenee Paul.

(He points down, and shows by pantomime how he buried Paul.)

SCUD. The Injiun means that he buried him there! Stop! Here's a bit of leather. (Drawing out the mail-bags.) The mail-bags that were lost! (Sees the tomahawk in Wahnotee's belt—draws it out and examines it.) Look! here are marks of blood—look thar, red-skin, what's that?

WAHNOTEE. Paul!

(Makes a sign that Paul was killed by a blow on the head.)

M'CLOSKY. He confesses it; the Indian got drunk, quarrelled with him, and killed him.

(Re-enter Lafouche, with smashed apparatus.)

LAFOUCHE. Here are evidences of the crime; this rum-bottle half emptied—this photographic apparatus smashed—and there are marks of blood and footsteps around the shed.

M'CLOSKY. What more d'ye want—ain't that proof enough? Lynch him!

OMNES. Lynch him! Lynch him!

SCUD. Stan' back, boys! He's an Injiun—fair play.

JACKSON. Try him, then—try him on the spot of his crime.

OMNES. Try him! Try him!

LAFOUCHE. Don't let him escape!

RATTS. I'll see to that. (Drawing revolver.) If he stirs, I'll put a bullet through his skull, mighty quick.

M'CLOSKY. Come, form a court then, choose a jury—we'll fix this varmin.

(Enter Thibodeaux and Caillou.)

THIBODEAUX. What's the matter?

LAFOUCHE. We've caught this murdering Injiun, and are going to try him.

(Wahnotee sits, rolled in blanket.)

PETE. Poor little Paul—poor little nigger!

SCUD. This business goes agin me, Ratts—'t ain't right.

LAFOUCHE. We're ready; the jury's impanelled—go ahead—who'll be accuser?

RATTS. M'Closky.

M'CLOSKY. Me?

RATTS. Yes; you was the first to hail Judge Lynch.

M'CLOSKY. Well, what's the use of argument whar guilt sticks out so plain; the boy and Injiun were alone when last seen.

SCUD. Who says that?

M'CLOSKY. Everybody—that is, I heard so.

SCUD. Say what you know—not what you heard.

M'CLOSKY. I know then that the boy was killed with that tomahawk —the red-skin owns it—the signs of violence are all round the shed— this apparatus smashed—ain't it plain that in a drunken fit he slew the boy, and when sober concealed the body yonder?

OMNES. That's it—that's it.

RATTS. Who defends the Injiun?

SCUD. I will; for it is agin my natur' to b'lieve him guilty; and if he be, this ain't the place, nor you the authority to try him. How are we sure the boy is dead at all? There are no witnesses but a rum bottle and an old machine. Is it on such evidence you'd hang a human being?

RATTS. His own confession.

SCUD. I appeal against your usurped authority. This lynch law is a wild and lawless proceeding. Here's a pictur' for a civilized community to afford; yonder, a poor, ignorant savage, and round him a circle of hearts, white with revenge and hate, thirsting for his blood: you call your-selves judges—you ain't—you're a jury of executioners. It is such scenes as these that bring disgrace upon our Western life.

M'CLOSKY. Evidence! Evidence! Give us evidence. We've had talk enough; now for proof.

OMNES. Yes, yes! Proof, proof!

SCUD. Where am I to get it? The proof is here, in my heart.

PETE. (Who has been looking about the camera.) 'Top, sar! 'Top a bit! O, laws-a-mussey, see dis! here's a pictur' I found stickin' in that yar telescope machine, sar! look, sar!

SCUD. A photographic plate. (Pete holds his lantern up.) What's this, eh? two forms! The child—'t is he! dead—and above him—An! an! Jacob M'Closky, 't was you murdered that boy!

M'CLOSKY. Me?

SCUD. You! You slew him with that tomahawk; and as you stood over his body with the letter in your hand, you thought that no witness saw the deed, that no eye was on you—but there was, Jacob M'Closky, there was. The eye of the Eternal was on you—the blessed sun in heaven, that, looking down, struck upon this plate the image of the deed. Here you are, in the very attitude of your crime!

M'CLOSKY. 'T is false!

SCUD. 'T is true! The apparatus can't lie. Look there, jurymen. (Showing plate to jury.) Look there. O, you wanted evidence—you called for proof—Heaven has answered and convicted you.

M'CLOSKY. What court of law would receive such evidence? (Going.)

RATTS. Stop! *this* would! You called it yourself; you wanted to make us murder that Injiun; and since we've got our hands in for justice, we'll try it on *you*. What say ye? shall we have one law for the red-skin and another for the white?

OMNES. Try him! Try him!

RATTS. Who'll be accuser?

SCUD. I will! Fellow-citizens, you are convened and assembled here under a higher power than the law. What's the law? When the ship's abroad on the ocean, when the army is before the enemy, where in thunder's the law? It is in the hearts of brave men, who can tell right from wrong, and from whom justice can't be bought. So it is here, in the wilds of the West, where our hatred of crime is measured by the speed of our executions—where necessity is law! I say then, air you honest men? air you true? Put your hands on you naked breasts, and let every man as don't feel a real American heart there, bustin' up with freedom, truth, and right, let that man step out—that's the oath I put to ye—and then say, darn ye, go it!

OMNES. Go on! Go on!

SCUD. No! I won't go on; that man's down. I won't strike him, even with words. Jacob, your accuser is that pictur' of the crime—let that speak —defend yourself.

M'CLOSKY. (Drawing knife.) I will, quicker than lightning.

RATTS. Seize him, then! (They rush on M'Closky, and disarm him.) He can fight though he's a painter: claws all over.

SCUD. Stop! Search him, we may find more evidence.

M'CLOSKY. Would you rob me first, and murder me afterwards?

RATTS. (Searching him.) That's his programme—here's a picket-book.

SCUD. (Opening it.) What's here? Letters! Hello! to "Mrs. Peyton, Terrebonne, Louisiana, United States." Liverpool postmark. Ho! I've got hold of the tail of a rat—come out. (Reading.) What's this? A draft for eighty-five thousand dollars, and credit on Palisse and Co., of New Orleans, for the balance. Hi! the rat's out. You killed the boy to steal this letter from the mail-bags—you stole this letter, that the money should not arrive in time to save the Octoroon; had it done so, the lien on the estate would have ceased, and Zoe be free.

OMNES. Lynch him! Lynch him! Down with him!

SCUD. Silence in the court: stand back, let the gentlemen of the jury retire, consult, and return their verdict.

RATTS. I'm responsible for the crittur—go on.

PETE. (To Wahnotee.) See, Injiun; look dar. (Showing him the plate.) See dat innocent; look, dar's de murderer of poor Paul.

WAHNOTEE. Ugh! (Examining the plate.)

PETE. Ya! as he? Closky tue Paul—kill de child with your tomahawk dar: 't wasn't you, no—ole Pete allus say so. Poor Injiun lub our little Paul. (Wahnotee rises and looks at M'Closky—he is in his war paint and fully armed.)

SCUD. What say ye, gentlemen? Is the prisoner guilty, or is he not guilty?

OMNES. Guilty!

Scud. And what is to be his punishment?

Omnes. Death! (All advance.)

Wahnotee. (Crosses to M'Closky.) Ugh!

Scud. No, Injiun; we deal out justice here, not revenge. 'T ain't you he has injured, 't is the white man, whose laws he has offended.

Ratts. Away with him—put him down the aft hatch, till we rig his funeral.

M'Closky. Fifth against one! O! if I had you one by one alone in the swamp, I'd rip ye all.

(He is borne off in boat struggling.)

CALIFORNIA, HERE I COME!

The California legal situation in the early 1840's left judges with the responsibility of creating a state jurisprudence from scratch—of creating a system out of chaos. San Francisco was transformed from a town of barely nine hundred people into a city of ten thousand within the single year 1848–1849. The city had grown too rapidly and was beset with difficulties: no less than six fires broke out between 1849 and 1851. Lawlessness, however, was San Francisco's greatest problem. The government was corrupt and failed to curb a large vicious element. In 1851, and then again in 1856, citizens organized as committees of vigilance, and rid the town of many criminals. The situation was deteriorating in 1855 when only seven of thirty-five homicides resulted in convictions. Aroused by James King's demands for reform in his paper, The Evening Bulletin, *the citizenry of San Francisco reached a breaking point when King, after attacking specific policies and people, was shot down in the street. Vigilance committees rounded up murderers, thieves, and ballot stuffers, executed four of the first group, and banished the others. When the state threatened to intervene the group disbanded in August, 1856, after two more hangings and a parade to commemorate its achievements. Politics in San Francisco continued in this informal state until the triumph of a reform movement in 1906. Reading more like a declaration of independence than a constitution, the following excerpt sets out the Committee's grievances, goals, and good intentions.*

Into this situation came David Smith Terry and Stephen Johnson Field. Terry, who was born in Kentucky, moved to California in 1849 to study law. In 1855, running on the Know-Nothing ticket, he was elected to the California Supreme Court. The very next year, the erratic Terry stabbed and almost killed an official of the San Francisco Vigilance Committee in an attempt to halt its extra-legal actions.

Field was born in 1816. After studying law in the office of his brother, David Dudley Field, in New York City, he became his brother's partner in a firm which lasted till 1848. In 1849, he cut the ties with his powerful family by setting sail for California. Here he encountered an environment as different from New York as conceivable—as his charge to the jury reveals—and he could find himself.

Terry became Chief Justice in 1857 in the same year that Field was elected to the Court. In Ex parte Newman *he held that a law which forced the Sabbath closing of business establishments discriminated against the free exercise of religion. Field dissented sharply, stating that this law was not religious in content, but rather an attempt to protect health and morals. The tension between Field and Terry began. Some years later Terry denounced Field for his public retraction of charges against one Harvey Lee. Terry's tempestuous nature is further revealed during this period by his feud with Senator David Broderick; a duel resulted, in which Broderick was fatally wounded. Nor was Field's the most stable of personalities. Although in later years he was the very embodiment of judicial dignity, complete with flowing beard and patriarchal mien, his early California career included a feud with a state judge in the course of which he was disbarred, reinstated, disbarred again, sent to jail for contempt, fined, and involved in a duel.*

Hostility between Terry and Field came to a head in 1886 when Field (now on the United States Supreme Court) ruled against a client of Terry in a divorce case; Terry and the client had been married during the proceedings. Both Terry and his new wife were imprisoned following a violent outburst after Field's decision. Terry then threatened to shoot Field upon his release. The United States Attorney General assigned David Neagle as a bodyguard to Field. On August 14, 1889, while Field and Neagle were dining in a California restaurant, Terry entered and assaulted Field. Neagle shot Terry, killing him instantly. Neagle was indicted for murder, but the Supreme Court held the killing to be justifiable since it was performed in the line of duty.

We Shall Spare No Effort to Avoid Bloodshed

COMMITTEE OF VIGILANCE

THE COMMITTEE OF VIGILANCE, placed in the position they now occupy by the voice and countenance of the vast majority of their fellow-citizens, as executors of their will, desire to define the necessity which has forced this people into their present organization. . . .

Organized gangs of bad men, of all political parties, or who assumed any particular creed from mercenary and corrupt motives, have parcelled out our offices among themselves, or sold them to the highest bidders;

Constitution and Address of the Committee of Vigilance of San Francisco (1856), Treasure Room, Harvard Law School, p. 5.

Have provided themselves with convenient tools to obey their nod, as Clerks, Inspectors and Judges of election;

Have employed bullies and professional fighters to destroy tally-lists by force, and prevent peaceable citizens from ascertaining, in a lawful manner, the true number of votes polled at our elections;

And have used cunningly contrived ballot-boxes, with false sides and bottoms, so prepared that by means of a spring or slide, spurious tickets, concealed there previous to the election, could be mingled with genuine votes.

Of all this we have the most irrefragable proofs. Felons from other lands and States, and unconvicted criminals equally as bad, have thus controlled public funds and property, and have often amassed sudden fortunes without having done an honest day's work with head or hands. Thus the fair inheritance of our city has been embezzled and squandered —our streets and wharves are in ruins, and the miserable entailment of an enormous debt will bequeath sorrow and poverty to another generation.

The Jury-box has been tampered with, and our Jury trials have been made to shield the hundreds of murderers whose red hands have cemented this tyranny, and silenced with the Bowie-knife and the pistol, not only the free voice of an indignant press, but the shuddering rebuke of the outraged citizen.

To our shame be it said, that the inhabitants of distant lands already know that corrupt men in office, as well as gamblers, shoulder strikers, and other vile tools of unscrupulous leaders, beat, maim and shoot down with impunity, as well peaceable and unoffending citizens, as those earnest reformers who, at the known hazard of their lives, and with singleness of heart have sought, in a lawful manner, to thwart schemes of public plunder or to awaken investigation.

Embodied in the principles of republican governments are the truths that the majority should rule, and that when corrupt officials, who have fraudulently seized the reigns of authority, designedly thwart the execution of the laws and avert punishment from the notoriously guilty, the power they usurp reverts back to the people from whom it was wrested.

Realizing these truths, and confident that they were carrying out the will of the vast majority of the citizens of this county, the Committee of Vigilance, under a solemn sense of the responsibility that rested upon them, have calmly and dispassionately weighed the evidences before them, and decreed the death of some and banishment of others, who by their crimes and villainies, had stained our fair land. With those that were banished this comparatively moderate punishment was chosen, not because ignominious death was not deserved, but that the error, if any, might surely be upon the side of mercy to the criminal. There are others scarcely less guilty, against whom the same punishment has been decreed, but they have been allowed further time to arrange for their final departure, and with the hope that permission to depart voluntarily might induce repentance, and repentance amendment, they have been suffered to choose within certain limits their own time and method of going.

Thus far, and throughout their arduous duties, they have been, and will be guided by the most conscientious convictions of imperative duty; and they earnestly hope that in endeavoring to mete out merciful justice to the guilty, their counsels may be so guided by that Power before whose tribunal we shall all stand, that in the vicissitudes of after life, amid the calm reflections of old age and in the clear view of dying conscience, there may be found nothing we would regret or wish to change.

We have no friends to reward, no enemies to punish, no private ends to accomplish.

Our single, heartfelt aim is the public good; the purging, from our community, of those abandoned characters whose actions have been evil continually, and have finally forced upon us the efforts we are now making. We have no favoritism as a body, nor shall there be evinced, in any of our acts, either partiality for, or prejudice against any race, sect or party.

While thus far we have not discovered on the part of our constituents any indications of lack of confidence, and have no reason to doubt that the great majority of the inhabitants of the county endorse our acts, and desire us to continue the work of weeding out the irreclaimable characters from the community, we have, with deep regret, seen that some of the State authorities have felt it their duty to organize a force to resist us. It is not impossible for us to realize, that not only those who have sought place with a view to public plunder, but also those gentlemen who, in accepting offices to which they were honestly elected, have sworn to support the laws of the State of California, find it difficult to reconcile their supposed duties with acquiescence in the acts of the Committee of Vigilance, since they do not reflect that perhaps more than three-fourths of the people of the entire State sympathize with and endorse our efforts, and as that all law emanates from the people, so that, when the laws thus enacted are not executed, the power returns to the people, and is theirs whenever they may choose to exercise it. These gentlemen would not have hesitated to acknowledge the self-evident truth, had the people chosen to make their present movement a complete revolution, recalled all the power they had delegated, and re-issued it to new agents, under new forms.

Now, because the people have not seen fit to resume *all* the powers they have confided to executive or legislative officers, it certainly does not follow that they cannot, in the exercise of their inherent sovereign power, withdraw from corrupt and unfaithful servants the authority they have used to thwart the ends of justice.

Those officers whose mistaken sense of duty leads them to array themselves against the determined action of the people, whose servants they have become, may be respected, while their errors may be regretted; but none can envy the future reflections of that man who, whether in the heat of malignant passion, or with the vain hope of preserving by violence a position obtained through fraud and bribery, seeks under the color of law to enlist the outcasts of society as a hireling soldiery in the service of the State, or urges criminals, by hopes of plunder, to continue at the cost of civil war, the reign of ballot-box stuffers, suborners of witnesses, and tamperers with the jury-box.

The Committee of Vigilance believe that the people have entrusted to them the duty of gathering evidence, and, after due trial, expelling from the community those ruffians and assassins who have so long outraged the peace and good order of society, violated the ballot-box, overridden law and thwarted justice. Beyond the duties incident to this, we do not desire to interfere with the details of government.

We have spared and shall spare no effort to avoid bloodshed or civil war; but undeterred by threats or opposing organizations, shall continue peaceably if we can, forcibly if we must, this work of reform, to which we have pledged our lives, our fortunes and our sacred honor.

Our labors have been arduous, our deliberations have been cautious, our determinations firm, our counsels prudent, our motives pure; and while regretting the imperious necessity which called us into action, we are anxious that this necessity should exist no longer; and when our labors shall have been accomplished, when the community shall be freed from the evils it has so long endured; when we have insured to our citizens an honest and vigorous protection of their rights, then the Committee of Vigilance will find great pleasure in resigning their power into the hands of the people, from whom it was received.

If I Felt Guilty of Any Crime

DAVID SMITH TERRY

San Francisco June 30, 1856

DEAREST NEAL

I received yours just now. Next to seeing you it is my greatest comfort to know that you are well and still keep up your spirits under the most distressing circumstances in which we are placed.

I have today been engaged in taking the testimony of the witnesses against me. The testimony is very conflicting as must always be the case when a no. of persons differing in temperament & excitabillity [sic] detail occurrences which they all witnessed.

David S. Terry, Letter, June 30, 1856, in Russell Buchanan, *David S. Terry of California* (1956), p. 44.

Before any important tribunal even upon the evidence already adduced I would be held blameless—but it is not in human nature to judge our enemy fairly and impartially & the result must be as God wills. I have tried with a great deal of anxiety to read the characters of those who are at once my judges and accusers. I am inclined to think that a majority of them are men who desire to do right but considering the infirmity of human nature they are assuming an awful responsibility in sitting in judgment on a man against whom so much has been said to excite their prejudices. You desire to know if I am well & in Spirits. I am well & keep up my Spirits as well as could be expected. Do not fear that I will despond. My mind has been relieved from care for the future of my boy & I am now equal to any fortunes.

If I felt guilty of any crime I would despond but upon this point I am invulnerable. I know that I acted not from any feeling of malice towards any human being but solely from regard to a sacred principle, from a desire to prevent the consumation in my presence of an act which (though it may have been attempted from good motives & would certainly have worked no injury to the community, (as the man sought to be removed was a bad man)) was a violation of the Constitution of this state which I had *sworn* to support as well as the Constitution of the United States to secure the blessings of which to their posterity both my grandfathers fought & bled & toiled & suffered. I was educated to believe that it is the duty of every American to support the Constitution of his Country to regard it as a sacred instrument not to be violated in its least provision—& if necessary to die in its defense. The meanest criminal is under that instrument guaranteed the same rights as the noblest citizen & cannot without a violation of its provisions be deprived of his liberty, except by legal process—It was at this holy principle and the obligation of my oath I looked and not at the demerrits (?) of the man whom I knew to be a bad man—& I believe even those who are my self constituted judges will do me the justice to believe I would not defend him for his own sake. The matter stands thus with me actuated by the principles taught me in my childhood. I have done certain acts about the merrits [sic] of which men who are perhaps equally honest and patriotic differ. This must always be the case as long as mens minds are differently constituted. I feel that I am right & so feeling would lay down my life rather than deny these principles the same conciousness [sic] of the Justice of my cause which sustained old Nat Terry when wounded & a prisoner in Charleston & which nerved the heart of David Smith to refuse to release his fathers brother who had supported his tottering steps [in] infancy & whom he had made prisoner at King's Mountain must support me in this trial. If need be I can go out of this world feeling that I have done nothing in this life which would cause the spirits of those patriots & heroes to blush for their descendant.

So My Darling dont fear that I will falter.

Attempted Bribery

STEPHEN J. FIELD

"Gentlemen, we have not endeavored to influence your judgment except by the evidence; we have not approached you secretly and tried to control your verdict. . . . But the other side have not thus acted . . . They have said that you were so low and debased that although you had with uplifted hands declared that so might the ever-living God help you, as you rendered a verdict according to the evidence, you were willing, to please them, to decide against the evidence, and let perjury rest on your souls. I know that you [pointing to one of the jurors] have been approached. Did you spurn the wretch away who made a corrupt proposal to you, or did you hold counsel, sweet counsel with him? I know that you [pointing to another juror] talked over this case with one of the other side at the house on the hill last night, for I overheard the conversation—the promise made to you and your pledge to him. . . . I was there and overheard the foul bargain." At this thrust there was great excitement, and click, click, was heard all through the room, which showed a general cocking of pistols; for every one in those days went armed. I continued: "There is no terror in your pistols, gentlemen; you will not win your case by shooting me; you can win it only in one way—by evidence showing title to the property; you will never win it by bribery or threats of violence. I charge openly attempted bribery, and if what I say be not true, let the jurors speak out now from their seats. Attempted bribery, I say—whether it will be successful bribery, will depend upon what may occur hereafter. If, after invoking the vengeance of Heaven upon their souls should they not render a verdict according to the evidence, the jurors are willing to sell their souls, let them decide against us."

Stephen J. Field, *Personal Reminiscences of Early Days* (1877), p. 100.

3. *The Principles of Natural Law*

JUS NATURÆ ET GENTIUM, A REVIEW

North American Review

IT IS EVIDENT, HOWEVER, that our author does not pretend to have discovered any royal road to legal learning. He manifestly contemplates a long
course of assiduity for his student, and while he would lessen the fatigue, he
would extend the sphere of his acquisitions. He aims chiefly to give his
labors the right direction, and to solve for him the problem, not how to
read the least (which seems to be the more common one), but how he may
compass the most, and with the most understanding, in the shortest time.
Thus he traces indeed each path distinctly, but he carries it far and high
into the recesses of jurisprudence; he disentangles the topography, but he
does not contract the limits of this particular domain of learning; he even
makes excursions into contiguous regions. He has an enlarged conception
of the duties and of the qualifications of the lawyer, and seeks therefore to
extend his views beyond the limits of mere positive and municipal jurisprudence, so as to embrace those original principles in which it has its birth,
and by which it must always be controlled and illustrated. He has accordingly devoted this first volume of his "Legal Outlines," the only one which
has yet appeared, to a consideration of the elements of Natural and Political
Law. He treats of the nature of the being who is the subject of this law; of
his supposed condition before the institutions of civil society, and of the
rights arising in that condition, and independent of civil government; of the
origin of the latter, its true foundation, and its effects upon natural rights;
of the general properties of law, and of the source and sanction of that
universal "law of nature," which is itself the fountain and standard of all
other law; of political, as distinguished from civil law; and of the various
forms of government. . . . As there are many able accountants, who know
nothing of transcendental mathematics, and many skilful workmen equally
ignorant of mechanics; so are there many clever attorneys that drive a good
business, who may marvel to see Mr. Hoffman beginning legal education at
so remote a point as the nature of man. The point is certainly not necessary

---

"Review of Professor Hoffman's *Legal Outlines*," *North American Review* (1830),
XXX, p. 135.

for gaining a suit, nor need we quarrel with those who think it therefore useless. But when the question is about forming able advocates, wise judges, and perspicacious lawgivers, it is plain that this ordinary education will do no longer. When the file affords no precedent; when we are to travel out of the record; when the index presents no case in point; we are obliged to revert to first principles, and spin for ourselves that thread of ingenious deduction, which is not ready made to our hands. It is this kind of legal education that our author contemplates in his different publications, and in the work under review. . . .

It may not, indeed, be very obvious at first sight to a student, why he is detained, for example, in the outset of his studies, with an examination into the unity of the species, and whether this be reconcilable with its variety of color; or into the true origin of political power, whether from divine right, inheritance, prescription, or consent of the governed; or into the actual existence and true meaning of the state of nature; or into the distinction between perfect and imperfect rights; or the extent of the right of extreme necessity, &c. &c. Yet a wrong understanding of some of these points, we doubt not, has had its share in diffusing some of the greatest moral calamities, and exciting some of the most violent political convulsions, which have desolated the race. The history of the slave trade may induce a doubt whether the victims of this tyranny could have been deemed by their oppressors to be of the same rank of being with themselves; nay, we believe it has been justified on a presumed inferiority, of which their color and shape were seriously asserted to be the badge. It will hardly be denied, that the absurd notions which have been upheld, of the origin and sanction of political power, have contributed to the number of unwise and arbitrary kings, and of brutish and servile subjects; while false notions of what is called the state of nature, and of the rights of nature, may have added something to the folly and fury of popular and revolutionary delusions. . . .

How else than by the principles of the natural law, are we to discuss the questions of religious toleration; the obligation of mere positive laws, with the distinction between *mala prohibita* and *mala in se*; the alleged omnipotence of parliament; the rights of extreme necessity (a branch of which has been already alluded to), and of harmless profit; the nullity of *ex post facto* and retroactive laws; the right to pursue fugitives and their abducted property into the territories of other nations, upon the ocean, or into regions where jurisdiction is unknown; the extra-territorial operation of civil laws; the right of capital punishment, and the true theory of punishment in general; the nature and effects of occupancy, whether particular or in gross; the appropriation of the ocean, and the doctrine of *mare clausum aut mare liberum*; the extra-patrimonial nature of certain things, such as air, running waters, &c., and the limitations of the same? How, the legality of usury, independently of positive laws; the right of parents to disinherit their offspring; the perpetuity of the marriage contract; the exclusion of aliens from inheriting or holding lands within the territory of a nation; the like exclusion in the case of personal property, and the validity of the *droit d'aubaine*; the extent of parental power, with the crime of infanticide; the numerous questions of intestacy; questions of insanity, and others in medical jurisprudence; the validity of foreign marriages; the nullity of marriages for incest, natural or civil, with the effect on this contract of prior or supervenient frigidity? How ascertain the right and extent of eminent domain, and the limitations of despotic sovereigns? All these questions of grand consideration can be solved only by a reference to the principles of the *jus naturæ et gentium*, and those also of human physiology and mental philosophy. . . .

A different train of considerations will suggest themselves to those whose views and objects in the law are of a more enlarged kind. The code of natural equity is a body of rules deduced from the constitution and natural condition of man; or it may be considered in another aspect, as that body of rules which is the best adapted to promote his moral happiness. But innumerable accidents give rise to peculiar policies which, however adapted to instant emergencies, may thwart in some degree the true aims of political society; and as these particular policies have also their peculiar principles, as their laws are fashioned to promote their ends, the impress of their institutions is felt long after the causes have passed away to which they owed their birth. The rule remains, though the reason of it has ceased; and the facility is wonderful, and not fully conceived by ourselves, with which we become reconciled to institutions which shock, or ought to shock, the natural justice of the mind. It is thus that the feudal nations established, and transmitted to us, the barbarous right of primogeniture, the ungentle law of baron and feme, the cruelty of escheat and attainder, the iniquitous exemption of lands, in most cases, from liability for debt; the injustice of all which, we forget from habit, or excuse because, forsooth, they have a nice consistency with the general aim of the feudal system. A student rises from the elementary writers of the common law so struck with this general coherence, that he forgets the original barbarousness of the system from which the alleged doctrines are drawn. . . .

It is not within our scope to inquire, how far this system of natural jurisprudence has been revealed in the works of those who have written upon it. It has been objected to them, that they reason concerning laws too abstractly, and without sufficient reference to "the particular circumstances of society to which they meant their conclusions should be applied." Bentham remarks that, "if there are any works of universal jurisprudence, they must be looked for within very narrow limits"; and that writer would have those of the expository kind to be confined wholly to *terminology*, that is, to the explanation of words connected with law, as *power, right, obligation*, &c. in order to be susceptible of a universal application. Stewart's censure of this opinion must be admitted to be sufficiently light, when he says, "He certainly carries this matter too far." Bentham's description of Natural Law is but too just, if we confine it to the manner in which the science has often been treated by writers. He calls it "an obscure phantom, which points sometimes to *manners*, sometimes to *laws*, sometimes to what the law *is*, sometimes to what it *ought to be*." This is eminently true of the treatise *De Jure Belli ac Pacis*. But if the description be designed, remarks Stewart, "for the Law of Nature, as originally understood among ethical writers, it is impossible to assent to it without abandoning all the principles on which the science of morals ultimately rests." While it may be accorded to these two writers, that an abstract code of *laws* is unphilosophical in design as well as useless in execution, the same objections can by no means be made to works professing to treat of the *principles* of legislation. We confess, then, we do not understand why the Scottish philosopher, while he admits the utility of a comparative view of the municipal institutions of various nations, should doubt "whether this can be done with advantage by referring these institutions to that abstract theory called the *Law of Nature*, as to a common standard." He would have "the code of some particular country fixed on as a groundwork for our speculations; and its laws studied, not as consequences of any abstract principles of justice, but in connexion with the circumstances of the people among whom they originated." On the contrary, such works as we have adverted to, examining and embodying such general principles as should pervade all laws, and illustrating them by a comparison with municipal laws, when either they coincided or differed, would, it seems to us, possess very obvious utility. For whether our aim was to determine the reasonableness of particular institutions, or to compare the merit of corresponding laws in different nations, it would be necessary to have some standard of comparison. How else arrive at any conclusion, either as to the reasonableness of an institution, or the respective merits of the laws compared? However philosophical it may be to estimate the policy of laws by reference to the peculiar circumstances of nations, it will hardly be denied that there are some principles quite independent of these, and which must therefore be common to all.

We think it will scarcely be denied that in one branch of jurisprudence, that part of international law we mean, which is commonly called conventional and customary, some such standard is requisite for appeal and correction. Rights have been set up on the ground of these, by the powerful and ambitious, which have been resisted on those broader grounds which are furnished by the law of nature as applied to the transactions of independent communities; and there have been writers who have insisted that the decrees of natural justice, as applied to nations, vary from its injunctions as regards man and man. To estimate aright this opinion, which has been found so convenient to long subsisting usurpation, it is necessary to advert to the distinction between the *necessary* and the *positive* law of nations; the first of which is that general and fundamental standard to which we have so often referred, and which, in the words of Hobbes, can suffer no necessary change; while the latter being, or supposed to be, founded on the first, or not to contradict it at least, must be judged by its correspondence with, or deviation from it. This positive law of nations is of three kinds, the *voluntary*, the *conventional*, and the *customary*; the two last being those compacts which have either been positively established, or have been tacitly admitted, between the nations, and are therefore obligatory only between the parties; while the first, being such general rules as have been found convenient for the welfare and common safety of nations, is on the contrary of universal obligation. Now these conventional and customary parts of public law may, or may not, be repugnant to the necessary; and whatever may have been the practice, the compacts, or the customs of power, they must be judged by a superior law, and resisted, when wrong, by a paramount right. Examples of such usurpations, and of such resistance to them, will suggest themselves to the reader; and in order to measure that resistance, it is necessary to refer to the principles of that universal justice arising out of the constitution of men and states, and serving therefore as a test of the acts of both. Nay, as the voluntary law of nations itself must sometimes tolerate what is inconsistent with the necessary, because the vindication of the latter might interfere with general liberty and reciprocal independence, it cannot be regarded as actually and always immutable. It is a principle, for example, arising out of an obvious policy, that one nation shall not interfere with another in its internal regulations, however unjust; yet perhaps the interposition of the European Powers in behalf of Greece is not in the strictest conformity, in this respect, with the voluntary, however consistent with the necessary law of nations.

It is observed by the distinguished writer whom we have so often quoted, that the alliance established between the law of nature and the conventional law of nations, by the writers on these subjects, had the effect of presenting more enlarged and philosophical views to the minds of speculative statesmen, and led to more liberal doctrines respecting commercial policy, and the other relations of states. . . .

In every country, ancient and modern, positive laws, as we have before remarked, must fall very short of the aims of government, and of distributive and commutative justice. . . .

It is manifest, therefore, that the laws of England and of this country are not to be found in the statute books only, nor in the superadded volumes of judicial reports, nor in Plowden nor Coke; nor would they be found in the most elaborate codes that could be formed. We must still draw from that exhaustless fountain of reason and abstract justice, the code of natural law, much of which is reflected in the pages of Grotius, Wolfius, Puffendorf, Vattel, Bynkershoek, and others. This code, and these authorities, have been often appealed to, and will continue to be, we hope, by British and

American judges; and we have pride in perceiving that some of our American jurists have been warmly praised by their trans-Atlantic brethren, for their exertions to make jurisprudence in this country a science more equitable and philosophical than it has been regarded in England. This they conceive is to be promoted, as Mr. Du Ponceau has declared, by establishing it as a maxim, "that pure ethics and sound logic are also parts of the common law." The parallelism of the Roman code with the natural law has been the boast of its admirers; and it has been the aim of some American jurists, among whom our author is to be numbered, to draw the attention of students to the consideration of that great body of wisdom, less jealousy of which in the common lawyers would have been fortunate for the improvement of the common law.

SUNDAY CLOSING LAWS

David Smith Terry and Stephen J. Field

The concept of natural law, with its undertones of divine law, which is argued in the following case, is characteristic of the thought and rhetoric of the period. It is striking that the subject of judicial division between those perennial antagonists, Terry and Field, should have reached the Supreme Court—and divided it—so recently as Gallagher v. Crown Kosher *in 1962. The selections which follow further illustrate the variety of contexts in which bench and bar resorted to natural-law arguments as conclusive of the issues before them.*

TERRY, C. J.—The petitioner was tried and convicted before a justice of the peace for a violation of the act of April, 1858, entitled "An Act for the better observance of the Sabbath," and, upon his failure to pay the fine imposed, was imprisoned.

The counsel for petitioner moves his discharge, on the ground that the act under which these proceedings were had is in conflict with the first and fourth sections of the first article of the State Constitution, and therefore void.

The first section declares "all men are by nature free and independent, and have certain inalienable rights, among which are those of enjoying and defending life and liberty; acquiring, possessing, and protecting property, and pursuing and obtaining safety and happiness."

Ex Parte Newman, 9 *Calif.* (1858), p. 502.

The fourth section declares "the free exercise and enjoyment of religious profession and worship, without discrimination or preference, shall for ever be allowed in this State."

The questions which arise in the consideration of the case, are:

1. Does the act of the Legislature make a discrimination or preference favorable to one religious profession, or is it a mere civil rule of conduct?

2. Has the Legislature the power to enact a municipal regulation which enforces upon the citizen a compulsory abstinence from his ordinary lawful and peaceable avocations for one day in the week?

There is no expression in the act under consideration which can lead to the conclusion that it was intended as a civil rule, as contradistinguished from a law for the benefit of religion. It is entitled "An Act for the better observance of the Sabbath," and the prohibitions in the body of the act are confined to the "Christian Sabbath."

It is, however, contended, on the authority of some of the decisions of other States, that notwithstanding the pointed language of the act, it may be construed into a civil rule of action, and that the result would be the same, even if the language were essentially different.

The fault of this argument is that it is opposed to the universally admitted rule which requires a law to be construed according to the intention of the law-maker, and this intention to be gathered from the language of the law, according to its plain and common acceptation.

It is contended that a civil rule requiring the devotion of one-seventh of the time to repose is an absolute necessity, and the want of it has been dilated upon as a great evil to society. But have the Legislature so considered it? Such an assumption is not warranted by anything contained in the Sunday law. On the contrary, the intention which pervades the whole act is to enforce, as a *religious institution*, the observance of a day held sacred by the followers of one faith, and entirely disregarded by all the other denominations within the State. The whole scope of the act is expressive of an intention on the part of the Legislature to require a periodical cessation from ordinary pursuits, not as a civil duty, necessary for the repression of any existing evil, but in furtherance of the interests, and in aid of the devotions of those who profess the Christian religion.

Several authorities, affirming the validity of similar statutes, have been cited from the reports of other States. While we entertain a profound respect for the Courts of our sister States, we do not feel called upon to yield our convictions of right to a blind adherence to precedent; especially when they are, in our opinion, opposed to principle; and the reasoning by which they are endeavored to be supported is by no means satisfactory or convincing. . . .

Now, does our Constitution, when it forbids discrimination or preference in religion, mean merely to guaranty toleration? For that, in effect, is all which the cases cited seem to award, as the right of a citizen. In a community composed of persons of various religious denominations, having different days of worship, each considering his own as sacred from secular employment, all being equally considered and protected under the Constitution, a law is passed which in effect recognizes the sacred character of one of these days, by compelling all others to abstain from secular employment, which is precisely one of the modes in which its observance is manifested and required by the creed of that sect to which it belongs as a Sabbath. Is not this a discrimination in favor of the one? Does it require more than an appeal to one's common sense to decide that this is a preference? And when the Jew, or Seventh-Day Christian complains of this, is it any answer to say, your conscience is not constrained, you are not compelled to worship or to perform religious rites on that day, nor forbidden to keep holy the day which you esteem as a Sabbath? We think not, however high the authority which decides otherwise.

When our liberties were acquired, our republican form of government adopted, and our Constitution framed, we deemed that we had attained not only toleration, but religious liberty in its largest sense—a complete separation between Church and State, and a perfect equality without distinction between all religious sects. "Our Government," said Mr. Johnson, in his celebrated Sunday-mail report, "is a civil and not a religious institution; whatever may be the religious sentiments of citizens, and however variant, they are alike entitled to protection from the government, so long as they do not invade the rights of others." And again, dwelling upon the danger of applying the powers of government to the furtherance and support of sectarian objects, he remarks, in language which should not be forgotten, but which ought to be deeply impressed on the minds of all who desire to maintain the supremacy of our republican system: "Extensive religious combinations to effect a political object, were, in the opinion of the committee, always dangerous. The first effort of the kind calls for the establishment of a principle which would lay the foundation for dangerous innovation upon the spirit of the Constitution, and upon the religious rights of the citizen. If admitted, it may be justly apprehended that the future measures of the Government will be strangely marked, if not eventually controlled by the same influence. All religious despotism commences by combination and influence, and when that influence begins to operate upon the political institution of a country, the civil power soon bends under it, and the catastrophe of other nations furnishes an awful warning of the consequences. . . . What other nations call religious toleration, we call religious rights; they were not exercised in virtue of governmental indulgence, but as rights of which the government cannot deprive any portion of her citizens, however small. Despotic power may invade those rights, but justice still confirms them. Let the National Legislature once perform an act which involves the decision of a religious controversy, and it will have passed its legitimate bounds. The precedent will then be established, and the foundation laid for that usurpation of the divine prerogative in this country, which has been the desolating scourge of the fairest portions of the old world. Our Constitution recognizes no other power than that of persuasion for enforcing religious observances."

We come next to the question whether, considering the Sunday law as civil regulation, it is in the power of the Legislature to enforce a compulsory abstinence from lawful and ordinary occupation for a given period of time, without some apparent civil necessity for such action; whether a pursuit, which is not only peaceable and lawful, but also praiseworthy and commendable, for six days in the week, can be arbitrarily converted into a penal offence or misdemeanor on the seventh. As a general rule, it will be admitted that men have a natural right to do anything which their inclinations may suggest, if it be not evil in itself, and in no way impairs the rights of others. When societies are formed, each individual surrenders certain rights, and as an equivalent for that surrender has secured to him the enjoyment of certain others appertaining to his person and property, without the protection of which society cannot exist. All legislation is a restraint on individuals, but it is a restraint which must be submitted to by all who would enjoy the benefits derived from the institutions of society.

It is necessary, for the preservation of free institutions, that there should be some general and easily recognized rule, to determine the extent of governmental power, and establish a proper line of demarkation between such as are strictly legitimate and such as are usurpations which invade the reserved rights of the citizen and infringe upon his constitutional liberty. The true rule of distinction would seem to be that which allows to the Legislature the right so to restrain each one, in his freedom of conduct, as to secure perfect protection to all others from every species of danger to person, health, and property; that each individual shall be required so to use his own as not to inflict injury upon his neighbor, and these, we think, are all the immunities which can be justly claimed by one portion of society from another, under a government of constitutional limitation. For these reasons, the law restrains the establishment of tanneries, slaughter-houses, gunpowder depots, the discharge of fire-arms, etc., in a city, the sale of drugs and poisons, and the practice of physic by incompetent persons, and makes a variety of other prohibitions, the reason and sense of which are obvious to the most common understanding.

Now, when we come to inquire what reason can be given for the claim of power to enact a Sunday law, we are told, looking at it in its purely civil aspect, that it is absolutely necessary for the benefit of his health and the restoration of his powers, and in aid of this great social necessity, the Legislature may, for the general convenience, set apart a particular day of rest, and require its observance by all.

This argument is founded on the assumption that mankind are in the habit of working too much, and thereby entailing evil upon society, and that without compulsion they will not seek the necessary repose which their exhausted natures demand. This is to us a new theory, and is contradicted by the history of the past and the observations of the present. We have heard, in all ages, of declamations and reproaches against the vice of indolence, but we have yet to learn that there has ever been any general complaint of an intemperate, vicious, unhealthy or morbid industry. On the contrary, we know that mankind seek cessation from toil from the natural influences of self-preservation, in the same manner and as certainly as they seek slumber, relief from pain, or food to appease their hunger.

Again, it may be well considered, that the amount of rest which would be required by one-half of society may be widely disproportionate to that required by the other. It is a matter of which each individual must be permitted to judge for himself, according to his own instincts and necessities. As well might the Legislature fix the days and hours for work, and enforce their observance by an unbending rule which shall be visited alike upon the weak and strong. Whenever such attempts are made, the law-making power leaves its legitimate sphere, and makes an incursion into the realms of physiology, and its enactments, like the sumptuary laws of the ancients, which prescribe the mode and texture of people's clothing, or similar laws which might prescribe and limit our food and drink, must be regarded as an invasion, without reason or necessity, of the natural rights of the citizen, which are guarantied by the fundamental law.

The truth is, however much it may be disguised, that this one day of rest is a purely religious idea. Derived from the Sabbatical institutions of the ancient Hebrew, it has been adopted into all the creeds of succeeding religious sects throughout the civilized world; and whether it be the Friday of the Mohammedan, the Saturday of the Israelite, or the Sunday of the Christian, it is alike fixed in the affections of its followers, beyond the power of eradication, and in most of the States of our Confederacy, the aid of the law to enforce its observance has been given, under the pretence of a civil, municipal, or police regulation.

But it has been argued that this is a question exclusively for the Legislature; that the law-making power alone has the right to judge of the necessity and character of all police rules, and that there is no power in the judiciary to interfere with the exercise of this right.

One of the objects for which the judicial department is established is the protection of the constitutional rights of the citizen. The question presented in this case is not merely one of expediency or abuse of power; it is a question of usurpation of power. If the Legislature have the authority to appoint a time of compulsory rest, we would have no right to interfere with it, even if they required a cessation from toil for six days in the week instead of one. If they possess this power, it is without limit, and may extend to the prohibition of all occupations at all times.

While we concede to the Legislature all the supremacy to which it is entitled, we can not yield to it the omnipotence which has been ascribed to the British Parliament, so long as we have a Constitution which limits its powers, and places certain innate rights of the citizen beyond its control. . . .

It is the settled doctrine of this Court to enforce every provision of the Constitution in favor of the rights reserved to the citizen against a usurpation of power in any question whatsoever, and although in a doubtful case, we would yield to the authority of the Legislature, yet upon the question before us, we are constrained to declare that, in our opinion, the act in question is in conflict with the first section of article first of the Constitution, because, without necessity, it infringes upon the liberty of the citizen, by restraining his right to acquire property.

And that it is in conflict with the fourth section of the same article, because it was intended as, and is in effect, a discrimination in favor of one religious profession, and gives it a preference over all others.

It follows that the petitioner was improperly convicted, and it is ordered that he be discharged from custody. . . .

FIELD, J.—After a careful and repeated perusal of the opinions of my associates, I am unable to concur either in their reasoning or in their judgment. I can not perceive any valid ground for declaring the Act of 1858, for the better observance of the Sabbath, unconstitutional. In ordinary cases, I should be content with refraining from a concurrence, or expressing a simple dissent, but, in the present case, I feel compelled to state the reasons of my dissent, as the opinions of my associates appear to me to assert a power in the judiciary never contemplated by the Constitution, and of dangerous consequences; and to adopt a construction of constitutional provisions, which must deprive the Legislature of all control over a great variety of subjects, upon which its right to legislate, in the promotion of the public weal, has never been doubted.

The enactment in question is held to conflict with the first and fourth sections of the first article of the Constitution. . . . The petitioner is an Israelite, engaged in the sale of clothing, and his complaint is, not that his religious profession or worship is interfered with, but that he is not permitted to dispose of his goods on Sunday; not that any religious observance is imposed upon him, but that his secular business is closed on a day on which he does not think proper to rest. In other words, the law, as a civil regulation, by the generality of its provisions, interrupts his acquisitions on a day which does not suit him. The law treats of business matters, not religious duties. In fixing a day of rest, it establishes only a rule of civil conduct. In limiting its command to secular pursuits, it necessarily leaves religious profession and worship free. It is absurd to say that the sale of clothing, or other goods, on Sunday, is an act of religion or worship; and it follows that the inhibition of such sale does not interfere with either. . . .

As to the forms in which that profession or worship shall be exhibited, the law is silent; it utters no command, and it imposes no restraint. It makes no discrimination or preference. . . . *It does not even allude to the subject of religious profession or worship, in any of its provisions.* It establishes, as a civil regulation, a day of rest from secular pursuits, and that is its only scope and purpose. Its requirement is a cessation from labor. In its enactment, the Legislature has given the sanction of law to a rule of conduct, which the entire civilized world recognizes as essential to the physical and moral well-being of society. Upon no subject is there such a concurrence of opinion, among philosophers, moralists, and statesmen of all nations, as on the necessity of periodical cessations from labor. One day in seven is the rule, founded in experience, and sustained by science. There is no nation, possessing any degree of civilization, where the rule is not observed, either from the sanctions of the law, or the sanctions of religion. This fact has not escaped the observation of men of science, and distinguished philosophers have not hesitated to pronounce the rule founded upon a law of our race.

The Legislature possesses the undoubted right to pass laws for the preservation of health and the promotion of good morals, and if it is of opinion that periodical cessation from labor will tend to both, and thinks proper to carry its opinion into a statutory enactment on the subject, there is no power, outside of its constituents, which can sit in judgment upon its action. It is not for the judiciary to assume a wisdom which it denies to the Legislature, and exercise a supervision over the discretion of the latter. It is not the province of the judiciary to pass upon the wisdom and policy of legislation; and when it does so, it usurps a power never conferred by the Constitution.

It is no answer to the requirements of the statute to say that mankind will seek cessation from labor by the natural influences of self-preservation. The position assumes that all men are independent, and at liberty to work whenever they choose. Whether this be true or not in theory, it is false in fact; it is contradicted by every day's experience. The relations of superior and subordinate, master and servant, principal and clerk, always have and always will exist. Labor is in a great degree dependent upon capital, and unless the exercise of the power which capital affords is restrained, those who are obliged to labor will not possess the freedom for rest which they would otherwise exercise. The necessities for food and raiment are imperious, and the exactions of avarice are not easily satisfied. It is idle to talk of a man's freedom to rest when his wife and children are looking to his daily labor for their daily support. The law steps in to restrain the power of capital. Its object is not to protect those who can rest at their pleasure, but to afford rest to those who need it, and who, from the conditions of society, could not otherwise obtain it. Its aim is to prevent the physical and moral debility which springs from uninterrupted labor; and in this aspect it is a beneficent and merciful law. It gives one day to the poor and dependent; from the enjoyment of which no capital or power is permitted to deprive them. It is theirs for repose, for social intercourse, for moral culture, and, if they choose, for divine worship. Authority for the enactment I find in the great object of all government, which is protection. Labor is a necessity imposed by the condition of our race, and to protect labor is the highest office of our laws.

But [it] is urged that the intention of the law is to enforce the Sabbath as a religious institution. This position is assumed from the description of the day and the title of the act, but is not warranted by either. The terms "Christian Sabbath or Sunday," are used simply to designate the day selected by the Legislature. . . . The power of selection being in the Legislature, there is no valid reason why Sunday should not be designated as well as any other day. Probably no day in the week could be taken which would not be subject to some objection. That the law operates with inconvenience to some is no argument against its constitutionality. Such inconvenience is an incident to all general laws. A civil regulation can not be converted into a religious institution because it is enforced on a day which a particular religious sect regards as sacred. The Legislature has seen fit, in different enactments, to prohibit judicial and various kinds of official business on Sunday, and yet it has never been contended that these enactments establish any religious observances, or that the compulsory abstinence from judicial or official labor is a discrimination or preference in favor of any religious sect. . . . The prohibition of secular business on Sunday is advocated on the ground that by it the general welfare is advanced, labor protected, and the moral and physical well-being of society promoted. The Legislature has so considered it, and the judiciary can not say that the Legislature was mistaken, and, therefore, the act is unconstitutional, without passing out of its legitimate sphere, and assuming a right to supervise the exercise of legislative discretion in matters of mere expediency. Such right, as I have already observed, does not belong to the judiciary. Its assumption would be usurpation, and well calculated to lessen the just influence which the judiciary should possess in a constitutional government.

"Questions of policy and State necessity," says Sedgwick, "are not to be assigned to the domain of the Courts; and I can not but think it unfortunate for the real influence of the judiciary that this authority has ever been claimed for them." (Interp. of Statutory and Cons. Law, 182.)

"We can not declare," says Mr. Justice Baldwin of the Supreme Court of the United States, "a legislative act void, because it conflicts with our opinions of policy, expediency, or justice. We are not the guardians of the rights of the people of the State, unless they are secured by some constitutional provision which comes within our judicial cognizance. The remedy for unwise or oppressive legislation, within constitutional bounds, is by appeal to the justice and patriotism of the representatives of the people. If this fail, the people in their sovereign capacity can correct the evil, but Courts can not assume their rights." (Bennett v. Boggs, 1 Bald., 74.)

I am of opinion that the "Act for the better observance of the Sabbath," is constitutional, and that the petitioner ought to be remanded.

THE RHYTHMS OF NATURAL LAW

An End to Private Property

DANIEL WEBSTER

IF AT THIS PERIOD there is not a general restraint of legislatures, in favor of private rights, there is an end to private property. Though there may be no prohibition in the constitution, the legislature is restrained from committing flagrant acts, from acts subverting the great principles of republican liberty, and of the social compact.

The Inherent Rights of Man

J. GOLDTHWAITE

BY THIS IT APPEARS, not only that the rights asserted in this instrument, are reserved out of the general powers of government, but also that this enumeration shall not disparage others not enumerated; and that any act of the legislature which violates any of these great principles of civil liberty, or inherent rights of man, though not enumerated, shall be void.

Implicit Restraints

J. HOSMER

IT IS UNIVERSALLY ADMITTED, and unsusceptible of dispute, that there may be retrospective laws impairing vested rights, which are unjust, neither according with sound legislation, nor the fundamental principles of the social compact. If, for example, the legislature should enact a law, without any assignable reason, taking from A. his estate, and giving it to B., the injustice would be flagrant, and the act would produce a sensation of universal insecurity. . . . With those judges, who assert the omnipotence of the legislature, in all cases, where the constitution has not interposed an explicit restraint, I cannot agree. Should there exist, what I know is not only an incredible supposition, but a most remote improbability, a

Wilkinson v. Leland, 2 *Peters* (1829), pp. 627, 646.
In Re Dorsey, 7 *Porter's Reports (Ala.)* (1838), pp. 293, 378.
Goshin v. Stonington, 4 *Conn.* (1822), pp. 209, 221, 225.

case of the direct infraction of vested rights, too palpable to be questioned, and, too unjust to admit of vindication, I could not avoid considering it as a violation of the social compact, and within the control of the judiciary.

The Legislature and Property Rights

WYNEHAMER V. NEW YORK

No DOUBT, it seems to me, can be admitted of the meaning of these provisions. To say, as has been suggested, that "the law of the land," or "due process of law," may mean the very act of legislation which deprives the citizen of his rights, privileges or property, leads to a simple absurdity. The constitution would then mean, that no person shall be deprived of his property or rights, unless the legislature shall pass a law to effectuate the wrong, and this would be throwing the restraint entirely away. The true interpretation of these constitutional phrases is, that where rights are acquired by the citizen under the existing law, there is no power in any branch of the government to take them away; but where they are held contrary to the existing law, or are forfeited by its violation, then they may be taken from him—not by an act of the legislature, but in the due administration of the law itself, before the judicial tribunals of the state. The cause or occasion for depriving the citizen of his supposed rights must be found in the law as it is, or, at least it cannot be *created* by a legislative act which aims at their destruction. Where rights of property are admitted to exist, the legislature cannot say they shall exist no longer; nor will it make any difference, although a process and a tribunal are appointed to execute the sentence.

Mischiefs of an *Ex Post Facto* Law

JAMES KENT

A RETROACTIVE STATUTE would partake in its character of the mischiefs of an *ex post facto* law, as to all cases of crimes and penalties; and in every other case relating to contracts or property, it would be against every sound principle. It would come within the reach of the doctrine, that a statute is not to have a retrospective effect; and which doctrine was very much discussed in the case of *Dash* v. *Vankleeck*, and shown to be

---

13 *N.Y.* (1856), pp. 378, 392, 393.
James Kent, *Commentaries on American Law*, I (1826), p. 426.

founded, not only in English law, but on the principles of general jurisprudence.

The Dictates of Reason

J. PECK

BUT CERTAIN LIMITS to the exercise of legislative power have been recognized from the earliest times. It is a principle of the English common law,
as old as the law itself, that a statute, even of the omnipotent Parliament
of Great Britain, is not to have retrospective effect. Why was it so considered by the English courts? They had no written constitution, with express restrictions upon the legislative power. It was so considered because
there are eternal principles of justice which no government has a
right to disregard. It does not follow, therefore, because there may be no
restriction in the constitution prohibiting a particular act of the legislature,
that such act is therefore constitutional. Some acts, although not expressly
forbidden, may be against the plain and obvious dictates of reason. The
common law, says Lord Coke, (8 Co. 118a) adjudgeth a statute so far
void.

A Fundamental Principle

STUYVESANT V. THE MAYOR

[IT IS] . . . a fundamental principle of civilized society, that private property shall not be taken even for public use without just compensation.

No Odious Exceptions

VAN ZANT V. WADDEL

THE IDEA OF A PEOPLE through their respresentatives making laws whereby
are swept away the life, liberty and property of *one* or a *few* citizens, by
which neither the representatives nor their other constituents are willing to

---

Bank *v.* Cooper, 2 *Yerg. (Tenn.)* (1831), pp. 599, 603.
7 *Cow.* (1827), pp. 585, 606.
2 *Yerg. (Tenn.)* (1829), pp. 260, 270.

be bound, is too odious to be tolerated in any government where freedom has a name. Such abuses resulted in the adoption of Magna Charta in England, securing the subject against odious exceptions, which is, and for centuries has been, the foundation of English liberty.

A Natural Right of Universal Obligation

BORDEN V. STATE

BUT NOTICE OF THE CONTROVERSY is necessary in order to become a party. And it is a principle of natural justice, of universal obligation that, before the rights of an individual be bound by a judicial sentence, he shall have notice either actual or implied of the proceedings against him. In face of these authorities, embracing the opinions of the most distinguished and profound jurists in the highest English and American courts, including their latest published opinions, can it be said that this right to be heard in defence of property is not a "natural right of universal obligation"?

No Arbitrary Legislation

WHITE V. WHITE

I MAINTAIN, THEREFORE, that the security of the citizen against such arbitrary legislation rests upon the broader and more solid ground of natural rights, and is not wholly dependent upon these negatives upon the legislative power contained in the constitution. It can never be admitted as a just attribute of sovereignty in a government, to take the property of one citizen and bestow it upon another. The exercise of such a power is incompatible with the nature and object of all government, and is destructive of the great end and aim for which government is instituted, and is subversive of the fundamental principles upon which all free governments are organized. This was a power repudiated by the Romans during the whole reign of imperial despotism, and has ever been a maxim of the civil law. And the right of the subject against the exercise of such arbitrary power was asserted in England as one of the sovereign rights of the citizen, and forms a part of the 29th chapter of Magna Charta.

11 *Arkansas* (1851), pp. 519, 558.
5 *Barb. (N.Y.)* (1849), p. 484.

LAW AND THE AMERICAN CONSCIOUSNESS

The man of letters—novelist, philosopher, social critic—tends to express his sense of truth and justice in abstract, metaphysical terms. To the usual gallery of ideal conceptions the early American writers added yet another: Natural Law. This, rather than the Common Law, was used as the standard against which they measured the mores of the country, the standard to which they referred when criticizing the tendency of their society toward materialism and opportunism.

Walt Whitman, disciple of American democracy and nineteenth-century liberalism, looked upon the law as an instrument for the protection of the rights of man, as an aid in the advancement of individualism, and as a weapon against privilege. His attitude toward the law is summed up in his vigorous opposition in 1854 to an act of the Brooklyn City Council prohibiting the operation of public transportation or the opening of restaurants on Sunday. The Council had in this way hoped to enforce observation of the Sabbath; Whitman denounced the ruling as a violation of man's individual rights, the most sacred possession to be defended (not usurped) by his elected representatives.

Whitman became disillusioned during and after the Civil War, but unlike Thoreau he did not pack up his philosophy and retreat from society. In Democratic Vistas, *despite a bitter indictment of the society of the Grant era, Whitman urged young men to enter politics and to restore the government and the law to their rightful roles in the advancement of individual democracy.*

Man Must Become a Law

WALT WHITMAN

THE PURPOSE OF DEMOCRACY—supplanting old belief in the necessary absoluteness of establish'd dynastic rulership, temporal, ecclesiastical, and scholastic, as furnishing the only security against chaos, crime and ignorance—is, through many transmigrations and amid endless ridicules, arguments, and ostensible failures, to illustrate, at all hazards, this doctrine or theory that man, properly train'd in sanest, highest freedom, may and must become a law, and series of laws, unto himself, surrounding and providing for, not only his own personal control, but all his relations to other individuals, and to the State; and that, while other theories, as in the past histories of nations, have proved wise enough, and indispensable

Walt Whitman, *Democratic Vistas* (1871), p. 17.

perhaps for their conditions, *this*, as matters now stand in our civilized world, is the only scheme worth working from, as warranting results like those of Nature's laws, reliable, when once establish'd to carry on themselves.

Fast-Fish and Loose-Fish

HERMAN MELVILLE

BUT THOUGH NO OTHER NATION has ever had any written whaling law, yet the American fishermen have been their own legislators and lawyers in this matter. They have provided a system which for terse comprehensiveness surpasses Justinian's Pandects and the By-laws of the Chinese Society for the Suppression of Meddling with other People's Business. Yes; these laws might be engraven on a Queen Anne's farthing, or the barb of a harpoon, and worn round the neck, so small are they.

I. A Fast-Fish belongs to the party fast to it.

II. A Loose-Fish is fair game for anybody who can soonest catch it.

But what plays the mischief with this masterly code is the admirable brevity of it, which necessitates a vast volume of commentaries to expound it.

First: What is a Fast-Fish? Alive or dead a fish is technically fast, when it is connected with an occupied ship or boat, by any medium at all controllable by the occupant or occupants,—a mast, an oar, a nine-inch cable, a telegraph wire, or a strand of cobweb, it is all the same. Likewise a fish is technically fast when it bears a waif, or any other recognized symbol of possession; so long as the party waifing it plainly evince their ability at any time to take it alongside, as well as their intention so to do.

These are scientific commentaries; but the commentaries of the whalemen themselves sometimes consist in hard words and harder knocks —the Coke-upon-Littleton of the fist. True, among the more upright and honourable whalemen allowances are always made for peculiar cases, where it would be an outrageous moral injustice for one party to claim possession of a whale previously chased or killed by another party. But others are by no means so scrupulous.

Some fifty years ago there was a curious case of whale-trover litigated in England, wherein the plaintiffs set forth that after a hard chase of a whale in the Northern seas; and when indeed they (the plaintiffs) had succeeded in harpooning the fish; they were at last, through peril of their lives, obliged to forsake not only their lines, but their boat itself. Ultimately

Herman Melville, *Moby Dick* (1851), p. 365.

the defendants (the crew of another ship) came up with the whale, struck, killed, seized, and finally appropriated it before the very eyes of the plaintiffs. And when those defendants were remonstrated with, their captain snapped his fingers in the plaintiffs' teeth, and assured them that by way of doxology to the deed he had done, he would now retain their line, harpoons, and boat, which had remained attached to the whale at the time of the seizure. Wherefore the plaintiffs now sued for the recovery of the value of their whale, line, harpoons, and boat.

Mr. Erskine was counsel for the defendants; Lord Ellenborough was the judge. In the course of the defence, the witty Erskine went on to illustrate his position, by alluding to a recent crim. con. case, wherein a gentleman, after in vain trying to bridle his wife's viciousness, had at last abandoned her upon the seas of life; but in the course of years, re- penting of that step, he instituted an action to recover possession of her. Erskine was on the other side; and he then supported it by saying, that though the gentleman had originally harpooned the lady, and had once had her fast, and only by reason of the great stress of her plunging viciousness, had at last abandoned her; yet abandon her he did, so that she became a loose-fish; and therefore when a subsequent gentleman re-harpooned her, the lady then became that subsequent gentleman's property, along with whatever harpoon might have been found sticking in her.

Now in the present case Erskine contended that the examples of the whale and the lady were reciprocally illustrative to each other.

These pleadings, and the counter pleadings, being duly heard, the very learned judge in set terms decided, to wit,—That as for the boat, he awarded it to the plaintiffs, because they had merely abandoned it to save their lives; but that with regard to the controverted whale, harpoons, and line, they belonged to the defendants; the whale, because it was a Loose-Fish at the time of the final capture; and the harpoons and line because when the fish made off with them, it (the fish) acquired a prop- erty in those articles; and hence anybody who afterwards took the fish had a right to them. Now the [defendants] afterwards took the fish; ergo, the aforesaid articles were theirs.

A common man looking at this decision of the very learned Judge, might possibly object to it. But ploughed up to the primary rock of the matter, the two great principles laid down in the twin whaling laws previously quoted, and applied and elucidated by Lord Ellenborough in the above cited case; these two laws touching Fast-Fish and Loose-Fish, I say, will on reflection, be found the fundamentals of all human juris- prudence; for notwithstanding its complicated tracery of sculpture, the Temple of the Law, like the Temple of the Philistines, has but two props to stand on.

Is it not a saying in every one's mouth, Possession is half of the law: that is, regardless of how the thing came into possession? But often possession is the whole of the law. What are the sinews and souls of Russian serfs and Republican slaves but Fast-Fish, whereof possession is the whole of the law? What to the rapacious landlord is the widow's last mite but a Fast-Fish? What is yonder undetected villain's marble mansion with a door-plate for a waif; what is that but a Fast-Fish? What is the ruinous discount which Mordecai, the broker, gets from poor Woebegone, the bankrupt, on a loan to keep Woebegone's family from starvation; what is that ruinous discount but a Fast-Fish? What is the Archbishop of Savesoul's income of £100,000 seized from the scant bread and cheese of hundreds of thousands of broken-backed laborers (all sure of heaven without any of Savesoul's help) what is that globular 100,000 but a Fast-Fish? What are the Duke of Dunder's hereditary towns and hamlets but Fast-Fish? What to that redoubted harpooneer, John Bull, is poor Ireland, but a Fast-Fish? What to that apostolic lancer, Brother Jonathan, is Texas but a Fast-Fish? And concerning all these, is not Possession the whole of the law?

But if the doctrine of Fast-Fish be pretty generally applicable, the kindred doctrine of Loose-Fish is still more widely so. That is internationally and universally applicable.

What was America in 1492 but a Loose-Fish, in which Columbus struck the Spanish standard by way of waifing it for his royal master and mistress? What was Poland to the Czar? What Greece to the Turk? What India to England? What at last will Mexico be to the United States? All Loose-Fish.

What are the Rights of Man and the Liberties of the World but Loose-Fish? What all men's minds and opinions but Loose-Fish? What is the principle of religious belief in them but a Loose-Fish? What to the ostentatious smuggling verbalists are the thoughts of thinkers but Loose-Fish? What is the great globe itself but a Loose-Fish? And what are you, reader, but a Loose-Fish and a Fast-Fish, too?

Unjust Laws

HENRY DAVID THOREAU

UNJUST LAWS EXIST: shall we be content to obey them, or shall we endeavor to amend them, and obey them until we have succeeded, or shall we transgress them at once? Men generally, under such a government as this, think that they ought to wait until they have persuaded the

---

Henry David Thoreau, *Civil Disobedience* (1849), pp. 144, 164.

majority to alter them. They think that, if they should resist, the remedy would be worse than the evil. But it is the fault of the government itself that the remedy *is* worse than the evil. *It* makes it worse. Why is it not more apt to anticipate and provide for reform? Why does it not cherish its wise minority? Why does it cry and resist before it is hurt? Why does it not encourage its citizens to be on the alert to point out its faults, and *do* better than it would have them? Why does it always crucify Christ, and excommunicate Copernicus and Luther, and pronounce Washington and Franklin rebels?

One would think, that a deliberate and practical denial of its authority was the only offense never contemplated by government; else, why has it not assigned its definite, its suitable and proportionate penalty? If a man who has no property refuses but once to earn nine shillings for the state, he is put in prison for a period unlimited by any law that I know, and determined only by the discretion of those who placed him there; but if he should steal ninety times nine shillings from the state, he is soon permitted to go at large again.

If the injustice is part of the necessary friction of the machine of government, let it go, let it go: perchance it will wear smooth,—certainly the machine will wear out. If the injustice has a spring, or a pulley, or a rope, or a crank, exclusively for itself, then perhaps you may consider whether the remedy will not be worse than the evil; but if it is of such a nature that it requires you to be the agent of injustice to another, then, I say, break the law. Let your life be a counter friction to stop the machine. What I have to do is to see, at any rate, that I do not lend myself to the wrong which I condemn.

As for adopting the ways which the state has provided for remedying the evil, I know not of such ways. They take too much time, and a man's life will be gone. I have other affairs to attend to. I came into this world, not chiefly to make this a good place to live in, but to live in it, be it good or bad. A man has not everything to do, but something; and because he cannot do *everything*, it is not necessary that he should do *something* wrong. It is not my business to be petitioning the Governor or the Legislature any more than it is theirs to petition me; and if they should not hear my petition, what should I do then? But in this case the state has provided no way: its very Constitution is the evil. This may seem to be harsh and stubborn and unconciliatory; but it is to treat with the utmost kindness and consideration the only spirit that can appreciate or deserves it. So is all change for the better, like birth and death, which convulse the body.

I do not hesitate to say, that those who call themselves Abolitionists should at once effectually withdraw their support, both in person and property, from the government of Massachusetts, and not wait till they constitute a majority of one, before they suffer the right to prevail through them. I think that it is enough if they have God on their side, without waiting for that other one. Moreover, any man more right than his neighbors constitutes a majority of one already.

I meet this American government, or its representative, the state government, directly, and face to face, once a year—no more—in the person of its tax-gatherer; this is the only mode in which a man situated as I am necessarily meets it; and it then says distinctly, Recognize me, and the simplest, the most effectual, and, in the present posture of affairs, the indispensablest mode of treating with it on this head, of expressing your little satisfaction with and love for it, is to deny it then. My civil neighbor, the tax-gatherer, is the very man I have to deal with,—for it is, after all, with men and not with parchment that I quarrel,—and he has voluntarily chosen to be an agent of the government. How shall he ever know well what he is and does as an officer of the government, or as a man, until he is obliged to consider whether he shall treat me, his neighbor, for whom he has respect, as a neighbor and well-disposed man, or as a maniac and disturber of the peace, and see if he can get over this obstruction to his neighborliness without a ruder and more impetuous thought or speech corresponding with his action. I know this well, that if one thousand, if one hundred, if ten men whom I could name,—if ten *honest* men only,— ay, if *one* HONEST man, in this State of Massachusetts, *ceasing to hold slaves*, were actually to withdraw from this copartnership, and be locked up in the county jail therefor, it would be the abolition of slavery in America. For it matters not how small the beginning may seem to be: what is once well done is done forever. But we love better to talk about it: that we say is our mission. Reform keeps many scores of newspapers in its service, but not one man. If my esteemed neighbor, the State's ambassador, who will devote his days to the settlement of the question of human rights in the Council Chamber, instead of being threatened with the prisons of Carolina, were to sit down the prisoner of Massachusetts, that State which is so anxious to foist the sin of slavery upon her sister,— though at present she can discover only an act of inhospitality to be the ground of a quarrel with her,—the Legislature would not wholly waive the subject the following winter.

Under a government which imprisons any unjustly, the true place for a just man is also a prison. The proper place to-day, the only place which Massachusetts has provided for her freer and less desponding spirits, is in her prisons, to be put out and locked out of the State by her own act, as they have already put themselves out by their principles. It is there that the fugitive slave, and the Mexican prisoner on parole, and the Indian come to plead the wrongs of his race should find them; on that separate, but more free and honorable ground, where the State places those who are not *with* her, but *against* her,—the only house in a slave State in which a free man can abide with honor. . . .

Webster never goes behind government, and so cannot speak with authority about it. His words are wisdom to those legislators who contemplate no essential reform in the existing government; but for thinkers, and those who legislate for all time, he never once glances at the subject. I know of those whose serene and wise speculations on this theme would soon reveal the limits of his mind's range and hospitality. Yet, compared with the cheap professions of most reformers, and the still cheaper wisdom and eloquence of politicians in general, his are almost the only sensible and valuable words, and we thank Heaven for him. Comparatively, he is always strong, original, and, above all, practical. Still, his quality is not wisdom, but prudence. The lawyer's truth is not Truth, but consistency or a consistent expediency. Truth is always in harmony with herself, and is not concerned chiefly to reveal the justice that may consist with wrong-doing. He well deserves to be called, as he has been called, the Defender of the Constitution. There are really no blows to be given by him but defensive ones. He is not a leader, but a follower. His leaders are the men of '87. "I have never made an effort," he says, "and never propose to make an effort; I have never countenanced an effort, and never mean to countenance an effort, to disturb the arrangement as originally made, by which the various States came into the Union." Still thinking of the sanction which the Constitution gives to slavery, he says, "Because it was a part of the original compact,—let it stand." Notwithstanding his special acuteness and ability, he is unable to take a fact out of its merely political relations, and behold it as it lies absolutely to be disposed of by the intellect,— what, for instance, it behooves a man to do here in America to-day with regard to slavery,—but ventures, or is driven, to make some such desperate answer as the following, while professing to speak, absolutely, and as a private man,—from which what new and singular code of social duties might be inferred? "The manner," says he, "in which the governments of those States where slavery exists are to regulate it is for their own consideration, under their responsibility to their constituents, to the general laws of propriety, humanity, and justice, and to God. Associations formed elsewhere, springing from a feeling of humanity, or any other cause, have nothing whatever to do with it. They have never received any encouragement from me, and they never will."

They who know of no purer sources of truth, who have traced up its stream no higher, stand, and wisely stand, by the Bible and the Constitution, and drink at it there with reverence and humility; but they who behold where it comes trickling into this lake or that pool, gird up their loins once more, and continue their pilgrimage toward its fountain-head. . . .

The authority of government, even such as I am willing to submit to,—for I will cheerfully obey those who know and can do better than I, and in many things even those who neither know nor can do so well,— is still an impure one: to be strictly just, it must have the sanction and consent of the governed. It can have no pure right over my person and property but what I concede to it. The progress from an absolute to a limited monarchy, from a limited monarchy to a democracy, is a progress toward a true respect for the individual. Even the Chinese philosopher was wise enough to regard the individual as the basis of the empire. Is a democracy, such as we know it, the last improvement possible in government? Is it not possible to take a step further towards recognizing and organizing the rights of man? There will never be a really free and enlightened State until the State comes to recognize the individual as a higher and independent power, from which all its own power and authority are derived, and treats him accordingly. I please myself with imagining a State at last which can afford to be just to all men, and to treat the individual with respect as a neighbor; which even would not think it inconsistent with its own repose if a few were to live aloof from it, not meddling with it, nor embraced by it, who fulfilled all the duties of neighbors and fellowmen. A State which bore this kind of fruit, and suffered it to drop off as fast as it ripened, would prepare the way for a still more perfect and glorious State, which also I have imagined, but not yet anywhere seen.

4. *The Laboratory of the States: American Experimentalism*

NO LONGER PUPILS OF THE ENGLISH

American Jurist

THERE IS NO COUNTRY in which some medium of legal communication and intelligence between the different parts is more necessary than in the United States, since the frequent migrations and active commerce among the different states, and the consequent intermixture of the interests and affairs of the subjects of distinct jurisdictions, make it important, and indeed necessary, that the members of the profession in one state should have some knowledge of the legislation and legal administration in the others, and much of this knowledge can be most conveniently and economically obtained through a periodical journal.

Such a work may be no less useful and important as affording the means of information wanted by every practising lawyer and liberal student, respecting the legal proceedings and publications of foreign countries. Until very recently, a great part of our law, as well as our law books, were made in England; we followed the decisions of the English courts with a deference little short of servility, insomuch that our courts have, in some instances, felt themselves to be so strictly bound by their authority, as to reject very cogent and conclusive arguments against them, continuing to decide upon the old doctrine even after it had, in fact, been overruled and exploded by the English courts; until afterwards, by the subsequent publication of their reports, our judges felt themselves at liberty to decide in conformity to the demonstrated law of the case, without deeming it a violation of the respect due to those foreign tribunals, or apprehending the reproach of dangerous innovation. The maxim was, and indeed is, that the courts must administer the law as they find it; not make it; and as many doctrines of the law are the logical deductions from principles acknowledged both in England and this country, the practical application of the maxim was, that our courts were as much bound by the logic of the English judges, as by the principles of the common law. The means afforded us by a community of language to resort directly to the richly-stored repositories of English law, are, no doubt, of immense advantage, and will always continue to be so; but the time for implicitly adopting the English books, and servilely following the English administration of the law, is fast passing by; and the period of our pupilage is almost expired. "I do not like," says an eminent American jurist in a private letter now before us, "this everlasting copying of British publications, this everlasting waiting for the word of the fugelman beyond sea"; and he expresses what we believe to be the universal sentiment of the profession. If the time is not already arrived, it is very near, when the British jurists, ceasing to be our masters and oracles, will only be our fellow-laborers in the common field of legal science; and the more we cease to adopt implicitly, and in the gross, their books and their law, the greater will be the necessity and utility of a work, one of the objects of which may be to direct the attention of the profession to such parts of the legal literature of Great Britain, as well as of the nations of the continent, as shall shed the most light upon our own system.

LABORS LIGHTENED BY PREDECESSORS

Law Commissioners' Report

IN THE OUTSET OF OUR LABORS we considered the very important question whether it would be advantageous to abolish the court of chancery, and the different forms of actions, and provide that all litigation, whether of a legal or equitable nature, should be conducted according to the same forms of procedure. After a careful inquiry into the practical operations of the New York code, where that plan has been adopted, by sweeping away the whole of their old system, and introducing an entire new code of great length, we were entirely satisfied that it would be extremely unwise to follow their example; we feel fully persuaded that by so doing, instead of "rendering the administration of justice more simple, speedy and economical," we would vastly increase the doubts, uncertainties, and delays of the law, and add immensely to the costs of litigation.

Law Commissioners, *Report to the New Jersey Legislature* (1855), p. 25.

Such is the uncertainty of language, so liable is it to different constructions, even when carefully used by accurate scholars and logicians, so short-sighted are the most far-seeing, that the wisest men and ablest lawyers would find it impossible to frame an entire new code of laws, that would provide for hundreds of new cases continually arising, or that would be so clear and explicit in all its details as to leave no room for opposite opinions and conflicting decisions. As an example, the New York code begins by defining an action in these words:

"An action is an ordinary proceeding in a court of justice, by which a party prosecutes another for the enforcement or protection of a right, the redress or prevention of a wrong, or the punishment of a public offence."

Simple and intelligible as this appears, their courts have been several times called upon to tell what it means, and have given various and conflicting interpretations.

A judge in one district decides one way, and in another district an opposite rule is established. We might add similar illustrations from almost every part of their code.

The first code was adopted in eighteen hundred and forty-eight, and an amended one in eighteen hundred and forty-nine; they will be fortunate if the process of amending and perfecting does not furnish employment to their legislature for the next generation.

The reported decisions of practice cases arising under their new code, have already, in six years, outnumbered all the previous reported practice decisions in their law courts, and all the reported law decisions, upon all questions, in our own state. It will be many years before the practice under this code can be considered as at all in a settled state, and by that time the code itself will be well nigh buried under the accumulated mass of amendments and conflicting decisions.

All the delay, vexation, and expense, of settling their system, must fall upon such of their citizens as may unfortunately be obliged to invoke the aid of their courts. . . .

We have carefully examined the reports of the commissioners appointed for similar purposes in our sister states, and England, and our labors have been lightened by theirs' who have preceded us. Wherever we considered it best, we have used both their language and ideas.

There is manifest advantage in so doing; we will have the benefit of the cotemporaneous judicial constructions of other courts, which will relieve us in a measure from an evil always incident to even the most salutary reforms. Although we felt unwilling to adopt the New York plan of codifying, yet justice demands of us to acknowledge the many valuable provisions and suggestions in their code, of which we have availed ourselves so far as applicable to a common law system.

JURISPRUDENCE AS A PHILOSOPHICAL SCIENCE

Peter S. Du Ponceau

Peter Stephen Du Ponceau (1760–1844), born in France, was brought to America by Baron Steuben as his secretary in 1777. After serving in the Continental Army, Du Ponceau became a highly successful attorney. He was also Provost of the Law Academy of Philadelphia, founded in 1821.

His European background put him in a unique position in a country rapidly developing international ties. It could not but strengthen the morale of the opposers of codification when a man of such authority on international and comparative law, himself the translator of the French Commercial and Penal Codes, came to their support.

THERE IS among the members of the legal profession in this country a disposition to extend the bounds of our science, and to improve our jurisprudence by the study of that of other nations, ancient and modern, which has not been sufficiently observed. We have a Law Journal, of which seven volumes have already been published in this city by John E. Hall, Esq. the contents of which bear ample testimony to this fact. Mr. Wheaton, the official reporter of the decisions of the Supreme Court of the United States, has placed at the end of each of the eight volumes that have hitherto appeared of his Reports, an appendix of learned notes, giving comparative views of the laws of different countries on the various subjects which are treated of in the body of the work. We understand that his ninth volume is to contain an epitome of the laws of *Spain.* A great number of the works of eminent foreign authors, such as Roccus, Bynkershoek, Martens, Schlegel, Pothier, Emerigon, Valin, Jacobsen, and others have been translated by our jurists from various languages, and published, some of them with valuable notes. Two different translations have appeared of the French commercial code, and one of the criminal code, all with copious notes by different authors. Judge Cooper has published Justinian's Institutes, with a translation, and a large body of annotations, in which he ably compares the Roman system of jurisprudence with our own. All these things are hardly known, except by a few, even in this country. They nevertheless shew the inclination of our professional men to cultivate jurisprudence as a philosophical science, and the result may be easily anticipated.

Peter S. Du Ponceau, *A Dissertation on the Nature and Extent of the Jurisdiction of the Courts of the United States* (1824), p. xx.

THE NEW AND PECULIAR RELATIONS
OF OUR SYSTEM

Joseph Story

THE PROGRESS OF JURISPRUDENCE since the termination of the War of Independence, and especially within the last twenty years, has been remarkable throughout all America. More than 150 volumes of reports are already published, containing a mass of decisions which evinces uncommon devotion to the study of the law, and uncommon ambition to acquire the highest professional character. The best of our reports scarcely shrink from a comparison with those of England in the corresponding period; and even those of a more provincial cast exhibit researches of no mean extent, and presage future excellence. The danger, indeed, seems to be, not that we shall hereafter want able reports, but that we shall be overwhelmed with their number and variety.

In this respect our country presents a subject of very serious contemplation and interest to the profession. There are now twenty-four States in the Union, in all of which, except Louisiana, the common law is the acknowledged basis of their jurisprudence. Yet this jurisprudence, partly by statute, partly by judicial interpretations, and partly by local usages and peculiarities, is perpetually receding farther and farther from the common standard. While the States retain their independent sovereignties, as they must continue to do under our federative system, it is hopeless to expect that any greater uniformity will exist in the future than in the past. Nor do I know that, so far as domestic happiness and political convenience are concerned, a greater uniformity would in most respects be desirable. The task, however, of administering justice in the state as well as national courts, from the new and peculiar relations of our system, must be very laborious and perplexing; and the conflict of opinion upon general questions of law in the rival jurisdictions of the different States, will not be less distressing to the philosophical jurists, than to the practical lawyer. . . .

Some of the prominent features of state jurisprudence, do, as I think, justify the suggestion already made, that American jurisprudence can never acquire a homogeneous character; and that we must look to the future rather for increasing discrepancies than coincidences in the law and the administration of the law. This is a consideration of no small moment to

Joseph Story, *A Discourse on the Past History, Present State, and Future Prospects of the Law* (1835), p. 20.

us all, lest, by being split up into distinct provincial bars, the profession should become devoted to mere state jurisprudence, and abandon those more enlightened and extensive researches which form the accomplished scholar, and elevate the refined jurist; which ennoble the patriot, and shed a never dying lustre round the statesman. The establishment of the national government, and of courts to exercise its constitutional jurisdiction, will, it is to be hoped, in this respect, operate with a salutary influence. Dealing, as such courts must, in questions of a public nature; such as concerns the law of nations, and the general rights and duties of foreign nations; such as respect the domestic relations of the states with each other, and with the general government; such as treat of the great doctrines of prize and maritime law; such as involve the discussion of grave constitutional powers and authorities;—it is natural to expect, that these courts will attract the ambition of some of the ablest lawyers in the different states, with a view both to fame and fortune. And thus, perhaps, if I do not indulge in an idle dream, the foundations may be laid for a character of excellence and professional ability, more various and exalted than has hitherto belonged to any bar under the auspices of the common law; a character in which minute knowledge of local law will be combined with the most profound attainments in general jurisprudence, and with that instructive eloquence, which never soars so high, or touches so potently, as when it grasps principles which fix the destiny of nations, or strike down to the very roots of civil polity.

A COMMUNITY OF INTEREST

Law Magazine

OUR COUNTRY has no general and common system of national jurisprudence. That which is furnished by the legislation of Congress, and the decisions of the Supreme Court of the United States, is limited in its character, and restricted in its application. On the other hand, no less than thirty-one distinct systems, founded upon the legislation and judicial decisions of as many different States, subject to continual change and contradiction, baffle all attempts to master their various details, harmonize and reconcile their multitudinous incongruities and contradictions, or trace the new forms and features which they assume in almost each successive year. Yet some degree of knowledge of all these systems is necessary for the advocate and jurist before he is master of his profession, and for the judge before he is fully competent to meet all the questions which may

"National Jurisprudence," *U.S. Law Magazine* (1851), III, p. 125.

come before him for decision. For the tribunals of each State are liable to be called upon to consider the laws of every other; nor are the occasions of such liability by any means unfrequent. There may have been a reason for this want of uniformity, at the commencement, in the nature and origin of our political institutions, and an excuse for it in the comparatively slight inconvenience which it at first occasioned. But at the present time, when all our interests are so closely interwoven and united, the reason and the excuse can hardly exist, or at all events weigh against the more powerful considerations which seem to demand an uniform national jurisprudence, prevailing, and administered alike in every State. . . .

"*The Union*," is a term which we most often use to designate our common country. This union signifies something more than a mere political compact. In the first place it represents unity of language. . . .

This *Union* also reminds us of an identity of race. In every State are the endearing monuments of our common origin, significant of indomitable energy, commanding talents, and unparalleled enterprise. Nor do the occasional intermingling and contact of other races in any respect destroy this identity. We invite among us the exiles of the world—they are received in our midst, and become part and parcel of ourselves. . . .

But there is yet a closer union than that of race. The ties of kindred and blood embrace the inhabitants of every State. Fathers, sons and brothers are scattered from Maine to California, from Georgia to Oregon. . . .

From this identity of language and race, and from this scattering abroad of kindred and friends, springs a community of interest, whose influence knows no limit either of extent or power. We are united for a common protection and defence—how effectually, has been proved in many a well-fought field. We are united in all the interests of literature, science and the arts. It is a national measure that secures to the author the profit of his works, and to the inventor the benefit of his discoveries. Yet in the end the profit and the benefit, if any there be, are not confined to one, but enjoyed by all. But more intimate still are the interests of trade, commerce and business. These penetrate and pervade every state, county and village. No inhabited spot, however remote, is exempt from their influence. Nor is this the less so, because the inhabitants of some sections are engaged in pursuits of trade, those of others in agriculture, and those of others still in manufactures or mechanic arts. These pursuits materially depend upon and support each other. The cotton, sugar, rice and tobacco of the South, the products of the teeming fields of the West, and the various fabrics of the North and East, meet daily upon some common ground. The princely merchant of the city, and the smaller dealer of the country, are daily brought into communion. The proud ship of the ocean receives its lading from the little bark, or pigmy car of the distant interior, and freights the bark and car back again in return. All these interests grow and expand by each others aid. They are the pride and power of our country, and more glorious than the imperial legions and subject provinces of ancient Rome. They are not confined to any one community or exclusive limits, and the facilities for their development and expansion, are continually growing more perfect and extended. Memory runs back but a brief space of time, when the slow moving coach bore us in our painful and halting journey for days and weeks to another State—then to us as a distant and foreign country, or the lazy sloop, ever at the mercy of adverse winds, carried us on a lingering, sea-sick voyage, from port to port, or we were, and indeed are sometimes now, compelled to wait for annual floods, to bear ourselves and the products of our industry down rapid and dangerous rivers to seek a market. After weeks and months the slow mail brought replies to our letters, from distant friends. Now, the swift car wheels the traveller over the iron track, and the distant city is reached in a day. Now, the traveller puts himself, at night, upon some palace of the deep, and during the hours of repose a long voyage is accomplished. Now, we seek converse with a friend a thousand miles remote; sooner than the words can be formed the message flies, and swift as thought the answer returns. The neighbor is no longer confined to the next door, the next street, or the next farm. What seemed great distance a few years since, is but small now. Friends and kindred separate for distant places, but the separations seems slight. The calls of business are heard from distant points, but they occasion no extraordinary stir; they are obeyed with the same facility, as if made in the same town. Intervening space seems scarcely longer to exist. The vast and complicated details of business, every day, make a wide circle. They constantly operate to diminish the distinctness of state lines, and obliterate geographical divisions and distinctions. Despite the threatening portents, which are sometimes seen in the political sky, our country is all the time becoming more as one, and the necessity of union is increasing in an equal ratio with the increase of facilities for travel, communication, and mutual intercourse.

But that which has been predicated of almost every other interest of our country, cannot truly be said of our jurisprudence. In this respect, there seems to be no sympathy, intercourse or communion between the different States. The jurisprudence of the country enters into, and indeed forms a part of all its business relations. These business relations are everywhere extended, interwoven and connected together; yet they are subject in each different State to the application of a different legal system. There is no man of considerable business, but has experienced the inconvenience and evil of this state of things.

It is not necessary or desirable to interfere with the more local police regulations of the States, or trample upon their sovereign rights. But there are certain general principles applicable to legislation, and judicial systems, which should prevail everywhere alike. Nor is it less necessary, so far as practical results are concerned, that the details of legal proceedings, through a country like ours, should be everywhere the same. The like may be said of many of those arbitrary regulations which have no inherent foundation in right or wrong, but which should, in some form or other, be adopted in every government.

Of this character is the rate of interest upon the loan or forbearance of money, which is universally fixed, and some restriction upon the taking of usury imposed by law. In the different States are no less than four different rates. In nineteen, the rate is six per cent.; in five, seven; in four, eight; and in one, five. This difference is no slight embarrassment to our commercial intercourse. Besides the legal questions to which it gives occasion, it tends to direct capital from the States where the lower rates of interest prevail, to those in which the rates are higher. The one State is deprived of its necessary and proper capital, and the other by offering a bounty upon its importation, in the higher rate of interest, stimulates enterprise and business to an unnatural degree. . . .

There is also a want of uniformity in the tenure of lands, and the rules which govern the descent, transmission, and distribution of property. There is a diversity even in the formalities of a conveyance, the mode of proof or acknowledgement, and the proper officer to take the same. This is not merely an inconvenience, it is a positive evil. It embarrasses the interchange of property, leads to defective titles, and in the end engenders expensive litigation. Citizens of one State become owners of land in another, but are never certain without much trouble and expense of the nature and conditions of the title they acquire; and if they seek to dispose of such land, they are subjected to the same or greater difficulties in making the proper conveyance with the proper formalities. . . .

But there are still other vexations and difficulties, to which the citizen of one State is subject, who has business intercourse in another. He finds, in that intercourse, if it ever requires resort to legal proceedings, a different mode of administering justice from that to which he has been accustomed. The courts to which he is compelled to apply, exercise a different jurisdiction, and are governed by different rules of practice and procedure. He finds different laws relating to frauds, to the limitation of actions, to insolvency, and other matters relating to remedial justice—in all which, as in the commercial law of the country, there should be universal uniformity. The various, multiplied, and often vast commercial dealings between the citizens of different States, the constantly increasing advantages for commercial intercourse, and the immense interests involved, render it indispensable that the utmost facility should be afforded in the pursuit of remedies for every wrong or breach of good faith. This facility cannot exist, unless he who has suffered injury, shall be entitled to avail himself of the same exercise of jurisdiction, and the same remedies in the courts of every part of the Union. But this is not, at present, the case. In some States, a summary process is allowed which at once affords a creditor security for his debt. In others, he is subjected to such delays, that the debtor, if dishonestly disposed, conceals, disposes of, or squanders his property to the defeat of a just claim. In some, the creditor can compel a sale of property to the ruin of his debtor. In others, he can only get satisfaction out of the rents and profits of his debtor's estate. In some, the law secures to the debtor, from liability for debts, sufficient property for a competence. In others, it sacrifices almost everything to the claim of the creditor. In addition to individual inconvenience, this state of things begets evils of a political character, which seem never to have been contemplated by statesmen or politicians. It fixes upon the States subject to these differences, different characters for credit, responsibility, morals, and security for property. Those States which afford the best facilities for enforcing the obligations of contracts, good faith, and the various duties owing from one man to another, ever enjoy a higher character in these particulars. In such States property is more secure, and moral and business integrity stands higher. On the other hand, in those States whose systems are lax in compelling those obligations, and afford opportunity for evasion, or delay, there is less confidence, credit is at a lower ebb and pays a higher premium. In the former States those who are impatient of the restraints of good laws, thoroughly enforced, seek refuge in the latter, while in the latter, those who are disposed to perform all their obligations, are compelled to resort to the former. The laxity or stringency of laws to compel the duties of citizens has not a little to do with public and private morals. When these laws are stringent within the proper limits and rigidly enforced, good morals are more generally found. On the contrary, extreme laxity and leniency in such laws, either in their letter or enforcement, result in public degeneracy. . . .

There is the same variety to be found in the criminal, as in the civil codes of the several States, often giving rise to serious questions of jurisdiction, and involving the States themselves in bitter and re-criminating controversies. It is therefore a reasonable subject of enquiry, whether, among States whose citizens are in habits of such common and familiar intercourse, they should not be subject to one common criminal code, at least, except so far as locality or circumstances, may require a difference. There is, and there can be no substantial reason why an act innocent in one State, should be criminal in another, except it be in relation to some subject existing in the former and not in the latter; why an act constituting one degree of crime in one State, should be of a different degree in another; why the same offence should be punished by death in one State, and by a milder penalty in another; why one mode of trial and certain rules of evidence should prevail in one state, and other modes of trial and different rules of evidence in another. It was frequently said when Dr. Webster was found guilty of the murder of Dr. Parkman in Boston, that had the trial been in New York, the result would have been different. If this be so, then innocence is either unjustly pursued and punished in Massachusetts, or crime is unjustly and injuriously suffered to triumph in New York; justice is too certain and too sure in the former, and too slow and uncertain in the latter; honesty incurs the penalties due to crime in the one, while the reckless criminal escapes in the other. These differences indeed, except in the degree of punishment, belong rather to the *mala prohibita*, than the *mala in se*; though it is not out of the latter that serious difficulties generally arise. But in respect to the former we not only have embarrassing questions of comity, jurisdiction, and constitutional obligations, but all the evils which flow from tolerating in one State, practices which are prohibited in another. Acts which are really offences against society anywhere, are equally so everywhere. If innocent and beneficial anywhere, they are equally so everywhere; and when they are allowed in one place and restricted in another, the former becomes the abode of all those in the latter, who desire to practice them. The citizen of one State should not, when he steps into another, find himself subject to punishment for an act which in his own would be entirely innocent. There may be some regulations required by the peculiar situation or circumstances of a State to which these principles will not apply, but in regard to all acts which are really offences against society at large, there can be no exception. Uniformity of criminal codes, however, although desirable, is not indispensable, and does not necessarily enter into the plan which it is the object of this article to suggest. It would certainly tend to render the system more harmonious and perfect, and render stronger and more entire, that unity which is so essential to the perfection of every system.

The foregoing are a few of the legal topics out of which spring that variety, contrariety, and conflict of laws, which tend to embarrass the business, restrict the intercourse, and obstruct the justice of the country. All, or nearly all legal questions and titles, are subject to the same difficulties as those which have been mentioned. To obviate these difficulties, to advance legal science and philosophy and to promote universal justice, it is proposed to have in this country but one legal system in its principles or its details; or rather that all legal systems should be founded upon the same model, and pursue the same plan, embracing every principle of universal application, and every subject upon which a conflict of laws can arise. Thus may we hope to realize for the several States of our Union, the more enlarged aspirations of a writer deeply and ardently imbued with the sound and conservative spirit of legal philosophy, progress, and reform,—"such a similarity of laws and institutions as will favor inter-communion, diminish State jealousies, lessen the causes of discord and prepare the American family, if not for one religious and political faith, at least for such an approximation as will greatly enlarge the sphere of reciprocal usefulness and of national and individual enjoyment." *Hoffman's Legal Studies.*

It is true that by the general maxims of jurisprudence, every State possesses exclusive sovereignty and jurisdiction within its own territory; that no State can by its laws directly affect or bind property out of its own territory, or bind persons not resident therein; and that whatever force and obligation the laws of one State have in another, depend solely upon the laws and regulations of the latter. *Story's Conflict of Laws*, § 18, 20, 23. Yet that comity which has become a part of every enlightened system of jurisprudence, in many instances gives force and effect to the laws and judicial proceedings of other States. Still there are many instances in which this comity is not applicable, and does not prevail. That such is the case, is owing to the existing diversity of laws and legal systems. Do away with this diversity, and adopt the principle of uniformity, and every State in the exercise of its proper jurisdiction, will accord to the laws of every other the same respect that is conceded to its own.

Next to the obligations which men are under to their maker, are those which they owe to one another, growing out of and embracing all the social relations. The comprehensive injunction upon whose sublime morality those obligations are founded—"what ye would that men should do to you, do ye likewise to them,"—it is the sole object of law to enforce. The circumstances under which men are placed in relation to each other, constitute an infinite variety; the details of intercourse and business, are intricate and almost limitless. To understand and apply the principles of justice to all this variety, and harmonize these various details, is in some degree the office of the science of jurisprudence. To reduce to practice and enforce the duties and obligations of mankind, is the object and design of laws and municipal regulations. The study of these obligations and duties is next to the highest in which man can engage, and to apply them in all the varied intercourse and transactions of life, calls forth the profoundest knowledge, the highest degree of moral power, and the most varied wisdom of the most gifted mind. To perfect and improve the knowledge of these obligations and duties, and facilitate their application to all the affairs of life, is among the noblest of human pursuits, and not the least among the objects which tend to the happiness and enjoyment of mankind. If therefore, we can divest existing legal systems of even a few of the vexed questions, which hide the fountains and obscure the streams of justice, we shall have accomplished something towards these ends.

The present diversity of legal systems in our country, and their entire independence of each other, lead to a contrariety of judicial decisions, and cause an apparent if not real conflict of legal principles. What is pronounced legal, equitable, and just, in one State, is adjudged the very reverse in another. Under an uniform system of laws, these difficulties, at least in a measure, would be obviated. Judicial investigation, every where directed to the same enquiries, and pursuing the same general course, unembarrassed to a great degree with questions of local legislation and local practice, will tend to greater certainty and more correct results. As the case now is, the courts and legislatures of thirty-one different States are devising and maturing separate systems of their own, some striking out new and unheard of paths, and others copying the latest inventions engrafted with new and incongruous features of their own.

Each State is exploring the region of experiment, and whatever is novel seems to find most favor with those who talk loudest of reform. Indeed, instead of the closer assimilation of practice and principle, which we might expect from our character, situation and circumstances, we see but increasing differences. In this state of things, how can we ever expect to create a jurisprudence that is national and American?

On the other hand, suppose each of the thirty-one States to adopt the same legal and judicial system, subject to no change which shall not be adopted by all, or at least a majority, how will many of our doubts, difficulties and uncertainties disappear! How much learning will be no longer necessary! What study and toil of the jurist, the judge, the legislator and the student may be dispensed with! To what perfection may not American legal science, thus adopting some degree of unity and simplicity, be brought! The legal learning and talent of the thirty-one States, instead of being devoted to as many different systems, will be concentrated on one, and it will ill accord with our character in other respects if they do not produce a body of jurisprudence as perfect as the world has ever seen. National, not sectional, in its character, and universal, if not in the obligations it shall impose, at least, in the respect it shall win from the civilized world. It is true that there can be no appellate jurisdiction to control these systems, and correct their errors, and that each must in general be supreme in its own State. Yet the defect will be in a measure supplied by the Supreme Court of the United States. That court now administers and expounds the laws of the several States as it finds them, adopts the practice, and is governed by the decisions of the courts of the States, in which the questions to be decided arise. The hitherto divided labors of that court, therefore, will become more concentrated, and consequently tend to greater certainty, uniformity and perfection.

But it is not the desirableness and necessity of uniformity in our legal systems that require demonstration. The only question is as to its feasibility. We shall be met with the ever active jealousy of encroachment on State rights. We shall be told, that there nowhere resides the power to effect the object. But it is not necessary to interfere with State sovereignty, nor is it desirable to exercise compulsion. The whole scheme can be accomplished by voluntary action. Let a correspondence be opened by and with the proper authorities of the several States, recommending the appointment of a commissioner, or commissioners, from each State, not exceeding three, whose duty it shall be to meet from time to time, and frame a code of statute law, embracing only these provisions which shall be equally applicable in every State, and shall not interfere with the constitutional provisions of any. This commission will, of course, examine and scrutinize carefully the statute codes of each State, and enquire into the operations and defects of each particular law. Nor will the enquiry be confined to the codes of our own States, but those of every civilized country may be brought into requisition, and the best features of all, so far as they may be in harmony with the genius of our government and institutions, contribute to the perfection of the plan to be adopted. When any branch of the labors of this commission have been finished, let it be submitted to the Legislatures of the several States, for such corrections and improvements as they, in their wisdom, may deem it necessary to make, and let it then be again recommitted, for the final action of the commission, when they shall have completed their plan. When all the heads and titles of statute law shall have been subjected to this process, and framed into a complete body by the commission, in that form, let it be adopted by the Legislature of each State. In carrying out this plan, it is not necessary to overturn existing systems, or make great and radical changes. The grand features, and fundamental principles of each present system, may be preserved, and yet the whole be reduced to harmonious uniformity. It is not recommended to strike out new paths, to seek new inventions, or even disturb ancient prejudices. Neither is it expected, that this is to be the work of a day, or even a year. Such are the checks against sudden innovations, that no change can be effected, without the most thorough scrutiny, and every needful preparation on the part of the public mind. The system may require five, or even ten years for its perfection. Nor is it proposed to stop when the system is once adopted. Like all human productions, it will be liable to imperfections, and the many changes and improvements which grow out of the progressive spirit of the age, will call for corresponding change and adaptation in the laws. The commission should therefore be continued or re-appointed from time to time, for the purpose of remedying imperfections, and recommending the necessary improvements and reforms.

The scheme of uniting every State in some uniform system of jurisprudence, is herein shadowed forth, for it does not profess to be complete. But the task of its accomplishment, will devolve upon those who see, in the science of law, something more than the daily routine of professional duty; something more than the mere means of acquiring a livelihood, or even wealth; who see in it a profound and sublime philosophy, teaching mankind the source of their rights and obligations, and the means by which those rights and obligations are to be maintained. "Jurisprudentia est divinarum atque humanarum rerum notitia, justi atque injusti scientia." *Institutes*. "While the splendid victories of Justinian, which would perhaps have immortalized his name, had his fame depended upon them alone, are forgotten, the system of jurisprudence created by his code, his pandects and his institutes, will bear his name with the highest honor to the latest time." *Gibbon*. That system at once became the fountain of justice, for a boundless empire; has been perpetuated through centuries of darkness to the present age, and now prevails in a large portion of the civilized world. It is not indeed confined to the continent upon which it originated, but it has crossed the ocean, and has in a measure displaced, or at all events modified, our venerable common law, which runs back to an antiquity almost as remote. Our systems of laws are now in a worse condition than were those of the Roman empire in the age of Justinian, and labor under the same evils. If an imperial despot, in an age of ignorance, could command the labors of Tribonian and his associates, to collect the scattered, various and contradictory fragments of statutes, edicts, rescripts and decisions of his vast empire, embracing the people of every habit and every language, in one compact, harmonious and beautiful system, why may not our thirty-one States, inhabited by one race, speaking the same language, and possessed of the highest degree of civilization, learning and intelligence, by a concentrated effort, effect the same, or even a greater result. Instead of conflict, variety and contradiction of statutes and decisions, we should then have harmony and uniformity; instead of doubt and uncertainty, permanence and stability. Instead of a path-way through obscurity and darkness, to him who pursues the stream and seeks the fountains of justice, he would find it illumined by cheering light, agreeably shaded, perhaps, by the systems of old, yet never be compelled to grope his way through impenetrable mazes, that no eye can pierce and no industry remove.

The success of the system which is here recommended, has no less importance in a political view. How would it tend to connect the bonds of union? How would it operate to dissipate the enmities, the prejudices and jealousies which so often threaten our national existence? Might we not reasonably hope for the day, when one section, arrayed against the other, will no longer study and strive, how to get and maintain a political supremacy over the other, but the sole study and the sole strife shall be, in the spirit of comity to suggest and perfect measures for the universal and common good; when the States, while they remain in all that pertains to individual interests, several, shall yet deem themselves in all that concerns national greatness, glory and happiness, one. Then,—to borrow and apply to our country, the prediction of Cicero, which Story has so beautifully applied to his subject, in his commentaries on the conflict of laws,—"Non erit alia lex Romae, alia Athenis, alia nunc, alia posthuc; sed et omnis gentis, et omni tempore, una lex et sempiterna, et immortalis continebit."

ENVOI: A PERSONAL NOTE

In himself the lawyer embodied the compromise that American society worked out—public service, involvement in national affairs, participation in reform, together with hard work toward personal fulfillment and enrichment. Contrast the attitudes of Harden and Shaw in the following pages on reaching the pinnacle of the profession.

MANY HIGHLY COMPLIMENTARY NOTICES

Edward Randolph Harden

When Edward Randolph Harden graduated from the University of Georgia, he joined his father's legal practice. In 1854 he received an appointment as judge of the first court in Nebraska Territory. He was apparently a successful judge despite a lack of firmness and authority. Although he was originally enthusiastic about Nebraska, and intended to bring his family from Georgia for permanent settlement, he suddenly changed his mind and returned to his native state.

Ringgold, June 29th, 54

MY DEAR MOTHER

I have rec'd the appointment out of Eight hundred applicants of Judge of the Supreme Court of Nebraska. I am told that the salary is three thousand Dollars per annum, and twenty Dollars mileage for every hundred miles going to the place—It is the same position in the territories, that Judge, Nichol's in Sav: is in the States. I can go from here to Nashville Tenn: in 6 hours pr RRoad, and thence by steam Boat all the way to Nebraska—can accomplish the trip in 8 days, and at an expense of 35$—I am rejoiced that I rec'd this appointment, instead of Utah, which would have taken 2 months, & which I had made up my mind to decline, had it been offered to me—If my poor father was alive how proud he would be at my success—and I am sure that you and Conta ought to be proud—It is the first Judge that we have ever had in the family. . . .

Many of my prominent friends in Geo—in congratulating me—give it

Judge Edward R. Harden, Letter, June 29, 1854, *Nebraska History*, XXVII (1946), p. 20.

as their opinion that if I live now, in a few years I may be in the United States Senate. . . . My name is in the papers every where—the only appointment from Georgia—and many highly complimentary notices, among those who know—me—I think our old Athens paper ought to speak out for me— . . .

ON BECOMING A JUDGE

Lemuel Shaw

Governor Levi Lincoln offered Shaw the appointment as Chief Justice of Massachusetts on the death of Isaac Parker in 1830. Webster, then at the height of his power and repute, was commissioned to persuade Shaw. He later reported, "I guess he smoked a thousand cigars while settling the point." Shaw accepted after drawing up the following balance sheet, although it meant giving up a practice of $15,000 to $20,000 a year for an annual salary of $3,500.

WHETHER I SHALL ACCEPT the appointment of Judge.

Against it:—

I shall in some measure sacrifice ease and independence; it will be more laborious. I shall lose something in part of present emolument. I shall be more absent from my family at a time when my presence might be useful to my children. I shall miss the opportunity of travelling, of making tours and journeys, and be confined principally to the pale of the Commonwealth.

In favor:—

Although I shall have a good deal of labor I do not know that it is more irksome—in many respects it is less so—than that of the Bar. There will be considerable intervals of leisure. Although the emolument will not be so great as that which I have been receiving, yet it is more regular, permanent, and secure.

At fifty the labors of the Bar begin to become irksome, and many a man who has in early life enjoyed a full practice is apt to decline after that period.

The situation is a highly honorable and useful one, which, if the duties of it are ably and acceptably discharged, will lay the foundation of an honorable lasting name.

Lemuel Shaw, "Memorandum," Samuel Shaw, *Memoir of Lemuel Shaw* (1885), p. 21.

The above "if" is with me the great cause of apprehension and alarm.

Upon this I confess I am influenced more by the judgment of others than by my own. I am conscious that I cannot thus discharge the duties; they assure me that I can. I have only one consolation, that I have often thought the same in regard to other arduous undertakings and yet upon trial have found my strength equal to the occasion. If I undertake this great office, God grant it may be so here.

THE GATHERED WISDOM

OF A THOUSAND YEARS

Joseph Story

In his inaugural discourse at the Harvard Law School in 1829, Judge Story outlined a truly mammoth course of learning for the would-be lawyer. The lecture embodies the restrictive side of professionalism—the stress on specialized knowledge (even a deliberately specialized terminology) which marks the separation of the elect from the common run of mankind. But it equally expresses the positive aspect. To Story, that perfection of skill and the excellence he praises can only be achieved by immense labors. The regal dignity of the law rests on an arduous course of learning. The lawyer, stationed as a "public sentinel," must be armed with reason, to curb both anarchy and despotism. The profession, thus, is open to talent rather than to birth or wealth—though the latter need provide no obstacle.

I KNOW NOT, if among human sciences there is any one, which requires such various qualifications and extensive attainments, as the law. While it demands the first order of talents, genius alone never did, and never can, win its highest elevations. There is not only no royal road to smooth the way to the summit; but the passes, like those of Alpine regions, are sometimes dark and narrow; sometimes bold and precipitous; sometimes dazzling from the reflected light of their naked fronts; and sometimes bewildering from the shadows projecting from their dizzy heights. Whoever advances for safety must advance slowly. He must cautiously follow the old guides, and toil on with steady footsteps; for the old paths, though well beaten, are rugged; and the new paths, though broad, are still perplexed. To drop all metaphor, the law is a science, in which there is no substitute for diligence and labor. It is a fine remark of one, who is himself a brilliant example of

---

Inaugural Address at the Harvard Law School (1829).

all he teaches, that "It appears to be the general order of Providence, manifested in the constitution of our nature, that every thing valuable in human acquisition should be the result of toil and labor." But this truth is nowhere more forcibly manifested than in the law. Here, moderate talents with unbroken industry have often attained a victory over superior genius, and cast into shade the brightest natural parts.

The student, therefore, should, at his first entrance upon the study, weigh well the difficulties of his task, not merely to guard himself against despondency on account of expectations too sanguinely indulged; but also to stimulate his zeal, by a proper estimate of the value of perseverance. He, who has learned to survey the labor without dismay, has achieved half the victory. I will not say, with Lord Hale, that "The law will admit of no rival, and nothing to go even with it"; but I will say, that it is a jealous mistress, and requires a long and constant courtship. It is not to be won by trifling favors, but by a lavish homage.

Many causes combine to make the study of the common law, at the present day, a laborious undertaking. In the first place, it necessarily embraces the reasoning and doctrines of very remote ages. It is, as has been elegantly said, "The gathered wisdom of a thousand years"; or, in the language of one of the greatest of English judges, it is not "the product of the wisdom of some one man, or society of men, in any one age; but of the wisdom, counsel, experience, and observation of many ages of wise and observing men." It is a system having its foundations in natural reason; but, at the same time, built up and perfected by artificial doctrines, adapted and moulded to the artificial structure of society. The law, for instance, which governs the titles to real estate, is principally derived from the feudal polity and usages, and is in a great measure unintelligible without an intimate acquaintance with the peculiarities of that system. This knowledge is not, even now, in all cases easily attainable; but must sometimes be searched out amidst the dusty ruins of antiquity, or traced back through blacklettered pages of a most forbidding aspect both in language and matter. The old law, too, is not only of an uncouth and uninviting appearance; but it abounds with nice distinctions, and subtile refinements, which enter deeply into the modern structure of titles. No man even in our own day, can venture safely upon the exposition of an intricate devise, or of the effect of a power of appointment, or of a deed to lead uses and trusts, who has not, in some good degree, mastered its learning. More than two centuries ago, Sir Henry Spelman depicted his own distress on entering upon such studies, when at the very vestibule he was met by a foreign language, a barbarous dialect, an inelegant method, and a mass of learning, which could be borne only upon the shoulders of Atlas; and frankly admitted, that his heart sunk within him at the prospect. The defects of a foreign tongue, and barbarous dialect, and inelegant method, have almost entirely disappeared, and no longer vex the student in his midnight vigils. But the materials for his labor have in other respects greatly accumulated in the intermediate period. He may, perchance, escape from the dry severity of the Year-Books, and the painful digestion of the Abridgments of Statham, Fitzherbert, and Brooke. He may even venture to glide by the exhausting arguments of Plowden. But Lord Coke, with his ponderous *Commentaries*, will arrest his course; and, faint and disheartened with the view, he must plunge into the labyrinths of contingent remainders, and executory devises, and springing uses; and he may deem himself fortunate, if, after many years' devotion to Fearne, he may venture upon the interpretation of that darkest of all mysteries, a last will and testament. So true it is, that no man knows his own will so ill, as the testator; and that over-solicitude to be brief and simple ends in being profoundly enigmatical. "Dum brevis esse laboro, obscurus fio."

In the next place, as has been already hinted, every successive age brings its own additions to the general mass of antecedent principles. If something is gained by clearing out the old channels, much is added by new increments and deposits. If here and there a spring of litigation is dried up, many new ones break out in unsuspected places. In fact, there is scarcely a single branch of the law, which belonged to the age of Queen Elizabeth, which does not now come within the daily contemplation of a lawyer of extensive practice. And all these branches have been spreading to an incalculable extent since that period, by the changes in society, wrought by commerce, agriculture, and manufactures, and other efforts of human ingenuity and enterprise.